Rethinking Environmental Security

RETHINKING POLITICAL SCIENCE AND INTERNATIONAL STUDIES

This series is a forum for innovative scholarly writing from across all substantive fields of political science and international studies. The series aims to enrich the study of these fields by promoting a cutting-edge approach to thought and analysis. Academic scrutiny and challenge is an essential component in the development of political science and international studies as fields of study, and the act of re-thinking and re-examining principles and precepts that may have been long-held is imperative.

Rethinking Political Science and International Studies showcases authored books that address the field from a new angle, expose the weaknesses of existing concepts and arguments, or 're-frame' the topic in some way. This might be through the introduction of radical ideas, through the integration of perspectives from other fields or even disciplines, through challenging existing paradigms, or simply through a level of analysis that elevates or sharpens our understanding of a subject.

Titles in the series include:

Rethinking International Relations
Bertrand Badie

Rethinking International Political Economy
Benjamin J. Cohen

Rethinking Environmental Security
Simon Dalby

Rethinking Environmental Security

Simon Dalby

Professor, Balsillie School of International Affairs, Wilfrid Laurier University, Canada

RETHINKING POLITICAL SCIENCE AND INTERNATIONAL STUDIES

Cheltenham, UK • Northampton, MA, USA

© Simon Dalby 2022

All rights reserved. No part of this publication may be reproduced, stored in a retrieval system or transmitted in any form or by any means, electronic, mechanical or photocopying, recording, or otherwise without the prior permission of the publisher.

Published by
Edward Elgar Publishing Limited
The Lypiatts
15 Lansdown Road
Cheltenham
Glos GL50 2JA
UK

Edward Elgar Publishing, Inc.
William Pratt House
9 Dewey Court
Northampton
Massachusetts 01060
USA

Paperback edition 2023

A catalogue record for this book
is available from the British Library

Library of Congress Control Number: 2022932891

This book is available electronically in the **Elgar**online
Political Science and Public Policy subject collection
http://dx.doi.org/10.4337/9781800375857

ISBN 978 1 80037 584 0 (cased)
ISBN 978 1 80037 585 7 (eBook)
ISBN 978 1 0353 1892 6 (paperback)

Printed and bound by CPI Group (UK) Ltd, Croydon, CR0 4YY

Contents

Preface

Half a century after delegates from some members of the United Nations first gathered to discuss the Human Environment in 1972 in Stockholm the matters they addressed now need much more urgent attention. In late 2020 the Secretary-General of the United Nations posed matters in terms of emergency; the United Nations Human Development report highlighted the appropriate contextualization for urgent action in terms of living in the new geological period of earth's history, the Anthropocene. The Intergovernmental Panel on Climate Change (IPCC) and numerous scientists have started talking in medical terms of a global code red, a matter of an imminent potentially fatal situation.

The matters that were initially raised in 1972 in terms of human survival have been added to by other considerations of global change since and were gathered under the rubric of environmental security in the aftermath of the cold war. What is clearly needed now from policy makers, social scientists and financial managers are initiatives to rapidly accelerate the transition to a world where global ecology is taken seriously as the necessary premise for public policy and investment decisions; and consequently the use of fossil fuels is phased out quickly. Time is, as the Secretary-General has made very clear repeatedly, running out. The longer we wait, the worse it will get.

Rethinking environmental security requires first and foremost this shift in terms of temporality. Where climate change and extinction have long been understood as matters for the future, this is no longer the case. To borrow a phrase from Dan Smith, director of the Stockholm International Peace Research Institute, the future that delegates to the 1972 United Nations meeting on the Human Environment hoped to avoid is what we are now living in. Political and policy thinking about security has to start from that premise; climate change and extinction are accelerating, no longer a matter for future consideration.

Thinking in these terms is a tall order in a world where the rich and powerful still mostly understand environment as something external to their affairs, a source of resources, a playground for their recreation, and out of sight, a sink for their wastes. Climate change!? Well that is, they still apparently frequently think, a matter for future generations to worry about later. Or perhaps, in a common but more worrisome formulation, something that their wealth can enable them to ignore, given that the nasty consequences will presumably fall elsewhere. Where climate activists pose the problem as one of system change or climate change, the rich and powerful still, it seems, prefer the latter as a better option than the former.

It is thus necessary to explore the modes of thought that have led to this situation as well as those that might offer novel formulations that lead towards a different future. Until fairly recently, as Amitav Ghosh (2016) argued, there was a "great derangement" in Western culture where the dramatic story of climate change, and the current reconfiguration of the earth system caused by the expansion of the fossil fueled global economy, was absent from most novels and cultural productions in the West. This has begun to change as the zeitgeist slowly registers the point that we no longer live in the relatively stable conditions of the Holocene that humanity has known throughout its history. Novelists are increasingly starting to engage themes of climate change, extinction and the possibilities of both dystopian and better futures for humanity in a rapidly changing world (Andersen 2020).

A key point for the arguments that follow in the chapters of this book is that the overall culture within which climate is being considered is starting to shift and novels and larger cultural issues matter in how what is dangerous is framed. This matters in terms of what is considered within academic analyses of security. Not only are scientific and political matters involved, but the popular imagination of what is to come is important in shaping political discourse, and cultural matters related to climate are especially fraught (Hulme 2009). This is especially the case where energy innovations and the connections between climate change, disasters and the possibilities of better lives in the future powered by novel electrical systems after fossil fuels are part of the discussion.

In Sheila Jasanoff's (2015, 2021) terms the socio-technical imaginaries that underpin political discourse need to explicitly engage with this new context with much more humility, recognizing the importance of the earth system as something modernity can no longer pretend to ignore. It is also the case that popular culture is increasingly being engaged by political scientists and other disciplines in terms of teaching and the interpretation of cultural politics. Popular political tropes draw on the larger cultural vocabulary in circulation, and hence matters of rethinking political things, in this case environmental security, need to draw on the larger cultural repertoire, and not just academic analyses of the traditional themes of international relations. Hence the periodic mention of novels and movies in the pages that follow here.

Part of the problem of dealing with matters of environmental security and the future dangers presented by species extinction and climate change is precisely that academic disciplines of the social sciences, and not just international relations, have been slow to grapple with the novel geophysical and biological circumstances of our times (Clark and Szerszynski 2021). But the current generation of students, both when on climate strike in the streets or when in their classrooms, are owed a much better range of intellectual and pedagogic options, ones that require rethinking both security and environment simultaneously while engaging with the international dimensions of both in light of the new insights of earth system science (Rockström and Gaffney 2021). This volume offers a few modest suggestions as to how this might be done.

This book is to a substantial extent a product of the COVID-19 pandemic. Initially conceived in the early weeks of the pandemic in 2020, when staying home and worrying about the disease, more so than many volumes, this book is a product of long confinement in the professorial study. Brooding over global catastrophes and the failure of "security" to provide for the basics of life for many vulnerable people, not least the elderly confined in "care" facilities, or impoverished people without medical assistance, added impetus to rethinking security on the large scale. Headlines about megafires in Australia and California, storms in numerous places, and both "heat domes" and, a few months later, an "atmospheric river" bringing severe floods to British Columbia focused attention on the consequences of climate change and the failures to anticipate their arrival, as well as the policy disconnects in a province where resource extraction still dominates policy making despite rising human vulnerabilities.

The ongoing opposition to the political economy of raw extractivism in the province is linked to attempts to decolonize academic understandings of the province's history, as well as rethink the legacy of colonization and the fate of violently dispossessed indigenous peoples. So many of these processes set in motion by the expansion of European colonization, powered frequently by fossil fuels, have parallels elsewhere, that the larger story needs to be incorporated into academic discussions of environmental security. Likewise the importance of ecological disruptions elsewhere, and not just climate change, has been sharpened by a focus on the COVID-19 pandemic, the mutating virus, its modes of transmission through complex artificial ecologies and the sometimes bizarre politics surrounding vaccines. All these themes have shaped this volume.

But while confinement to the professorial study reduced in-person contacts, important inputs to my thinking have come from many Balsillie School of International Affairs colleagues and students on Zoom, email and various other electronic media. In particular thanks to Alan Whiteside for conversations about viruses and the role of expertise and Neil Craik on geoengineering. Zhenzhong Si helped on China and eco-security. Randy Wigle and Alex Suen's engagement with me on economic damage estimates related to climate change led me to realize that most of that discussion was a distraction from the core concerns of environmental security. Tamara Lorinz's work on military emissions and Roger Boyd's on energy and geopolitics has all helped too.

University of Kansas professor John Head has been a visiting fellow at the School and his work on rethinking agriculture, law and ecostates has been especially inspiring even if he is cited less frequently in the pages that follow than perhaps he ought to be.

Also in Kansas, Shannon O'Lear helped with our ongoing discussion of environmental geopolitics. Long ago Derek Orosz collected material for me on the debate about the legacy of the 1970s *Limits to Growth* discussion, and a subsequent inspiring meeting in Oslo, before the pandemic, with one of the original authors, Jorgen Randers, focused my attention on this legacy once again. Cara Stewart's media sleuthing has, as usual, kept me in the loop on current climate events. Julia Trombetta and Ray Silvius helped with China. Dialogue with Luke Ashworth on his parallel efforts on the Anthropocene and how to teach about the end of the world, Rome and the history of international relations has helped too. David Long saved me from an embarrassing faux pas related to E.H. Carr. My ongoing conversation on all these topics with Thomas Homer-Dixon and Tom Deligiannis has provided very useful reality checks. Virtual participation in the Planet Politics Institute (planetpolitics.org) also connects me to innovative scholarship and commentary by colleagues around the world on the themes in this volume. My thanks to you one and all. Given the very diverse sources drawn on in the following pages, more so than usual, the normal disclaimer applies exonerating everyone listed here from any responsibility for my foibles and errors. Finally thanks to Harry Fabian and all the crew at Edward Elgar for getting this text into print.

Abbreviations

AMOC	Atlantic Meridional Overturning Current
COP	Conference of the Parties
GDP	Gross Domestic Product
GNP	Gross National Product
IMF	International Monetary Fund
IPBES	Intergovernmental Science-Policy Platform on Biodiversity and Ecosystem Services
IPCC	Intergovernmental Panel on Climate Change
NASA	National Aeronautics and Space Administration
NATO	North Atlantic Treaty Organization
OPEC	Organization of Petroleum Exporting Countries
SDG	Sustainable Development Goal
SUV	Sports Utility Vehicle
UNCED	United Nations Conference on Environment and Development
UNCHE	United Nations Conference on the Human Environment
UNEP	United Nations Environment Programme
UNESCO	United Nations Educational, Scientific and Cultural Organization
UNFCCC	United Nations Framework Convention on Climate Change

Introduction to *Rethinking Environmental Security*

The politics of planetary peril

OUR COMMON FUTURE

While numerous inquiries into the human prospect have long pondered the prospects for humanity, in the latter part of the twentieth century, as knowledge of the planetary system rapidly expanded, both the external dangers to our species and the novel self-imposed threats to civilization coalesced into a discussion of what became known as environmental security. Its impetus has usually been global scale threats to civilization and global human activity, but much of the practical attention has been on smaller issues of environment as a cause of local conflict, the dangers of pollution in numerous forms, and the implications of resource shortages, water and food in specific contexts. Most recently the rapidly advancing science of the earth system has highlighted looming catastrophic and existential risks at the global scale, which international relations as a scholarly enterprise, like the institutions and political arrangements it studies, has been very slow to effectively address.

The key document that codified environmental security as a focus for policy and scholarly concern, the World Commission on Environment and Development's 1987 report on *Our Common Future*, explicitly stated that environmental insecurity needed to be addressed by change in numerous aspects of economic life and security provision. The implications were that societies needed to pursue sustainable development rather than modern patterns of economic growth. Sustainable development would, so the argument in *Our Common Future* went, deal with environmental insecurities. This crucial innovation was neglected in subsequent decades where the rapid expansion of fossil fueled globalization was given policy priority even if the rhetoric of sustainable development was widely invoked. But the current climate crisis, the rapid loss of many species in the current planetary extinction event and renewed concerns about disease highlighted by the COVID-19 pandemic have revived concerns about global environmental insecurity and given them a renewed urgency.

This now requires rethinking how the scholarly field of international relations, and more specifically the security studies component of it, might effectively grapple with the rapidly changing material context that is shaping global politics. It also requires addressing how the changes, both in how security is formulated and in how sustainable development policies are crafted, that *Our Common Future* insisted were necessary might be implemented now. To do so requires reworking both the assumptions underlying the economic trajectories that have underpinned "development" in recent decades, and the arrangements of international politics that, despite the supposed priority given to global security, have radically endangered both people and the planetary system in which we all now live. We are in new times, captured in the discussion of a new geological era caused by human action, now commonly called the Anthropocene.

Given the danger of superpower nuclear arsenals and related weapons systems, international relations as a scholarly enterprise in the Anglosphere was formerly primarily concerned with survival in the nuclear age, but now survival is threatened by another series of political and technical arrangements. Traditional notions of state rivalries, and the struggles for power as supposedly the source of insecurity, are now part of the problem in terms of climate change and the extinction crisis. Precisely the fossil fueled industrial systems that power the economy and military capabilities that supposedly provide security are undermining the ecological conditions for their existence. This is the crisis of environmental security that requires rethinking many things, and the framework for security thinking in international relations in particular. The new sources of danger to humanity in general, and to specific populations in particular places, are now very different from the traditional international relations focus on armed conflicts. The dangers of nuclear war have not disappeared, but these new concerns need urgent attention. All this is not to forget that a major nuclear war would also be an environmental disaster of global scope, and as this book suggests, these interconnections are important in revisiting the environmental security discussion.

International relations as a discipline has not been effective at dealing with the climate crisis, partly because many of the political divisions that matter in this case are between the contemporary fossil fueled model of economy and future human generations. Those generations will need a functional biosphere to live in if a human civilization of multiple billions is to survive, never mind thrive, but they don't have an effective voice in the corridors of power. The geopolitical divisions marked by climate change also run in complicated ways between states that produce and consume fossil fuels and those, frequently former colonies with underdeveloped economies dependent on agriculture, that are subject to the largest disruptions caused by climate change, and which have no obvious policy or military options to deal with these threats to their security.

Neither are the modes of thinking related to regime formation, interdependence and cooperation, a dominant stream in international relations thinking after the cold war, all that helpful. Much of the focus in climate negotiations, and in international relations literature dealing with regime formation, has been on greenhouse gas emissions as a pollution problem, a matter of curtailing the amounts of methane and carbon dioxide coming from industrial and agricultural activities. So far these institutions, namely the United Nations Framework Convention on Climate Change (UNFCCC), the Kyoto Protocol and the Paris Agreement, have failed to grapple effectively with climate change, being in effect empty or decoy institutions (Dimitrov 2020). They simply don't deal with the causes of the crisis, namely the massive use of fossil fuels and the expansionist mode of contemporary economy. The Paris Agreement didn't mention fossil fuels, and until recently, key investment decisions that shape the future of the global economy were made without much consideration of climate matters. This has begun to change, as the discussions of coal, fossil fuel subsidies and investments at the Glasgow Conference of the Parties (COP) in 2021 indicates. Discussions within global environmental politics studies focused mainly on regime construction and related matters, and have been slow to grapple with the existential risks involved in the global economy.

One important exception is the matter of ozone depleting substances, namely chlorofluorocarbons and related chemicals, where ending their production has been a priority, and considerable academic attention has focused on this regime, albeit not explicitly as a climate change issue. The model of side payments to compensate Southern states for the forgone benefits of using these chemicals has been important as a precedent for climate change negotiations where common but differentiated responsibilities have been a key principle. The attempts to construct international regimes to deal with climate change, under the auspices of the UNFCCC, have not noticeably slowed, much less reversed, the trajectory of fossil fuel use and the resultant temperature changes in the earth system. Nonetheless, despite repeated international conferences, the annual (until COVID-19 disruptions intervened in 2020) COP to the UNFCCC and dramatic statements by the United Nations Secretary-General (2020) about the imminent dangers of climate change, greenhouse gas emissions continue ever upward.

But mostly, international relations thinking has simply taken the environment for granted as the context for the rivalries of states that are its subject matter, and as such ignores the huge transformations of both natural and human systems currently underway (Burke, Fishel, Mitchell et al. 2016). This is not a new trend; as Lucian Ashworth (2014) has noted, the predecessors to contemporary international thinking mostly overlooked the importance of nineteenth century industrialization and its material consequences. The material context of states, and the contexts their industrial systems are reshaping, need a much more explicit treatment in international relations thinking. Politics and administrative arrangements may indeed shape policy making and institutional innovation, but the larger social contexts, remade by the production processes of the global economy, are key to the current crisis. This requires rethinking what both security and environment might mean in contemporary circumstances.

Hence international relations scholars are mostly not asking the kinds of questions that are needed to reshape the global economy to make it sustainable. Realists assume inevitable power struggles among elites; institutionalists that cooperation may deal with the worst aspects of rivalries. So called constructivists point to the importance of identity in the fault lines that divide peoples and might be used to mobilize support for conflict. But the Anthropocene requires that other analytical priorities get attention, and given the rapidly changing earth system, it implies that security cannot be provided by ever more dominance games between state elites. While the threat of nuclear war has long endangered humanity, now the *firepower* of the contemporary economic system has become an additional urgent global security problem.

If the long term survival of human civilization is of concern, power now has to be reinterpreted in ecological terms and focused on the flourishing of adaptable ecological systems rather than physical domination and the imposition of particular modes of conduct on both humans and what is increasingly inaccurately termed the natural world. This is necessary because both climate change and a rapid reduction of biodiversity in the current global extinction event are upon us. Focusing on both as matters for the distant future has to be replaced by a focus on the urgent and immediate (Rockström and Gaffney 2021). In particular this book emphasizes the urgency of dealing with both: greenhouse gases are accumulating in the atmosphere and "locking in" future heating and hence meteorological disruptions; biodiversity losses are reducing the species available for the future, removing numerous evolutionary possibilities for the planetary system. Decisions made in the immediate future about how to grapple with this context, or failure to do so, will have dramatic long term repercussions.

Related to this is the necessity of realizing that the past is no longer a reliable indication of likely future weather conditions. This assumption of stationarity has to be abandoned; non-stationarity, where the range of likely meteorological conditions in a place can no longer be reliably imputed from historical records, is the new normal (Milly, Betancourt, Falkenmark et al. 2008). Assumptions of climate stability as the backdrop for human affairs cannot be the basis for useful politics. This is about much more than traditional discussions of environmental regulation, international treaties to limit trade or damage to wildlife, pollution standards and other matters under the rubric of global environmental politics. All these remain important, but how they play out in a more dynamic and changeable earth system increasingly shapes the context for future politics, and the rivalries of states as well as corporations. Climate instability, without appropriate social and policy innovations to grapple with these new circumstances, threatens future conflicts, disruptions and much future avoidable human suffering. Greta Thunberg (2019) and her youthful colleagues in the Fridays for Future and Extinction Rebellion (2019) movements understand this even if many of their elders apparently don't.

Thinking about climate change as a pollution problem, and negotiating agreements to constrain emissions, hasn't worked effectively, not least because of the classic notions of free riders and collective action problems. But the larger political struggles are about the future modes of urban life, and extensive consumption that is based on the widespread use of fossil fuels. The inertia in this system is used to legitimize such things as fossil fuel subsidies from governments. Governments would be much better off taxing fossil fuels in the short run and phasing them out in the medium term (Coady, Parry, Sears and Shang 2017). As of 2020 numerous financial institutions had at last begun to wake up to the vulnerabilities of many supply chains to climate disruptions, and simultaneously to the potential of a shift away from fossil fuels towards an economy based on renewables and alternative modes of production, only most obviously such things as hydrogen as a source of heat for industrial processes.

The question of environmental security now is how fast these transitions will happen, because if they don't move ahead quickly then the disruptions to weather systems, water supplies, agriculture and infrastructure will become ever more severe in coming decades. In the process these will increasingly challenge the capabilities of the urban systems, that now house the majority of humanity, to function effectively. The political disruptions set in motion by these difficulties are likely to cause all sorts of security problems in numerous places. Failure to grapple with the causes of these disruptions ensures that, as greenhouse gases accumulate in the atmosphere, the disruptions will get ever larger further into the future. Regardless of how much credence is put in looming tipping points in the earth system (Steffen, Rockström, Richardson et al. 2018), it is clear the earth system or "ecosphere", the complex combination of the atmosphere, cryosphere, lithosphere, hydrosphere and biosphere, is being radically altered by the novel artificial entities that industrial humanity has made, an ensemble of materials and processes now frequently called the technosphere (Donges, Lucht, Müller-Hansen and Steffen 2017). Its future configuration is now key to humanity's prospects, and whether collectively humanity can secure the conditions for our future thriving is precisely the question posed in contemporary discussions of environmental security.

ONLY ONE EARTH

It is important to note that in some ways this isn't a new debate. In the 1970s extensive discussions about environmental problems spilled over into the international arena. The United Nations Conference on the Human Environment (UNCHE) was held in Stockholm in 1972, the same year as the first computer simulations of the earth system were published in *The Limits to Growth* (Meadows, Meadows, Randers and Behrens 1972). The background report for UNCHE, which included a discussion of the technosphere, was called *Only One Earth* (Ward and Dubos 1972), and at least the British version had a NASA picture of the earth on its cover. At the end of the major period of decolonization, discussions of a new international economic order were in the air, and the possibilities of development to rapidly tackle poverty in the former colonies structured much of the international agenda. At least it did in those parts of international politics not preoccupied by the Vietnam war and the dangers of superpower confrontation.

What wasn't clear back then were the precise details of the operation of the earth system, where thresholds might be or whence the greatest dangers to human civilization might lie. Half a century later this contextual information is much clearer, and the decades in-between, when sensible economic arrangements that take ecology seriously might have been put in place, have been squandered. Early concerns about climate change were eclipsed in part by the geopolitical consequences of the Organization of Petroleum Exporting Countries (OPEC) oil embargo following the October 1973 war between Israel and an alliance of Syria and Egypt. The focus on fuel supplies and vulnerabilities replaced much of the concern in Western states about pollution, but it also generated an extensive discussion of how to replace oil as a fuel in modern economies (Lovins 1977).

Tied into this was a confusing academic and political discussion of resources and their shortage, seen in the *Limits to Growth* framework as a constraint on economic growth. Growth, the key focus in so much economic thinking, was, many economists argued, not constrained by shortages of key materials, and erroneous claims on that score by ecologists were used to ridicule the larger concerns about limits on a finite planet. Economic growth, usually understood in terms of Gross National Product (GNP), or sometimes the slightly different formulation of Gross Domestic Product (GDP), was the benchmark measure for progress. Growth was supposedly the solution to the ills of poverty worldwide. Usually environmental concerns, with pollution in particular, were seen as an unnecessary constraint on growth, and in the politics of these matters, appeals to workers in particular industries are made on the grounds that economics is more important than conservation. It is easy to reduce conservation, or environment in these terms, to a matter of affluent peoples' recreation preferences for parks, and then contrast this to the economic necessity of earning a living.

Here the politics of knowledge enters into the discussion, and arguments about who was competent to pronounce on which policy were as much about disciplinary turf as they were about ecological realities. Reduced to an argument about resources, the larger ecological concerns about species elimination, soil depletion, pollution of natural systems and damaged health, not to mention large scale climate destabilization, were often sidelined. As will be seen in the following chapters in this book, which expert discourse frames policy discussion matters greatly, although politics usually trumps the claims of expertise. This is especially the case when notions of national security enter the picture, as in discussions of climate and security in particular and environment and security more generally. Where nationalist politicians wish to brandish military technologies and use fossil fuels as a token of state capability, climate change concerns get short shrift. Likewise in recent years the reproduction of earlier modes of Western security thinking in the claims of a new cold war with China is easy to do, but it distracts attention from the much more serious looming threats of climate disruption (Lieven 2020).

Part of the argument in what follows is about the need to shift the contextualization that frames security thinking to grapple with the novel circumstances that are now clear as a result of the rapid advances in earth system sciences in the last few decades, a matter explored in detail elsewhere (Dalby 2020a, 2020b). But to understand how difficult it is to change the politics of knowledge, and to think through the implications for policy that follow on from a drastic recontextualization of security, it is necessary to revisit some of the earlier debates, about the *Limits to Growth* and the formulations at the UNCHE, to understand their limited efficacy. The intense debates then about growth, pollution, resource shortages and development are now a matter of historical interest mostly, but because the arguments then are precursors to how attempts are being made to deal with the twenty first century ecological crisis, they need renewed attention.

But much of this debate in the 1970s, about environment, resources and new international economic orders (Lean 1978), was forgotten in the early 1980s. The revived cold war contest between the superpowers, when nuclear warfare replaced environmental matters as the primary cause of political anxiety, pushed matters of energy supplies and nuclear power controversies in particular off the policy agenda in the United States and in Europe. Neoliberal arguments about deregulation, public sector spending reductions and a limited state involvement in economic matters beyond key military concerns further worked to displace discussions of existential risks and long term sustainability (Harvey 2005). The New International Economic Order aspirations of the

1970s were also swept aside by the reassertion of corporate power and the militarization of superpower politics.

Many of the contradictions in the *Limits to Growth* debates were elaborately fudged in the 1980s in the establishment of sustainable development as the overarching rhetoric for tackling environmental matters and the appropriation of this by numerous corporate actors apparently more anxious to maintain their power and privilege in the world order than to tackle the consequences of their material status (Chatterjee and Finger 1994). This formulation, articulated in the World Commission on Environment and Development's report *Our Common Future* (1987), was the basis for the 1992 United Nations Conference on Environment and Development (UNCED) "Earth Summit" in Rio de Janeiro which produced the conventions on both climate change and global biodiversity. While these agreements focused on the key issues in rapid changes in the earth system, they didn't generate substantive policy changes in the years that followed.

Crucially for the argument in the following pages, *Our Common Future* premised the necessary conditions for sustainable development as a matter of dealing with issues of "environmental insecurity", to use the phrasing that structured much of its text. Without those necessary conditions sustainable development wasn't likely to be successful, but if it were successful it would in turn provide environmental security for the future. Conflict, and the dangers of nuclear war in particular, was highlighted as a major obstacle to the achievement of environmental security; the money wasted on weapons would, the report's authors argued, be much better spent on development, health care and ecological restoration.

Sustainable development also provides the overarching rhetorical framework for the 2015 Sustainable Development Goals (SDGs), widely adopted as the policy desiderata for the United Nations system, but which present numerous contradictory projects and don't resolve many of the difficulties of contemporary global governance (Dalby, Horton, Mahon and Thomaz 2019). This series of aspirational goals and multiple subsidiary policy targets do, despite being contradictory in key places, nonetheless set out a framework for a desirable future for all of humanity. To provide the conditions necessary for their achievement however requires rethinking both climate change strategies and the global problem of species extinction that are reducing the options for the future quite drastically. Environmental security requires addressing all these if the aspirations expressed by the SDGs are to be reached, if not by the target date of 2030, then soon after.

The current trajectories of fossil fueled economic activity imperil many things that are necessary for future environmental security. The massive accumulation of wealth on the part of a small part of humanity is now the key to the destruction and the endangerment of peoples in many marginal environments.

Consumption drives both climate change and the rapidly accelerating extinction crisis. This is so both because, directly, the extraction activities required to appropriate resources lead to the destruction of habitats and, indirectly, processes are set in motion by ecological disruption, only most obviously climate change, which can lead to very grave long term dangers arising from ocean acidification caused by excess carbon dioxide being absorbed from the atmosphere. Bluntly put, contemporary patricians are accumulating wealth at the expense of much of the human population (Piketty 2014), and are playing consumption status games at the cost of the impoverishment of plebeians more or less everywhere. Highlighted by the responses of the rich to the perils of COVID-19, mostly escaping its direct impacts and using the crisis for further enrichment, this pattern of wealth accumulation suggests forcefully that this mode of economy is unsustainable. It also suggests that the security of the very rich comes at the cost of impoverishment and vulnerability for many others; hence the now extensive discussion of matters of climate justice.

Putting all this together suggests an analysis that links four themes. First, environmental security is an aspirational discourse, aspiring to a future that is a sustainable ecological context for humanity. This is in doubt because of military and political efforts that endanger it by a focus on economic expansion and the forceful preservation of this trajectory in the name of national security. The trajectories of the last few centuries have already disrupted and destroyed numerous peoples and their habitats; environmental security hasn't been supplied for them (Grove 2019). Now the question is for whom can it be supplied in coming decades, and whether a liveable planet in perpetuity, the implicit goal in most of this discussion, can be shaped by policy actions and economic change in coming decades.

To reach this goal of a liveable planet, second, careful analysis of the earth system, humanity's place in it, and how it has changed in the past and is now being rapidly transformed is necessary. So too is an investigation of how the contemporary changes are related to past human actions and the colonization of ecological niches by an expanding humanity, a species that has uniquely adopted the use of fire to change key parameters in the earth system. Focusing on this generates, third, considerable anxiety about contemporary and future threats to the human enterprise, and these need careful contextualization to understand the causes of human insecurity. Having appropriate responses to these anxieties clearly requires, fourth, advocacy of sensible economic, security and ecological policies to generate a sustainable ecosphere as humanity's habitat in future. Political strategies for achieving this end are also an unavoidable part of any serious discussion of the future of environmental security.

THE BOOK

To work through these four interconnected themes the book is organized into eight chapters with each two chapters roughly focused on, in turn, traditional notions of security which contrast with aspirations for a sustainable earth, analysis of the earth system, anxieties about ecological dangers and, finally, advocacy for a secure human future.

The rationale for this volume, and the context of rethinking issues of our common future half a century after the first UNCHE, is set out in this introduction. The urgency for addressing these matters is now unquestioned, but how to reframe matters is far from easy to articulate effectively for scholars of international studies and others in the social sciences.

Chapter 1 starts with questions of security which are at the heart of contemporary international relations thinking. While much of the recent literature focuses on regimes, interdependence, hegemony, constructivism and related matters, at the heart of the international relations enterprise historically have been questions of great powers, their rivalries, the causes and consequences of inter-state warfare and, in the aftermath of the invention of nuclear weapons, how inter-state rivalries and the larger questions of world order can be addressed to prevent the global catastrophe of major nuclear war. Aggression has to be deterred, and nuclear risks managed by the architecture of international order to tackle the self-imposed existential risk to humanity, that of massive technological devastation to the whole planet by the unleashing of nuclear firepower. But now another series of self-imposed existential risks are looming, caused as a consequence of the success of other forms of firepower, the successful manipulation of combustion to power modern societies. Climate change is now a matter of security too, and international relations thinking needs an overhaul to deal with this new category of threat.

Chapter 2 tackles the precursors to the current discussion, first in terms of the rise of environmental concerns in the 1960s and 1970s in the West, crystallized in the 1972 UNCHE with its influential conference statements as well as the debate around the contemporaneous *Limits to Growth*. In parallel there was a discussion in the international relations literature on how to grapple with these emergent issues, one that has potential for informing current debates, but which was then at best a marginal contribution to the international relations discipline. Subsequent sections in the chapter outline the follow on discussion in the 1980s leading to the publication of *Our Common Future*, the debate around the UNCED and the emergence of environmental security as a focal point in the discussions of post-cold war security issues. The sustainable development rhetoric structured the United Nations development goals a quarter of a century later, just as earth systems science was charting in detail the scale of ecological transformations.

These insights into earth history and the place of humanity in the earth systems require a more fundamental rethinking of categories such as environment, the topic of Chapter 3. The earth is a much more dynamic place than is frequently recognized, and this requires both a reassessment of the premises in environmental thought and a recognition that humanity is now, as a result of its appropriation of processes of combustion, a key geophysical player in the future configuration of planetary systems. Firepower is the key here; the ability to do ignition in numerous modes lies at the heart of technological innovation that has remade both humanity and the planet, facilitating numerous human endeavours while simultaneously generating new dangers in the remade geographies humans now inhabit.

Which also requires us to look much more closely in Chapter 4 at the history of human colonization and the legacy of imperialism and capitalism in shaping the global rivalries of international relations and the structures of security that now confront disruptive global changes. Given this legacy of imperial rivalries, the formulations of security that aim to perpetuate these unsustainable ways of life are easily seen as part of the problem. The expansion of colonization and the extension of commercial arrangements into rural areas disrupts both traditional social patterns and ecologies. In the process the violence on the colonial frontier comes into focus as a key dimension of environmental insecurity. The implicit imperial premises in this need more explicit attention in the literature on environmental security, because the transformation of nature into property is key to modernity.

As Chapter 5 indicates, these patterns of theory and administrative practice are the lenses through which much of the discussion of resources, conflict, security and sustainability are viewed, and may be singularly unhelpful in tackling the major threats of our times. The case of Syria and the possible role of climate change in causing its civil war has garnered much attention, but the situation there suggests that climate was much less important than maldevelopment. Crucially both the biodiversity and climate crises require a reconsideration of modernity and its assumptions of humanity as apart from nature rather than part of a nature that industrial systems are rapidly changing. Likewise the implicit geopolitical categories in the rapidly proliferating discourse of climate security often focus on symptoms rather than causes, and as such narrowly constrain policy options while focusing on military matters. Contrasting endangered, entangled and extractivist views of the world highlights the implicit representations of the world that shape security policy discourse.

Chapter 6 looks at matters of threats to climate, biodiversity loss, pandemics and other existential threats facing humanity, including the persistent dangers of nuclear warfare and related modes of extremely destructive human activities which conventional notions of national security in particular have mostly aggravated in recent decades rather than ameliorated. The contrast with the policy formulations that have emerged in terms of the financial risks implied by climate change to the global economy is noteworthy in terms of what is endangered. At the largest scale, which matters most in terms of environmental security, the key question is whether contemporary trajectories will lead to societal collapse, or whether a rapid reorganization of the global economy to rapidly reduce the use of fossil fuels will avoid this outcome.

Persisting with attempts to use technological modes of intervention as a response to these threats frequently leads, Chapter 7 shows, to discussions of geoengineering and attempts to use force to reshape at least parts of the planetary system. In contrast whole earth security understands the interconnections between ecologies and human habitats as the essential framework for living appropriately within the vulnerable context of a fragile planet. Whereas Chapter 5 deals with the contrasting perspectives of endangered, entangled and extractivist worlds, this chapter looks to the debates about a future engineered world, one of geoengineering, and the potential security implications of these novel geopolitical possibilities. An alternative focus on ecology and the flourishing of ecosystems, as in regenerative agriculture and permaculture modes of food production, suggests possibilities for living within nature, inhabiting the world rather than exploiting it, a matter of taking eco-security, in Chinese terms, seriously.

Finally Chapter 8 thinks through the contemporary debates about how to rework security and policies of peacemaking and peacebuilding as an alternative series of activities that may foster a flourishing ecosphere, the key necessity for any notion of long term environmental security, but a notion substantially removed from traditional international relations thinking focused on either the rivalries of great powers or the institutional arrangements of trading and regulatory regimes in a liberal order. National security understood in these terms is anathema to flourishing societies in the long run, but rethinking security now requires confronting these implicit assumptions quite directly. Taking ecology at various scales seriously requires nothing less than rethinking assumptions of force controlling territory as the basis of security.

The conclusion offers some reflections on the links between international relations and these novel formulations and the need to escape narrow disciplinary modes of thought and policy formulations if environmental security is to be rethought in the comprehensive terms that present circumstances urgently require.

1. Realism, firepower and insecurity

INTERNATIONAL RELATIONS

In the 1930s in Britain E.H. Carr (1939) pondered the causes of the First World War and many other wars that European states had been plagued with over the previous few centuries. His book, *The Twenty Years' Crisis*, which contained his ruminations on the failures of international politics and the catastrophe of war, is often conveniently looked to by international relations scholars, anxious to provide undergraduates with a simple potted history of the discipline, as one of the founding texts of the field. Coupled with Hans Morgenthau's (1948) *Politics Among Nations: The Struggle for Power and Peace* published a decade later on the other side of the Atlantic, these texts are the core of the so called realist interpretations of international politics. Supposedly these analyses debunk the naïve hopes of idealists that international cooperation, peaceful norms and global institutions can provide material security for citizens and states. Power in the form of military and economic capabilities is the ultimate arbiter, and security must be sought in these terms.

These canonical disciplinary statements about the fate of humanity suggested that we are always in danger of conflict. Power promised peace but frequently led to conflict; this is the tragedy of the human condition that can at best be managed to minimize the damage, but never entirely eliminated as the ontological condition of human being. How then, these thinkers pondered, might security be achieved in a world of rival powers and mutual suspicion, plagued by politicians seeking for primacy first and foremost, and in the process creating security dilemmas (Herz 1950)? What role might international agreements and organizations play, and how might peace be maintained as some states grow in strength and ambition while others fall into decline? All of which became much more complicated in 1945 when American nuclear weapons destroyed Hiroshima and Nagasaki and threatened to wreak havoc in future wars (Mandelbaum 1981) or, perhaps, to make future wars unthinkable precisely because the sheer scale of that likely havoc required cooperation in the interests of common survival.

The intellectual history of international relations is of course much more complicated than these simple renditions of realism and idealism that conveniently organize matters for undergraduate textbooks (Ashworth 2014). But one key theme that is fundamental to this concerns the questions of war, peace and the survival of states. Nuclear weapons posed these questions in stark terms. In the period of the cold war, in Western states security was linked to these dangers, the sheer destructive power of nuclear weapons demanding attention from scholars, policy makers and the growing ranks of think tank employees applying new models of social science to numerous problems of the modern human condition. In the case of warfare, the irony that the firepower that supposedly provided security had suddenly also become the source of existential danger presented all sorts of dilemmas encapsulated by the phrasing of the standoff between the superpower arsenals in the cold war as a matter of mutually assured destruction. The British journal established as the flagship for the Institute of International and Strategic Studies in London was for good reason simply and aptly named *Survival*.

The dangers of an overabundance of firepower, the ability to incinerate and radiate large parts of the civilized world, loomed over international politics throughout the period of the cold war, a four decade long period of dangerous standoff between the Soviet Union and the United States. Obliteration became possible in a matter of hours once intercontinental ballistic missiles with nuclear warheads populated the arsenals of those superpowers. The possibilities of misunderstanding, accident or just bad luck leading to the use of these weapons preoccupied thinkers on security for much of those four decades, and shaped the discourse of the discipline that emerged as international relations, with its core elements focused on "strategic" or "security" studies. This discourse also functioned as a mode of coordination for policy discussions in the Western alliance, a mode of knowledge that shaped how it was possible to think about security, and reinforced American hegemony in the process (Klein 1995).

That the Soviet Union was an expansionist power was mostly taken for granted in the "West", and strategies of deterrence to militarily contain its ambitions were the logical corollary (Leffler 1984). That Soviet planners, reflecting on the history of the first half of the twentieth century, might assume that capitalism was inherently war prone, and that in the event of further hostilities Western powers might yet again invade its territory, and hence they should plan accordingly, was only rarely taken seriously in Western strategic thinking (MccGwire 1987). The superpower standoff ended at the end of the 1980s and the Soviet Union dissolved in a relatively peaceful transition in 1991, an eventuality more or less unforeseen by the international relations field prior to the event. But the lessons that were taken from this event were mostly articulated in narratives of Western success. Apparently George Kennan's long telegram strategy dating from the 1940s (X 1947), advocating a patient exercise in containment, had paid off; strength and nuclear deterrence were vindicated and, as he predicted, the Soviet Union had disintegrated because of its own internal contradictions.

Subsequent developments have added numerous additional themes to international relations. The period of superpower détente in the 1970s suggested that complex interdependence and the international regimes that structured these arrangements constituted a key theme in understanding geopolitics and the role of hegemony in maintaining order among states. International economics too became increasingly important both in terms of development and international trade theories, and as the cold war gave way to what was soon named the era of globalization, political economy featured more prominently. Much of this literature took the environmental context within which the great game of states was played for granted, although the rise of concerns with global environmental issues, perhaps most obviously the discovery of the depletion of stratospheric ozone in the 1980s, led to the development of global environmental politics as a theme in international relations too (Hoffman 2005). But while it has become a thriving subdiscipline, highlighted by papers in the journal *Global Environmental Politics* and the MIT Press book series on the theme, the topic is much less obviously present in the mainstream journals of the discipline. That said, it is important to note too that climate change is about much more than what is conventionally understood as environmental politics (Goldstein 2016). Likewise the global extinction crisis.

Mostly, during the cold war, these concerns with security, weapons, strategy and geopolitics were studied by men. The gendered dimensions of both the practice of international politics and how it was studied drove scholars in the later stages of the cold war to investigate how power works in these modes too (Cohn 1987). The practices of security were tackled from much more critical perspectives focused on the ironies that the provision of security so frequently left people and regimes in states of insecurity. Voices from the Global South, and marginalized peoples in the North, insisted that the whole edifice of international relations needed to be decolonized to recognize that the great powers were edifices of empire and the world order has been shaped profoundly by the colonization practices of European and subsequently American power. International relations was, as Stanley Hoffman (1977) asserted, mostly an American discipline. Extending Klein's (1995) point, it is not too large a stretch to suggest that international relations as an intellectual enterprise effectively is the conceptual infrastructure of the liberal order established by American power in the cold war period.

The failure to anticipate the rapid peaceful end to the cold war nuclear standoff remains a black mark on the intellectual trajectory of a discipline that purports to provide policy advice to all and sundry concerning the appropriate measures to be taken by states to provide security. Regardless, humanity survived a very dangerous few decades where the possibilities of nuclear annihilation had loomed over all policy decisions and the dangers of firepower in its most concentrated form threatened the end of civilization. However the lessons that were frequently not learned concerned the dangers of accidental nuclear war and the narrow escapes in the most dangerous episodes during the cold war, only most obviously the Cuba crisis in 1962 (Sherwin 2020), the alerts in 1973 in the October war in the Middle East, and the Able Archer exercise a decade later in 1983. Assumptions of dominance and the ability to control events imputed a rationality to the cold war that these episodes suggest were more about luck.

Rather than recognize these dangers, after the Soviet Union collapsed American policy makers, in particular, framed the results as a victory for the West. The reassertion of military capabilities in the first Gulf war, viewed as an overcoming of the Vietnam Syndrome, where American interventions in the Global South had been constrained because of the failures to prosecute the Vietnam intervention to a successful conclusion, led to the use of force in various places in the 1990s and, after the events of 9/11, a remilitarization of American security thinking (Bacevich 2013). Where NATO had mostly been on the defensive, at least in Europe during the cold war, and arguably successful precisely because it had been (Lieven 2021), initial promises to Soviet and then Russian leaders as the cold war ended that NATO would not expand eastward were quickly forgotten. The subsequent accession of Eastern European states to the alliance eventually fed into renewed confrontation with Russia as its policy makers feared American encroachment in what they understood to be their sphere of interest (Toal 2017). While the Warsaw Pact dissolved, NATO did not. Nuclear deterrence remains as the bedrock doctrine of Western security; dominance and threats of extreme violence undergird the political arrangements of international politics.

Lost in this were some of the insights in the 1980s in the Soviet Union "New Thinking" on security that nuclear weapons were simply too dangerous to use as the basis of a security strategy (MccGwire 1991). The corollary that international cooperation and novel security arrangements were needed was swept aside and realist assumptions of the inevitability of force in human affairs and the specification of the world as a dangerous place in need of, at least the threat of, American violence to maintain order were reasserted in the global war on terror and the subsequent formulations of a rapidly growing Chinese economy as a threat in need of containment. The geopolitical logic of rivalries continues to feed into arms races, and the never ending technological innovations by the military industrial complex that retiring President Eisenhower warned against in his farewell speech in 1961. Security this obviously isn't if the safety and well-being of ordinary citizens in numerous places is what matters, but security in terms of maintaining American control of much of the world it just might be. Nuclear firepower undergirds this international arrangement. So too does the widespread use of fossil fuels.

FIREPOWER

But now some decades after the end of the cold war, firepower once again, in a different form this time, threatens the future survival of contemporary civilization. This time the dangers of firepower come both directly in some places in terms of the rising incidence of wildfire, and indirectly from the byproduct of the routine use of fire, mostly in the form of the combustion of fossil fuels (Dalby 2018). Climate change is accelerating and destabilizing many of the ecological and geographical contexts within which contemporary civilization operates, and in the process endangering people in numerous places, albeit mostly indirectly. Should contemporary trajectories not change soon, they are potentially leading to major runaway accelerations as natural positive feedbacks kick in, and in the worst case scenarios these may lead to an end of civilization itself, a matter of *Collapse* in Jared Diamond's (2005) terms. In popular literature the question as to whether runaway climate change might indeed lead to the extinction of our own species has sounded alarm bells, notably in David Wallace-Wells' *New York Magazine* article in 2017 that garnered much attention when he posited the possibility of a future earth rendered uninhabitable by human actions.

Over the last few decades a large literature has grown on many of these themes, under the umbrella term "environmental security" from the 1980s onwards. Recently this has morphed into a focus on climate security more specifically, and concerns that climate change is a cause of conflict has generated a series of research projects on the fringes of the international relations discipline. In 2020 this sense of environmental insecurity was suddenly added to by a focus on other related dangers of biodiversity loss and habitat disruption once the vulnerability of humans to novel zoonotic diseases was made unavoidably clear by the COVID-19 pandemic. The palpable failures of security planning on the part of many states to render their populations safe from the dangers of disease highlight the vulnerabilities of people to dangers in an interconnected world (Dalby 2020a, 2022). The policy debate about how to rebuild disrupted economies after the pandemic has subsided has once again linked environmental matters with development thinking, and highlighted both the 2015 adoption of the Sustainable Development Goals (SDGs) and the subsequent Paris Agreement on Climate Change (Falkner 2016). Now climate security looms as an overarching threat to the future of civilization even though the core themes of the international relations discipline have been slow to engage these dangers.

The argument in what follows in the rest of this book takes these points about the failure of firepower to provide the security that its technological innovations so frequently promised and uses them to rethink the context for both security studies and the practical application of its modes of thought to policy making in the international system. The focus now on environment, climate, habitat disruption, ocean acidification and related matters requires a rethink of the contextual assumptions that underlie international relations. The historical analogies with previous episodes are far from exact replications of present circumstances, but the argument in what follows suggests that there are enough commonalties to offer a novel way of thinking about both environment and security.

Especially in the case of climate change, increasingly rapid changes are already happening, and while many militaries, including the American one, are well aware of the likely consequences, the warnings about rapid destabilizing change that they have been issuing since the middle of the 2000s are only beginning, as of 2021, to penetrate either the corporate boardrooms of major finance and investment institutions or the political forums where major decisions are made about industrial and energy policy. In the years since the Paris Agreement on Climate Change in 2015 this has begun to change, but the overarching "extractivist" assumptions of an external world to be used to provide resources for ever larger modes of economic activity, and as a repository for its wastes, have yet to effectively grapple with the insights of earth system science which make it clear that the earth is a much more dynamic and fragile system than the hegemonic modern assumptions of it as a taken for granted substrate for human actions have long assumed (Rockström and Gaffney 2021).

The implicit assumption of a quiescent earth that underlies modernity's quest for security is no longer tenable, but planetary social thought is relatively novel, and as yet not integrated into the much more profound rethinking that is urgently needed in the new circumstances of the Anthropocene (Clark and Szerszynski 2021). In historical perspective this is ironic given that one of the key events in European history that set in motion some fundamental reconsiderations of the human condition, and freed much critical thinking from the formerly theological frameworks, was the huge Lisbon earthquake of 1755. This disaster forced a fundamental reconsideration of the role of natural events in the human condition, and as Carol Dumaine (2021) notes in her arguments for a similar dramatic reconsideration of the modes of security thinking in light of the COVID-19 pandemic, now once again catastrophe should stimulate a reconsideration of the practical conditions for both human safety and state survival. Whatever the earth may be, it is not quiescent.

At the heart of these issues are some fundamental themes about the human condition, and crucially how scholars and policy makers think about the human context, many of these themes being related to the ambiguities implicit in the human appropriation of firepower in quests for security. Like the sorcerer's apprentice, some sections of humanity have gained a partial ability to control the powerful forces of combustion, but lack of foresight and limited skill have unloosed these forces in ways that may yet lead to our immolation. Avoiding that fate is now the necessary task in rethinking environmental security. No longer can assumptions of environment as a stable backdrop to human affairs be used as the basis of international relations thinking (Dalby 2020b); the novel material circumstances of what is now called the Anthropocene require new modes of thought about security and international politics.

The surface of the earth has long been convulsed by earthquakes, volcanoes and the occasional meteor strike. The climate has flipped rapidly from one configuration to another in the past, especially in the highly changeable period immediately prior to the remarkably stable one, the Holocene in geological science parlance, of the last twelve thousand years. What is new in all this, captured in the term Anthropocene, the age of humans, is that the scale of human activity is now, in its consequences for how the earth system operates, akin to the celestial mechanics that have until recently determined the climate's configuration (Lewis and Maslin 2018). Now humanity, and its proclivity for burning things, has taken on the role of deciding the future configuration of the climate. In fire historian Steven Pyne's (2021) terms, we have shed the ice ages and are now in the fire age, what he suggests we call the Pyrocene.

These new circumstances require rethinking many things, including the relationship between fire and security. But to formulate these new modes of thought requires an understanding of both the implicit assumptions in the traditional modes and the contradictions that have made security both an essential concept in modern modes of political conduct and one that simultaneously encompasses the dilemmas that comprise contemporary geopolitics and supposedly offers the ultimate political desideratum, safety from many dangers.

SECURITY AND ITS DILEMMAS

In a world divided into multiple states, which are the entities that supposedly provide security but find themselves in rivalries with each other, preparing to protect one's own state from rivals, whose capabilities and intentions are obscure, is always in danger of causing suspicion among rivals, and responses in turn to build further capabilities. The dilemma lies in that in preparing to protect oneself one triggers responses elsewhere (Herz 1950). This in turn appears threatening and hence requires further preparations which in turn confirm in the minds of potential antagonists that you are dangerous and need to be countered. Rivalry among polities can frequently give rise to this dynamic, and a history of prior conflict can feed resentment on the part of losers and a desire to redress the losses imposed by a previous peace settlement. So too the obvious political utility of having an antagonist to both blame for difficulties and mobilize against in a crisis can aggravate these dynamics.

In the twentieth century in particular, security dilemmas were tied into the rapid pace of technical innovation (Buzan 1991). In the decade prior to the First World War the naval arms race between Germany and Britain was accelerated by the arrival of the new Dreadnought class battleships, and the emergence of long range submarines as a novel mode of naval action. The emergence of tanks changed how land warfare was to be fought and the swift introduction of air forces and tactical innovations in their use led to a rapid extension of the speed, range and capabilities of airplanes. In the aftermath of the Second World War the extension of air power, nuclear weapons, missiles capable of intercontinental ranges and nuclear powered submarines that could remain submerged for weeks accelerated the capabilities of military forces and in each case forced the development of countermeasures in a constant ratcheting up of firepower in new configurations. Fear of "the other side" getting an overwhelming advantage because of a technological innovation drove this arms race in a perpetual escalation that could never accomplish a state of security in terms of a permanent decisive advantage.

The temptations to pre-empt in a situation where a rival is growing in power and the opportunity for a military attempt to stop their ascendance may be limited in time also apply in these situations of rivalry. Realist scholarship usually refers to Thucydides in these situations, and to his account of the fear evoked in Sparta by the growing power of Athens as a cause of the Peloponnesian war. This argument has been reworked in recent years by American scholars wondering about the implications of China's recent growth, and the challenge that presents to America's hegemony (Allison 2017). In a world of rapid technological change and scientific innovation, not only is the number of weapons and potential combatants an issue, but the changing capabilities of the weapons—their range, destructive power, accuracy and control systems—also plays on fears that "the other side" may gain a decisive technological advantage.

Assumptions of the role of states in these arrangements also draw on a theme highlighted by Thomas Hobbes where the ruler of a state has an implicit, and sometimes fairly explicit, obligation to provide safety for subjects as the price of their loyalty. The provision of order internally is connected to the need to prepare to defend the realm too, although modern states have usually nuanced this arrangement so that policing is a matter of domestic security within boundaries and military preparations and actions are concerned with external threats and the dangers of the use of armed force in the case of an insurrection. These divisions are never absolute, and subversion, espionage and interference in the internal affairs of one state by another, or by international non-state actors, have blurred these distinctions frequently. But nonetheless the basic assumptions of liberal order are of independent states where citizens look to their own affairs, a matter of territorial sovereignty in which freedom resides within states (Jackson 2000).

In addition to this basic set of geographical arrangements at the heart of the formal thinking about security there are multiple international relationships, alliances, treaties and informal rules of the road for militaries and diplomats. The United Nations in theory at least provides an overarching structure to all this and a forum to prevent conflict, or attenuate it should it occur. Implicit in the United Nations system is the clear understanding that aggressive war is illegal, and that while national defence is permitted, the use of other forms of military action is not unless it is authorized by the United Nations, and the Security Council in particular. As a measure to facilitate conflict resolution, and provide a face saving invocation of authority greater than that of a state ruler, it has considerable utility, even if, as so often is the case, these rules are circumvented. That said it is noteworthy that the decision making body in the United Nations is called the Security Council and not the Peace Council and the permanent members of the body that have a veto over its decisions are the five major nuclear weapons states.

But there is much more to these notions of security than these ideal case formulations encompass. The history of nation states is relatively recent, and many states, those specified in many textbooks as great powers, are much more obviously empires than something resembling a clear national population living on a discrete territory. Powerful states project power far from their boundaries, and navies in particular often range far afield, while military interventions abroad and the stationing of troops in both hostile territory and allied countries happens in numerous complex arrangements. In Barry Buzan and Ole Wæver's (2003) terms there are numerous geographical "security complexes" in the current world system, with overlays of force projection by larger powers over smaller ones providing forms of political order, or at least enforcing tacit arrangements in particular places. Clearly the cold war liberal order in parts of the world, and its extension to much of the rest of the world in the aftermath of the collapse of the Soviet Union, has long been undergirded by series of military arrangements that provide a form of order, if not security, in many parts of the world (Latham 1997).

While this might be understood as an overarching imperial order, these intersecting security complexes are in many places fraught and at best only temporarily stable. This order, which makes simple assumptions of autonomous territorial states as the basis of the system untenable, has been underpinned by American military might since the end of the Second World War. This is the only organized military force capable of operating around the globe. Matters are confused when this is understood, as it usually is in the United States, as a matter of American "national security". The origins of this formulation come from the 1940s, and while American forces were involved in fighting the Axis powers, American planners were thinking about the future world order and how to shape it so that no obvious future contender for world power could endanger American security once again as the Japanese had done in 1941 (Leffler 1984). To prevent the emergence of a peer competitor it seemed an American military presence and a series of alliances in Asia and Europe would be needed along with a system of bases to rapidly move American air power, in particular to distant places.

With this went the need for much more detailed information about the states and societies in these regions as well as the economic resources to be found around the world which might be put to use by American corporations anxious to expand their reach after the war. Likewise those planners thinking about the political order for the post war years were anxious to ensure that the disastrous economic downturns of the great depression, part of the cause of the rise of Nazi power in Europe, didn't recur. The Bretton Woods system of international financial arrangements likewise was constructed as the basis of a trading order, and one with international arrangements in terms of the World Bank and the International Monetary Fund dominated by American interests to oversee financial stability among members of that nascent liberal order. In Panitch and Gindin's (2012) terms these arrangements made the world safe for capitalism and in the process enhanced the power of American business in that world.

Underpinning this system, although frequently simply taken for granted, was the growing importance of petroleum as the energy source to keep everything moving (Yergin 2011). The rapid mobilization of the American and to a lesser extent the Canadian economies in the Second World War to provide huge amounts of war material, and vast numbers of vehicles and airplanes, changed the transportation systems and gave rise to modern logistics, tying trading and technology together in new long distance relationships. The subsequent post war rise of American style consumer societies, and the rapid spread of the necessary technology and the ubiquitous and iconic symbol of that lifestyle, the individually owned automobile, was mostly fueled by gasoline. Subsequently earth system science has dubbed this period the beginning of the great acceleration (McNeill and Engelke 2016), a doubly apt designation given the speed of economic expansion based on this new mode of individual locomotion. To keep it all moving petroleum supplies had to be secured, and as later chapters will explain in more detail, this was to have profound geopolitical effects. American national security was tied into the global political economy of petroleum in numerous important matters, and subsequently into military adventures in the Middle East.

One other crucial innovation matters in this period. As the Second World War ended and confrontations with the Soviet Union morphed into what was soon called the cold war, American military planners realized that they needed to know much more about what was now a global arena of potential conflict. Submarine warfare in both the Atlantic and the Pacific had extended the range of naval operations. Likewise the rapid expansion of the American Air Force and its new global system of bases raised questions of global weather patterns, and the finer points of atmospheric conditions for long range aircraft. The advent of nuclear weapons also raised matters of global geophysics, and as nuclear testing in the atmosphere revealed the interconnected nature of the atmosphere, with radioactive fallout being tracked round the globe (Masco 2015), as well as the importance of the ozone layer and the potential of the ionosphere for radio communications, scientific enquiry into the atmosphere and hydrosphere rapidly expanded as the military tried to learn as much as it could about its new arenas of operation. In scientific terms all this led to an emergent sense of globality, of the world as a series of interconnected realms (van Munster and Sylvest 2016).

The possibilities of using those environments as part of their combat operations, and of weaponizing natural systems, as well as learning to fight in extreme environments, was all part of the expansion of these new agendas, and an integral part of American cold war culture with its fascination with technology and futuristic visions (Farish 2010). Large scale weather modification possibilities and thinking through the use of nuclear explosives for massive engineering operations were part of this research agenda. The advent of intercontinental ballistic missiles and the use of orbital satellites for military reconnaissance extended further both the capabilities for understanding the earth system and the abilities to monitor changes. Computation and the development of digital data collection and processing capabilities fed into all this too, linking sensors and modelling together intimately (Edwards 2010). Weather satellites are now taken for granted and the use of their data in climate modelling is a key part of contemporary science, but all this has its origins in cold war research and these connections are morphing once again in the contemporary discussions of the possibilities of geoengineering technologies as a mode of dealing with rapidly accelerating climate change (Surprise 2020).

The apotheosis of this expansion of American military reach happened in the aftermath of the events of 9/11 when a global war on terror was launched by the Bush administration. In parallel the combatant commands map was once again updated, this time to include Antarctica so that the whole earth system was now incorporated into the remit of American military operations. Crucial to all this is the ability to surveil distant places as a potential preliminary to military action. The whole world is potentially a battle space, one that in the planning documents of the US military distinguishes geographical regions partly in terms of their distance from the homeland, with the assumption in the war on terror that peripheral locations and failed states were the primary source of potential danger (Dalby 2009a). That has more recently given way to higher priority being paid to China and Russia as potential military antagonists, but these mappings of danger, and the implicit assumption that the environment is an external entity to be monitored, technologically dominated and controlled in the extension of military power to provide "security" to the American homeland, constitute a powerful and persistent set of epistemological practices. These modes of knowing the world have also shaped how climate change came to be a matter of concern too (Allan 2017), and they now shape much of the discussion about environmental security.

NUCLEAR REALISM

In parallel with the expansion of American power and the extension of its reach into all parts of the world and into orbital space too, numerous critics were alarmed by the scale of the weapons systems and the cavalier attitude to nuclear risks. As the arsenals rapidly increased in the 1950s, alarm about the dangers of nuclear technologies and weapons in particular accelerated. The British too built nuclear weapons and in the process generated a reaction most notably in the form of the Campaign for Nuclear Disarmament with its annual protest walks to the Atomic Weapons Research Establishment at Aldermaston and its campaign to "ban the bomb" with its iconic peace symbol.

Nuclear anxiety arose both from the immediate dangers of warfare and from the numerous above ground tests of nuclear devices that the superpowers conducted in the 1950s. The enormous destructive power of the thermonuclear weapons, the largest of which dwarfed the destructive capabilities of the bombs used on Hiroshima and Nagasaki, raised alarms. If even a small part of the rapidly growing arsenals were to be used in a war, then the destruction would obviously be so large and the indirect disruption of economies and societies so widespread that the successful continuation of these economies and societies was highly doubtful. The destruction of Pacific atolls used as testing grounds and the suffering of the local residents forcefully removed and subjected to radioactive fallout downwind of the explosions foreshadowed a much larger series of potential future catastrophes (Masco 2015). They also emphasized the fate of indigenous peoples whose islands have been occupied by foreign military power in the Pacific just as national independence movements were dismantling the former European empires in Asia and Africa. Fears of nuclear fallout and the illnesses from radiation and cancers were encapsulated in popular culture in various mediums, from *Godzilla* to Nevil Shute's ruminations about the last surviving humans after a nuclear war in his novel *On the Beach*.

With the emergence of intercontinental missiles and submarine based missile systems, as well as long range bombers, a situation of mutually assured destruction ensued. While nuclear strategists argued over the finer points of how these systems might be used, and conflicts in some sense won, more level headed commentators realized that this wasn't war as traditionally understood but something akin to a doomsday situation. Mutually assured destruction wasn't security in any meaningful sense, however many theorists of deterrence argued that the threat actually maintained something called peace. Intellectual notables in the 1950s including Lewis Mumford, Albert Einstein and Bertrand Russell argued against the deployment of nuclear devices, suggesting that their enormous firepower was simply too great to be gambled with given the destruction that would result should they actually be used (van Munster and Sylvest 2014). The possibilities of error and assumptions of rational control of the weapons should hostilities commence were, they argued, such that it simply wasn't realistic to gamble with these systems. Hence another form of realism, one which demanded that security for all humans be supplied in the form of disarmament so that no combination of accident and miscalculation, much less deliberate aggression, could endanger the survival of humanity.

The sense of an endangered world, due to the enormous potential destructive power of this novel technology, shaped much of the discussion about global affairs, at least in NATO countries including the United States. As noted above, Soviet thinking, influenced by Leninist formulations, was very concerned about the inherent tendencies to expansion, crisis and conflict that plagued capitalist states and their empires in the first half of the twentieth century. The Soviets were mostly concerned with their own survival, and maintaining some form of socialism should another major war eventuate, and built weapons systems designed so that they would not lose a war should it happen (MccGwire 1991). This involved plans to capture Western Europe to prevent an American beachhead on the continent, but those plans looked immensely threatening when viewed from Washington.

Thus misperception and the security dilemma raised the stakes in the cold war standoff until the reappraisal of Soviet thinking in the 1980s. Then Soviet "New Thinking" revised the Leninist interpretation of long term historical trajectories and concluded that a political rapprochement with the United States was possible in a world where the contradictions of global capitalism didn't necessarily any longer presage inevitable wars. Subsequently the dissolution of the Soviet Union obscured the fact that this was what had happened. Instead many American interpretations invoked a triumphalist narrative of victory. This in turn then vindicated the continuation of the American search for technological dominance in strategic affairs and perpetuated the implicit geopolitical assumptions of external dangers to a supposedly peaceful American order (Bacevich 2010).

Part of the Soviet New Thinking in the 1980s included a focus on environment and the need to take it seriously as part of the larger ambit of security. These ideas were introduced in the United Nations in 1987 and reiterated in international discussions (Timoshenko 1992). In part this too was related to the Soviet reconsiderations of global geopolitics. The explosion of the Chernobyl reactor in 1986 emphasized the vulnerabilities of contemporary nuclear technologies. A military strategy involving attempts to occupy Western Europe, something that could not be contemplated without major combat operations in a region that is home to hundreds of reactors, looked increasingly dangerous. It was hard to imagine a war scenario in Europe that left most of the reactors intact and, given prevailing wind patterns, the radioactive consequences of meltdowns and explosions would be carried over the western Soviet Union. This added another link between traditional military concerns and a growing awareness of environmental dangers.

Given the appalling environmental record of the Soviet Union in previous decades and its frequently cavalier attitude to pollution, radiation and environmental degradation (see Komarov 1980 for a widely circulated exposé, and Feshbach and Friendly 1992), it was easy for Western thinkers to dismiss these newfound concerns with environmental security as being at best disingenuous or at worst deliberately deceptive. What was not easy to see, given the ideological filters through which all Soviet actions were viewed in the cold war (Cohen 1985), was the possibility that precisely because of this awful record, a new generation of policy makers might think it necessary to come to terms with this legacy and attempt to rethink security and development in ways that precluded further destruction. The link to the rethinking of Soviet strategy was also occluded given that the Leninist premises in traditional Soviet thinking were not widely understood among Western analysts. Because of this the Soviet assumption that occupying Western Europe was a necessary military step to prevent the defeat of the Soviet Union in a war caused by Western dynamics wasn't likely to be considered either. But read this way the introduction of concerns about environmental security by the Gorbachev administration in the 1980s makes logical sense as part of their "New Thinking".

On the other side of the cold war divide in the 1980s there were revived concerns with themes that had preoccupied Bertrand Russell, Albert Einstein and Lewis Mumford, of technology run amok and the consequent dangers to all of humanity of trying to live with and manage nuclear arsenals. Given the fractious nature of twentieth century politics the realistic policy was to get rid of nuclear weapons. But in the late 1970s, as the cold war became more confrontational and arsenals were enhanced by new missile systems, including the SS-20 intermediate range weapons of the Soviet Union and the Pershing 2 and new cruise missiles of the United States, in the European theatre peace activists once again focused on the immense potential destruction of these weapons and the dangers of hair trigger alerts, errors and misunderstandings (Johnstone 1984).

Notable among the prominent voices was Edward Thompson, who penned numerous essays pointing out the dangers of nuclear weapons and the completely inadequate efforts to prepare for the worst in terms of civil defence. His rejoinder to British government programs to "protect and survive" was titled "protest and survive" (Thompson 1980). In a more theoretical mode he analyzed the nuclear arms race and its escalation in Europe in the late 1970s in terms of a logic of exterminism, a term that highlighted the dangers of strategies of nuclear deterrence that ultimately presented themselves as mutually assured destruction (Thompson 1982). Isomorphic replication, in Thompson's (1982) terms, led to the ever larger production of military means of extermination, based on ever larger and more sophisticated modes of firepower. The geopolitical division of Europe effectively made all Europeans insecure given the dangers of warfare using these huge arsenals, and the political program of the European Nuclear Disarmament movement, debated at length in the pages of its eponymous journal in the 1980s, explicitly focused on dealignment (Dalby 1991), removing both the superpower forces from the continent and eliminating some of the potential causes of accidental nuclear war in the process.

BEYOND REALISM, EXTENDING SECURITY

The formulations of firepower as the ultimate arbiter in human affairs have thus never been unchallenged. Attempts to manage the superpower relationship and prevent accidental warfare due to miscalculation or misadventure followed from the Cuban missile crisis (Blight and Lang 2018). The "hotline" modes of communication between Moscow and Washington were designed to allow rapid communication to prevent conflicts escalating. Détente followed in the 1970s as both superpowers had accumulated massive nuclear arsenals and the standoff of earlier years had settled into a stalemate. Arms control agreements followed this, and if they didn't quite stabilize the arsenals and the delivery systems for the weapons, they shaped their numbers and capabilities. National technical means of surveillance were institutionalized as a mode of inspection to ensure that both sides were abiding by the agreements. But in the early 1980s tensions rose and proxy conflict was extended into Afghanistan. The logic of exterminism once again raised the danger of conflict by misadventure as the Soviet fears that the 1983 NATO exercise Able Archer was a dress rehearsal for a nuclear assault on the Soviet Union showed all too clearly in retrospect.

Simultaneously various efforts were made both to extend notions of détente and to rethink security concepts and their policy applications. A United Nations document in 1986 identified eight concepts of security that were in use in various contexts, suggesting that numerous innovations were being considered (Report of the Secretary-General 1986). The eighth concept is one of common security formulated by the Palme Commission in the early 1980s focusing on the common vulnerabilities of all states in the case of a nuclear war, and making the case for disarmament as the logical policy to deal with shared vulnerabilities (Independent Commission on Disarmament Issues and Security 1982). The commission, although not providing any detailed analysis, enlarged the compass of threats to security to include mention of resource shortages and environmental degradation in addition to the dangers of both conventional and nuclear arms races.

Simultaneously, in the United States the notion of national security was under increasing scrutiny by scholars concerned about its narrow focus on military matters and the neglect of political and diplomatic modes of thinking and conduct. Richard Ullman (1983, 133) offered the following suggestion:

> A more useful (although certainly not conventional) definition might be: a threat to national security is an action or sequence of events that (1) threatens drastically and over a relatively brief span of time to degrade the quality of life for the inhabitants of a state, or (2) threatens significantly to narrow the range of policy choices available to the government of a state or to private, nongovernmental entities (persons, groups corporations) within the state.

This is clearly a much more nuanced definition, and one starkly at odds with the expansive view of what constituted the conventional American cold war view, with its focus on global matters and its concerns with military power.

Crucially, nonetheless, this focus on national security is about responding to threats, and implicitly a situation in which external actions impinge on a supposedly autonomous state. What is not here is an engagement with potential antagonists, who are to be secured against. Security is, as Mick Dillon (1996) put it, about modern thought as metaphysics. In contrast understanding things in terms of tragedy, rather than metaphysics, focusing on the failures to consider the consequence of actions on others, and to understand how others see us, assuming conflict rather than compassion and engagement, suggests very different political possibilities. Likewise, for those who insist that nature, and human nature too, is intrinsically competitive, and that force is the ultimate arbiter, tragedy is unavoidable, and all one can do is prepare for the worst. For those who believe it is possible to use reason to avoid this fate, security is rather different, but it requires politics and discussions about how to coexist, not the use of force to impose one's will on others who may have other desires.

Crude forms of realism simply assume that what is must be protected, thus has it always been in human affairs and that nothing else is possible, and if violence is the ultimate arbiter in human affairs, that is a matter of unavoidable tragedy. The rules of the game are given; only how well you play it matters. In a world of large nuclear arsenals this is, the nuclear realists would argue, suicidal, given that errors and accidents are inevitable. What then is security?

Force clearly arbitrates many things, but in a world of nuclear firepower it ultimately endangers both humans and the ecosystems they inhabit.

These dilemmas were especially clearly spelled out in the 1980s as the reaction to the second cold war highlighted the impossibilities of massive destruction providing any meaningful condition of security. The rearticulation of who was in need of security and how it might be provided generated a substantial discussion of human security focused on the various dangers faced by people in the world of states and nuclear weapons. But in doing so the discussion of human security adumbrated so many sources of danger and vulnerability as to make it very difficult to formulate any clear policy for its application. The codification of human security in the widely cited United Nations Development Report of 1994 included environmental threats to human well-being, and emphasized that such threats were mostly the unintended consequences of economic and social activities, not the deliberate actions of overtly hostile entities.

In such circumstances both the sources of insecurity and their counter, by some agent or policy, stretched the formulation of security so far as to render it effectively inchoate, and to so muddy the waters in terms of who was responsible for its provision that while it provided a focus for much political and policy discourse it offered anything but clarity. Emma Rothschild summarized the 1990s discussion as involving four extensions.

> In the first, the concept of security is extended from the security of nations to the security of groups and individuals: it is extended downwards from nations to individuals. In the second, it is extended from the security of nations to the security of the international system, or of a supranational physical environment: it is extended upwards, from the nation to the biosphere. The extension, in both cases, is in the sorts of entities whose security is to be ensured. (1995, 55)

This involves expanding the scope of security in many new ways, well beyond either the traditional liberalism relating security to social order, and the order of property in particular, or the larger international concerns with state security and the collective security of alliances that classical realism emphasized. Third, Rothschild suggested that

> … the concept of security is extended horizontally, or to the sorts of security that are in question. Different entities (such as individuals, nations, and "systems") cannot be expected to be secure or insecure in the same way; the concept of security is extended, therefore, from military to political, economic, social, environmental, or "human" security. (1995, 55)

Given these multiple extensions, clearly states alone are no longer the sole repositories of institutions to provide security. Hence fourth,

> … the political responsibility for ensuring security (or for invigilating all these "concepts of security") is itself extended: it is diffused in all directions from national states, including upwards to international institutions, downwards to regional or local government, and sideways to nongovernmental organizations, to public opinion and the press, and to the abstract forces of nature or of the market. (1995, 55)

This is clearly a term with a broad scope, one that suggests that states alone are not the sole arbiters of security, nor their sole providers. If security is a widely accepted political desideratum then the question of priorities inevitably arises, once again making security an essentially contested term at the heart of much political discourse.

A crucial further twist to this series of arguments came in attempting to define who had the obligation to provide for security. In the subsequent discussions the principle of the responsibility to protect emerged and was widely acceded to in the United Nations system (International Commission on Intervention and State Sovereignty 2001). A corollary to the traditional Hobbesian notion of a social contract between ruler and subjects where loyalty is traded for security, in a system of supposedly autonomous sovereignties, came in the form of a responsibility to protect wherein membership in the international system was deemed to be contingent upon the state providing for the safety of its members. Failure in this provision was then linked to a requirement for the international community to intervene should the rulers of a member state prove unwilling or unable to prevent genocide, crimes against humanity and related atrocities against their country's residents.

The subsequent invocation of this principle to justify intervention in supporting Libyan insurgents in their attempt to overthrow the Gaddafi regime there, and the intervention's spectacular failure to provide protection for much of the Libyan population, has thrown this notion into disrepute, but the attempt to reorder the responsibilities of both states and the international system is nonetheless an additional extension of the traditional formulations of security that matters, not least because it points to the obligations of states to act in terms of collective benefits beyond the United Nations notions of collective defence. As to whether this principle can or should be extended to the global environment, and how that is now reimagined in light of the current biodiversity and climate crises, is one of the key ongoing issues in rethinking environmental security.

SECURITIZATION, ONTOLOGY AND SURVIVAL

A related question then is who can effectively posit things as a matter of security. While entities may be in need of protection, who can do the protecting, and against what supposed, or real, threat, is a matter of politics. While numerous fears and threats to identity may be in circulation, in so far as security is a matter primarily for states, then which threats are accepted as a matter of priority for states to protect against is a profoundly political question. Thus in the aftermath of the cold war and in light of the numerous extensions to the security concept that appeared in the 1980s and 1990s, Buzan, Wæver and de Wilde (1998) offered "A New Framework for Analysis of Security". They suggested that only some political arguments about threats became state policy, and that the processes whereby matters become security concerns, the process of securitization, required the clear articulation of a threat to some specified identity, that is, a referent object that is threatened, an audience willing to accept this specification of affairs, and shifts in state policy to address the threat. Mostly these threats are understood as having external sources, although, as was the case throughout much of the cold war, external threats are frequently linked to fears of internal subversion.

This focus on securitization links loosely to additional innovations in more recent security studies focusing on this question of what entity needs to be secured. In this line of thinking, what it is that needs to be secured is a matter of ontological security (Mitzen 2006), invoking entities, and more specifically political identities, that need to be defended from external threat. Nationalist rhetoric obviously works effectively here, invoking a community that is both unique and endangered from outside. So called populist politicians have of late used this rhetorical strategy to bolster support and done so by constructing threats to an imagined but often nostalgic invocation of a national community.

What is much harder to do is to think about the implicit threat that one's own identity and practices of securing it might present and how this would endanger others. Ethnocentrism has long bedeviled strategic thinking (Booth 1979). As noted above, this failure of insight into the key assumptions being made on the other side of the cold war divide was one of the things that made this period of history so dangerous. Understanding the modes of thought that potential antagonists are using is a key to international cooperation, and to negotiating agreements. Reassurance that hostile intent is not part of the security calculation is a key to dealing with the security dilemma. This requires acting in ways that don't raise concerns among others who have no good reason to believe the claims of benign intent used in shoring up self-identity.

Changing the overarching narratives of ontological security is a fraught political matter (Subotic 2016), frequently requiring nimble political maneuvering and successful rearticulation of parts of a national identity. This has been done in cases of major political realignments, as in the end of the cold war, but also in terms of finding resolutions to longstanding conflicts and resolving political tensions. These rearticulations are also a necessary part of creating the conditions required for quality peace, and ensuring that in the aftermath of a conflict the conditions that caused it in the first place do not recur and reactivate it (Wallensteen 2015). But as the Brexit case has also demonstrated, nostalgic populist formulations with implicit assumptions of autonomy as a political desideratum persist too (Agnew 2020), something that fits with "fortress" formulations of security that are frequently much less than helpful with environmental issues (White 2014). Once again distant phenomena are portrayed as a threat to Western order while downplaying the consequences of that order for those places. As much of the rest of this book points out, the causes of environmental insecurity now lie in the massive use of fossil fuels, not in supposedly stingy natures on the periphery of the global economy.

In John Herz's (1950, 157) phrasing, his original formulation of the security dilemma wasn't about biology: "The condition that concerns us here is not a biological or anthropological but a social one." But now the argument in this book suggests that humanity faces a new security dilemma, one also brought about as an indirect result of the ever larger use of firepower in the broader sense. More specifically the argument in what follows in the rest of this volume suggests that, whereas traditional notions of a security dilemma were concerned with the actions of potential antagonists, and that the source of the dilemma lay in social arrangements, firepower, understood in its broader sense involving combustion and its use as a key mode of power in human affairs, is now endangering numerous communities because of its geophysical consequences. This isn't a matter of social actions, nor strictly biology in Herz's terms. It is a matter of geophysics, of actions having indirect consequences, and the formulation of security in terms of attempts to shape supposedly external contexts in ways that are endangering precisely what is supposedly being secured. Hence an extended notion of the security dilemma structures the argument that follows in the rest of this volume.

INTERNATIONAL RELATIONS?

All these complicated themes raise the key question as to whether this larger discussion of the fate of humanity is really a topic suitable for a discipline, or subdiscipline, called international relations at all? If one takes the term literally, always accepting the implicit fudge in substituting nation for state, then the topic is about the relationships between states, not about the larger questions of planetary habitability for our species. And yet the rapid rise of the international relations discipline during the cold war, and security studies as its central focus, was driven by a concern for the survival of major states in a system endangered by the prospect of nuclear warfare. Nuclear war posited the possibility of the destruction of civilization itself; climate change, ocean acidification and the extinction crisis also now threaten the same fate unless firepower in its more general sense is reined in soon.

After the initial cold war and during the period of 1970s détente, when nuclear warfare seemed much less of a threat, the discipline turned its attention to regimes, governance and the functioning of an increasingly integrated global economy. So while the key foci of the discipline over the last few generations has been on issues of conflict, governance and economy, it is fair to say that these intellectual engagements are not far off the central questions of survival for at least civilization, if not humanity in some form. But what has been relatively neglected in both the security studies literature of the cold war and the globalization literature subsequently is the material context of this civilization; mostly it has been taken for granted. As with economics which has taken a relatively stable climate and cheap energy as a given context, so too has much of international relations (Albert 2020).

What is new now in the third decade of the third millennium is the growing realization that this assumption of a stable backdrop for humanity is no longer tenable as a premise. Gradually through the cold war period, as the dangers of nuclear fallout percolated into many cultures, and then other forms of pollution as well as ongoing famines in some parts of the world, apparently related to the rapid growth of population, questions about the global environment as such emerged. They provided the tentative beginnings of an understanding of the planetary context as much more vulnerable than had been assumed, and challenged the modern dichotomies of humanity and nature too. Now the new thinking of *Planetary Social Thought* (Clark and Szerszynski 2021) requires engaging with earth system science and *Breaking Boundaries* (Rockström and Gaffney 2021) in the sense of transcending divisions between disciplines too. Given international relations' concerns with security and survival, clearly it needs to rethink many things in grappling with the current crisis, one that is to a substantial extent a result of previous efforts to provide security, based on firepower in both its senses.

2. Sustainable development/ environmental insecurity

ONTOLOGICAL SECURITY

Stories of disaster, epic struggles and human survival provide foundational myths for many peoples. Famine frequently stalked our ancestors most of whom long ago became dependent on agriculture for food supplies, a series of processes vulnerable to droughts and floods in the short term and climate variability on the longer timescale related to volcanic activity in particular (Jenkins 2021). Disease likewise; pandemics are nothing new in human history, and as the COVID-19 episode has reminded us all again recently, inept political responses have frequently rendered numerous people insecure. Assumptions of vulnerability and insecurity are related to narratives of scarcity, inevitable conflict and the need for leadership to protect some community or nation. Ontological security, the matter of maintaining a coherent narrative of a collectivity (Mitzen 2006), weaves these themes together in numerous political discourses, only most obviously in those of war and struggles against external antagonists in a dangerous world. Modernity's promise that the use of firepower and technology could insulate societies from the vagaries of a fickle nature is, it turns out, coming back to haunt humanity's future in the form of global environmental disruption.

War has long been linked to matters of environmental change too, only most obviously in European discussions of the fall of the Western Roman empire caused, Thomas Malthus (1798/1970) asserted, by climate fluctuations in Asia leading to the western migration of numerous tribes that eventually overran Roman defences. Similar concerns about food, fodder and climate limitations have shaped Chinese history in particular too, the rise and fall of various dynasties being linked to famine and attempts to ameliorate the worst vagaries of natural fluctuations. This was highlighted in the 1950s by famine once again striking the Chinese population, largely as a result of the economic misadventures as part of the great leap forward and the political convulsions related to misconceived attempts to force very rapid economic transformation in China's rural areas in particular.

Many of the themes that show up in contemporary discussions of environmental security have their forerunners in nineteenth century discussions of resources, pollution and conflict, a point worth remembering in considering the multiple claims that environmental security is a new concern in global politics (Hough 2019). The origins of the discourses of contemporary international relations are tied into industrialization in Europe in the nineteenth century, even if that part of their history is frequently overlooked (Ashworth 2014). But it was only in the twentieth century that it became clear that human actions on a global scale, as opposed to the disruptions of particular empires and ecosystems in the process of colonization, were part of the causal mechanisms that induced human insecurity. In the second half of the twentieth century, themes from earlier discussions of political economy, of Thomas Malthus's pessimistic prognostications about the human fate in particular, coalesced with the larger discussions of international politics and nascent ideas of global governance to generate a discourse that linked these things together in what subsequently became known as environmental security.

These themes came together in 1972 against the backdrop of the first photographs of earth from the Apollo program's missions to the moon suggesting a fragile planet in an inhospitable solar system. The United Nations Conference on the Human Environment (UNCHE) was held in Stockholm in June that year. The background report to the conference was simply titled *Only One Earth*, reprising the theme so powerfully articulated in the NASA photographs of the "blue marble" set against a black backdrop (Cosgrove 1994). In the United States a study with the first computer simulations of the earth as a single system was published called *The Limits to Growth.* While there are numerous precursors to all this, the conjunction of space exploration, computer modelling, widespread angst about the future and a United Nations conference on the theme suggests that what became the discourse of environmental security can fairly be said to have started in 1972. The origins of the United Nations Environment Programme (UNEP) lie in the 1972 Stockholm conference too.

The term environmental security itself became part of the policy deliberations of international politics fifteen years later with the publication of the World Commission on Environment and Development's report on *Our Common Future*. Commonly called the Brundtland report, after the Norwegian former prime minister who chaired the commission, *Our Common Future* popularized the term sustainable development. But it forcefully argued that for sustainable development to be successful, conditions of "environmental insecurity" had to be removed. The argument was neatly circular: sustainable development could, so the report argued, provide conditions of environmental security for future generations. These two concepts were essential complements to each other even if sustainable development was the term that got most of the attention. It still is getting that priority, as the 2015 United Nations

Sustainable Development Goals (SDGs) highlight (Dalby, Horton, Mahon and Thomaz 2019).

Some key works in international relations did grapple with the environment and resource agenda in the 1970s, but much of the discussion about international security remained focused on nuclear warfare and matters of international development. These were highlighted in the aftermath of the October 1973 war when Egypt and Syria launched a coordinated military assault on Israeli forces in the Golan Heights and the Sinai Peninsula. When the United States and some European states began resupplying Israeli forces, members of the Organization of Petroleum Exporting States (OPEC) began suspending petroleum exports to those states and the price of oil quadrupled. Fuel supply issues quickly dominated American and European geopolitical discussions, and the larger discussion of resource constraints to development in general became entangled with the specifics of oil supply. The knock on effects of the rapid OPEC increase in petroleum prices both subsequently caused the debt crisis in many developing countries and partly derailed international efforts to formulate a new international economic order to deal with global economic inequalities. But the environmental questions kept returning onto the policy agendas of major states.

HUMANITY AND NATURE

Clarence Glacken's (1967) magisterial survey of Western discussions of humanity and nature poses matters in terms of three questions. First, is the earth, so obviously a conducive place for humanity, a purposive creation, a pristine nature into which humanity has subsequently been placed? The second question is one about how the varied geographic regions of the world have shaped specific human cultures, with climate and cohabiting species offering possibilities for societal formation. Third is the matter of how humanity, by its cultural actions, agriculture and modes of life, has changed nature. While the first question is now mostly the preserve of theological discussions, the supposition of a pristine nature prior to human intervention is very persistent and structures the dominant dichotomy of modernity, one that specifies humanity as separate, superior and in some senses above nature. While the second of Glacken's questions is frequently dismissed, often far too quickly, as a matter of dubious environmental determinism with numerous racialized presuppositions dating from the worst excesses of European and subsequently American colonization, there nonetheless remain many constraints on what humans can do where.

The third question Glacken (1967) raised, that of how humanity is changing nature, is now the preoccupation of numerous research efforts. These issues were, as Ashworth (2021) suggests, major preoccupations of political geographers in the 1930s and 1940s, but as he notes, the emergent realist consensus in international relations in the early years of the atomic age ignored this mode of thought and focused instead on human psychology and power. The material context as it was being changed by human activity wasn't a pressing priority for thinkers trying to work through the implications of the enormous expansion of firepower that had suddenly become available to the larger states in the international system. While this focus on the pressing issues of the time, given the advent of nuclear weapons and the then recent history of aggressive warfare as a mode of state policy, made sense in those times, the longer legacy is one where much of international relations has been mostly blind, until recently, to the pressing issues of the human transformation of the earth (Burke, Fishel, Mitchell et al. 2016).

But this discussion has been underway in numerous other forums both within the academy and outside of it, longstanding discussion in economics about resources and shortages of supplies of numerous things, perhaps only most obviously in the long history of humanity that of food. The chaos of the 1930s and 1940s, with famine, war, conquest and the mobilization of immense industrial productive forces to supply the war machines, emphasized the vulnerabilities of societies to economic disruptions. The starvation of millions in the Bengal famine in India during the Second World War likewise focused attention on political economy and the importance of political decisions in terms of the fate of the poor. In the aftermath of the war, as decolonization led to the dismantling of European empires and the presence of communist parties challenged the efficacy of capitalism to provide economic necessities, discussions of development emerged as the dominant framing of what needed to be done. While the Soviet model promised development led by planning, and the spread of industrialization, the capitalist model promised much the same, with private ownership driving innovation. Both however required policy, technological innovation and rapid growth in energy use to shape the future for the provision of prosperity.

While the period that has in retrospect become known to earth system scientists as the "great acceleration", the post world war long economic boom that spread consumer culture and its economics to many parts of the world, was premised on American notions of technological progress and economic growth (Farish 2010), worries about resource shortages provided a persistent, if minor counter narrative to the enthusiasm for "development". *The Road to Survival* (Vogt 1948) for machine civilization was indeed the *Challenge of Man's Future* (Brown 1954), to use the phrasing from two popular books that posed matters in terms of a predicament of technology, resources, pollution and social adaptability. The proceedings of a major symposium (Thomas 1956) on "Man's Role in Changing the Face of the Earth" in 1955 summarized the state of contemporary knowledge of human driven transformations.

Much of the expansion of modernity depended on cheap energy, in the form of coal for industry, petroleum for many things and, in many cases, water for generating hydroelectricity. The downsides of these were pollution in terms of combustion products and numerous chemicals let loose as byproducts of industrial activity. Pesticides promised to rapidly expand the productivity of agriculture and lead in gasoline the power of internal combustion engines, but both soon turned out to have dangerous unintended ecological consequences. In the case of hydropower the inundation of land and the displacement of river valley residents this supposedly clean power entailed had numerous ramifications. Hanging over all this discussion of the environmental disruptions of modernity was the fear of nuclear fallout, both in terms of the actual spread of radioactive residues from tests in the atmosphere and in terms of the potential for future damage from nuclear wars yet to come.

But development did, it seemed at the time, have tremendous promise, something that the very rapidly growing populations of the second half of the twentieth century were going to need. If, that is, the resources could be found to feed the expanding industrial system that was supposed to provide all manner of consumer products deemed essential to the good life. In Europe at least, alarms about resource supplies came into focus in the aftermath of the Suez crisis of 1956 when war disrupted petroleum supplies. Rachel Carson (1962) warned of a *Silent Spring* when pesticides designed to kill insects would also kill off bird populations, eliminating their songs and silencing nature. Paul Erhlich (1968) raised the alarm about a forthcoming *Population Bomb*, rhetorically linking anxieties about nuclear catastrophe to a formulation of disaster due to subsistence crises. R.F. Dasmann (1971) posed matters in terms of a question regarding a *Planet in Peril?* while summarizing the initial work of the United Nations Educational, Scientific and Cultural Organization (UNESCO) “Man and the Biosphere” program established following the 1968 scientific conference on these themes.

In the 1960s, famines in India in particular, and pollution as a result of rapidly expanding industries and mass consumption, fed into a widespread concern about the environment in at least some so called developed countries. Air and water quality in the United States became a major issue as fears of pollution overwhelming progress rearticulated narratives of environmental degradation and societal decline (Rienow and Rienow 1969). In addition the spectre of mass annihilation caused by the use of even a small portion of the superpower nuclear arsenals raised the issue of human survival, or at least civilizational survival. The related matter of environmental concerns stretching round the globe was focused on the dangers of nuclear fallout from the atmospheric dispersal of radioactive elements generated in the 1950s and early 1960s weapons tests (Masco 2015). A sense of global vulnerability emerged from these events as tracking fallout made it clear that the atmosphere was a single complex entity where pollution in one place could show up on the other side of the world in a matter of weeks.

This rise of concern over fallout, resources, pollution and shortage of food, especially in India in the 1960s when emergency international grain shipments were needed to stave off famine, coalesced in a rising concern at least in Western states about global environmental matters. Concerns over pollution and population combined in an environmental social movement in the United States and subsequently in Europe in the 1960s. Anxiety over how to frame these matters in international politics in the 1960s gave rise to discussions about who was responsible and how policy might be formulated (Boroway 2019). While in retrospect this all might seem to be obviously a matter of environment, and the need for some international agreements to deal with the matter, this wasn't clear in the 1960s when discussions of development, technology, war and the potential for nuclear destruction intersected with concerns about pollution and resource shortages, as well as matters of the role of science, as both the source of many of the problems and potentially a major player in the potential for solutions, for all these issues.

Matters crystallized in 1972 when the Swedish government hosted the UNCHE in Stockholm, out of which emerged a new agency, the UNEP. The Soviet Union boycotted the Stockholm conference over an argument about granting East Germany delegate status at the conference, and this and other superpower disputes marked the event. But in retrospect, despite the international controversies, this conference is seen as marking the emergence of contemporary global environmental concern and the beginnings of comprehensive international efforts to grapple with ecological matters that were then being considered as properly global concerns (Conca 2015). Not least is the now taken for granted argument that states have the right to use resources for their development, but should not do so in ways that impinge on the rights of other states because of the generation of cross boundary pollution. This rearticulation of standard liberal notions of property and responsibility was scaled up, as it were, to states and hence to the international arena in the 1972 Stockholm Declaration.

The one head of state who did make it to Stockholm was Indira Gandhi, Prime Minister of India, and her speech to the conference is in some ways a watershed in international politics, and one that is still repeatedly cited (Gandhi 1972). It is so because she explicitly argued that poverty was the worst form of pollution and warned against the dangers of developed states using arguments about environment to constrain the development that poor states needed to address issues of poverty. This key argument, reinterpreted subsequently as a matter of "environmental colonialism" (Agarwal and Narian 1991) where the poor in the South get to pay for the consumption of the rich, persists to this day in discussions of climate change and, in the formulation widely used under the aegis of the United Nations Framework Convention on Climate Change (UNFCCC), common but differentiated responsibilities (Brunnée and Streck 2013).

What is much less cited in the retrospectives on Stockholm is the point that the conference declaration is very blunt about the need for nuclear disarmament. The dangers of nuclear war were seen as a major concern, and eradicating this was explicitly pointed to in the final item in the conference declaration. A sense of global vulnerability as well as numerous concerns about injustice, apartheid and poverty shape the declaration, marking its historical origins but also linking environmental deliberations into a much larger discussion of the politics of human insecurity. Western worries about resource shortages were highlighted once again a little later by the disruptions to the international petroleum trade as OPEC raised prices in the aftermath of the October war between Syria, Egypt and Israel in 1973. How the rich world and the poor world could coexist, and what might be done to deal with the tensions in the global system and the persistence of gross inequities in trade and development, the legacies of centuries of colonialism, shaped demands for a "New International Economic Order" in subsequent years (Lean 1978).

Simultaneously with the rise of environmental concern in the 1960s, the crises of resources and pollution generated critiques of the conventional economic assumption that growth was key to future prosperity, and the implicit assumption that it could go on forever. Most high profile in this discussion was the debate about a report for the Club of Rome published in 1972 that identified what it called *The Limits to Growth* (Meadows, Meadows, Randers and Behrens 1972). Based on a simple computer model of the global problematique, with industrialization, population, malnutrition, resources and a deteriorating environment the five key interacting variables, the various runs of the model forecasted disaster if then current trajectories were maintained. Contrary to many popular misconceptions of the report, disaster wasn't projected as inevitable, and the time frame pointed to the decisive time period, then many decades in the future, of the early decades of the twenty first century.

Nonetheless it generated vehement objections on numerous grounds, especially from economists anxious to defend the key credo of their canon, the unquestioned benefits of economic growth and the related assertion that technological innovation could handle whatever problems came along (Cole, Freeman, Jahoda and Pavitt 1973). Now half a century later we are living in the period that the *Limits to Growth* report identified as key decades when the trajectories it identified would converge in crisis. The rapidly escalating climate change crisis and the loss of biodiversity suggest that, tragically, those initial crude forecasts of planetary trajectories were fairly close to the mark, and are so precisely because the warnings from that period in this report and others weren't heeded (Turner 2014). As the fiftieth anniversary of the report is reached, humanity is living in the period where *The Limits to Growth* predicted things would go wrong if action wasn't taken!

The discussion of the *Limits to Growth* was part of a larger political and cultural transformation, one marked by the emergence of the annual earth day in April each year following on from the initial one in 1970 in the United States. It was also a time where politics was especially fraught in the United States, with the civil rights movement and the anti-Vietnam war movement being especially high profile. In Europe the student actions in 1968 and the Prague Spring shook up conventional political assumptions. Simultaneously the so called space race between the superpowers generated a fascination with technology, and a cultural innovation too when the first pictures of the whole earth from space were taken by the Apollo astronauts going to the moon (Cosgrove 1994).

Notable books from the time specified various combinations of political economy and technology as key to the crisis (Commoner 1971). In Britain *The Ecologist* (1972) published its *Blueprint for Survival* and established its magazine as part of the larger cultural discussion. In the United States Richard Falk published a lengthy volume examining *This Endangered Planet* which started with a blunt discussion of the ecological imperative that required "... the development of an ecological politics, whose essence is a political embodiment of man-in-nature, as the ideological underpinning for an adequate conception of world order" (1971, 21). Subsequently Jon Barnett (2001) was to claim this particular volume as the appropriate starting point for what has since become environmental security, although the term itself doesn't appear in Falk's text. The unofficial background report for the Stockholm conference used images of the earth from space to emphasize earthly vulnerability in specifying matters in terms of *Only One Earth* (Ward and Dubos 1972). Given the concerns about nuclear warfare in the Stockholm Declaration, Barnett's timing seems very appropriate. The agenda of what has subsequently been known as environmental security can be dated clearly from the early 1970s and the explicit attempts to conjoin concerns about military dangers and environmental disruptions.

The crisis of the 1970s arising from the increase in concern about environmental destruction, and then once again in the West after the disruptions in oil supply triggered by OPEC action following the October war of 1973 in the Middle East, generated numerous efforts to think through alternative economic models that might be both less vulnerable to petroleum supplies and less demanding on environments. Alternative development movements, the widespread popularity of discussions of Fritz Schumacher's (1974) economic critiques of conventional growth models in *Small is Beautiful* and technological innovation all promised at least partial resolutions to the global crisis. A decade before *Our Common Future*, Amory Lovins (1977) suggested that a "soft energy path" offered possibilities for dealing with climate matters and national security in the United States in particular in very different ways. He suggested that much better technology, ending wasteful use of energy by dramatically increasing efficiencies in buildings, production systems and vehicles, offered a much easier path to a sensible future than continued extraction of fossil fuels from, among other places, a volatile Middle East.

The Carter administration tackled many of these issues and compiled a major report providing an overview of the state of the environment (United States Department of State and Council on Environmental Quality 1980). It established a Solar Energy Research Institute as a major research initiative, and symbolically put solar panels on the White House roof. But these initiatives were swept aside by the subsequent Reagan administrations' focus on fossil fuels and economic growth during the rise of neoliberalism and the acceleration of globalization. The cultural politics of the Reagan slogan of "it's morning in America", with the emphasis on consumption as the key to the American way, justified policy that sidelined many initiatives that had promised a more sustainable United States. The Reagan administration closed the Solar Energy Research Institute and moved to deregulate many industries that had been subject to the clean air and water legislation of the Nixon era. In Lovins' terms (1977) they chose the hard path and combustion as the key energy source, and with that made a major contribution to the current climate crisis. Solar panels disappeared from the White House roof when the Reagans moved in, only to return later when the Obamas were in residence then disappear once again during the Trump presidency. They are clearly very symbolic of the larger American cultural dimensions of energy (Daggett 2018).

ECOPOLITICS AND INTERNATIONAL RELATIONS

These discussions found their way into at least some of the international relations journals of the time, but remained a minor concern in the major journals in the 1970s. Richard Falk's (1971) formulation suggested four major causes for the dangerous predicament that the planet finds itself in: the war system; population pressure; the insufficiency of resources; and environmental overload. Exponential growth and complacent assumptions that political and economic systems can adjust seemed on a collision course to Falk, and having laid out these four causes of imminent danger he wondered as to whether a civilizational crash was looming. The failure to think about the larger context, and the collapse of previous empires, whose rulers didn't foresee their demise too, offers, he suggested, a cautionary tale requiring some serious rethinking of world order and the incorporation of these themes into discussions of politics. The disconnection between the size, function and authority of political units is one of Falk's concerns, and this doesn't lead to sensible efforts to grapple with the looming dangers. The discrepancy between state sovereignty and the universal precepts of the United Nations Charter on the use of force are among the additional concerns that Falk worried about. Clearly the existing arrangement of states and international organizations wasn't up to the job.

Across the Atlantic Hedley Bull (1977) was worrying about some similar themes of world order, and in his synthesis of the "English School" literature, *The Anarchical Society*, a few years later, he addressed Falk's concerns, taking him to task for simultaneously complaining about the inadequacy of states and contemporary institutions and the need for urgent action. Bull suggested that if urgency was required there was little choice but to act using existing institutions even if they didn't appear very efficacious, the implication being that waiting for new political forms to address these issues would delay action too long. While Bull was willing to concede that a greater sense of solidarity might engender global innovations, his argument suggests that states, as the provider of what semblance of order there is in the world, were going to be an essential institution for tackling environmental problems. But that said, Bull only addressed a few pages in his book to environmental matters.

In the United States Dennis Pirages (1978) devoted a whole book to *Global Ecopolitics*, what he termed *The New Context for International Relations*. This text, suggested as being both an overview of the issues and an introduction to the new themes looming in international relations, posited matters in terms of an impending revolution in global politics. Looking back in human history, Pirages suggested that there were two great revolutions in history, first the agricultural one, and second the industrial one which defined modernity. Tentatively he suggested that numerous scarcities emerging at the time he was writing challenged the pattern of resource extensive industrial development that marked modernity. The possibilities of extending this mode of economic life to the developing world seemed impossible. Hence Pirages suggested an incipient revolution in the human condition, one that would require new modes of governance in this new world of emerging ecopolitics. The dominance paradigm, of human societies pitted against each other and the natural world, would have to give way to something novel, as the carrying capacities of the natural world were being exceeded by rising human numbers and economic activity.

While comparisons between these three books should not be taken too far, it is clear that over the decades since, Bull's themes have dominated international relations to a much greater extent than those of either Falk or Pirages. In June 2021 Google Scholar listed less than one hundred citations for Pirages, nearly five hundred for Falk, and as a canonical text in international relations, Bull's volume, reprinted in multiple editions in subsequent decades, had nearly twelve thousand. These numbers are only roughly indicative of their relative importance within the discipline, but they do emphasize the point made much later in critiques of international relations which argue that the material context of planetary systems has been remarkably absent from deliberations in the field (Burke, Fishel, Mitchell et al. 2016). Much more recently Hans Guenter Brauch (2021) and Ursula Oswald Spring (2020) have led substantial efforts to engage with the changing material context and how sustainable transitions relate to matters of peace in the Anthropocene (Oswald Spring and Brauch 2021). It's notable that Brauch sometimes extends Pirages's formulations of the revolutions in human history too in his discussion of the need for new thinking of ecology and peace (Brauch 2021), but Oswald Spring and Brauch's multiple volume edited book series has had little noticeable impact in the core Anglo-American international relations literature (Brauch, Oswald Spring, Grin and Scheffran 2016). In part this is probably a matter of their geographical locations and intellectual roots outside the Anglo-American mainstream, and the focus on peace rather than power in how they formulate security.

Within international relations in the 1970s the focus on realist issues of war and peace was challenged by literature suggesting that the relationships between states were more complicated than the simple formulations of realism allowed. While military force might be the ultimate arbiter in politics, the strictures of mutually assured destruction, rapidly growing international trade and the emergence of numerous international organizations had given rise to a situation of complex interdependence in which many more actors had to be considered, and governance of many matters was increasingly happening in complex regimes where rules, actors, norms and procedures intersect to shape conduct (Keohane and Nye 1977). Both regime theory and the emergent concerns with global political economy occasionally tackled matters of environment and resources, and spun off a subdiscipline of global environmental politics, along with its eponymous scholarly journal. But much of this scholarship worked within the loose ambit of regime theory and with concerns with trade and political economy and how these shaped the finer points of environmental governance, or frequently failed to effectively do so (Laferrière and Stoett 1999).

These political economy, trade and regime theory texts mostly didn't grapple with the large transformations of the earth system that the extraordinary expansion of the global economy had set in motion in the twentieth century. In addition much of the discussion of pollution and ecosystem management focused on technical fixes and regulation, not on the questions of the driving forces of production in the first place. If pollution was identified as the problem, then clearly modernizing industrial technology to prevent it was the solution. Ecomodernism, as this response to environmental difficulties came to be called (Mol 2001), didn't call into question the larger context of production or consumption; business could continue as usual once technology had solved the immediate problems with toxicity. In Peter Dauvergne's (2016) terms, this "environmentalism of the rich" is not capable of dealing with either the disruptions caused by the total throughput of energy and materials in the earth system or the history of the destruction of indigenous peoples and their lands caused by the expansion of European imperialism and now the global economy.

SUSTAINABLE DEVELOPMENT

What was missing in all this discussion in the 1970s was an agreed upon succinct way of linking environment and development, and dealing with the contradiction that Indira Gandhi had eloquently expressed in Stockholm. While the two were linked in numerous ways as part of an overall discourse, fifteen years after Stockholm the Brundtland report on *Our Common Future* provided the synthesis that has dominated discussions ever since, the notion of sustainable development. This has turned out to be amenable to a nearly infinite number of interpretations and has acted as the ideological infrastructure for ecomodernist initiatives of numerous sorts, including most recently various efforts to facilitate both the mitigation of climate change and adaptation efforts to it in many places (Sovacool and Linner 2016).

Much of the discussion of sustainability since stems from *Our Common Future*, and the attempts, five years after its publication, at the United Nations Conference on Environment and Development (UNCED) in Rio de Janeiro in 1992 to implement some of its key themes in novel arrangements of global governance. Two key conventions were agreed upon there: the United Nations Framework Convention on Climate Change (UNFCCC) and the Convention on Biological Diversity (CBD). In addition an ambitious program called Agenda 21, as in an agenda for the twenty first century, was discussed, but the practical innovations that it implied for new forms of sustainable development were quickly pushed aside by corporations and governments enthralled by the logic of neoliberalism with its narrow focus on economic growth and the supposed benefits for all of globalization (Chatterjee and Finger 1994). While both key conventions established in Rio in 1992 have evolved into formal institutions of environmental governance, as the current global environmental crisis makes clear, neither has yet effectively constrained the destruction of natural systems or the rapidly accumulating greenhouse gases in the atmosphere.

The arguments for sustainable development are remarkably persistent, not least precisely because they are loosely compatible with the neoliberal logics of private sector expansion, at best loose government regulation, and the priority given to growth measured in financial metrics. The term is part of the overarching SDGs adopted by the United Nations in 2015 (Dalby, Horton, Mahon and Thomaz 2019). As climate change in particular accelerates, notions of sustainability have become ever more important in global politics. While the Rio conference, which happened after the cold war ended, downplayed the term environmental security, the premise of environmental insecurity had been a key theme in *Our Common Future*. The report emphasized both the dangers of warfare disrupting development and the potential conflicts that might erupt if development were not done in a sustainable fashion. Environmental security concerns have been heightened more recently by the discussion of climate change as many military institutions worry about the disruptions it causes and possible conflicts that will ensue (Klare 2019). This is now especially important as the insights of earth system science make it clear just how much human actions are changing the planet, how fast this is happening and, if present trajectories are maintained, the likely increasingly severe disruptions to the biosphere that will result (Intergovernmental Panel on Climate Change 2018).

Globalization and its acceleration in recent decades means in practical terms that the global economy has expanded so much that it is now causing environmental change on the scale of major climate and geomorphological forces. The rapidly expanding technosphere is a new element in the earth system, a product of the extraordinary expansion of the global economy, one that is changing how that earth system functions (Zalasiewicz, Williams, Waters et al. 2017). While critics of globalization have frequently invoked deleterious local consequences of global processes as the problem that needs to be addressed, it is clear that in many matters the assumptions of bordered national states as the key to human fulfilment and the appropriate mode of governing human affairs are now also being challenged fundamentally by ecological change. Autonomy may appeal to nationalist politicians and environmentalists trying to protect particular places from development sourced in distant cities and their investment banks, but sustainability now has to be considered at the global scale if it is to grapple with key economic transformations that are pushing the earth system into previously unknown configurations. Welcome to the new age of human dominance in biophysical matters, this new geological epoch now frequently called the Anthropocene (Lewis and Maslin 2018).

Traditional notions of conservation, of parks, ecological reserves and pollution restrictions in particular places, have to be complemented by considerations of global impacts and the connections across distant and disparate places. While such management devices as treaties to try to ensure bird migration pathways are maintained are not new, the scale and speed of ecological change now means that assumptions of relatively stable geographies, and of the past as a reasonable guide for predictions of future environmental conditions, no longer hold. Globalization has become a major force of biophysical transformation and sustainability thinking has to incorporate this new situation into analysis and policy making (Kareiva and Fuller 2016). State rivalries and struggles for power and prestige in international politics likewise are playing out in these changing circumstances, and those circumstances are in part a consequence of those same processes; geography is increasingly what states and corporations make it as the Anthropocene unfolds. In these circumstances sustainability cannot mean keeping things the same, or preserving ecologies in situ. A much more dynamic series of processes must necessarily be involved, and what precisely needs to be sustained and how is now much more complicated.

The famous definition of sustainable development at the beginning of the second chapter of *Our Common Future* reads: "Sustainable development is development that meets the needs of the present without compromising the ability of future generations to meet their own needs" (World Commission on Environment and Development 1987, 43). This has become the standard definition of one of the most widely used terms in contemporary international politics. The authors of *Our Common Future* went on to elaborate on the definition, stating that it involved two key concepts. The first is "the concept of 'needs', in particular the essential needs of the world's poor, to which overriding priority should be given" (World Commission on Environment and Development 1987, 43). The second concept is "the idea of limitations imposed by the state of technology and social organization on the environment's ability to meet present and future needs" (World Commission on Environment and Development 1987, 43). The report's authors went on to emphasize that the social and the physical are inextricably interconnected: "Even the narrow notion of physical sustainability implies a concern for social equity between generations, a concern that must logically be extended to equity within each generation" (World Commission on Environment and Development 1987, 43). How to do this is not exactly easy; claims to inter-generational and intra-generational equity persist in discussions of sustainable development, and are a key theme in the current SDGs (United Nations 2015), but the dramatic trajectory of economic change since *Our Common Future* was published has apparently not operated on the report's principles, despite the repeated invocation of the term sustainable development.

Bluntly put, the term was at best a compromise. It was an attempt to incorporate Northern concerns with environment with Southern concerns about development. Fifteen years after Indira Gandhi called poverty the worst kind of pollution at the UNCHE in Stockholm, the necessity of dealing with rapid environmental change and with impoverishment in many parts of the world required that some compromise between development and environmental protection be articulated in international forums (Conca 2015). At the time, alarm about the depletion of stratospheric ozone and concerns about industrial accidents—with the Chernobyl nuclear meltdown and the Bhopal chemical leak very much on people's minds—was coupled with worries about deforestation and the limited possibilities of expanding agricultural production. Ozone depletion in particular made it clear that some environmental vulnerabilities were in fact widely shared and global cooperation was necessary to deal with these matters.

Southern leaders, rearticulating Indira Gandhi's concerns expressed in Stockholm, were adamant that Northern environmental issues should not be used as a method for constraining what they saw as essential Southern economic growth (Kjellen 2008). Given that most of the big environmental problems of the time were caused by Northern activities, simple matters of justice required that those who had caused the problems be the ones to pay for the solution. At the time of the Rio conference environmentalists posed matters bluntly in terms of "Whose Common Future?" (*The Ecologist* 1993). Where ozone depleting substances were a problem, Southern leaders insisted that Northern economies help provide technological alternatives to compensate for what they portrayed as forgone development opportunities. Such principles linking environment to development have subsequently been key to much of the diplomatic discussions about aid and development. More recently, these themes have been key to international discussions of climate change where technology transfer and development aid are part of the negotiations under the rubric of common but differentiated responsibilities (Brunnée and Streck 2013). This terminology has become the taken for granted language for discussing many international political matters, not just obviously and immediately "environmental" matters.

ENVIRONMENTAL (IN)SECURITY

At the heart of *Our Common Future* was a concern that shortages of resources would lead to conflict, and that sustainable development was the answer to prevent it, precisely by anticipating potential resource shortages and building economies that were sustainable in the sense of using resources so that they didn't run out. *Our Common Future* also expressed concerns about the arms race and the financial resources expended on military matters in the cold war, monies that could be much more usefully spent on development, health and environmental management. The report's authors also bluntly warned that warfare was likely to stymie efforts to implement sustainable development. Development for most societies requires peace. Environmental security is an essential prerequisite for sustainable development and in the long run sustainable development is necessary for environmental security.

In the early 1980s, as alarm grew about the dangers of nuclear warfare, environmental research on the effects of nuclear explosions was raising alarm about the likely second order effects of nuclear weapons beyond the immediate fire and shock wave destruction. While fallout was a major issue and the long term illnesses from radioactivity at least tentatively understood, other effects, such as the disruption to electronic systems caused by the electromagnetic pulse given off by nuclear detonations and, in the case of high altitude detonations, damage to the stratospheric ozone layer, continued to be examined (Peterson 1983). A crucial innovation in this thinking came in 1983 with the publication of a couple of papers clearly delineating the potential for climate disruptions should multiple nuclear detonations and firestorms loft large amounts of smoke, soot and dust into the upper atmosphere during the Northern Hemisphere growing season (Crutzen and Birks 1983).

The possibilities of an extended "nuclear winter" disrupting agriculture by changing growing conditions for crops added to the list of likely adverse consequences of a nuclear conflict (Turco, Toon, Ackerman et al. 1983; Ehrlich, Harte, Harwell et al. 1983; see also Sagan and Turco 1990). In the process it became abundantly clear that humanity could potentially cause an abrupt if mostly temporary change in the earth's climate. This added one more reason to rethink security given that the scale of firepower now available made everyone, regardless of whether they were combatants or not, vulnerable to warfare. Environmental insecurity on a global scale presented an obvious existential threat to much of humanity. As the nuclear winter discussion suggested, this might come indirectly through rapid onset catastrophic climate change.

Diverting funds from military preparation to create such an event was a key additional theme in *Our Common Future*; challenging the arms culture and offering much more useful alternatives for funding health care, environmental remediation and development suggested making a safer and more healthy world as the key to environmental security in the future. While the term environmental security itself only appears in passing in *Our Common Future*, environmental insecurity is clearly articulated as the problem to be addressed. Environmental security is obviously the condition that has to be established if absent, or protected if it already exists. The term appears explicitly in subsequent discussions, and simultaneously as part of the extended United Nations engagement with environmental issues in the 1980s.

The term explicitly appears as part of the Soviet Union's ideas of *New Thinking* in this period too. Alexandre Timoshenko's (1992) subsequent summation of much of this emphasizes the need for international law to grapple with what he specifically terms "ecological security" issues, and to do so in a non-competitive way given that common interests should generate common concerns with flourishing ecologies. Focusing on the common heritage of mankind as well as inter-generational equity, Timoshenko links these to United Nations resolutions in the 1980s where climate was noted as a common concern as well as alarm expressed by Soviet thinkers, including Mikhail Gorbachev (1988) in the 1980s, about the dangers of major industrial and nuclear accidents as an ecological dimension of international security. Not least Timoshenko suggests that ecological security shifts the focus from traditional "react and correct" environmental regulations to a "forecast and prevent" framework, and as such ought to redistribute resources in the security sector away from military matters and towards anticipating and avoiding likely future dangers.

While *Our Common Future* did not offer an explicit definition of environmental security, focusing more on sustainable development as the solution to environmental insecurities, the 1992 Olaf Palme lecture, which was delivered by Gro Harlem Brundtland on the theme of "The Environment, Security and Development" and published in the annual yearbook of the Stockholm International Peace Research Institute in 1993, led to a fairly clear articulation. The lecture's text is accompanied by a technical appendix by Richard Moss which offers a definition of environmental security in which it is suggested that "Environmental security is defined as the condition which exists when governments are able to mitigate the social and political impacts of environmental scarcity of resources, drawing on their own capabilities as well as the capabilities of inter-governmental organizations and non-governmental organizations" (Moss 1993, 27). This clearly links adequate supplies of needed resources to the notion of security, an economic definition which implies that effective extraction from environmental sources is the key consideration. Crucially it also includes government and other agency capacity to deal with scarcities, which was specified as the key problem. This definition is fairly close to the subsequent use of the term eco-security by environmental managers in China concerned to think through regional environmental impacts and ecological sustainability (Zhao, Zou, Cheng et al. 2006).

But the 1993 definition attached to Brundtland's name is very expansive and includes environmental services too:

> Environmental resources include not only (a) non-renewable resources such as oil and minerals and (b) renewable resources such as fisheries products, biomass and fresh water, but also (c) environmental services such as waste assimilation, nutrient recycling, generation of soils, regulation of atmospheric conditions and climate, and the creation and maintenance of genetic diversity. (Moss 1993, 27)

Thus ecological functions in cleaning up messes made by human activities, including climate change, are worked in here too. But in linking these together in a summary statement, Moss (1993, 27) emphasizes all this in terms of scarcity: "Environmental security is thus a function of three sets of factors: (a) current and projected levels of resource exploitation; (b) the social and political impacts of scarcity, and (c) the response capabilities that are available to mitigate the effects of scarcity."

What is not in this final articulation of the concept is a matter of environmental services to deal with pollution and the consequences of consumption. Clearly in the case of climate change in particular the problem isn't scarcity, it's just the opposite. The widespread availability of relatively easy to access fossil fuels is generating greenhouse gases and hence climate change. There is far too much fossil fuel, not too little. Scarcity overall is precisely the opposite of the problem. Which is why climate campaigners frequently use the phrase "keep it in the ground". The environmental services needed to deal with the effects of resource consumption frequently slide out of the picture with this focus on scarcity. It is of course possible to stretch Moss's (1993) definition and argue that what is now scarce are intact landscapes and ecosystems that can capture the excess carbon in the atmosphere, but this convolution is in danger of shifting the focus away from the causes of climate change in the excessive consumption activities of urban-industrial economies and blaming rural residents and those in the Global South of mismanaging landscapes that "we" urban consumers "need" to absorb our waste products, reiterating things in terms of an imperial view of the world (Brand and Wissen 2021). But, as the latter parts of this book suggest, these ecosystem services, and their active construction and reconstruction as part of regenerative ecological activities, are now a key part of what needs attention in rethinking environmental security in the next phase of the Anthropocene, always assuming that the firepower creating climate change dangers can be rapidly constrained.

These ambiguities, both including renewable and non-renewable resources as "environmental" and including pollution cleanup in with resources scarcities, have long plagued much of the discussion of environment and the various social movements that adopt the terminology of environmentalism (O'Riordan 1976). But none of this helps clarify matters, especially as overarching policy goals are concerned. Moss (1993), citing Homer-Dixon's (1991) early work among others, also noted that environmental difficulties may lead to conflict or to social mobilization demanding government reform. The opposition to the Soviet system in Eastern Europe around pollution and health issues is noted as a source of the nationalism that was in part responsible for the collapse of Eastern European regimes in the late 1980s. There, clearly environmental matters profoundly influenced politics. Even if they were not an explicit source of conflict, clearly mobilization around these issues had in part undermined the security of the Soviet modelled governments in Eastern Europe.

THE WORLD IN 2022

Now, as noted in the preface to this volume, in Dan Smith's terms we live in the world that the *Limits to Growth* warned about and that the Stockholm conference attendees had mostly hoped to avoid; we live in a world of "Anthropocene (In)securities" to use the title of the Stockholm International Peace Research Institute (SIPRI) report reflecting on the half century since the 1972 meeting (Lövbrand and Mobjörk 2021). As later chapters in this volume will discuss in some detail, the legacy of the failed or inadequate efforts to grapple with the agenda laid out in Stockholm, and subsequently in more detail in *Our Common Future*, now in part requires rethinking environmental security by shifting the focus from only preventing future difficulties to doing so while simultaneously working out how to live with the results of the failure to do so over the last half century. Key to this is reimagining the context for humanity, of us as part of a rapidly changing dynamic ecosphere where decisions made by the rich and powerful about the constitution of the technosphere in coming decades will be key to future trajectories.

Thinking in terms of ecologies, and their flourishing as key to security, rather than purely in terms of states or their inhabitants, is an essential part of this rethinking (McDonald 2021). Where much unnecessary damage has been done to living systems, now the tasks are to think about rewilding, about facilitating the reconstruction of flourishing systems. Integrating them into human activities is part of what needs to be done. These new ecological arrangements also have to be resilient in the sense of being able to adapt to a much wider range of climate circumstances than was the case in the twentieth century. Rather than a focus on protection of separate stable spaces from encroachment, now the tasks at hand are about producing flexible arrangements that allow human activities without destroying ecological possibilities in particular places. Tackling the practices of extractivism across many modes of economic activity and thinking instead of closed systems, permacultures and novel modes of urban living are parts of this new agenda, because as the last few decades have shown, development as practiced isn't sustainable (Buck 2021). Living in a dynamic changing world means that species have to be able to migrate as circumstances change, and this too requires relaxing the strict territorial demarcations that have so often been what environmental policies of parks and ecosystem protection have been about.

Above all, the focus on dynamic geographies also requires a recognition that in many ways the most extreme and rapid changes to the ecosphere are happening where discussions of environmental security half a century ago never considered, in the Arctic regions of the world, what can reasonably be called the north of the north where dramatic change has long been in evidence (Dalby 2003). Yes, perhaps the worst suffering caused by the over-consumption of fossil fuels in particular will be caused in the climate disrupted regions of what is called the Global South, but the most dramatic heating is in the Arctic region with all the dangers of accelerating permafrost melting and enhanced greenhouse gas emissions. The possibilities of runaway climate change, where methane and carbon dioxide emissions from this melting and increased boreal forest wildfires generate a powerful positive feedback mechanism that accelerates climate change, is one of the nightmare scenarios that worries climate scientists. Even if the evidence for such an eventuality hasn't yet appeared conclusively, current trajectories are exceedingly worrisome.

All of which requires a reconsideration of the scope of human activity, and a reconsideration of what was until recently more or less taken for granted as a separate backdrop to human affairs. While sustainable development accepted, at least rhetorically, the enmeshment of economic activity within a larger ecological realm, too often it has worked to suggest that the reliable provision of resources for future economic exploitation is what matters in considerations of environmental security. Climate change and the growing problems of extinction have demonstrated both that this isn't adequate and that humanity is an integral part of the earth system, not just an appendage on a separate and stable environment. This requires conceptual innovations that challenge the most persistent dichotomies of modernity. Now climate and extinction require scholars to amalgamate geology and history, earth and humanity, in what Bruno Latour (2014) suggested might best be termed "geostory".

3. Geostory: deep time and history

DIVIDING NATURE

The discussion of sustainable development and environmental security mostly takes the notions of development and environment for granted. These categories however have histories; they are, despite their prevalence, not the only possible categorizations. While much of human history in many civilizations has some notion of nature, the more specific category of environment is, in the Western world, a construction of the late nineteenth century and a formulation that intruded as such on global politics only in the latter half of the twentieth (Conway 2019). While environment carries numerous connotations, clearly it is a formulation of something that surrounds something else, an entity that is environed. As such it codifies the division between humanity and the rest of the cosmos, or more specifically the planet. Linked to parallel considerations of the emergence of territory as a category of governance, it also facilitates the processes of enclosure and commodification that drive the great transformation at the heart of modernity (Blomley 2019).

As nature is turned into property, it can be divided, owned, financialized and privatized in processes of transformation that frequently are termed development (Moore 2015). But, and the catch is important, failure to do this in sensible ways leads to pollution, degradation and scarcities, and as the twentieth century unfolded, this led to a growing sense of an environmental crisis that could be understood to be global. Resource management has to be part of successful development, conserving supplies and ensuring that development can thus be sustainable. Too much pollution, failure to use ecosystems wisely and the exhaustion of resources all lead to trouble and, in the more alarmist formulations, conflict. In at least one critical commentary, nature has simply become a battlefield (Keucheyan 2016). Scarcities supposedly lead to conflict, although the historical record suggests that most resource conflicts are a result of their exploitation for distant economic actors rather than strictly local disputes (Le Billon 2012). The lack of clarity and specification of what is environment, what is a resource and which scarcity matters to whom has been a powerful source of ideological confusion, and has given rise to environmental alarmism, as well as utopian promises, based on assumptions of ever more sophisticated technological innovations, of ever more appropriations of the natural world to supply unlimited economic growth.

Most recently climate change and growing concerns about the rapidly rising rates of species extinction have added to earlier concerns about resource shortages, pollution and ecological collapse. The sheer scale of human modifications to the planetary system has suggested not only that humanity has taken its fate into its own hands, but that the notion of environment itself may not be adequate to grapple with what needs to be done to shape the future in a manner that will ensure the long term survival of human civilization. Critics suggest that the violent practices of appropriation and exploitation that have led to the current crisis mean that the notion of civilization is premature, but the productive powers now in existence might yet lead to a more sensible and humane mode of existence for all humanity.

The Anthropocene as a concept encompasses this sense of global capitalism as a planet altering force, one that will have long term consequences for the planetary system, and for future modes of life. But the rapidly proliferating discussion of the Anthropocene, how it might be specified, whether it is useful as a scientific or political term, focuses attention on how the current crisis is contextualized (Moore 2016). In the debate about when it might be said to have begun, there lies a larger question about the role of humanity as a planet shaping force. If humanity is in fact a novel "forcing agent" in the earth system, then when it first became one, and how, is a key question. But of course not all humanity has played an equal part in shaping the system, and critics of the notion of an Anthropocene are quick to insist that it is only recent global appropriations of environment by the rich and powerful elements in the capitalist system that are responsible for the dangers that most of the rest of humanity now face.

All this matters greatly for the consideration of what environmental security might now mean. In particular climate change is at the heart of this discussion as growing storms, droughts, wildfire, floods and related disruptions raise questions of security in many ways. But these disruptions require thinking about both geological scale transformation and historical change together, a matter of conflating the scientific and the human, geology and history in Bruno Latour's (2014) terms, a matter of geostory. Framing matters in these terms refuses to take environment as a given backdrop to the human drama, and insists instead on embedding humanity in its context, one understood over geological timescales, and understanding humanity as a geological scale change agent, among which the rich and powerful are initiating a very rapid transformation of the earth system with potentially disastrous consequences for planetary life (Barnosky, Hadly, Bascompte et al. 2012).

The argument in this volume is focused on trying to link up the scientific discussion of these matters but think through the human consequences in terms of security, and the possible connections between environmental change and violence. The link between these matters is most obviously about firepower, a category at the heart of concerns about warfare and dominance in geopolitics, but also, as the rest of this chapter will explicate, one that is essential to much else in the rise of humanity to become the dominant species in the planetary system. Teasing out these linkages more explicitly is key to rethinking environmental security. Earth system science makes it clear that there is no taken for granted backdrop to human activities that is a given context for humanity. Humanity as a form of life is an ecological actor, changing its habitat, as so many other animals do as a consequence of their activities. But now this is having planet wide consequences which are the new context for considering what has become called environmental security.

THE GEOLOGICAL CONTEXT

Thinking in terms of geology and the human context in the longer term evolution of the planet and the ecosphere in particular suggests that we are part of a very dynamic, and at times dangerous, system. Indeed some of the historical compilations of previous human calamities, famines, pandemics and wars suggest that the dynamism of the planetary system is such that humanity's survival, never mind its extraordinary expansion in recent centuries, is at best a fluke event (Jenkins 2021). Existential threats loom, and in the past could easily have rendered humanity extinct (Ord 2020). The assumption that humanity is here as part of the biosphere and will continue to be in perpetuity is just that, a very large assumption. The related modern assumption, that the planetary context is stable, predictable and likely to remain so, is likewise an assumption, one that the rapidly accelerating disruptions of climate change in particular and environmental transformation in general render highly dubious. But the cultural assumptions in modernity, of human mastery of its environmental circumstances, have dominated the social sciences for a long time, and in part shape the failure of international relations to grapple with the human material context. Removing this cultural myopia and looking more clearly at the history of the planet suggests that contextual matters are much more dynamic than the social sciences usually assume, and once that is done and the condition of planetarity (Clark and Szerszynski 2021) substituted as the ontological framework, matters of security take on new interpretations.

Popular culture with its disaster movies and speculative fictions sometimes offers a corrective to assumptions of stationarity with the premise that the past is an accurate indication of future conditions. The discussion of the fate of the dinosaurs highlights ecosystem fragilities. A huge meteor strike apparently led to the extinction of the dinosaurs, or at least was a contributing factor in their demise. Some accounts suggest instant immolation for animals close to the impact and slower starvation elsewhere as food supplies were promptly destroyed, or as plants failed to grow in the cooling period that followed due to skies darkened by dust and debris. But that said, of course some dinosaurs did survive; their descendants are what humans now call birds.

There is a long history of meteor impacts, and indeed the current formation of the earth and the moon was apparently a result of a massive impact in the early history of the solar system. Mars, Mercury and the moon, without oceans, biospheres or mobile crustal plates that might obscure the evidence, are pock-marked with impact craters. Fortunately in recent decades space monitoring systems have been carefully tracking asteroids and comets that have trajectories that potentially intersect with earth. Apparently there are few obvious risks of dangerous collisions in the near future, although numerous very minor ones frequently generate shooting stars in the night sky. If a dangerous trajectory is discovered, the possibilities of using spacecraft to nudge the asteroid into a safer orbit arise, although early warning long in advance would be key to an appropriate response. With due apologies to Bruce Willis movie fans, blowing them apart with nuclear weapons is not likely to be an effective response.

Volcanos have in the past generated earth shaping changes both globally and on the immediate scale as in Mount Toba's eruption and the more recent detonations of Tamboro in 1815 and the well documented case of Krakatoa (Winchester 2003). Mount St Helens exploded in 1980 in the Western United States, and eleven years later in the Philippines, Mount Pinatubo's eruption lofted aerosols into the stratosphere with a pronounced cooling effect on global temperatures (McCormick, Thomason and Trepte 1995). This subsequently generated speculation about the possibilities of artificially cooling the world by using stratospheric aerosol injection, a form of solar "geoengineering" to mimic the "Pinatubo effect". Apart from the immediate effects close to the eruption, humans frequently note their consequences when airplane routes are disrupted. Jet engines are vulnerable to damage from volcanic dust.

The debate about the cause of the demise of the dinosaurs also considers the possibility that volcanic action triggered fatal climate disruptions. And while science fiction authors, and Star Trek fans in particular, may speculate about controlling volcanic action, at least for the foreseeable future this is way beyond plausible human capabilities. The possibility of a major long lasting eruption exists, and that might have dramatic effects on the climate system as has been the case in the past; the massive lava ejection into the so called "Siberian traps" probably caused climate disruptions that led to the largest recorded mass extinction in the planet's history at the end of the Permian.

Another potential hazard is a supernova type stellar explosion somewhere in the galactic vicinity which could cause atmospheric disturbances due to large gamma radiation and, among other things, disrupt the earth's ozone layer. Although the chances of this are probably exceedingly remote, such speculation is useful in that it also emphasizes the importance of thinking of the earth as a dynamic celestial body, not a given stable habitat for humanity. This is the planetarity context that matters in considering contemporary trajectories. One additional inference is the point that, should future human colonization of planets and asteroids occur, and conflict break out between those societies, redirecting asteroids or comets to use as a weapon to impact earth would be relatively easy for those colonists, and much more difficult for earth based societies given the much greater "gravity well" of earth (Deudney 2020). In the long run, space colonization cannot escape security dilemmas and inter-entity conflict dynamics either, as Kim Stanley Robinson's fictional speculations about Mars colonization in his *Mars* novel trilogy suggests, another reason to treat such projects skeptically when considering the long run human future.

Much of the contemporary discussion of global change, climate crisis, the sixth extinction and questions of human survival is now formulated in terms of the new geological age in which it is widely asserted we are now living. The Anthropocene is first and foremost a geological term, one that denotes a major change in the earth system. The finer points of the debate among earth system scientists and geologists about its appropriateness and how it fits into the larger construction of earth history are beyond the scope of this volume (see Zalasiewicz, Waters, Williams and Summerhayes 2019), but the broad outline of the discussion is key to understanding this new contextualization, and with it the implications for international relations in general and the environmental security discussion in particular. The crucial point is that we are now living in new circumstances, ones wrought by human activity, and the massive combustion of fossil fuels in particular. Historical analogies may help interpret matters, but the novel dimensions of the Anthropocene require a rethink of the human condition and who is securing what where.

It is noteworthy that while climate change and the larger ecological predicament is highly ranked by international relations scholars as an important matter, as of the middle of the second decade of this millennium few scholars in the field were taking it as their prime research concern (Harrington 2016). Robert Keohane (2015) made a similar argument more generally about political science in his 2014 James Madison lecture. More specifically the field has been slow to adopt the Anthropocene formulation as the appropriate contextualization for contemporary investigations (Pereira 2017; Simangan 2020). Peace research likewise (Kelly 2021). Much of this is a matter of disciplinary specialization; international relations is about states, institutions, world orders and discussions of war and peace, not a matter of geology. As Hardt (2021) notes, the debates about climate change in the United Nations have likewise, as of 2020, mostly not embraced these new scientific contextualizations either, although in contrast the United Nations Development Programme (2020) has recently begun using the Anthropocene to contextualize what needs to be done in terms of development in the novel circumstances of the twenty first century. But, as this book and these other recent interventions make clear, the implicit contextualization of a stable backdrop to human affairs that much of international relations works within is increasingly out of date and as a result a rethink is urgently needed.

UNIFORMITARIANISM AND CATASTROPHISM

While the history of the geological sciences since the early nineteenth century has been one first of a recognition of how old the earth is, and how to unravel its history from the accumulated sedimentary rocks with their fossil assemblages, more recent concerns have incorporated numerous novel scientific methods both to accurately date rocks and fossils and to connect up seemingly disparate geological features (Lewis and Maslin 2018). Nineteenth and early twentieth century thinking frequently suggested a fairly stable earth with uniformitarianism as a key principle; contemporary processes were an accurate guide to how geological processes had worked in the distant past, and gradual changes were a matter of evolution by natural selection in ways outlined by Darwin. The counter argument, that the world had been subject to dramatic catastrophes in the past, with relatively stable periods in-between, the so called catastrophist theories, suggested a very different history of the earth and its modes of life, with huge, albeit infrequent, disruptions repeatedly reshaping evolution.

In the second half of the twentieth century the gradual acceptance of theories of plate-tectonics, and the consequent confirmation of continental drift, suggested a dynamic earth where landmasses moved and continents coalesced and broke apart, and did so leaving the evidence in rocks that were to be found in widely dispersed locations. The movement of continents also implied shifting ocean currents, and while much of geology is focused on the landmasses above sea level, it is always worth remembering both that life started in the oceans and that they cover 70 percent of the earth's surface, a matter naval personnel understand even if land based security thinkers sometimes forget. Ocean acidification due to the rapid rise in atmospheric carbon dioxide which is being absorbed by seawater looms over discussions of the future of the earth system, and whether it will trigger a global extinction catastrophe.

As the history of the planet has gradually been pieced together in recent decades, what has become clear is that conditions have fluctuated dramatically in the past and life has nearly been extinguished on a number of occasions (Rockström and Gaffney 2021). In events involving dramatic episodes of volcanic action as well as the extension of ice over much of the planet, a so called snow ball world in the distant past, the planet's physical configuration and the chemical composition of its atmosphere and oceans have undergone dramatic changes. These dramatic transformations are part of the earth's history, and remain so. Climate change is highlighting this point; the earth is a dynamic system, and one that faces various rapid transitions in the foreseeable future both in terms of climate disruptions and in terms of the ongoing dramatic alterations to the species mix on land and in the oceans.

Once life established itself in the oceans it has persisted, and sometimes become a significant player in changing how the earth system works. In the 1970s James Lovelock and Lynn Margulis posited that life itself played a key regulatory function in keeping the overall system broadly within parameters that allowed life itself to continue. This so called Gaia Hypothesis (Lovelock 1979) has been broadly confirmed in recent decades, and the significance it has for how environmental security might now be understood is profound. Living things have a role in removing carbon dioxide from the atmosphere, and when they die they sometimes sequester it in sediments on land and on the ocean floor. Volcanoes emit carbon dioxide among other gases, and the amount of carbon dioxide and oxygen in the atmosphere fluctuates, with climate consequences. Now that humanity is rapidly adding carbon dioxide to the atmosphere, and doing so much more rapidly than previous geological transformations have done, the consequences are likely to be quick and dramatic in geological terms.

Life itself is a participant in the earth system, but not the only one. Moving continents, the gradually growing intensity of solar radiation, the intricacies of celestial mechanics and the fluctuation of planetary orbits as well as volcanic action are obviously also key, but these constitute the context within which life evolves, and in doing so it changes the chemistry of the system. The term system here is key, as the lithosphere, atmosphere, hydrosphere, cryosphere and biosphere are all interconnected in complicated and changing ways, best encapsulated in the term ecosphere. There are feedback loops too where changes in one component amplify or negate trends in others. No longer is it possible to posit the planet as a given substrate on which life lives. If all the world is a stage, to borrow the Shakespearian formulation, then it's one with props and characters repeatedly changing the structure of that stage. This is the overall contextualization that now needs to be incorporated into discussions of environmental security.

Crucial for the current discussion is the point that the Isthmus of Panama closed about three million years ago, separating the Atlantic from the Pacific and in the process changing ocean circulation and much of the world's climate. It's about then that ice started collecting on Greenland and that the planet adopted a climate pattern that has been fairly consistent throughout the period since known as the Pleistocene. The more recent part of this was marked by a long term ice age, with large masses of ice on the Northern continents much of the time. But this was interrupted periodically by shorter term "inter-glacial" warming periods where rapid warming led to the temporary retreat of the ice sheets.

This system has come to an end very recently. The period since the last retreat of the ice sheets, with the dramatic flooding events and rapid climate fluctuations between twelve and ten thousand years ago, has been remarkably stable in comparison to the previous million years. This recent period of the Holocene has been when humanity flourished and came to be the dominant species in the earth system. In part this related to the very stable atmospheric conditions that have prevailed over this period, and the fairly consistent level of atmospheric carbon dioxide, the crucial greenhouse gas.

But no longer; human actions have dramatically altered this, and the consequences are starting to play out in ways that are already unsettling the largely predicable climates in most parts of the world as well as the assumptions we make about the future of the planet and how we can live as a result. Much of this is because of the widespread use of fire by humans to change many things. In the process we have introduced something novel into the earth system, a collection of materials, technologies and waste best simply called the technosphere, and the future of this is now key to human security in this now increasingly artificial ecosphere (Zalasiewicz, Williams, Waters et al. 2017). Human actions have also dramatically changed the mix of terrestrial species and their locations, a process of habitat disruption and artificial migration on a planetary scale analogous to earlier rapid geological transformations.

To put this larger context into the environmental security discussion requires a brief but essential digression into matters of ecology and geophysics, the latter at least being familiar to at least the more technical branches of security studies. Indeed some of the key insights into how the earth system operates have their origins in cold war science investigations. The carbon dioxide monitoring station on Moana Lao in Hawai'i dates from the International Geophysical Year in the late 1950s, a time of scientific collaboration in, among other places, Antarctica, despite the obvious military dimensions to contemporaneous research in both the United States and the Soviet Union. The widely seen plots of rising carbon dioxide in the atmosphere, that iconic upward curve that has come to symbolize climate change, date from 1958. In this crucial sense some of the science that explains planetary geophysics is a result of military research, and it is perhaps no accident that militaries around the globe have long been more worried about climate change than many other institutions.

The most obvious points sometimes are the most important in linking environmental matters, security and the human place in the earth system, and this is clearly the case in relation to fire, geology and life (Pyne 2012). The emergence of fire as a geophysical phenomenon in the earth system is dependent on both atmospheric oxygen and fuel to burn. That fuel in the earth system in the detritus from terrestrial life mostly, because what burns is organic matter, rich in carbon. Hence life is fuel for combustion; timber, grass and other vegetation suck carbon dioxide out of the atmosphere in the process of photosynthesis, and provide the fuel supply both for animals to eat and metabolize and for combustion to burn, which returns carbon dioxide to the air. Prior to life emerging from the oceans and colonizing terrestrial surfaces there wasn't fuel to burn. Life itself has produced the oxygen in the atmosphere that we breath and that burns things.

Life itself pulls carbon dioxide out of the atmosphere, reversing the processes of volcanoes that, among other things, expel carbon dioxide into the air. Volcanoes do other things too, not least injecting aerosols into the upper atmosphere and cooling the planet's surface. But terrestrial life is a crucial regulator of atmospheric carbon dioxide levels. Once life in the form of trees in particular colonized land surfaces and subsequently got buried prior to decaying, then fossil fuels were the result, deeply buried and stored carbon as part of the geological processes of carbon sequestration. Other life forms buried in the processes of sedimentation gave rise to petroleum and natural gases, locking large quantities of carbon into the ground. At least this was part of the natural history of the planet until *Homo sapiens* figured out how to reverse the process and, in using fossil fuels for numerous combustion technologies, started rapidly turning rocks back into air. Quite literally.

The climate of the earth system isn't all about carbon dioxide levels, but they matter not least because increases in carbon dioxide levels are clearly related to perturbations of the earth system in the geological past. Severe extinction events in the past have been related to rises in carbon dioxide levels and their fall related to episodes of glaciation. Other factors such as the fluctuations in the earth's orbit and how the earth's axis tilts in relation to the sun over long periods have a profound effect on climate. These so called Milankovich cycles, named after the astronomer who worked out their periodicity and how they interconnect, have shaped the major glacial and inter-glacial fluctuations in the planetary system over the last few million years. But the earth is a dynamic system and the continents move, and with them the ocean currents too; only in the last few million years, since the Isthmus of Panama closed and prevented equatorial flows of ocean currents, has the configuration of the climate system approximated what humanity has known throughout its history.

Crucial to this configuration is the role of the Gulf Stream in the North Atlantic, pushing warm water north to give Europe a relatively mild climate, and sucking carbon dioxide from surface waters in the North Atlantic down into the depths prior to recirculating those waters deep below the surface into the rest of the oceans. In 2021 alarm was expressed once again over the slowing of that current and the possibility that melting Greenland ice is changing the density of the surface waters and slowing this Atlantic Meridional Overturning

Current (AMOC) "conveyor belt" (Caesar, McCarthy, Thornally et al. 2021). While its abruptly stopping, the scenario in the Hollywood disaster movie *The Day After Tomorrow*, is unlikely, if it slows substantially then Europe, ironically, may temporarily suffer colder weather if the Gulf Stream's waters don't warm the continent as they have done throughout human history.

Antarctica has been over the southern pole for much longer, accumulating ice slowly for tens of millions of years there. White surfaces, ice and snow, reflect much more sunlight back into space than darker ones, oceans or land surfaces, and this affects the overall heat balance of the planet too. Melting ice in the Arctic in particular is worrisome because of the enhanced albedo effect of darker water surfaces and their presence in Northern regions for longer parts of the year. Both Greenland and Antarctic ice cores have recorded changes in climate over the last million years, trapped atmospheric gases revealing the complex changes over this period, one that has seen repeated advances and retreats of ice sheets over the Northern Hemisphere landmasses. Driven by Milankovich cycles, and enhanced heating and cooling as greenhouse gas levels rose and fell as vegetation spread and retreated with the glaciers, the geological history can be traced by examining this frozen record.

But no longer do the Milankovich cycles drive the climate system in the way they have done since before the emergence of *Homo sapiens*. Now the most important driver of climate change is the extraordinarily rapid rise in carbon dioxide in the atmosphere. Methane and nitrous oxide too, as well as other gases given off by human activities, notably the ozone depleting chlorofluorocarbons, contribute to heating the planet, but carbon dioxide is the most significant trace gas in the atmosphere that traps heat. Human activities are now the key to its rapidly growing presence. On current trajectories it is set to double its concentration later this century, and one of the key scientific quests of the moment is calculating exactly how sensitive the global temperature change is to this rising level of the leading greenhouse gas. This climate sensitivity, as it is known, is fundamental to projections of future disruptions. The question is how hot will it get, and how fast? That all this recently added gas will increase temperatures notably in coming decades is clear, but policy decisions to curtail combustion will slow this down. The sooner combustion is rapidly reduced the slower the increase in temperature and the easier it will be for human systems to adapt to new circumstances. This is key to numerous forms of security in the twenty first century.

If much of the realist literature that shaped international relations, and more specifically strategic studies, since the middle of the twentieth century is focused on the importance of power, then the Anthropocene discussion requires consideration of the material processes involved in its operation. Power in human terms is about the ability to shape circumstances and force others to act in ways that they might not wish to. Coercion involves the threats of violence and force and, when it meets resistance, the use of that violence to either eliminate others or overcome resistance and force them to do your bidding. Technology has been key to this in recent centuries, and the ever larger application of industrial production systems to the production of the mode of violence produced the mass conscript armies of the first half of the twentieth century armed with ever more violent modes of firepower. Subsequently the destructive capabilities of nuclear weapons in turn dwarfed these technologies, and missiles extended their range and speed dramatically too, threatening all life on the terrestrial surfaces.

Now power is about the ability to shape the configuration of many of the key planetary systems, not least the climate one. Determining how hot the planet will get is a key part of global politics, and the Paris Climate Change Agreement, with its aspirational statements about keeping the planet's average temperature increase to close to one and a half degrees Celsius, is about precisely this power. Who decides how hot it will get, and hence with what consequences for humans in various parts of the planet, is now the most important question of which forms of human power are applied how and where, with specific consequences for human security depending on wealth and crucially geography.

Perhaps the most alarming aspect of all this is that the rise in concentration of atmospheric carbon dioxide is causing the acidification of the oceans. Already this is part of the problem coral reefs face, in addition to rising water temperatures. The rapid acidification of ocean waters is happening at a rate for which there is no obvious parallel in the geological history of the planet. "The only thing that comes close to this is the Paloecene-Eocene Thermal Maximum shock 55 million years ago—a major extinction event, particularly in the ocean—but that happened over a much longer period" (Rockström and Gaffney 2021, 80). Given that life is predominantly an aqueous phenomenon, this is especially ominous for the future even if humanity, as a terrestrial rather than oceanic species, is slow to understand how fundamental such a shift in the earth system actually is. The possibility of such drastic disruptions to the earth system looms if humanity continues burning fossil fuels into the future.

COMBUSTION AND FIREPOWER

Steven Pyne's (2012) discussions of fire history offer the key here in linking the historical and the geological. His argument is simple and profound for rethinking environmental security. In all the discussions of what makes humanity unique among other species, he suggests that fire is the key. Historians frequently look to other things: culture, language, technology, even bipedal locomotion, habitat making and so on. But clearly animals have the rudiments of language, and the ability to communicate and learn socially. Whales and elephants obviously learn, and cooperate over large distances, changing migration paths in relation to changing ecological conditions, food supplies and threats from humans. Birds, squirrels and other animals build substantial and intricate nests. Ants and termites build complex communal habitats. Beavers are fine hydrological engineers that have substantial ecological transformation capabilities, their dams changing many landscapes for other species. But only humans have learned to start and partially control fire. Some birds do try to move smoldering embers from wildfire to start other fires to flush out prey, but only humans have learned what Pyne calls the ignition trick.

Our ancestors learned to start fires, and keep them burning by providing them with fuel. That changed everything for our species. It allowed us to keep warm in places where survival without additional heat was difficult. Fire led to cooking, and in the process, by changing diets and allowing humans to effectively pre-digest various foods, extended what we could eat and hence our ecological range. Fire offered a weapon against other animals, and against other humans too. Driving animals into a killing ground by using fire is organized human violence on a substantial scale. Scorched earth is a tactic in hunting as well as in warfare. Fire allows the hardening of spear tips, which also helps in contests with large animals, and as a mode of hunting for food too. Hunting has over time reduced animal populations in numerous places and is a contributing cause of the elimination of large species in the aftermath of the last ice age. This was a large scale ecological change in many parts of the world. Fire allowed humans to range widely as the glaciers retreated, and the ecological consequences were profound as humans were able to eliminate potential competitors in numerous places.

As more settled communities emerged, fire helped with deforestation, as well as grassland regeneration and numerous other useful ecological processes. Land clearing for agriculture is facilitated by burning forests, a phenomenon that is still part of the process of expanding agriculture in tropical forests to this day, and a matter of contentious politics, only most obviously in Indonesia and Brazil, although caution needs to be exercised in attributing all fires to forest clearing in these cases. Fires also allowed for the crucial innovation of smelting metals, and with that the expansion of all sorts of technologies, not only the obvious ones of weapons. Tin, bronze, iron and subsequently steel have been key technologies of war, as well as much else in human history, but smelting is a key geological process, effectively a new mode of metamorphosis in geological terms where heated rocks transform their minerals as a result of chemical transformation under pressure. And more recently heat is crucial to the construction of that key new artificial rock that we know as concrete. Here too military as well as civilian uses of this novel geological form matters.

Most recently humanity has taken these smelted forms and used them to construct ever more sophisticated spaces for the controlled use of fire. Mostly this is key in military terms, in terms of cannon, muskets and rifled weapons as well as the propulsion systems of rockets, a matter of firepower literally. But elsewhere, in what Pyne (2021) calls a pyric transition, ever more sophisticated uses of fire have been harnessed in the technological transformation that is usually called the industrial revolution. First in the form of the combustion spaces of steam engines, concentrating heat to make steam and hence converting heat into mechanical energy. This allowed for railways and what are still called steam ships, using those engines to transform shipping and rapidly expand global trade, European imperial reach and the processes of colonization in the nineteenth century. Then subsequently, in what are correctly termed internal combustion engines, fire was made to generate much more efficient mechanical energy in the cylinders of those engines, setting weapons in motion in tanks and armoured cars, and all the rest of us in motion in the extensive expansion of suburbanization of the twentieth century, made possible by the private automobile. And, despite the recent increasingly popular use of electric vehicles, nearly all of those are still powered by gasoline and diesel engines years after the signing of the Paris Agreement on Climate Change.

All of this is a matter of the ever more sophisticated utilization of combustion, the power made possible by controlling fire. This firepower, to extend the conventional use of the term to encompass these larger related processes, is key to the extraordinary extension of humanity in recent generations. In terms of the geological part of geostory, this is key, because at the heart of the rapidly escalating climate crisis of our times, combustion is what is directly causing greenhouse gases to rise and indirectly at the heart of most of the other processes that are changing the atmosphere rapidly and dangerously. Military power and ecological transformation go hand in hand, and therein lies one key to the current crisis of global environmental insecurity. The other is the matter of the extensive use of similar technologies for civilian use in the last three quarters of a century.

In Barry Buzan's (1991) synthesis of security studies he focuses on the importance of arms races and both the quantity and the quality of weapons in the hands of rival powers. Competition for a technical edge over adversaries is a key dynamic in modern military rivalries. While this matters in terms of particular historical circumstances, it is also worth noting that fire has long been a weapon of war, even if the modes of starting it have changed. Scorched earth tactics are as old as warfare; depriving rivals of resources, food, shelter and fuel is a key to winning a conflict. In the history of the technologies of violence, innovations in combustion with the invention and use of gunpowder both to destroy things directly and, in the form of rockets, to propel projectiles added to military capabilities (Crosby 2002). Ever more sophisticated explosives are based on combustion, and the destruction they make possible is key to combat capabilities for most military forces. Rockets have been updated into guided missiles, and at the largest scale intercontinental ballistic missiles, all requiring sophisticated fuels to burn for propulsion.

Fire too has made ever more sophisticated weapons possible. Smelting metals and shaping swords, spears and armour requires metallurgy based on combustion. Combined with gunpowder, metallurgy provides mortars, cannons and ever more sophisticated muskets, rifles and subsequently machine guns. Land based cannons of ever greater power required dramatically changing the configuration of fortifications; high medieval walls provided easy targets, and had to be replaced by structures that resisted or deflected cannon balls. Naval gunnery grew ever more sophisticated as metallurgy improved in the nineteenth century in particular. As cannons gave way to breech loading weapons and rifled barrels, the range and capabilities of these weapons gave us iron clads, dreadnoughts and then battleships.

Key to these innovations was the development of the other use of firepower, the industrial application of technology to turn heat energy into mechanical energy, crucially in the iconic machines of the industrial revolution, steam engines. Using coal or wood to heat water and generate pressure in boilers allowed pistons and cylinders to generate mechanical force. Once that trick was mastered, and James Watt's more sophisticated versions of John Newcomen's designs could govern their power output, numerous things became possible. Industrial power generation mechanized production, notably first in the Lancashire cotton mills, as industrialists used these machines to greatly increase their control over their labourers (Malm 2016). Put in motion as railway locomotives and then propulsion units in ships, steam ships replaced sail and dramatically enhanced long distance transport in the nineteenth century.

Further control over combustion, moving the fire itself into the cylinders of engines in the aptly called "internal combustion engines" powered by diesel and gasoline, led to dramatic extensions of the range and power of transportation. Airplanes followed too, with piston engines and then jet engines making the atmosphere a whole new arena for combat. Incendiaries could now set distant cities and factories afire, but most of these new weapons still relied on combustive explosions to do their damage, even if secondary fires consumed enemy people, equipment and buildings. The firestorms in European and Japanese cities demonstrated this all too clearly in the 1940s.

The rise of modernity has been about both colonization and industrialization, the former frequently providing the raw materials for key parts of the production processes that were accelerated by industrial production systems. The rise of industrial states is not unrelated to the growth of imperial power in the nineteenth century, first in Britain and subsequently in other empires, of which the American and Russian expansions in the late nineteenth and early twentieth centuries were especially notable. The partly thwarted rise of

Germany and the constrictions of geography in Europe are part of the story of how these expansions turned to war with all the tragic consequences in the first half of the twentieth century. It is also worth remembering that imperial policies stymied economic innovation in many of the colonies, and delayed their "development" into modern states. Amitav Ghosh (2016) notes that if Britain hadn't stopped Indian experimentation with steam engines in the early nineteenth century, and the industrial revolution had spread there then, the upshot might well have been that the current climate crisis might have occurred some decades earlier!

GEOPOLITICS

Crucial to the story of firepower and its role in the current security crisis is the link between the increasingly sophisticated control of combustion and geopolitics; energy systems are tied to struggles for political dominance much more so than to the market forces that economic explanations for growth frequently suggest (Daggett 2021). Steam ships were powered by coal in the nineteenth century, and as steam power was gradually introduced into nautical affairs following the initial naval engagements in the American civil war, coal was the fuel used. But engineering innovations made possible the use of oil as a much more effective fuel for ships. In the case of Britain, whose Royal Navy did for a while rule the waves, coal was to be had in substantial quantities at home. Petroleum was in short supply domestically and hence, while it might be a better fuel, securing its reliable supply for the navy would require foreign sources which might be at risk of enemy interdiction in the event of hostilities.

Thus the decision to change the navy from coal to oil came with huge geopolitical consequences. As one of the key players in the British admiralty, Winston Churchill was part of the decision making to take the risk. As he wrote a couple of decades later:

> The oil supplies of the world were in the hands of vast oil trusts under foreign control. To commit the navy irrevocably to oil was indeed to take arms against a sea of troubles. If we overcame the difficulties and surmounted the risks, we should be able to raise the whole power and efficiency of the navy to a definitely higher level; better ships, better crews, higher economies, more intense forms of war power—in a word, mastery itself was the prize of the venture. (Churchill 1923, as cited by Dahl 2001, 51)

The British involvements in what was then called Persia are tied into this search for fuel supplies and the subsequent history of the region is in part a result of this decision. Daniel Yergin's (1991) history of petroleum is named *The Prize* in recognition of Churchill's formulation of the importance of petroleum in this mastery of the geopolitics of the modern world. The Middle East has been a key supplier of petroleum since then, and much of the history of the last few decades is tied to this geography; so too is the pattern of violence, the incidence of wars and the fluctuating price of petroleum (Bichler and Nitzan 2004). The industrial infrastructure and logistics for both weapons systems and fossil fuel extraction are interconnected in numerous complex ways.

A further extension of the connections between firepower, domination and danger came with nuclear technology, once again offering greatly expanded capabilities for destruction. The fission weapons that destroyed Nagasaki and Hiroshima were puny in comparison with the subsequent fusion or thermonuclear weapons that were built and tested in the 1950s. While the initial detonation isn't technically combustion, the secondary effects of nuclear weapons include widespread incineration and damage caused by fires (Peterson 1983). Combustion remains at the heart of military capabilities; the technical innovations in the Second World War with engines, vehicles and aircraft extended the capabilities of firepower dramatically and in the process set in motion the expansion of mobility that marked the second half of the twentieth century, the period that earth system scientists aptly term the great acceleration (McNeill and Engelke 2016). Nuclear technology has also enhanced naval mobility, with reactors powering many of the large naval vessels as well as submarines currently in service.

But the sheer scale of the potential destruction in the cold war arsenals of the superpowers threatened complete destruction should they ever be detonated in a conflict. The rapid expansion of the superpower arsenals amounted to a logic of exterminism, in Edward Thompson's (1982) phrasing, where the competitive logic of building ever larger nuclear arsenals in the pursuit of some chimera of security leads to annihilation. The arms culture that *Our Common Future* criticized explicitly warned of this logic, one that threatened to make environmental insecurity the future condition for all. The apotheosis of firepower is the threat of nuclear winter and the destabilization of the ecosphere to such an extent that civilized life becomes impossible. Firepower has become an existential threat to the civilization that has used it so extensively. Understanding security in terms of power, the key to understanding it in terms of dominance, has in a world altered by fire come to render humanity insecure in novel ways, precisely due to the search for these forms of "security".

Given these connections between firepower in the conventional military sense of the ability to bring destruction to an enemy, and the technologies of modernity, industrial and transportation related that are all reliant on combustion, it's not too much of a stretch to suggest that the term firepower can be extended to this larger assemblage of technologies. The ability of combustion based technologies to transform environments rapidly is part of the current stage of the Anthropocene, one that is destabilizing the earth system. Fire is still used to clear forests, as the concerns about tropical rain forest destruction in numerous places in Africa as well as the headline cases of the Amazon and Indonesia highlight, but a key part of this transformation involves the use of chainsaws, mostly powered by that ubiquitous technology of modernity, the internal combustion engine.

Concrete too requires the large use of combustion to generate the heat needed to make it. Most industrial processes use heat in some form. Bulldozers and excavators that are remaking landscapes and transforming ecosystems into monoculture agricultural spaces likewise. Boats, planes and trains as well as vehicles nearly all rely on firepower in this application to move. Modernity may be epitomized by mobility, but much of this is a matter of applied power provided by the technological control of fire. "Firepower" quite literally. Now, as carbon dioxide levels rise in the atmosphere, we have come to realize that one of the consequences of all this firepower is climate change. History now is about geological scale changes, hence the necessity of thinking about geostory (Latour 2014), geology and history combined into one contextualization, one narrative that emphasizes the fact that the future of the planet depends on how firepower is shaped in coming decades.

In Pyne's (2021) terms the first fires, of nature burning organic material, were supplemented by second fires, humans working with fire to change landscapes and, using organic materials, usually wood, to extend their range and technological capabilities. All this changed when, in his terms, third fire or lithic fire, using the long sequested carbon in rocks, in what are called fossil fuels, powered novel industrial arrangements and unleashed a new geological situation where fire now dominates the climate system, not the ice of the Pleistocene period. Coupled with attempts in many parts of the world to suppress first fires—where fire is a natural part of ecosystems, facilitating their regeneration—and colonial attempts to prevent native peoples in parts of the world using their traditional fire practices to shape landscapes, now climate disrupted spaces are generating much more intense and larger wildfires, only most obviously in California, Australia, Greece and Portugal's "Mediterranean" climate zones, but also across the boreal forests of the Northern Hemisphere. The implications in terms of ocean acidification are especially ominous for the future of humanity.

There is simply far too much firepower now loose in the earth system. Stephen Pyne (2021) suggests that we are living in the Pyrocene, a geological period where fire now dominates the earth system in ways that, until recently, ice used to. Precisely what has allowed the enormous expansion of humanity, and the removal of most ecological competitors, is now endangering the future success of the mode of human society powered by fossil fuels. Where security dilemmas in the past have been about military preparations to provide security for some, hence raising the alarm among those supposedly being defended against, now the environmental security dilemma poses the issue of unintended backwash effects at the global scale. The development and deployment of firepower is endangering all by the disruptions of the climate system and the eradication of biodiversity, with as yet unforeseen potential hazards. In the words of Walt Kelly's cartoon character Pogo from the 1960s, "we have seen the enemy and he is us"!

4. The geopolitics of colonizing nature

IMPERIAL LEGACIES

George Perkins Marsh, writing in the 1860s when he was an American diplomat in Rome, focused attention on the third of Clarence Glacken's (1967) three questions, that of the human impact on the earth. March pondered the legacy of the Roman empire and its impact on environments across the Mediterranean area. There was little pristine left when the Western empire expired, and the legacy of that empire impressed Marsh fifteen centuries later. Marsh (1864/1965, 11) suggested that:

> … the primitive source, the *causa causarum*, of the acts and neglects which have blasted with sterility and physical decrepitude the noblest half of the empire of the Caesars, is, first, the brutal and exhausting despotism which Rome herself exercised over her conquered kingdoms, and even over her Italian territory; then, the host of temporal and spiritual tyrannies which she left as her dying curse to all her wide dominium, and which in some form of violence or of fraud, still brood over almost every soil subdued by the Roman legions.

This empire, with its patterns of settling retired legionnaires in newly conquered lands and its fascination with using exotic animals in spectacles and "games", clearly transformed much of its region. That Marsh could see this legacy a millennium and a half later suggests that the long term transformation of the earth is just that—a long term human project.

But it is also the case that the expansive nature of the empire is replicated in numerous other human histories, a matter of environmental history being part and parcel of colonizing processes where frontiers are pushed back from metropolitan centres precisely in the process of extracting resources to feed, fuel and supply those centres. Prior occupants, both human and other species, frequently resist these intrusions, but the dynamic of imperial expansion is a repeated pattern in human history; environmental change has to be understood in these terms, if the novel patterns of the Anthropocene are to be understood in context. Assumptions of a pristine nature usurped by humanity ignore the long history of colonization and its ecological transformations. While European colonists, and the naturalists who often accompanied naval expeditions of exploration, may have viewed what they came across as more or less pristine (Grove 1995, 1997), and the peoples who inhabited their new colonies in the Americas and Africa as primitive, in that they didn't live in European ways, the long history of human habitation had changed landscapes and species mixes in numerous ways prior to their incorporation into the global economy.

Looking further back in human history suggests that current changes can be understood in terms of the expansion of our species over the period of the Holocene to fill numerous ecological niches and, simultaneously, develop numerous modes of life that interconnected in complex ways with the rest of the ecologies that humans intruded upon. As Chapter 3 has indicated, being the fire species allowed this spread in ways that other species could not emulate. In the process the human influence has spread and dramatically altered landscapes along with, more recently, seascape—where fishing has extended the reach of human appropriations of nature—and the wider oceans as they acidify. The expansion of humanity through the Holocene has been an extended process. Iceland was first colonized a millennium ago, and likewise some of the Pacific Islands on a broadly similar timescale.

One could argue that this process of reaching all the continents has only recently been completed, when, in the twentieth century, permanent settlements were finally established in Antarctica. But, and this is a crucial point in the whole process of colonization, in this case, even more than others, these communities are dependent on supplies of food, fuel and building materials brought from a great distance. Crucially humanity has both brought with it various biota, and in the process changed ecologies fundamentally wherever it has gone, although once again Antarctica is an extreme case. Permanent settlements on the moon, and perhaps later on Mars, are now being actively discussed by aficionados of space exploration, suggesting that the colonizing impetus is far from over (Davenport 2018). Curiosity about what's over the horizon combined with ever more capable technologies and the search of novel ways to make a living persist as a powerful combination in human affairs. Now, ironically, fear of catastrophe on earth is providing justification for space exploration; having only one planet is apparently a dangerous gamble for the human species.

SLOW VIOLENCE

In much of human history, however, colonization hasn't been just about humans using ingenuity to spread to uninhabited places. The first peoples to inhabit a place have frequently been displaced, conquered and in some cases eliminated by subsequent arrivals. This is only most obviously the case in terms of the expansion of European colonization in the last half millennium, a matter of slow violence in Rob Nixon's (2011) terms, where landscape transformation is tied into the spread of novel forms of economy, and where the peoples are displaced, often violently, in the process. In the history of colonization, in the Americas in particular, native peoples have suffered destruction and displacement, not least by the introduction of diseases to which they had little or no immunity.

But, and this is crucial for how environmental security is now being rethought, it is nearly always the colonists who get to tell the stories of the places and societies they have occupied, stories of conquest and victory told mostly by white men. Those eliminated by the processes of colonization have only rarely got to tell their stories of violence, dispossession and lost cultures, a matter in need of correction by contemporary social scientists (O'Lear 2021). The current movements to decolonize social sciences and recoup the lost stories of the violence of colonization are attempts to retell the histories obliterated by the triumphalist settler narratives. In the process the places in these narratives, and how they fit into the larger scheme of things, are being reimagined, and who endangers who or what where is being reconsidered. The people without history (Wolf 1982) are starting to reclaim their silenced pasts and in the process both challenging the triumphalist colonial narratives of the past and raising key questions of how the transformation of landscapes is an integral part of those histories (Graeber and Wengrow 2021).

Environmental history research has been recouping these understandings while also charting the ecological consequences of colonization at the global scale (Hornborg, McNeill and Martinez-Alier 2007). Aided by both better dating techniques and innovations in forensic archaeology it is now possible to reconstruct the histories of colonization and also the diseases that afflicted societies. Clearly empires are about much more than battles, conquest and the glory of emperors; the human history of these events is also very much the ecological history of their context, something George Perkins Marsh understood in general terms about Rome, but which contemporary historians can now reconstruct in much greater detail. In the case of Rome this is being done, and the interconnections between climate and disease add crucial additional insights into the fate of the empire (Harper 2017).

All this matters because at the heart of much of the concern about environmental security are fears of resource shortages and potential dangers that lurk on the frontier, or at least at a distance from the metropolitan centres where so many of the texts on environmental danger are written. The geographical imaginations implicit, and sometimes explicit, in these discourses shape the policy prescriptions because designations of the attributes of places, which "require" certain modes of conduct, are a key part of how this political discourse works. As later sections of this book will elaborate, the technical practices of development, frequently now rephrased in terms of climate adaptation as a potential solution to environmental insecurities, specify landscapes and their inhabitants in ways that are frequently in danger of perpetuating colonizing practices that fail to grapple with the complicated ecological and social contexts of human vulnerability in the processes of development (Taylor 2014).

Human populations have been in what is now Australia for sixty millennia or so and learned to live in a landscape where fire and El Nino climate cycles shaped life in ways very different from what the European colonists knew when they, and their biota, arrived in the eighteenth century. This incorporation of European colonists and their biota dramatically accelerated ecological change in places where mines, roads, deforestation, plantations and other forms of agriculture intruded, but the prior cultivation and hunting practices, as well as forestry, meant that these were far from "pristine" landscapes. The indigenous inhabitants had used fire as a mode of adjusting landscapes for numerous millennia, although the mostly British settlers would take a very long time to begin to understand the very different landscapes and ecological conditions that the aboriginal peoples had lived in and worked with for so long prior to the disastrous disruptions of the colonization (Flannery 1995). But these European colonies were understood as sources of resources for the metropolitan countries more than anything else, and "developed" as such. Danger on the colonial frontier frequently came from the efforts of the dispossessed to resist their displacements, as well as from unknown ecological phenomena such as animals, plants and ecological conditions that were unknown to the settlers, if not to the dispossessed local inhabitants.

In the Americas the disease burden brought by the settlers worked in their favour at least in the higher latitudes, with smallpox, measles and other diseases causing the death of many millions of indigenous inhabitants there. In Africa and some other tropical locations, diseases often limited the influx of colonists; yellow fever in particular shaped military strategies in the Caribbean, where European forces needed to move quickly while their soldiers still could, prior to being afflicted by the disease (McNeill 2007). What has been crucial in all this is the movement of fauna and flora around the world; the Columbian exchange of plants and animals has effectively meant that natural evolution of landscapes is over; the artificial movement of species has changed ecologies dramatically. The process goes on; the very tasty fish eaten on the shores of Lake Titicaca high in the Andes are a Canadian trout species introduced, successfully, as a food supply in the middle of the twentieth century. The history of introduced species in Lake Victoria has been less successful; the story of Asian Carp in America's rivers quite easily qualifies as an ecological disaster (Kolbert 2021). The processes of natural evolution have been dramatically altered by the human movement of numerous species, sometimes intentionally with locally beneficial effects for local societies, sometimes disastrously. These increasingly artificial landscapes are now the context in which security and environment have to be considered.

The disruptions of ecologies and landscapes which so alarm both activists in particular places and scientists concerned with the overall state of biodiversity are the other side of the colonizing coin. While settlers in much of imperial history may have sought agricultural lands for their subsistence, their colonization of uncultivated lands, or their occupation of places where populations have been eliminated or relocated, is also tied into the larger economies from which they came (Crosby 1986). While much agricultural produce may be consumed locally, some of it is a matter of production for trade, and for supplying the urban centres of empire. But colonization has also been about seeking other resources, whether fish, wildlife, timber, fuel or minerals, to feed and supply urban centres. This geopolitics of plundering (Le Billon 2012) is a key part of imperial histories; supplying the economy and the war machines of great powers with key supplies is, as the discussion of firepower in Chapter 3 emphasized, a longstanding matter of military and imperial history. This is the key context for thinking through twenty first century transformations.

THE EUROCENE

But while military innovation and demands for supplies are a key part of history, they should not be overemphasized as the prime cause of ecological disruption. World system thinkers have of late been rethinking the ecological dimensions of the rise of the global economy, and the importance of examining the history of capitalism in Europe and the implications this has had for the subsequent transformation of the earth system. Jason Moore (2015) points to the long processes of gradual expansion of European economies to suggest that the key causes of the contemporary earth system crisis have their roots there. Hence his suggestion that the term Capitalocene might be more appropriate than that of Anthropocene given the power of economic forces generated by the logic of accumulation that drives capital accumulation. The expansion of Europe in search of materials and markets is a key point in all this and the source of much of the contemporary global economy. While the bulk of these transformations may have initially been in Europe, the long distance consequences in terms of imperialism and the search for new sources of materials and wealth were a key part of the emergence of a world system.

The conquest of the Americas also led to the "great dying" of the American native peoples. While some of the destruction was as a consequence of direct military violence, and the use of musketry and cannons using forms of firepower that were unknown in the Americas prior to the Europeans' arrival, the dislocations caused by epidemics were key to the dissolution of prior civilizations. The agricultural systems feeding these societies collapsed in many places, and abandoned fields were widely reforested. Lewis and Maslin (2018) suggest that this reforestation removed enough carbon dioxide from the atmosphere to be noticeable in the climate records, where 1610 marks the lowest point. They suggest this point as a likely candidate for the start of the Anthropocene because it simultaneously marks the unintended climate effects of the conquest of the Americas, the incorporation of the whole world into a single global economy, and the beginning of what has been a rise in carbon dioxide levels in the atmosphere ever since. They suggest this "Orbis hypothesis", a synthesis of natural and human actions, marks the appropriate starting point for the Anthropocene.

As to whether this dip in the carbon dioxide levels is the key to the beginning of the Little Ice Age in Europe at least, paleoclimate experts might disagree; some estimates suggest that the Little Ice Age in Europe, while regionally significant, wasn't a global climate event (Neukom, Steiger, Gómez-Navarro et al. 2019). Hence the implication is that the Orbis hypothesis is a regional rather than global artifact, and hence that it's not a good starting point for the Anthropocene. But clearly the calamities of the seventeenth century, which were worldwide, did shape the beginnings of the emergence of the modern state system in Europe (Parker 2013), a system that has subsequently been extended worldwide, but which fits uneasily with other historical civilizations, only most obviously China. Conventional histories of the modern state arrangements date them to the settlements that ended the thirty years war, the popularly called Treaty of Westphalia, where exclusive territorial jurisdiction was established as a principle at least in terms of religious observance. But the other social and military transformations of the period hastened by the emergence of novel economic arrangements shaped modern modes of governance with their territorial states, professional bureaucracies, taxation schemes, financial administration, policing and standing armies.

Jarius Grove (2019) suggests that these profound transformations, and the destruction of the native peoples of the Americas in particular, require naming the contemporary period as the Eurocene rather than the Anthropocene. The key mover, he suggests, was European imperialism, and the technological innovations related to its violence have reverberated through the earth system ever since. The catastrophes faced by indigenous peoples whose societies were in many cases effectively destroyed, and some of which were eliminated altogether, suggest that the period of the Anthropocene has been disastrous for many societies. The conclusion from this is that the current alarms about climate change and other imminent disruptions is nothing new for many of the world's peoples. What is new is that the rich and powerful among the states that did the colonizing are now starting to worry that their future is threatened.

Hence the implication is that the Anthropocene discussion is merely a matter of novelty for Europeans and Americans, but that much of the rest of the world has long been dealing with massive dangerous disruptions, caused by those self-same Europeans and Americans. Much of the Global South is thus preoccupied with justice while the Europeans and Americans are looking to technological innovations to render themselves secure from the disruptions that their prior activities have set in motion. Security thus means very different things depending on where you are in the global economy, and the endless arguments about climate finance in international forums and the annual Conferences of the Parties of the United Nations Framework Convention on Climate Change (UNFCCC COPs) bear out both its importance and the great reluctance on the part of rich states, not to mention their corporations, to pay for the indirect consequences of their profligate use of fossil fuels.

The Global South faces a double vulnerability, both as a periphery in the global power structure and as places in harm's way as climate disruptions accelerate. They face a situation of "climate terror" where climate science warns that accelerating disruptions are likely, while they are mostly powerless to influence the trajectories of fossil fuel combustion, and unable to get effective compensation and aid from those who have caused their difficulties (Chaturvedi and Doyle 2015). National security for these states is being compromised by the direct impact of storms and droughts and indirectly by the disruptions these cause to agriculture and rural economies more generally. Even if a plausible case could be made to justify their going to war as an attempt to ensure their survival (Martin 2020), they don't have military options to deal with the sources of their insecurity and hence their security is entirely dependent on persuasion and international diplomatic efforts, which have—despite promising developments in the Paris Agreement in 2015, at least as of 2021, and the endless promises of *future* action to constrain fossil fuel use, reiterated once again at the Glasgow COP in 2021—yet to deliver meaningful global reductions in fossil fuel use.

In grappling with these transformations and in posing security in terms of nation states, one of the key difficulties in climate politics emerges very clearly. In Paul Harris's (2021) terms one of the pathologies of climate governance is precisely this division of the world into supposedly autonomous states, an arrangement that stymies effective action to deal with matters that cross national boundaries. This is an old problem in discussions of global environmental matters, but one that is now much more urgent given rapid climate change and the biodiversity crisis.

TERRITORIES, SOVEREIGNTIES, JURISDICTIONS

Crucially the dynamics of capitalism require the ever larger appropriation of nature to provide the raw materials to be processed into products that are sold to accumulate yet more wealth. With that goes the property systems that demarcate who owns what and facilitate the enclosure of spaces for exclusive use by economic actors. The extension of property relationships in land requires more sophisticated systems of surveying, demarcating and delimiting territories (Blomley 2019). While the contemporary notions of territory have a long lineage, their dominance in how the world is divided up and the implicit assumptions of this as the appropriate mode of governance are relatively recent (Elden 2013). The precise demarcations of territory were frequently a key part of the expansion of European empires and the colonization of the Americas. The geometric shapes of many of the states that constitute the United States, and likewise those of the Prairie provinces in Canada, remain a cartographic reminder of this. Africa's borders too; they were formally agreed upon by European colonizers in a Berlin conference in the 1880s.

This imposition of territorial and, on the smaller scale, property relations on the landscape, frequently in ignorance of the precise physical geographies, is the governance framework used for grappling with numerous ecological changes, and the discrepancy between the maps and ecologies remains a major obstacle to sensible environmental governance in numerous places (Head 2019). The subsequent decolonization of some of the colonial states likewise leaves a series of territorial and governance mechanisms that are at odds with ecological circumstances, compounding the difficulties. The integration of these post colonial states into the global economy, mostly as a source of commodities for export, perpetuates practices of extractivism, and in the process enhances vulnerabilities both economically and ecologically.

The expansion of European empires involved the extension of resource extractions and the conversion of relatively wild landscapes as well as subsistence based agriculture into plantations and commercial farms. While the extension of commercial relationships, making farmers dependent on global food prices rather than local conditions, is part of the story of accelerated colonization in the nineteenth century (Davis 2001), the extension of the agricultural frontier in the Americas in particular is a key part of the growth of imperial economies. Most obviously in those regions that Alfred Crosby (1986) terms the neo-Europes, the temperate grasslands of the Americas as well as Southern Africa, Australia and New Zealand, sheep and cattle raising displaced both indigenous peoples and the grazing animals that thrived in those ecosystems. In the case of Australia and New Zealand the invention of effective refrigeration in the latter part of the nineteenth century made meat exports to Britain possible, emphasizing once again the link between technological innovation and the growth of what was by then, despite imperial trade restrictions in many places, a global economy.

The conversion of the American prairies into farms and ranches generated agricultural produce and led to the rise of Chicago as "nature's metropolis" in Cronon's (1991) terms, as the centre for the cattle trade. The small wars on the frontier, and the destruction and displacement of indigenous peoples once again, remind historians that this was a violent process. Progress this might be, but only for those who manage to take possession of the colonized spaces and have some luck with frontier agriculture. These processes also subsequently gave the world the culturally ambiguous character of the cowboy, as well as Upton Sinclair's classic novel of the suffering of immigrant workers in the city of Chicago, *The Jungle*. Development is a very uneven process, one that both incorporates distant lands into metropolitan consumption and drives innovation in cities, which in turn creates demands for new sources of materials and energy in distant places connected by trading links (Taylor 2016).

These processes of dispossession and the privatization of land in the hands of settlers and corporations continue in many parts of the world, accelerating land use change and habitat destruction in numerous places, usually justified in terms of economic growth and the supposedly inevitable processes of development (Buxton and Hayes 2016). In the early decades of the twenty first century these processes have also involved the use of extensive fires to clear forests, most notably in Brazil and Indonesia. Clearing these landscapes, for cattle grazing, palm oil plantations and other commercial activities, contributes to both biodiversity loss and climate change, both immediately in terms of the fires and subsequently in the reduction of carbon sequestration because the forests are no longer there to act as carbon sinks. These "shadows of consumption" (Dauvergne 2008) both hide the impacts of metropolitan consumption from those consumers and, because of the territorial divisions involved, frequently assign responsibility for the damage to local authorities while occluding the consequences of long supply chains.

The crucial point in all this in terms of security is that what is being secured is the legal order of property, and the commercial arrangements that facilitate the expansion of the modern economy. The processes of economic growth are about enclosures, privatization and the extension of property arrangements ever further into terrestrial landscapes, as well as into the oceans, and, as discussions of mining asteroids and setting up permanent settlements on the moon and eventually Mars suggest, ever more distant arrangements for the extraction of resources to support economic expansion (Davenport 2018). This economy and its dynamics of contested expansion suggest permanent states of economic insecurity, but also, simultaneously, the need to secure these economic arrangements which provide the consumer goods of modernity.

Some of the roots of modern notions of security lie in the rise of commercial society and the search by nascent capitalists for social and political guarantees that their wealth would not be subject to arbitrary appropriation by governments (Rothschild 1995). The legal arrangements to protect property and guarantee contracts are key to notions of security, and with them go the operations of most national agencies to maintain this order. On the larger scale this is the bedrock of the liberal international order that American notions of national security are tied into (Latham 1997). The explicit formulations of these things in terms of the free world, or in recent rearticulations, matters of democracy, may obscure the importance of these arrangements, but the global environmental crisis highlights the fact that this expansion of economic activity is what is being secured, at the cost of the functional biosphere. Both climate change and the current global extinction event are the ecological manifestations of the expansion of this technosphere into most parts of the ecosphere.

The elaborate attempts to deal with these contradictions are what much of the discourse of sustainability is about, and the repeated attempts to commodify ecosystems and monetize "ecosystem services" as commercial efforts to "sink" emissions in tropical forests or elsewhere extend this logic. The certification processes whereby ecosystems are incorporated into this process, including such dubious ideas as using eucalyptus forestry schemes as ecological sinks, perpetuates the colonizing processes (Lansing 2010). This reinvention of plantation agriculture extends the long term pattern of commercial extraction systems that feed urban markets at great distance. Understanding climate finance and ecological sinks in these terms also suggests clearly that the ecological arrangements that are commercialized in these manners need to be secured into the future so that they can continue to deliver what the original contracts suggested. But, given the speed of climate change, and the larger political and economic dynamics of many states, these may be highly dubious arrangements, at least in terms of the promises about ecological services that they are premised upon (Dehm 2021). In many cases its far from clear that trees or other species planted today will have the necessary weather conditions or water supplies to thrive long into the future. Neither is it clear that the rapidly changing rural property markets and commercial arrangements, or dispossessed rural populations, will ensure the continued existence of plantations and ecosystem reserves into the long term future.

Likewise the extension of commercial property arrangements in rural areas continues and, to use the term popularized in the early twenty first century, "land grabbing" (Sassen 2013), where commercial and state enterprises appropriate land from indigenous peoples or subsistence farming communities, is now aggravated by international efforts to outsource food and raw material sources as part of climate adaptation. The globalization of agriculture and rural property markets drives these processes and extends the logic of colonization ever further into rural areas in the Global South in particular. Land has become a new global asset class driving financial initiatives (Fairbairn 2020). Where this process extends the frontier into forested places, then, as the high profile discussions of Indonesia attest, deforestation to provide supplies of palm oil for global urban markets simultaneously extends extraction further into rural areas but also commercializes land and by removing forests demolishes habitat for numerous species (Davis, Koo, Dell'Angelo et al. 2020). Where domestic sources of food are imperilled by climate change, water shortages or other problems, then sourcing food from abroad makes economic and security sense. But if it is done at the expense of local communities elsewhere, then their displacement simply changes the location of human insecurity from domestic situations to those abroad where the land is purchased and repurposed for export production.

Not least, all this is made even more complicated by the fact that the worst labour conditions, indentured contract arrangements, and what is technically termed slavery in many cases, involve workers engaged in the extractive industries that supply the fuel and materials for the global economy:

> Whether slaves are extracting gold from Ghana, granite from India, or graphite from China, the impact of modern slavery on the natural climate is immense. From Eastern Congo to the Bangladeshi Sundarbans to the Brazilian Amazon, slave labor is routinely utilized by some of the most ecologically toxic industries on earth, like brick making, clear-cut deforestation, precious-woods logging, and strip mining. (Bales and Sovacool 2021, 1)

The irony here is that various environmental protection arrangements often facilitate the invasion of protected spaces by criminal operations operating to grab trees or other resources in spaces where legal operations have been curtailed but enforcement mechanisms are inadequate. Dealing with these matters of illegal logging and the criminal appropriation of resources for sale on various illegal or quasi legal international markets adds an additional criminal enforcement dimension to discussions of environmental security, matters of "ecoviolence" that are usually missing from the social science literature on environmental security (Stoett and Omrow 2021), but which are an essential part of any attempt to think about global governance related to long term sustainability.

For those expelled from their landscapes, the ecologically marginalized in Homer-Dixon's (1994) terms, and forced to migrate because of these processes of resource capture, often into the informal settlements surrounding Southern megacities, the outcome is frequently more insecurity. This is part of the larger processes of modernization which, by the expansion of global production systems and supply chains around the world, are in Sassen's (2014) terms expelling workers and farmers from numerous traditional modes of employment. This globalization process is both rendering national economies more vulnerable to economic actions in distant places and expelling smallholder farmers and traditional subsistence modes of livelihood in places where commercial monocultures colonize landscapes. These dramatic transformations now form the context within which people are rendered insecure, and it's not surprising that in many cases traditional landholders and indigenous peoples act to resist commercial encroachments, whether they are mines, forestry extractions, commercial plantations or dam construction projects (Menton and Le Billon 2021).

PANDEMICS, DISEASES, ECOLOGY

These processes of landscape transformation and the increased contact of people with previously relatively remote regions also highlights the dangers of zoonotic diseases. Ebola, SARS, Zika, AIDS and most recently COVID-19 have emphasized the role of landscape disruptions and the possibilities of viruses jumping species from wild animals to human populations. They have also reminded everyone that these things spread, and that geographical distance and the use of border controls isn't going to stop future epidemics. This isn't a newly recognized problem. Laurie Garrett's magnum opus from the 1990s on *The Coming Plague* clearly identified the dangers of new zoonotic diseases emerging from what she called a world out of balance:

> Ultimately, humanity will have to change its perspective on its place in Earth's ecology if the species hopes to stave off or survive the next plague. Rapid globalization of human niches requires that human beings everywhere on the planet go beyond viewing their neighbourhoods, provinces, countries, or hemispheres as the sum total of their personal ecospheres. Microbes, and their vectors, recognize none of the artificial boundaries erected by human beings. (Garrett 1995, 618)

But, these warnings aside, the practices of security in the contemporary world have been revealed as seriously inadequate for dealing with these circumstances by the spread of COVID-19 and the failures to contain it effectively. This all requires much more attention in the process of rethinking environmental security. The COVID-19 pandemic has revealed once again how ill prepared international health systems are for coping with the consequences of an infectious outbreak. Human insecurity is highlighted here too by the lack of medical care available for the poor and marginal in most societies where survival odds are also compromised by poverty and lack of access to safe drinking water and good nutrition. Likewise health infrastructures are also vulnerable to climate disruptions as the World Health Organization (2021) recognizes; it has begun preparing climate vulnerability checklists for health care facilities, lists that include extreme weather vulnerabilities as well as sea level concerns!

In Garrett's (1995) terms the world is out of balance, and not only are humans moving into new areas but climate change and habitat disruption are also causing other species to move, both away from areas being deforested, but also towards areas that may be more suitable as climate change causes conditions to change. Migration towards the poles as the planet heats might be a general summation, but more detailed patterns include upwards on hillsides to cooler conditions. Both processes change the pattern of human encounters with wildlife. In addition the spread of patterns of eating wild animals, both as a necessity by local peoples and in exotic consumption practices among the wealthy who pay a premium for status consumption experiences, changes ecological interactions. Concerns about ecological fragmentation and deforestation are clearly related to matters of zoonotic disease emergence (Gibb, Redding, Chin et al. 2020). Habitat fragmentation and the routine penetration of humans into relatively wild areas increases the opportunities for viruses to jump from animals to people (Bloomfield, McIntosh and Lambin 2020). Further disruption of relatively remote areas may generate yet more zoonotic hazards for humans as the processes of "development" intrude on more remote places.

As the Intergovernmental Science-Policy Platform on Biodiversity and Ecosystem Services (IPBES) workshop on biodiversity and pandemics summarized matters late in 2020:

> The underlying causes of pandemics are the same global environmental changes that drive biodiversity loss and climate change. These include land-use change, agricultural expansion and intensification, and wildlife trade and consumption. These drivers of change bring wildlife, livestock, and people into closer contact, allowing animal microbes to move into people and lead to infections, sometimes outbreaks, and more rarely into true pandemics that spread through road networks, urban centres and global travel and trade routes. The recent exponential rise in consumption and trade, driven by demand in developed countries and emerging economies, as well as by demographic pressure, has led to a series of emerging diseases that originate mainly in biodiverse developing countries, driven by global consumption patterns. (IPBES 2020, 2)

Care needs to be taken here with colonial interpretations of landscapes and disease origins; it is all too easy to revert to simple arguments about the failure of Southern states to manage their environments effectively, or resort to stereotyping of mysterious threats emanating from the unruly spaces in the Global South, without investigating the processes that have shaped the landscapes in the first place.

These old familiar invocations of fortress thinking, where dangers to civilization lurk in dark spaces of the Global South, are in many cases seriously misleading in terms of the causes of disease and what needs to be done in a globalized world to deal with health emergencies, not least because the driving forces that have displaced many smallholder farmers in recent decades are key to the processes that have fragmented forests and opened up the ecosystems to human encroachment. "The colonial plantation connected to the metropole through telegram and precarious shipping has morphed into networks of digitized financial capital and transit corridors moving germplasm, animals, plants, and humans across vast distances in a fraction of the time" (Liebman,

Perfecto and Wallace 2020). Traditional smallholder farming may be much more productive in terms of food for local consumption, even if it doesn't fit well with the international commodity circuits of agribusiness (Clapp 2020). But here too the specific ecologies are part of the larger processes of investment shaping landscape ecologies, and disease emergence is tied to these patterns in some cases.

While clearly the dangers of wild species causing zoonotic hazards need attention and provide another good reason to think seriously about ecological change and conservation, many zoonotic diseases are a result of modes of agriculture that involve human and animal proximity. The long term scourge of smallpox originated from domesticated cattle, and numerous other diseases are related to farming rather than wild animals. While the wet markets of China, widely criticized as a source of the COVID-19 virus, may indeed be hazardous in terms of potential zoonotic diseases, this focus overlooks the complex artificial ecologies constructed by industrial farming. The dangers there were highlighted during the COVID-19 pandemic by the Danish case of mink farms and virus mutation (Leste-Lasserre 2020). In 2020 the virus was transmitted from farmers to the mink in Northern Denmark, and apparently mutated in the mink. Fearing further spread of a novel mutation back to the human population, the decision was taken to slaughter the millions of mink living in the industrial facilities.

As to why human societies need to farm mink by the millions to provide furs for status clothing was rarely part of the conversation, but it once again emphasizes the sheer scale of the global economy which generates such demands on what can no longer be reasonably called natural systems. Agriculture and the mass breeding of numerous species for food and fur no longer rely on hunting in the wild, and the mass use of food supplements and antibiotics to try to limit the diseases in these incarcerated animals adds another dimension to the increasingly artificial circumstances of the Anthropocene. The destruction of mink in Denmark is far from the first attempt to deal with potential pandemic diseases by mass extermination; the case of H5N1 in Asian factory farms illustrated this process years earlier, highlighting the international connections within animal production corporations and the complexity of the political economy of biosecurity efforts in the face of very different production systems (Hameiri and Jones 2015). Prior to the disruptions of the COVID-19 pandemic the annual influenza outbreaks were usually sourced in the agricultural regions of China and South East Asia, another reminder that animal agriculture is hazardous in ways that are often forgotten.

A POST COLONIAL WORLD?

While formal decolonization has, with the notable exception of many of the indigenous lands of the former settler colonies, been accomplished, and national sovereignty asserted in most terrestrial spaces, this formal mode of governance frequently obscures the economic relationships that dominate the global system. Much of this still works in terms of transfers of wealth from the Global South to the North. While these geographical designations are very rough, nonetheless the overall patterns of wealth accumulation and the discrepancies between metropolitan peripheral states are clear. There remain major wealth transfers from the poor to the rich, and from rural resource supply areas to the urban centres of consumption. Calculating these patterns with precision is a fraught exercise, but the overall transfer, established with the expansion of European empires in previous centuries, has been maintained in many places. Resources and cheap labour in the Global South remain key parts of the global economy, while at the other end of those long supply chains human production systems have allowed an extraordinary expansion of consumption so that human biomass and the farm animal populations that support us are now massive in comparison with the remaining "wild" animals.

The processes of transforming the biosphere, accelerated so dramatically first by the expansion of the European empires and their trading schemes and then by the rise of industrial production systems, have now so transformed things that humanity is clearly the dominant species in much of the world, and has consequently become the key biomass in the biosphere (Elhacham, Liad, Grozovski et al. 2020). This is now a very different world from that inhabited by humans even a few centuries back (Ellis 2011); now humanity is producing vast quantities of material in novel forms, a rapidly expanding technosphere that is shaping the world dramatically and within which policies to deal with growing vulnerabilities in this artificial world have to be considered.

The continued appropriation of wealth, including billions of tons of materials, and the use of cheap labour to produce commodities for Northern consumption continues the patterns established in colonial times (Hickel, Sullivan and Zoomkawala 2021). Obviously this is now much more complicated with the rise of Asian economies in the period of the great acceleration, and the recent rise of Chinese production systems in the global economy in particular, but the wide discrepancies in wealth and life chances for populations in many places remain. The COVID-19 pandemic has highlighted these discrepancies both within states and between them; this global pattern underlies the processes that are now rendering environments vulnerable in numerous ways. In Richard Falk's (1999) apt phrasing, the world has been living through a period of predatory globalization where the rich get richer at the expense of the poor around the world.

While formal slavery has supposedly been ended in the global economy by nineteenth century innovations in Europe, and after the civil war in the United States, numerous forms of indentured labour and related patterns of economic coercion remain. This is, it seems, especially the case in extractivist industries, and artisanal mining operations where many of the key minerals in the current global economy are sourced (Bales and Sovacool 2021). While the finer terminological points of who is technically a slave may obscure the argument, it is clear that the worst jobs, with the highest rates of illness and accidental death, coincide with key extractivist tasks. Ironically the root source of the materials that are causing climate change and biodiversity reduction are directly linked to the worst labour practices and the poverty in marginal places. Human insecurity is most palpable at the heart of the harshest extractivist economic processes.

Not surprisingly local inhabitants and marginalized workers resist these processes and the dispossession involved in land clearing, mining and other forms of "development", and are often subject to violence and assassination in the process. Violence on the frontier isn't new, but now it's part of international environmental politics too, as human rights monitors and journalists repeatedly suggest, sometimes at the cost of their lives (Menton and Le Billon 2021). In terms of security these processes raise the crucial questions of security for whom and of what. If the planetary system is being damaged by these extensions of extractivist activity, then the local land defenders and their international supporters in human rights, environmental and indigenous peoples movements are protecting the ecological integrity of the earth system.

When, as is frequently the case, these activists are termed dangers to national security (Matejova, Parker and Dauvergne 2018), criminalized and punished as agents of foreign powers threatening national sovereignty, the contradictions between global and national security are palpable. In the case of mining companies despoiling indigenous peoples' territories, the resistance to their activities generates similar dynamics, once again highlighting the conflictual processes of contemporary colonization and the need to think about both security and environment in ways that challenge the ever larger spread of extractivist activities. What is being secured here in the use of violence against indigenous peoples and environmentalists is the property "rights" and territorial arrangements of commercial society, not the ecological integrity of these landscapes.

These struggles frequently don't fit easily into traditional political notions of left and right, nor do they necessarily map well onto nationalist agendas. In the case of Ecuador (Riofrancos 2020), struggles between national governments anxious to use national resource revenues gained from exporting oil and minerals run afoul of indigenous and rural peoples resisting the expropriation of land and the destruction and pollution of petroleum and mineral extraction processes. The complexities of these conflicts and the possibilities of using non-violent resistance to proposed developments depend in part on local political circumstances, but rural conflict is frequently violent in struggles over what Markus Kroger (2020) calls "investment politics". Mass protests and peaceful opposition are often met with violence on the part of governments, corporations and paramilitaries, or attempts to criminalize opposition.

These contradictions have spilled over into opposition to supposedly renewable and sustainable developments too, not least where windfarms and dams are imposed on rural populations without consultation and without the economic benefits flowing at least in part to local communities. Fights over proposals to establish windfarms in rural Mexico have turned violent, with complex conflicts leading to attacks on local opponents (Dunlap 2017). In contrast research in the rather different circumstances of Scotland has suggested that consultations with local communities, and efforts to ensure that local employment at the facilities and revenue streams from the electricity generated by the windfarms go to those local communities, can be useful modes of rural regeneration (Mackenzie 2013). The connections between violence on the frontier and urban consumption, whether it is of electricity or material commodities, are now an inescapable part of the larger discussion of environmental security, and the related matters of how environmental justice might be reconsidered (Ryder, Powlen, Laituri et al. 2021) and conflicts decolonized (Oswald Spring and Brauch 2021).

WAR AND CITIES

One interesting argument in this process is the suggestion that such patterns are in fact very old, and link violence directly to extraction and to urban processes (Taylor, O'Brien and O'Keefe 2020). Conventional archaeology and history suggests the gradual growth of populations linked with domestication of plants and animals, leading to first villages and then gradually to larger urban settlements as surplus production made more sophisticated societies possible. But Taylor, O'Brien and O'Keefe (2020) suggest instead that this gradual increase in economic surplus may have been driven by conflict and the demands that this made for supplies of food and weapons. Their rethinking of early urban settlements suggests that violence and competition among early humans led to the warfare and the need to accumulate resources to support military operations. Trading to provide these was related to raiding and conquest; protected spaces in the forms of fortified camps are nascent urban arrangements. To this day expanding empires and colonizing states build forts and observation facilities as part of the colonization process to survey and control spaces before they become formally integrated into permanent territorial arrangements.

Crucially, Taylor, O'Brien and O'Keefe (2020) argue, these early urbanization processes led to the extraction of resources at distance, and the impetus for innovation to supply warriors based in nascent cities. Urbanization, they argue, was about fortification, violence and logistics, with long distance indirect trading consequences right from the beginning. Trading is an urban phenomenon mostly, and as such it is key to invention and travel. Food, fuel, weapons and clothes draw resources from distance, and this is, so they argue, key to understanding the trajectories of human transformations of environments. Drawing on Jane Jacobs' (1994) ideas of innovation as the key to economic growth, they argue that is still the case today with ever larger appropriations from distance to feed the metropolitan demand. Thus the key to climate change is urban demand, and how cities are rebuilt and reimagined is key to future climates.

The geography of all this doesn't fit well with territorial states, but clearly the question of urban demand is fundamental to the processes linking the global economy together and now shaping the overall use of fossil fuels, and the matter of rural transformations as development and industrial agriculture rework rural areas. The point about this is that resource extraction to fuel metropolitan demand is not new, but now in the Anthropocene it has reached such a scale that it is destabilizing the earth system. The rapidly growing technosphere, which is the global economy understood in material terms, is now a novel entity linking places and processes together in new topological patterns, but ones which have long historical antecedents in the extension of imperial powers and the disruption and denudation of more realms than those of the Caesars.

How all this is interpreted as a matter of security is important for current reconsiderations. Likewise it is a concern in the discussion of the Anthropocene and its origins. The key point in this discussion is the matter of who is insecure where and how. The genesis of insecurity is tied to the transformations of the Anthropocene, and in terms of the current alarm about climate and biodiversity, this discussion is unavoidably about who is to blame for current difficulties. The widespread assumption in Europe and North America that these are technical matters that can be fixed by innovation contrast dramatically with perspectives from parts of the world that are former colonies or whose societies were disrupted by the rise of European and subsequently American power. There the matters of climate and biodiversity are seen as matters of justice, and of the need for those who became wealthy by exploiting colonies and extracting wealth from the Global South to recognize that this is what they did and act to help the most vulnerable cope with the disasters that they are suffering but which are not of their making.

5. Global security/environmental conflict

ENVIRONMENTAL CONFLICT

The more alarmist arguments about climate change and coming disruptions paint dystopian pictures about the future which also feed into larger narratives about conflict and the supposed need to prepare for violent situations brought about by environmental disruption. Popular culture reinforces widespread alarms in media, drawing on a wide repertoire of disaster narratives in tackling the consequences of climate change, although only sometimes assuming that major disruptions will cause warfare. All this matters because the politics of security is about fears, foes and anxieties and where these can be marshalled to shape state actions. Environmental matters have long been discussed in terms of securitization, as a threat requiring emergency action, and hence in some circumstances involving military activity (Buzan, Wæver and de Wilde 1998). But the precise modalities of environmental change that might lead to conflict are much less than clear in the academic research literature and the relationships between small scale conflicts and larger security concerns no better understood.

Contemporary concerns with climate security and the growing policy focus on the relationships between climate change and conflict raise questions of global security policy and the matter of whether climate change will cause conflict and if so where and when. More specifically issues arise as to if and when climate disruptions lead to warfare or, as is frequently discussed in these cases, simply aggravate or accelerate tendencies to violence. Most of this research and academic discussion has recently dealt with analyses of conflicts in Africa and Asia, with attempts to trace links between climate change and the onset or persistence of violence. Claims about climate change causing war in Sudan (Mamdani 2009), and more recently in Syria (Kelley, Mohtadi, Cane et al. 2015), have been prominently used in policy discourses arguing that climate is thus a matter for consideration in the field of global security. Resource scarcities, and most notably worries about water supplies, populate the narratives, many of which suggest that warfare is inevitable as conditions worsen. And climate models suggest that more extreme weather is likely in many places.

But the empirical record on the relationships between environmental change and conflict is far from clear, and much of the alarmist literature, while possibly effective at raising concern and gaining a hearing in policy circles, is misplaced because of, as this volume emphasizes, its inadequate focus on both the specific contexts invoked in these narratives, and the failure to consider the long term transformations of landscapes by the patterns of human colonization that have marked recent history. Detailed research into recent conflicts in which water is ostensibly a cause suggest that institutions and infrastructure are key rather than water per se (Zografos, Goulden and Kallis 2014). There is little doubt that through much of human history weather changes, often as a result of volcanic action and El Nino/La Nina cycles, as well as longer term climate trends have been profoundly disruptive of agricultural societies. The political turmoil, famines and epidemics that often follow from crop failures have also influenced religious movements in numerous ways. But as Jenkins (2021) emphasizes in the case of both religious and large scale political changes, what has been crucial in recent history is the rise of stronger states in Europe in particular, with both institutions partly capable of dealing with food shortages due to the use of industrial scale farming and artificial fertilizers, as well as huge quantities of fossil fuels, and security apparatuses much better able to stifle large scale dissent and potential insurrections. Ironically its precisely the success of these efforts in recent centuries in providing enhanced security to their populations, if not to their colonial subjects, that now presents people in the twenty first century with crises of climate change and global extinction that require rethinking environmental security.

This point about political institutions is key to the environmental change and conflict issue, and as later chapters in this book suggest, it needs to be worked into both national and international adaptation strategies to cope with climate change (Benzie and Persson 2019). Grappling with how environment has been and continues to be invoked as a dangerous cause of conflict requires noting both the empirical realities in particular places and the conceptual framing that security narratives bring to bear in providing interpretations. This chapter does just this, making the point that both are related to issues of security ontology, the sense of who we are and what threatens that identity, and hence who gets to write texts that portray threats that require policy responses. Knowledge and politics are, as usual, deeply entwined with larger cultural formations and climate imaginaries. The role of states and their efficacy in dealing with dangers has been highlighted by the COVID-19 pandemic, where some states have been able to initiate substantial measures to buffer their populations from the worst effects of the virus and measures to cope with it, while others have not (Tooze 2021).

Given the scale of the current transformations it is noteworthy that much of Western culture has had what Amitav Ghosh (2016) terms a crisis of imagination, a great derangement in which the contemporary culture industries, and novelists in particular, apart from those writing specifically in the science fiction genre, have been very slow to grapple with climate change and the sheer scale of what has been set in motion in the period of the great acceleration. This has changed in the second decade of the third millennium as novelists and other cultural productions have begun to grapple with the rapidly transformed world that we now live in, and in turn generated numerous works of eco-criticism grappling with the representations of climate catastrophe (Andersen 2020), as well as other Anthropocene concerns (Dell'Agnese 2021).

Part of the reason for the relative silence in thinking through climate change in larger political and cultural modes until recently is the representation of climate as a technical matter of science. Focusing on the complex global circulation models, and interpreted through the arcane scientific language in the Intergovernmental Panel on Climate Change (IPCC) reports, much of the discussion of climate change in the Global North has narrowed the matter to technical discussions (O'Lear 2016). This happens while excluding the larger questions of modes of political and economic life that have generated the climate crisis in the first place, and which need to be drastically transformed to stop the massive production of carbon dioxide that support them. Related to this is the key assumption in modern socio-technical imaginaries that climate catastrophes and their societal disruptions are a thing of the past in "modern" societies where industrial systems, agricultural innovations and international trade in food have rendered famines only of concern in the Global South.

The popular imaginations tend to assume either catastrophic violence in climate futures or gradual peaceful transitions to a post carbon fueled future (Benner, Rothe, Ullstrom and Stripple 2019). Prior concerns with catastrophe, and the 1980s discussions of nuclear winter in particular, have morphed into fears of climate change. The possibilities of nuclear war induced climate chaos, dramatized in the 1983 movie *The Day After*, were reprised in a movie title two decades later on rapid climate change, *The Day After Tomorrow*. One of the notable scenes in the 2004 disaster movie is of American refugees heading south trying to cross the border into Mexico, neatly reversing common fears of Latin Americans "invading" the United States. Despite the fact that scholarship suggests that, while climate migrants are obviously an issue in many places, massive sudden displacements over long distances are unlikely (Selby and Daoust 2021), disaster scripts persist. Images from Europe in 2015 of refugees walking from Turkey towards Western Europe quickly became iconic in these discussions, linked to generalized fears of the other and that destination states would be unable to cope with the social disruptions.

These violent imaginaries link fairly directly to assumptions of environmental causes of conflict, and popular images feed into securitizing moves where climate disruptions abroad are portrayed as threats to domestic peace and security. While this theme has been a popular mode of mobilizing attention to the importance of climate change, in so far as it is then framed as an external threat, it's less than helpful in tackling the sources of climate change or providing efficacious policy measures (Miller, Buxton and Akkerman 2021). It links quite directly to discussions of climate as a threat multiplier, a formulation that has come to dominate American discussions of climate security since it appeared in think tank reports in 2007 and was reworked in the 2009 United Nations Secretary-General's discussions of climate risks to security (CNA Corporation 2007). The most high profile case in the second decade of this century was clearly Syria, and the discussion about the relationship between drought and conflict highlights the difficulties with proving causation.

CLIMATE AND CONFLICT IN SYRIA

The case of Syria and climate change generated media headlines, alarmist suggestions of this as a case of a climate caused war, and considerable scholarly dispute over the claims of such a linkage as well as how such claims have been substantiated (Gleick 2014; Kelley, Mohtadi, Cane et al. 2015; Werrell, Femia and Sternberg 2015; Ide 2018). The argument is that severe drought in Eastern Syria in the final few years of the first decade of the new millennium caused much hardship among farmers. Many were, through lack of adequate rainfall and hence crop failure, forced to leave their land and seek sustenance in the rapidly growing cities. Unhappiness with the state failure to provide aid led to protests, and in turn to violent state repression of the protestors. This in turn escalated as protestors resisted police and military actions and the result was a series of increasingly violent confrontations that morphed into ongoing violence and eventually a full scale civil war. If this is in fact what happened, then it is not hard to make the case that climate change causes war. That being the case, then it follows that if it happened in Syria as a result of a climate change induced disruption, it likely will happen elsewhere, and hence this is a matter of global significance and a clear warning of future trends.

But is, the critics argued, this really what happened, or is the climate security narrative being foisted on a situation that might be better interpreted in other ways, ones that do not lead to conclusions that climate causes conflict (Selby, Dahi, Fröhlich and Hulme 2017). As the scholarly research has grown, the skepticism has increased, and while there very obviously was rural distress and unemployment in Syria in the period coinciding with the start of the Arab Spring, it has, so the critics argue, much more to do with flawed government policies, the bungled transition to grain farming, and larger political economy matters, including the removal of subsidies on fuel needed for pumps for wells at a crucial moment, than any direct connection with climate (Daoudy 2020). That there was serious rural distress and unemployment in Eastern Syria as the Arab Spring unfolded isn't in doubt, but did it cause conflict?

To make the case for climate caused conflict a number of key links in the causal chain have to be verified, and the case for most of them is empirically weak, in some cases derived from media reports rather than on the ground investigations. First the drought has to be linked to clear indications that climate change caused it. Climate modellers may argue about this causation, and regional variations are hard to attribute to macro scale changes, but if it is the case as determined by climate modelling, then the supposed initial cause is established. But establishing what is actually a drought isn't so simple. Detailed rainfall figures as well as temperature and evapotranspiration measurements are needed to establish conditions that are far from the norm. A drought doesn't matter if farmers aren't trying to grow crops that can't survive in those conditions. Seasonal average rainfall figures aren't key either; what matters is if there is rainfall when crops need it to mature. Inadequate rainfall may not matter either if there are either river or lake sources for irrigation or groundwater supplies available along with pumps to get it to the surface, combined with irrigation systems to get it on fields, to compensate for lack of rainfall.

An additional complication in this initial part of the argument is simply that there were worse droughts in previous decades. Hence why, if drought is a cause of migration and conflict, did the earlier ones not lead to violence? The earlier more severe droughts would seem to have been more likely triggers for disruptions and hence violence. Did large numbers of farmers move to cities in earlier droughts? Even if they did they didn't apparently protest in ways that might have brought about conflict. At least in part the answer might be that changes on the ground had made people more vulnerable in some ways in the later drought, and indeed the growth of grain farming and increased reliance on pumps for irrigation may explain much of this (Selby 2019a). In the later drought episode the Syrian regime removed subsidies for diesel fuel to run pumps, and this apparently made at least some farms financially unsustainable. As a consequence, widespread layoffs of farm labourers may have generated migration to the cities in search of employment.

But a further link in the causal chain needs to be demonstrated here, because if migrants to the city are to be seen as a key part of the whole process, then they need to have been involved in protests which the regime then repressed. Or perhaps indirectly they need to be seen as a cause of unrest in the cities, causing residents to resent the migrants or perhaps the failure of the regime to provide housing and other assistance which, because of the rural influx, was then in even shorter supply. But the empirical evidence from Syrian cities seems weak on this point too; many rural residents apparently left the cities either when it became clear that there were no opportunities there, or once the violence started, fleeing back to the country for safety.

Perhaps the most important point in all this is that what the simple climate causing conflict argument overlooks are the processes of rural change that were underway prior to the drought, in the extension of commercial agriculture, and the role of the state in promoting particular modes of farming. Likewise the corruption and failure to supply good quality seed and fertilizer may have left farmers vulnerable, and also resentful of the regime (Schwartzstein 2021). Here the point is about the particular modes of development in rural areas and the failure to consider the local needs of rural populations struggling with multiple difficulties, which drought compounded. Climate here is indeed a factor, a conflict multiplier, but it is inadequate governance and neglect, corruption and incompetence that are key to turning stresses into larger political problems. More specifically the Syrian case reinforces Baechler's (1998) earlier focus on maldevelopment and conflict related to these difficulties, now in places enhanced by the stresses of less predictable weather patterns and extreme events.

The Syrian case garnered headlines, and attention from the burgeoning think tank and policy community on climate security (Mabey, Gulledge, Finel and Silverthorne 2011), but the critical research on this case suggests that establishing causation linking climate change to the Syrian civil war is at best difficult, and it may simply be wrong, or at least misleading in terms of the policy implications. But given that numerous researchers have been investigating relationships between environmental change and conflict, there are numerous other cases that might be more illuminating, and that might establish the causal links that were imputed but not proved in the Syrian case. The debate about climate as a cause of conflict is in some ways a reinvention of the debate about environment and conflict from the 1990s, although at times it seems that these earlier discussions have either been forgotten or ignored in the focus specifically on climate.

ENVIRONMENT AND CONFLICT: EMPIRICAL EVIDENCE

In the 1990s, following the focus in *Our Common Future* on environmental insecurity as a cause of conflict, and the emergence of the environmental security policy discussions in American publications (Mathews 1989; Renner 1989), Thomas Homer-Dixon (1991) and others pondered the empirical case for linking environment and security, and at least initially concluded that while there might be much low level conflict there was little plausible evidence to suggest that environmental scarcities were likely to be a cause of large scale inter-state warfare (Homer-Dixon 1994). In February 1994 journalist Robert Kaplan brought high level attention to this discussion with his cover story in *Atlantic Monthly* on "The Coming Anarchy". There might be some important exceptions to this suggestion, but nowhere was there a plausible alliance system of environmentally vulnerable states that might engage in combat as a result of strictly environmental causes. For all the headlines about water wars, empirical examinations of historical records suggested that wars over water were mostly fiction not established historical fact (Wolf 1999). As to whether that will change as climate change accelerates remains a key but open question, partly a matter of the specific geographies involved.

In parallel, Daniel Deudney (1990) argued vehemently that linking ecology and security was a bad idea, not least because of the obvious incompatibility between environmental issues and the dominant modalities of security forces. They were not equipped or trained to deal with ecological restoration, pollution controls, agricultural innovations or wildlife management. The record of the US military a couple of decades previously in massive defoliation efforts in South East Asia suggested that they were the last agency to invoke in environmental matters. Matthias Finger (1991) suggested that the military, and the industrial system supplying it with weapons, fuel and all the other paraphernalia of warfare, was a prime cause of environmental degradation; providing "security" in these terms was anathema to ecological sanity.

Where major warfare on environmental matters might be highly unlikely the questions then turned to smaller scale disturbances and civil wars, and the relationships between resources, environmental change and conflict. Defining what was a resource made matters difficult here, as did what constituted scarcity and how it might be linked to conflict. Thomas Homer-Dixon (1999) concluded that there were links between environmental scarcities and conflict, but ones that usually required additional factors to be considered. While migration caused by environmental scarcity might trigger conflict in destinations where newcomers clashed with locals, or possibly with previous migrants anxious not to be economically undercut by recent arrivals, nonetheless this wasn't a matter of major warfare. The opportunistic actions by political elites in a crisis to gain access to resources, a matter of resource capture in Homer-Dixon's terms, might also lead to displacements and the ecological marginalization of disadvantaged people forced either on to marginal land or into cities in search of sustenance. Structural scarcity is clearly a factor too in these circumstances where access to resources is restricted by elite control.

Guenter Baechler (1998) led a European initiative looking at the relationships between conflict and environment and concluded that while there were linkages, many of them occurred in regions that were undergoing what he termed maldevelopment, and in marginal locations between major ecological systems, ecotone boundaries on the large scale, and notably in mountainous areas. In a formulation loosely parallel with Homer-Dixon's he suggested that discrimination in terms of resource access was a frequent problem, and that conflict often happened in ecotones between large biomes. The displacements along with failures of governments to handle the unfortunate consequences of development projects were part of the problem, but once again little of this was likely to lead to traditional security problems in terms of inter-state warfare, however much intra-state violence might be implicated. Colin Kahl's (2006) empirical follow up looking at a comparison of Kenya and the Philippines suggested that much rural violence was generated by elites trying to extract resources and being resisted by locals, rather than being a matter of scarcity per se.

Two major counter arguments emerged in the 1990s. The first was from political ecologists and critical development researchers, mainly geographers and anthropologists who objected that there was a longstanding literature on violence in rural areas, and much of the research showed that a fair amount of the violence related to the expropriation and displacements of peoples by colonization and more recently development (Peluso and Watts 2001). There was little cause, so the argument went, to reinvent neo-Malthusian concerns about population and scarcity when the established frameworks for investigating conflicts around resource capture and violent dispossession were well understood, at least in those disciplines. Watts' (2013) work in Nigeria had long shown that in cases of extreme scarcity, what resulted was famine, and that state actions, or in fact inaction, frequently was a contributing cause of the suffering and death.

The second counter argument, drawing in part on the discussions of new wars (Kaldor 1999) and the failures of development in many places, pointed to resources, where they were in enough abundance to be worth fighting over, as a much more significant source of conflict in the Global South. Here the longstanding patterns of conflict over the sources of resources, part and parcel of the long term European expansion (Le Billon 2012), were replicated in struggles to control the rents from land and the revenue streams that came from the export of resources to global markets. In the case of the new wars, combat, control over territory, access to resources and international financial and weapons trading were tied into low grade violence where controlling territory and extracting wealth were obviously more important than victory. Insurgent forces need supplies and funds, and these too can come from the control over mines, oil wells and forestry.

An especially chilling variation on this theme at the larger scale emerged in Shimshon Bichler and Jonathan Nitzan's (2004) analysis of the political economy of violence in the Middle East. They noted an empirical pattern in the differential accumulation rates between the weapons and logistics companies and the rest of the economy, where low oil prices tended to predict the imminence of war in the region. Logistics companies provide support for oil industries, who need their services most when prices are high and exploration and construction of petroleum related facilities are underway. With low prices in that sector, profitability suffers for those in the "petro dollar weapon dollar" portion of the global economy; warfare reverses this trend as logistics are key to modern warfare, and the disruptions also may have the effect of heightening oil prices once again. While the precise mechanisms whereby low oil prices necessarily trigger wars aren't clear, the correlation in this data is certainly suggestive.

One of the implications of this analysis is a clear refutation of the argument that US policy is simply about intervening in the Middle East to ensure access to oil supplies; the situation is much more complicated than such simple arguments suggest (Meierding 2016a). Key to this isn't access but profitability, and that has been the key factor in the long term history of petroleum politics (Yergin 1991). It was an issue in the 1950s too, as petroleum was promoted as a fuel in Europe, in part as a policy to break the hold of coal on energy supplies, but also to expand the automobile industry and increase the control of American companies over energy markets (Mitchell 2011). Likewise this argument has ramifications for the transition off oil to renewable energy that is a key part of mid twenty first century geopolitics. There is a long history of political instability in oil producing states, where drops in prices are often related to unrest (Vadlamannati and de Soysa 2020). A sustainable future has to require that much of the remaining fossil fuel resources remain in the ground, and the consequences of transitions and declining oil revenues in the region connect directly to matters of security. Transition strategies related to international climate policy that requires the reduction in fossil fuel production are thus part of future geopolitics quite directly, a matter that will be discussed again in Chapter 8.

CLIMATE WARS?

Much of the discussion of resources and conflict and the role of environmental change in causing violence has been reworked in the more recent debate about whether climate causes conflict. Much of this too is focused on the Global South, where people are widely engaged in agriculture, which is obviously the economic sector most directly impacted by changing climatic conditions, but at best the numerous attempts to quantify the putative links between climate and conflict have produced ambiguous results, not least because of the narrow focus on conflict as an outcome (Meierding 2016b; Selby 2014). As already mentioned in the previous chapter, many of the rural areas of the world have been remade by the processes of colonization and the rapid introduction of agricultural innovations which changes both production methods and property relationships in rural areas. Both of these things can cause conflict, especially where subsistence modes of economy are replaced by commercial ones. It is a sad fact that those who die first in famines are farmers and their families. This happens precisely because their wealth is tied up with land and when that fails to produce they are bereft of economic resources; commercial relationships are usually more flexible, allowing trading to provide essential food and other necessities.

Not all farmers are sedentary; in some parts of the world, and the Sahel region of Africa in particular, migratory herders continue to be a substantial part of rural economies and their animals a source of wealth and food, as well as status. Harmonious relationships with pastoralists, whose fields are sometimes grazed by herders' animals after harvest, can work to mutual benefit, but if the rhythms of planting and migration are interrupted, conflict is frequent. Likewise cattle raiding is common in some places, but made much more lethal by the addition of modern firearms. Climate change on top of the rapid spread of modern commercial economic development adds additional stresses to these complex relationships. Not surprisingly some of the obvious empirical relationships that have been investigated linking climate to conflict focus on these rural areas.

But these small scale disputes in rural areas are a long way from major inter-state warfare. Given the relative paucity of international combat in recent decades, researchers have looked to longer term historical studies in search of answers to questions linking climate and conflict. There is a notable passage in Thomas Malthus's (1798/1970) *Essay on the Principle of Population* in which he claims that it was absence of grazing in Asia that set nomadic peoples in motion west into Europe and to the eventual fall of Rome following repeated migrations and conflicts with the declining empire (Heather 2006). Geopolitics and climate are implicitly related here but in circumstances that are very different from those pertaining to the twenty first century. The barbarians are not at the gates, and as much of this volume suggests, it's not clear exactly who they actually are, a theme explored in exquisite detail in Iain Pears' novel on the theme *The Dream of Scipio*.

Historical analysis has to be treated very carefully in terms of drawing lessons applicable to a global economy of nearly eight billion people, the majority of whom now live in cities. Territorial states now claim all the terrestrial surface of the globe with the exception of Antarctica, and much of the aqueous world too. Satellite surveillance, air power, naval forces and all the other paraphernalia of modernity makes historical analogy difficult. As noted in Chapter 3, the disruptions of the seventeenth century, which might be traced to the temporary cooling of much of the earth following the reforestation of the Americas, did indeed involve much conflict (Parker 2013). Famines and disruption followed poor harvests and then made farming more difficult too, but those circumstances are not an obvious analogy with present times, not least because temporary cooling was at least part of the problem then, whereas now it is rapid heating that is causing disruptions. But as Parker (2013) also makes clear, dealing with the violence and disruption of the seventeenth century led to innovation in state structures, and the emergence of both political theories about states and practical innovation in terms of bureaucracy, taxation and permanent military institutions too. International relations textbooks frequently refer to the Treaty of Westphalia as the origin of the modern international system, even if they don't connect it to the climate disruptions of the period.

Some of the most comprehensive historical records of calamities and wars come from China, with its very long history of continuous civilization. Harry Lee (2018) has carefully assembled these records and, using statistical analyses, tried to tease out the relationships between climate change, disasters and conflict in the form of internal wars within agrarian China through the last half millennium. "Generally, socio-ecological catastrophes are the proximate triggers of internal wars. Specifically, internal wars are triggered by epidemics in the wheat region, while ignited by famines in the rice region in historic China. Furthermore, internal wars in the two agro-ecological zones are revealed to be context-dependent" (Lee 2018, 1079). Lee makes the point that disasters lead first to economic disruptions and social failures, not directly to wars, which may come later. The analysis is complicated to say the least, but the findings suggest that while climate change may be a background factor, internal wars within China are more obviously related to short term disasters. As is to be expected in an agrarian society, food supplies are a key part of this history, with famine as one trigger for conflicts. While this history is suggestive, care has to be taken in applying these insights to the twenty first century, where industrial farming techniques and international food aid, as well as global markets, add novel complexities to such analyses. Likewise, as other longitudinal studies suggest, complex causalities are intertwined with shifting agricultural practices related both to subsistence strategies and to commercial opportunities, making clear causal claims difficult (Deligiannis 2020).

Despite all these difficulties, the repeated invocation of security dangers in policy debates and the use of securitizing rhetoric to raise the profile of climate dangers has meant continuing research efforts grappling with some of these issues. Not surprisingly the results have been mixed (Scartozzi 2021). Statistical correlations between climate fluctuations have been claimed as proof of climate as a cause of conflict (Hsiang, Meng and Cane 2011; Hsiang and Burke 2014). Analyses from Africa dispute these findings (O'Loughlin, Witmer, Linke et al. 2012). Equally other studies have suggested that if not spurious, such correlations are just that—correlations—and don't provide proof that climate is a cause of conflict (Selby 2014). Part of the problem is also a matter of scale; data crudely aggregated may suggest things that don't make sense once the detailed cases are investigated. Likewise disputes over the appropriate threshold in terms of numbers of casualties needed to qualify as a conflict or a war complicate conclusions. Is average temperature a reasonable proxy of climate change, and how is that to be reliably ascertained prior to contemporary standardized thermometers being widely available? Aggregate rainfall statistics aren't much help either because what matters in terms of agricultural productivity is whether reasonable amounts of rain arrive at crucial stages in planting and crop maturity. In pastoral economies raiding and conflict are more likely in good years when herds are prolific than when attention is focused on trying to find forage in drought conditions to keep at least some animals alive. But the statistical interpretations remain murky, making attempts to synthesize the research for policy makers a fraught exercise (Buhaug 2015; Detges 2017).

In attempting to tease out what can be learned from these numerous studies, which are often at odds with one another because of differing definitional, scale and statistical assumptions, recent efforts at expert elucidation have come to at least some tenuous conclusions (Mach, Kraan, Adger et al. 2019). Clearly, underdeveloped regions are at greater risk, although even here climate change is, at least so far, less of a driver of conflict than many other social and economic factors. But clearly too, much additional research work on the precise relationships between climate and conflict will be needed, both to evaluate the links and to think through what interventions can prevent conflict even in cases where climate has generated conditions of severe social instability (Mach, Adger, Buhaug et al. 2020). All of which suggests that longstanding concerns about good governance and equitable development are key to shaping more resilient societies that are likely to be less conflict prone.

In trying to resolve some of the difficulty with empirical cases, Josh Busby's (2022) attempt at a synthesis analyses comparison cases, trying to find situations where climate disruptions apparently caused conflict, and some where they didn't. Such comparative studies ought to clarify what factors are involved in making causal links between the two. While no two cases are identical, if at least broadly similar sets of circumstances yield different outcomes, then the factors that differ in these paired cases may provide clues to what is most important in determining which trajectory results. But there is more to security problems than acute conflict and therefore Busby chose to include large scale humanitarian disasters in his security case studies. He compared Somalia, where famine killed hundreds of thousands, and Ethiopia, where it didn't at the same time, as well as looking at historical comparisons with earlier famine in Ethiopia, pointing to governmental capacity as key to avoiding major death tolls. International aid also matters: people died when aid wasn't allowed into the country. Droughts in Lebanon and Syria are compared in another paired case comparison, pointing to the inadequacy of the Assad regime's response but a better performance in Lebanon.

A third case comparison in terms of responses to cyclones in Bangladesh, Myanmar and India adds another dimension to the discussion focused on rapid onset disasters, in contrast to slow onset drought events. There the key factor in the death toll from cyclones was once again government capacity, and a willingness to accept international assistance, in the case of Bangladesh over the long term to build disaster preparedness and resilience. Failure on the part of the Myanmar government to either prepare or allow international assistance into the country led to large numbers of deaths in 2008. Busby also notes that attempts to respond to climate change may cause conflicts and difficulties too, and that thinking about the future, where past histories are not necessarily appropriate models for a climate altered world, has to be part of the research agenda for the future on climate security. Climate insecurities are now a major matter in international politics even if the traditional themes in the international relations discipline have been slow to grapple with these novel circumstances of the Anthropocene.

European policy formulations of these matters have tended to think in terms of a broad formulation of security, understanding it as more than a matter of conflict and thinking about strategies to avoid the worst possible futures. A key report from the Adelphi think tank in Berlin commissioned by the G7 posed matters in terms of "A New Climate for Peace", looking at the need to take action to reduce the dangers of climate change and in particular the fragility of many institutions in the face of coming disruptions (Rüttinger, Smith, Stang et al. 2015). Subsequently the United Nations Environment Programme (UNEP) and the European Union collaborated on programs to try to tackle environmental matters in crisis ridden states, combining development, disaster reduction and peacemaking efforts to better anticipate and hence avoid potential conflicts and disruptions (Rüttinger 2017). Disaster planning, international aid and careful foresight all matter, and are frequently in short supply where they might be most useful, in poor states with limited infrastructure and management capabilities (Moran, Busby, Raleigh et al. 2018). Dealing with those fragilities is understood as a key theme in climate security and a key matter for climate diplomacy as well as the larger discussions under the United Nations Framework Convention on Climate Change (UNFCCC) on adaptation and the fraught matters of loss and damage compensation funding, not to mention the rising frequency of litigation on these matters (Byers, Franks and Gage 2017).

THE NEW GEOPOLITICAL LANDSCAPE

While the initial years of the war on terror, in the aftermath of the events of 9/11, were preoccupied in international relations with American concerns about terrorism and military interventions in Afghanistan, and subsequently in Iraq, behind the scenes in various think tanks and university research efforts the debate about environmental security continued. One report, in the form of a scoping exercise on likely climate and conflict futures (Schwartz and Randall

2003), caused a flurry of media attention in 2004, in part arguing that the Bush administration was so preoccupied by Iraq that it was ignoring climate dangers. But it is noteworthy in that it suggested that climate change might happen abruptly with obviously disruptive consequences, rather than as a matter of gradual environmental change. This scenario was based on the possibility that the Gulf Stream in the Atlantic might stop flowing, with numerous climate disruptions resulting on a much larger scale than the empirical investigations of rural African violence caused by climate change discussed above suggest.

In 2007, after years of relative public neglect during the global war on terror period, a number of reports appeared pointing to the potential for violence related to climate change in particular. In 2007 the CNA corporation (formerly the Center for Naval Analyses) released a report arguing that while climate itself might not be a direct cause of conflict, the disruptions it was starting to cause were likely to be a "threat multiplier". Instabilities and distress, especially in rural areas in Africa, would, so the report contended, provide fertile recruitment areas for insurgent groups, especially so where they could pay or at least feed recruits in economic situations where few other options existed. Connected to Al Qaeda or other "terrorist" organizations, the report suggested that climate multiplied the possibilities for conflict and as such vulnerable regions needed to be taken seriously because of the enhanced risks of political violence. Other similar publications followed quickly (Campbell, Gulledge, McNeill et al. 2007), and European efforts to draw these links proceeded too, with a high profile German report on climate security risks pointing to numerous dangers that needed attention in terms of security more broadly defined (German Advisory Council on Global Change 2008).

Seven years after their initial report on threat multipliers, the military advisory committee to the CNA corporation (CNA Military Advisory Board 2014) released an update where they suggested that climate change was already a "catalyst of conflict". Throughout this period the US military became increasingly concerned that climate change was a factor driving both conflict and increasingly disasters, and as such a factor that was changing their operational environments and requiring them to undertake more emergency relief and disaster response missions (Briggs and Matejova 2019). In addition they became increasingly concerned that climate change would directly threaten operations because of rising sea levels threatening naval facilities in particular, and storms and droughts threatening bases and training facilities; the major naval base at Norfolk, Virginia is already suffering regular high tide flooding (Klare 2019). A report from the US Army War College also noted that climate change will put increased strain on the national electrical grid in the United States, making the Army vulnerable to service interruptions, and emphasized that environmentalist political pressures may constrain its activities, not least because of objections to its large use of fossil fuels (Brosig, Frawley, Hill et al.

2019). It is a notable irony that the US military is the largest single institutional user of fossil fuels, and the carbon footprint of its worldwide military operations is a substantial contributor to climate change (Belcher, Bigger, Neimark and Kennelly 2020). Reports on climate security now frequently mention this point, but fewer of them, at least those generated in Washington, suggest that this global military footprint needs to be fundamentally rethought as part of tackling climate insecurity.

The view from the think tank world in Washington has generated numerous reports, particularly from the Center for Climate and Security, but their 2017 report on "Epicenters of Climate and Security" was tellingly subtitled "The New Geostrategic Landscape of the Anthropocene" (Werrell and Femia 2017). Trying to encapsulate this novel landscape suggested some clear focal points of concern, which they defined in terms of three criteria: critical for global security, vulnerable to a rapidly changing climate, and categories of risk present in multiple centres. These criteria are obviously about much more than specifying particular places or states as the problem, and the analysis is noteworthy in its attempts to think through the ripple effects of climate induced difficulties running through the global security system. Local events may have complex consequences elsewhere, and this requires analyses that focus on systemic risks, and specifically, to use the chapter titles in the report, "eroding sovereignty, water towers, disappearing islands, dire straits, nuclear and climate, health security, coastal megacities, water weaponization, melting Arctic, fish and conflict, the coffee belt as well as migration and displacement".

The report also focuses on some relevant management tools, including the use of foresight and early warning systems, mapping and earth observation tools, that might be useful. Worried about the declining effectiveness of states in many places as well as the rapidly changing political and economic circumstances of many places beyond the stable metropoles of the global economy, this list of potential difficulties and their complicated geographies offers a smorgasbord of policy concerns with the danger of spillover effects. The key point is that while climate is changing and making rural life less predictable, the huge transformation wrought by colonization and subsequently globalization in the period of the great acceleration means that climate plays out on this novel stage. It isn't an exogenous variable acting on a stable environment; it's a variable that has to be understood as a factor in the larger transformations of the Anthropocene. Now the task for security policy makers is to try to shape the transformations to increase the resilience of increasingly artificial ecosystems, while avoiding social breakdowns that stymie attempts to adapt. As with so many of these reports there is little discussion of the causes of climate change, and from whence the driving forces that are making these epicentres a matter of concern in Washington come.

WHOSE SECURITY?

Which brings the argument back to the questions of security ontology and the issue of who is that "we" that is threatened (Mitzen 2006; Rossdale 2015). Much of the discussion of climate security, and the American variation on it in particular, is about threats from rural peripheries in the global system, and climate threat multipliers enhancing terrorist and insurgent activities in Africa and Asia in the earlier formulations, and now with the "Epicenters" formulation, more complex interconnected risks (Werrell and Femia 2017). The who that is threatened here is the American world order, and its embeddedness in a "liberal" trading and financial order premised on endless economic growth. Threats to this are about peripheral disruptions, whether in terms of extreme meteorological events disrupting supply chains or extremists attacking those supply chains in insurgent actions, or some combination of both. Maintaining this geopolitical arrangement has long been seen as essential to national security planners and policy makers in the United States.

But if it is to be maintained into the long term future then clearly, in the face of accelerating climate change, it can no longer be powered by fossil fuels. The accelerating disruptions will clearly come home too; hurricanes, wildfires and extreme weather events are already overwhelming infrastructure in the United States. Water shortages in the American South West and in California in particular are now routine, as are huge wildfires, and more extremes will only aggravate the stresses on existing systems, not least the air conditioners needed to keep the housing and businesses there liveable in summer. This model of using technology to change environments, replumbing rivers, irrigating deserts and golf courses to maintain a particular lifestyle, and a sense of who "we" are as consumers of luxury items and recreational activities, is increasingly difficult to sustain. Failure to do so could lead to nightmare scenarios like Paolo Bacigalupi suggests in *The Water Knife*.

A very different set of priorities in terms of who that "we" might be looms in the campaigns for green new deals and justice in the face of glaring inequities in the polity accentuated by the rapid roll out of emergency funds to deal with COVID-19. These struggles are key to the future and to what kind of "we" becomes the subject of security policy (Holthaus 2020). The "ever larger technological control over environment" model that has been key to the expansion of American modes of life throughout the period of the great acceleration is now seriously in doubt as it confronts its own limits and generates discussions of degrowth and related economic initiatives (Kallis 2018). Simply changing the technology and running it on "renewable" energy has been much of the focus among American elite thinkers focused on placating and assuring middle class consumers that climate change is manageable (see for example

Bloomberg and Pope 2017, Gates 2021 and even Mann 2021). But no longer is this adequate in the United States, as mounting disasters make it clear that extreme weather is a hazard at home as well as one that may cause dangerous complications abroad; storms and disasters as well as the COVID-19 pandemic have very clearly raised the question of who is being secured in present circumstances (Buck 2019).

Viewed from elsewhere this preoccupation with preserving the resource intensive lifestyle that advertising agencies have been defining as the good life and the aspiration for all has long been under challenge. In the early enthusiasm for tackling climate change in the 1990s one of the most effective critiques of climate policy and the "we are all in this together" line on the need to deal with climate change was the argument from India that a distinction had to be made between subsistence and luxury emissions (Agarwal and Narain 1991). Suggesting that carbon dioxide from rural farming for immediate sustenance in the Global South and emissions from luxury vehicles or recreational equipment in the North should be treated as equivalent in carbon dioxide policy making brought charges of colonialism, and arguments that those who had created the problem and who generated the most emissions needed to be those that solved it, or at least moved first in terms of policy response.

Viewed from Bangladesh, the Mekong Delta, or other places facing imminent inundation, these suggestions that emissions from recreational vehicles in the North are the equivalent of their agricultural emissions make no sense. The most vulnerable people in these places have done little to cause climate change and what minimal carbon dioxide and methane they do add to the atmosphere is to provide food and sustenance, not for status and thrill seeking. "The Anthropocene, however, indicates that injustice is now global in the most literal sense. Extending human presence to the far corners of the earth, and doing so in ways that reward the already rich and powerful and punish the poor and voiceless, has created the spectre of both grinding injustice and planetary fragility" (Wapner 2019, 224). Worse, when those people are forced to move and are then portrayed as a threat to the places they aspire to move to, they are rendered doubly vulnerable. And when informed that there is little they can do to ameliorate their condition they face a condition of what Chaturvedi and Doyle (2015) call climate terror, where forces beyond their control require that they stay put and suffer the consequences of climate change.

The most basic mode of adaptation in the face of disaster is to move, but in a world of hardening borders this is now all the more difficult (McLeman 2019). If the projected need to migrate as a result of increased temperatures in numerous places comes to pass, then the human insecurities as borders are closed become ever greater. Discerning likely migration patterns is a fraught business, but at the largest scale as global heating progresses, clearly some parts of the planet will become ever more difficult to live in, and heat waves may drive people to move. At least it may do so in places where farmers can no longer grow food due to drought and temperatures too hot for crops to mature. If climate patterns migrate towards the poles, then up to a point agricultural patterns may do so too (Xu, Kohler, Lenton et al. 2020). As residents in Phoenix in the United States who own air conditioners, as well as long term inhabitants of various deserts, show however, there is a danger of climate determinist type arguments where average temperatures are linked to migration patterns without the careful consideration of the adaptive capabilities that local cultures may have to cope (Horton, de Sherbinin, Wrathall and Oppenheimer 2021). Many of the areas most likely to face extreme heat are among those where the poorest societies live, and clearly at least some of these populations will seek to move in coming decades.

But in so far as these potential migrants are then portrayed as threats to their destination areas, and a "fortress" mentality of security invoked to keep them out, then fences, walls and armed patrols become part of the security imaginary (White 2014). Linked to white supremacy or white nationalist movements in the United States in particular, nativist narratives rework climate change into a matter of external threats to domestic landscapes (Hultgren 2015). In Europe such xenophobic concerns have a long history, not only in the romantic fantasies of racially pure homelands in Nazi thinking (Snyder 2015), but also in other more recent articulations, including in Jean Raspail's novel *The Camp of the Saints* reflecting on the European response to starvation in India in the 1960s, which has circulated in right wing circles in various versions since its original publication in France.

These questions of racial purity and spatial boundaries invoked in border narratives are precisely what concerns Alex Alvarez (2021) in warning that climate change narratives carry with them potentially genocidal implications. "Such spatiality has meant that border zones are regions that have often been swayed by belief systems and popular movements defining specific population groups as a source of contamination and pollution and deciding to remove the offensive physical presence of the group so designated" (Alvarez 2021, 139). In the case of American security narratives, Reece Jones has recently reminded us once again that American borders have frequently been defined in terms of whiteness (2021). Notions of climate apartheid fit all too neatly into these formulations of external dangers to white populations from tropical peoples set in motion by rising sea levels, droughts and agricultural disruptions. This focus on the symptoms of climate disruption neatly evades considerations of causation.

ENDANGERED, ENTANGLED, EXTRACTIVIST

In making sense of the multiple conflicting interpretations of the various narratives linking environment and global politics in the Anthropocene, Lövbrand, Mobjörk and Soder (2020) suggest that three dominant modes of discourse can be discerned in current academic discussions, those of endangered worlds, entangled worlds, and extractivist worlds. These categories are largely self-explanatory, but they add a key dimension to the questions of ontological security, and the question of what identities are invoked in the discussions of global security. They also emphasize the importance of shifting the focus from the narrow one in many versions of sustainable development discourse on resource scarcities to environmental security understood much more broadly (Pirages and Cousins 2005).

The endangered world discourse engages with the discussion of the Anthropocene and earth system science concerns that human actions have changed humanity's relationship with the earth. "The endangered world presents a global scene where new environmental threats and dangers are causing socioeconomic turbulence and gradually altering the geopolitical map" (Lövbrand, Mobjörk and Soder 2020, 3). Citing Dumaine and Mintzer (2015), Lövbrand, Mobjörk and Soder state that

> … traditional security thinking makes little analytical sense in a world bound together by complex, non-linear and closely coupled environmental risks. In the Anthropocene security analysts must move beyond the assumption that the main purpose of defense is to secure the nation against external, state-based, mainly military threats. In order to respond to the dangers of a radically transformed global environment, states need to cultivate a shared view about common threats and improve collective capacities for early warning, rapid response, and disaster mitigation … (2020, 3)

The entangled world is a discourse drawing more explicitly from international relations themes and less focused on a series of problems that can be solved. It "instead represents a new reality where humans, nonhumans, things and materials coexist in complex relations of life and non-life. … In a world marked by melting ice caps, thawing permafrost, acidified oceans, accelerating deforestation, degraded agricultural lands and dramatic species loss, human activity and nature are so enmeshed that they are existentially indistinguishable" (Lövbrand, Mobjörk and Soder 2020, 4). The implications of this for security thinking are profound. "Security cannot be achieved by resolute actions grounded in expression of power targeting 'external' threats, but only by re-embedding modern humanity in the multi-species world that we now are remaking" (Lövbrand, Mobjörk and Soder 2020, 4). This requires a different politics, one that makes other species part of the discussion and understands security in terms of a functional biosphere, not a matter of domination and force.

The third Anthropocene discourse focuses on justice and the social-ecological consequences of the expansion of a capitalist world economy. "In the extractivist world the center of concern is instead the global capitalist system and the monumental damage and injustice done by its ceaseless need for expansion, accumulation and extraction" (Lövbrand, Mobjörk and Soder 2020, 4). Drawing from Saskia Sassen (2016), Lövbrand, Mobjörk and Soder suggest that

> (T)he development of capitalism has, since its origins, been marked by violence, destruction, and appropriation. By digging up and burning large reserves of fossilized carbon, industrialized economies have long done damage to the biosphere and people living on the edges of the Western world. However, the past three decades of petroleum-powered economic globalization have reorganized human-nature relations on the largest possible scale. The extraordinary growth in industrial production, commodity markets, technological innovation and consumerism is now remaking the entire ecological context for humanity. (2020, 4)

Dealing with this world requires rapid changes in political economy and abandoning both a simple conflation of all of humanity as a single actor in the earth system and assumptions that fiddling with market arrangements will bring about appropriate economic innovation to produce a sustainable future for all.

Clearly numerous things are endangered in this world, and the climate discussion highlights many of them. Hence the general alarm about many climate issues and the importance of considering policy actions. The entangled formulation suggests long distance connections, and the fact that simple policy solutions working in silos or stovepipes, focusing on just one aspect of a problem, are often likely to make things worse precisely because they don't think about the entanglements. The extractivist world is in many ways the antithesis of the endangered world, because it posits a separate world as a source of resources for use by humanity, rather than a world whereby the disruptions set in motion by extractivist activities are the source of the endangerments. Clearly extractivist activities are entangled in the global economy, but the focus on one at the expense of the other is likely to miss key connections between the two (Bales and Sovacool 2021).

Crucially what is most concerning in all this is the interconnections between all three and the fact that extractivism is occurring in an entangled world that precisely by the interconnections is now endangering numerous things. The entanglements suggest tele-connections too, between systems that at least until recently were understood to be relatively separate (Benzie and Persson 2019). In Clive Hamilton's (2017) terms the epistemological rupture that marks the difference between the Anthropocene and earlier formulations relates to this interconnection at a global scale. But more than this is the fact that the sheer amount of human activity is now shaping the future configuration of the earth system, and in the process raising the spectre of catastrophic or existential risks, not just for individual civilizations or societies, as has been the case in the past, but now for the survival of the species itself.

The expanding awareness of interconnections and the recognition that in total human actions are now potentially leading to our extinction puts matters of catastrophic and existential risk back into the security frame. They have been there in the past, prior to the 1980s and 1990s focus on smaller scale issues of overt conflict and environmental change in particular locales. Now in a return to the discussions in 1972 and 1987, in the United Nations Conference on the Human Environment (UNCHE) and around *Our Common Future*, new earth system science research is once again raising the possibility of making the planet uninhabitable due to some combination of the extinction crisis (Ceballos, Ehrlich and Dirzo 2017), climate change (Steffen, Röckstrom, Richardson et al. 2018) and ocean acidification. These questions of environmental security at the largest of scales are the focus of Chapter 6.

6. Catastrophic and existential risks

EXISTENTIAL THREATS

In 2017 David Wallace-Wells published an article in *New York Magazine* that galvanized attention to the potential disastrous effects of continued global warming, posing the question as to whether climate change might in fact lead to humanity's own extinction. Read by millions of readers, it clearly had an effect in changing American attitudes at least to the seriousness of climate change and posed the question starkly in terms of likely future events in a climate disrupted system. If there is an existential question for humanity it is this one. At least the Biden presidential campaign in the United States in 2020 talked in terms of climate as an existential issue, and undoubtedly gained youthful support in the American electorate by doing so. But while the journalistic flourishes and campaign rhetoric are clearly important politically, the larger questions about the likelihood of extinction and disaster ahead concern numerous scientific disciplines. What are the lessons from prior catastrophes and extinction events? These are issues much bigger than traditionally understood in terms of environment and resource management issues.

On the other side of the Atlantic, and more or less at the same time as Wallace-Wells was getting attention too, David Bendell (2018) generated controversy with a paper and subsequent edited book on what he called deep adaptation (Bendell and Read 2021). When the paper was rejected by a journal he self-published it online, arguing that contemporary trajectories, especially melting permafrost and methane releases in the Arctic, were happening much faster than conventional analyses were suggesting. The acceleration of climate change suggested to Bendell that conventional assumptions about climate adaptation were underestimating what was coming and that civilization was unlikely to cope without dramatic social and economic change. These he saw as unlikely to transpire in a timely manner, hence societal collapse looms in the near term future. Some of these arguments were influential with parts of the Extinction Rebellion movement in Britain in particular.

One notable point in Bendell's argument is that his paper was rejected on the grounds that it didn't engage the contemporary social science literature. But, he argued, that was his point; conventional social science assumes that the future will be more or less the same as the present, hence it doesn't generate the kind of material that Bendell is concerned about, a rapid climate transition that is outside what conventional projections, and economic analyses in particular, are assuming. Not surprisingly there wasn't much of a social science literature for him to engage! While Bendell doesn't use Michael Albert's (2020) formulation of social science as committed to "continuationism", the argument is loosely consistent with the use of this term. Projections into the future assume that social patterns change gradually, not abruptly.

The case of international relations as a discipline failing to anticipate the demise of the Soviet Union in the early 1990s suggests linearity and persistence as key assumptions in security studies. What both Wallace-Wells and Bendell suggest is that current trajectories are likely to lead to non-linear responses, both in terms of natural change and in terms of social change. Gradual linear changes are what one assumes if market mechanisms and technical innovation form the policy framework for tackling climate change. But, and this is a key point, it's mostly rapid severe and unexpected shocks, and tipping points in natural and social systems, that worry people thinking about climate as a security problem.

Failure to respond appropriately and in time to indications of likely future risks may indeed lead to catastrophe. In security studies at least, histories of war suggest that militaries are usually preparing to fight previous wars, or at least frequently find themselves ill equipped for novel circumstances. This was the case most recently when the United States fought the war on terror in the aftermath of 9/11 mostly with an organization and armaments which had been designed to fight the Soviet Union decades earlier (Dalby 2009a). Likewise it seems that the military now are ill equipped to deal with the challenges that climate change and biodiversity decline present. As noted earlier, Daniel Deudney (1990) pointed out at the beginning of the environmental security discussion that given its training, missions and equipment, the military is hardly the appropriate institution to tackle ecological matters. Its equipment is frequently useful in responding to disasters, but the huge use of fossil fuels involved in military transport, frequently not counted in greenhouse gas emission calculations, is part of the problem (Belcher, Bigger, Neimark and Kennelly 2020). Prevention is key; drastic reactions after the fact are an indication of failure. To paraphrase the key argument from classical Chinese strategist Sun Tsu, if you have to fight your strategy has failed. In the case of climate change this adage is directly applicable; avoiding catastrophic climate change is the only security strategy that is feasible, and a functional civilization of many billion people in a radically destabilized climate system is simply not possible.

There is a very considerable social science literature engaging with the dangers of environmental collapse and the lessons that might be learned from historical cases of empires and societies disappearing as a result of calamities, some of which they brought upon themselves. Jared Diamond's (2005) volume *Collapse* is an especially high profile example. What is new in the case of Wallace-Wells and Bendell is the projections that climate change and radical disruptions caused by humanity will be the likely cause of civilizational collapse in coming decades. While much of the discussion about historical cases of societal collapse has focused on naturally occurring climate change, or in many cases on the exhaustion of agricultural resources by either ill-considered farming and irrigation practices or natural limitations in particular ecosystems, the current apocalyptic framing doesn't focus on resource shortages or direct poisoning by pollution. The 1970s discussion of the *Limits to Growth* too focused on resource shortages as a cause of the collapse of industrial civilization (Herrington 2021). The formulation of environmental security derived from *Our Common Future* likewise suggests that resource shortages are a key problem. But now, with both the extinction crisis and climate change, the discussion is focused on the opposite argument: the consequences of too much economic growth based on the dramatic expansion of firepower in the period of the great acceleration.

In contrast climate disasters are projected as the indirect result of disruptions caused by greenhouse gas emissions, and the response of such things as melting permafrost and the slowing of the Gulf Stream, and, in Bendell's case, alarm about collapsing marine methane clathrates which might cause a huge spike in methane in the atmosphere with disastrous rapid global heating as the outcome. At the worst these disruptions and the failure to deal with them might, so these narratives of doom suggest, lead to the elimination of humanity *in toto*. Science fiction writers have explored these scenarios too. John Barnes in *Mother of Storms* offers a cautionary tale of rapid heating caused by military action; Frank Schatzing's nightmare scenario in his novel *The Swarm* focuses on other dangers from clathrates but cautions against military attempts to destroy environmental threats. While both are excellent entertainment, there is little in the scientific literature to suggest that disintegrating ocean bed clathrates offer immediate threats of destabilizing the earth system.

A failure to anticipate such concerns with possible dramatic destabilizations of the earth system in time, or instigate actions to slow climate change and make societies much more adaptable, might lead to elites struggling to maintain control, in the process leading to major wars. If they went nuclear, which given the number of nuclear arsenals currently in existence is quite possible, then once again nuclear winter raises its head as civilization's fate. Glikson (2017) makes the argument that we might better term present circumstances the Plutocene, because of the future persistence of plutonium and the long lasting isotopes that it generates. In this context the concerns raised by the delegates at the 1972 conference in Stockholm about the need to eliminate nuclear weapons as part of any serious attempt to grapple with global environmental issues seem prescient, even if they were dropped from the sustainable development discourse once the cold war ended.

Human extinction looms over this discussion and has led to more recent systematic discussions of this possibility, and a larger scholarly engagement with the question of long term human survival (Bostrom 2013). This now provides the largest scale contextualization for security studies, and in terms of how environmental security might be rethought, is an essential part of the discussion for a discipline that has survival as its core concern. But this isn't just a matter of human extinction: earth system trajectories in motion suggest that fossil fueled civilization is already causing the sixth overall extinction event in the planet's history (Ceballos, Ehrlich and Dirzo 2017). The potential for major biosphere disruption because of ocean acidification looms over much of this discussion too. This is now the key context for engaging with environmental security, rather than the narrow focus on resource shortages as putative causes of conflict in the Global South.

EXTINCTIONS, AND MERE CATASTROPHES

While there are some technical arguments about what counts as a global extinction event and whether we are living in the sixth one at the moment, conventional wisdom counts five major extinction events in the geological record. As noted in Chapter 3, the most famous is the episode ending the age of the dinosaurs, with a massive asteroid collision with earth being a key part of this story. Reconstructing such episodes is key to stratigraphy, the study of the layers of rocks that tell the story of the planet in the history of sediments and volcanic episodes, and paleontology, the study of fossil life that charts the rise and demise of forms of life in the biosphere, the living part of the planetary system. The major periods of earth history are designated in terms of the dominant forms of life that lived in those times. Now the dominant form is human, the Anthropos is us; hence we now live in the Anthropocene.

The discussion of the Anthropocene highlights the simple but profound fact that humanity is now causing geological scale transformations of the earth, something that is not intuitively obvious to most people, and something that is clearly well beyond the scope of many politicians to grasp, and also beyond most efforts, at least so far, at global governance. While climate change is mostly discussed in terms of more extreme weather, potential violence and the costs of storms and floods, that larger context is more fundamental once one considers the long term fate of humanity. Hence the growing use of terms such as existential crisis, even if it is frequently far from clear precisely whose existence is threatened and hence what kind of security policy is needed for whom where. The David Wallace-Wells (2017) article posed the question of whether all of humanity might be eliminated by climate change and the disruptions likely to follow from failures to anticipate what might be coming and act in time to prevent calamity. His subsequent book (Wallace-Wells 2019) may have been less apocalyptic in tone, but the question hangs over the discussion of climate change, and work in the field of environmental security simply has to confront it even if conventional international relations analyses have been slow to engage these larger questions.

Because one thing is clear: the prior climate history of the planet demonstrates that popular journalistic and policy maker assumptions of gradual climate changes, of slowly rising temperatures and weather patterns shifting in predicable trajectories towards the poles, are unlikely to be correct (Barnosky, Hadly, Bascompte et al. 2012). While clearly climate systems will move, and where soils can accommodate plants from distant places, agricultural opportunities may open up (Xu, Kohler amd Lenton 2020), the newly ice free parts of Greenland being a case in point, assuming that these transitions will be either smooth progressions or predictable sequences has long been recognized as assuming too much (Alley 2004; Schneider 2004). These possibilities are key to thinking about global security, a very different set of assumptions than those that have long populated economic risk analyses relating to climate, with linear projections far into the future (Keen 2021), and implicit assumptions of the inevitability of economic growth.

One particular worrisome scenario that has engaged popular culture is the matter of the dangers of the Gulf Stream stopping, or at least slowing noticeably (Caesar, McCarthy, Thornally et al. 2021). If substantial meltwater from Arctic ice changes the density of water in the North Atlantic then it will not sink as it has been doing since the end of the last glaciation. If this occurs, in technical terms the Atlantic Meridional Overturning Current (AMOC) stops, then the global circulation of ocean currents would stop, and this would have numerous ecological effects. Should that happen, then European climates are likely to be very substantially cooler in the short run (farmers in Greenland will have their hopes disappointed) and agriculture there will be disrupted. (This too has been presented in hugely exaggerated form in the 2004 Hollywood disaster movie *The Day After Tomorrow*.) If the AMOC slows or stops it might temporarily slow melting in Greenland, but presumably heating would intensify further south as the warm waters no longer move heat to higher latitudes. More than this, the various crucial parts of the earth system that may be destabilized as the earth heats are not independent, and if one crosses a tipping point and begins to operate differently, others may follow (Wunderling, Donges, Kurths and Winkelmann 2021). Cascade disruptions make predicting these interactions difficult, and because there is lack of clarity in terms of what amount of heating is required for tipping points to be crossed, predictions are difficult. But that doesn't mean these dangers aren't foreseeable, and if rapid decarbonization of the global economy is set in motion, they might be avoided.

The crucial point in all this is that regional consequences are likely from global climate change, and average temperature changes over the whole system aren't helpful as indications of how conditions in particular places are likely to be affected. All of which means that risks to specific places, as with specific economic systems, need to be evaluated in much more detail, and in the case of supply chains in the global economy, points of vulnerability identified. Policies over the next few decades need to grapple with the disruptions, extreme weather and heat waves that are likely, rather than assume a smooth transition to a future stable state (Albert 2020). The key question for consideration specifically of security is whether states, societies and economies with production systems, and crucially infrastructure designed for one set of circumstances, will be flexible enough to handle disruptive transitions.

Failure to do so, leading to social breakdown and conflict and violence on a large scale, is the nightmare scenario that environmental security researchers wish to convince policy makers that they need to avoid. It doesn't help when these considerations are refracted through security discussions that emphasize fortress formulations of distant threats to metropolitan prosperity (White 2014) and that there has been a rise in survivalist literatures and fantasies on the part of the rich and powerful that they can hide from the ecological disruptions that are coming (Katz-Rosene and Szwarc 2021) or, as critics of conventional climate security discussions suggest, protect themselves by building walls and securitizing climate migration rather than tackling the source in terms of fossil fuel emissions (Miller, Buxton and Akkerman 2021).

In his warning about possible extinction, Wallace-Wells was following in the footsteps of Jonathan Schell (1982), who had ruminated over the possibilities of major nuclear war causing human extinction in his bestseller book *The Fate of the Earth*. As van Munster and Sylvest (2021) emphasize, what was especially interesting in this volume was speculations about the ecological consequences of a major nuclear conflagration, which suggested that more than immediate destruction, firestorms and nuclear fallout were the dangers. This came the year before the "nuclear winter" discussions (Turco, Toon, Ackerman et al. 1983), and highlighted the then emergent recognition in nascent earth system thinking that humanity had, with its technological capabilities, become an earth system scale transformative force. The possibility of human extinction, as a direct outcome of the enormous destructive capabilities of technology, posed nuclear war as an existential threat to the whole of humanity, and hence a compelling argument for rethinking the logics of deterrence and the assumption that as these weapons had apparently kept the superpowers in check so far, they would continue to do so in perpetuity.

But as noted above, this is only a new condition for some peoples; notably it is new for those who actually built and now operate nuclear weapons systems. In that sense the claim that this is an existential threat for all of humanity simply shifts the referent object somewhat to, in this case ironically, those societies whose leaders built the weapons. One of the key counter arguments to adopting the Anthropocene as a novel condition for humanity points to the fact that extreme dangers, and the wholescale elimination of peoples in warfare and by imperial conquest, only most obviously by Europeans and Americans in the last few centuries, are far from new. In political terms many colonized peoples have already faced catastrophe, violence and displacement, whether it's native North Americans, Pacific Islanders or Palestinians. Hence Jarius Grove's (2019) suggestion that the last few centuries might better be termed the Eurocene to highlight the destruction and disruption, and the wholescale elimination of many millions of humans particularly in the Americas, as a result of conquest. The Beothuk people of what is now called Newfoundland simply don't have a say in the future—they are already extinct.

It is also worth noting that, until recently, at least Western cultures hadn't considered the possibility of human extinction (Moynihan 2020). If there was a divine plan then humanity had little concern with such things; we were here since creation apparently and were likely to remain until end times of some sort or other, but the possibility of our elimination, whether by geological misadventure or due to human folly, simply wasn't a consideration. But following the acceptance of Darwinian notions of evolution and the widespread understanding of fossils as the remnants of once existent life forms that were no longer living, the question of the future of the species becomes unavoidable. Nuclear angst in the aftermath of Hiroshima and Nagasaki makes this question palpable; now this is revisited by discussions of climate change and the elimination of numerous species in what is increasingly understood as a current extinction crisis, now usually considered the sixth in the planet's history (Kolbert 2014).

These reassessments of humanity's place in the larger order of things raises questions of environmental insecurity at the global scale, and does so because these concerns now impact the global political and economic system. Climate justice advocates often focus on the short term distributional consequences of regional climate vulnerabilities, which in terms of security studies unavoidably raises the key political question, the matter of "whose security?" (Walker 1997). Much of the security discussion of climate is, as this book highlights, about the survival of Americans and Europeans, and in particular the relatively affluent parts of those societies whose lifestyles are obviously potentially affected directly by storms, floods, wildfires and droughts. Likewise the politics of this insecurity is tangled up in fears of government actions to deal with these hazards, in the process constraining aspects of this consumption driven lifestyle which has come to be equated with "freedom".

While this may lead to particular invocations of what exactly is in need of securing, as previous chapters have made clear, the earth system sciences have made major advances in understanding the dynamics of the earth system, and the dangers to many species in addition to humans, that are unfolding as climate change accelerates on an already radically altered earth. At the largest scale the analyses of existential risks have identified potential terminal events that endanger the future of humanity *in toto*. And this now presents the largest canvass for considering environmental insecurity, and for considering who might respond how to shape the future in less dangerous directions.

NATURAL, ANTHROPOGENIC AND FUTURE RISKS

Following in the path of earlier work on major risks to humanity (Smil 2008; Al-Rodhan 2009), Toby Ord (2020) uses a threefold categorization of the dangers: natural ones that arise from being part of a small planet; artificial ones already created by the actions of the rich and powerful among us; and possible future ones, that at least in part could be avoided by wise action and sensible policies. The natural risks have been discussed in Chapter 3; the artificial risks are part of the larger considerations of environment that now have to be integrated into discussions of security if the newly understood risks to humanity that the Anthropocene entails are to be worked into a revised agenda for international relations.

In terms of artificial risks, Ord's (2020) overview suggests three very obvious ones that we understand in at least broad outline, those of nuclear war, climate change and other forms of environmental degradation. All three of these are within the ambit of the initial concerns at the Stockholm United Nations Conference on the Human Environment (UNCHE) in 1972, and were detailed in *Our Common Future* fifteen years later. Ord emphasizes the dangers of accidental nuclear warfare and includes a listing of nuclear accidents, some of which in the context of the cold war confrontation and hair trigger alert systems could well have caused a major nuclear war between the superpowers. The subsequent historical analysis of the Cuban missile crisis of 1962 has suggested that there were serious misunderstandings on the part of the major protagonists, and failures to comprehend the actual situation on the ground (Blight and Lang 2018), either or both of which could easily have led to rapid escalation and nuclear war. It is also worth noting that a key link between these risks is the danger of a nuclear winter caused in the aftermath of multiple nuclear explosions by the cooling effect that smoke and soot would have over an extended period if that material was lofted into the stratosphere. Climate change and the biodiversity crisis likewise are now key to the global ecological crisis to which the whole discussion about environmental security is at least a putative response.

The third category of existential risks that Ord (2020) focuses on are likely future ones, caused by human activity in part. Crucially he notes that scientists have frequently been wrong about novel technologies. Practical engineers likewise. He instances the case of Wilbur Wright, who thought heavier than air flight was many decades in the future, two years before he actually proved that it could be done. Ord warns that predicting technological innovations and their dangers accurately is nigh on impossible, but something that clearly has to be attempted, even if only in rough outline, in a world being rapidly remade by the growing technosphere.

In light of subsequent events, Ord is clearly right to list pandemic dangers as a key risk that humanity faces; the COVID-19 pandemic has proven how interconnected humanity is, the importance of public health preparation and, not least, the possibilities of medical science generating vaccines relatively quickly. The history of pandemics and infectious diseases is one of a huge toll of human casualties, and one often linked to climate disruptions too (McMichael 2017). The possibilities of major disease events can't be ruled out, and the disruption of relatively wild spaces by the ever larger colonization and intrusion of agricultural populations and those hunting for food around the world heightens the dangers of zoonotic disease outbreaks. As COVID-19 has shown, once one is widespread in the world, containing it is nigh on impossible. Ebola, SARS, Zika and MERS have been contained, or turned out not to spread in pandemic fashion; the world has not been so lucky with COVID-19. Ironically the success in partly containing SARS, Ebola, MERS and Zika in the years prior to the COVID-19 may have lulled security experts into falsely believing that diseases distant from Europe and North America would stay in their regions of origin.

The possibilities of both a deadly and a highly infectious disease dramatically reducing human population has been amply illustrated by the Black Death in Europe, and the demise of Native American populations after the introduction of European diseases following the colonization of the Americas. The possibilities of a bioweapon escaping a laboratory or being used in a conflict offers one potentially deadly risk for the future (Ord 2020). The possibilities of DNA sequencing linked to the rapid spread of the technological knowledge to make use of it poses risks that are far from clear. Biological threats are many, and while there have been successes in eliminating diseases, and smallpox in particular, there is no guarantee that future biological dangers can be dealt with effectively, as the COVID-19 event makes very clear. That said, it is also the case that innovations with mRNA technologies that facilitated the rapid roll out of COVID-19 vaccines may offer promise of further health improvements, at least for those living in the wealthy parts of the world that can pay for them if they are made by private corporations.

At least as unknowable are the effects of artificial intelligence and possible threats from its getting loose, or being weaponized in as yet unknowable ways. Linked to an interconnected cyberspace where all sorts of viruses and weaponized software are already lurking, the possibilities of disaster mount. Already, directed attacks on public utilities, either as a criminal act in the case of ransomware attacks or for geopolitical leverage as in attacks to switch off electrical utilities in moments of heightened confrontation, have become relatively commonplace. The potential to link these to environmental disasters suggests compounding risks where infrastructure merges with environmental factors to increase vulnerabilities (Briggs and Matejova 2019). Environmental security is now also about preventing hostile disruptions of infrastructure, and questions about digital governance are linked here quite directly to questions of human vulnerability to "artificial" disasters.

The widespread prevalence of microplastics in both human bodies and the wider environment is but one additional worry in how the technosphere is changing the context for life, both human and other (Amarel-Zettler, Zettler and Mincer 2020). The sheer amount of artificial materials that constitute the new technosphere, and potentially compromise the operation of numerous parts of the biosphere, is worrisome to anyone thinking intelligently about the future of the planetary system (Mitchell 2015). Such formulations are now an unavoidable part of security thinking because the expanding technosphere is the context for human societies, and as such built and digital environments provide security and vulnerability.

The failure to anticipate the seriousness of the COVID-19 pandemic, and the scramble to provide basic public health measures in the face of the rapid spread of the disease, makes very clear that the state systems, surveillance systems and security planning in the contemporary world are ill equipped to deal with the kinds of threats that medical experts have been warning about for decades (Elbe 2009; Price-Smith 2009). In part this is because specialized knowledge is compartmentalized and frequently not easy to communicate in culturally appropriate ways. Likewise political authority is frequently challenged by expertise that requires acting in ways that disrupt "normal" life, and in the process challenges the prerogatives of politicians who are used to making decisions. The intense lobbying by corporate and institutional interests in the face of crises likewise shapes public agendas, and the perpetual desires to be in control have played their part in stymying innovation (Stoddard, Anderson, Capstick et al. 2021). Nowhere is this clearer than in the current climate crisis, where in so many instances existing institutional and corporate entities have responded by either denying the severity of the situation (Speth 2021) or trying to shape the response so that the consequences are born elsewhere.

CLIMATE RISKS

While these academic discussions of catastrophic and existential risks encompass the largest scale environmental insecurities that humanity as a whole faces, much of the discussion in the West in recent years has been about the financial risks that climate disruptions might entail. One key point in the climate risk discussion that has to be emphasized is that climate risk on the planetary scale doesn't fit the conventional schemes used in risk analysis. Usually these operate on the assumption that there are frequent small scale risks at one end of the scale and few high consequence ones at the other end. Insurance and other financial calculations frequently operate on such premises in calculating likelihoods and consequences. But climate risk doesn't operate this way. Climate change is a certainty, and the longer effective policies to deal with it are delayed the greater the long term disruptions will be (Mabey, Gulledge, Finel and Silverthorne 2011). This is not least because carbon dioxide is very persistent in the atmosphere, hence the urgency in curtailing its accumulation. Failure to do so will obviously threaten to disrupt economic activities, and considerable intellectual energy has gone into working out the likely economic risks of a warming world.

One of the key methodological issues in economic evaluations of risk is the use of simple calculations of risk related to future average temperature estimates and such questions as to how to add in losses from disasters, which may not follow linearly from average temperature increases (Howard and Sterner 2017). How one specifies future conditions is of course a key to estimating what disruptions might cost. And given the rapidity of technological change too, and the presumed ability of economic production systems to incorporate risk calculations and move facilities and supply sources in the face of changing circumstances, projections are fraught with assumptions. This isn't a new problem, but nonetheless estimates of climate induced costs vary widely. Projections far into the future make matters even more uncertain, but this hasn't stopped various think tanks and academic research projects trying to make forecasts!

Some of these look to total estimated costs, and others calculate things in terms of reductions to future GDP. Once one digs into this literature it is also clear that different reports highlight different aspects of the economy, and financial consultants, banks and research agencies connected to particular economic sectors look at matters through sector specific lenses. Early attempts to think through the costs of adaptations to deal with these risks likewise struggled with huge uncertainties both in terms of how to calculate risks and in terms of what would be needed to cope with them (Parry, Arnell, Berry et al. 2009). Not least, in the early years of this century, data on the costs of disasters frequently ignored small events and focused on the insurance payouts which emphasize large scale economic operations and not the frequently uninsured smallholders in rural areas. Estimates from central top down global calculations didn't necessarily mesh with local or sectoral estimates from the bottom up.

All such estimates of course have to make assumptions about how societies and investors will choose to work future potential dangers into their calculations, and as with so much of risk communication in environmental matters, the whole point is to try to make sure that such future costs are avoided by timely investments to pre-empt them. Wei and colleagues (2020) suggest that if states do follow through with their declared nationally determined contributions to the Paris Agreement, then they will have a net economic benefit. Failure to follow such "self-preservation strategies" might cost the world anywhere from 150 to 792 trillion dollars by the end of this century. A working paper from the International Monetary Fund (IMF), looking back at past fluctuations in temperature and linking them to productivity, suggests that temperature fluctuations have a pronounced effect, and that failure to abide by the Paris Agreement will over the course of this century reduce real per capita GDP worldwide by 7 percent (Kahn, Mohaddes, Ng et al. 2019).

Analysis of particular countries is likewise dependent on numerous assumptions. In one study of the United States detailed estimates of the vulnerabilities to particular climate change induced hazards, such as increasing hurricane damage, were coupled with attempts to categorize them geographically. This was an attempt to provide insights into likely risks while trying to add consistency between bottom up and top down estimation methods (Hsiang, Kopp, Jina et al. 2017). Estimates in this case of cumulative damage by mid century, which might include social conflict induced by climate disruptions, suggest that between 1 and 3 percent of GNP might be forgone due to climate disruptions. One key point in this analysis highlights the discrepancies between likely vulnerabilities. Relatively speaking the United States has a very small part of its labour force and economy directly supported by agriculture, so unlike many states in the Global South, climate disruptions are much less likely to induce direct costs than they are in countries with a large agricultural sector. The inequity of those causing climate change not feeling its most direct consequences is once again clear in such estimates.

While the detailed financial calculations continue to be made, the political attention to them has escalated. This is clear in the repeated suggestions from World Economic Forum meetings in Davos and their global risk assessments that climate is an increasingly severe risk (World Economic Forum 2020), in addition to statements from G7 and G20 meetings emphasizing the need to act. The United Nations Secretary-General (2020) in particular has made climate action a priority. In doing so the politics of this is clearly taking the risks much more seriously than many of the financial calculations suggest would be the case if purely financial matters were the criteria for judgement. After all, if a few percent reductions of GDP many years in the future are all that are in play, then the case for acting is minimal. If economic growth is a few percent per annum, then a few percent per annum cost of climate change simply means reaching a particular GDP goal a year or two later decades in the future. On the other hand, if climate change only implies a slight slowing of economic growth, then policy makers focused on GDP increase as the overarching social goal are unlikely to be concerned. As with so much of contemporary economics, the potential for dramatic geophysical disruptions, and the need to either integrate the biophysical transformations of the present into its calculations or think very differently, is manifest (Gopel 2016).

Beyond these global estimates of danger, the Paris Agreement and ever more alarming warnings on the part of scientists, researchers and policy makers in specific segments of the economy have also been evaluating both the risks to existing investments and the possibilities of practical policies to minimize exposure to both climate damage and the likely policy responses that such policies are likely to face. In the aftermath of the Paris Agreement on Climate Change, investors and central bank operatives have gradually paid increasing attention to the risks to their systems from climate disruptions (Diringer and Perciasepe 2020). Real estate in vulnerable coastal locations subject to rising sea levels and storm exposure presents problems for the insurance industry, and here novel, if dubious, forms of insurance linked securitization have emerged in the financial sector in response to growing hazards (Taylor 2020). Fire risks in California likewise have been highlighted in recent years as the risks from wildfire have escalated. Here too, because of high housing prices, many people have been forced to live in rural areas vulnerable to fires and where insurance may simply not be available, emphasizing the difficulties that climate change enhances for economically marginal citizens (Flavelle 2020).

By the beginning of 2020, climate risks and the implications for investors were clearly penetrating the corridors of high finance, and investment houses were taking note. High profile director of BlackRock Corporation, Larry Fink (2020), penned an open letter to CEOs in January 2020 warning that climate risks were setting in motion a substantial reconsideration of investment strategies and anticipating that sustainability would become a key criterion for future capital allocations. The following month the *Guardian* newspaper obtained an internal report generated by the JP Morgan financial corporation, which has invested large amounts of money in fossil fuels, suggesting that the world was on course for climate disaster and the corporation needed to address the related risks (Greenfield and Watts 2020). Simultaneously McKinsey's consulting group was thinking along similar lines (McKinsey Global Institute 2020), pondering the climate risks to many corporations which had not thought through the likely disruptions that climate change will bring (Kormann 2020).

In the last few years these formulations have begun to shape a new discourse on climate and economics that looks to the possibilities of remaking the economy after fossil fuels, one that looks to investments in green energy and innovation to deal with social and economic ills while simultaneously slowing the rate of climate change. The arguments about climate risks and their complex interconnections (Yokohata, Tanaka, Nishina et al. 2019) have permeated the World Bank, the IMF, and even the International Energy Agency (2021), which abandoned its focus on fossil fuels in at least one prominent report to suggest that an energy transition was necessary and financially feasible given the reduction in renewable energy prices and the urgency of tackling climate change. The IMF *Economic Outlook* in the Fall of 2020, which highlights risks, concludes that while the window of opportunity for transition to renewable energy and limiting global heating to less than 2 degrees Celsius is closing, it is still possible to do this globally (Barrett, Bogmans, Carton et al. 2020). This transition will have to involve carbon pricing, which is essential to shift energy systems away from carbon fuels. But they argue that with sensible policies to use revenue from carbon fees to cushion the impacts on poorer consumers and enhance transitions for displaced workers, it is possible to facilitate a structural economic transition to a post carbon future. Doing so should make avoiding the nightmare scenario of climate induced civilizational collapse possible.

WHICH RISK TO WHAT FUTURE?

While the pandemic disruptions of 2020 and 2021 partly shifted these concerns to focus on short term disruptions, the fiscal stimulus provided to many economies to tackle the economic shutdowns suggests a more active role for governments in directing economies than had been the case in previous years (Tooze 2021). Risks to the financial system drove these innovations, but raise the question as to whether other risks now might generate similar responses.

Key to this is the formulation of climate as a risk to the existing economic system, and how this thinking tries to bridge the gap between the physical science of climate and the economic calculations in global estimates of losses and economic costs, as well as think through the variable geography of risk (Hedlund, Fick, Carlsen and Benzie 2018). There are numerous epistemological incongruities between these fields, and at least part of the discussion about climate and risk is explained by the different assumptions brought to bear. Steve Keen's (2021) full scale assault on William Nordhaus's widely influential climate models suggests that their major flaw is simply that they don't consider the geophysical realities of climate change in any detail. Keen (2021) suggests that the expert elicitation used to calibrate the costs of change came mainly from economists' estimates of what has come to be known as the social cost of carbon, rather than from any attempt to engage with physical scientists' methods or data, much less serious projections of climate trajectories or tipping points (Lenton, Rockström, Gaffney et al. 2019).

In particular the assumptions that disruptions can be dealt with by ever more affluent future societies, and that major discontinuities in the climate system are not forthcoming, skew the policy making framework towards minor tinkering and pricing carbon rather than more transformative reorientation to deal with the novel geophysical context of the Anthropocene. In terms of security most of the climate models assume that relative social stability persists, in Albert's (2020) terms, continuationism, and the possibilities of major social discontinuities are not worked into the projections. Which suggests another discrepancy between economic models and physical ones which are much more concerned with discontinuities, and the difficult to predict interactions between parts of the earth system.

Where economists assume the continuity of economic growth and the potential for technological innovation, earth system scientists are concerned about destabilization of the earth system. Climate models that suggest a gradual movement of weather systems towards higher latitudes and to higher altitudes are premised on gradual change and evolutionary adaptations, not a rupture or phase shift transition in the climate system, precisely what most worries climate scientists (Asefi-Najafabady, Villegas-Ortiz and Morgan 2020). Climates are not likely to migrate smoothly, and the disruptions in the Arctic regions in particular, due to melting permafrost and sea ice, complicate matters greatly. This suggests very clearly that while in theory the warming Arctic region may increase access to petroleum and gas resources, extracting them and getting them to market will not be easy in many places. Doing so would exacerbate climate change inducing positive feedback loops that make everything more difficult, and the likelihood of collapsing societies greater.

Projections into the future and fears about imminent collapse have a long history, and the discussion of the *Limits to Growth* in the 1970s is a salutary tale about misconceptions and assumptions not meshing across disciplines (Turner 2014). Not least in the case of the *Limits to Growth* discussion is the failure of early critics to engage with the long term forecasts that were at the heart of the models, ones that suggested that the crunch decades would be in the 2020s and 2030s, not in the 1970s or 1980s (Cole, Freeman, Jahoda and Pavitt 1973). The *Limits to Growth* suggested that rising population growth and with it resource usage would encounter limits in terms of shortages of supply, and also rising levels of pollution. But the key focus was on resource shortages. The economics response is that rising resource prices will encourage innovations and hence resources never actually run out because new resources, novel technologies and processes substitute for shortages and change how economies operate prior to complete exhaustion.

But in the case of current discussions of environmental security, resources aren't the main issue; the indirect effects of elevated greenhouse gases are. This point is frequently obscured when the disruptions of climate change are folded into standard scarcity narratives, especially about water supplies as a likely cause of conflict in many places. It is noteworthy that the iconic graph of the "standard run" of the limits to growth computer model suggested that subsequent to the rapid decline of industrial production when resources shortages caused economic disruptions, pollution would fairly quickly drop too as ecological processes recycled materials (Meadows, Meadows, Randers and Behrens 1972). But at least in the case of carbon dioxide, the key substance driving climate change, this obviously is not going to be the case, and disruptions as a result of climate change are likely to be long lasting as the stability of the Holocene period, and the larger ice age dominated period of the Quaternary, is overturned by the new climate systems of a hothouse world. Nonetheless it is also worth noting that Jorgen Randers (2012), one of the original *Limits to Growth* authors, suggested forty years after the initial publication, using the updated World3 model, that despite these difficulties there was still a substantial chance that industrial humanity could survive the contemporary global crisis (Herrington 2021).

Time is a key matter in climate change, mostly because carbon dioxide is accumulating in the atmosphere much faster than either terrestrial or oceanic systems can remove it. Carbon dioxide remains in the air for centuries and as such the longer effective action in reducing emissions is delayed, the worse the consequences will be in terms of climate disruptions (Funk 2021). These are already kicking in; the policy questions are now about how quickly to act to slow the pace of climate change and attempt to reduce the impact of what is already unavoidable. Time also matters here in terms of economic forecasts, because the future doesn't send any market signals; the consequences of today's actions will show up in future economic activities, but potential hazards in decades hence are not usually integrated into purchasing or investment decisions. In former governor of both the Bank of Canada and the Bank of England Mark Carney's formulation: "Once climate change becomes a clear and present danger to financial stability it may already be too late to stabilize the atmosphere at two degrees" (cited in Gaffney, Crona, Dauriach and Galaz 2018, 3). What is uncertain is how fast policies, market forces or technological change will influence the production of greenhouse gases or further either the deforestation or the regeneration of key ecosystems. These are policy dependent up to a point, hence the importance of politics and policy actors moving to shape investment choices and regulate dangerous activities. These social tipping points (Otto, Donges, Cremades et al. 2020) are the other side of the climate change risk issue; if and how fast they will operate is key to shaping the future.

In terms of risk, the cultural framing of the climate discussion clearly plays a key role. While environmentalists are looking at the science of the earth system and the repeated warnings of the scientific community about looming hazards, thresholds and tipping points in the earth system, it seems that many business people and entrepreneurs operate in a cultural frame that often precludes taking these warnings seriously. In Jane Jacobs' (1994, 43) apt summary:

> As a generalization, people with a commercial cast of mind find it almost impossible to believe they're headed willy-nilly into irreversible environmental disaster. They can't believe there's no way out. It doesn't ring true emotionally. Instead, what does grab commercial people, emotionally as well as practically, is ingenious ways to forestall disaster.

Hence the endless search for technological innovation and assumptions that some new technical fix will emerge so that the social order that has created the climate change crisis will be the one to solve it.

COLLAPSE OR REFORM?

The overarching conclusion from such deliberations is that there is a multitude of dangers which might threaten long term human survival. The exhaustion of resources and dramatic changes in ecological circumstances raise the issue of the collapse of civilizations, a theme that is highlighted by Jared Diamond's (2005) book simply called *Collapse*. Crudely put the collapse arguments suggest that ever larger use of limited resources and ever more complexity in societies lead to eventual demise as innovations fail to engineer a way out of the social traps that limit possibilities (Tainter 1988). Attempts to perpetuate traditional ways of doing things in the face of changed circumstances may lead to disaster. In terms of security understood as the perpetuation of modern modes of fossil fueled industrial society and dealing with threats to these modes from outside, this then seems likely to be civilization's fate. Hence the rallying cry of young protesters, climate strikers, extinction rebels and others that demands a change of course before it's too late, and a refusal to accept that reform isn't possible despite the reluctance of their elders to contemplate social change and essential novel economic models.

But there is another possible trajectory, one where environmental troubles cause radical reform in how resources are used or societies organized (Holthaus 2020; Rudel 2019). In the face of accelerating climate change, species extinction, ocean acidification and all the other issues identified by contemporary ecological science, the possibilities of radical and rapid changes in policy and a reconsideration of what environmental security might mean open up as necessities, if, that is, the traps that Tainter (1988) and other scholars of collapse suggest are a looming danger can be avoided. If however these dangers exacerbate international tensions, or even as Allison (2017) has suggested, present the United States with a situation in which its elites think events are slipping out of control, could they lead to war?

It is important to note that Jared Diamond emphasizes that our current civilization has one large advantage over its predecessors: it knows what happened to previous ones. We both understand some of the causes of failure and live in a social system that innovates with technology rapidly, hence the possibilities of learning our way out of potentially deadly trajectories exist. But to tackle this requires focusing explicitly on what needs to be done to function in a dynamic world where human decisions about what to produce are a key component shaping the future of the technosphere, and with it the other key components of the earth system. Can the flexibility of the global supply chains and the sheer capabilities of science, technical innovation and social learning avoid Tainter (1988) style collapses, as Diamond suggests is possible? Or will disasters provoke defensive parochialism, as some climate politics in response to disasters suggests (Cohen 2021), and a return to a geopolitics dominated by security dilemmas and fortress politics where threats are seen as external hence obviating domestic responses (White 2014)?

Or is the complexity of the global economy reaching such a state that with so many potential choke points in the supply chains, should a number of them be disrupted simultaneously, chaos would result and the complex edifice of international trading would unravel? The situation in early 2021 when the *Ever Given* container ship ran aground in the Suez Canal, further disrupting an international shipping system that was already reeling from the pandemic, suggests the brittleness of much of the economy so heavily dependent on just in time deliveries. The priority in just in time deliveries is efficiency understood in terms of minimizing costs, and effectively having inventories on board ships rather than in warehouses. Contingency planning in terms of "just in case" preparation implies redundancy, in the sense of having supplies on hand in case of disruptions, but this increases storage costs. The logics of cost and security do not align.

But this discussion too may be misleading. While Diamond's and even more so Tainter's discussions relate to historical and archaeological cases, what is noteworthy in Diamond's account is how immensely tenacious many societies actually are in the face of profound challenges to their ecological context. Subsequent historical and archaeological research may dispute or refute their analyses, but as in the case of the persistence of the Greenland Norse in particular, the more important question in terms of security may be how, despite the odds, they survived for as long as they did, not the question of what finally caused their society to die out. As McNeill (2010) points out in his rejoinder to Diamond, the Norse settlement there survived longer than most modern settler colonies have so far done. Three centuries into that Norse history, it would have been judged to be a success for having survived that long. While in this case Diamond suggests their failure to adapt technologies and practices that allowed indigenous peoples to live in these circumstances caused their eventual demise, their tenacity in terms of the centuries long survival of an isolated society in very marginal ecological conditions may have more important lessons to teach.

McNeill's (2010) additional suggestion is a key to considering all this in terms of security. He poses the question of what survives through long periods of history. No states that existed fifteen hundred years ago are now extant. Chinese civilization stretching back nearly four millennia is more or less a continuous society, but the numerous dynastic changes, the rise to power of the communist party in the mid twentieth century being only the latest one, were frequently violent collapses out of which a novel ruling elite gained temporary control. Is it culture that should be made to survive, its future secured by political methods and the threat of violence if necessary? Once again the key question is "whose security?"

What is clear from earth systems research is that the current global economy based on the massive energy subsidy from the past in the form of fossil fuels is destabilizing many things, and the current imperial mode of life, to use Brand and Wissen's (2021) terms, of the affluent part of the world's population, based on consumption using resources from all over the world, is unsustainable. In Diamond's terms the collapse of this particular social order would seem to be essential for the long term survival of many human cultures. What then is being secured by whom and for what purpose? How might a rapid transition to a post carbon fueled global civilization be facilitated? From the perspective of many in the Global South, the collapse of the affluent fossil fueled SUV driving capitalism of the Global North would seem to be essential to slow global ecological transformation and give them a chance to thrive, a view that is anathema to traditional Northern security thinking which is premised on modernity and consumption as the key economic process that is to be sustained.

Likewise, given the scale of the global economy and the enormous speed of technological innovation in particular, it's an open question as to whether the lessons from many of these prior histories are directly applicable. The world isn't running out of fossil fuels any time soon; their abundance and the ease of access to them has generated the climate problems we face. Clearly a lack of social flexibility matters greatly in terms of adaptation, but the ability to substitute products and technologies in the present global economy is on an unprecedented scale. So too of course is the scale of ecological transformation and the abilities to use massive amounts of firepower to both fight and produce novel things. Hence the human induced existential risks are now global in scale, where prior to this they were largely a matter of geology and biology, and disease in particular in specific regions.

In current circumstances, one of an interconnected human and natural world, one that is ever more modified by engineering of both artifacts and ecologies, clearly the most important thing that needs to be secured is the ability of societies to adapt, both in terms of rapidly moving away from fossil fuels and in terms of coping with the changes that are already "baked in" to the earth system by the recent overabundant use of firepower. Securing this requires simultaneous recognition of the necessity of contextualizing the human predicament in terms of a whole earth, contextualizing firepower as the threat to security, and thinking through how to facilitate preventing conflict, or ending it where it occurs, as the precondition for long term survival. Chapter 7 addresses this contextual question; Chapter 8 the institutional one.

7. Whole earth security: an engineered world

THE ANTHROPOCENE

Human actions have already transformed the world fundamentally. This is the key point about the Anthropocene, one that needs to be clearly integrated into how environmental insecurity is now understood. In practical terms, as Chapter 6 has suggested, investment decisions in coming decades will determine how the earth system functions long into the future. Our fire age circumstances, or to use Stephen Pyne's (2021) formulation, the Pyrocene, mean that the future is being shaped by fire ecology, and the domestication of combustion, much more than celestial and orbital mechanics. The Milankovich cycles that used to determine the earth's climate have been replaced by combustion processes as the driving force shaping future climates. This is the world that colonization and firepower has wrought. It's the circumstances within which scholars and policy makers now have to rethink security and environment. How these are formulated and acted upon in coming years will shape the future of the earth system profoundly. Living in the Anthropocene means just this, and the implications for how security is rethought need to be integrated into international relations and many other disciplines.

While Lövbrand, Mobjörk and Soder (2020) have outlined the dominant geopolitical formulations that appear in the scholarly analyses of the Anthropocene, what is needed now, this chapter suggests, is another one that explicitly deals with the future and how to shape it. The rich and powerful among us are effectively designing the future world even if they don't understand that this is what they are doing. What gets made, how, with what materials, powered by what energy and where is being decided by investment decisions and government policies. This is a matter of engineering on the planetary scale, and as this chapter suggests, we now need to engage matters of environment and security in terms of an engineered world. This doesn't necessarily mean a dystopian world of ever more drastic chemical and mechanical interventions in the atmosphere, the scenarios of solar geoengineering that so concern many environmentalists; but as the largest climate forcing agent in the earth system at present, industrial actions are charting the future configuration of the earth's climate and, as such, in practice engineering the future.

The alternative socio-technical imaginary, of ecological actions involving working with ecosystems, planting, nurturing and living in flourishing habitats, of permacultures and agroecology, rather than extractivist projects to supply resources from afar to consume, is key to thinking about global environmental security once the modernist premises of endlessly manipulating an external environment are abandoned. On a smaller scale, decisions about what to plant where, reforestation, carbon sequestering farming techniques and rewilding projects shape the earth system too. Thinking about these too as forms of engineering, matters of design and the application of particular ecological techniques, is congruent with thinking in terms of reshaping the technosphere in particular and the earth system in general.

This chapter first revisits some key points about traditional environmentalism, then addresses conventional matters of geoengineering in terms of solar radiation management, before moving on to discuss passive modes of "albedo modification". Then the chapter focuses on the need to not only protect environments and hence, as traditional sustainable development thinking assumes, ensure resources for future societal needs, but also to think about dramatically enhancing the ecosystem functions of landscapes, both rural and urban. This is necessary both to attempt to reduce greenhouse gas concentrations and to buffer existing systems from the more extreme events that will result from the levels of greenhouse gases that are already in the atmosphere. These efforts are novel forms of ecological engineering, but engineering nonetheless in the sense of shaping new habitats for numerous species, not only for humans. Crucially these considerations now require a focus on China, where the scale of urbanization and industrialization shapes the planetary future and where considerations of "eco-security" are becoming part of the planning process there—one more twist in the environmental security story which concludes this chapter.

ENVIRONMENTALISM REDUX

What is needed now is to think about how to arrange legal matters in a rapidly changing world, one where given the speed and trajectory of current transformations, preserving the past as a matter of stability is not what is most important (Kareiva and Fuller 2016). Substantial rethinking, especially when it comes to matters of how geoengineering might be governed, is now essential (Reynolds 2019b). Much of the environmentalist criticism of geoengineering proposals, and fears of further attempts to manipulate nature, draws on longstanding concerns with the hubris of humanity attempting to dominate or manipulate natural phenomena that would be much better left alone (Baskin

2019). The oxymoron "wildlife management" epitomizes this fear of hubris, of attempting to manage things that are very imperfectly understood. More importantly, however, the discussion of geoengineering is understood as a dangerous distraction from undertaking the climate change mitigation actions that are urgently needed to tackle the crisis (Biermann, Oomen, Gupta et al. 2022).

But the point of the Anthropocene is that actions by the rich and powerful among humanity are already on the scale of geological forcing mechanisms. While this may be regretted, it's the context within which decisions have to be made; we live in an increasingly artificial world where the technosphere is changing key aspects of the ecosphere, and as summarized in Elizabeth Kolbert's (2021) musings on geoengineering, there are growing fears of living "under a white sky". But as yet there is nothing approaching a single coherent plan or governance structure for all this, and the key point is that the disruptions already set in motion have to be coped with in the world of non-stationarity. Experiments with rewilding, ecological regeneration and agroecology in particular will be ongoing in coming decades (Lorimer 2015). While in some cases protected areas may be a key part of these experiments, clearly they cannot be isolated or cordoned off from the rest of the ecosphere, and adaptations will have to be sensitive to large scale contexts rather than just local ecologies. Given the jurisdictional divisions of territorial space that are used in contemporary governance, this is anything but easy. The popular imagination in many Western states of environmental disruptions as something distant from their concerns, and matters for containment rather than a reduction of luxury consumption and lifestyles, is an especially difficult aspect of this politics (Gough 2017).

The term engineering also conjures up futures of geoengineering with stratospheric aerosol injections, artificially cooling the planet by fiddling with the chemical composition of the upper atmosphere. The dangers of doing so, and the potential for conflicts should some states or corporations try this unilaterally, are very considerable. The logic of traditional American national security formulations also lead inevitably in this direction, attempting to use technology to maintain some form of control over the whole planet (Surprise 2020). Cold war technostrategic discourse was all about nuclear bombs, missiles and force, a matter of firepower writ large. The subject of security was reified into arcane considerations of missiles, megatonnage and game theory, and in the process people and ecologies were occluded. But, as this book emphasizes, this mode of thinking is now precisely the problem; force, firepower and state rivalry lead to insecurity in so many ways that new modes of thought, and a focus on altogether different modes of life for the future, have to be the basis of rethinking environmental security. In McDonald's (2021) terms, the focus has to be on ecology.

It is also the case that artificially altering both urban spaces and rural landscapes to make them much less dependent on fossil fuels, or political economies of extractivism, monocultural industrial agriculture included, is a form of engineering, but engineering that takes ecology seriously, a shift from physics and force to biology and life effectively. This shift requires looking to different sources of knowledge too to inform security policies, one that also has had resistance in the American academy in particular, where physics and engineering have so long dominated the knowledge practices brought to bear in security thinking (Lahsen 2008). In contrasting old fashioned cold war vintage technological tinkering and security focused on force and firepower with the novel considerations of agricultural innovation, including ideas of regenerative farming, permacultures and agroecology, as well as carbon neutral and negative building linked to renewable energy sources, what is at stake in terms of securing futures for many societies is clarified.

The title for this chapter picks up on Daniel Deudney's formulation from a Worldwatch Institute paper written in 1983 suggesting that the planetary system itself was what needed to be secured. Peacefully that is! Worried about the spread of nuclear weapons and the focus on orbital space as a potential battle space as well as the neglect of planetary perspectives in revived cold war thinking in the 1980s, he suggested that the whole earth was what was in need of securing. The focus in earth system thinking in recent years suggests that this formulation was indeed prescient. Eight years later Jeremy Rifkin (1991) posed similar matters in terms of "Biosphere Politics", sharply contrasting traditional notions of security and containment strategies linked back as far as Halford Mackinder, with the need to reformulate security thinking in terms of the biosphere rather than traditional geopolitics. The contrast between ecopolitics and geopolitics has long been highlighted by other scholars too (see Dalby 2002), but those discussions now have to be revisited and updated in light of climate change and biodiversity loss, and discussions about their relationships to global security, and now to proposals to artificially alter the composition of the atmosphere in a deliberate attempt to "shade" the earth.

GEOENGINEERING

If the whole earth is understood in terms of the ecosphere, or as an arena for conflict arbitrated ultimately by the threat of the use of firepower, then dramatically different notions of security inform policy. Underlying these are simple but powerful matters of geopolitical assumptions. Loosely these distinctions also parallel Amory Lovins' 1970s formulations of soft paths involving renewable energy, carefully calibrated task appropriate technologies and energy efficiencies, or hard paths involving the ever larger use of nuclear and fossil fuel energies with all the geopolitical difficulties resulting from world spanning vulnerable supply chains, nuclear proliferation and climate change. More recently this contrast has been reworked in terms of the formulation of a security paradox that Jonna Nyman (2018) posed in terms of the discrepancy between energy security in terms of reliable fossil fuel supplies in the short run, and the possibilities of a sustainable climate policy for the long term future. Short term rivalries may be facilitated by firepower, but long term survival of a relatively stable climate system requires an altogether different understanding of the human context as part of an ecosphere, and as a result a drastic reduction in the use of firepower. This contrast is now sharply refracted through the discussion of geoengineering, and the definitional issues related to what it is that needs to be done by whom and how to offer security in various forms (Hamilton 2013).

Key to all this is a matter of time; slowing climate change requires rapid reductions in the use of fossil fuels (Intergovernmental Panel on Climate Change 2018), and the wholesale rethinking of agriculture and land use, as well as water systems for human use. Or, at least, it does if the long term future for a habitable planet is taken seriously as the premise for security thinking. Failure to do this may lead to political elites trying to use extraordinary measures to shape the future in ways that maintain their control, looking to technological fixes rather than social change as modes of security provision to prevent social breakdown. Top of the list seems to be ideas of solar radiation management and stratospheric aerosol injection to cool the planet by shading the surface from sunlight, a matter of "albedo modification" in technical terms preferred by the National Research Council (2015). In June 1991 Mount Pinatubo in the Philippines erupted and lofted large amounts of material and gases into the upper atmosphere, allowing for fairly detailed measurements of the global cooling effect over the following few years (McCormick, Thomason and Trepte 1995). Solar geoengineering is thus frequently understood as artificially mimicking "the Pinatubo effect". And yet once these forms of active interventions in the earth system are investigated in detail they, not surprisingly, potentially present more problems than solutions (Pierrehumbert 2019), only most obviously the fact that cooling would be uneven geographically, and key systems like the Asian monsoon might be affected in unpredictable ways. Dreaming of a designer climate, in Oomen's (2021) terms, may be easy, but the implementation would be fraught with practical and political difficulties.

The terminology used in the discussion of geoengineering is far from consistent, but a basic division between solar radiation management and carbon dioxide removal is widespread. The former involves active attempts to reduce insolation and hence cool the planet, an active mode of intervention in the immediate problems of heating. Carbon dioxide removal might be understood as a passive response, focused on removing the cause of the heating and hence dealing with the problem by removing its source. Avoiding excessive heating precludes the need for geoengineering, hence the longstanding insistence by climate activists that mitigation, as in reducing the causes of climate change in the first place, is job one. The sheer complexity of the earth system makes thinking in system terms essential for policy making related to geoengineering proposals (Chris 2016), but given the numerous uncertainties about how the climate might react to aerosol injections, thinking in those terms is no guarantee that either the physics is understood adequately or the governance mechanisms that might be invoked to cope with solar engineering could cope with the complexities (Burns and Strauss 2013). In a rapidly changing earth system, where massive use of fossil fuels is the key source of heating, and the conversion of land for agricultural purposes an important secondary source, whatever policies are adopted and production systems introduced in coming decades will have to be on a large enough scale to make a difference. But in these terms carbon dioxide removal is a form of climate change mitigation; hence some of the difficulties with the terminology in this discussion! In general terms there are many fewer objections to carbon dioxide removal than to albedo modification by adding reflective substances to the atmosphere.

Reframing this in the innocuous language of "Reflecting Sunlight", as the title of a subsequent National Academies of Science report did in 2021 (National Academies of Sciences, Engineering, and Medicine 2021), may be good public relations, but the ecological consequences are hard to predict whatever terminology is used. Unilateral research into solar geoengineering likewise generates increasing suspicion and potential political conflict too in the absence of widely agreed governance arrangements (Stephens, Kashwan, McLaren and Surprise 2021). Much initial attention was paid to the possibilities of using sulfur dioxide, which ought to be relatively easy to manufacture and, with some minor modification to existing airplanes, easy to disperse in the upper atmosphere (Keith 2013). The immediate concern with this technology is that this chemical turns into sulfuric acid in the air and would, when it eventually falls into the lower atmosphere, become acid rain. Other suggestions to use finely ground calcium carbonate, in effect limestone, should at least solve the acidification problem because this is an alkaline chemical.

While laboratory experiments can explore some of the parameters of such technologies, field testing would seem to be essential to get a clear sense of what might be possible if stratospheric injections are tried in future. Preliminary efforts to calibrate monitoring equipment needed to run field experiments of this technology have run afoul of indigenous peoples' objections to these activities being carried out on their territories without their consent. In Arizona and subsequently in Sweden, failure on the part of would be experimenters to gain local consent for their tests using high altitude balloon based measurements stymied their efforts (Greenfield 2021a). But there is a long history of such objections to geoengineering experiments, a matter aggravated by the absence of any clear governance mechanisms that might oversee experiments, never mind the actual implementation of some of these proposed techniques with their plethora of ethical, political and governance issues (Preston 2016; Talberg, Christoff, Thomas and Karoly 2018; Blackstock and Low 2019).

Stratospheric injections of suitable chemicals to shade the earth could be started on a small scale with a small fleet of aircraft operating in the stratosphere. An alternative might be to use tethered balloons with chemicals pumped up to them for release in various parts of the atmosphere. In the stratosphere the rate of exchange of air masses with the lower level troposphere is relatively slow, allowing chemicals a long residence time in the upper reaches of the atmosphere. Eventually chemicals will fall out of the stratosphere and this requires repeatedly "injecting" substances into the stratosphere as long as such geoengineering programs are carried out. But assuming that preliminary demonstrations prove their efficacy, for the use of these technologies on the large scale to be effective, at least in theory, once it was started it would have to be continued for as long as shading was considered necessary. If carbon dioxide levels in the atmosphere continue to increase then to maintain an even average temperature would require increased stratospheric injections in lockstep with the accumulation of carbon dioxide. The planes would effectively have to keep flying, or if balloons were used, assuming it were possible to continuously pump chemicals up many kilometres, the pumps would have to keep pumping effectively in perpetuity.

If for whatever reason these "injections" were to stop, than very rapid heating would result. This so called termination shock, where heating would rapidly accelerate once "injection" ceased, would induce potentially catastrophic weather disruptions. Hence, once started, so the argument goes, this will have to be continued until such time as carbon dioxide levels are low enough for it to be safely discontinued. As this is a matter for many decades or centuries into the future, while this isn't a huge investment relatively speaking to other human industrial activities, the necessity to keep it going regardless of political, economic or budgetary conditions for the operating states or corporations make it a dangerous gamble. Apart from this very obvious concern with a termination problem, the more immediate security dimensions of this problem could emerge if one state starts to use geoengineering technologies unilaterally regardless of international opinion or a collective effort to regulate the process. In this case it is plausible that a weather disaster in one state could be blamed on the geoengineering activities by another. Gwynne Dyer posed these questions in terms of possible confrontations between India and Pakistan over disputed geoengineering efforts in his 2008 book *Climate Wars* (Dyer 2008). Demands for compensation, or demands that the program be halted, might easily lead to conflict should the state doing the geoengineering reject the imputation of causation, or even if that is accepted, refuse to supply the remedy.

The arguments don't stop there, however, because even if one state's leaders don't take military action in the face of what is judged to be a hostile act by another state, countermeasures might be taken instead. The possibilities of counter-geoengineering, where one state, unhappy with another's geoengineering efforts, takes countermeasures, perhaps even ramping up the use of fossil fuels, adds further potential security dimensions to this discussion (Parker, Horton and Keith 2018). Most obviously where states disagree as to how much cooling or how much heating is optimal, conflict is possible. Scenarios where military action is taken against the infrastructure used in climate engineering projects are not far-fetched; the sabotage of Iranian nuclear efforts by the use of the Stuxnet virus to wreck engineering control mechanisms, and numerous other episodes of bad or explicitly aggressive behaviour in cyberspace causing disasters of various kinds (Briggs and Matejova 2019), make this kind of conflict possible even without direct "kinetic" interventions.

All of which suggests clearly that climate engineering proposals need to be carefully considered by the international community, and unilateral geoengineering rendered anathema prior to any state trying to do it in coming decades. Similar reasoning applies to any proposals to use space based mirrors to reflect some solar radiation and hence cool the earth. Given how much material would have to be put into space, and perhaps transported to the appropriate solar LaGrange points distant from the earth, it seems unlikely that such engineering options will be seriously considered in coming decades. The environmental disruptions involved in making and launching the necessary rockets to lift mirrors into space might well be more severe than the putative benefits of such sun dimming efforts.

Regional efforts, among other things to refreeze the Arctic Ocean and in the process reflect more sunlight from the planet, a procedure that involves chemical injections of substances to whiten Arctic waters and enhance freezing, offer other possibilities which, given the interconnected nature of the planetary hydrosphere, might present numerous other potential hazards. Might it be possible to use mega-engineering projects to slow or halt the movement of major glaciers in Greenland or Antarctica towards the sea, hence protecting coastal cities from the most rapid sea level rises? More innocuous efforts, such as making ship wakes whiter, or injecting seawater into low lying clouds to enhance their scale, might provide some shading or enhanced reflectivity of the atmosphere and hence cooling of the surface too.

Simply painting buildings, roads and other infrastructure would likewise marginally change the planet's albedo. White buildings both reflect more sunlight and, in winter, emit less waste heat, so these on a small scale help too. In the process they would also reduce the energy needed to cool them in summer and heat them in winter, so too slightly assisting with both local climate extremes, energy costs and conservation. These innovations are in that sense forms of geoengineering too, ones that are mostly innocuous in ecological terms. All of which emphasizes the point that decisions made about how to shape the technosphere matter, but distinguishing all these from deliberate artificial attempts to manipulate the earth's temperature by using stratospheric injection in terms of their overall impact is a matter of degrees.

The prehistory of geoengineering, as it were, is the earlier discussion in the cold war of weather modification as a potential weapon of war. Cloud seeding techniques, where silver iodide or similar chemicals are used to "seed" clouds to provide condensation nuclei and hence form rain droplets, were tried in the United States. Then these ideas were weaponized in South East Asia with efforts to make it rain on the Ho Chi Minh trail that North Vietnamese forces were using to send supplies to the war in the South. Combined with the widespread use of aerial spraying of pesticides, and the notorious Agent Orange in particular, these initiatives led to international efforts to curtail the use of environmental modification techniques in warfare and the Convention on the Prohibition of Military or Any Other Hostile Use of Environmental Modification Techniques ("ENMOD" Treaty) resulted (Juda 1978). The peacetime use of cloud seeding is still widely used in China in attempts to make it rain in agricultural areas and, famously, not rain on the Beijing Olympic Games in 2008. Repeated efforts to modify rainfall patterns in China persist, and in late 2020 an announcement of expanded efforts suggests that this will be continued (State Council of the People's Republic of China 2020). But given that this is specifically aimed at rainfall patterns, once again the question of whether this qualifies as geoengineering raises its head.

The difference between solar radiation management proposals and many more conventional conservation projects, and why so many doubts about geoengineering the planet keep appearing, is in part about the active nature of stratospheric injection, and the necessity of keeping the systems running once they have been started. More passive measures, such as painting buildings white, planting more trees in urban areas and certifying forestry plantations as carbon sinks, in complicated arrangements to monetize "ecosystem services", generate less open opposition, even if their ecological impacts may be dubious beyond temporarily sequestering carbon dioxide.

The point seems to be that deliberate engineering for climate control is just one step too far for most activists and many scientists as well as security thinkers. The largely unknowable global consequences are especially worrisome, and the danger of excessive cooling or unanticipated effects in particular regions suggests large scale strategic uncertainty (Abatayo, Bosetti, Casari et al. 2020). The counter argument that present trajectories are heading for a world of precisely these kind of dangers is of course precisely the longstanding case for doing albedo modification experiments (Keith 2013). If all else fails in terms of preventing climate change, then precisely these technologies may be needed as a last resort to buy time while methods of removing carbon dioxide in particular from the atmosphere are worked out and implemented.

The suggestion that solar radiation management is doing the marginalized peoples of the Global South a favour (Keith 2021), because they are likely to suffer worst from climate change, is easily countered by the ethical argument that they are not being consulted, and full consultation and informed consent principles are not applicable. This perpetuates colonial power relations, with rich Northern engineers once again deciding what is good for people in the Global South or, in the case of the Stratospheric Controlled Perturbation Experiment (SCoPEx) programs in Arizona or Sweden, the indigenous peoples of those regions. Very little of the discussion so far on climate engineering has involved active participation by researchers from the Global South (Biermann and Moller 2019), and the implications are that once again those in the North will make consequential decisions without the input of those most obviously in harm's way. Many of those people are obviously in the Global South, where climate model projections are suggesting they may be living in places where it will soon become impossible to live without extensive air conditioning technologies (Xu, Kohler, Lenton et al. 2020; Horton, de Sherbinin, Wrathall and Oppenheimer 2021).

More importantly this discussion focuses on how the issue of crisis is framed, and what options are thus considered appropriate policy "solutions" (Peoples 2021). It is worth remembering that the construction of a climate crisis as an epistemological project in the first place is to a substantial extent a matter of states focusing on the geophysics of climate, and carbon as a key entity in this, rather than on the larger political economy of environmental transformation (Allan 2017). These limitations in problem definition are now at the heart of the political discussion of climate change and efforts to limit it to technical matters beyond politics, a matter of post politics (Swyngedouw 2013) wherein the continued technological expansion of economic growth is taken as a given and only technical details are up for discussion.

As Jasanoff (2021) puts it, there is an absence of humility in the Anthropocene, where less physical engineering and more engagement with politics and ethics are sorely needed to chart the future. But in the present geopolitical circumstances of inter-state rivalry and the unquestioned centrality of economic growth as a necessity, such humility is in short supply among political elites, even if such considerations are actively being engaged by civil society, in particular by a youthful generation in Western states worried about what current trajectories may mean for their future later this century.

ECOSYSTEM ENGINEERING

Many of the major rivers on earth have been dammed. Highways and cities cover an increasingly large portion of the terrestrial surface. Agriculture has transformed much of the fertile landscape of the planet into monocultures; the Aral Sea has been reduced to the status of a small lake. All of which suggests that the scale of human activities is already a matter of mega-engineering in some senses; numerous individual large scale projects are shaping the earth profoundly (Brunn 2011). So, in this context, what is geoengineering and what isn't, and how might this discussion be suitably contextualized? Is deliberately introducing relatively small amounts of calcium carbonate into the upper atmosphere really qualitatively different?

Major tree planting initiatives to reduce carbon dioxide, or industrial scale efforts at carbon capture through "enhanced weathering" or other techniques, are considered in terms of geoengineering too (Herzog 2018). But such carbon dioxide reduction techniques are much less obviously direct interventions into the atmosphere, and as such, while they are more difficult and perhaps expensive than stratospheric injection, are less likely to raise environmental alarm. Not least this is so because they tackle the key issue of carbon dioxide levels in the atmosphere, rather than trying to mask its effects. Tree planting and ecosystem regeneration efforts are also feasible at the local level, a matter of enhancing existing efforts at resource management and conservation, and as such familiar practices with, in at least some cases, tangible local benefits likely to garner political support.

As more extreme weather and less predictable rain patterns stress traditional agricultural systems as well as the commercial arrangements of industrial farming, the urgency of doing practical environmental management in particular places has revived longstanding environmental concerns with food supplies and the dangers of famine. The 2021 famine in Madagascar, as is so frequently the case, may only be partly a consequence of climate change driven rainfall reductions, but it emphasizes the point. Failures of governance are also part of the long story of famine, where ironically it is food producers who are usually the first to die when crops fail and governments fail to provide sustenance (Watts 2013).

Given that much of humanity in the Global South depends on small scale production systems, there are widespread fears that food security will be increasingly compromised. Simultaneously the appropriation of traditional lands for commercial megafarms, many of which supply global markets rather than local ones, suggest increasingly dangerous trajectories both for food supplies and local ecologies and water supplies (Clapp 2020). The attempts to "modernize" agriculture and commercialize and regulate it have generated protest throughout history, only perhaps most obviously in the 2021 high profile protests in India, where smallholder and traditional farming practices are once again under legal assault from Delhi, in processes designed to modernize agriculture. Struggles elsewhere over access to land and subsistence, in particular the Brazilian Landless Workers Movement appropriating land for food production, reprise long histories of peasant struggles and resistance to enclosures and commercialization of land. Given the rising impacts of a disrupted climate, these are once again a key issue in governance; land reforms and rural economy are intertwined with notions of sustainability, and challenged by "land grabbing" for industrial monoculture cultivations to feed global markets (Sassen 2013), or for that matter to supply greenhouse gas emission offsets.

This is about much more than tree plantations, which while they may work in the short term to capture carbon, operate as offsets for metropolitan fossil fuel consumers (McCall 2016). These practices, which are in some ways a reinvention of plantation agricultural systems, have been popular as a mode of supposedly "sinking" carbon dioxide emissions and hence making consumption carbon neutral (Dehm 2021). They have also generated novel modes of mapping and certifying the ecological services provided by these territories (Lansing 2010). But if they are to work they require long term property and payment arrangements, as well as growing conditions into the future that ensure the trees continue to absorb carbon dioxide. Neither of these conditions is a certainty in the face of climate disruptions to both economic and ecological conditions. If they are to fulfil the related matter of protecting biodiversity by providing habitat for numerous species, then monocultural plantations are not suitable, especially if they are such things as eucalyptus plantations, with their voracious appetite for water which deprives other parts of ecosystems of hydrological resources.

How agriculture might be reformed and rethought so that the unsustainable monocultural practices of large scale fossil fuel driven farming are replaced by ones that simultaneously produce nutritious food while conserving water, sequestering carbon, protecting species diversity and buffering ecosystems from extreme weather is now a key question under the rubric of environmental security. Numerous ideas about regenerative practices have emerged in recent years to go beyond conserving traditional resources and think about how to make ecologically flourishing systems that also provide livelihoods for local people (Rhodes 2017). This focus on producing fecund landscapes goes beyond renewable resource supplies. Now ecosystem services need to be added both to suck up carbon and to regenerate ecologies so they can buffer humans from climate impacts, provide flood mitigation and enhance soil fertility all simultaneously. More than sustainable development, this is literally developing sustainability where modernity has undercut traditional modes of ecology, but now adding ecological benefits too.

Permaculture experiments provide one key to how to remake rural landscapes (Krebs and Bach 2018). The monocultures of crop farming, where planting and harvesting are an annual event and the soil is ploughed and treated with pesticides and fertilizers annually, have become the taken for granted mode of crop production, one which is hugely ecologically disruptive, and involves the massive use of fossil fuels both directly in farm operations and indirectly in terms of fertilizers and the global transportation system used in industrial food processing systems. Initial land clearing is a major ecological disruption because of habitat destruction and hence the loss of species from those areas. It also leaves the land open to soil erosion, and downstream areas vulnerable to flooding due to the lack of "sponge" functions soaking up rainfall and releasing it slowly. The use of fossil fuels to both run the machinery and produce vast amounts of fertilizer contribute to climate change, as do the nitrous oxides that fertilizers emit from fields. When crops are used to feed cattle in feedlots in particular, there too methane and carbon dioxide is generated on a large scale.

All these aspects of industrial agriculture are extractivist processes that simultaneously reduce ecological functions of their landscapes while generating greenhouse gases. While eating crops directly might be understood to be beneficial by vegans, the larger ecological disruptions of monoculture industrial agriculture has to be tackled both to reduce greenhouse gas emissions directly and to reconstruct rural landscapes to provide multiple ecological benefits. Hence the increasing interest in regenerative agriculture and the possibilities of permacultures where food is produced without the need to strip the land each harvest season and start over, and its adoption by some marginalized peoples struggling with food security too (Hernandez 2020). The question all this raises is how to rebuild ecologies using traditional knowledge of ecosystems in many places as well as innovations with crop mixes and innovations with plant and animal combinations.

With these considerations go obvious matters of jurisdiction over land and water, and the key question of how to move away from fortress conservation thinking towards regimes that facilitate fecundity while being both socially and ecologically adaptable too. As earlier chapters have emphasized, questions of resource shortages and rural environmental "security" are tied into matters of property and access to land and water as well as the fuel, fertilizer and other inputs to agriculture. Ecological systems are only rarely coextensive with jurisdictional systems of state and property boundaries, leading to complicated arrangements and overlapping jurisdictions where water management and allocations in particular are concerned. Numerous conservation areas, ecological preservation reserves and wildlife management schemes crisscross property and state boundaries, and as such provide complex legal arrangements for thinking about the ecological innovations that are needed for both biodiversity protection and climate change policies.

As though this wasn't complicated enough, climate change in particular is now upsetting the relatively stable ecological circumstances of the Holocene period, and setting species in motion towards more conducive locations. Ecological thinking now has to incorporate these larger transformations; protection of particular places and climate refugia in particular matters greatly, but facilitating migration now also has to be part of the policy picture (Kareiva and Fuller 2016). This upsets the implicitly stable cartographic arrangements of traditional jurisdictions and as such adds an additional complexity to planning. All of which suggests to John Head (2019) that novel notions of "ecostates" designed to accommodate these changes are necessary to provide legal and administrative arrangements appropriate for our new circumstances. The stationarity assumption, where past meteorological patterns are used to predict the range of future conditions, is no longer adequate for planning; neither are the fixed boundaries of traditional conservation practices.

While sophisticated monitoring devices and artificial intelligence offer the prospects of much more comprehensive ecological monitoring than has been possible in the past, the question of whose interests are being served by these innovations is unavoidable (Bakker and Ritts 2018). Peter Dauvergne (2021) warns about the potential of technocratic environmentalism, allowing monitoring of ecological matters but also of environmental activists campaigning against the further extension of extractivist projects. If artificial intelligence simply extends the control of extractivist corporations and state projects then, for all its scientific sophistication, it may further undercut ecological sustainability in favour of sustaining corporate power. In short, who decides what data is needed and who controls the data that is produced matters in terms of how the ecosphere is shaped in coming decades.

While renewable energy is key to futures that deal with climate change, these technologies too involve complex rural ecological systems. Dams which are used to generate electricity have long been touted as renewable energy sources, but the disruptions to human communities "in the way" of the flooding of valleys (Baviscar 2005), as well as the ecological problems of rotting vegetation, the release of mercury and other substances from the flooded landscape, and fish migration disruptions, are very considerable.

Likewise with large scale windfarms, especially when they are imposed on rural communities without their input or a share in the revenue streams. In these circumstances rural resistance to what are seen as further colonial intrusions on traditional communities and their landscapes aggravate the politics of sustainability (Dunlap 2017). Where local societies and their complex property arrangements are taken into consideration, siting and traditional land use arrangements respected, and revenue from windmills fed back to local communities, the possibilities for rural regeneration and linking high technology with community economic initiatives open up. Doing this requires a reimagining of what rural, or more particularly "wild", spaces involve; there is a complex cultural politics to this which is a key part of thinking about sustainability as much more than a matter of technical fixes (Mackenzie 2013). That politics will have to be part and parcel of any serious attempt to generate new administrative arrangements on the lines that Head (2019) suggests are necessary for future ecostates.

ECOLOGICAL SECURITY

Rethinking what "wild" spaces entail has also led to experiments with "rewilding" ecosystems in attempts to allow nature to regenerate in ways that might not be obvious if deliberate efforts are made to rebuild spaces that have been drastically altered by modern land clearance and resource extraction. In some ways this is the reverse of fortress conservation, where instead of trying to maintain an ecosystem and its animal inhabitants by eliminating poaching and human intrusions while managing "wildlife", rewilding excludes humans altogether and allows "nature" to take its course (Lorimer 2015). Given the limited ecological range for animals in what is effectively a large enclosure, it isn't surprising if there are population surges and then crashes, a matter that generates political pressures to intervene to keep animals alive when they are in danger of starvation. The crucial point here is that animals need to move as environmental conditions fluctuate and small scale fenced arrangements preclude this. Once again the geography matters, and ecological connections over long distances have to be a key consideration in how "wilding" is practiced, a matter clearly understood in proposals that half of the earth be given over to wild processes from which humans are excluded (Wilson 2016).

If such efforts are to be attempted, a form of ecological geoengineering on the large scale, then thinking about them in planetary terms is essential. This is exactly what the United Nations Decade of Ecosystem Restoration, launched in 2021, is attempting to do with numerous efforts around the world to restore degraded ecosystems (Greenfield 2021b). While this isn't what is normally understood as a matter of geoengineering, nonetheless replanting forests, cleaning up waterways to allow for fish populations to recover, slowing the profligate spread of plastic waste and numerous efforts to reestablish animals in their previous habitats add up to deliberate efforts to shape the ecosphere at a global level. Clearly they fall into the category of carbon dioxide removal, the second major categorization conventionally used in discussing geoengineering, but they encompass more than this too. As such this is a very different mode of earth system modification, but one that clearly recognizes that a biodiverse flourishing ecosphere is what is needed to prevent the worst existential threats to the future of humanity (Mitchell 2016). None of this is likely to work without a rapid reduction in the use of fossil fuels and preventing the destruction of remaining relatively intact "natural" ecosystems to slow the extinction of numerous species.

Crucial to this at the planetary scale is the recognition that the Stockholm Environment Institute's planetary boundaries have to be respected for a sustainable future (Steffen, Richardson, Rockström et al. 2015). Numerous calculations suggest that humanity either has already transcended some of these boundaries or is in danger of transcending them soon. Key to thinking about them effectively is recognizing that the initial specification of the boundaries disaggregated them for analytical simplicity, but that the urgency of acting to prevent their transcendence is emphasized when their dynamic interactions are taken into account (Lade, Steffen, de Vries et al. 2020). Simultaneously the political considerations of all this suggest that sustainability thinking needs to work in the provision of the basic necessity for life for all humans as a lower limit too; hence Kate Raworth's (2017) reformulation of the iconic planetary boundaries diagram as a doughnut, where the outside represents the planetary boundaries and the innermost part of the ring the social safety net that humanity requires. Technocratic efforts that fail to grapple with the practical lives of the poor are always in danger of undercutting their political legitimacy, hence the importance of linking ecological sustainability to the provision of life's necessities for all.

Such considerations require refocusing on the subject of security and, in Matt McDonald's (2021) terms, focusing specifically on ecological security, and hence on ecology, and in particular the resilience of ecosystems, as that which is in need of securing. While at first blush this is very similar to classic discussions of *Our Common Future*, and its notions of sustainable development premised on appropriate long term resource management, this focus shifts from environment as a source of materials and sustenance to ecological resilience as the crucial factor. The shift away from how to perpetuate resource supplies to one that focuses on keeping ecologies intact may in some cases be subtle, but the focus on ecology rather than environment is key to rethinking security once the larger natural context is focused on explicitly.

Drawing on ethical thinking, McDonald points to the importance of what it is that is deemed necessary to secure in political practices, but also highlights responsibilities to vulnerable and marginal people and species. Here the key point is that ecological resilience as a necessary condition for human life comes to the fore, but raises the question of whose human life is being secured, and simultaneously poses the matter of whether ecological systems should be secured because they have intrinsic value, regardless of their utility for humans. If security is about survival, then what is deemed worthy of being made to survive is an unavoidable one, made complicated by humans' embeddedness in multiple ecological systems.

But ecological systems adapt to changes all the time, and this needs to be worked into thinking about security in ecological terms. In focusing on ecological systems and their resilience McDonald (2021, 118) notes a contrast here with earlier formulations from Dennis Pirages (2005) where the emphasis was on balance and equilibrium. One of the key themes of the Anthropocene and the focus on resilience is the importance of understanding ecological change as key rather than operating on the assumption that security is in some sense stasis. "Ecological security can be defined as a concern with the resilience of ecosystems. Viewed through this lens, climate change constitutes a direct security threat through undermining this resilience and functionality, in turn creating harms for a multitude of living beings" (McDonald 2021, 121).

Facing this situation in current circumstances then raises the issues of accountability and the responsibility to act. Clearly here too those with the greatest capabilities to act have considerable responsibilities, even if they have not been historically responsible for making the dangerous circumstances that call for climate security policies.

> A national security discourse remains dominant, a product (at least significantly) of the nation state constituting our default answer to the question of whose security matters in global politics. But, clearly, protecting or insulating powerful institutions from manifestations of climate change, while accepting the exposure of the most vulnerable to these same effects, is ethically indefensible by almost any standard. (McDonald 2021, 191)

Those with the historic record of changing the climate clearly have the most obvious ethical obligations even if the political leaders of the United States, Australia and Canada have been especially tardy in living up to these responsibilities. But given the scale of current fossil fuel use, these historical producers of carbon dioxide alone cannot solve the problem. Thinking in terms of ecological security, and the global connections that are so frequently elided by the political geography of separate territorial states, requires efforts in numerous places, and conceptual frameworks that work with humanity enmeshed in ecological processes, not the traditional modern ones premised on a disconnection between humans and the larger ecosphere.

ECO-SECURITY WITH CHINESE CHARACTERISTICS

Of particular interest here is that in China notions of eco-security have been invoked in thinking about regional ecological matters, and whether particular regions and cities are operating in a way that is sustainable, at least in terms of local water, pollution and landscape ecological functions. This is now being extended into a larger consideration of how to facilitate the production of an ecological civilization which requires a more comprehensive environmental management system (Zhang and Shao 2019). This eco-security framework borrows its definition from *Our Common Future*, albeit sometimes without attribution: "ecologically sustainable development that meets the environmental and ecological needs of the present generation without compromising the ability of future generations to meet their own environmental and ecological needs" (Lai and Xiao 2020, 24915). While the attempts to quantify the ecosystem connections with urban spaces and link these to the regional scale are beyond the scope of the discussion here, the point that is significant is their attempt to think through the practical implications of this thinking for how cities and regions can be planned to fit the sustainability criteria.

The key question is whether these Chinese ideas about eco-security, mostly focused on the footprints of cities and ecological capabilities of particular regions, can be scaled up to consider eco-security at the planetary scale (Zhao, Zou, Cheng et al. 2006). Much of this literature focuses on the urban and regional indicators of the ecological impacts of urban and industrial activities, and attempts assessments of whether these exceed the carrying capacities of the relevant ecosystems. Lai and Xiao's (2020) analysis warns of the brittleness of the ecological underpinnings for the urban system and suggests that the speed with which the COVID-19 virus spread emphasizes the importance of focusing on this vulnerability. Scaling this framework up to think in terms of an ecological civilization is far from easy, but clearly drawing on ecological literature in various genres is now part of the discussion. In some formulations ecological is interpreted as a condition where an ecosystem maintains its integrity under external stress. Using this definition one attempt to think about ecological security at the global scale comes to the alarming conclusion that 57 percent of the global land surface will be insecure by the end of the century (Huang, Yu, Han et al. 2020).

To put this in the context of earlier points made in this book, if one takes the nuclear realist position seriously (van Munster and Sylvest 2014, 2021) and recognizes that security in the form of nuclear weapons is potentially self-destructive, and then extends it into considerations of the other form of firepower, in terms of the control and use of combustion to shape economies and ecologies, then the corollary needs to be considered in terms of global security. Constraining firepower, in both its forms, rather than worrying about scarcities causing conflict, is key to making a sustainable ecosphere at the planetary scale. This is the challenge involved in rethinking environmental security, and developments in Chinese thinking, where the Mao era war with nature thinking has long since been transcended by Xi thinking in terms of harmony with nature, is a substantial step in the right direction.

The initial Chinese interventions at the United Nations Security Council debates about climate security in 2007 were not supportive of this framing of climate issues (Ku 2018). But much more favourable recent interpretations suggest that climate security ideas may now effectively engage with the eco-security discussion at smaller scales in China (Vuori forthcoming). How this connects to larger matters of both economic policy in China and the larger conceptualizations of ecological civilization matters greatly now on the global stage given the massive industrial infrastructure that has been built there in the last few decades. A rising China is clearly one that plays a key role in the future configuration of the ecosphere.

The frequent insistence that China's rise is a peaceful one, if taken seriously, connects to the larger issues of international security, and how the future is shaped by technological innovation and energy policy. But likewise the realist concerns with rivalry and potential conflict keep intruding on the agenda, as confrontations in the South China Sea and over other off shore territorial claims suggest. Likewise concerns about trade rules, currency exchange rates, capital movements, 5G networks, espionage, human rights in China, the development strategies in Western China and the Uighur people in particular suggest a troublesome relationship between the two superpowers, one that has the potential to undermine climate initiatives, especially if China fears international energy blockades and sanctions from the United States (Boyd 2021). Cooperating on climate while ignoring these other issues is a fraught matter, but one that is key to peaceful and sustainable futures.

As this book has made clear repeatedly so far, humans now live in a system that the rich and powerful have been changing dramatically for a long time. There is no longer a stable given context to be protected, albeit key species and ecosystems need to be maintained, as the sheer scale of human activity is now shaping the future. Hence the importance of who gets to decide what gets made and which landscapes are used for what purposes. Carbon dioxide removal by regenerating landscapes and integrating agriculture with the construction of biodiverse landscapes has very considerable promise. But if this is to be the future of the ecosphere, then rapid policy and financial innovation is essential: "To put it baldly: in the face of what is to come, we cannot continue to believe in the old future if we want to have a future at all" (Latour 2017, 245).

This suggests the necessity to rethink many things, to come to terms with the great reckoning with world security in Booth's (2007) terms. All this amounts to making ecological matters a macro-securitization issue, to borrow Buzan and Wæver's (2009) formulation, which need to be dealt with by mobilizing multiple states for a common cause. Returning to Hedley Bull's (1977) criticism of Richard Falk (1971), discussed in Chapter 2, dealing with the urgency of climate change requires working with whatever institutions are available (Harris 2021), however inadequate they may be. Given the explicit invocation of states as the key actors in the Paris Agreement, is a realist world of states the only option in terms of governing climate (Lieven 2020), even if this actually requires abandoning the core understanding of realism as undergirded by modern industrial states relying on firepower? If so, then what role might international peacemaking and diplomacy play in constraining firepower if climate change and biodiversity protection become the overarching macro-securitization framework? These are the themes for Chapter 8 with its focus on peace and peacemaking.

8. Environmental peacebuilding

ENVIRONMENTAL PEACE?

The logic of sustainable development requiring environmental security, and sustainable development as a strategy to provide environmental security, sketched out in *Our Common Future* remains a key to the discussions of global governance thirty years later. The discussion about climate change and potential conflict repeatedly reiterates these themes (Bretthauer 2017; Rothe 2016). Focused more explicitly on peacemaking and peacebuilding, the logic is the same: warfare is antithetical to sustainable development (Busby 2018; Ide 2018; Ide and Detges 2018). The additional question is how peacemaking and peacebuilding might facilitate sustainable futures (Krampe 2017), because there is no guarantee that once peace allows economic activity to happen it will do so in sustainable ways or that development might not reignite prior conflict dynamics. Thinking through how to work on peacemaking and sustainability simultaneously is an emerging policy and academic discussion (Swain and Öjendal 2018), part of the larger scholarly discussions about how to implement the United Nations Sustainable Development Goals (SDGs; Dalby, Horton, Mahon and Thomaz 2019).

Much of the environmental security discussion in the 1980s and 1990s focused on fears of environmental scarcities causing conflict, and the detailed empirical research on this concluded that while environmental difficulties were in some cases related to conflict, matters of institutions, governance and prior conflicts were key to understanding the dynamics around resources. Where much of the early work on environmental security focused on the dangers of change, possible conflicts over resource scarcity and, later on, the possible role of climate change as a threat multiplier or catalyst for conflict, another parallel set of arguments reversed the alarmist fears of conflict and suggested that environmental change offered the prospects of promoting peace (Conca and Dabelko 2002). Peace parks and demilitarized borders, in addition to resource management cooperation across borders, offer possibilities for building peace and removing border irritants that might escalate to conflict. At least they could do if the worst excesses of militarized conservation (Duffy 2014, 2016) and tourist exploitation are avoided (Buscher 2013; Dunlap and Fairhead 2014). More recently the converse has become a focus for policy and research, suggesting that dealing with environmental matters may be a useful way of resolving conflict.

In all this discussion it is helpful to note that the rising concerns are now more about the conditions of life than matters of, in the social science jargon, biopolitics, life itself (Dalby 2013a). Geopower in terms of the conditions of life is key to the Anthropocene discussion, and the governmental strategies invoked in campaigns to constrain climate change focus there rather than only on traditional issues of politics focused on populations and their conduct (Beuret 2021). But these considerations of geopower remain constrained by the division of the world into territorial states, and hence the governmental pathologies that come from competition and blame games, assigning responsibilities and invoking threats as beyond "our borders, over there" (Harris 2021). The legacy of colonization and the enclosure, privatization and designation of exclusive sovereignty at various scales stymies efforts to think about the earth as a single place (Deudney 2018), an entity that has to be secured as such in terms of planetary boundaries rather than a hodgepodge of fiefdoms with conflicting priorities (Dalby 2021).

This chapter turns first to the matters of territorial security and potential water wars, and then to the matter of peacebuilding, much of which is related to smaller scale rural disruptions and insurgencies and how these might be resolved. Climate change has added an important dimension to this work, and one of the key issues in this is the potential for climate adaptation measures to backfire, mostly due to a failure to consider local conditions and apply appropriate policies to specific places. But now, as climate change accelerates, another parallel twist to this discussion has emerged focusing on the question as to whether policies to deal with climate change, and especially those aimed at dramatically reducing the use of fossil fuels, will generate conflict.

TERRITORIES, BORDERS, SECURITIES

In the case of putative water wars the historical research has suggested that they simply didn't happen; water simply wasn't a *casus belli*. Much of the historical research also suggested that in times of water stress, cooperation was more likely than conflict (Wolf 1999). This is especially so where shared waterways, dams, canals and other infrastructure need cooperation to be used effectively. Even in situations of conflict both parties have a shared interest in not destroying infrastructure that they both need; water treaties have tended to be robust even in difficult political times (Dinar and Dinar 2017). The converse may yet turn out to be the case, where upstream riparians use water as they please and weaker downstream states are powerless to do much about the disruptions to their historical sources. But at least so far fears of international conflict over water are not borne out by the historical record. Making sure that remains the case is a key matter for climate change diplomacy and ensuring that peace reigns even when climate disruptions become severe.

This is not to say that water infrastructure isn't a target in some conflicts; English writers of Second World War histories frequently extoll the engineering virtuosity of the Royal Air Force "dam buster" bombing operations which destroyed a number of German dams in 1943 with considerable loss of life downstream in the valleys of the Ruhr region. These were targeted as a method of indirectly disrupting industrial production by removing hydropower supplies and flooding downstream areas. In the history of warfare such things are relatively isolated, even if in recent years there have been threats by Egypt to destroy the Ethiopian Grand Renaissance Dam, and insistence that negotiations should determine the water management regime of the dam. Ethiopia has proceeded to start filling the dam as part of its efforts to extend its infrastructural power and use the precipitation in the highlands for power and irrigation (Verhoeven 2021). But this too is not a new issue; Gwyn Prins (see Prins and Stamp 1991) used this case in the early 1990s in his documentary on environmental security, *Top Guns and Toxic Whales*, speculating on Egyptian military action to prevent dam construction as a likely future cause of war. His scenario's timing was off by at least fifteen years, but the conflict dynamics implied by a downstream state worried about its water supplies coming from an upstream state persist.

Thomas Homer-Dixon (1994) noted that in many such cases downstream states were simply weaker than upstream states and as such didn't have a military option if they suffered from water shortages caused by upstream states. The case of Iraq and the Turkish dams upstream on the Tigris and Euphrates as well as the case of the Mexicans being powerless to do much about American diversions of the Colorado waters are noteworthy. So too, the case of the Mekong, where Chinese dams have disrupted the historical patterns of water flow through Laos and Cambodia and in the process damaged both river fishing and agriculture as well as enhanced salinization of the delta in Vietnam, doesn't lend itself to military response from downstream states. Likewise waters running off the Himalayas, both in terms of India and Pakistan, are rivers where the headwaters are in China (Huda and Ali 2018).

In circumstances of non-stationarity, where past patterns aren't a reliable indicator of things to come, protocols on existing agreements to agree in advance on what happens in extreme circumstances are likely to be a useful innovation to prevent future conflict. If the rules and procedures, agreed in advance, are clear as to who gets which allocation of what water is available in a drought, or how flood waters will be dealt with if they exceed normal flows, then the potential for future conflict is minimized. The failure to anticipate and provide new modes of sharing what water is available leads to dystopian nightmares of conflict, displacement and enhanced inequalities as elites appropriate what they can and leave the rest to fend for themselves in the new wild zones of ecological scarcity, epitomized in Paolo Bacigalupi's novel about a possible future Western United States, *The Water Knife*.

Focusing on national priorities and invoking territorial sovereignty in the face of supposedly external threats highlights one of the interesting ironies in the discussion of environmental and specifically climate security. While the focus on globalization is frequently on how processes transcend national boundaries, as noted in Chapter 4, many of the economic practices that constitute globalization are about the construction of new borders and bounded spaces that exclude traditional peoples and their occupations. The expansion of industrial agriculture involves the construction of formal property arrangements in many places where informal commercial or subsistence arrangements have functioned. Production for export frequently involves the construction of pre-clearance areas for trade goods, and numerous, often violent efforts to secure the transport of commodities worldwide (Cowen 2014). The attempts to patent seeds and traditional knowledge are another form of enclosure. Economic trade zones and the enclaves the rich construct to separate themselves, both horizontally in gated communities and now sometimes vertically in high-rise luxury buildings, are increasing separations and partitions of social and economic spaces as part of the globalization process (Graham 2016).

These processes frequently emphasize the point that the global economy has grown rapidly in recent decades but in many cases has done so by accentuating inequalities both within states and between them (Piketty 2014). The SDGs explicitly aim to reduce inequalities and poverty, and, particularly because of the rapid transformation of China, some poverty reduction has been accomplished, but the larger question of how to transform economies so they can deal with poverty while not transcending the planetary boundaries is now a key theme at the heart of sustainability discussions. The COVID-19 pandemic, and the complicated efforts to reboot the global economy following the initial shutdowns, has emphasized the point that the neoliberal consensus on austerity and inflation control has been scrapped by the new focus on central banks as economic agents (Tooze 2021).

The pandemic has simultaneously exacerbated the inequalities in many societies, while rising concerns about climate change pose big questions of how to invest in renewable energy while also thinking effectively about transition strategies for labour. All this can't avoid dealing with the need to think through how to regulate the long commodity chains that link the global economy together, which were seriously disrupted by the pandemic response, but in the process require large amounts of fossil fuels to keep the whole system moving. Territorial thinking and fortress mentalities (White 2014), whereby threats are assumed to be of external origin, simply gets the geography all wrong when it comes to both climate and the economic consequences of the pandemic (Dalby 2022).

Failure to think these things through, and simultaneously a focus only on the formal economy rather than the context within which it is structured, is likely to lead to serious ecological disruptions. These disasters are increasingly artificial, and as such security policy is in part about dealing with them, a matter that has been clear in the United States at least since the Katrina inundation of New Orleans in 2005 (Dalby 2009b). But few remain within state borders, and the causes of climate disruptions in particular are obviously beyond any particular state, even if it is fairly obvious that the emissions from particular states are crucially important in the history of the causes of climate disruptions. At the largest scale globalization has produced a situation where planetary boundaries loom as limits to the human endeavour, ones that at least some political elites are apparently uninterested in respecting, presumably because they either think that nothing can be done or think that they and their families can ride out the disruptions due to their wealth and power (Katz-Rosene and Szwarc 2021).

Formulating the politics of climate in these terms, a climate apartheid of drastic divisions of people into the rich who can somehow ride out the apocalypse and the poor who must suffer the consequences is how numerous politicians and activists in the Global South view matters (Chaturvedi and Doyle 2015). Hence the endless appeals for climate justice and aid to deal with the disruptions caused by the historical patterns of Northern fossil fuel consumption. The actions of fossil fuel emitting states are a major security threat to many poorer and Southern states. In the case of Tuvalu, its people face imminent inundation because of this "warming war" (Pita 2007), and their migration to some other higher altitude locations is a matter of physical survival. They don't have any security policy in the face of the imminent disappearance of their territory. Preventing that is key to the survival of a national entity, and that can only be done by rapidly decarbonizing the global economy. Tuvalu doesn't have any military options!

Another political division that is increasingly sharp in many parts of the world is between climate change activists and the fossil fuel industry that is willing to spend large quantities of cash to influence popular attempts to legislate climate actions and convert the economy into a post fossil fuel one. The divestment movement has focused attention on the particular corporations who still, despite the consequences of their business model, persist in exploring for yet more resources when it is clear that those that are already known can't all be burnt if the planet is to have a climate loosely analogous to that of the last ten thousand years (Mangat, Dalby and Paterson 2018). Borders are no protection to these hazards. For states dependent on petroleum production, unless substantial rethinking is undertaken and new policies formulated, national security involves the continuation of a fossil fueled economic strategy despite the long term disasters that will ensue. For many poorer and low lying states, Tuvalu included, disasters are already occurring as a result of climate change, and their short term, never mind long term, security is already being compromised.

While security threats have traditionally been seen in terms of cross boundary violations, now the biggest threats are precisely as a result of the success of capitalism in remaking the world. Hence the ambiguity relating globalization and its enhanced connectivity across distance to questions of sustainability. Globalization is about transformation and yet its functioning depends on not transcending planetary boundaries (Steffen, Richardson, Rockström et al. 2015). The post political premises of most policies preclude grappling with these new circumstances; actions are to be taken within the market economy, and security is about preserving this mode of social life. Larger political questions are frequently silenced in the policy discourse that focuses on incremental change and minor adjustments and posing matters as "problems" to which there are obvious scientific "solutions" (Cockerill, Armstrong, Richter and Okie 2017). But these are not what is needed in the face of rapid climate change and the other disruptions of the latest phase of globalization. In these circumstances sustainability now requires securing the ability to adapt effectively to rapid change, a very different formulation of security from that which has dominated global politics for the last few decades.

The difficulty here is that the spatial language of contemporary politics doesn't help in linking global and local issues effectively, and defensive formulations which so frequently operate in environmental politics to privilege particular places link poorly with global transformations that the earth system research makes clear has to be the context for thinking about politics in the Anthropocene. Robyn Eckersley (2017) nuances these matters in her call to think about geopolitan democracy rather than cosmopolitan politics, precisely because the larger geological context has to be part of the engagement with the conditions of life that the Anthropocene demands. This geopower isn't a matter of either local control or global governance; both have to be articulated somehow to prevent the dangers of a global technocratic elite trying to enforce rules and regulations by decree. "Therefore we cannot simply substitute the political fantasy of rational Earth systems steering led by scientific elites with a political fantasy of local or national self-rule led by political forces which are ignorant of their vulnerability to (and roles in producing) the life-threatening changes to Earth systems processes that are underway" (Eckersley 2017, 995–996). But things have to work in reverse too: "The minimization of world risks depends on a local understanding of how local practices are inserted into, and bear upon, larger Earth systems processes and vice versa" (Eckersley 2017, 995–996).

This is obviously a tall order in the face of global crisis, but these are the challenges of rethinking security in the novel circumstances of the Anthropocene; formulations of isolated states in competition and potentially threatening each other may offer historical solace to confused social scientists, but they do not form the ontological framework that is needed for grasping the dilemmas of governance in a rapidly changing world. Yes, this is partly about how to rethink notions of development and progress in the sense of increased capacities for human flourishing, but as Chapter 7 has indicated, these now have to follow new models, not those of fossil fueled industrialization and urbanization that set the great acceleration in motion in the twentieth century, nor the neat separate spaces of the world political map that fail to provide an appropriate framework for governance (Harris 2021). The possibilities for cities and their governing structures to innovate rapidly may be one source of hope (Bernstein and Hoffman 2018), but in so far as urban centres lead on climate innovation, they further challenge the traditional international relations focus on states as the providers of security.

The security dilemmas of the twenty first century require thinking about material production in conjunction with threats to use force while considering these in terms of a dynamic earth system destabilized by previous efforts to secure various things. Simultaneously it is necessary to recognize that globalization is mostly about topological connections however much governance efforts may try to grapple with these using topographically based reasoning (Dalby 2021). Traditional notions of national security, and power understood in terms of industrial capabilities and military firepower, are anathema to ecological security in a world where climate change and species extinctions are accelerating.

ENVIRONMENTAL PEACEBUILDING

While, as noted in Chapter 5, much of the discussion of climate and security focuses on potential social disruptions caused by environmental change and extreme events, the other side of the discussion is getting much more attention of late. If environmental change is a stressor, or threat multiplier, then thinking through how to prevent conflict, or perhaps better still make peace by using environmental cooperation as a tool, would seem to be a promising way to think about constructive policy. At least it can potentially do so if regenerating ecological systems, rather than extending extractive activities, is understood as the key task of ecological security (McDonald 2021), one made increasingly difficult by global earth system scale changes that impact on local ecologies. Resilience now has to be about building back better after local disruptions, rather than reverting to a status quo ante (Dalby 2020c).

This discussion however is mostly conducted outside the mainstream international relations journals, which have been slow to make links between environmental matters and peace research (Kelly 2021). As with mainstream international relations, which has been mostly uninterested in the rapidly changing planetary context and the Anthropocene debate in particular (Simangan 2020), discussions of peace and environment draw from both practitioner perspectives and disciplinary representatives from diverse sources. Development studies, geography, environmental studies and other social sciences focus on these themes. Perhaps this is an appropriate division of academic labour, but given the importance of conflict prevention as a theme in security studies, further developments of this field might reasonably be expected in the leading journals in the field in coming years (Ide, Bruch, Carius et al. 2021).

Environmental peacebuilding has to confront both cross border difficulties and situations of internal conflict within notional nation states. But as much of this book has emphasized, the dramatic expansion of European imperialism and the subsequent spread of globalization has been far from peaceful. The processes of extractivism are also those of dislocation and displacement, and much of the violence on the resource frontiers of modernity have been about attempts to remove indigenous peoples, or previous generations of settlers, to make way for new mines, plantations and infrastructure (Menton and Le Billon 2021). Local communities, "the people in the way", frequently resist, and as international human rights workers continue to document, assassination squads and killing is part of these processes; Chico Mendes, the Brazilian rubber tapper activist murdered in 1988, was only one (Hecht and Cockburn 1990), albeit especially high profile, case of a longstanding problem. His case is especially interesting however because the rubber tappers were struggling to maintain the intact ecosystems on which their livelihood depended in the face of encroaching agricultural interests and forest destruction to facilitate monocultural production.

Where people resist external impositions, low grade warfare and the use of "security" forces to extend "development" is part of the problem of peace. The ongoing violence in Colombia is related to these processes too, albeit in complicated ways that are challenging the attempts to finally resolve the lengthy civil war in that country. Indeed the post settlement arrangements after the peace accord between the government and the Revolutionary Armed Forces of Colombia (FARC) has seen larger violent displacements of numerous local people and has led to some of the most uneven land distribution arrangements in the continent (Koopman 2020). Sometimes these processes of "slow violence", in Rob Nixon's (2011) terms, involve very fast violence in the form of the deliberate killing of activists.

When, as is frequently the case, resistance to these kinds of "development" is linked to international human rights campaigns, then here too governments can invoke "national security" as a mode of justifying repression and violence. External influences are apparently at work, and local people that connect their struggles to international organizations can easily be portrayed as traitors providing aid to sinister foreign forces (Matejova, Parker and Dauvergne 2018). Thus the complicated geographies of local opposition to developments designed to feed international markets continue the long term patterns of colonial dispossession. Nonetheless it is also clear that by now integration of most parts of humanity into the global economy is a fait accompli. What now matters, given the scale of the transformations that have already occurred, is what comes next and how these dislocations can be dealt with in ways that are deemed legitimate by rural populations facing simultaneous climate and environmental disruptions, as well as novel health dangers and related economic uncertainties linked to pandemics and the periodic convulsions of the global economy. Making the slow violence involved in these processes of dislocation visible is part of the scholarly task of tackling climate politics (O'Lear 2021).

Many states are simply unable to provide the necessities for much of their population and modern assumptions of the responsibility to protect require development assistance, not to mention climate adaptation funding too, a matter where getting states that have long histories of extensive greenhouse gas emissions to live up to their commitments has been a source of seemingly endless frustration at annual COPs. In linking these things up the broadly construed practices of environmental peacebuilding are coming to the fore, encompassing at least five themes (Ide 2020): efforts to prevent or mediate environment related conflicts; efforts to deal with resource management issues in post conflict situations; efforts focusing on resilient livelihoods as a mode of coping with climate change; disaster risk reduction strategies related to community cohesion associated with environmental change; and finally, environmental peacebuilding where joint problem solving facilitates improved intergroup relations.

Peacebuilding focuses on solutions, inverting the conflict focus of much of the earlier work.

> As a concept, it illustrates the deep intertwinement of environmental change and security in the Anthropocene .... At the same time, environmental peacebuilding challenges the conflict-centred ontologies and determinist connotations shared by parts of the environmental (and now climate) conflict discourse for quite some time .... It does so by highlighting that the scarcity (or abundance) of natural resources is often produced by specific political ecologies, and that environmental change can also catalyse peaceful adaptation and increased solidarity rather than facilitate violence. (Ide 2020, 2)

How these landscapes, their property relations and access to land, water and other resources are changed in the peacebuilding processes shapes future political possibilities. Key literature on climate adaptation as well as peacebuilding operations links these contextual matters quite directly together. While reworking landscapes in ways that are both ecologically sustainable and likely to promote peace is the overall goal of peacebuilding projects, they may not succeed if they follow some of the traditional modes of development. But efforts to facilitate cooperation are not without their potential pitfalls, and these reprise some of the themes highlighted earlier in this volume about how the contexts within which climate change in particular plays out are constructed by prior human occupation, the modification of environments and the property arrangements that shape adaptation possibilities.

THE POLITICAL ECONOMY OF ADAPTATION

In attempting to respond to these new circumstances and the rising impacts of climate change there have been increasing efforts to address climate adaptation. Many of these are national efforts but linked to attempts by states to extract funds from novel green financing arrangements. While the adage that mitigation is global and adaptation is local effectively summarizes the situation, in that local environments are impacted in specific ways, nonetheless it is notable that there is relatively little international coordination of these efforts. National efforts are frequently linked directly to existing development strategies, and funding channelled through international aid programs. The dangers here are that these perpetuate existing patterns of ecological transformation without clearly distancing themselves from the ecologically unsustainable practices of the past.

In particular Sovacool and Linner (2016) use a political economy framework to itemize four common problems with climate adaptation projects that prevent their being sustainable. Summarized in terms of four "E"s, enclosure, exclusion, encroachment and entrenchment, they argue that implementing adaptation projects, especially when engineering is the main focus, leads to numerous failures to think through the social and economic impacts. While ostensibly climate adaptation is supposed to help those most vulnerable to climate change, in many cases the projects aggravate inequities and promote social change that benefits the better off, the socially well-connected, donor agencies, political elites in capital cities and the corporate agendas of those who get the engineering contracts.

More specifically enclosures involve economic aspects of adaptation where resources are transferred from public domains into private hands. Exclusion relates to the political marginalization of stakeholders where adaptation decisions are taken without considering local conditions and subsistence and peasant economies. Damage to ecosystems and biodiversity comes from encroachment on landscapes and interference with ecosystem services, while the entrenchment suggests that adaptation can have the perverse effect of increasing inequality, and disempowering women and minorities. Avoiding these outcomes requires thinking carefully about both the ecology and economy of areas where adaptation projects are being considered, but also about political inclusion, something that is especially difficult in fractured or divided societies. Failure to do these things may well aggravate the problems of "maldevelopment" to use Baechler's (1998) term from some of the 1990s studies of the environmental sources of conflict.

Tobias Ide (2020) offers a similar list of cautionary tales, in this case specifically focusing less on adaptation than on things that may cause environmental peacebuilding efforts to fail. Given that efforts at peacebuilding are increasingly likely to have to take matters of climate adaptation into account if they are to be successful, it is worth noting the parallels between these two studies. Emphasizing the important point that resources and environmental matters are frequently part and parcel of ongoing political and economic cleavages in most societies, Ide suggests that environmental peacebuilding efforts need to be carefully crafted to avoid six difficulties that may derail their initiatives. In many cases the transformations undertaken in peacebuilding efforts have winners and losers, and costs may lead to resentments and conflict among those who are disadvantaged. "(E)xternally derived, 'one size fits all' solutions are likely to facilitate depoliticization, conflicts (between locals as well as between locals and externals) and state delegitimization" (Ide 2020, 7).

More specifically Ide's (2020) six "D"s are depoliticization, displacement, discrimination, deterioration into conflict, delegitimization of the state and degradation of the environment. Depoliticization refers to the frequent preference for focusing on technical and scientific matters at the expense of dealing with the political causes of conflict. Focusing on increasing water supplies from dams, or novel seeds to deal with drought, may well exclude dealing with issues of grievances and poverty which are frequently the underlying causes of vulnerability. Large scale engineering projects such as dams involve displacing people, often on the large scale, and failure to think through how they are to be adequately relocated and compensated leads to political difficulties. Peace parks that remove residents are an especially contradictory mode of activity. If these practices work along existing ethnic schisms in a society they may add to the discrimination experienced by marginal peoples, making the potential for conflict greater.

Likewise thinking through the specifically gendered aspects of development is needed to ensure greater inequities on those grounds don't increase vulnerability. Failure to deal with such issues may lead to social deterioration and conflict, especially when large projects designed to enhance development don't consider the needs of local inhabitants. Where projects are contracted out and run into opposition, the absence of effective government oversight may delegitimize the state, further weakening social cohesion. Finally short term thinking and enhanced resource extraction as a method of development may lead to long term degradation of environments and such things as the overexploitation of groundwater leading to further agricultural difficulties when the wells run dry.

If what is being secured here is the extension of conventional development projects and the further colonization of vulnerable landscapes, then peacebuilding might be much less than environmentally oriented. All these things are even more difficult in places where lengthy conflicts have endured and social fractures, histories of violence and injustice, as well as claims that past crimes must be accounted for in peaceful settlements, are involved (Kleinfeld 2018). But in terms of Wallensteen's (2015) insistence that a "quality peace" has to ensure that the conditions that generated conflict in the first place are removed in post conflict settlements, environmental peacebuilding has to think through these issues. Where uneven access to land, water and commons is involved, complex issues of property, redistribution and equity also have to be considered.

As earlier chapters in this volume have emphasized, the processes of development, and the extension of settler and commercial farming arrangements into numerous landscapes, are frequently fraught affairs. It is no surprise if attempts at low carbon development too generate security problems. As noted in Chapter 7, windfarms in particular have frequently been opposed by local communities, not least because of the failure of local consultations and the imposition of these facilities without their benefiting from the revenue generated by the windmills (Dunlap 2017). Much of this is a matter of failure to consider local conditions, and failures to understand that inadequate governance mechanisms to ameliorate social stresses are more frequently to blame for resulting conflicts linked to changing environmental conditions than those conditions themselves (Mirumachi, Sawas and Workman 2020).

BACKDRAFTS AND BOOMERANGS

In terms of security the more worrisome point is that, while trying to initiate policies to address climate change at the global scale, failures to think through the local context and changing ecological circumstances will in fact "boomerang" back on the state trying to provide climate adaptation, making conflict worse rather than better, a matter of the unintended consequences of ill-considered policies, ones that ignore the particularities of local context and in particular land use issues (Swatuk and Wirkus 2018). "Thus, before state-initiated, biosphere-oriented climate actions are taken, policy makers must be able to answer the following question: what will be the impacts of these actions at the point of intervention?" (Swatuk, Thomas, Wirkus et al.

2021, 61). Given the complex local property arrangements, resource attributes of particular places, and local histories which are often effectively unknown in state capitals, never mind in the offices of global development agencies, this practical geography of climate adaptation is tricky at best. As the saying in climate change circles frequently has it, mitigation is global but adaptation is local.

The dangers of these problems, termed "backdrafts" in the Wilson Center Environmental Change and Security Program (Dabelko, Herzer, Null et al. 2013), add another complicated dimension to thinking about the relationships of peace and conflict related to climate in that where they occur they both make matters worse and in the process discredit efforts to tackle climate change. In so far as climate mitigation on the global scale is, as outlined in Chapter 7, likely to need fairly drastic rural change in many places to regenerate landscapes, including introducing agroecologies and polycultures as well as other ecological innovations to simultaneously buffer the worst effects of climate change while hopefully sequestering carbon and facilitating species migration, then peacebuilding thinking clearly has to avoid simple technical fixes while working sensitively with local contexts.

Dealing with these matters effectively is a complex matter, but at least three key elements for success seem to be clear. First, contacts across social and political divides to build clarity and trust are important, as, second, are transnational norms of good governance in the resource sector. Third is the necessity of having effective state action to address the instrumental needs of communities, which in the process can build trust and improve the legitimacy of the local state (Krampe, Hegazi and VanDeveer 2021). But this does involve local on the ground efforts and state action designed for the long term pacification of troubled regions. Failure to involve local actors, and the assumptions that international organizations, including projects run by the United Nations Environment Programme (UNEP), should have ownership of these initiatives and can impose good governance and peace in the aftermath of conflict, simply replicates the problems of top down projects imposed from a distance with local input rendered less important than the international policies (Krampe 2021).

All of which is now aggravated by the increasing vulnerabilities of many landscapes to extreme events; the non-stationarity condition is now what societies have to live with for the foreseeable future. Climate change may be making peacebuilding all the more difficult, as has been suggested in the case of Mali, where ongoing conflict isn't helped by climatic fluctuations that add pressures to the already fraught relationships between and within agricultural communities in many rural areas (Hegazi, Krampe and Smith 2021). The likelihood of increased rural stresses of this kind in coming years makes peacemaking efforts urgent as Anthropocene changes accelerate.

How this is all to be turned into arrangements that provide what Head (2019) calls ecostates, and how the provision of sustainable extraction finance arrangements is to be organized, are major policy issues raised by environmental peacemaking. While peacebuilding efforts are fraught with difficulties, the larger point about environmental peace is simply that, while there may be numerous small scale conflicts over resource issues, mostly the world is a relatively peaceful place. As Barnett (2019) cogently argues, if climate was to cause wars, or large scale conflicts, then the last few decades, when the world has noticeably warmed, weather is getting less predictable and population continues to grow, should have seen a noticeable increase in conflicts related to these matters. But headlines from Syria, Yemen, Iraq and various parts of Africa notwithstanding, while there has been an increase in hostilities, and international arms sales figures climbed in the second decade of this century, there has not been a large increase in hostilities in line with the determinist assumptions that frequently drive the more alarmist versions of the climate security narrative. The impetus for peacemaking projects is precisely to make sure this condition prevails in coming decades.

What are increasing are extreme events, and human vulnerabilities have yet to be comprehensively addressed by governments and the corporations that shape policy agendas. This results in widespread vulnerabilities (Mobjörk, Smith and Rüttinger 2016), and as such insecurity for numerous populations, but it hasn't generated warfare. Insecurity is widespread, but it is in forms that are mostly not amenable to military action, even if in some cases it is in fact a threat multiplier, and in many cases emergency aid by armed forces is needed in disaster situations. The COVID-19 pandemic has had perverse consequences in many places, reinforcing state controls through the use of lockdowns and migration controls, while also undermining their legitimacy in places where they have patently failed to protect vulnerable populations. But as of the time of writing for this volume, late in 2021, its far from clear as to whether this will connect up with climate disaster responses or the continued dramatic disruptions of economic change in ways that generate overt conflict and further state fragility, or will lead to political reforms more conducive to thinking about ecostates and novel modes of ecological security.

Fragile states clearly need help in terms of climate adaptation, and in doing these things avoiding the pitfalls that Ide (2020) and Sovacool and Linner (2016) identify. Resilience is important, albeit this has to be interpreted as much more than facilitating the ability to bound back after disruptions, and is a crucial consideration at the global scale (Dalby 2020c). The ability to cope with enhanced dangers and rapidly changing circumstances is now key to security broadly understood; this isn't about rival powers, but about vulnerabilities built into the landscapes and infrastructures that feed and supply most human needs. These are changing and dealing with rapid transitions is what preparing to live in the Anthropocene now implies for all planners, but most importantly those dealing with ecological change and landscape management (Kareiva and Fuller 2016).

The really difficult question in all this discussion is whether peace can be linked to regenerative agriculture and other ecological restoration practices such as widespread tree planting and the reconstruction of traditional water conservation measures which can help buffer ecologies and human supply systems from the worst extremes of climate change. As Chapter 7 has suggested, rethinking rural political economy is essential as part of serious efforts to tackle climate change and buffer ecosystems from more extreme weather while regenerating capabilities to feed a still growing human population. The continued destruction of the Amazon rainforest by extractivist agriculture and fears of similar damage being done by proposed petroleum extraction in Central Africa, highlighted by Greta Thunberg and other climate activists in 2021, likewise suggest things will get worse before rural political economy moves in sustainable directions. The political economy of extractivism has to be challenged as part of efforts to use environmental matters as a peacemaking project, if, that is, long term sustainability is the goal and notions of justice are applicable to these policies (Stoett 2019).

TRANSITION STRATEGIES AND CONFLICT

An additional key consideration in environmental security discussions at the global scale is whether the necessary rapid transitions off fossil fuels will trigger conflict (Vakulchuk, Overland and Scholten 2020). Will states that fail to think through effective transition strategies be vulnerable to collapse, or, fearing eclipse by those that have moved ahead in the new post fossil fuel economies, be tempted to resort to military action to thwart rivals while they still have the capabilities? Fears in particular focus on the Middle East and the possible demise of petro states there once the revenue streams from petroleum and natural gas dry up (Global Commission on the Geopolitics of Energy Transformation 2019). The impetus to pump as much oil as possible prior to reductions in global demand also perpetuates dependence on petroleum revenues in the short term. If these are used to facilitate a transition to renewable sources and novel economic activities the outcome is likely to be peaceful (Rabinowitz 2020). But the fear is that failure to anticipate the transition may leave states with severe fiscal crises and in danger of political turmoil once state support for economic activities is removed. Given the sheer complexity of energy and its key role in contemporary societies, transition strategies are clearly needed (Newell 2021). Environmental peacemaking as large scale preventative diplomacy would seem to fit the bill to grapple with the geopolitical dimensions of transition.

These academic discussions are related to the growing policy discussions of these matters. Concerns about fragile states and how to facilitate a "climate of peace" were complemented by European discussions of green new deals and recovery strategies from the COVID-19 pandemic, suggesting a shift in economic thinking away from the austerity narratives that dominated Europe after the 2008 financial crisis. Security conferences in Bonn and Berlin as well as initiatives by the Netherlands and Sweden to move discussions of environment and peace forward have highlighted the links between climate, environmental change and the possibilities of peace actions. The European Union and the UNEP weighed in with projects that focus on climate security. The American Center for Climate Security has highlighted these issues and, in anticipation of the fiftieth anniversary of the Stockholm conference, the Stockholm International Peace Research Institute launched a project on "Environment of Peace". Issues of peacebuilding are clearly getting attention.

Other security concerns have been raised about shortages and disruptions of energy supplies, especially where grids are interconnected across national borders. Likewise concerns about shortages of key minerals needed for batteries and windmills have been expressed, reprising the Malthusian fears related to gas and petroleum supplies. What clearly is of concern is the conditions under which many of these substances are mined. Many of the worst working conditions in the global economy are in extractivist sectors and in mining in particular. The indentured labour arrangements and practical dangers as well as chemical hazards from mining operations mean that human insecurity is a major problem, but one that usually gets short shrift in considerations of global energy systems (Bales and Sovacool 2021).

The most obvious point in all this is precisely that renewable energy systems, with the notable exception of some biomass combustion generation facilities, which despite the rhetoric are far from renewable, don't involve fuel. Energy security has long been understood to be a matter of a reliable supply of fuel at a reasonable price, but in the case of renewable energy systems, the fuel component of this is absent. Reliability is a matter of grid performance and storage facilities, not a matter of tankers, pipelines and potential international disruptions every time political tensions rise in the Middle East. Many rare earth elements, which are used in small quantities in electronic devices, are widespread in geological formations, and while difficult to mine, not something that is in any way physically analogous to the constant supply of fuels involved in combustion technology (Overland 2019). Firepower needs fuel; renewable electricity doesn't; and the physics in all this is very different, hence fear of supply shortages don't transfer well from fossil fuels to novel energy systems.

While much of the discussion of renewable energy suggests that a transition off fossil fuels and into an electric future is occurring, at least up until 2021, and in the economic rebound after the worst disruptions of the COVID-19 pandemic, it is clear that renewables have mostly added so far to the energy mix, rather than replacing fossil fuels. Energy systems in the past have been shaped by political decisions, and usually by commercial ones too, that enhance the power of certain sectors (Daggett 2021). In the case of the industrial revolution in England, the use of steam engines, and their appetite for coal, was driven to a very substantial extent by the desire of industrialists to increase their control over the labour force in the cotton textiles business (Malm 2016), rather than by any inevitable expansion of the economy of fuel use. Myths of inevitable growth of energy use in modern societies frequently obscure these political decisions, a matter that is of great importance in considering responses to climate change and how novel energy systems may be created while fossil fuel use is drastically curtailed, or not.

An additional consideration in terms of energy transitions relates to the pattern of violence in the Middle East over much of the latter part of the twentieth century. There has been a clear correlation between low oil prices and warfare in the region, a matter which suggests a complicated relationship between differential accumulation within global capitalism and the relative performance of logistics companies, arms merchants and oil companies (Bichler and Nitzan 2004). While the relationship is complex, the pattern of shifting investments in logistics from weapons to petroleum and back again clearly links the violent politics of the region to the patterns of wealth gained from the extraction of oil and the rivalries of numerous state actors, both local and those at a distance. The intriguing question here is whether an overall reduction in the importance of petroleum exports in the region will be related to a reduction in weapons sales, and in activities by logistics companies, or whether price collapses and further volatility in the region will feed conflict dynamics.

As the early chapters in this book suggest, national security for the great powers has long been about the search for ever more military capabilities. Fossil fuels dramatically altered these dynamics in the nineteenth century as trains and ships powered by steam engines changed geopolitical calculations. Drahos (2021, 2) is blunt in linking this also to matters of state power: “Price didn’t entrench coal and oil as fuels. States entrenched these fuels because they increased their military capabilities.” In so far as states and capitalism are so closely intertwined in the current world order (Nitzan and Bichler 2009), these dynamics are perpetuated and shape how the political future will unfold. In Susan Strange’s (1999) classic formulation, this Westfailure system, the combination of capitalism and states, has failed to handle both global finances and ecological problems, or generate some balance between rich and poor, and as such is failing global civil society too. But climate change and its dangers are adding novel elements to this discussion, with the prospects of increasing insecurities demanding a reduction in the use of the key fuels that have driven the strategies of domination that this combination of states and capitalism has generated. To prevent further dramatic climate disruption large parts of the existing inventory of fossil fuel reserves simply have to remain in the ground (Welsby, Price, Pye and Ekins 2021). They can't be burnt if atmospheric levels of carbon dioxide are to remain low enough to prevent accelerating climate disruptions.

Which is why the future of China, the largest state using fossil fuels, has become a key consideration in geopolitics, not in terms of the ongoing rivalry with the United States, which gets so much policy attention in security circles, but in terms of how the future climate is shaped by technological and political innovation there too (Drahos 2021), and whether the economy will draw on those fossil fuel reserves or transition to novel energy systems to power the growing urban civilization along ecological lines. The global consequences of the future investment strategies of the Chinese state, the forms of urbanization that appear and whether they take the eco-security framework seriously in their planning, will be a key to the future shape of the ecosphere, and with it the fate of peoples in numerous places (Taylor, O'Brien and O'Keefe 2020). Will the eco-security framework invoked in urban and regional planning there shape future considerations of an ecological civilization, recognizing that sustainability has to function at a global level too within planetary boundaries? Or does it become merely a rhetorical device cloaking the operation of brute power (Goron 2018)?

The planetary boundary framework is premised on the idea that only in the Holocene have conditions been such that humanity could thrive in complex civilizations (Steffen, Richardson, Rockström et al. 2015). There is always a danger here that this slides into a determinist argument that the Holocene produced civilization, and that a hothouse world will necessarily lead to its end, presumably violently. But a more nuanced possibilist argument focusing on necessary conditions suggests that relatively stable climate conditions are necessary for organized agriculture that is needed to feed urban populations. While small scale farming is key to food security in numerous places, and it can be flexible in the face of disruptions, and large scale commercial farming can, by moving food internationally, offer food security up to a point too, what the limits to this current system, in terms of climate variations intersecting with the existing corporate structure, are is not clear (Clapp 2020). They of course relate to what kinds of food production become common in coming decades and whether polycultures, agroecology and regenerative agricultural practices become widely adopted to buffer landscapes and infrastructure from the worst extreme events that a climate disrupted world will present.

One other key point in these prognostications for the future relates to the need to anticipate where climate will most severely impact human populations.

While forecasts of rising sea levels can suggest fairly clearly which coastal areas are in immediate danger of inundation, and hence where evacuation and migration will be essential, it's not so easy in terms of temperature. While climate models can predict where temperatures will rise, and the likelihood of extreme droughts and other disturbances, human responses will be very varied. It is simply not possible to read human response in a simple determinist fashion from climate projections. Responses depend on numerous factors, and the resilience of particular peoples in specific places will be a complex matter of political economy and cultural adaptation, not a simple matter of moving when it gets too hot (Horton, de Sherbinin, Wrathall and Oppenheimer 2021).

If, as seems likely, the weather systems and larger trajectory of climate changes make agriculture, as has been practiced since the fertilizer and green revolution innovations of the twentieth century, increasingly difficult, and food prices repeatedly but unpredictably spike dramatically as they did in 2008 and 2010, then can the global trading system and the political regimes that regulate it in particular places maintain control (Homer-Dixon, Walker, Biggs et al. 2015)? Or will the shocks to the system be on such a scale that conflict breaks out? Might nuclear war lead to temporary cooling, a nuclear winter that will simply pause warming until the dust, soot and smoke dissipate, and then, with elevated carbon dioxide levels and a discontinuation of possible geoengineering efforts due to the war, to an additional "termination" shock to the climate system, making the hothouse even more volatile? Such speculations quickly lead to discussions of human extinction, and pessimistic prognostications about the human fate epitomized by David Wallace-Wells' 2017 *New York Magazine* article, discussed in Chapter 6. Avoiding such disastrous outcomes has to be the primary concern of any serious policies related to environmental security.

Tying these considerations to old fashioned notions of national security is not helpful. If security is understood as maintaining the status quo and mobilizing against external threats, then in these circumstances it seems highly unlikely that anything except exacerbated conflict will result. Daniel Deudney's (1990) warning about this remains entirely apposite. In a world armed with nuclear weapons, and presumably facing rising uncertainties about the efficacy or effects of geoengineering experiments, mistrust and conflict seem ever more likely in the absence of concerted efforts to cooperate on transition strategies. Is there a role for scaling up the peacebuilding processes to facilitate the reform of the global economy and its political systems to ensure a peaceful progression into a policy regime designed to avoid a future hothouse world? This is a tall order, but this is the kind of question that is now looming on the horizon in the discussion of environmental security, and a matter for serious engagement in the discipline of international relations.

On the other hand, in so far as the leaders of the Soviet Union can be understood to have come to their senses in the 1980s and realized that their notion of security in terms of military preparations was simply too dangerous, the possibilities of drastic rethinking of the larger context for global security does have a precedent, albeit one that is usually dismissed when viewed through Western ideological lenses. The subsequent collapse of the Soviet Union means that this key moment has been forgotten, lost in tales of American victory and the triumphalism of the 1990s. The security ontology that matters in the next phase of the Anthropocene is of a functional global biosphere, one that is partly but judiciously enmeshed with a coevolving technosphere. Strategies to enhance adaptability while quickly reducing fossil fuel use and facilitating ecological regeneration have to be at the heart of environmental security understood as a global priority. This is starkly at odds with the colonizing premises of modernity and the long term trajectory of increased firepower in human affairs. Focusing on elites as major climate change agents likewise shifts the focus from the poor and marginal as potential destabilizing triggers of conflict to the key driving forces of the global economy that shape the technosphere; environmental security is a problem of investment, not of marginal agricultural scarcity.

Clearly if human institutions are carefully crafted with these insights in mind then disastrous or self-imposed existential threats are a fate that it is possible to avoid. But this seems unlikely without some fairly drastic rethinking of how security is formulated, and societies restructured to be both more flexible and more just, so that legitimacy is widespread and reinforced by practical capabilities to ensure human thriving, even in the face of a much more volatile climate system. But to do these things will also require a recognition of the human condition that is at odds with some of the fondest held assumptions of modernity. Ecological thinking challenges modernity's presumption of the virtues of autonomy, the social necessity of property, and the widespread use of fossil fuels. In the Anthropocene this is no longer the social order that should be "secured"; it's increasingly the source of contemporary security problems.

Conclusion

Security after firepower?

ENVIRONMENTAL SECURITY REVISITED

Discussions about peaceful transitions to a sustainable society are driven by an often implicit understanding that humanity ought to live in a planetary system that is at least broadly similar to the geological circumstances of the last ten thousand years. It provided the ecological conditions that facilitated the emergence of human civilization (Lewis and Maslin 2018). Now recent research into the earth system, and a growing recognition of the sheer scale of human transformation of many environments, suggests that the assumption of a relatively stable geological context for humanity is at best misleading, and at worst a dangerous failure to think carefully about the new context that humanity is creating for itself in this new epoch of the Anthropocene. Failure to take this recontextualization seriously is likely to lead to rapid disruptive changes in the earth system, which if not addressed could lead to runaway climate change and a planet with surface conditions not seen on earth since the Cretaceous period when there were no icecaps and the climate was very much hotter than humanity has known.

Now as Asian economies grow relative to the rest of the world, and China in particular has boosted production of renewable energy sources, although not, at least yet, substantially constrained its use of coal powered electricity generation, the geopolitics of energy is changing. Nonetheless there are already substantial climate changes underway as tropical storms, increasing wildfires and rapid melting of Arctic environments emphasize. Sustainability now requires taking this dynamic situation as its benchmark condition and working from there; we live in a world where "non-stationarity" is now the background condition for planning. Slowing down climate change is key to making adaptation easier. Preventing runaway climate change, and a hothouse earth future, is key to the long term survival of a global civilization capable of feeding and housing more than seven billion humans. How to do this is now a major question for global governance, even if the leaders of some states still seem more or less fixated on their own national priorities regardless of the larger consequences. Rethinking environmental security requires rethinking both the stationarity and territorial assumptions in contemporary governance thinking and practice. This is a tall order, but present circumstances require nothing less if the future survival of human civilization is to be assured.

As the first draft of this chapter was being keyboarded in February 2021, the United Nations was hosting a virtual Security Council session on climate security. The newly installed Biden administration in Washington was making statements about foreign policy strategies, considering the fragility of many states and linking them to the issues of climate change and the political dangers that result from climate disruptions. While such statements have been made since the end of the cold war, now they are done with a renewed urgency. Perhaps finally this new contextualization for security will become the overarching concern for international security? The following May a statement from the G7 coincided with a major change of direction by the International Energy Authority, which issued a report stating that investments in fossil fuel infrastructure had to be stopped more or less forthwith if there was any chance of keeping average global warming to under 1.5 degrees Celsius, the aspirational target established at the 2015 Paris meetings that formalized the Paris Agreement on Climate Change. In September of 2021 President Xi of China announced to the United Nations General Assembly that it would no longer finance the building of coal powered electricity generation plants abroad and would instead support renewable energy projects.

In Glasgow, at the COP 26 conference in November 2021, further statements were forthcoming on limitations of future fossil fuel subsidies, or at least those specified as inefficient. For the first time fossil fuels were explicitly mentioned as part of the problem of climate change, and following last minute squabbles about wording, the final conference declaration agreed to a phase down of coal usage. Loss and damage also emerged as a topic for consideration, although funding from developed countries for climate adaptation still fell short of previous promises. Methane too finally made it onto the agenda as a problem, and further rules for international carbon markets and forest protection initiatives were discussed. As to whether this constitutes definitive evidence that the world has reached a policy tipping point, and will transition rapidly to a post fossil fueled world, as Rockström and Gaffney (2021) hope, it is too soon to tell. Although it would be conveniently timely in the lead up to the fiftieth anniversary of the Stockholm conference, it is clearly too soon to confirm that the world had reached a social tipping point on the climate issue (Otto, Donges, Cremades et al. 2020).

While expressions of concern have clearly grown in volume and urgency, nonetheless the global use of fossil fuels has not shrunk, apart from a small decrease due to the pandemic caused economic disruptions in 2020. Emissions of greenhouse gases need to be rapidly reduced and eliminated in coming decades if the dangers of firepower are to be effectively tackled. This is the challenge of climate security and a topic that needs urgent attention from all sectors of government and corporate policy making. Key to this is the direction of investment funds; further expansion of fossil fuel infrastructure, locking in future fossil fuel consumption, only makes the dangers of firepower worse.

REALISM'S NEW CONTEXT

But, at least by 2020, there was little evidence that such matters were penetrating to the heart of the international relations discipline (Simangan 2021). Is it once again going to be bypassed by events, committed to a set of assumptions about continuation and stability in the international order that is changing far more rapidly than its assumptions allow it to engage (Albert 2020)? Simultaneously the numerous novel investigations that critical international relations in its various forms engage are frequently in danger of distracting attention away from the core concerns that animated the security studies in the first few decades of the cold war. Survival was then a matter of constraining firepower, of limiting the potential use of nuclear weapons, and invoking restraint on the part of those who possessed the ability to launch the missiles. Now too once again, constraining firepower in terms of what combustion facilitates has to be the key focus.

In Daniel Deudney's (2007) terms a negarchy, a series of enforced restrictions, governed international relations among the superpowers throughout the cold war period and since. Attempts to use firepower to impose human will on antagonists came up against the potential for self-destruction, thus necessitating the need for more circumspect actions. The attempts to use firepower to coerce external antagonists reached its limits in mutually assured destruction, but firepower in terms of fossil fuel combustion is still clearly being used on the large scale to remake the ecosphere, forcing it to do the will of corporations and governments, despite the obvious future consequences; the environmental security dilemma is being enhanced not ameliorated by continued investments in fossil fuels and spin off industries.

The extensive use of firepower in its various forms is precisely the problem that is causing insecurity. This is the case because the products of combustion are the greenhouse gases causing the earth to heat and disrupting the climate system. Once again external forces are pushing back against the overuse of firepower, only most obviously by the increasing incidence of wildfires, not only in the lands with Mediterranean style climates, but in other forested areas, not least the boreal forests of the sub-Arctic. Summers in Siberia recently have been marked by massive wildfires and anomalous heat waves. While climate change increasingly disrupts the stable geographical circumstances of the Holocene, the politics of self-imposed vulnerabilities are beginning to challenge the mode of economic life that has dominated for the last few centuries. In the process the overarching formulations of modernity, postulating a separation of humanity and environment, nature and culture, are collapsing. The shift from security as protection to a focus on making new worlds, from environmental protection to ecological production, is encapsulated in the discussion of the Anthropocene.

The ontological shift that the Anthropocene formulation implies, a matter of carefully inhabiting a small planet rather than carelessly expropriating materials from a big one, requires nothing less than a fundamental reformulation of global politics if a stabilized earth system is to be the world of the future (Rockström and Klum 2015). Without the emergence of modes of governance actively making flourishing ecosystems at all scales, the prospects for human civilization in the long run are bleak. This change of focus towards inhabiting a small vulnerable planet requires overcoming at least the worst aspects of the autistic geopolitics of the present, the protectionism, xenophobia and assumptions of autonomy and "firepower" as the premise of security provision. Extending notions of mutual restraint, a negarchy relating in particular to fossil fuels, and to related extractivist activities for key ecological services, will probably have to be complemented with production coordination well beyond existing trading and environmental agreements. Simply banning the mining and burning of coal would be a good start, and a treaty to that effect is clearly in order (Burke and Fishel 2020). But beyond this a clear focus on eliminating the use of fossil fuels *tout court* is key; much of the discussion of net zero emissions by 2050 is more about net rather than zero, allowing much wriggle room and arguments about offsets, carbon removal technologies and related matters (Buck 2021).

While these policy issues are fairly obvious, the future of international relations as an intellectual concern, and as a scholarly agenda, is very much in doubt. The formulations of security at the heart of Carr's (1939) and Morgenthau's (1948) notions of power are premised on a world without an overarching authority, a matter technically of anarchy. But if the climate crisis and the other dimensions of the planetary inhabitability dilemma are to be solved, then this premise, of the inevitability of faction, the perpetuation of territorially circumscribed entities as those primarily in need of security, has to be challenged by scholarly researchers as well as activists. While Thucydides may have been historically accurate in the Melian dialogue, where, to roughly paraphrase, he suggested that the powerful do what they want and the weak suffer what they must, the question this implies is how to change this order of things now that the scale of human activities clearly endangers civilizational continuity in the long run?

Carr (1939) and Morgenthau (1948) may have been skeptical about international institutions and notions of law without global enforcement, but nuclear weapons, ecological disruption and the dangers of technology pose the question once again now in the aftermath of the COVID-19 pandemic, in especially pressing terms. While classical realists might assume that states rise and fall, strive for primacy and are defeated in the great game of power, they were able to assume that the setting for the game would persist. That, as the discussion of the findings of earth system science in this volume shows, is no longer a valid assumption. As Reynolds (2019a) argues, Morgenthau's response to hydrogen bombs was to insist that in these new circumstances states had to cooperate on key issues of common interest, and in terms of climate change such a realist response now requires cooperative system preservation, and as such, ambitious efforts at low carbon innovation.

Rethinking environmental security thus requires rethinking many other things, and crucially shifting the primary formulation of ontological security to the planet itself, rather than territorially bounded entities with a supposedly common identity. This isn't a matter of reworking idealism and invoking some universal humanity; now it's simply recognizing the novel ecological context for powers, great and small. Playing the great game of power requires a functional earth system in which to operate. But that is now in danger precisely because of the current modes of playing the game, and the multiple forms of power that operate to stymie innovation and perpetuate dangerous modes of fossil fuel powered modernity (Stoddard, Anderson, Capstick et al. 2021). This is not just the issue of nuclear weapons and the destructive capabilities of firepower in military mode, but is also the issue of the destructive capabilities of firepower in civilian mode too; mass consumption societies based on fossil fuels, with built in obsolescence in its products, are calling into question a functional earth system.

One of the most difficult parts of the discussion about environmental security lies precisely here in the need to reconsider key elements of the identities of Western consumers (Gough 2017) and their construction in terms of status consumption and freedom represented in terms of the "right" to an affluent lifestyle premised on using vast quantities of energy and frequently discarding numerous "disposable" or "single use" products. But in terms of foreign policy and climate change these will need to be addressed by many state leaders if security in any meaningful sense is to be provided in the novel circumstances of the Anthropocene. As much of this book suggests, technology alone will not provide security from what is coming, and the identities that security discourse engages need to be rearticulated to consider citizenships in new ecological ways too.

International relations has mostly addressed these issues by focusing on the construction of regimes and institutions that ostensibly govern global environmental matters. But Radoslav Dimitrov's (2020) argument about empty and decoy institutions points to the limits of this as an effective mode of governance and poses the question of what else international relations scholars ought to investigate if they are to take seriously the premises of planetary social thought. Such recontextualizations suggest clearly that modes of inquiry inherited from the past in academic institutions need an update, and quickly. In so far as international relations is an Anglo-American academic preoccupation, it is not unreasonable to argue that effectively this mode of thought has functioned as the conceptual infrastructure of American hegemony. As that hegemony erodes, not least with the rise of China beginning to challenge world order, it may also be the case that new modes of intellectual engagement are now timely. If international relations cannot encompass the challenge of the Anthropocene (Burke, Fishel, Mitchell et al. 2016), then it may well be that novel interpretations from outside its canon are what will replace it. It is especially noteworthy that Clark and Szerszynski's (2021) engagement with planetary social thought doesn't cite any international relations scholarship. The mutual silence, where international relations ignores the Anthropocene discussion (Kelly 2021) and planetary thinking ignores international relations, works both ways apparently!

The overarching argument in this book is one that shifts the focus from security as protection, with its implicit geographical formulations of "our" spaces as threatened from "outside", to security as production, on literally what kind of world is being made by human actions. Hence the need to focus on how financial investments are directed to make specific things. Economic security isn't just a matter of ensuring supplies and access to markets any more; now it has to be about taking the larger questions of an increasingly artificial world into consideration and thinking about how economic activity is shaping the ecosphere so that it can continue to function as a habitat for humans in the long run. Failure to do so raises all the prospects of conflict and the nightmare scenarios of war over access to food, water and other materials.

A crucial question hanging over all this discussion is whether lessons from small scale peacebuilding efforts can be scaled up. If premodern states frequently disintegrated as a result of natural catastrophes, as some of the discussion in Chapter 4 suggested, the worrisome thing is that hothouse world transitions might lead to the same kind of disintegration of the global system (Homer-Dixon, Walker, Biggs et al. 2015), and the resort to force as things fall apart in attempts by elites to maintain control over at least some parts of the earth. In a world of nuclear arsenals, artificial intelligence and genetic engineering, clearly the lessons of environmental peacemaking on the small scale have to be scaled up to the international system. And in the longer run Deudney's (2020) warning about interplanetary warfare may have to be considered too as the reverse side of the space colonization argument. While colonization suggests existential risks have to be tackled by humanity becoming a spacefaring civilization with multiple planetary homes, Deudney warns that the long term potential for conflict among them, with earth at a serious disadvantage because of its relatively large gravity well, needs consideration too.

More so than this however is the large question of changes in world order in contemporary times, and whether the end of the American world order can be comprehended in international affairs as an opportunity to rethink at least some of the cultural premises of intrinsic rivalry that structure so much of global security thinking (Acharya 2014). One wonders if the Chinese notions of ecocities and ecoregions can be scaled up to the global reconsideration of environmental security (Yanarella and Levine 2021) while simultaneously accelerating the reduction of the use of coal in particular in its energy mix. While the Biden administration's accession to the White House promised a new beginning in international politics, what was on offer was clearly in many ways a return to the past when the United States as a superpower ran an international order very much to its benefit. In Andrew Bacevich's (2010) pithy formulation it was a return to *Washington Rules*, although one encouraging development from the Glasgow COP in 2021 was an announcement that China and the United States would cooperate on international climate change issues regardless of their other disagreements.

A more nuanced foreign policy, one that doesn't assume zero sum games on so many themes, might be welcomed, but the response to the oddly inconsistent Trump administration has in many ways been an attempt to return to the status quo ante, albeit with somewhat more coherence on the theme of climate, if not energy (Selby 2019b). Whether this is understood as nostalgia or stubbornness is much less important than recognizing that the novel circumstances of climate change and related disruptions require a more fundamental shake up of global politics to deal with shared dangers. But to do so will need a rethink of security, in particular where assumptions of great power rivalries as the name of the game are challenged by a more comprehensive reevaluation of the sources of American insecurity. The long term existential threat to much of the Western world isn't a rising China; it's a destabilized climate system and the nightmare of a runaway series of positive feedback loops in that system that leads down the path to a radically destabilized hothouse earth.

An American fixation on China as a geopolitical rival precludes a more comprehensive engagement with the novel ecological circumstances that now present both immediate threats of local disasters and longer term possibilities of major disruptions. But this is clearly what any political doctrine worthy of the name realism now requires (Dalby 2013b). Likewise, where much of the discussion about catastrophic disruptions from climate change and biodiversity loss, as well as pollution, ozone depletion and other earth system disruptions, links up with speculations about civilizational collapse, it is fairly obvious that some key facets of modernity will collapse, one way or another. Most obviously this relates to fossil fuels and the energy system that powers much contemporary human life. The activists pushing the divestment movement in the West in recent years are quite clear about the fact that the fossil fuel industry presents an existential threat, one that needs to be countered directly precisely to prevent future accelerating disruptions that endanger one and all (Mangat, Dalby and Paterson 2018). In so far as environmental security is concerned, the collapse of the fossil fuel industry is to be welcomed, assuming that it can be done peacefully to minimize the harm done in the process.

While the much cited Joseph Tainter (1988) formulation of societies collapsing when they lose complexity suggests that security should be about maintaining that complexity and preserving the existing social order, in the case of environmental security, endangered not by resource shortages but by the indirect consequences of greenhouse gas pollution, this formulation would not seem to fit present circumstances. Ever greater complexity appears more likely to make societies more brittle in the face of this challenge. Larger resource throughputs make supply chains ever more vulnerable to disruptions, as the pandemic response confusion in the global economy in 2020 demonstrated. The blockage of the Suez Canal in 2021 when the *Ever Given* container ship ran aground emphasized the simple fact that this level of complexity may be unsustainable, especially when pressures compound as ecological disruptions become more severe.

Once again, what needs to be secured is the ability to adapt, and overly complex systems, while efficacious for some purposes, are vulnerable to disruptions precisely because so many things have to work correctly for the whole system to function. Likewise the COVID-19 pandemic has shown clearly that the tradeoff between efficiency and resilience leaves societies vulnerable (Dalby 2022). Just in time deliveries revealed the absence of robustness, and a complete lack of "just in case" security planning. Security can no longer be about perpetuating past practices; non-stationarity requires flexibility and robust institutions not reliant on firepower.

FUTURE GEOPOLITICS

At the largest of geopolitical scales too there is a need to think through questions of global order and the possibilities of an Eastphalia as China, India and other growing states try to shape what will hopefully be a new peaceful global order (Uesugi and Richmond 2021). A rising China and dramatic changes elsewhere in Asia pose the question of how the larger future order may be shaped. While historically the Western nations have been responsible for setting climate change in motion, and the wealthy among their populations for using the majority of fossil fuels, now as China rapidly urbanizes, and uses vast amounts of concrete in the process, in addition to coal powered electricity, the future is increasingly a matter of Asian actions. How the future of the global energy economy is shaped is increasingly being driven by Chinese decisions about urbanization (Taylor, O'Brien and O'Keefe 2020). In the lead up to the 2021 COP in Scotland, President Xi of China did announce an end to foreign investments in coal electricity generation projects, a move welcomed by climate activists, but the larger trajectory of Chinese energy futures remained murky despite their announcements that fossil fuel use would peak in coming decades. Building the promised ecocities would seem to be essential both to make them resilient to extreme weather and to reduce fossil fuel use to power them.

These decisions about energy futures are in part also being shaped by fears of geopolitical confrontation with the United States, and the need for energy security in the face of possible sanctions or possible coercive trade restriction attempts by a declining American hegemon (Boyd 2021). This in turn raises the largest questions of the future of global order, and whether Western notions of an international peace architecture are likely to hold in coming decades or whether the traditional Westphalian schemes may be transcended by novel Asian initiatives to provide global leadership in the absence of transition initiatives from elsewhere in the system. There are few indications that this will be forthcoming in the near future. Nonetheless it is clearly the case that if the continued relative rise of Chinese economic capabilities persists, this is key to the future configuration of geopolitics, something that now has to be understood as both changing the relative importance of political actors on the playing field of international relations and, simultaneously, dramatically altering that field itself.

Leo Panitch and Sam Gindin (2012) end their overview volume on the history of global capitalism by focusing on the possibilities of remaking international financial architecture to organize the global economy in a much more sustainable mode. As the financial crisis of 2008 suggested, and the extraordinary interventions by central banks in response to the shutdown of large parts of the global economy in early 2020 in response to the COVID-19 pandemic confirmed, there are all sorts of financial possibilities available once the prevailing neoliberal assumptions about the limited role of central banks in constraining inflation are abandoned and shaping financial arrangements becomes the priority instead (Tooze 2021). While this new role for central banks mostly played to the advantage of large corporations and the wealthy during the pandemic, the point is that such measures could be reoriented to link money supply to climate related matters, and to the reduction of carbon fuels and the making of ecologically fecund landscapes.

Major financial institutions are key to the large scale investments that create future political orders, and as such, now in the Anthropocene, are shaping much more than just a political economy that combines states and capitalism (Nitzan and Bichler 2009). But that said, central banks and investment institutions have been slow to concern themselves with the largest matters of planetary sustainability and tackle ecological changes as more than tangential risks in investment calculations. Likewise climate change discussions have frequently been dominated by the fossil fuels part of the energy industry, as the large delegations to the COP in Glasgow in late 2021 illustrated once again, and their dominance in the policy debates has to be challenged directly in attempts to rethink environmental security. The gap between the amount of fossil fuels being produced and what is needed to constrain rapid climate change remains very large (Stockholm Environment Institute 2021). Survival of resilient ecosystems now has to be the prize, not the mastery over either nature or putative political rivals.

Hanging over all of this discussion of environmental security is the question of how to build economies that allow humans to live well without burning stuff to do so. Security is now about the ability to adapt to changing circumstances and to simultaneously shape economic activity to focus on human needs within planetary boundaries (Raworth 2017), not about the ever larger appropriation of firepower to dominate external environments. In terms of the scholarly study of international relations, where earlier generations of realists worried about the firepower of nuclear arsenals, the current generation now has to worry about the consequences of the unrestricted use of firepower in its other sense, as lithic fire and extensive burning of fossil fuels. Environmental security now requires engaging with firepower in all its manifestations; human survival depends on coming to terms with the consequences of partially domesticating combustion, a key geophysical force in the planetary system, and dramatically reducing its future use in the novel circumstances it has recently wrought.

References

Abatayo, A.L., Bosetti, V., Casari, M. et al. (2020). Solar geoengineering may lead to excessive cooling and high strategic uncertainty. *Proceedings of the National Academy of Sciences*, 117(24), pp. 13393–13398.

Acharya, A. (2014). *The End of the American World Order*. Cambridge: Polity.

Agarwal, A. and Narain, S. (1991). *Global Warming in an Unequal World: A Case of Environmental Colonialism*. New Delhi: Centre for Science and Environment.

Agnew, J. (2020). Taking back control? The myth of territorial sovereignty and the Brexit fiasco. *Territory, Politics, Governance*, 8(2), pp. 259–272.

Albert, M. (2020). Beyond continuationism: climate change, economic growth and the future of world (dis)order. *Cambridge Review of International Affairs*, Latest Articles.

Allan, B.B. (2017). Producing the climate: states, scientists, and the constitution of global governance. *International Organization*, 71, pp. 131–162.

Alley, R. (2004). Abrupt climate change. *Scientific American*, November, pp. 62–69.

Allison, G. (2017). *Destined for War: Can America and China Escape Thucydides's Trap?* New York: Houghton Mifflin.

Al-Rodhan, N.R.F. ed. (2009). *Potential Global Strategic Catastrophes*. Zurich: Lit.

Alvarez, A. (2021). *Unstable Ground: Climate Change, Conflict, and Genocide*. Lanham, MD: Rowman and Littlefield.

Amarel-Zettler, L., Zettler, E. and Mincer, T. (2020). Ecology of the plastisphere. *Nature Reviews: Microbiology*, 18, pp. 139–151.

Andersen, G. (2020). *Climate Fiction and Cultural Analysis: A New Perspective on Life in the Anthropocene*. London and New York: Routledge.

Asefi-Najafabady, S., Villegas-Ortiz, L. and Morgan, J. (2020). The failure of integrated assessment models as a response to "climate emergency" and ecological breakdown: the emperor has no clothes. *Globalizations*, 18(17), pp. 1–11.

Ashworth, L. (2014). *A History of International Thought: From the Origins of the Modern State to Academic International Relations*. London and New York: Routledge.

Ashworth, L. (2021). A forgotten environmental international relations: Derwent Whittlesey's international thought. *Global Studies Quarterly*, 1(2), ksab006.

Bacevich, A.J. (2010). *Washington Rules: America's Path to Permanent War*. New York: Metropolitan.

Bacevich, A.J. (2013). *The New American Militarism: How Americans Are Seduced by War* (updated edition). Oxford: Oxford University Press.

Baechler, G. (1998). Why environmental transformation causes violence: a synthesis. *Environmental Change and Security Project Report 4*, pp. 24–44.

Bakker, K. and Ritts, M. (2018). Smart earth: a meta-review and implications for environmental governance. *Global Environmental Change*, 52, pp. 201–211.

Bales, K. and Sovacool, B. (2021). From forests to factories: how modern slavery deepens the crisis of climate change. *Energy Research and Social Science*, 77, 102096.

Barnett, J. (2001). *The Meaning of Environmental Security: Ecological Politics and Policy in the New Security Era*. London: Zed Books.

Barnett, J. (2019). Global environmental change I: climate resilient peace? *Progress in Human Geography*, 43(5), pp. 927–936.

Barnosky, A.D., Hadly, E., Bascompte, J. et al. (2012). Approaching a state shift in earth's biosphere. *Nature*, 486, pp. 52–58.

Barrett, P., Bogmans, C., Carton, B. et al. (2020). Mitigating climate change—growth and distribution-friendly strategies. *IMF Economic Outlook*, October, pp. 85–113.

Baskin, J. (2019). *Geoengineering, the Anthropocene and the End of Nature*. London and New York: Palgrave Macmillan.

Baviscar, A. (2005). *In the Belly of the River: Tribal Conflicts over Development in the Narmada Valley* (2nd edition). Oxford: Oxford University Press.

Belcher, O., Bigger, P., Neimark, B. and Kennelly, C. (2020). Hidden carbon costs of the "everywhere war": logistics, geopolitical ecology, and the carbon boot-print of the US military. *Transactions of the Institute of British Geographers*, 45(1), pp. 65–80.

Bendell, J. (2018). *Deep Adaptation: A Map for Navigating Climate Tragedy*. IFLAS Occasional Paper 2.

Bendell, J. and Read, R. eds (2021). *Deep Adaptation: Navigating the Realities of Climate Chaos*. Cambridge: Polity.

Benner, A.-K., Rothe, D., Ullstrom, S. and Stripple, J. (2019). *Violent Climate Imaginaries: Science-Fiction-Politics*. Hamburg: University of Hamburg Institute for Peace Research and Security Policy.

Benzie, M. and Persson, Å. (2019). Governing borderless climate risks: moving beyond the territorial framing of adaptation. *International Environmental Agreements: Politics, Law and Economics*, 19, pp. 369–393.

Bernstein, S. and Hoffman, M. (2018). The politics of decarbonization and the catalytic impact of subnational climate experiments. *Policy Sciences*, 51, pp. 189–211.

Beuret, N. (2021). Containing climate change: the new governmental strategies of catastrophic environments. *Environment and Planning E: Nature and Space*, 4(3), pp. 818–837.

Bichler, S. and Nitzan, J. (2004). Dominant capital and the new wars. *Journal of World Systems Research*, 10(2), pp. 255–327.

Biermann, F. and Moller, I. (2019). Rich man's solution? Climate engineering discourses and the marginalization of the Global South. *International Environmental Agreements: Politics, Law and Economics*, 19, pp. 151–167.

Biermann, F., Oomen, J., Gupta, A. et al. (2022). Solar engineering: the case for an international non-use agreement. *WIRES Climate Change*, Early View.

Blackstock, J.J. and Low, S. eds (2019). *Geoengineering Our Climate? Ethics, Politics, and Governance*. London: Routledge.

Blight, J. and Lang, J. (2018). *Dark beyond Darkness: The Cuban Missile Crisis as History, Warning and Catalyst*. Lanham, MD: Rowman and Littlefield.

Blomley, N. (2019). The territorialization of property in land: space, power and practice. *Territory, Politics, Governance*, 7(2), pp. 233–249.

Bloomberg, M. and Pope, C. (2017). *Climate of Hope: How Cities, Businesses, and Citizens Can Save the Planet*. New York: St. Martin's Press.

Bloomfield, L.S.P., McIntosh, T.L. and Lambin, E.F. (2020). Habitat fragmentation, livelihood behaviours, and contact between people and nonhuman primates in Africa. *Landscape Ecology*, 35, pp. 985–1000.

Booth, K. (1979). *Strategy and Ethnocentrism*. London: Croom Helm.

Booth, K. (2007). *Theory of World Security*. London: Routledge.

Boroway, I. (2019). Before UNEP: who was in charge of the global environment? The struggle for institutional responsibility 1968–72. *Journal of Global History*, 14(1), pp. 87–106.

Bostrom, N. (2013). Existential risk prevention as global priority. *Global Policy*, 4(1), pp. 15–31.

Boyd, R. (2021). *The Combined Transitions of Great Power Politics and the Global Energy System: A Comparative Analysis of China, the United States and Russia*. Wilfrid Laurier University. Unpublished Ph.D. Dissertation.

Brand, U. and Wissen, M. (2021). *The Imperial Mode of Living: Everyday Life and the Ecological Crisis of Capitalism*. London: Verso.

Brauch, H.G. (2021). Peace ecology in the Anthropocene, in U. Oswald Spring and H.G. Brauch, eds. *Decolonizing Conflicts, Security, Peace, Gender, Environment and Development in the Anthropocene*. Cham: Springer, pp. 51–185.

Brauch, H.G., Oswald Spring, U., Grin, J. and Scheffran, J. eds (2016). *Handbook on Sustainability Transition and Sustainable Peace*. Cham: Springer.

Bretthauer, J.M. (2017). *Climate Change and Resource Conflict: The Role of Scarcity*. London: Routledge.

Briggs, C.M. and Matejova, M. (2019). *Disaster Security: Using Intelligence and Military Planning for Energy and Environmental Risks*. Cambridge: Cambridge University Press.

Brosig, M., Frawley, P., Hill, A. et al. (2019). *Implications of Climate Change for the U.S. Army*. United States Army War College.

Brown, H. (1954). *The Challenge of Man's Future*. New York: Viking.

Brundtland, G.H. (1993). The environment, security and development, in *World Armaments and Disarmaments*, SIPRI Yearbook. Oxford: Oxford University Press, pp. 15–26.

Brunn, S. (2011). *Engineering Earth: The Impacts of Megaengineering Projects*. Dordrecht Springer.

Brunnée, J. and Streck, C. (2013). The UNFCCC as a negotiation forum: towards common but more differentiated responsibilities. *Climate Policy*, 13(5), pp. 589–607.

Buck, H.J. (2019). *After Geoengineering: Climate Tragedy, Repair, and Restoration*. London: Verso.

Buck, H.J. (2021). *Ending Fossil Fuels: Why Net Zero Is Not Enough*. London: Verso.

Buhaug, H. (2015). Climate–conflict research: some reflections on the way forward? *WIREs Climate Change*, 6(3), pp. 269–275.

Bull, H. (1977). *The Anarchical Society: A Study of Order in World Politics*. London: Macmillan.

Burke, A. and Fishel, S. (2020). A coal elimination treaty 2030: fast tracking climate change mitigation, global health and security. *Earth System Governance*, 3, 100046.

Burke, A., Fishel, S., Mitchell, A. et al. (2016). Planet politics: a manifesto from the end of IR. *Millennium*, 44(3), pp. 499–523.

Burns, W.C.G. and Strauss, A.L. eds (2013). *Climate Change Geoengineering: Philosophical Perspectives, Legal Issues and Governance Frameworks*. Cambridge: Cambridge University Press.

Busby, J. (2018). Taking stock: the field of climate and security. *Current Climate Change Reports*, 44(4), pp. 338–346.

Busby, J. (2022). *States and Nature*. Cambridge: Cambridge University Press.

Buscher, B. (2013). *Transforming the Frontier: Peace Parks and the Politics of Neoliberal Conservation in Southern Africa*. Durham, NC: Duke University Press.

Buxton, N. and Hayes, B. eds (2016). *The Secure and the Dispossessed*. London: Pluto.
Buzan, B. (1991). *People, States and Fear: An Agenda for International Security Studies in the Post-Cold War Era*. Boulder, CO: Lynne Rienner.
Buzan, B. and Wæver, O. (2003). *Regions and Powers: The Structure of International Security*. Cambridge: Cambridge University Press.
Buzan, B. and Wæver, O. (2009). Macrosecuritisation and security constellations: reconsidering scale in securitisation theory. *Review of International Studies*, 35, pp. 253–276.
Buzan, B., Wæver, O. and de Wilde, J. (1998). *Security: A New Framework for Analysis*. Boulder, CO: Lynne Rienner.
Byers, M., Franks, K. and Gage, A. (2017). The internationalization of climate damages litigation. *Washington Journal of Environmental Law and Policy*, 7(2), pp. 264–319.
Caesar, L., McCarthy, G.D., Thornally, D.J.R. et al. (2021). Current Atlantic Meridional Overturning Circulation weakest in last millennium. *Nature Geoscience*, 14, pp. 118–120.
Campbell, K.M., Gulledge, J., McNeill, J.R. et al. (2007). *The Age of Consequences: The Foreign Policy and National Security Implications of Global Climate Change*. Washington, DC: Center for Strategic and International Studies.
Carr, E.H. (1939). *The Twenty Years' Crisis: An Introduction to the Study of International Relations*. London: Macmillan.
Carson, R. (1962). *Silent Spring*. Boston, MA: Houghton Mifflin.
Ceballos, G., Ehrlich, P.R. and Dirzo, R. (2017). Biological annihilation via the ongoing sixth mass extinction signalled by vertebrate population losses and declines. *Proceedings of the National Academy of Sciences*, 114(30), pp. E6089–E6096.
Chatterjee, P. and Finger, M. (1994). *The Earth Brokers: Power, Politics, and World Development*. London: Routledge.
Chaturvedi, S. and Doyle, T. (2015). *Climate Terror: A Critical Geopolitics of Climate Change*. London and New York: Palgrave Macmillan.
Chris, R. (2016). *Systems Thinking for Geoengineering Policy*. London: Routledge.
Churchill, W.S. (1923). *The World Crisis*. New York: Scribner's.
Clapp, J. (2020). The problem with growing corporate concentration and power in the global food system. *Nature Food*, 2, pp. 404–408.
Clark, N. and Szerszynski, B. (2021). *Planetary Social Thought: The Anthropocene Challenge to the Social Sciences*. Cambridge: Polity.
CNA Corporation (2007). *National Security and the Threat of Climate Change*. Alexandria, VA: CNA Corporation.
CNA Military Advisory Board (2014). *National Security and the Accelerating Risks of Climate Change*. Alexandria, VA: CNA Corporation.
Coady, D., Parry, I., Sears, L. and Shang, B. (2017). How large are global fossil fuel subsidies? *World Development*, 91, pp. 11–27.
Cockerill, K., Armstrong, M., Richter, J. and Okie, J. (2017). *Environmental Realism: Challenging Solutions*. London: Palgrave Macmillan.
Cohen, D.A. (2021). New York City as "fortress of solitude" after Hurricane Sandy: a relational sociology of extreme weather's relationship to climate politics. *Environmental Politics*, 30(5), pp. 687–707.
Cohen, S.F. (1985). *Rethinking the Soviet Experience: Politics and History since 1917*. New York: Oxford University Press.
Cohn, C. (1987). Sex and death in the rational world of defense intellectuals. *Signs: Journal of Women in Culture and Society*, 12, pp. 687–718.

Cole, H.S.D., Freeman, C., Jahoda, M. and Pavitt, K.L.R. eds (1973). *Models of Doom: A Critique of the Limits to Growth*. New York: Universe.
Commoner, B. (1971). *The Closing Circle*. New York: Knopf.
Conca, K. (2015). *An Unfinished Foundation: The United Nations and Global Environmental Governance*. Oxford: Oxford University Press.
Conca, K. and Dabelko, G. eds (2002). *Environmental Peacemaking*. Baltimore, MD: Johns Hopkins University Press.
Conway, P.R. (2019). *The Historical Ontology of Environment: From the Unity of Nature to the Birth of Geopolitics*. Aberystwyth University. Unpublished Ph.D. Dissertation.
Cosgrove, D. (1994). Contested global visions: one-world, whole earth, and the Apollo space photographs. *Annals of the Association of American Geographers*, 84(2), pp. 270–294.
Cowen, D. (2014). *The Deadly Life of Logistics: Mapping Violence in Global Trade*. Minneapolis, MN: University of Minnesota Press.
Cronon, W. (1991). *Nature's Metropolis: Chicago and the Great West*. New York: Norton.
Crosby, A. (1986). *Ecological Imperialism*. Cambridge: Cambridge University Press.
Crosby, A. (2002). *Throwing Fire: Projectile Technology through History*. Cambridge: Cambridge University Press.
Crutzen, P.J. and Birks, J.W. (1983). The atmosphere after a nuclear war: twilight at noon, in J. Peterson, ed. *The Aftermath: The Human and Ecological Consequences of Nuclear War*. New York: Pantheon, pp. 73–96.
Dabelko, G.D., Herzer, L., Null, S. et al. (2013). *Backdraft: The Conflict Potential of Climate Change Adaptation and Mitigation*. Washington, DC: Woodrow Wilson International Center for Scholars.
Daggett, C. (2018). Petro-masculinity: fossil fuels and authoritarian desire. *Millennium: Journal of International Studies*, 47(1), pp. 25–44.
Daggett, C. (2021). Energy and domination: contesting the fossil fuel myth of fuel expansion. *Environmental Politics*, 30(4), pp. 644–662.
Dahl, E.J. (2001). Naval innovation: from coal to oil. *Joint Forces Quarterly*, 27, pp. 50–56.
Dalby, S. (1991). Dealignment discourse: thinking beyond the blocs. *Current Research in Peace and Violence*, 13(3), pp. 140–155.
Dalby, S. (2002). *Environmental Security*. Minneapolis, MN: University of Minnesota Press.
Dalby, S. (2003). Geopolitical identities: Arctic ecology and global consumption. *Geopolitics*, 8(1), pp. 181–203.
Dalby, S. (2009a). Geopolitics, the revolution in military affairs and the Bush doctrine. *International Politics*, 46(2/3), pp. 234–252.
Dalby, S. (2009b). *Security and Environmental Change*. Cambridge: Polity.
Dalby, S. (2013a). Biopolitics and climate security in the Anthropocene. *Geoforum*, 49, pp. 184–192.
Dalby, S. (2013b). Realism and geopolitics, in K. Dodds, M. Kuus and J. Sharp, eds. *The Ashgate Research Companion to Critical Geopolitics*. Farnham: Ashgate Publishers, pp. 33–47.
Dalby, S. (2018). Firepower: geopolitical cultures in the Anthropocene. *Geopolitics*, 23(3), pp. 718–742.
Dalby, S. (2020a). National security in a rapidly changing world. *Balsillie Papers*, 3(2), 10pp.

Dalby, S. (2020b). *Anthropocene Geopolitics: Globalization, Security, Sustainability*. Ottawa: University of Ottawa Press.

Dalby, S. (2020c). Resilient earth: Gaia, geopolitics and the Anthropocene, in D. Chandler, K. Grove and S. Wakefield, eds. *Resilience in the Anthropocene: Governance and Politics at the End of the World*. New York: Routledge, pp. 22–36.

Dalby, S. (2021). Unsustainable borders? Globalization in a climate disrupted world. *Borders in Globalization Review*, 2(2), pp. 26–37.

Dalby, S. (2022). Pandemic geopolitics in the Anthropocene, in S.D. Brunn and D. Gilbreath, eds. *COVID-19 and an Emerging World of Ad Hoc Geographies*. Cham: Springer.

Dalby, S., Horton, S., Mahon, R. and Thomaz, D. eds (2019). *Achieving the Sustainable Development Goals: Global Governance Challenges*. London: Routledge.

Dasmann, R.F. (1971). *Planet in Peril?: Man and the Biosphere Today*. Harmondsworth: Penguin.

Dauody, M. (2020). *The Origins of the Syrian Conflict: Climate Change and Human Security*. Cambridge: Cambridge University Press.

Dauvergne, P. (2008). *Shadows of Consumption: Consequences for the Global Environment*. Cambridge, MA: MIT Press.

Dauvergne, P. (2016). *Environmentalism of the Rich*. Cambridge, MA: MIT Press.

Dauvergne, P. (2021). The globalization of artificial intelligence: consequences for the politics of environmentalism. *Globalizations*, 18(2), pp. 285–299.

Davenport, C. (2018). *The Space Barons: Elon Musk, Jeff Bezos and the Quest to Colonize the Cosmos*. New York: Public Affairs.

Davis, K.F., Koo, H.I., Dell'Angelo, J. et al. (2020). Tropical forest loss enhanced by large-scale land acquisitions. *Nature Geoscience*, 13, pp. 482–488.

Davis, M. (2001). *Late Victorian Holocausts: El Nino Famines and the Making of the Third World*. London: Verso.

Dehm, J. (2021). *Reconsidering REDD+: Authority, Power and Law in the Green Economy*. Cambridge: Cambridge University Press.

Deligiannis, T. (2020). *Environmental and Demographic Change and Rural Violence in Peru: A Case Study of the District of Chuschi, Ayacucho*. University of Toronto. Unpublished Ph.D. Dissertation.

Dell'Agnese, E. (2021). *Ecocritical Geopolitics: Popular Culture and Environmental Discourse*. London and New York: Routledge.

Detges, A. (2017). *Climate and Conflict: Reviewing the Statistical Evidence, A Summary for Policymakers*. Berlin: Adelphi.

Deudney, D. (1983). *Whole Earth Security: A Geopolitics of Peace*. Washington, DC: Worldwatch Institute, Worldwatch Paper 55.

Deudney, D. (1990). The case against linking environmental degradation and national security. *Millennium*, 19, pp. 461–476.

Deudney, D. (2007). *Bounding Power: Republican Security Theory from the Polis to the Global Village*. Princeton, NJ: Princeton University Press.

Deudney, D. (2018). All together now: geography, the three cosmopolitanisms, and planetary earth, in L. Cabrera, ed. *Institutional Cosmopolitanism*. Oxford: Oxford University Press, pp. 253–276.

Deudney, D. (2020). *Dark Skies: Space Expansionism, Planetary Geopolitics, and the Ends of Humanity*. Oxford: Oxford University Press.

Diamond, J. (2005). *Collapse: How Societies Choose to Fail or Succeed*. New York: Viking.

Dillon, M. (1996). *Politics of Security: Towards a Political Philosophy of Continental Thought*. London: Routledge.
Dimitrov, R. (2020). Empty institutions in global environmental politics. *International Studies Review*, 22(3), pp. 626–650.
Dinar, S. and Dinar, A. (2017). *International Water Scarcity and Variability: Managing Resource Use across Political Boundaries*. Berkeley, CA: University of California Press.
Diringer, E. and Perciasepe, B. (2020). The climate awakening of global capital. *Bulletin of the Atomic Scientists*, 76(5), pp. 233–237.
Donges, J.F., Lucht, W., Müller-Hansen, F. and Steffen, W. (2017). The technosphere in earth system analysis: a coevolutionary perspective. *The Anthropocene Review*, 4(1), pp. 23–33.
Drahos, P. (2021). *Survival Governance: Energy and Climate in the Chinese Century*. Oxford: Oxford University Press.
Duffy, R. (2014). Waging a war to save biodiversity: the rise of militarized conservation. *International Affairs*, 90(4), pp. 819–834.
Duffy, R. (2016). War by conservation. *Geoforum*, 69, pp. 238–248.
Dumaine, C. (2021). The health of nations in an age of global risks: COVID-19's implications for new paradigms of human rights and international security and cooperation. *Georgetown Journal of International Affairs*, 22, pp. 153–161.
Dumaine, C. and Mintzer, I. (2015). Confronting climate change and reframing security. *SAIS Review of International Affairs*, 35, pp. 5–16.
Dunlap, A. (2017). The "solution" is now the "problem": wind energy, colonisation and the "genocide-ecocide nexus" in the Isthmus of Tehuantepec, Oaxaca. *The International Journal of Human Rights*, 22(4), pp. 550–573.
Dunlap, A. and Fairhead, J. (2014). The militarisation and marketisation of nature: an alternative lens to "climate-conflict". *Geopolitics*, 19, pp. 937–961.
Dyer, G. (2008). *Climate Wars*. Toronto: Random House of Canada.
Eckersley, R. (2017). Geopolitan democracy in the Anthropocene. *Political Studies*, 65(4), pp. 983–999.
Edwards, P.N. (2010). *A Vast Machine: Computer Models, Climate Data, and the Politics of Global Warming*. Cambridge, MA: MIT Press.
Ehrlich, P. (1968). *The Population Bomb*. New York: Ballantine.
Ehrlich, P., Harte, J., Harwell, M.A. et al. (1983). Long-term biological consequences of nuclear war. *Science*, 222(4630), pp. 1293–1300.
Elbe, S. (2009). *Security and Global Health*. Cambridge: Polity.
Elden, S. (2013). *The Birth of Territory*. Chicago: University of Chicago Press.
Elhacham, E., Liad, B.-U., Grozovski, J. et al. (2020). Global human-made mass exceeds all living biomass. *Nature*, 588, pp. 442–444.
Ellis, E.C. (2011). Anthropogenic transformation of the terrestrial biosphere. *Philosophical Transactions of the Royal Society A*, 369, pp. 1010–1035.
Extinction Rebellion (2019). *This Is Not a Drill*. London: Penguin.
Fairbairn, M. (2020). *Fields of Gold: Financing the Global Land Rush*. Ithaca, NY: Cornell University Press.
Falk, R. (1971). *This Endangered Planet: Prospects and Proposals for Human Survival*. New York: Random House.
Falk, R. (1999). *Predatory Globalization: A Critique*. Cambridge: Polity.
Falkner, R. (2016). The Paris Agreement and the new logic of international climate politics. *International Affairs*, 92(5), pp. 1107–1125.

Farish, M. (2010). *The Contours of America's Cold War*. Minneapolis, MN: University of Minnesota Press.

Feshbach, M. and Friendly, A. (1992). *Ecocide in the USSR: Health and Nature under Siege*. New York: Basic Books.

Finger, M. (1991). The military, the nation state and the environment. *The Ecologist*, 21(5), pp. 220–225.

Fink, L. (2020). *A Fundamental Reshaping of Finance: A Letter to CEOs*. BlackRock Corporation.

Flannery, T. (1995). *The Future Eaters: An Ecological History of the Australasian Lands and People*. New York: George Braziller.

Flavelle, C. (2020). Wildfires hasten another climate crisis: homeowners who can't get insurance. *New York Times*, 2 September.

Funk, C. (2021). *Drought, Flood, Fire: How Climate Change Contributes to Catastrophes*. Cambridge: Cambridge University Press.

Gaffney, O., Crona, B., Dauriach, A. and Galaz, V. (2018). *Sleeping Financial Giants: Opportunities in Financial Leadership for Climate Stability*. Stockholm: Stockholm Resilience Centre.

Gandhi, I. (1972). Address to the United Nations Conference on the Human Environment, Stockholm, 14 June.

Garrett, L. (1995). *The Coming Plague: Newly Emerging Diseases in a World out of Balance*. New York: Penguin.

Gates, B. (2021). *How to Avoid a Climate Disaster: The Solutions We Have and the Breakthroughs We Need*. New York: Knopf.

German Advisory Council on Global Change (2008). *Climate Change as a Security Risk*. London: Earthscan.

Ghosh, A. (2016). *The Great Derangement: Climate Change and the Unthinkable*. Chicago: University of Chicago Press.

Gibb, R., Redding, D.W., Chin, K.Q. et al. (2020). Zoonotic host diversity increases in human-dominated ecosystems. *Nature*, 584, pp. 398–402.

Glacken, C. (1967). *Traces on the Rhodian Shore*. Berkeley, CA: University of California Press.

Gleick, P. (2014). Water, drought, climate change, and conflict in Syria. *Weather, Climate and Society*, 6, pp. 331–340.

Glikson, A. (2017). *Plutocene: Blueprints for a Post-Anthropocene Greenhouse Earth*. Berlin: Springer.

Global Commission on the Geopolitics of Energy Transformation (2019). *A New World: The Geopolitics of Energy Transformation*. International Renewable Energy Agency.

Goldstein, J. (2016). Climate change as a global security issue. *Journal of Global Security Studies*, 1(1), pp. 95–98.

Gopel, M. (2016). *The Great Mindshift: How a New Economic Paradigm and Sustainability Transformations Go Hand in Hand*. Berlin: Springer.

Gorbachev, M. (1988). *Perestroika*. New York: Harper and Row.

Goron, C. (2018). Ecological civilization and the political limits of a Chinese concept of sustainability. *China Perspectives*, 2018(4), pp. 39–52.

Gough, I. (2017). *Heat, Greed and Human Need: Climate Change, Capitalism and Sustainable Wellbeing*. Cheltenham, UK and Northampton, MA, USA: Edward Elgar Publishing.

Graeber, D. and Wengrow, D. (2021). *The Dawn of Everything: A New History of Humanity*. London: Allen Lane.

Graham, S. (2016). *Vertical*. London: Verso.

Greenfield, P. (2021a). Balloon test flight plan under fire over solar geoengineering fears. *The Guardian*, 8 February.

Greenfield, P. (2021b). World must rewild on massive scale to heal nature and climate, says UN. *The Guardian*, 3 June.

Greenfield, P. and Watts, J. (2020). JP Morgan economists warn climate crisis is threat to human race. *The Guardian*, 21 February.

Grove, J. (2019). *Savage Ecology: War and Geopolitics at the End of the World*. Durham, NC: Duke University Press.

Grove, R. (1995). *Green Imperialism: Colonial Expansion, Tropical Island Edens, and the Origins of Environmentalism, 1600–1800*. Cambridge: Cambridge University Press.

Grove, R. (1997). *Ecology, Climate and Empire: Colonialism and Global Environmental History, 1400–1940*. Cambridge: White Horse Press.

Hameiri, S. and Jones, L. (2015). *Governing Borderless Threats: Non-Traditional Security and the Politics of State Transformation*. Cambridge: Cambridge University Press.

Hamilton, C. (2013). *Earthmasters: The Dawn of the Age of Climate Engineering*. New Haven, CT: Yale University Press.

Hamilton, C. (2017). *Defiant Earth: The Fate of Humans in the Anthropocene*. Cambridge: Polity.

Hardt, J.N. (2021). The United Nations Security Council and the forefront of (climate) change? Confusion, stalemate, ignorance. *Politics and Governance*, 9(4), pp. 5–15.

Harper, K. (2017). *The Fate of Rome: Climate, Disease, and the End of an Empire*. Princeton, NJ: Princeton University Press.

Harrington, C. (2016). The ends of the world: international relations and the Anthropocene. *Millennium: Journal of International Studies*, 44(3), pp. 478–498.

Harris, P. (2021). *Pathologies of Climate Governance: International Relations, National Politics and Human Nature*. Cambridge: Cambridge University Press.

Harvey, D. (2005). *A Brief History of Neoliberalism*. Oxford: Oxford University Press.

Head, J. (2019). *A Global Corporate Trust for Agroecological Integrity: New Agriculture in a World of Legitimate Ecostates*. New York: Routledge.

Heather, P. (2006). *The Fall of the Roman Empire: A New History of Rome and the Barbarians*. Oxford: Oxford University Press.

Hecht, S. and Cockburn, A. (1990). *The Fate of the Forest: Developers, Destroyers and Defenders of the Amazon*. Harmondsworth: Penguin.

Hedlund, J., Fick, S., Carlsen, H. and Benzie, M. (2018). Quantifying transnational climate impact exposure: new perspectives on the global distribution of climate risk. *Global Environmental Change*, 52, pp. 75–85.

Hegazi, F., Krampe, F. and Smith, E.S. (2021). *Climate-Related Security Risks and Peacebuilding in Mali*. Stockholm: Stockholm International Peace Research Institute, Policy Paper 60.

Hernandez, A. (2020). The emergence of agroecology as a political tool in the Brazilian Landless Movement. *Local Environment*, 25(3), pp. 205–227.

Herrington, G. (2021). Update to limits to growth: comparing the World3 model with empirical data. *Journal of Industrial Ecology*, 25(3), pp. 614–626.

Herz, J. (1950). Idealist internationalism and the security dilemma. *World Politics*, 2(2), pp. 157–180.

Herzog, H.J. (2018). *Carbon Capture*. Cambridge, MA: MIT Press.

Hickel, J., Sullivan, D. and Zoomkawala, H. (2021). Plunder in the post-colonial era: quantifying drain from the Global South through unequal exchange, 1960–2018. *New Political Economy*, 26(6), pp. 1030–1047.
Hoffman, M.J. (2005). *Ozone Depletion and Climate Change: Constructing a Global Response*. Albany, NY: State University of New York Press.
Hoffman, S. (1977). An American social science: international relations. *Daedalus*, 51, pp. 41–59.
Holthaus, E. (2020). *The Future Earth: A Radical Vision for What's Possible in the Age of Warming*. New York: Harper Collins.
Homer-Dixon, T. (1991). On the threshold: environmental changes as causes of acute conflict. *International Security*, 16(2), pp. 76–116.
Homer-Dixon, T. (1994). Environmental scarcities and violent conflict: evidence from cases. *International Security*, 19(1), pp. 5–40.
Homer-Dixon, T. (1999). *Environment, Scarcity, and Violence*. Princeton, NJ: Princeton University Press.
Homer-Dixon, T., Walker, B., Biggs, R. et al. (2015). Synchronous failure: the emerging causal architecture of global crisis. *Ecology and Society*, 20(3), 6.
Hornborg, A., McNeill, J.R. and Martinez-Alier, J. eds (2007). *Rethinking Environmental History: World System History and Global Environmental Change*. Lanham, MD: AltiMira Press.
Horton, R.M., de Sherbinin, A., Wrathall, D. and Oppenheimer, M. (2021). Assessing human habitability and migration. *Science*, 372(6548), pp. 1279–1283.
Hough, P. (2019). Back to the future: environmental security in nineteenth century global politics. *Global Security, Health, Science and Policy*, 4(1), pp. 1–13.
Howard, P.H. and Sterner, T. (2017). Few and not so far between: a meta-analysis of climate damage estimates. *Environmental Resource Economics*, 68, pp. 197–225.
Hsiang, S. and Burke, M. (2014). Climate, conflict, and social stability: what does the evidence say? *Climatic Change*, 123, pp. 39–55.
Hsiang, S., Kopp, R., Jina, A. et al. (2017). Estimating economic damage from climate change in the United States. *Science*, 356, pp. 1362–1369.
Hsiang, S.M., Meng, K.C. and Cane, M.A. (2011). Civil conflicts are associated with the global climate. *Nature*, 476, pp. 438–441.
Huang, J., Yu, H., Han, D. et al. (2020). Declines in global ecological security under climate change. *Ecological Indicators*, 117, 106651.
Huda, M.S. and Ali, S.H. (2018). Environmental peacebuilding in South Asia: establishing consensus on hydroelectric projects in the Ganges-Bramaputra-Megna (GBM) Basin. *Geoforum*, 96, pp. 160–171.
Hulme, M. (2009). *Why We Disagree about Climate Change: Understanding Controversy, Inaction and Opportunity*. Cambridge: Cambridge University Press.
Hultgren, J. (2015). *Border Walls Gone Green: Nature and Anti-Immigrant Politics in America*. Minneapolis, MN: University of Minnesota Press.
Ide, T. (2018). Climate war in the Middle East? Drought, the Syrian civil war and the state of climate-conflict research. *Current Climate Change Reports*, 4, pp. 347–354.
Ide, T. (2020). The dark side of environmental peacebuilding. *World Development*, 127, 104777.
Ide, T., Bruch, C., Carius, A. et al. (2021). The past and future(s) of environmental peacebuilding. *International Affairs*, 97(1), pp. 1–16.
Ide, T. and Detges, A. (2018). International water cooperation and environmental peacemaking. *Global Environmental Politics*, 18(4), pp. 63–84.

Independent Commission on Disarmament Issues and Security (1982). *Common Security: A Programme for Disarmament*. London: Pan.
Intergovernmental Panel on Climate Change (2018). *Global Warming of 1.5°C*. Geneva: World Meteorological Organization.
Intergovernmental Science-Policy Platform on Biodiversity and Ecosystem Services (2020). *Workshop Report on Biodiversity and Pandemics of the Intergovernmental Platform on Biodiversity and Ecosystem Services*. Bonn: IPBES secretariat.
International Commission on Intervention and State Sovereignty (2001). *The Responsibility to Protect*. Ottawa: International Development Research Center.
International Energy Agency (2021). *Net Zero by 2050: A Road Map for the Global Energy Sector*. International Energy Agency.
Jackson, R. (2000). *The Global Covenant: Human Conduct in a World of States*. Oxford: Oxford University Press.
Jacobs, J. (1994). *Systems of Survival: A Dialogue on the Moral Foundations of Commerce and Politics*. New York: Vintage Books.
Jasanoff, S. (2015). Future imperfect: science, technology, and the imaginations of modernity, in S. Jasanoff and K. Sang-Hyun, eds. *Dreamscapes of Modernity: Sociotechnical Imaginaries and the Fabrication of Power*. Chicago: University of Chicago Press, pp. 1–33.
Jasanoff, S. (2021). Humility in the Anthropocene. *Globalizations*, 18(6), pp. 839–853.
Jenkins, P. (2021). *Climate, Catastrophe, and Faith: How Changes in Climate Drive Religious Revival*. Oxford: Oxford University Press.
Johnstone, D. (1984). *The Politics of EuroMissiles: Europe's Role in America's World*. London: Verso.
Jones, R. (2021). *White Borders: The History of Race and Immigration in the United States from the Chinese Exclusion to the Border Wall*. New York: Penguin.
Juda, L. (1978). Negotiating a treaty on environmental modification warfare: the convention on environmental warfare and its impact upon arms control negotiations. *International Organization*, 32(4), pp. 975–991.
Kahl, C. (2006). *States, Scarcity, and Civil Strife in the Developing World*. Princeton, NJ: Princeton University Press.
Kahn, M.E., Mohaddes, K., Ng, R.N.C. et al. (2019). *Long-Term Macroeconomic Effects of Climate Change: A Cross-Country Analysis*. Washington, DC: IMF, Working Paper No. 19/215.
Kaldor, M. (1999). *New and Old Wars*. Stanford, CA: Stanford University Press.
Kallis, G. (2018). *Degrowth*. Newcastle: Agenda.
Kaplan, R.D. (1994). The coming anarchy. *Atlantic Monthly*, 273(2), pp. 44–76.
Kareiva, P. and Fuller, E. (2016). Beyond Resilience: how to better prepare for the profound disruption of the Anthropocene. *Global Policy*, 7(S1), pp. 107–118.
Katz-Rosene, R. and Szwarc, J. (2021). Preparing for collapse: the concerning rise of "eco-survivalism". *Capitalism Nature Socialism*, Latest Articles.
Keen, S. (2021). The appallingly bad neoclassical economics of climate change. *Globalizations*, 18(7), pp. 1149–1177.
Keith, D. (2013). *A Case for Climate Engineering*. Cambridge, MA: MIT Press.
Keith, D. (2021). What is the least bad way to cool the planet? *New York Times*, 1 October.
Kelley, C., Mohtadi, S., Cane, M.A. et al. (2015). Climate change in the fertile crescent and implications of the recent Syrian drought. *Proceedings of the National Academy of Sciences*, 112(11), pp. 3241–3246.

Kelly, R. (2021). Avoiding the "Anthropocene"?: an assessment of the extent and nature of engagement with environmental issues in peace research. *Peace and Conflict Studies*, 27(3), 3.

Keohane, R. (2015). The global politics of climate change: challenge for political science. *PS: Political Science and Politics*, 48(1), pp. 19–26.

Keohane, R. and Nye, J. (1977). *Power and Interdependence: World Politics in Transition*. Boston, MA: Little, Brown.

Keucheyan, R. (2016). *Nature Is a Battlefield*. Cambridge: Polity.

Kjellen, B. (2008). *A New Diplomacy for Sustainable Development: The Challenge of Global Change*. New York: Routledge.

Klare, M. (2019). *All Hell Breaking Loose: The Pentagon's Perspective on Climate Change*. New York: Metropolitan.

Klein, B.S. (1995). *Strategic Studies and World Order*. Cambridge: Cambridge University Press.

Kleinfeld, R. (2018). *A Savage Order: How the World's Deadliest Countries Can Forge a Path to Security*. New York: Pantheon.

Kolbert, E. (2014). *The Sixth Extinction: An Unnatural History*. New York: Henry Holt.

Kolbert, E. (2021). *Under a White Sky: The Nature of the Future*. New York: Crown.

Komarov, B. (1980). *The Destruction of Nature in the Soviet Union*. London: Pluto.

Koopman, S. (2020). Building an inclusive peace is an uneven socio-political process: Colombia's differential approach. *Political Geography*, 83, 102252.

Kormann, C. (2020). Will big business finally reckon with the climate crisis? *The New Yorker*, 4 February.

Krampe, F. (2017). Toward sustainable peace: a new research agenda for post-conflict natural resource management. *Global Environmental Politics*, 17(4), pp. 1–8.

Krampe, F. (2021). Ownership and inequalities: exploring UNEP's Environmental Cooperation for Peacebuilding Program. *Sustainability Science*, 16, pp. 1159–1172.

Krampe, F., Hegazi, F. and VanDeveer, S. (2021). Sustaining peace through better resource governance: Three potential mechanisms for environmental peacebuilding. *World Development*, 144, 105508.

Krebs, J. and Bach, S. (2018). Permaculture—scientific evidence of principles for the agroecological design of farming systems. *Sustainability*, 10, 3218.

Kroger, M. (2020). *Iron Will: Resisting Extractivist Exploitation in Brazil and India*. Ann Arbor, MI: University of Michigan Press.

Ku, C. (2018). The UN Security Council's role in developing a responsibility to respond to the climate change challenge, in S.V. Scott and C. Ku, eds. *Climate Change and the UN Security Council*. Cheltenham, UK and Northampton, MA, USA: Edward Elgar Publishing, pp. 162–185.

Lade, S.J., Steffen, W., de Vries, W. et al. (2020). Human impacts on planetary boundaries amplified by earth system interactions. *Nature Sustainability*, 3, pp. 119–128.

Laferrière, E. and Stoett, P. (1999). *International Relations Theory and Ecological Thought: Towards Synthesis*. London: Routledge.

Lahsen, M. (2008). Experience of modernity in the greenhouse: a cultural analysis of a physicist "trio" supporting the backlash against global warming. *Global Environmental Change*, 18, pp. 204–219.

Lai, X. and Xiao, Z. (2020). A research on urban eco-security evaluation and analysis: complex system's brittle structure model. *Environmental Science and Pollution Research*, 27, pp. 24914–24928.

Lansing, D. (2010). Carbon's calculatory spaces: the emergence of carbon offsets in Costa Rica. *Society and Space*, 28, pp. 710–725.
Latham, R. (1997). *The Liberal Moment: Modernity, Security, and the Making of the Postwar International Order*. New York: Columbia University Press.
Latour, B. (2014). Agency at the time of the Anthropocene. *New Literary History*, 45, pp. 1–18.
Latour, B. (2017). *Facing Gaia: Eight Lectures on the New Climatic Regime*. Cambridge: Polity.
Le Billon, P. (2012). *Wars of Plunder: Conflicts, Profits and the Politics of Resources*. London: Hurst.
Lean, G. (1978). *Rich World, Poor World*. London: Allen and Unwin.
Lee, H.F. (2018). Internal wars in history: triggered by natural disasters or socio-ecological catastrophes? *The Holocene*, 28(7), pp. 1071–1081.
Leffler, M.P. (1984). The American conception of national security and the beginnings of the cold war, 1945–48. *American Historical Review*, 89(2), pp. 246–281.
Lenton, T., Rockström, J., Gaffney, O. et al. (2019). Climate tipping points—too risky to bet against. *Nature*, 575, pp. 592–595.
Leste-Lasserre, C. (2020). Pandemic dooms Danish mink—and mink research. *Science*, 270(6815), p. 754.
Lewis, S. and Maslin, M. (2018). *The Human Planet: How We Created the Anthropocene*. London: Pelican Books.
Liebman, A., Perfecto, I. and Wallace, R. (2020). *Whose Agriculture Drives Disease?* Agroecology and Rural Economics Research Corps.
Lieven, A. (2020). *Climate Change and the Nation State: The Case for Nationalism in a Warming World*. New York: Oxford University Press.
Lieven, A. (2021). NATO is best when it is doing nothing. *Responsible Statecraft*, 12 April.
Lorimer, J. (2015). *Wildlife in the Anthropocene: Conservation after Nature*. Minneapolis, MN: University of Minnesota Press.
Lövbrand, E. and Mobjörk, M. eds (2021). *Anthropocene (In)Securities: Reflections on Survival 50 Years after the Stockholm Conference*. Stockholm: Stockholm International Peace Research Institute/Oxford University Press.
Lövbrand, E., Mobjörk, M. and Soder, R. (2020). The Anthropocene and the geo-political imagination: rewriting earth as political space. *Earth System Governance*, 4, 100051.
Lovelock, J.E. (1979). *Gaia: A New Look at Life on Earth*. Oxford: Oxford University Press.
Lovins, A.B. (1977). *Soft Energy Paths: Toward a Durable Peace*. Harmondsworth: Penguin.
Mabey, N., Gulledge, J., Finel, B. and Silverthorne, K. (2011). *Degrees of Risk: Defining a Risk Management Framework for Climate Security*. London: E3G.
Mach, K.J., Adger, N., Buhaug, H. et al. (2020). Directions for research on climate and conflict. *Earth's Future*, 8(7), EF001532.
Mach, K.J., Kraan, C.M., Adger, N.W. et al. (2019). Climate as a risk factor for armed conflict. *Nature*, 571, pp. 193–197.
Mackenzie, A.F.D. (2013). *Places of Possibility: Property, Nature and Community Land Ownership*. Oxford: Wiley.
Malm, A. (2016). *Fossil Capital: The Rise of Steam Power and the Roots of Global Warming*. London: Verso.
Malthus, T. (1798/1970). *An Essay on the Principle of Population*. Harmondsworth: Penguin.

Mamdani, M. (2009). *Saviors and Survivors: Darfur, Politics and the War on Terror*. New York: Pantheon.
Mandelbaum, M. (1981). *The Nuclear Revolution: International Politics before and after Hiroshima*. Cambridge: Cambridge University Press.
Mangat, R., Dalby, S. and Paterson, M. (2018). Divestment discourse: war, justice, morality and money. *Environmental Politics*, 27(2), pp. 187–208.
Mann, M. (2021). *The New Climate War: The Fight to Take Back Our Planet*. New York: Public Affairs.
Marsh, G.P. (1864/1965). *Man and Nature: Or, Physical Geography as Modified by Human Action*. Cambridge, MA: The Belknap Press of Harvard University Press.
Martin, C. (2020). Atmospheric intervention? The climate change crisis and the jus ad bellum regime. *Columbia Journal of Environmental Law*, 45(S), pp. 331–417.
Masco, J. (2015). The age of fallout. *History of the Present: A Journal of Critical History*, 5(2), pp. 137–168.
Matejova, M., Parker, S. and Dauvergne, P. (2018). The politics of repressing environmentalists as agents of foreign influence. *Australian Journal of International Affairs*, 72(2), pp. 145–162.
Mathews, J.T. (1989). Redefining security. *Foreign Affairs*, 68(2), pp. 162–177.
McCall, M. (2016). Beyond "landscape" in REDD+: the imperative for "territory". *World Development*, 85, pp. 58–72.
MccGwire, M. (1987). *Military Objectives in Soviet Foreign Policy*. Washington, DC: Brookings Institute.
MccGwire, M. (1991). *Perestroika and Soviet National Security*. Washington, DC: Brookings Institute.
McCormick, P., Thomason, L.W. and Trepte, C.R. (1995). Atmospheric effects of the Mt Pinatubo eruption. *Nature*, 373, pp. 399–404.
McDonald, M. (2021). *Ecological Security: Climate Change and the Construction of Security*. Cambridge: Cambridge University Press.
McKinsey Global Institute (2020). *Climate Risk and Response: Physical Hazards and Socioeconomic Impacts*. McKinsey Global Institute.
McLeman, R. (2019). International migration and climate adaptation in an era of hardening borders. *Nature Climate Change*, 9, pp. 911–918.
McMichael, A.J. (2017). *Climate Change and the Health of Nations*. Oxford: Oxford University Press.
McNeill, J.R. (2007). Yellow jack and geopolitics: environment, epidemics, and the struggles for empire in the American tropics, 1640–1830, in A. Hornborg, J.R. McNeill and J. Martinez-Alier, eds. *Rethinking Environmental History: World System History and Global Environmental Change*. Lanham, MD: AltiMira, pp. 199–217.
McNeill, J.R. (2010). Sustainable survival, in P.A. McAnany and N. Yoffee, eds. *Questioning Collapse: Human Resilience, Ecological Vulnerability and the Aftermath of Empire*. Cambridge: Cambridge University Press, pp. 355–366.
McNeill, J.R. and Engelke, P. (2016). *The Great Acceleration: An Environmental History of the Anthropocene since 1945*. Cambridge, MA.: Harvard University Press.
Meadows, D.H., Meadows, D.L., Randers, J. and Behrens W.W. III (1972). *The Limits to Growth*. New York: Universe Books.
Meierding, E. (2016a). Dismantling the oil wars myth. *Security Studies*, 25(2), pp. 258–288.

Meierding, E. (2016b). Disconnecting climate change from conflict: a methodological proposal, in S. O'Lear and S. Dalby, eds. *Climate Change: Constructing Ecological Geopolitics*. London: Routledge, pp. 52–66.

Menton, M. and Le Billon, P. eds (2021). *Environmental Defenders: Deadly Struggles for Life and Territory*. London and New York: Routledge.

Miller, T., Buxton, N. and Akkerman, M. (2021). *Global Climate Wall*. Transnational Institute.

Milly, P.C.D., Betancourt, J., Falkenmark, M. et al. (2008). Stationarity is dead: whither water management? *Science*, 319(5863), pp. 573–574.

Mirumachi, N., Sawas, A. and Workman, M. (2020). Unveiling the security concerns of low carbon development: climate security analysis of the undesirable and unintended effects of mitigation and adaptation. *Climate and Development*, 12(2), pp. 97–109.

Mitchell, A. (2015). Thinking without the circle: marine plastic and global ethics. *Political Geography*, 47, pp. 77–85.

Mitchell, A. (2016). Beyond biodiversity and species: problematizing extinction. *Theory, Culture, and Society*, 33(5), pp. 23–42.

Mitchell, T. (2011). *Carbon Democracy: Political Power in the Age of Oil*. London: Verso.

Mitzen, J. (2006). Ontological security in world politics: state identity and the security dilemma. *European Journal of International Relations*, 12(3), pp. 341–370.

Mobjörk, M., Smith, D. and Rüttinger, L. (2016). *Towards a Global Resilience Agenda: Action on Climate Fragility Risks*. The Hague: Clingendael—the Netherlands Institute for International Relations.

Mol, A.P.J. (2001). *Globalization and Environmental Reform: The Ecological Modernization of the Global Economy*. Cambridge, MA: MIT Press.

Moore, J. (2015). *Capitalism in the Web of Life: Ecology and the Accumulation of Capital*. London: Verso.

Moore, J. ed. (2016). *Anthropocene or Capitalocene? Nature History, and the Crisis of Capitalism*. Oakland, CA: PM Press.

Moran, A., Busby, J., Raleigh, C. et al. (2018). *The Intersection of Global Fragility and Climate Risks*. Washington, DC: USAID.

Morgenthau, H. (1948). *Politics Among Nations: The Struggle for Power and Peace*. New York: Knopf.

Moss, R.H. (1993). Appendix lA. Resource scarcity and environmental security, in *World Armaments and Disarmaments*, SIPRI Yearbook. Oxford: Oxford University Press, pp. 27–36.

Moynihan, T. (2020). *X-Risk: How Humanity Discovered Its Own Extinction*. Cambridge, MA: MIT Press.

National Academies of Sciences, Engineering, and Medicine (2021). *Reflecting Sunlight: Recommendations for Solar Geoengineering Research and Research Governance*. Washington, DC: The National Academies Press.

National Research Council (2015). *Climate Intervention: Reflecting Sunlight to Cool Earth*. Washington, DC: National Academy of Sciences.

Neukom, R., Steiger, N., Gómez-Navarro, J.J., Wang, J. and Werner, J.P. (2019). No evidence for globally coherent warm and cold periods over the preindustrial Common Era. *Nature*, 571, pp. 550–554.

Newell, P. (2021). *Power Shift: The Global Political Economy of Energy Transitions*. Cambridge: Cambridge University Press.

Nitzan, J. and Bichler, S. (2009). *Capital as Power: A Study of Order and Creorder*. London: Routledge.

Nixon, R. (2011). *Slow Violence and the Environmentalism of the Poor*. Cambridge, MA: Harvard University Press.

Nyman, J. (2018). *The Energy Security Paradox: Rethinking Energy (In)Security in the United States and China*. Oxford: Oxford University Press.

O'Lear, S. (2016). Climate science and slow violence: a view from political geography and STS on mobilizing technoscientific ontologies of climate change. *Political Geography*, 52, pp. 4–13.

O'Lear, S. (2021). *A Research Agenda for Geographies of Slow Violence*. Cheltenham, UK and Northampton, MA, USA: Edward Elgar Publishing.

O'Loughlin, J., Witmer, F.D.W., Linke, A. et al. (2012). Climate variability and conflict risk in East Africa 1990–2009. *Proceedings of the National Academy of Sciences*, 109(45), pp. 18344–18349.

Oomen, J. (2021). *Imagining Climate Engineering: Dreaming of the Designer Climate*. New York and London: Routledge.

Ord, T. (2020). *The Precipice: Existential Risk and the Future of Humanity*. New York: Hachette.

O'Riordan, T. (1976). *Environmentalism*. London: Pion.

Oswald Spring, U. (2020). *Earth at Risk in the 21st Century: Rethinking Peace, Environment, Gender, and Human, Water, Health, Food, Energy Security, and Migration*. Cham: Springer.

Oswald Spring, U. and Brauch, H.G. eds (2021). *Decolonizing Conflicts, Security, Peace, Gender, Environment and Development in the Anthropocene*. Cham: Springer.

Otto, I.M., Donges, J.F., Cremades, R. et al. (2020). Social tipping dynamics for stabilizing earth's climate by 2050. *Proceedings of the National Academy of Sciences*, 117(5), pp. 2354–2365.

Overland, I. (2019). The geopolitics of renewable energy: debunking four emerging myths. *Energy Research and Social Science*, 49, pp. 36–40.

Panitch, L. and Gindin, S. (2012). *The Making of Global Capitalism: The Political Economy of American Empire*. London: Verso.

Parker, A., Horton, J.B. and Keith, D. (2018). Stopping solar geoengineering through technical means: a preliminary assessment of counter-geoengineering, *Earth's Future*, 6(8), pp. 1058–1065.

Parker, G. (2013). *Global Crisis: War, Climate Change and Catastrophe in the Seventeenth Century*. New Haven, CT: Yale University Press.

Parry, M., Arnell, N., Berry, P. et al. (2009). *Assessing the Costs of Adaptation to Climate Change: A Review of the UNFCCC and Other Estimates*. London: International Institute for Environment and Development.

Peluso, N. and Watts, M. eds (2001). *Violent Environments*. Ithaca, NY: Cornell University Press.

Peoples, C. (2021). Global uncertainties, geoengineering and the technopolitics of planetary crisis management. *Globalizations*, Latest Articles.

Pereira, J.C. (2017). The limitations of IR theory regarding the environment: lessons from the Anthropocene. *Revista Brasileira de Politica Internacional*, 60(1), e018.

Peterson, J. ed. (1983). *The Aftermath: The Human and Ecological Consequences of Nuclear War*. New York: Pantheon.

Pierrehumbert, R. (2019). There is no Plan B for dealing with the climate crisis. *Bulletin of the Atomic Scientists*, 75(5), pp. 215–221.

Piketty, T. (2014). *Capital in the Twenty-First Century*. Cambridge, MA: Harvard University Press.

Pirages, D. (1978). *Global Ecopolitics: The New Context for International Relations.* North Scituate, MA: Duxbury Press.

Pirages, D. (2005). From limits to growth to ecological security, in D. Pirages and K. Cousins, eds. *From Resource Scarcity to Ecological Security: Exploring New Limits to Growth.* Cambridge, MA: MIT Press, pp. 1–20.

Pirages, D. and Cousins, K. eds (2005). *From Resource Scarcity to Ecological Security: Exploring New Limits to Growth.* Cambridge, MA: MIT Press.

Pita, A. (2007). *Statement to the United Nations Special Session of the Security Council.* New York, 17 April.

Preston, C.J. (2016). *Climate Justice and Geoengineering: Ethics and Policy in the Atmospheric Anthropocene.* London: Rowman and Littlefield.

Price-Smith, A. (2009). *Contagion and Chaos: Disease, Ecology and National Security in the Era of Globalization.* Cambridge, MA: MIT Press.

Prins, G. and Stamp, R. (1991). *Top Guns and Toxic Whales.* London: Earthscan.

Pyne, S.J. (2012). *Fire: Nature and Culture.* London: Reaktion.

Pyne, S.J. (2021). *The Pyrocene.* Berkeley, CA: University of California Press.

Rabinowitz, D. (2020). *The Power of Deserts: Climate Change, the Middle East, and the Promise of the Post-Oil Era.* Stanford, CA: Stanford University Press.

Randers, J. (2012). *2052: A Global Forecast for the Next Forty Years.* White River Junction, VT: Chelsea Green.

Raworth, K. (2017). *Doughnut Economics: Seven Ways to Think Like a 21st-Century Economist.* London: Random House.

Renner, M. (1989). *National Security: The Economic and Environmental Dimensions.* Washington, DC: Worldwatch Institute.

Report of the Secretary-General (1986). *Concepts of Security.* New York: United Nations Department of Disarmament Affairs.

Reynolds, J.L. (2019a). Realist climate ethics: promoting climate ambition within the classical realist tradition. *Review of International Studies*, 45(1), pp. 141–160.

Reynolds, J.L. (2019b). *The Governance of Solar Geoengineering: Managing Climate Change in the Anthropocene.* Cambridge: Cambridge University Press.

Rhodes, C.J. (2017). The imperative for regenerative agriculture. *Science Progress*, 100(1), pp. 80–129.

Rienow, R. and Rienow, L.T. (1969). *A Moment in the Sun: A Report on the Deteriorating Quality of the American Environment.* New York: Dial Press.

Rifkin, J. (1991). *Biosphere Politics: A New Consciousness for a New Century.* New York: Crown.

Riofrancos, T. (2020). *Resource Radicals: From Petro-Nationalism to Post-Extractivism in Ecuador.* Durham, NC: Duke University Press.

Rockström, J. and Gaffney, O. (2021). *Breaking Boundaries: The Science of Our Planet.* New York: DK Publishing.

Rockström, J. and Klum, M. (2015). *Big World, Small Planet: Abundance within Planetary Boundaries.* New Haven, CT: Yale University Press.

Rossdale, C. (2015). Enclosing critique: the limits of ontological security. *International Political Sociology*, 9(4), pp. 369–386.

Rothe, D. (2016). *Securitizing Global Warming: A Climate of Complexity.* London and New York: Routledge.

Rothschild, E. (1995). What is security? *Daedalus*, 124(3), pp. 53–98.

Rudel, T.K. (2019). *Shocks, States and Sustainability: The Origins of Radical Environmental Reform.* New York: Oxford University Press.

Rüttinger, L. (2017). *Climate-Fragility Risks: The Global Perspective.* Berlin: Adelphi.

Rüttinger, L., Smith, D., Stang, G. et al. (2015). *A New Climate for Peace: Taking Action on Climate and Fragility Risks*. Berlin: Adelphi.

Ryder, S., Powlen, K., Laituri, M. et al. eds (2021). *Environmental Justice in the Anthropocene: From (Un)Just Presents to Just Futures*. London and New York: Routledge.

Sagan, C. and Turco, R. (1990). *A Path Where No Man Thought: Nuclear Winter and the End of the Arms Race*. New York: Random House.

Sassen, S. (2013). Land grabs today: feeding the disassembling of national territory. *Globalizations*, 10(1), pp. 25–46.

Sassen, S. (2014). *Expulsions: Brutality and Complexity in the Global Economy*. Cambridge, MA: Harvard University Press.

Sassen, S. (2016). At the systemic edge: expulsions. *European Review*, 24(1), pp. 89–104.

Scartozzi, C.M. (2021). Reframing climate-induced socio-environmental conflicts: a systematic review. *International Studies Review*, 23, pp. 696–725.

Schell, J. (1982). *The Fate of the Earth*. New York: Knopf.

Schneider, S. (2004). Abrupt non-linear climate change: irreversibility and surprise. *Global Environmental Change*, 14, pp. 245–258.

Schumacher, E.F. (1974). *Small Is Beautiful: A Study of Economics as if People Mattered*. London: Abacus.

Schwartz, P. and Randall, D. (2003). *An Abrupt Climate Change Scenario and Its Implications for United States National Security*. GBN Corporation.

Schwartzstein, P. (2021). How we misunderstand the magnitude of climate risks—and why that contributes to controversy. *New Security Beat*, 12 January.

Selby, J. (2014). Positivist climate conflict research: a critique. *Geopolitics*, 19(4), pp. 829–856.

Selby, J. (2019a). Climate change and the Syrian civil war. Part II: the Jazira's agrarian crisis. *Geoforum*, 101, pp. 260–274.

Selby, J. (2019b). The Trump presidency, climate change, and the prospect of a disorderly energy transition. *Review of International Studies*, 45(3), pp. 471–490.

Selby, J., Dahi, O.S., Fröhlich, C.J. and Hulme, M. (2017). Climate change and the Syrian civil war revisited. *Political Geography*, 60, pp. 232–244.

Selby, J. and Daoust, G. (2021). *Rapid Evidence Assessment on the Impacts of Climate Change on Migration Patterns*. London: Foreign, Commonwealth and Development Office.

Sherwin, M.J. (2020). *Gambling with Armageddon: Nuclear Roulette from Hiroshima to the Cuban Missile Crisis, 1945–1962*. New York: Knopf.

Simangan, D. (2020). Where is the Anthropocene? IR in a new geological epoch. *International Affairs*, 96(1), pp. 211–224.

Simangan, D. (2021). Can the liberal international order survive the Anthropocene? Three propositions for converging peace and survival. *The Anthropocene Review*, Early View.

Smil, V. (2008). *Global Catastrophes and Trends: The Next Fifty Years*. Cambridge, MA: MIT Press.

Snyder, T. (2015). *Black Earth: The Holocaust as History and Warning*. New York: Duggan.

Sovacool, B.K. and Linner, B.-O. (2016). *The Political Economy of Climate Change Adaptation*. London: Palgrave Macmillan.

Speth, G.A. (2021). *They Knew: The US Federal Government's Fifty Year Role in Causing the Climate Crisis*. Cambridge, MA: MIT Press.

State Council of the People's Republic of China (2020). China to forge ahead with weather modification efforts. Beijing: Government of China, press release.

Steffen, W., Richardson, K., Rockström, J. et al. (2015). Planetary boundaries: guiding human development on a changing planet. *Science*, 347(6223), 1259855.

Steffen, W., Rockström, J., Richardson, K. et al. (2018). Trajectories of the earth system in the Anthropocene. *Proceedings of the National Academy of Sciences*, 115(33), pp. 8252–8259.

Stephens, J.C., Kashwan, P., McLaren, D. and Surprise, K. (2021). The dangers of mainstreaming solar geoengineering: a critique of the National Academies report. *Environmental Politics*, Latest Articles.

Stockholm Environment Institute (2021). *The Production Gap Report 2021*. Stockholm: Stockholm Environment Institute.

Stoddard, I., Anderson, K., Capstick, S. et al. (2021). Three decades of climate mitigation: why haven't we bent the global emissions curve? *Annual Review of Environment and Resources*, 46, pp. 653–689.

Stoett, P. (2019). *Global Ecopolitics: Crisis, Justice, and Governance* (2nd edition). Toronto: University of Toronto Press.

Stoett, P. and Omrow, D.A. (2021). *Spheres of Transnational Ecoviolence: Environmental Crime, Human Security and Justice*. Cham: Palgrave Macmillan.

Strange, S. (1999). The Westfailure system. *Review of International Studies*, 25(3), pp. 345–354.

Subotic, J. (2016). Narrative, ontological security, and foreign policy change. *Foreign Policy Analysis*, 12(4), pp. 610–627.

Surprise, K. (2020). Geopolitical ecology of solar geoengineering: from a "logic of multilateralism" to logics of militarization. *Journal of Political Ecology*, 27, pp. 213–235.

Swain, A. and Öjendal, J. eds (2018). *Routledge Handbook of Environmental Conflict and Peacebuilding*. London and New York: Routledge.

Swatuk, L.A., Thomas, B.K., Wirkus, L. et al. (2021). The "boomerang effect": insights for improved climate action. *Climate and Development*, 13(1), pp. 61–67.

Swatuk, L. and Wirkus, L. eds (2018). *Water, Climate Change and the Boomerang Effect: Unintentional Consequences for Resource Insecurity*. London and New York: Routledge.

Swyngedouw, E. (2013). The non-political politics of climate change. *Acme*, 12(1), pp. 1–8.

Tainter, J.A. (1988). *The Collapse of Complex Societies*. Cambridge: Cambridge University Press.

Talberg, A., Christoff, P., Thomas, S. and Karoly, D. (2018). Geoengineering governance-by-default: an earth system governance perspective. *International Environmental Agreements: Politics, Law and Economics*, 18, pp. 229–253.

Taylor, M. (2014). *The Political Ecology of Climate Change Adaptation: Livelihoods, Agrarian Change and the Conflicts of Development*. London: Earthscan.

Taylor, P. (2016). Geohistory of globalizations. *Protosociology*, 33, pp. 131–148.

Taylor, P.J., O'Brien, G. and O'Keefe, P. (2020). *Cities Demanding the Earth: A New Understanding of the Climate Emergency*. Bristol: Bristol University Press.

Taylor, Z. (2020). The real estate fix: residential insurance linked securitization in the Florida metropolis. *Environment and Planning A: Economy and Space*, 52(6), pp. 1131–1149.

The Ecologist (1972). *A Blueprint for Survival*. Harmondsworth: Penguin.

The Ecologist (1993). *Whose Common Future? Reclaiming the Commons.* London: Earthscan.
Thomas, W.L. ed. (1956). *Man's Role in Changing the Face of the Earth.* Chicago: University of Chicago Press.
Thompson, E.P. (1980). *Protest and Survive.* London: Campaign for Nuclear Disarmament.
Thompson, E.P. (1982). Notes on exterminism, the last stage of civilization, in *New Left Review*, ed. *Exterminism and Cold War.* London: Verso, pp. 1–33.
Thunberg, G. (2019). *No One Is Too Small to Make a Difference.* London: Penguin.
Timoshenko, A.S. (1992). Ecological security: response to global challenges, in E. Brown Weiss, ed. *Environmental Change and International Law: New Challenges and Directions.* Tokyo: United Nations University Press, pp. 413–456.
Toal, G. (2017). *Near Abroad: Putin, the West and the Contest over Ukraine and the Caucasus.* New York: Oxford University Press.
Tooze, A. (2021). *Shutdown: How Covid Shook the World's Economy.* New York: Viking.
Turco, R.P., Toon, O.B., Ackerman, T.P. et al. (1983). Nuclear winter: global consequences of multiple nuclear explosions. *Science*, 222(4630), pp. 1283–1292.
Turner, G. (2014). *Is Global Collapse Imminent?* Melbourne: Melbourne Sustainable Society Institute.
Uesugi, Y. and Richmond, O. (2021). The Western international peace architecture and the emergence of the Eastphalian peace. *Global Society*, 35(4), pp. 435–455.
Ullman, R. (1983). Redefining security. *International Security*, 8(1), pp. 129–153.
United Nations (2009). *Climate Change and Its Possible Security Implications.* Report of the Secretary-General (A/64/350).
United Nations (2015). *Transforming Our World: The 2030 Agenda for Sustainable Development.* United Nations (A/RES/70/1).
United Nations Development Programme (1994). *Human Development Report 1994.* New York: Oxford University Press.
United Nations Development Programme (2020). *The Next Frontier: Human Development and the Anthropocene.* New York: United Nations.
United Nations Secretary-General (2020). The State of the Planet. Address to Columbia University, 12 December.
United States Department of State and Council on Environmental Quality (1980). *Global 2000 Report to the President: Entering the Twenty First Century.* Washington: Government Printing Office.
Vadlamannati, K.C. and de Soysa, I. (2020). Oil price volatility and political unrest: prudence and protest in producer and consumer societies, 1980–2013. *Energy Policy*, 145, 111719.
Vakulchuk, R., Overland, I. and Scholten, S. (2020). Renewable energy and geopolitics: a review. *Renewable and Sustainable Energy Reviews*, 122, 109547.
van Munster, R. and Sylvest, C. (2014). Reclaiming nuclear politics? Nuclear realism, the H bomb and globality, *Security Dialogue*, 45(6), pp. 530–547.
van Munster, R. and Sylvest, C. eds (2016). *The Politics of Globality since 1945: Assembling the Planet.* London: Routledge.
van Munster, R. and Sylvest, C. (2021). Nuclear weapons, extinction and the Anthropocene: reappraising Jonathan Schell. *Review of International Studies*, 47(3), pp. 294–310.
Verhoeven, H. (2021). The Grand Ethiopian Renaissance Dam: Africa's water tower, environmental justice and infrastructural power. *Daedalus*, 150(4), pp. 159–180.

Vogt, W. (1948). *The Road to Survival*. New York: Sloan.

Vuori, J. (forthcoming). Climate security with Chinese characteristics, in J.M. Trombetta, ed. *Handbook of Climate Change and International Security*. Cheltenham, UK and Northampton, MA, USA: Edward Elgar Publishing.

Walker, R.B.J. (1997). The subject of security, in K. Krause and M.C. Williams, eds. *Critical Security Studies*. Minneapolis, MN: University of Minnesota Press, pp. 61–81.

Wallace-Wells, D. (2017). The uninhabitable earth. *New York Magazine*, 9 July.

Wallace-Wells, D. (2019). *The Uninhabitable Earth: Life After Warming*. New York: Duggan.

Wallensteen, P. (2015). *Quality Peace: Peace Building, Victory and World Order*. Oxford: Oxford University Press.

Wapner, P. (2019). The ethics of political research in the Anthropocene, in F. Biermann and E. Lovbrand, eds. *Anthropocene Encounters: New Directions in Green Political Thinking*. Cambridge: Cambridge University Press, pp. 212–227.

Ward, B. and Dubos, R. (1972). *Only One Earth: The Care and Maintenance of a Small Planet*. Harmondsworth: Penguin.

Watts, M. (2013). *Silent Violence: Food, Famine and Peasantry in Northern Nigeria* (2nd edition). Athens, GA: University of Georgia Press.

Wei, Y.M., Han, R., Wang, C. et al. (2020). Self-preservation strategy for approaching global warming targets in the post-Paris Agreement era. *Nature Communications*, 11, 1624.

Welsby, D., Price, J., Pye, S. and Ekins, P. (2021). Unextractable fossil fuels in a 1.5°C world. *Nature*, 597, pp. 230–234.

Werrell, C.E. and Femia, F. eds (2017). *The Epicenters of Climate and Security: The New Geostrategic Landscape of the Anthropocene*. Washington, DC: Center for Climate and Security.

Werrell, C., Femia, F. and Sternberg T. (2015). Did we see it coming? State fragility, climate vulnerability, and the uprisings in Syria and Egypt. *SAIS Review*, 35(1), pp. 29–46.

White, R. (2014). Environmental insecurity and fortress mentality. International Affairs, 90(4), pp. 835–851.

Wilson, E.O. (2016). *Half-Earth: Our Planet's Fight for Life*. New York: Norton.

Winchester, S. (2003). *Krakatoa: The Day the World Exploded*. New York: Harper Collins.

Wolf, A. (1999). "Water wars" and water reality: conflict and cooperation along international waterways, in S. Lonergan, ed. *Environmental Change, Adaptation, and Security*. Dordrecht: Kluwer Academic Press, pp. 251–265.

Wolf, E. (1982). *Europe and the People without History*. Berkeley, CA: University of California Press.

World Commission on Environment and Development (1987). *Our Common Future*. Oxford: Oxford University Press.

World Economic Forum (2020). *The Global Risks Report 2020*. Geneva: World Economic Forum.

World Health Organization (2021). *Checklists to Assess Vulnerabilities in Health Care Facilities in the Context of Climate Change*. Geneva: World Health Organization.

Wunderling, N., Donges, J.F., Kurths, J. and Winkelmann, R. (2021). Interacting tipping elements increase risk of climate domino effects under global warming. *Earth System Dynamics*, 12, pp. 601–619.

X (George Kennan) (1947). The sources of Soviet conduct. *Foreign Affairs*, 25(4), pp. 566–582.

Xu, C., Kohler, T.A., Lenton, T.M. et al. (2020). Future of the human climate niche. *Proceedings of the National Academy of Sciences*, 117(21), pp. 11350–11355.

Yanarella, E.J. and Levine, R.S. (2021). *From Eco-Cities to Sustainable City-Regions: China's Uncertain Quest for an Ecological Civilization*. Cheltenham, UK and Northampton, MA, USA: Edward Elgar Publishing.

Yergin, D. (1991). *The Prize: The Epic Quest for Oil, Money and Power*. New York: Simon and Schuster.

Yergin, D. (2011). *The Quest: Energy, Security and the Remaking of the Modern World*. New York: Penguin.

Yokohata, T., Tanaka, K., Nishina, K. et al. (2019). Visualizing the interconnections among climate risks. *Earth's Future*, 7, pp. 85–100.

Zalasiewicz, J., Waters, C.N., Williams, M. and Summerhayes, C.P. eds (2019). *The Anthropocene as a Geological Time Unit: A Guide to the Scientific Evidence and Current Debate*. Cambridge: Cambridge University Press.

Zalasiewicz, J., Williams, M., Waters, C.N. et al. (2017). Scale and diversity of the physical technosphere: a geological perspective. *The Anthropocene Review*, 4(1), pp. 9–22.

Zhang, Y. and Shao, C. (2019). Ideas and countermeasures for optimum design of environmental protection system based on ecological security. *IOP Conference. Series: Earth Environment. Science*, 267, 062011.

Zhao, Y.-Z., Zou, X.-Y., Cheng, H. et al. (2006). Assessing the ecological security of the Tibetan plateau: methodology and a case study for Lhaze County. *Journal of Environmental Management*, 80, pp. 120–131.

Zografos, C., Goulden, M.C. and Kallis, G. (2014). Sources of human insecurity in the face of hydro-climatic change. *Global Environmental Change*, 29, pp. 327–336.

Index

Printed and bound by CPI Group (UK) Ltd, Croydon, CR0 4YY

16/04/2025

14658485-0002

A Modern Guide to the Economics of Crime

Edited by

Paolo Buonanno

Professor of Economics, Department of Economics, University of Bergamo, Italy

Paolo Vanin

Professor of Economics, Department of Economics, University of Bologna, Italy

Juan Vargas

Professor of Economics, School of Economics, Universidad del Rosario, Bogotá, Colombia

ELGAR MODERN GUIDES

Cheltenham, UK • Northampton, MA, USA

© Paolo Buonanno, Paolo Vanin and Juan Vargas 2022

All rights reserved. No part of this publication may be reproduced, stored in a retrieval system or transmitted in any form or by any means, electronic, mechanical or photocopying, recording, or otherwise without the prior permission of the publisher.

Published by
Edward Elgar Publishing Limited
The Lypiatts
15 Lansdown Road
Cheltenham
Glos GL50 2JA
UK

Edward Elgar Publishing, Inc.
William Pratt House
9 Dewey Court
Northampton
Massachusetts 01060
USA

Paperback edition 2024

A catalogue record for this book
is available from the British Library

Library of Congress Control Number: 2022943001

This book is available electronically in the **Elgar**online
Economics subject collection
http://dx.doi.org/10.4337/9781789909333

ISBN 978 1 78990 932 6 (cased)
ISBN 978 1 78990 933 3 (eBook)
ISBN 978 1 0353 3898 6 (paperback)

Printed and bound by CPI Group (UK) Ltd, Croydon, CR0 4YY

Contents

Contributors

Pasquale Accardo, Leicester University

Paolo Buonanno, University of Bergamo

Joel Carr, University of Antwerp

Derek Christopher, Stanford University

Emanuele Colonnelli, University of Chicago

Giuseppe De Feo, Leicester University

Giacomo De Luca, University of Bozen and LICOS KU Leuven

Rafael Di Tella, Harvard Business School, CIfAR and NBER

Jennifer L. Doleac, Texas A&M University

Magdalena Domínguez, Uppsala University

Patricio Dominguez, Pontificia Universidad Católica, Chile

Eduardo Ferraz, Universidad del Rosario

Matthew Freedman, University of California, Irvine

Jorge Gallego, Universidad del Rosario

Evelina Gavrilova, NHH Norwegian School of Economics

Ben Lessing, University of Chicago

Magnus Lofstrom, Public Policy Institute of California

Olivier Marie, Erasmus University Rotterdam

Federico Masera, University of New South Wales

Daniel Mejía, Universidad de los Andes

Daniel Montolio, Universitat de Barcelona

Tommy E. Murphy, Universidad de San Andrés

Ervyn Norza, National Police of Colombia

Emily Owens, University of California, Irvine

Paolo Pinotti, Bocconi Univesity

Mounu Prem, Universidad del Rosario

Marcello Puca, University of Bergamo, CSEF, and Webster University Geneva

Steven Raphael, University of California, Berkeley

Sandra V. Rozo, World Bank

Ernesto Schargrodsky, CAF, UTDT and CONICET

Rodrigo Soares, Insper and Columbia University

Maria Micaela Sviatschi, Princeton University

Santiago Tobón, Universidad EAFIT

Martín Vanegas-Arias, Universidad EAFIT

Paolo Vanin, University of Bologna

Juan Vargas, Universidad del Rosario

Sunčica Vujić, University of Antwerp

1. The changing nature of economics of crime

Paolo Buonanno,[1] Paolo Vanin[2] and Juan Vargas[3]

1. INTRODUCTION

In 1968 Gary Becker published "Crime and Punishment: An Economic Approach" in the *Journal of Political Economy* (Becker, 1968). This is considered the seminal paper of the way modern economics conceptualizes criminal and illegal behavior, and so it gave birth to the field of "economics of crime." Becker applied, for the first time, the formal analytical elements of rational choice and utility maximization to the individual choice between committing a crime or work in the legal sector. Under this framework, criminal actions are not irrational or determined by mental illness but rather a choice that results from a rational cost-benefit analysis. The returns of crime are compared to the expected punishment (weighted by the probability of being caught) and to the opportunity cost of crime. Thus Becker highlighted the economic motives that tilt the balance for potential criminals toward either illegal or productive activities. Five years later, Isaac Ehrlich complemented Becker's insights with additional theoretical considerations as well as with an empirical test of these insights for the U.S. (Ehrlich, 1973).[4]

The field started by Becker and Ehrlich has grown very rapidly over time, gaining prominence and recognition. In a recent review paper on the literature on crime and economic incentives, Draca and Machin (2015) estimate that the number of economics of crime papers published in prominent economics journals grew, on average, 4.5 percent per year between the 1950s and the 2000s. More recently, Jennifer Doleac has compiled a thorough public repository of crime-related papers published in top general interest and top field journals, dating back to 1990.[5] Figure 1.1 plots the evolution of the number of published crime papers from 1990 to 2020, according to Doleac's repository. While the 1990s average was just over 5 papers per year, that of the 2010s was almost 40 papers. During this period, the number of published papers grew on average by 27 percent per year.

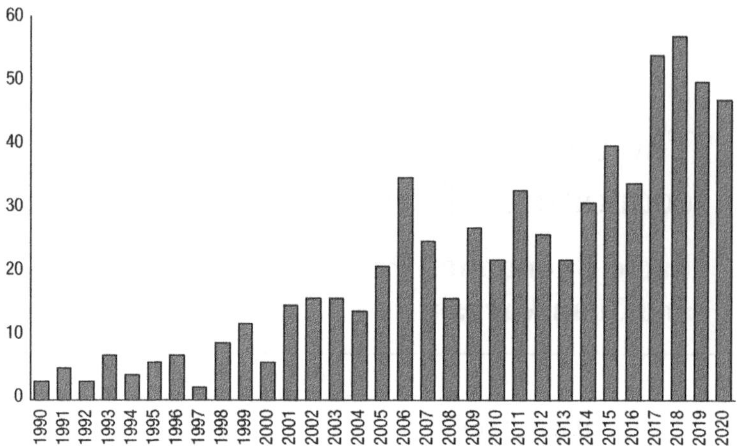

Source: Jennifer Doleac's "Crime Papers" repository, updated May–October 2021. The journals include *American Economic Review* (excluding P&P), *Quarterly Journal of Economics*, *Review of Economics Studies*, *Journal of Political Economy*, *Econometrica*, *Review of Economics and Statistics*, *Journal of the European Economic Association*, *American Economic Journal: Applied Economics*, *American Economic Journal: Economic Policy*, *American Economic Review: Insights*, *Economic Journal*, *Journal of Labor Economics*, *Journal of Public Economics*, *Journal of Law and Economics*, *Journal of Urban Economics*, *Journal of Policy Analysis and Management*, *Journal of Human Resources*, *Journal of Development Economics*, *Journal of Economic History*, *Explorations in Economic History* and *Journal of Health Economics*.

Figure 1.1 Forty years of publications of crime papers in top general interest and top field economics journals

What explains this remarkable trend? As argued by Cook et al. (2013), by offering a simple normative economic framework to evaluate crime-reduction policies, the Becker/Ehrlich model has surely contributed to it. These authors also highlight the role of two additional factors: the availability of more and better data from a variety of sources and the development of modern statistical tools to unveil causal relationships regarding the determinants of crime and to evaluate the impact of crime control policies.

On the availability of data, our own in-depth review of the crime papers published in top five economics journals in the last decade—using as a filter the *Journal of Economic Literature* (JEL) code of the area "Law and Economics," K—suggests that 85 percent of them use administrative data (instead of, for instance, self-collected survey data). Indeed, the increasing awareness of policymakers and public officials that accessible anonymized administrative information can help the design and evaluation of better policies has largely benefited all fields of applied microeconomics, not only the economics of crime. Moreover, the role of large-N datasets from other sources such as credit-card transactions or remote-sensing information and the use of statistical techniques to analyze such datasets have also contributed to the growth of the field.

The development of causal inference methodologies has also largely contributed to the growing attention that applied economists have placed on crime-related research topics. In 2010 Joshua Angrist and Jörn-Steffen Pischke coined the term "credibility revolution" to refer to the growing use of natural experiments in empirical economics to answer causal questions regarding key policy debates (Angrist and Pischke, 2010). A key example, which is still a source of policy and academic debate today, is whether a higher minimum wage affects employment levels.

Since the late 1980s the conjunction of natural experiments and research designs that address selection on unobservables—such as *instrumental variables* (IV), *difference-in-differences* (DiD) and *regression discontinuity design* (RDD)—has therefore improved the credibility of empirical economics and has boosted the publication share of empirical papers as a byproduct.[6] Further boosted by the growth of randomized control trials (RCT), since then hundreds of experimental and quasi-experimental impact evaluations on criminal justice and crime-reducing policies ranging from cash transfers and therapy to policing and incarceration have been produced. Our review of crime papers published in top five economics journals in the last decade suggests that, excluding papers that rely on structural estimation (15 percent of the total), 55 percent of the applied econometric papers identify causal effects using IV, DiD, RDD or RCT.

Before the credibility revolution, in the 1970s and 1980s, empirical economics was largely based on either time series or cross-sectional correlations, with limited attention to longitudinal variation in panel data models and little validity for policy design. Indeed, the development of new methods and tools coincided with Edward Leamer's view that economics lacked empirical credibility and that applied econometrics was largely leading to conclusions that could easily change by making small changes in models' specifications or parameters (Leamer, 1983). Incidentally, Leamer's critique is closely related to the early developments in the economics of crime. Indeed, to illustrate his point, Leamer challenged Isaac Ehrlich's conclusion that capital punishment in the U.S. deterred crime (Ehrlich, 1975, 1977). This finding proved to be driven by observations from the 1960, and thus was sensitive to changes in the sample period, as well as to the inclusion of controls and to changes in the model's functional form (Angrist and Pischke, 2010).

In addition to the causes highlighted by Cook et al. (2013), we propose three additional explanations of the boost experienced by the economics of crime literature. First, the increasing cross-fertilization of economics and other social sciences that have been traditionally interested in the incidence of crime and violence, such as criminology, sociology and political science. This spillover goes both ways, with sister disciplines providing research topics, policy debates and conceptual insights, and economics bringing its empirical toolkit. For instance, many studies now combine quantitative analysis with ethnographic work to understand the underlying determinants of criminal behavior in detail. If we were to include journals in other disciplines in our searches of economics of crime articles, the levels reported in Figure 1.1 would be substantially higher and the upward trend perhaps even more marked. This interdisciplinarity is also evident in the variety of topics addressed by the papers published in economics. Our in-depth reading of those published in top five journals over the last decade reveals themes as diverse and policy relevant as recidivism, racial bias, immigration, education, trial and sentencing, incapacitation, deterrence, policing, peer effects and rehabilitation, to mention just a few.

The second reason is the expansion of international academic workshops on the economics of crime. For at least a decade, venues such as the America Latina Crime and Policy Network (AL CAPONE) and Transatlantic Workshop on the Economics of Crime, have facilitated the integration and exchange of researchers from the Americas and Europe, and have increasingly witnessed participation of scholars from other parts of the world.

The third and final reason comes from the observation that, today, crime and violence levels worldwide are remarkably like those observed three decades ago.[7] There might be many reasons for the lack of sustained progress in curtailing crime, but most probably one of them is that, in most of the developing world, crime-reducing policies continue to be disassociated from empirical evidence. Even more worrisome, crime policy is perhaps one of the most vulnerable policy instruments to punitive populism. For example, legislators and policymakers around the world insist on increasing prison length, even in the presence of overcrowded systems. We hypothesize that this is perhaps one reason why economists are increasingly attracted to undertake research on crime-related topics. Economics has a lot to say about understanding criminal markets and developing and testing policies to reduce crime and violence.

Interestingly, many of these topics are being studied with analytical tools outside the static Beckerian framework, which suggests that the evolution of the field is concomitant with new theoretical insights. This is in part what motivated us to edit this volume on the new approaches to the economics of crime. In it, our goal is to highlight the variety of topics, conceptual frameworks and empirical approaches that the field is currently using. Many of these continue to be shaped, 50 years later, by the insightful idea that criminal behavior responds to incentives, but some others go beyond it.

Some of the most prolific contributors of the economics of crime literature have generously accepted our invitation and joined our effort. We are thrilled and honored to have such a diverse group—or should we say "gang" in agreement with the book's topic—of young scholars based in North America, Europe, Latin America and Australia who share their expertise.

2. THIS BOOK

The book is divided into four parts. As criminals' apprehension is a necessary premise for punishment or resocialization efforts, the first part starts by investigating the role of the police and its effectiveness against crime. In Chapter 2, Federico Masera reviews recent developments in the economics of policing and shows that the most credible estimates of the elasticity of crime to the size of police forces fall in the range –0.9 to –1.3 for violent crime and –0.3 and –0.8 for property crime. Masera also discusses the determinants of police effectiveness, ranging from gender and race composition to organization, oversight and technological endowment. The evidence about potential biases in policing is also discussed in this chapter.

In turn, Chapters 3 and 4 use longitudinal data to study the spatial and temporal distribution of crime and police forces (or policing activities). Each chapter focuses on a specific country. On the one hand, Matthew Freedman, Emily Owens and Derek Christopher document in Chapter 3 the evolution of crime and police in the U.S. since the 1980s. Among other things, they show that the general crime reduction observed at the national level has been more pronounced in cities with higher poor and black populations. And police forces have remained particularly concentrated in such areas.

On the other hand, Daniel Mejía, Ervyn Norza, Santiago Tobón and Martín Vanegas-Arias present in Chapter 4 an original investigation of the effects of "broken windows policing" for the case of Colombia. This refers to the strategy of intensifying police presence in low- and moderate-crime areas. The authors leverage highly disaggregated information on the spatial-temporal allocation of arrests and crime in 80 Colombian cities in 2019 and show that after a surge in unplanned arrests in a 2-by-2 block grid cell crime goes down both in "treated" and surrounding cells. The effect is more pronounced in areas with low crime rates and lower presence of organized crime. These findings complement the literature on "hot spot policing," namely the strategy of concentrating police efforts in high-crime areas.

The broad message emerging from these two chapters is that different groups in the population are exposed to highly heterogeneous interactions with police forces. This occurs for a variety of reasons including context-dependent policing strategies. Evaluating and improving such strategies, and more generally interactions between different population groups and the police, is extremely policy relevant, but it requires a better measurement of police activities. However, little data is generally available beyond manpower and arrests. Thus, collecting and analyzing new data sources is a promising avenue of future research.

Once a criminal is apprehended, different forms of punishment or correctional measures may be imposed. A prototypical sanction is incarceration, which is widely used due to its deterrent and incapacitation effects but may suffer from overcrowding and be itself criminogenic. Moreover, incarceration is generally very expensive to society. A large body of research has attempted to measure its effects on crime and has explored possible alternatives to it. Chapters 5 and 6 contribute to this debate by evaluating two reforms, one that reduced incarceration in California and one that substituted electronic monitoring for pre-trial prison in Argentina.

Patricio Dominguez, Magnus Lofstrom and Steven Raphael assess, in Chapter 5, the crime impact of reforms passed in 2011 and 2014 in California, which reduced by one-fourth the prison and jail population. The authors find small effects on violent crimes and an increase in property crime of the order of 5 percent. As the U.S. has become an outlier among OECD countries in terms of high incarceration rates, this research suggests that the cost of switching to alternative measures in terms of higher crime rates may be limited, while the savings may be substantial.

In Chapter 6, Rafael Di Tella and Ernesto Schargrodsky investigate a particular alternative to incarceration that is made possible by technological progress. This is the case of electronic monitoring (EM). The authors study a policy that, between 1998 and 2007, allocated some alleged offenders waiting for trial in the Province of Buenos Aires for EM, whereas others were sent to prison. Exploiting random assignment to judges, their conservative estimate suggests that allocation to EM halves recidivism rates. On top of this, EM clearly generates substantial savings, and so the cost-benefit analysis suggests that "the net welfare benefit of sending one alleged offender to EM, instead of prison, amounts to 2.4 times the average Argentine GDP per capita." Despite such large benefits, the policy was discontinued due to the mediatic resonance of a violent episode. This highlights both the potential for policy improvement and the vulnerability of good policies to political incentives.

While punishment probability and intensity are at the forefront of public strategies of law enforcement, they are not the only tools at hand. Several distinct socio-economic factors may induce individuals to commit crimes, and they have been explored by a large body of literature over the past half century. The second part of this volume summarizes the recent advances of this strand of the literature. Specifically, Chapters 7 to 10 reflect, in different contexts and with distinct perspectives, on the socio-economic determinants of crime.

Among those, education plays a prominent role among the potential deep roots of crime. It affects individual income and the income distribution, as well as cognitive and non-cognitive skills and traits. Yet, measuring the impact of education on crime is difficult because several potential omitted factors determine both the schooling and the crime choices of an individual. Joel Carr, Olivier Marie and Sunčica Vujić discuss in Chapter 7 the causal effect of education on crime. Reforms that raise school leaving age provide an important source of exogenous variations in educational attainment, but researchers have also exploited variation among twins and in free school days within a year. The evidence—which is mostly based on advanced economies—shows that being at school and finishing high school substantially reduce the propensity to commit crime and that investing in education is a very cost-effective crime-reducing endeavor. In the future we may expect a growing body of research on the effect of education on crime in developing countries and on trying to disentangle how different attributes of education affect different types of crime and through which channels.

While education is a permanent source of income, in the short run economic shocks may alter the balance between legality and crime. Eduardo Ferraz, Rodrigo Soares and Juan Vargas point out in Chapter 8 three characteristics of economic shocks that shape the way they translate into crime: the legality of the affected markets, the source of the income and contextual factors such as the overall institutional environment. While an increase in legal market wages raises the opportunity cost of crime, an increase in the revenues of concentrated and lootable natural resources or in the value of illegal markets may foster crime. This is especially so in contexts characterized by high inequality and poor institutions. The authors review the most recent evidence and provide a useful taxonomy, contrasting an "opportunity cost effect" and a "rapacity effect" of economic shocks. They also discuss how economic shocks may affect crime through non-Beckerian channels, such as those highlighted by social disorganization and strain theories, and they call for more research in this direction.

From a criminal's point of view, crime returns and costs have both an economic and a social component, so that the structure of social ties may interact with existing inequalities in determining crime choices. Social incentives are relevant for crime both theoretically and empirically. Their consideration allows the explanation of a large part of the variability of crime that otherwise remains unexplained and allows social multipliers to be quantified and better targeted interventions to be designed.

In Chapter 9, Magdalena Domínguez and Daniel Montolio address the possibility of fighting crime through "soft" interventions that increase community involvement and reduce inequalities. They present the literature on place-based policing and social capital and analyze a specific policy adopted in Spain between 2008 and 2014. The policy introduced, in quasi-random order, interventions aimed at improving health and reducing inequalities in disadvantaged neighborhoods of Barcelona, with a strong involvement of local communities. They show that such policy significantly increased association density, and through this channel it significantly reduced most forms of crime, confirming that well-targeted socio-economic interventions may usefully complement a deterrence-based approach based on punishment threats.

Over the last quarter century, economists have made substantial progress in modeling and estimating the effect of social interactions on crime choices. In Chapter 10, Evelina Gavrilova and Marcello Puca summarize the recent economics and criminology literature on peer effects and crime and discuss the associated identification difficulties. The authors point out that all empirical methods, from reduced-form regressions to the exploitation of quasi-exogenous sources of variation to controlled experiments, converge in documenting the existence of relevant peer effects in crime choices. This is true in both prisons and social networks, especially within relatively homogeneous groups. These findings may also help explain the effectiveness of EM documented in Chapter 6, as such an alternative to prison breaks criminogenic peer interaction behind bars.

The third part of this volume addresses issues related to crime in specific groups. Specifically, Chapters 11 to 13 focus on migrants, females and racial minorities respectively. The share of immigrants in the world roughly tripled over the last half century, and it disproportionately increased in high-income countries. This has often triggered harsh social and political reactions. Paolo Pinotti and Sandra V. Rozo document in Chapter 11 that host country populations hold widespread crime concerns about migration and investigate to what extent such concerns are justified by the data. Causal identification in this context is difficult because omitted ("pull") variables may drive both migration choices and local crime rates. To overcome this challenge, several studies rely on instruments based on shocks in the country of origin coupled with the geographical distribution of previous immigrants in the country of destination. Consistently, they find little or no effect of immigration on crime, with few exceptions depending on specific local conditions. Other studies exploit exogenous variation in immigrant legalization and document that it substantially reduces migrants' propensity to engage in criminal activities by providing access to legal jobs. This evidence is robust in developed countries, whereas it is weaker in developing countries, where the share of the informal sector is higher. The authors also highlight the negative effects of forced migration and deportation, and the fact that migrants' victimization rate tends to be higher than that of natives.

Just as migrants relative to natives, females relative to males show a higher victimization rate and lower rates of crime participation. In Chapter 12, Evelina Gavrilova documents that these gender differences have been shrinking over time in many high-income countries, and that in some countries the justice system seems biased in favor of women. The author reflects on the different incentives driving male and female crime choices, and on the need to pay closer attention to such aspects both theoretically and empirically.

Racial minorities need not always behave as majority groups, but for the same behavior they may also be treated differently by the criminal justice system. Jennifer L. Doleac documents in Chapter 13 the existing evidence of biased treatment of racial minorities by police, prosecutors and judges. She distinguishes between different possible drivers (animus, statistical discrimination and stereotypes) and reviews the natural experiments used to identify such bias. The chapter points out that the current research frontier lies in identifying how to reduce the existing—and well-documented—bias.

The fourth and final part of the book turns from individual to organized crime. Economists' interest in criminal organizations is as old as their interest in individual crime (Schelling, 1967, 1971; Buchanan, 1973). However, it has been increasing over the past half century, especially after Diego Gambetta's influential work on the Sicilian mafia (Gambetta, 1993). New datasets have been assembled to measure the origins and the effects of different criminal groups, and new models have been developed to study their operations.

In Chapter 14, Ben Lessing and Maria Micaela Sviatschi adopt an industrial organization perspective on the economics of organized crime. They portray the trajectories of some famous present and past gangs around the world and discuss their sources of revenues, internal organization and career paths. Gangs and criminal organizations produce a wealth of harmful effects, hindering important aspects of social and economic life. Hence, states often try to fight and curb organized crime. Criminal organizations may in turn fight back violently, hide or try to obtain more favorable treatment by the state. In Chapter 15, Pasquale Accardo, Giuseppe De Feo and Giacomo De Luca discuss how criminal organizations use bribes and violence to affect the selection of elected politicians and to distort public officials' choices. They highlight the impact of these strategies on self-selection into politics, on electoral outcomes and on policy choices. In turn, Emanuele Colonnelli, Jorge Gallego and Mounu Prem exploit in Chapter 16 Brazilian micro-data to show how novel machine learning models can be used to predict corruption. They find that the best predictors are measures of private sector activity, financial development and human capital. Understanding and fighting corruption, therefore, requires widening attention beyond the public sector and the political sphere to encompass also the "demand for corruption" posed by the private sector. Finally, Tommy E. Murphy and Paolo Vanin discuss in Chapter 17 the similarities between criminal organizations and states, and their fight for the legitimate monopoly of violence. They move beyond an industrial organization perspective and consider the role of violence in the emergence of both criminal organizations and states, their ability to extract resources, the harmful effects of extractive competition, the incentives to supply protection and the fight for the monopoly of violence and for legitimacy.

Overall, the different chapters give an overview of the tremendous progress made in recent years in the economic analysis of individual and organized crime. They do so while emphasizing the aspects that we discussed as driving the surge of this literature: the availability of novel and administrative microdata, the use of research designs that unveil causal relationships and the interdisciplinarity of approaches and theoretical frameworks.

Despite such progress, there are still many aspects of the economics of crime about which we know rather little. These are pointed out in detail in each chapter. Broadly speaking, however, although evidence from low- to middle-income countries has been increasing, we still need to understand better how different strategies of law enforcement work in different contexts. In the end, at half a century of age, the economics of crime remains a young, lively and promising field of research, both theoretically and empirically.

NOTES

1. Department of Economics, University of Bergamo.
2. Department of Economics, University of Bologna.
3. School of Economics, Universidad del Rosario.
4. Buonanno, Vargas and Tobón (2021) track the origins of this rational approach to criminal behavior to the utilitarian and redistributive theories of crime, respectively, put forward by Jeremy Bentham and Cesare Beccaria (1819) at the end of the eighteenth century. In particular, Bentham (1789) writes: "The profit of the crime is the force which urges man to delinquency: the pain of the punishment is the force employed to restrain him from it. If the first of these forces be the greater, the crime will be committed; if the second, the crime will not be committed" (p. 33). The Becker/Ehrlich model formalizes this old idea.
5. As of November 2021, the included journals are the *American Economic Review* (excluding P&P), *Quarterly Journal of Economics*, *Review of Economics Studies*, *Journal of Political Economy*, *Econometrica*, *Review of Economics and Statistics*, *Journal of the European Economic Association*, *American Economic Journal: Applied Economics*, *American Economic Journal: Economic Policy*, *American Economic Review: Insights*, *Economic Journal*, *Journal of Labor Economics*, *Journal of Public Economics*, *Journal of Law and Economics*, *Journal of Urban Economics*, *Journal of Policy Analysis and Management*, *Journal of Human Resources*, *Journal of Development Economics*, *Journal of Economic History*, *Explorations in Economic History* and *Journal of Health Economics*. The repository can be accessed here: https://docs.google.com/spreadsheets/d/1zyRB708QpsxG_8vNCRl7gv5FyrPE81w3mF_kMVJ1HbY/edit#gid=686724554.
6. In 2021, the Royal Swedish Academy of Sciences recognized the role of natural experiments in helping answer important questions for society and awarded the Sveriges Riksbank Prize in Economic Sciences in Memory of Alfred Nobel to David Card, Joshua Angrist and Guido Imbens.

7. This apparent stability, however, hides important regional heterogeneity: while regions such as Sub-Saharan Africa or Central Asia have made important progress, others such as Latin America and the Caribbean have much higher violence levels.

REFERENCES

Angrist, J. D. and Pischke, J. S. (2010). The Credibility Revolution in Empirical Economics: How Better Research Design Is Taking the Con out of Econometrics. *Journal of Economic Perspectives* 24(2):3–30.

Beccaria, C. (1819). An Essay on Crime and Punishments, second American edition published by Philip H Nicklin. Translated from the Italian: *Dei delitti e delle pene* (Livorno: Marco Coltellini, 1764).

Becker, G. S. (1968). Crime and Punishment: An Economic Approach. *Journal of Political Economy* 76(2):169–217.

Bentham, J. (1789). *An Introduction to the Principles of Morals and Legislation*. Oxford: Clarendon Press, 1907 (first published in 1789).

Buchanan, J. M. (1973). A Defense of Organized Crime? In *The Economics of Crime and Punishment*, ed. S. Rottenberg. Washington, DC: American Enterprise Institute for Public Policy Research, 119–32.

Buonanno, P., Vargas, J. and Tobón, S. (2021). Crime: Economics of, The Standard Approach. In A. Marciano and G.B. Ramello (Eds.) *Encyclopedia of Law and Economics*. Cham: Springer.

Cook, P., Machin, S., Marie, O. and Mastrobuoni, G. (2013). Crime Economics in its Fifth Decade. In P. Cook, S. Machin, O. Marie and G. Mastrobuoni (Eds.) *What Works in Reducing Offending? Lessons from the Economics of Crime*. Cambridge, MA: MIT Press.

Draca, M. and Machin, S. (2015). Crime and Economic Incentives. *Annual Review of Economics* 7:389–408.

Ehrlich, I. (1973). Participation in Illegitimate Activities: A Theoretical and Empirical Investigation. *Journal of Political Economy* 81(3):521–65.

Ehrlich, I. (1975). The Deterrent Effect of Capital Punishment: A Question of Life and Death. *American Economic Review* 65(3):397–417.

Ehrlich, I. (1977). Capital Punishment and Deterrence: Some Further Thoughts and Additional Evidence. *Journal of Political Economy* 85(4):741–88.

Gambetta, D. (1993). *The Sicilian Mafia: The Business of Private Protection*. London: Harvard University Press.

Leamer, E. (1983). Let's Take the Con Out of Econometrics. *American Economic Review* 73(1):31–43.

Schelling, T. C. (1967). Economics and the Criminal Enterprise. *Public Interest* 7:61–78.

Schelling, T. C. (1971). What is the Business of Organized Crime? *Journal of Public Law* 20:71–84.

2. The economics of policing and crime

Federico Masera[1]

1. INTRODUCTION

Two of the most basic functions of the state are the enforcement of its laws and ensuring the safety of its citizens. Modern states often use policing to achieve these goals. As shown in Figure 2.1, even in relatively safe countries, between 0.5 and 1 percent of annual GDP is spent on police services, which amounts to between 1 and 1.5 percent of overall state expenditure. In developing countries, the emphasis on policing is even more pronounced. South Africa offers one of the most extreme examples where around 6 percent of state expenditure is dedicated to policing. When focusing on the numbers of people employed in policing, the scale of this sector may be even more apparent: Among the countries represented in Figure 2.1, between 0.4 and 1.3 percent of the overall labor force is involved in policing.

The aim of this chapter is to explore the various effects of policing. In particular, I will explore recent advances in the economics literature that studies state-provided policing with a particular emphasis on the effects of policing on crime. It is important to note that, while the chapter is focused on state-provided policing, in most countries the state is not the sole provider of policing and law enforcement services. For example, private guards, criminal gangs and religious groups often play an even greater role in guaranteeing law enforcement. Additionally, although this chapter reviews the economic literature, most of the research on this topic is not carried out by economists. Criminology, sociology and political science, among many other disciplines, have also produced a large amount of high-quality scholarship.

2. OPTIMAL POLICING AND CRIMINAL BEHAVIOR

Economists view the decision regarding the optimal level of policing as determined by a trade-off: On the one hand, policing reduces overall crime while, on the other hand, policing is costly. In their most basic formulation, these costs include the costs of training and hiring police officers.[2]

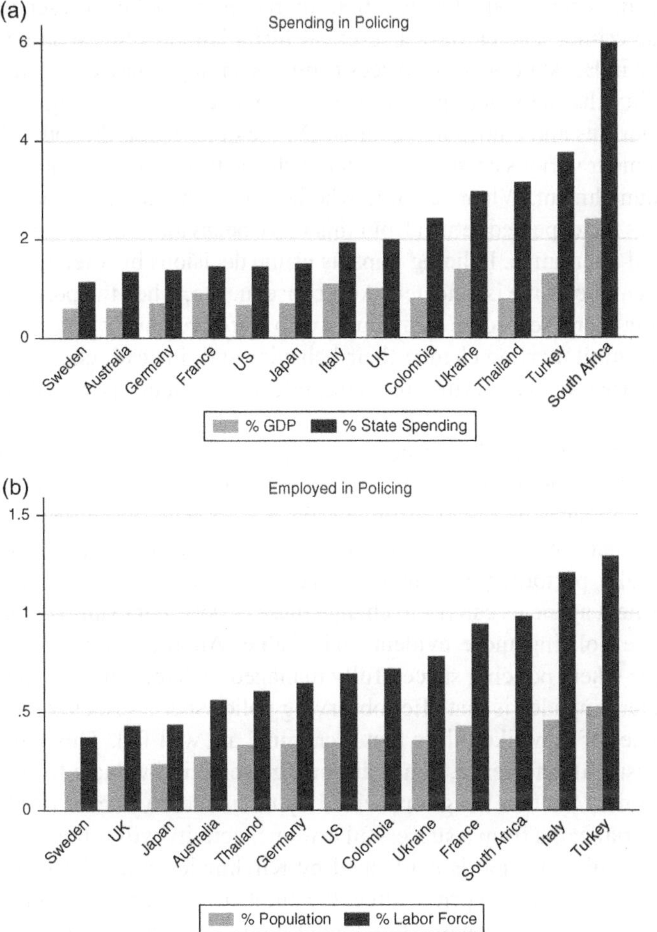

Sources (Top panel): US (Federal Reserve Economic Data), UK and Colombia (OECD) and the rest of the countries (IMF).

Sources (Bottom panel): US (Bureau of Justice), South Africa (South African Police Service), Japan, Australia, UK, Colombia, Thailand (UN) and for the remaining of the countries (EUROSTAT).

Figure 2.1 *Size of the police force by country. The top panel shows the amount spent on policing services as a percentage of GDP (light grey bars) and as a percentage of government spending (dark grey bars). The bottom panel shows the number of people employed in policing as a percentage of the total population (light grey bars) and the labor force (dark grey bars)*

Why do economists believe that increases in police presence should decrease crime? The earliest theoretical formulation of this relationship can be found in Becker (1968), who sees crime as a risky behavior. With a certain probability the individual performs a criminal act without being detected by the authorities and enjoys its rewards. On the other hand, the individual may fail and incur various costs. These include fines, time in jail and other forms of social punishment. When deciding whether to commit a crime, the individual compares the expected return from this risky behavior with the benefits of the best legal alternative. Policing impacts crime decisions by affecting the probability that the crime is detected. As a consequence, when the police presence in an area increases, some individuals who were previously optimally choosing to commit a crime change their behavior and, instead, choose their best legal alternative. This crime-reducing effect of policing is called the deterrence effect.

There are several other important insights regarding the determinants of crime that can be learned from this model. First, it is impossible to have a deterrent effect if potential criminals do not observe the increase in policing and, therefore, do not update their beliefs about how likely they are to successfully perform a criminal act. There are various ways in which law enforcement agencies can try to change these beliefs. For example, the agency can make policing more evident and visible. Another way is to publicize instances where policing successfully managed to detect an attempted crime. The underlying idea is that after observing police successes, citizens increase their belief of how likely it is that a criminal act will fail. This mechanism, called residual deterrence, could discourage some individuals from attempting a crime.[3] Another insight provided by the model in Becker (1968) is that the potential gains from a successful criminal activity will influence criminal behavior. This intuition is confirmed by Kirchmaier et al. (2020) that show how international metal prices affect the number of crimes involving the theft of those metals. Additionally, this model highlights that, when making decisions about committing a crime, individuals care about the expected costs they may incur if they are caught committing the act. This means that while increasing the probability of detecting a crime is a viable strategy to reduce overall crime, a similarly viable option is to increase the costs incurred by criminals when caught. This could be achieved without changing policing but instead increasing the harshness of the punishment delivered to criminals.

Policing may also have an effect on crime beyond the deterrence effect. For example, if a police officer detects a crime and apprehends the criminal, this will restrict the criminal's future actions. In particular, while the criminal is in jail or prison, he will be unable to commit new crimes. This is known as the incapacitation effect of policing. Whether incapacitation or deterrence are the main drivers of the effect that policing has on crime is often difficult to assess.

To do so, Mastrobuoni (2019) decomposes the elasticity of crime with respect to policing into two components: The elasticity of crime with respect to clearance rates and the elasticity of clearance rates with respect to policing. Doing so, he is able to identify the deterrence and incapacitation effects separately. In the context of robberies in Milan, Mastrobuoni (2019) finds that most of the effect that policing has on crime is due to the incapacitation effect.

3. EMPIRICAL LITERATURE

3.1. Policing Intensity and Crime

One of the most studied areas in the empirical literature on policing concerns determining and quantifying the effects that an increase in the size of the police force has on crime. As pointed out by Marvell and Moody (1996), even in the presence of high-quality data on crime and police deployment, studies need to overcome two issues. The first of these is the reverse causality problem generated by the fact that the police may be deployed in areas with a higher prevalence of crime. Because of this, a simple cross-sectional correlation could show no relationship between crime and the size of the police force, even though policing has a crime-reducing effect. The second issue is the potential correlation between the size of the police force and unobservable variables that influence crime. In order to control for time-invariant unobservable variables that influence crime, researchers have previously relied on panel data [Cornwell and Trumbull (1994)]. This type of analysis still leaves the estimates susceptible to time-varying unobservables that affect crime.

One of the first papers that attempted to address this endogeneity problem is Levitt (1997). Using the fact that increases in the size of the police force are concentrated in mayoral and gubernatorial election years, Levitt (1997) shows that the size of the police force negatively impacts violent and property crime. More recent examples in this literature are Di Tella and Schargrodsky (2004) and Draca et al. (2011) who exploit the fact that terrorist attacks in Buenos Aires and London, and the subsequent deployment of police in specific areas of these cities, can be used as an exogenous shock to policing. Both studies find negative and statistically significant effects of police deployments on crime. Similarly, based on the fact that changes in terror alert levels affect the police presence in Washington, DC, Klick and Tabarrok (2005) also highlight the crime-reducing effects of policing.

Another strand of the literature instead uses exogenous variation in the allocation of additional policing resources to certain cities. One source of variation often used in the literature is the US 'Violent Crime Control and Law Enforcement Act' that authorized US$8.8 billion in spending for grants directed to law enforcement agencies. After showing that time trends in crime rates were not related to the amount of grant money received by each municipality, Evans and Owens (2007) show that these grants were used to hire new police officers, which led to a reduction in crime. Weisburst (2019b) finds similar results for grants administered between 2000 and 2014, even after controlling for the police department's decision to apply for a grant. Another analysis of this grant is provided by Mello (2019), who instead uses the score cutoff rule in the grants distribution decision to show that a large spike in grants delivered in 2009 also reduced crime. Similarly, Machin and Marie (2011) studied the effect of the UK Street Crime Initiative, which, in 2002, distributed additional policing resources to only some specific areas of England and Wales. Also in this case an increase in policing resources reduced crime.

Other recent studies suggest a similar effect of policing on crime by exploiting shifts in policing intensity due to changes in patrolling routes and decisions. For example, Weisburd (2019) shows that some police patrol areas may be left unattended whenever a patrol car responds to a call from another police patrol area. Even in the few minutes when the area is left unattended, there is an increase in crime. This result shows how reactive criminal activity is to police presence. Mastrobuoni (2019) similarly explores what takes place during shift changes that disrupt policing. He shows that, although the likelihood of clearing the crime is considerably reduced in locations where police presence is lower due to shift changes, there is no increase in robberies in these locations.

Similarly, Blanes i Vidal and Kirchmaier (2018) make use of the fact that Manchester's police response times change discontinuously across division boundaries. Accordingly, if criminals are aware of these differences, they should target places with longer response times as they are less likely to be caught. In line with this prediction, crimes are less likely to be cleared in places with longer response times, thereby incentivizing crime in these areas.

One final method used to identify the causal effect of policing on crime is by exploiting the fact that fines are an important source of revenue for many city budgets. This suggests that policing may increase in moments when public finances are in difficulty. Makowsky and Stratmann (2011), using data from municipalities in Massachusetts, first instrument policing intensity regarding traffic violations with municipal budgetary shortfalls. As policing intensity increases, the number of motor vehicle violations and accidents decreases.

As shown in Table 2.1, a number of regularities emerge when comparing the elasticities of the effects of policing on crime. First, violent crimes are more reactive than property crimes to changes in policing. Second, elasticities are generally higher than –1, and in the few instances when they are lower than –1 they are not statistically different than –1. When reading Table 2.1, it is important to bear in mind that the elasticities in the third column, which relate to overall changes in crime, are expected to be similar to the elasticities for

Table 2.1 *Comparing effects of police on crime*

Paper	Elasticity property crime	Elasticity violent crime	Elasticity crime
Levitt (1997)	−0.3	−1	
Klick and Tabarrok (2005)			−0.3
Evans and Owens (2007)	−0.26	−0.99	
Draca et al. (2011)			(−0.3,−0.4)
Weisburst (2019)	−0.7	−1.3	
Mello (2019)	−0.8	−1.3	
Weisburd (2019)	−0.6	−0.9	
Mastrobuoni (2019)	−0.5		

Note: This table displays the estimates of the elasticity of crime to changes in the size of the police force. The first column displays the elasticity of property crime. The second column displays the elasticity of violent crime. The last column displays the elasticity of the overall crime rate.

property crimes because the vast majority of crimes are non-violent. Third, there are large discrepancies between estimates of elasticities. These differences may be due to peculiarities of the context studied or the identification strategy chosen.

An important factor to consider in this type of study is that the credibility of the size of the estimates relies upon the validity of the police and crime statistics. This issue is highlighted by Vollaard and Hamed (2012), who show how data issues may have important impacts on studies attempting to measure the effects of policing on crime. This is due to the fact that many criminal incidents are not reported to the police and, therefore, do not enter the statistics. This type of bias is not innocuous because this under-reporting depends on the size of the police force. Vollaard and Hamed (2012) show that when the number of police officers increases, a higher proportion of crimes enter the crime statistics. This phenomenon is especially present for violent crime statistics. This error in reporting ultimately generates an upward bias in the estimates. Chalfin and McCrary (2018) also highlight potential issues with measurement in US crime data and propose a method to solve these measurement errors. When using statistics corrected for these measurement errors, elasticities are larger and more precisely estimated. Therefore, it is important for researchers who study policing and crime to be aware of the limitations of the data used and attempt to either solve or correct these issues.

3.2. Spillovers

Beyond the direct effect that an increase in policing efforts may have on crime in that location, researchers have also hypothesized that policing could generate geographical spillovers. The reason underlying this proposition is that when potential criminals notice an increase in policing in a specific location, they may decide to move their activities to neighboring areas that offer similar criminal opportunities but have a lower police presence. The identification of these spillovers generally requires a special setting where policing differs between neighboring areas and the reasons for these differences are unrelated to unobservables that determine crime. Several recent studies have been able to overcome these constraints and study spillovers generated by policing.

For example, Maheshri and Mastrobuoni (2021) identify these geographical spillovers in the context of bank robberies in Italy. Bank guards substantially lower the probability that the bank they are guarding is robbed but increase the probability that unguarded neighboring banks are robbed. Also other types of crimes seem to display similar geographical spillovers. For example, Blattman et al. (2021) show that, in an experiment run in the city of Bogota, streets randomly assigned a double police patrol which subsequently saw a reduction in crime that was almost completely displaced onto neighboring areas. Additionally, displacement does not have to only be geographical. Yang (2008) shows that when the Philippines increased enforcement efforts on a particular method for avoiding import duties, this increased the use of alternative avoidance methods.

Not all studies have been able to find such spillover effects. Collazos et al. (2021) shows that street segments that were randomly assigned more police patrols experienced a decrease in crime. They find no evidence of consequent crime displacement and, if anything, they observe a decrease in crime in some untreated areas. Similarly, in a recent literature review, Braga et al. (2019) reveal that there is no evidence that policing efforts generally generate spillovers to surrounding areas.

More research is required to reconcile the results found in these studies. Understanding the existence of these spillover effects of policing is especially policy-relevant because of a common policing strategy called 'hot spot policing'. This strategy mandates concentrating policing efforts in particularly problematic areas. Importantly, the effectiveness of this type of strategy relies upon the fact that these extra policing efforts do not displace crime onto neighboring areas.

3.3. Policing Strategies and Policies

As with any other organization, the performance of police departments depends not only on the number of employees but also on many other factors that determine employee effectiveness. These factors include the composition of the employees and how they are monitored or compensated. Accordingly, the literature that studies the effects of policing on crime has looked not only at the effect of police officer numbers but also at the effects that various policing strategies and policies have on crime. This is of particular importance to policy-makers as many of these policies may provide an inexpensive way to decrease crime as compared to hiring and training new police officers.

A natural dimension of policing to study is the effect of the composition of the police force. One of the most striking imbalances in the composition of the police force is in terms of gender. While many improvements have been made in the last years, only a small minority of police officers are female. In the US, only 12.6 percent of police officers are women, while in Australia this number is 13.5 percent and in Europe it reaches 16.9 percent. To understand the effect of female representation in the police force, Miller and Segal (2019) study the integration of women into US police departments between the late 1970s and early 1990s. Their findings show that as the share of females in the force increases, violent crime rates toward women decrease. Importantly, these reductions are especially pronounced in rates of domestic violence.

An issue often highlighted in relation to the composition of the police force, especially in the US, is the racial dimension. As with gender, the racial composition of police forces does not reflect the demographic composition of the populations they police. In the US, a first push toward racial representation in the police force started in 1969, when courts started imposing affirmative action measures. As shown by McCrary (2007), in the decades that followed, these measures lead to an increase in the share of Black people employed in the police force. Although these affirmative action policies had no apparent effect on crime, they did lower the arrest per crime rate and the fraction of Black people arrested for the most serious offenses. In more recent work, Ba et al. (2021) have explored the effects of the identity of the police officer on various policing behaviors. Controlling for the fact that officers with different characteristics may be assigned to patrol different neighborhoods, they find that Black and Hispanic officers make fewer arrests and use force less often. These effects are particularly large when the citizen-officer interaction involves a Black civilian. Similarly, female officers make fewer arrests and use force less often.

Another aspect of policing, which has become particularly relevant following the emergence of the Black Lives Matter movement, is police oversight and the consequences that police face in cases of misconduct. While too much oversight may hinder the ability of police officers to do their jobs effectively, oversight is necessary to ensure discipline among police officers and ensure they are acting in the interests of the entire community. There are many sources of oversight over police behavior. First, police officers may be punished by the enforcement agency or even lose their job as a consequence of misconduct. However, as discussed by Cunningham et al. (2020), police unions are often able to shield officers from disciplinary action taken against them. Dharmapala et al. (2022) for the case of Florida and Cunningham et al. (2021) for the whole US show that, because of this, police unions affect police behavior. After the right to form a union is granted, enforcement agents are more frequently involved in violent incidents of misconduct and are more likely to use deadly force. These reforms have no effect on crime. Goncalves (2020) using a different identification strategy based on the staggered roll out of unions finds no effect on the behavior of police officers.

Another source of police oversight comes from the general public. Public attention may be particularly intense after a scandal involving the police, for example, due to the controversy generated by a police killing. Shi (2009) notes that in Cincinnati, after the public reaction to an infamous incident of police brutality in 2001 in which an unarmed Black adolescent was killed, police behavior changed. Arrests, especially in Black neighborhoods, decreased. In the same period, felony crimes increased. Similar results are found by Ba and Rivera (2019) who analyzed the effects of the increased oversight following the killing of a Black teenager by a Chicago police officer. This event generated considerable national media attention and led to a decrease in policing efforts and an increase in crime.

The authors contrast this event, which affected the oversight coming from the public, with changes in the perceived internal oversight imposed by the police department. To identify this effect, they use the publication of articles by the police union that shifted the perceived cost of receiving a misconduct accusation. They find that in this case increased oversight has no effect on crime. Finally, oversight from the public can also depend on how the media covers crime. Mastrorocco and Ornaghi (2020) explore the case of the acquisition of a TV station by the broadcasting group Sinclair, after which coverage of local crime decreased and crime became a less salient issue for civilians. This decrease in public oversight affects policing efforts as measured by a decrease in the clearance rate of various crimes.

As described in Section 3.1, the size of the police force has well-established effects on crime. Therefore, enforcement agencies often attempt to combat crime by increasing the number of police officers. This option may not always be available due to budgetary or legal reasons. Therefore, agencies have tried to find alternative sources to fulfill policing roles. One option is to hire from the private sector. Heaton et al. (2016) exploit the temporal and spatial variation of the University of Chicago Police Department jurisdiction, the largest private police department in Chicago, to estimate the effects of this type of policing. As with regular public police officers, private police officers decrease crime. In a similar fashion, another alternative policing strategy used by enforcement agencies is community monitoring. This strategy entails the use of members of the community to help with the policing effort. These individuals are not given policing powers but are only used for basic surveillance and crime reporting. McMillen et al. (2019) study the Chicago safe passage program that deployed civilian monitors on some routes that students use to travel from and to school. They find that these civilian guards reduced crime. Gonzalez and Komisarow (2020) confirm these results and, in addition, highlight how this program also generated important geographical spillovers. Finally, Cheng and Long (2018) researched the introduction of the 'French Quarter Task Force' in New Orleans. This program hired off-duty cops to proactively patrol some areas of the city. Officers employed through this program were also incentivized according to their performance and were monitored using a GPS tracking system. Also, in this case, the authors find a reduction in robberies, assaults and thefts in the areas patrolled by this task force as compared to other neighborhoods of New Orleans. Overall, these results show that, as with regular police officers, hiring officers in the private sector or recruiting policing forces from the community reduces crime.

Another strategy used to increase the effectiveness of scarce police resources is to concentrate policing efforts on particular types of crime while disregarding other less damaging, non-violent crimes. One of the most common proposals of this type is the depenalization of cannabis possession. The argument brought forward to defend this kind of policy is that police officers would be able to focus their efforts on more serious crimes generating an overall welfare improvement. Adda et al. (2014) study the effects of the implementation of this type of policy in London. They exploit the fact that the borough of Lambeth in London depenalized the possession of small quantities of cannabis and find that in this borough police reallocated their efforts toward other crimes. This change in the focus of policing entailed a reduction in non-drug crimes and general improvements in the effectiveness of police officers. In contrast, drug-related crimes increased, generating an overall decrease in the welfare of the citizens, as measured by house prices.

3.4. Technology and Policing

Recently, police have begun to extensively incorporate various modern equipment and technology to enhance their productivity. For example, surveillance cameras have become a common tool in combating crime. China is one of the most surveilled countries in the world with over 500 million surveillance cameras. The UK has an estimated 4 million surveillance cameras of which over half a million are in London alone. According to classical economic models of crime, we expect that surveillance cameras should decrease crime rates because they increase the probability that criminal behavior is detected and, therefore, increase the expected costs of committing a crime. Evidence from Priks (2015) confirms this intuition. When Stockholm introduced cameras in the subway system, crime decreased. Similar results were found by Gómez et al. (2021) when assessing a program that installed surveillance cameras in public areas of the city of Medellín, Colombia. The effects of the introduction of surveillance cameras tend to be geographically concentrated, and at least in the case of Priks (2015) they generate some spillovers to neighboring areas without cameras.

Another use of cameras in policing is for traffic control. As in the previous case, one would expect that traffic cameras reduce dangerous driving behavior and, therefore, also reduce traffic incidents. One important caveat related to traffic cameras is that drivers may drive more recklessly to avoid being detected by a camera. Overall, the results regarding traffic cameras are less conclusive than results on the effects of surveillance cameras used to detect other types of crime. For example, Chen and Warburton (2006) find some benefits from the introduction of speed cameras in British Columbia, while Gallagher and Fisher (2020) find, if anything, a negative effect from the introduction of electronic monitoring programs at road intersections.

One tool that is now omnipresent in policing around the world is the use of DNA databases. Starting at the end of the 1980s law enforcement agencies began creating databases containing information on the DNA profiles of criminals. This information could then be used to match crime scene evidence to individuals on this database. As with other technologies used in policing, this increases the expected cost of committing a crime for individuals in this database. One should therefore expect that these individuals would decrease the likelihood of perpetrating a crime. As shown by Doleac (2017) in the US case and Anker, Doleac and Landersø (2021) in the case of Denmark, DNA databases reduce recidivism and, therefore, overall crime.

Another source of new technology for the police is the military. The connection to the military does not stop at the equipment as often law enforcement uses military personnel and tactics for policing. For example, in developing countries, the military and a militarized police force are often used to police areas controlled by gangs and drug cartels. The rationale behind the use of this type of equipment is that the criminals themselves often use military-grade equipment and military tactics, which puts police officers in danger and renders them unable to police areas controlled by gangs. This militarized form of policing spread to most developed countries in the 2000s. This change was triggered by an increase in terrorist attacks in these countries and the subsequent perceived need to have a heavily armed police force to counteract this new risk. At the same time, troop withdrawal from the wars in Iraq and Afghanistan freed up large quantities of military equipment that have subsequently been used by the police. In no place is this more stark than in the US, where two-thirds of the population lives under the jurisdiction of an enforcement agency equipped with military weapons. Looking at the US case, Bove and Gavrilova (2017) find that the militarization of the police reduces crime.

Additionally, Harris et al. (2017) find that it reduces citizen complaints and assaults on officers. Masera (2021a) highlights the fact crime is displaced onto neighboring areas that are not militarized. This is particularly relevant given that the decision to militarize is left in the hands of individual law enforcement agencies, which are unlikely to take into account these negative spatial spillovers and may overmilitarize as a result. Masera (2021b) shows that the militarization of the police has increased police killings and, surprisingly, decreased police safety. Given the various costs and benefits of militarization, it is particularly difficult to assess the overall net benefits of this technology.

Finally, another important innovation now widely used in policing is predictive algorithms. This type of algorithm uses large datasets to predict where and when crimes are more likely to be committed. If implemented correctly, these algorithms should increase the productivity of the police and, therefore, decrease crime. Using the fact that in Milan not all police forces use predictive algorithms, Mastrobuoni (2020) shows that predictive policing increases police productivity. These algorithms are particularly effective because criminal groups tend to repeatedly operate in the same area and at the same time of the day, especially if they have been previously successful. In a similar fashion, predictive algorithms can be used to identify police officers who are misbehaving or are likely to be involved in police misconduct. In order to collect the data necessary for these predictions, many law enforcement agencies have created systems that allow civilians to report allegations of police misconduct. Rozema and Schanzenbach (2019) using data from the Chicago Police Department show that civilian allegations are a good predictor of future misconduct. Therefore, these types of systems can be hugely beneficial in the detection of problematic police officers.

3.5. Beyond Crime

The police may also affect the communities in which they operate beyond their impact on crime. One obvious effect of policing is the effects it can have on the illicit drug market. As described by Freeborn (2009) dealers and consumers of illicit drugs will respond to policing efforts by changing how the transactions of illicit drugs are made. For example, if policing efforts are focused on dealers, they will try to make quick and easy sales in order to avoid arrests. One way to achieve this is by reducing prices. On the other hand, if policing efforts are focused on the customers, they will accept high prices instead of shopping around for lower prices and increasing the risk of being arrested. This will increase equilibrium prices. Indeed, using US data, Freeborn (2009) finds that the relationship between policing efforts and illicit drug prices depends on the focus of the enforcement strategy. Moreover, policing the distribution of illicit drugs, by affecting drug use, may also impact health outcomes. To investigate this possibility Kelly and Rasul (2014) analyzed the decriminalization of the possession of small quantities of cannabis by the police force in the London borough of Lambeth. Their results show that this change in policing had a long-term effect on hospital admissions related to the use of hard drugs. Given that in the US, there is a substantial police presence in and around schools, policing could ultimately affect students' behavior. Weisburst (2019a) finds that an increased police presence in schools leads to more instances of disciplinary action taken toward students. This ultimately affects students' performance, especially in the case of Black students. Police may also have an effect on students even when they are not directly present at a school. In particular, incidents of police violence in a community may affect students' psychological well-being. Using data from Los Angeles County, Ang (2021) finds that the use of deadly violence by the police reduces students' school performance, school completion rates and emotional well-being. Gershenson and Hayes (2018) offer similar results based on a comparison between elementary school students' performance in Ferguson and in the greater St. Louis area following the infamous police shooting of Michael Brown.

3.5.1. Bias in policing

Many other areas can be affected by policing, but no discussion of policing would be complete without exploring how it can perpetuate pre-existing biases in society. In this subsection, I describe how scholars have tried to identify the existence of bias in policing and what factors can affect these biases.

The basic issue in this literature is that the over-representation of a particular group in the policed, stopped, arrested or jailed population is not sufficient evidence of biased policing. This is because this over-representation may be due to differences in the behavior of this group and not biased policing. To identify the existence and extent of any bias, researchers have applied various methods.

One of the first methods used was the hit-rate test, where bias in policing is identified by comparing the outcome of searches following police stops, across races. The underlying idea is that if the police are unbiased, the distribution of outcomes of police stops should be the same across races. This conclusion is based on the assumption that police officers make stop decisions to maximize arrests. Stashko (2022) shows that this assumption holds when using US data. Using this hit-rate test, Knowles et al. (2001) and Persico and Todd (2006) find no racial bias in police stops between races. Anwar and Fang (2006), using data from Florida, instead cannot reject the null that police officers do not exhibit racial prejudice.

Another popular method to identify bias involves controlling for many observable characteristics related to the policing incident. For example, when trying to identify bias in police stop decisions, researchers can control for the time of day, the location and the circumstance of the stop. According to this method, policing is biased if, even after controlling for these observables, citizens of different races are stopped at different rates. Using data from the Boston Police Department, Antonovics and Knight (2009) find that there are disparities in the search decisions of police officers along racial lines. Ba et al. (2021), after controlling for a large set of observables, find that Black and Hispanic officers in Chicago make fewer stops and use less force, especially toward Black citizens. Using datasets from various US cities, Fryer (2019) finds no racial differences in police use of force. It is important to highlight that some potential issues may hinder the ability to infer racial bias through this type of method. One complication, highlighted by Knox et al. (2020), is the existence of post-treatment bias. This may occur when racial bias is estimated by comparing how police officers behave after a stop. The issue comes from the possibility that the decision to make the stop could already have been biased. Accordingly, any researcher aiming to use this method to infer racial bias needs to choose a setting where post-treatment bias is unlikely.

Alternatively, instead of trying to control for observables related to police encounters, it is possible to identify racial bias by exploiting the random assignment of officers to some police encounters. For example, West (2018) uses the fact that automobile crash investigations are as good as random to show that US state police officers are racially biased toward drivers in their decisions to issue citations. Finally, some other researchers have exploited the particularities of the setting studied to infer racial bias. One common method is based on the fact that after sunset it is more difficult for a biased police officer to observe a citizen's race before a stop decision is made. Because of this, if the over-representation of a race decreases after sunset, it is possible to infer that the officer is racially biased toward this race. Using this method, Grogger and Ridgeway (2006) find no evidence that the police in Oakland, California, are racially biased. However, Horrace and Rohlin (2016) using data from Syracuse and Pierson et al. (2020) using data from the whole US find evidence for racial bias toward Black drivers. Using an alternative method, Goncalves (2020) instead exploits the fact that Florida highway patrol officers can choose to be lenient when issuing speeding tickets if the speed of the driver is close to a threshold. Using a bunching estimator technique, they show that minorities are less likely to receive this lenient treatment and leniency behavior is not equal across officers.

Other research instead has attempted to identify the factors that can affect bias in policing. Grosjean et al. (2021) focus on the 2015–16 Trump campaign and show that the probability that a police stop is of a Black driver increases after his rallies. The effects are largest among racially biased officers and in areas with more racist attitudes. Overall, more needs to be done on understanding what can affect bias in policing and the extent of this phenomenon beyond the US setting.

NOTES

1. University of New South Wales.
2. Beyond these basic requirements, policing may generate many other costs and benefits. These include effects on the mental health of citizens, overall economic activity and incarceration costs. In Section 3.5, I will discuss these additional consequences of policing in more depth.
3. Dilmé and Garrett (2019) provide a theory that describes how law enforcement agencies may use residual deterrence.

REFERENCES

Adda, J., McConnell, B., and Rasul, I. (2014). Crime and the depenalization of cannabis possession: Evidence from a policing experiment. *Journal of Political Economy*, 122(5):1130–202.

Ang, D. (2021). The effects of police violence on inner-city students. *The Quarterly Journal of Economics*, 136(1):115–68.

Anker, A. S. T., Doleac, J. L., and Landersø, R. (2021). The effects of DNA databases on the deterrence and detection of offenders. *American Economic Journal: Applied Economics*, 13(4):194–225.

Antonovics, K. and Knight, B. G. (2009). A new look at racial profiling: Evidence from the Boston police department. *The Review of Economics and Statistics*, 91(1):163–77.

Anwar, S. and Fang, H. (2006). An alternative test of racial prejudice in motor vehicle searches: Theory and evidence. *American Economic Review*, 96(1):127–51.

Ba, B. A. and Rivera, R. G. (2019). The effect of police oversight on crime and allegations of misconduct: Evidence from Chicago, Working Paper.

Ba, B. A., Knox, D., Mummolo, J., and Rivera, R. (2021). The role of officer race and gender in police-civilian interactions in Chicago. *Science*, 371(6530):696–702.

Becker, G. S. (1968). Crime and punishment: An economic approach. *The Journal of Political Economy*, 76(2):169–217.

Blanes, I., Vidal, J., and Kirchmaier, T. (2018). The effect of police response time on crime clearance rates. *The Review of Economic Studies*, 85(2):855–91.

Blattman, C., Green, D. P., Ortega, D., and Tobón, S. (2021). Place-based interventions at scale: The direct and spillover effects of policing and city services on crime. *Journal of the European Economic Association*, 19(4):2022–51.

Bove, V. and Gavrilova, E. (2017). Police officer on the frontline or a soldier? The effect of police militarization on crime. *American Economic Journal: Economic Policy*, 9(3):1–18.

Braga, A. A., Turchan, B., Papachristos, A. V., and Hureau, D. M. (2019). Hot spots policing of small geographic areas effects on crime. *Campbell Systematic Reviews*, 15(3):e1046.

Chalfin, A. and McCrary, J. (2018). Are US cities underpoliced? Theory and evidence. *Review of Economics and Statistics*, 100(1):167–86.

Chen, G. and Warburton, R. N. (2006). Do speed cameras produce net benefits? Evidence from British Columbia, Canada. *Journal of Policy Analysis and Management: The Journal of the Association for Public Policy Analysis and Management*, 25(3):661–78.

Cheng, C. and Long, W. (2018). Improving police services: Evidence from the French quarter task force. *Journal of Public Economics*, 164:1–18.

Collazos, D., García, E., Mejía, D., Ortega, D., and Tobón, S. (2021). Hot spots policing in a high-crime environment: An experimental evaluation in Medellin. *Journal of Experimental Criminology*, 17(3):473–506.

Cornwell, C. and Trumbull, W. N. (1994). Estimating the economic model of crime with panel data. *The Review of Economics and Statistics*, 76(2):360–66.

Cunningham, J., Feir, D., and Gillezeau, R. (2020). Overview of research on collective bargaining rights and law enforcement officer's bills of rights, Working Paper.

Cunningham, J., Feir, D., and Gillezeau, R. (2021). Collective bargaining rights, policing, and civilian deaths, Working Paper.

Dharmapala, D., McAdams, R. H., and Rappaport, J. (2022). Collective bargaining rights and police misconduct: Evidence from Florida. *The Journal of Law, Economics, and Organization*, 38(1):1–4.

Di Tella, R. and Schargrodsky, E. (2004). Do police reduce crime? Estimates using the allocation of police forces after a terrorist attack. *American Economic Review*, 94(1):115–33.

Dilmé, F. and Garrett, D. F. (2019). Residual deterrence. *Journal of the European Economic Association*, 17(5):1654–86.

Doleac, J. L. (2017). The effects of DNA databases on crime. *American Economic Journal: Applied Economics*, 9(1):165–201.

Draca, M., Machin, S., and Witt, R. (2011). Panic on the streets of London: Police, crime, and the July 2005 terror attacks. *American Economic Review*, 101(5):2157–81.

Evans, W. N. and Owens, E. G. (2007). Cops and crime. *Journal of Public Economics*, 91(1–2):181–201.

Freeborn, B. A. (2009). Arrest avoidance: Law enforcement and the price of cocaine. *The Journal of Law and Economics*, 52(1):19–40.

Fryer, R. G. (2019). An empirical analysis of racial differences in police use of force. *Journal of Political Economy*, 127(3):1210–61.

Gallagher, J. and Fisher, P. J. (2020). Criminal deterrence when there are offsetting risks: Traffic cameras, vehicular accidents, and public safety. *American Economic Journal: Economic Policy*, 12(3):202–37.

Gershenson, S. and Hayes, M. S. (2018). Police shootings, civic unrest and student achievement: Evidence from Ferguson. *Journal of Economic Geography*, 18(3):663–85.

Gómez, S., Mejía, D., and Tobón, S. (2021). The deterrent effect of surveillance cameras on crime. *Journal of Policy Analysis and Management*, 40(2):553–71.

Goncalves, F. (2020). *Do police unions increase misconduct.* Technical report, Working Paper.

Gonzalez, R. and Komisarow, S. (2020). Community monitoring and crime: Evidence from Chicago's safe passage program. *Journal of Public Economics*, 191:104250.

Grogger, J. and Ridgeway, G. (2006). Testing for racial profiling in traffic stops from behind a veil of darkness. *Journal of the American Statistical Association*, 101(475):878–87.

Grosjean, P. A., Masera, F., and Yousaf, H. (2021). Whistle the racist dogs: Political campaigns and police stops.

Harris, M. C., Park, J., Bruce, D. J., and Murray, M. N. (2017). Peacekeeping force: Effects of providing tactical equipment to local law enforcement. *American Economic Journal: Economic Policy*, 9(3):291–313.

Heaton, P., Hunt, P., MacDonald, J., and Saunders, J. (2016). The short-and long-run effects of private law enforcement: Evidence from university police. *The Journal of Law and Economics*, 59(4):889–912.

Horrace, W. C. and Rohlin, S. M. (2016). How dark is dark? Bright lights, big city, racial profiling. *Review of Economics and Statistics*, 98(2):226–32.

Kelly, E. and Rasul, I. (2014). Policing cannabis and drug related hospital admissions: Evidence from administrative records. *Journal of Public Economics*, 112:89–114.

Kirchmaier, T., Machin, S., Sandi, M., and Witt, R. (2020). Prices, policing and policy: The dynamics of crime booms and busts. *Journal of the European Economic Association*, 18(2):1040–77.

Klick, J. and Tabarrok, A. (2005). Using terror alert levels to estimate the effect of police on crime. *The Journal of Law and Economics*, 48(1):267–79.

Knowles, J., Persico, N., and Todd, P. (2001). Racial bias in motor vehicle searches: Theory and evidence. *Journal of Political Economy*, 109(1):203–29.

Knox, D., Lowe, W., and Mummolo, J. (2020). Administrative records mask racially biased policing. *American Political Science Review*, 114(3):619–37.

Levitt, S. D. (1997). Using electoral cycles in police hiring to estimate the effects of police on crime. *American Economic Review*, 87(3):270–90.

Machin, S. and Marie, O. (2011). Crime and police resources: The street crime initiative. *Journal of the European Economic Association*, 9(4):678–701.

Maheshri, V. and Mastrobuoni, G. (2021). The race between deterrence and displacement: Theory and evidence from bank robberies. *Review of Economics and Statistics*, 103(3):547–62.

Makowsky, M. D. and Stratmann, T. (2011). More tickets, fewer accidents: How cash-strapped towns make for safer roads. *The Journal of Law and Economics*, 54(4):863–88.

Marvell, T. B. and Moody, C. E. (1996). Specification problems, police levels, and crime rates. *Criminology*, 34(4):609–46.

Masera, F. (2021a). Violent Crime and the Overmilitarization of US Policing. *The Journal of Law, Economics, and Organization*, 37(3):479–511.

Masera, F. (2021b). Police safety, killings by the police, and the militarization of US law enforcement. *Journal of Urban Economics*, 124:103365.

Mastrobuoni, G. (2019). Police disruption and performance: Evidence from recurrent redeployments within a city. *Journal of Public Economics*, 176:18–31.

Mastrobuoni, G. (2020). Crime is terribly revealing: Information technology and police productivity. *The Review of Economic Studies*, 87(6):2727–53.

Mastrorocco, N. and Ornaghi, A. (2020). *Who Watches the Watchmen? Local News and Police Behavior in the United States*. University of Warwick, Department of Economics.

McCrary, J. (2007). The effect of court-ordered hiring quotas on the composition and quality of police. *American Economic Review*, 97(1):318–53.

McMillen, D., Sarmiento-Barbieri, I., and Singh, R. (2019). Do more eyes on the street reduce crime? Evidence from Chicago's safe passage program. *Journal of Urban Economics*, 110:1–25.

Mello, S. (2019). More cops, less crime. *Journal of Public Economics*, 172:174–200.

Miller, A. R. and Segal, C. (2019). Do female officers improve law enforcement quality? Effects on crime reporting and domestic violence. *The Review of Economic Studies*, 86(5):2220–47.

Persico, N. and Todd, P. (2006). Generalising the hit rates test for racial bias in law enforcement, with an application to vehicle searches in Wichita. *The Economic Journal*, 116(515):F351–67.

Pierson, E., Simoiu, C., Overgoor, J., Corbett-Davies, S., Jenson, D., Shoemaker, A., Ramachandran, V., Barghouty, P., Phillips, C., Shroff, R., et al. (2020). A large-scale analysis of racial disparities in police stops across the United States. *Nature Human Behaviour*, 4(7):736–45.

Priks, M. (2015). The effects of surveillance cameras on crime: Evidence from the Stockholm subway. *The Economic Journal*, 125(588):F289–305.

Rozema, K. and Schanzenbach, M. (2019). Good cop, bad cop: Using civilian allegations to predict police misconduct. *American Economic Journal: Economic Policy*, 11(2):225–68.

Shi, L. (2009). The limit of oversight in policing: Evidence from the 2001 Cincinnati riot. *Journal of Public Economics*, 93(1–2):99–113.

Stashko, A. (2022). Do police maximize arrests or minimize crime. Evidence from Racial Profiling in US Cities. *Journal of the European Economic Association,* Forthcoming.

Vollaard, B. and Hamed, J. (2012). Why the police have an effect on violent crime after all: Evidence from the British crime survey. *The Journal of Law and Economics*, 55(4):901–24.

Weisburd, S. (2021). Police presence, rapid response rates, and crime prevention. *Review of Economics and Statistics*, 103(2):280–93.

Weisburst, E. K. (2019a). Patrolling public schools: The impact of funding for school police on student discipline and long-term education outcomes. *Journal of Policy Analysis and Management*, 38(2):338–65.

Weisburst, E. K. (2019b). Safety in police numbers: Evidence of police effectiveness from federal cops grant applications. *American Law and Economics Review*, 21(1):81–109.

West, J. (2018). Racial bias in police investigations. Retrieved from University of California, Santa Cruz website: https://people.ucsc.edu/~jwest1/articles/West_RacialBiasPolice.pdf.

Yang, D. (2008). Can enforcement backfire? Crime displacement in the context of customs reform in the Philippines. *The Review of Economics and Statistics*, 90(1):1–14.

3. The geography of crime and policing

Matthew Freedman, Emily Owens and Derek Christopher[1]

1. INTRODUCTION

In this chapter, we explore changes in the geography of crime and policing in the US over the past four decades. Specifically, we document crime and policing's evolving relationships with poverty and race between 1980 and 2017. During this period, there were multiple large-scale structural shocks to crime and criminal justice in the US. These include shocks affecting potential root causes of crime, such as tax and welfare reform, workforce automation, the rise of free trade and the crack and opioid epidemics. They also include significant changes in the stance that governments in the US took toward both crime and crime control, including heightened federal involvement in drug control during the Reagan administration and increased federal funding of local police departments during the Clinton administration.

City-level crime rates and policing intensity are the product of a wide range of social, economic and contextual factors. Our focus on poverty and race is motivated by the theoretical and historical significance of these two demographic factors in crime and policing. From the standard economic perspective of the Becker (1968) model, poverty is a first-order determinant of criminal behavior. However, what it means to be poor in the US now is very different than in the 1970s (Chaudry et al. 2016). Therefore, we explore whether shifts in city-level poverty and inequality in the US over the past four decades have changed the importance of income in the criminal justice environment, in terms of exposure both to violent crime and to policing.

We also examine how crime and policing have changed in cities with larger Black populations. The percentage of a city's population that is Black and its poverty rate are positively correlated, and in fact wealth gaps between Black and White households in the US have not shrunk since 1980 (McIntosh et al. 2020). However, the history of policing, and conceptualization of crime, in the US cannot be separated from the history of Black people in America (National Academies of Sciences, Engineering, and Medicine 2018). This fraught history makes the geography of race, crime and policing critical to document on its own.

We illustrate and connect several broad facts regarding the spatial and temporal patterns of crime and policing in the US. First, against the backdrop of substantial declines in violent crime nationwide between 1980 and 2017, there was a flattening of the poverty-crime and race-crime gradients. The largest declines in violent crime occurred in cities with initially higher poverty rates and larger Black populations. As a result, poverty and race are weaker predictors of crime today than they were four decades ago.

Second, we show that the positive correlations between the number of police and poverty rates as well as the size of the Black population at the city level have been more persistent; the number of police per capita was, and remains, higher in higher poverty cities and cities with relatively large Black populations.

Third, arrests for violent and other crimes have fallen more per capita in cities with initially higher poverty rates and larger Black populations, and we observe a flattening of the poverty-arrest and race-arrest gradients over time. The statistical correlations between the arrest rate and poverty as well as race persist even after conditioning on city-level violent crime rates. Put differently, since 1980 the number of arrests made per resident, and per officer, has fallen more sharply in cities with initially higher poverty rates and in cities with initially larger Black populations.

The changing geography of crime and arrests, together with the stability of the geography of policing, suggests that police officers in cities with initially higher poverty and larger Black populations are spending relatively more time engaged in other, non-arrest activities today than 40 years ago. This reduction in time spent on arrest-focused officer activity creates the potential for policing in the US to be increasingly heterogeneous across place. While the reduction in exposure to violence, and the decreased concentration of violence in cities with larger disadvantaged populations, is something to celebrate,[2] the persistent city-level relationship between policing, poverty and race opens the possibility for growing spatial inequality in how people interact with the police.

This raises important questions about what police-civilian interactions look like and how they vary across different groups. Non-arrest activity by police officers is not currently measured in a systematic way that would allow for an evaluation of which police actions are the most effective at increasing social welfare. Some of these activities may actively reduce crime at minimal social cost, but others may impose substantial costs on society with only minimal benefits. One dataset that sheds some light on police operations in the US is the Law Enforcement Management and Administrative Survey (LEMAS). Using the 2016 LEMAS, we do not observe any clear cross-sectional relationship between race, poverty and the share of officers explicitly dedicated to community policing or community relations roles. We do observe a weak positive cross-sectional relationship between the fraction of a city's population that is Black or a city's poverty rate and a proxy for civilian demand for police presence. However, the same data suggest that this weak positive relationship is almost entirely explained by spatial differences in violent crime, rather than differences in preferences for police engagement that are correlated with race or poverty. While the LEMAS provides little visibility into why police presence is requested or what police-civilian interactions look like on the ground, these results further suggest that police may be engaged in a wider range of activities in cities with higher poverty rates and larger Black populations.

The observation that the breadth of what police do in a community has broadened after the Great Crime Decline of the 1990s is not new (e.g., Koper et al. (2020), Lum (2021), Brooks (2021)). Others have also documented the robust and persistent relationship between a city's police force size and the size of the local Black population (e.g., Carmichael and Kent (2014)). However, to the best of our knowledge, the link between the growth in the scope for 'non-traditional' policing and cities' poverty levels and racial compositions has not been explicitly documented.

We conclude with a discussion of how future research could help improve our understanding of the scope of officer activities and contribute to current policy discussions about the role of police. Identifying 'what works' in policing is not technically complicated but relies on measuring what police are actually doing. Researchers engaged in qualitative research and systematic field observation of the everyday operations of police departments and activities of officers are providing insights that could help to guide the development of data necessary for larger-scale quantitative analyses (Willis and Mastrofski 2016, Lum et al. 2020, Brooks 2021). Building on some departments' efforts in systematically generating and publicly disseminating records of officer tasks would also facilitate more compelling and generalizable cross-jurisdiction analyses. Finally, further exploration of the dynamics of policing, poverty and race across neighborhoods within cities could shed light on if and how the patterns we identify at the city level play out at more micro-geographic levels.

2. POVERTY, RACE AND CRIME ACROSS US CITIES, 1980–2017

In our first set of analyses, we examine how the violent crime-poverty gradient as well as the violent crime-race gradient at the city level have changed over time. We study the evolution of these gradients over the 37-year period between 1980 and 2017. The year 2017 is the most recent for which all necessary data for our analyses are available; the general pattern of results holds if we use 2010 or 2016 as end dates.[3] We include all cities in the US with at least 100 000 residents in 1980. Crime data for our city-level analyses are derived from the Uniform Crime Reports (UCR). We construct violent crime rates for each year at the city level using total known numbers of homicides, assaults, robberies and rapes (violent index crimes) and dividing by total population from the Decennial Census (for 1980) or the American Community Survey (for 2017). In subsequent analyses, we additionally leverage city-level data from the UCR on arrests (including both misdemeanor and felony arrests) as well as police force size (number of officers). We exclude cities that were missing information on crimes, arrests or number of officers in 1980 or 2017.

We begin by illustrating variation in poverty and violent crime over the entire 37-year time frame. The plots we show here and throughout this chapter are not weighted; the broad patterns are similar if we weight by city population. They are also qualitatively similar if, instead of using all violent index crimes, we use only homicides.

We first plot in Panel (a) of Figure 3.1 the relationship between violent crime rates (measured per 100 000 people) and poverty rates across the 151 cities in our sample in 1980 and in 2017. This figure makes clear both the broad decline in violent crime rates across cities as well as the general weakening of the relationship between city-level violent crime rates and poverty levels.

In Panel (b) of Figure 3.1, we explore the extent of each city's violent crime decline as a function of its initial (1980) poverty rate. Initially poorer cities witnessed relatively large declines in violent crime; for every 1 percentage point higher poverty rate in 1980, the number of violent crimes per 100 000 people declined by 33 between 1980 and 2017. This finding complements that of Friedson and Sharkey (2015), who document a similar spatiotemporal pattern of crime declines across neighborhoods within cities.

We conduct a similar analysis focusing on the racial composition of cities instead of poverty. In Panel (c) of Figure 3.1, we see that as violent crime rates dropped overall, the relationship between violent crime rates and the fraction of a city's population that is Black weakened. However, the relationship between violent crime rates and share Black in 1980 was not as pronounced as that between violent crime rates and poverty rates. In Panel (d) of Figure 3.1, we additionally see that the largest drops in crime occurred in cities with larger initial Black populations; every 1 percentage point higher share of the population that was Black in 1980 was associated with an additional 8 per 100 000 resident decline in violent crime between 1980 and 2017.

These findings corroborate prior work that highlights important cross-sectional relationships between poverty and crime as well as race and crime (e.g., Flango and Sherbenou (1976), Liska and Bellair (1995), Glaeser and Sacerdote (1996)). These results for the evolution of poverty-crime and race-crime gradients between 1980 and 2017 comport with Friedson and Sharkey

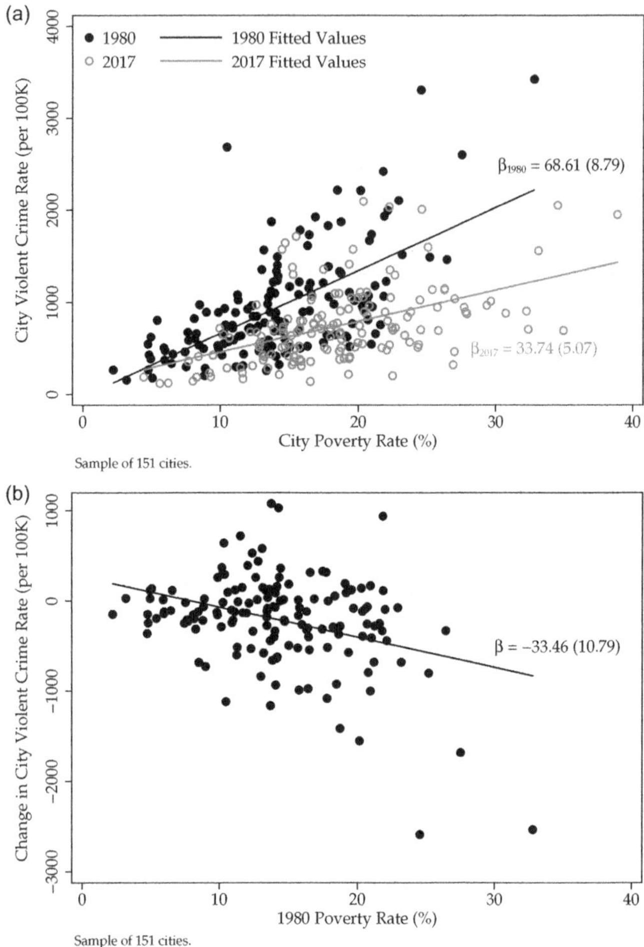

Notes: Data derived from the Uniform Crime Reports, Decennial Census and American Community Survey. The figure includes cities with populations of at least 100 000 in 1980 as well as complete data on crime, arrests and police force size in 1980 and 2017. Coefficients (βs) are from unweighted univariate regressions of the variable on the y-axis against the variable on the x-axis. Standard errors (in parentheses) are heteroskedasticity robust.

Figure 3.1 *Violent crime rates, poverty and race across US cities. (a) Crime and poverty, 1980 and 2017. (b) Changes in crime and poverty. (c) Crime and Black pop., 1980 and 2017. (d) Changes in crime and Black pop*

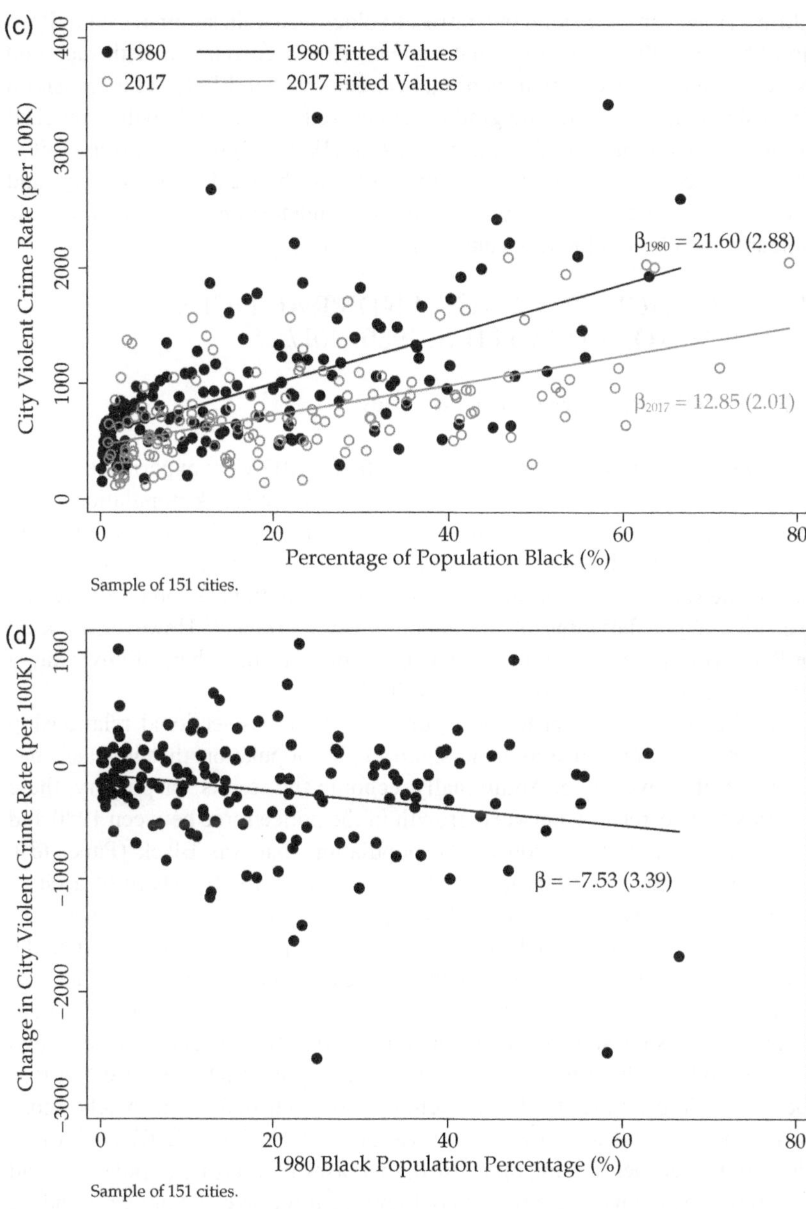

Figure 3.1 *(Continued)*

(2015). However, they stand in contrast to older research, summarized in Pratt and Cullen (2005), that finds that violent crime's correlation with race and poverty was stable, or strengthening, between 1950 and 1990. This transition from steepening to flattening gradients occurred concurrently with a reversal in overall crime rate trends from increasing (1950–90) to decreasing (1990–2017). The contribution of any specific policy to the weakening poverty- and race-crime gradients is currently empirically undetermined but could provide valuable insight into the root causes of violence.

3. POLICE PRESENCE AND PRACTICES ACROSS US CITIES, 1980–2017

3.1. Police Presence across US Cities

The largest declines in crime between 1980 and 2017 were experienced in the cities with initially higher poverty rates and larger Black populations. Did the size of local police forces change commensurately? To address this question, we examine changes in the number of police officers per 100 000 people across the same cities over the same 37-year period. In Panel (a) of Figure 3.2, we see a slight flattening of the police-poverty gradient. However, looking at Panel (b), those cities with higher initial poverty rates had, if anything, a greater number of police per capita by 2017.

As illustrated in Panel (c) of Figure 3.2, the cross-sectional relationship between police presence and the share of the population that is Black has changed little over time. Additionally, echoing the results for poverty, there is a positive correlation between growth in the police force between 1980 and 2017 and the initial fraction of the population that was Black (Panel (d)). Jackson and Carroll (1981) find that, cross-sectionally, the share of a city's population that was Black was a strong predictor of municipal police expenditures in the 1970s, and Derenoncourt (2022) presents evidence that the relationship between Black population shares and police spending is at least partially causal. To the extent that police force size proxies for police expenditures, our results suggest that the positive correlation observed 50 years ago persists today, which is consistent with existing correlational research (see Beck and Goldstein (2017) for a recent review). Our findings also echo those of Carmichael and Kent (2014) and Vargas and McHarris (2017), who find that, in the decades leading up to 2010, increases in minority populations and economic inequality relate positively to police force size and police spending in the US.

Against the backdrop of major changes in the geography of crime, the relatively stable geography of policing points to a degree of persistence in police force sizes. It also opens the door to changes in the breadth of police activities

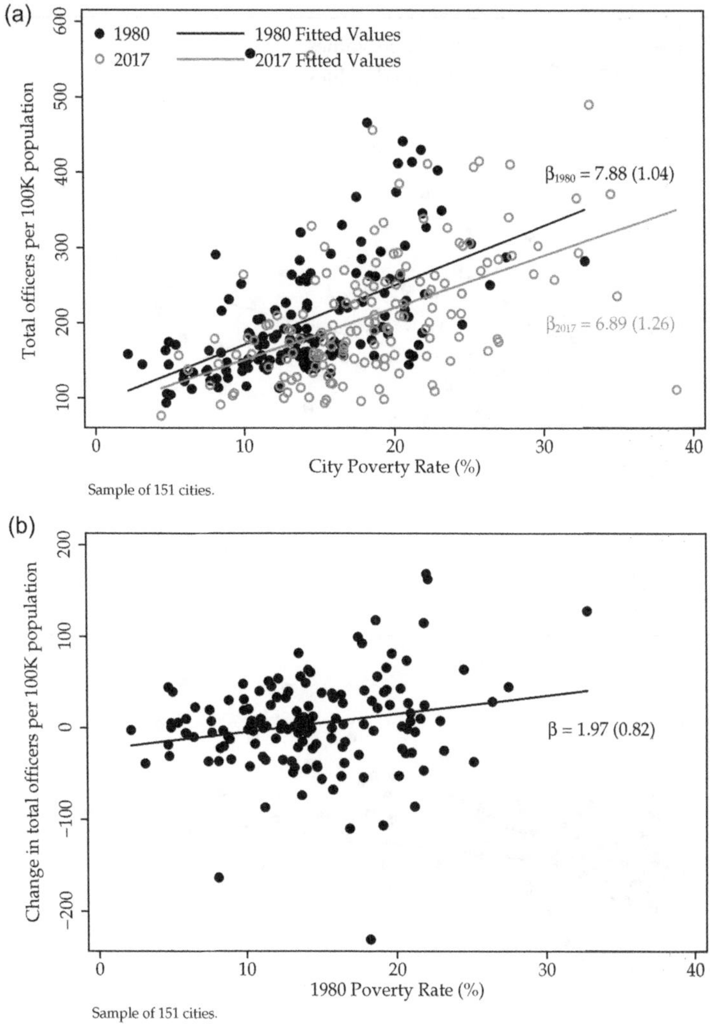

Notes: Data derived from the Uniform Crime Reports, Decennial Census and American Community Survey. The figure includes cities with populations of at least 100 000 in 1980 as well as complete data on crime, arrests and police force size in 1980 and 2017. Coefficients (βs) are from unweighted univariate regressions of the variable on the y-axis against the variable on the x-axis. Standard errors (in parentheses) are heteroskedasticity robust.

Figure 3.2 *Police presence, poverty and race across US cities. (a) Police and poverty, 1980 and 2017. (b) Changes in crime and poverty. (c) Crime and Black pop., 1980 and 2017. (d) Changes in crime and Black pop*

(c)

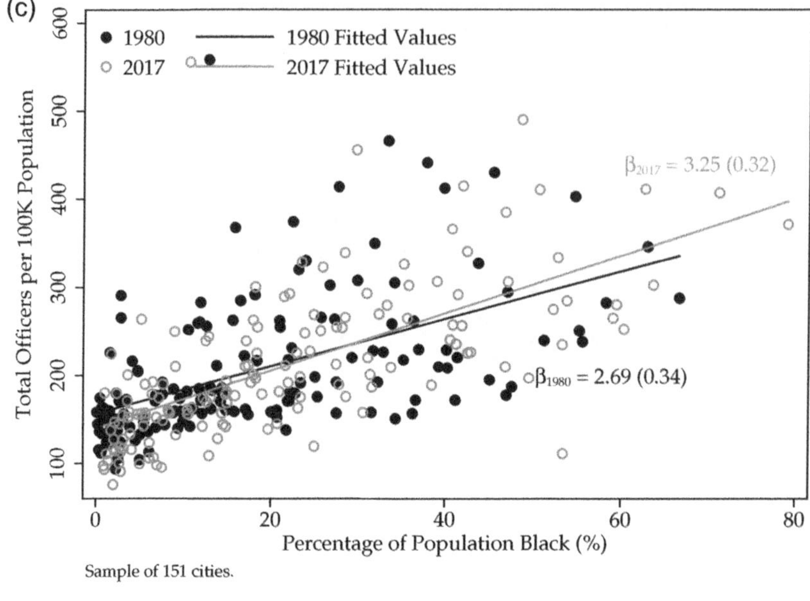

Sample of 151 cities.

(d)

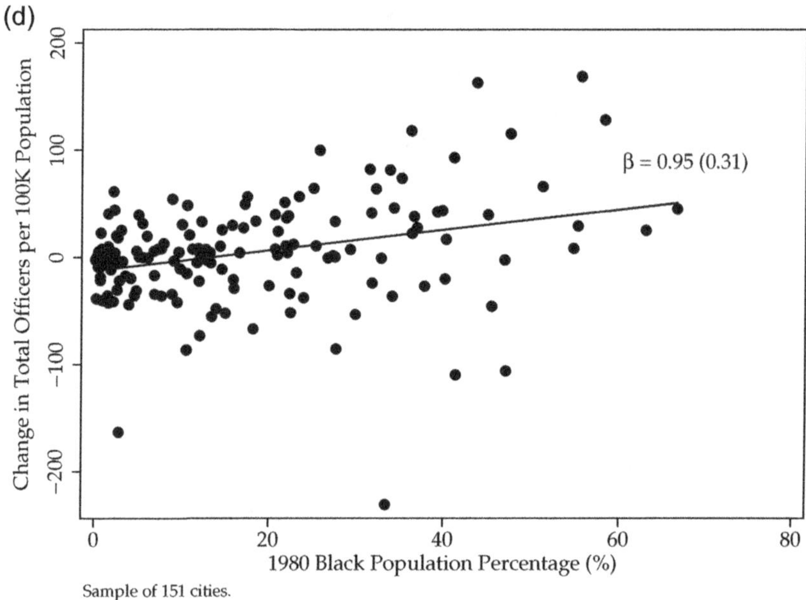

Sample of 151 cities.

Figure 3.2 (Continued)

that also vary across cities in a way that is correlated with poverty and racial composition. This builds on the cautious framing of the Great Crime Decline in Sharkey (2018). Exposure to violence is no longer a necessary fact of life in many US cities, but as also emphasized by Chetty et al. (2014), inequality in opportunities and experiences across places is stubbornly persistent. Larger police forces were an important contributor to the fall in crime, and cutting police forces is likely to lead to higher crime in the absence of any corresponding policy change (Weisburst 2018). However, the observation that cities with more Black and more lower-income residents remain more heavily policed when violent crime is (still) at relatively low levels leads to the question of what, exactly, the tasks of policing look like across US cities today.

3.2. Arrests across US Cities

Much of what police officers do in the field remains unobserved to researchers and to some extent their supervisors as well (Koper et al. 2020). While the capacity of police departments to monitor their officers' activities has grown enormously since the 1980s, when it could take months for a captain to learn about a felony arrest (Sherman 2000), departments regularly report only one on-the-job task of a sworn officer to the UCR: arrests made.

While levels of policing have remained stable with respect to cities' poverty levels and racial composition, arrests – the observed actions taken by officers – have fallen in ways commensurate with violent crime. Figure 3.3 shows plots similar to those in Figure 3.1, but using arrest rates as opposed to violent crime rates. Again, the correlations between arrest rates and poverty rates as well as between arrest rates and the share of the population that is Black have declined since 1980. That is, the arrest-poverty and arrest-race gradients flattened, and the cities with initially higher poverty rates and fractions of the population that were Black saw sharper declines in arrests per city resident.

Given the relationships depicted in the previous figures, a natural question is how arrest rates have evolved for cities with different poverty levels or racial composition *conditional* on changes in crime rates. If the propensity of each police officer to make arrests were fixed, then conditional on crime rates, we would expect to see more arrests happening in cities that were poorer and had larger Black populations, as those are the places that, still, have more police per resident. However, as Figure 3.4 shows, we see that if anything residualized arrest rates (i.e., the residual from a regression of arrest rates on violent crime rates) are negatively related to 1980 poverty rates and Black population shares.[4] The relationships are weak, though.

Hence, the data show that, in tow with crime rates, arrest rates have fallen more so in cities with initially higher poverty and with larger Black population shares. This has occurred despite the fact that police presence has not

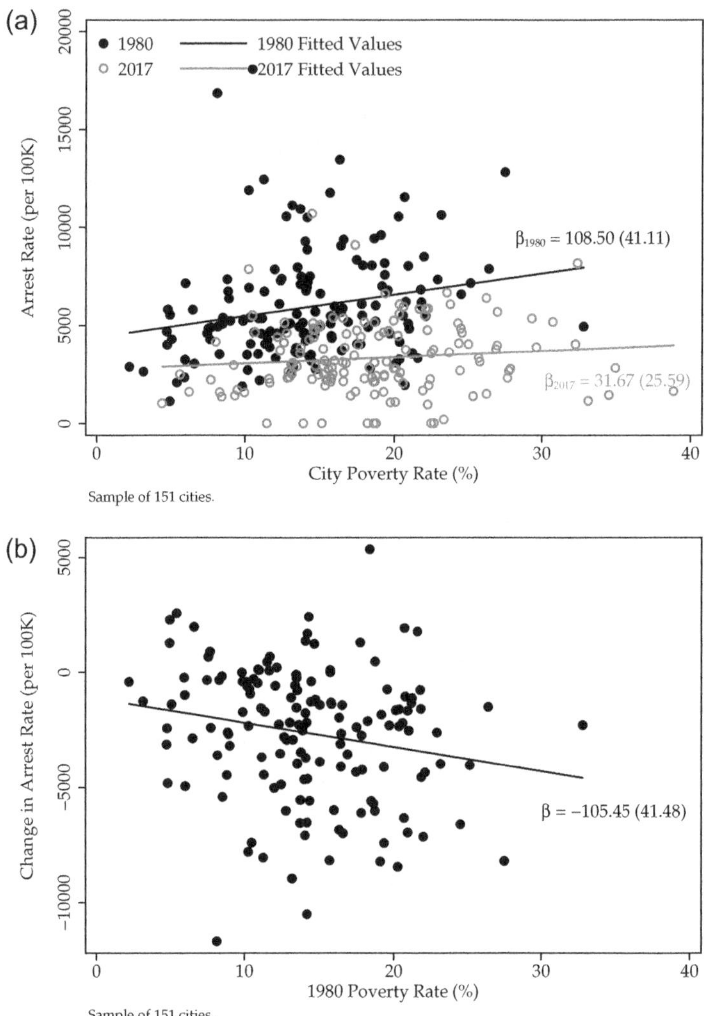

Notes: Data derived from the Uniform Crime Reports, Decennial Census and American Community Survey. The figure includes cities with populations of at least 100 000 in 1980 as well as complete data on crime, arrests and police force size in 1980 and 2017. Coefficients (βs) are from unweighted univariate regressions of the variable on the y-axis against the variable on the x-axis. Standard errors (in parentheses) are heteroskedasticity robust.

Figure 3.3 *Arrest rates, poverty and race across US cities. (a) Arrests and poverty, 1980–2017. (b) Changes in arrests and poverty. (c) Arrests and Black pop., 1980 and 2017. (d) Changes in arrests and Black pop*

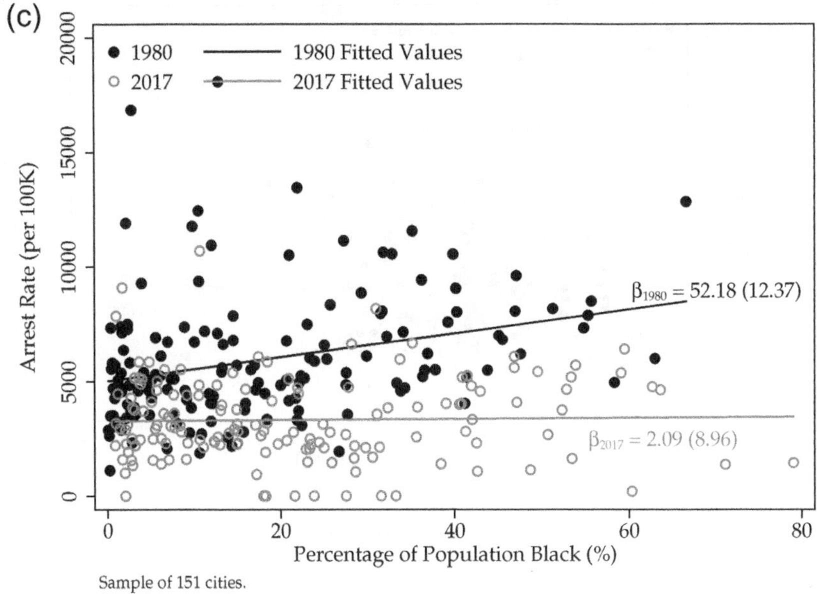

Sample of 151 cities.

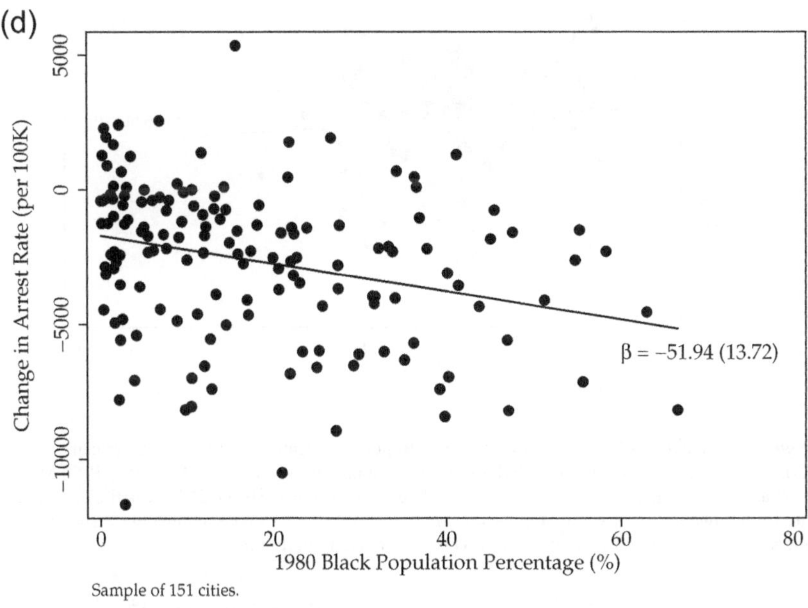

Sample of 151 cities.

Figure 3.3 *(Continued)*

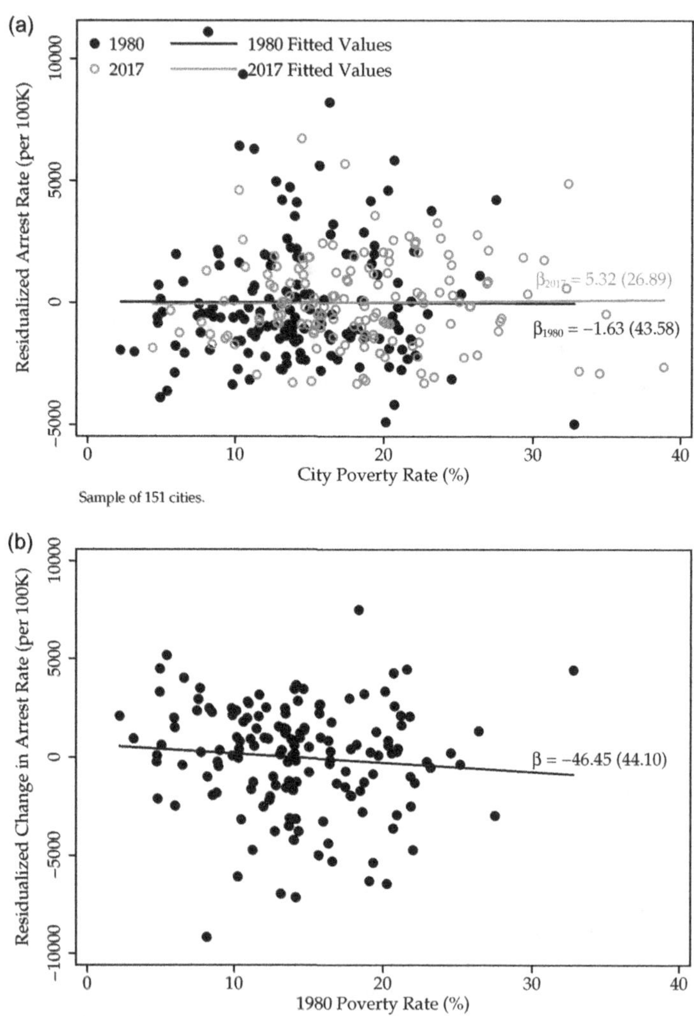

Notes: Data derived from the Uniform Crime Reports, Decennial Census and American Community Survey. The figure includes cities with populations of at least 100 000 in 1980 as well as complete data on crime, arrests and police force size in 1980 and 2017. Coefficients (βs) are from unweighted univariate regressions of the variable on the y-axis against the variable on the x-axis. Standard errors (in parentheses) are heteroskedasticity robust.

Figure 3.4 *Residualized arrest rates, poverty and race across US cities. (a) Res. arrests and poverty, 1980–2017. (b) Changes in res. arrests and poverty. (c) Res. arrests and Black pop., 1980 and 2017. (d) Changes in res. arrests and Black pop*

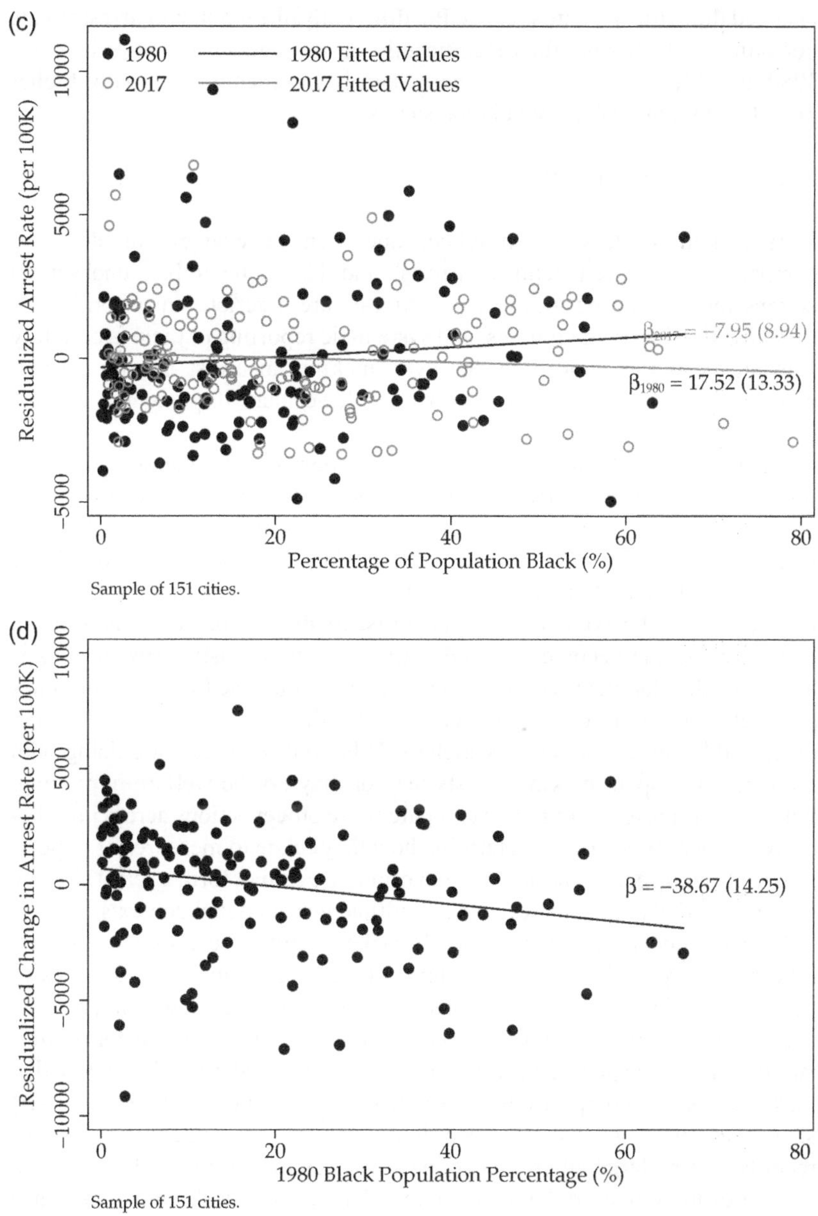

Figure 3.4 (Continued)

changed dramatically across cities. Put differently, the number of arrests made per officer, which has fallen significantly on average across cities between 1980 and 2017, has fallen even more sharply in cities with initially higher poverty and larger Black population shares.

3.3. Non-Arrest Activities

During their shift, what an officer does can be coarsely divided into comparable, observed actions (arrests) and less comparable, unobserved actions (everything besides arrests). Arrests are a serious intrusion by the state into the liberty of civilians, and systematic reporting of them is certainly warranted. At the same time, however, making an arrest is only a small component of an officer's job, occurring in fewer than 10 percent of civilian interactions (Owens et al. 2018).

The previously discussed changes in the geography of policing and arrests open the door to potentially more heterogeneity in the non-arrest activities of police officers across cities and point to particularly high levels of unobserved actions in cities with higher poverty rates and larger Black populations. Crime rates have fallen, and officers are relatively less likely to be making arrests in these cities. To the extent that fewer arrests, conditional on crime rates, mean that fewer people become involved with the criminal justice system, this is a positive development. However, a reduction in observed tasks also implies a reduction in the fraction of police activities that can be easily tracked and evaluated by supervisors or researchers. What police officers are doing with their time not spent making arrests may or may not be welfare improving; without a means to quantify and compare those officer actions across jurisdictions and over time, and to determine how they relate to measures of population well-being, economic activity and crime, we cannot form a scientific base of 'what works' at the city level or in multiple jurisdictional contexts.[5]

Individual departments increasingly make electronic records of non-arrest officer activity available to the public. These records include responses to 911 calls, traffic stops made, citations issued and instances in which force was used. However, these electronic records are generally produced for administrative use by a specific department and are not standardized in a way that makes cross-city comparisons informative. For example, Geller et al. (2021) show that different reasonable decisions about how to code administrative records in nine large cities change the size of estimated racial disparities in the use of force that are large enough to change the cities' relative rankings along this dimension.

One dataset that provides some insight into police operations nationwide is the Law Enforcement Management and Administrative Survey (LEMAS). The 2016 LEMAS does not ask specific questions about the types of non-arrest activity or community engagement in which police officers participated. However, it does provide information on the number of officers explicitly dedicated to community policing or community relations roles, which may be more focused on engaging the community in a positive, non-enforcement way. Using data from the 136 of the 151 cities in our data whose police departments are in the LEMAS,[6] we find a negative cross-sectional relationship between the percent of the jurisdiction that is Black and the percent of officers who are explicitly dedicated to community policing or community relations roles. However, the correlation is not strong ($\rho = -0.16$). The relationship between community policing and city-level poverty is even weaker ($\rho = 0.07$).

The persistence of policing in cities with larger lower-income and Black populations may also reflect different preferences across cities for police engagement in actions that are only tangentially related to crime. This could be particularly true in impoverished areas where other public goods and services are not available. In recounting her experience as an officer in Washington, DC, Brooks (2021) observed, 'When other social goods and services are absent or scarce, police become the default solution to an astonishingly wide range of problems' (152). Two different, but not necessarily mutually exclusive, mechanisms for this function creep have been noted by researchers. One is a story of governments actively transferring funds from social services to law enforcement (e.g., Hinton (2016)). A slightly different mechanism involves residents calling for more police to fill voids left by retreating service providers (e.g., Lum (2021)); in this model, the police are, in effect, the last government institution available to residents of particularly marginalized communities.

To shed some light on mechanisms, we use the LEMAS data to study how calls for service vary across cities. Here, we assume that the frequency with which civilians contact the police reflects their demand for police assistance in solving a problem, which may or may not be crime-related. We find that calls for service per capita are positively correlated with both the share Black and the poverty rate of a city. Panels (a) and (c) of Figure 3.5 illustrate these relationships. The positive correlations are driven in part by the lingering (albeit now weaker) positive correlation between crime and the poverty rate as well as the racial composition of cities (as depicted in Figure 3.1). Therefore, in Panels (b) and (d) of Figure 3.5, we use residualized calls for service per capita; i.e., the residual from a regression of calls for service per capita on violent crime rates (similar to in Figure 3.4). We find that even conditional on crime rates, cities with larger Black populations tend to have more calls for service per capita, but the relationship is not statistically significant. Further, we do not observe any meaningful relationship between residualized calls for service per capita and city poverty rates.[7] To the extent that calls for service proxy for demand for police presence, these results suggest that much of the city-level relationship between demographics and calls for service is driven

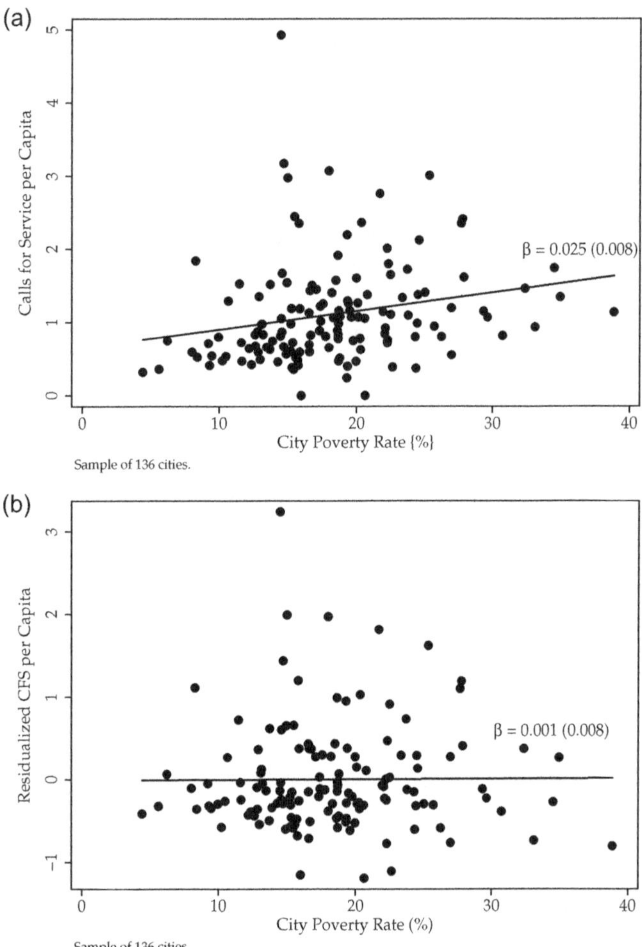

Notes: Data derived from the 2016 LEMAS and 2017 American Community Survey. The figure includes cities with populations of at least 100 000 in 1980 as well as complete data on crime, arrests, police force size and calls for service. Coefficients (βs) are from unweighted univariate regressions of the variable on the y-axis against the variable on the x-axis. Standard errors (in parentheses) are heteroskedasticity robust.

Figure 3.5 *Calls for service, poverty and race across US cities, 2016/17. (a) Calls for service and poverty. (b) Res. calls for service and poverty. (c) Calls for service and Black pop. (d) Res. calls for service and Black pop*

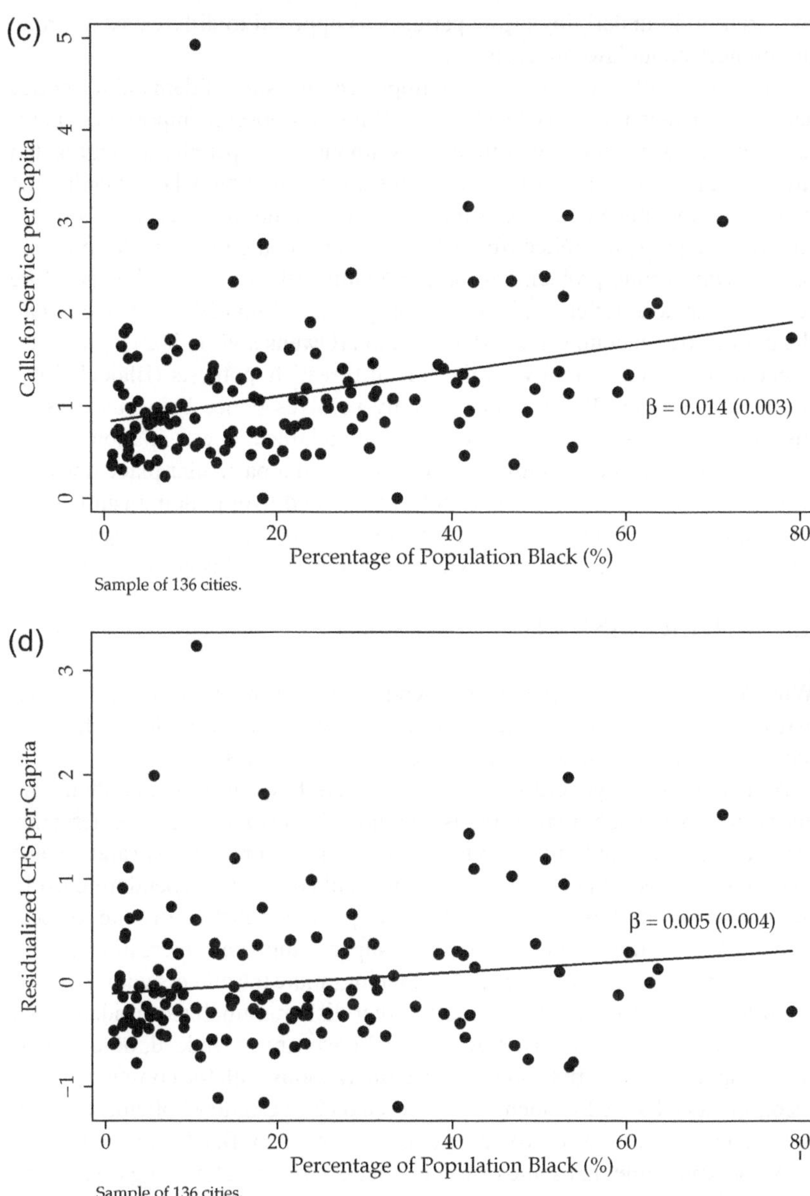

Figure 3.5 *(Continued)*

by variation in underlying crime patterns as opposed to differences in group preferences about law enforcement.

Of course, calls for service are an imperfect measure of demand for police services. Further, these city-level relationships may obscure important dynamics across neighborhoods within cities. Without more spatially disaggregated information on where the calls for service are originating, who is placing the calls and why police presence is requested, we cannot uncover these dynamics. More requests for police from Black residents could reflect under-policing of important crime problems in predominantly Black neighborhoods. More requests may also reflect an increased propensity of non-Black people to call the police after encountering a Black person (Owens and Ba 2021). The latter phenomenon is consistent with the 'racial threat' hypothesis (Blalock 1967, Stults and Baumer 2007), which broadly involves police being used as an instrument to support and entrench existing racialized power relationships in society. The existence of either of these forces in a particular place does not negate the existence of the other; both under- and over-policing can happen simultaneously. Quantitative research using geographically disaggregated data on who calls the police and who can shed light on this critical issue.

4. DISCUSSION

Why does it matter that police are spending more time in unmeasured, non-arrest activities in certain cities? The answer to this question lies in the myriad ways in which police engagement can affect civilians.

As agents of the government, police officers have information about and access to city services that civilians may not. Calls from police to emergency medical assistance or family services may be taken more seriously and receive a swifter response than calls from civilians. Police may also spend time working with communities proactively to solve problems that contribute to local crime, like cleaning up public spaces or supervising youth recreational centers. Non-punitive police officer efforts that ingratiate the officers with the communities they serve can also signal to otherwise marginalized residents that they are valued and supported by the local government. Indeed, officers participating in more positive, non-punitive interactions with the community was recommended by the President's Task Force on 21st Century Policing as a way to advance both crime control and police legitimacy in Black communities.

At the same time that some of what police do outside of making arrests can benefit civilians, police engagement that does not rise to the level of arrest can have negative consequences for directly engaged civilians, as well as for the persistence of poverty and racial disparities. For example, many low-level offenses are not punishable by arrest, but rather by citation – requiring the individual to pay a fine. Makowsky and Stratmann (2009, 2011) document a variety of extra-legal factors that influence the frequency with which police issue citations, including whether or not the individual lives nearby and the size of the local budget surplus. Makowsky et al.'s (2019) finding that citations of Black and Hispanic people appear to be particularly sensitive to local revenue needs highlights the need for further research on the causes and consequences of citations.

Additionally, the act of being stopped and searched by an officer can impose costs on a civilian, particularly if the civilian is not actually engaged in criminal behavior. Manski and Nagin (2017) explicitly include these costs in their model of optimal police activity. Research suggests that even these 'low-level' negative police encounters can have important social, psychological and physical health consequences (Rios 2011, Geller et al. 2014, Sewell et al. 2016, McFarland et al. 2019, Del Toro et al. 2019, Kerrison and Sewell 2020, Bandes et al. 2020).

It is also important to highlight that a reduced fraction of time devoted to observable, arrest-related activity is necessary, but not sufficient, for a growing divergence in what 'policing' means across cities. Indeed, while Lum et al. (2020) note that a large fraction of non-traditional proactive policing activities is not recorded, they also suggest that such practices are limited in scope in most departments, and largely homogeneous across agencies.

There is currently much more that we need to know about the net social impact of many non-arrest policing policies. In addition, the increased scope for variation in what police are actually doing, which has occurred as crime in general has fallen, has created a situation where a 'typical' police encounter may vary dramatically based on where that encounter takes place.

5. CONCLUSION AND AVENUES FOR FUTURE RESEARCH

In this chapter, we illustrate and connect several facts regarding changes in the geography of crime and policing across US cities in recent decades. Between 1980 and 2017, the correlations between violent crime and poverty as well as violent crime and race across cities have weakened. Against a backdrop of falling crime rates overall, cities with initially higher poverty rates and larger Black populations have witnessed disproportionately large drops in crime. This trend is a reversal from that observed between 1950 and 1990 (Pratt and Cullen 2005), when crime rates overall were increasing. However, our findings echo those from work studying within-city changes in the distribution of crime and crime reductions in recent decades; across neighborhoods within cities, the relationship between poverty and crime has also diminished but not disappeared entirely (Friedson and Sharkey 2015).

Changes in police presence across cities and over time have not mirrored changes in violent crime; if anything, despite their relatively large drops in crime, cities with initially higher poverty and larger Black populations have more police per capita now than they did in 1980. However, the relatively greater number of police in these cities has not translated into a disproportionate number of arrests; conditional on changes in crime rates, arrest rates are largely orthogonal to city poverty rates or racial composition.

Taken together, the results suggest that the geographic distribution of police with respect to city poverty and racial composition has remained stable in the face of substantial changes in the geography of crime. Given the fact that arrest rates have fallen in tow with violent crime rates across cities, our results point to potentially more heterogeneity in the non-arrest activities of police officers across cities. Further, there is substantially more scope for time spent in unobserved, non-arrest activities to increase in cities with higher poverty rates and larger Black populations. This time could be spent patrolling neighborhoods, interacting with citizens, responding to non-criminal justice-related calls or complaints, training, completing other administrative work and more. Hence, while there has been a convergence in exposure to violent crime across cities, there has been growing possibility for a divergence in people's experiences with police.

Our findings underscore the importance of investigating further how police officers use their time. Qualitative work in this area could be particularly helpful in guiding the development of data necessary for larger-scale quantitative work. In most departments, very little is recorded or measured about what police officers are doing when they are not making arrests. Some of their untracked activities could be welfare-improving, whereas others might not be. Further, the extent to which police activity is currently observed appears to be a function of the racial composition of a city, and patterns illustrated in this chapter suggest this is a growing, rather than stable or diminishing, problem. Rectifying this situation is a first-order issue for anyone serious about evidence-based policing.

More precise records of the tasks police undertake could improve our understanding of the ways in which different groups are interacting with the police across places in the US. To the extent that jurisdictions have provided more detailed records on, for example, police movements (Weisburd 2021) and officer-civilian encounters (Voigt et al. 2017), they have yielded important insights into police behavior and its impacts on relevant outcomes. However, data just for select agencies are less useful in characterizing broader, cross-jurisdictional patterns of police activities, and therefore we are still limited in our ability to assess past and present differences in different groups' experiences with the police. Even across similar cities, it is plausible that police engage in very different sets of activities, which in turn could have implications not just for crime control but also for relations with the public and police legitimacy.

At the same time, efforts to collect and disseminate detailed data on policing should be undertaken with consideration of the costs. Increased data collection and reporting requirements may require reallocations of resources within departments or more taxpayer funds. Time spent tracking officer behavior and recording information may be time that would otherwise be spent on activities that help to reduce crime or benefit the community in other ways. In some instances, greater monitoring and record-keeping could discourage inappropriate or unwarranted actions by officers, but in others they might alter police behavior in ways that are not socially desirable (Stuart et al. 2018). Data collection and reporting requirements that are viewed as overly burdensome could also affect compliance and the reliability of data made available.

Concerns about the costs of additional data collection and reporting have been raised in the context of recent efforts to increase data availability as well as officer and departmental accountability in certain jurisdictions. For example, the San Diego County Sheriff's Department estimated that officers spent six minutes per civilian stop complying with the reporting required by California's recent Racial and Identity Profiling Act, which mandated additional stop-data collection in order to help address racial disparities in law enforcement (San Diego County Sheriff's Department 2019). Even automated data collection can be costly; for example, the Massachusetts State Police estimated that it spends $50 000 per month to track and store data for 2900 cars using an Automated Vehicle Location system (Croteau 2020). Additionally, just as civilians report costs associated with surveillance, qualitative work suggests that officers bear psychic costs when their actions are monitored continuously by supervisors (Brayne 2021).

Finally, our results illustrating patterns over time across cities beg the question of whether similar patterns hold across neighborhoods within cities. Sharkey (2018) documents relatively large declines in crime in the poorest neighborhoods of six cities in recent decades. However, how the extent and nature of policing have changed across neighborhoods is not clear. One potential consequence of the spread of 'hot spots' policing, or 'focused deterrence', discussed in other chapters of this book, is the amplification of a city-level divergence in the relationships that police have with different groups of civilians that they serve.

NOTES

1. Freedman: Department of Economics, University of California, Irvine. Owens: Department of Criminology, Law, and Society and Department of Economics, University of California, Irvine. Christopher: Stanford Institute for Economic Policy Research (SIEPR), Stanford University. We thank the editors, Paolo Buonanno, Paolo Vanin and Juan Vargas, as well as Cynthia Lum and Patrick Sharkey for helpful comments.

2. Preliminary data for the first half of 2020 point to a substantial percentage increase in homicides relative to prior years. Of course, 2020 was an exceptional year in world history, which we believe suggests caution is currently warranted in interpreting 2020 crime data as informative about any specific social phenomenon or as signaling a broader trend reversal.
3. Notably, this analysis was undertaken prior to the COVID-19 pandemic. As of mid-2021, there is uncertainty about whether pre-pandemic trends in crime will persist. In particular, it is currently unclear whether increases in homicide rates in 2020 are a temporary shock related to the pandemic and protests in response to the murder of George Floyd, or if instead they represent the start of a more substantial shift in crime and policing. It is also unclear whether crimes besides homicides have increased.
4. We are not trying to measure police effectiveness, but rather people's exposure to the police and police activities. Therefore, instead of looking at arrests per crime (clearance rates), we examine arrests per capita and how they vary with city demographics conditional on city crime rates.
5. This is related to a note of caution raised in National Academies of Sciences, Engineering, and Medicine (2018): there are many randomized controlled trials run at the individual police department level that have shown specific proactive policing policies to be effective in reducing crime. However, these studies have focused on randomized treatments within a single jurisdiction and with generally short (less than one year) follow-up periods. The extent to which these credible results will generalize if implemented at scale and over a long time period is unknown (Blattman et al. 2021).
6. We further limit the LEMAS sample to departments with more than 100 officers, all of which receive LEMAS surveys. Small departments are surveyed via stratified sampling.
7. Similarly, we find positive, but weak correlations between the fraction of calls for which officers are dispatched and a city's poverty rate and the share of a city's population that is Black ($\rho = 0.095$ and $\rho = 0.104$, respectively).

REFERENCES

Bandes, Susan, Marie Pryor, Erin Kerrison, and Phillip Goff. 2020. "The mismeasure of Terry stops: Assessing the psychological and emotional harms of stop and frisk to individuals and communities." *Behavioral Sciences & the Law*, 37(2): 176–94.

Beck, Brenden, and Adam Goldstein. 2017. "Governing through police? Housing market reliance, welfare retrenchment, and police budgeting in an era of declining crime." *Social Forces*, 96(3): 1183–210.

Becker, Gary. 1968. "Crime and punishment: An economic approach." *Journal of Political Economy*, 76(2): 169–217.

Blalock, Hubert, Jr. 1967. *Toward a Theory of Minority-Group Relations*. John Wiley and Sons.

Blattman, Christopher, Donald Green, Daniel Ortega, and Santiago Tobon. 2021. "Place-based interventions at scale: The direct and spillover effects of policing and city services on crime." *Journal of the European Economic Association*, 19(4): 2022–51.

Brayne, Sarah. 2021. *Predict and Surveil: Data, Discretion, and the Future of Policing*. Oxford University Press.

Brooks, Rosa. 2021. *Tangled Up in Blue: Policing the American City*. Penguin Press.

Carmichael, Jason, and Stephanie Kent. 2014. "The persistent significance of racial and economic inequality on the size of municipal police forces in the United States, 1980–2010." *Social Problems*, 61(1): 259–82.

Chaudry, Ajay, Christopher Wimer, Suzanne Macartney, Lauren Frohlich, Colin Campbell, Kendall Swenson, Don Oellerich, and Susan Hauan. 2016. *Poverty in the United States: 50-year Trends and Safety Net Impacts*. Office of Human Services Policy, Office of the Assistant Secretary for Planning and Evaluation, U.S. Department of Health and Human Services.

Chetty, Raj, Nathaniel Hendren, Patrick Kline, and Emmanuel Saez. 2014. "Where is the land of opportunity? The geography of intergenerational mobility in the United States." *Quarterly Journal of Economics*, 129(4): 1553–623.

Croteau, Scott. 2020. "Nearly 2,900 Massachusetts State Police cruisers can now be tracked: Here's why." *MassLive*. https://www.masslive.com/boston/2020/01/nearly-2900-massachusetts-state-police-cruisers-can-now-be-tracked-heres-why.html

Del Toro, Juan, Tracey Lloyd, Kim S. Buchanan, Summer Joi Robins, Lucy Zhang Bencharit, Meredith Gamson Smiedt, Kavita Reddy, Enrique Rodriguez Pouget, Erin Kerrison, and Phillip Atiba Goff. 2019. "The criminogenic and psychological effects of police stops on adolescent black and Latino boys." *Proceedings of the National Academy of Sciences*, 116(17): 8261–68.

Derenoncourt, Ellora. 2022. "Can you move to opportunity? Evidence from the Great Migration." *American Economic Review*, 112(2):369–408.

Flango, Victor Eugene, and Edgar Sherbenou. 1976. "Poverty, urbanization, and crime." *Criminology*, 14(3): 331–46.

Friedson, Michael, and Patrick Sharkey. 2015. "Violence and neighborhood disadvantage after the crime decline." *The Annals of the American Academy of Political and Social Science*, 660: 341–58.

Geller, Amanda, Jeffrey Fagan, Tom Tyler, and Bruce Link. 2014. "Aggressive policing and the mental health of young urban men." *American Journal of Public Health*, 104(12): 2321–27.

Geller, Amanda, Phillip Atiba Goff, Tracey Lloyd, Amelia Haviland, Dean Obermark, and Jack Glaser. 2021. "Measuring racial disparities in police use of force: Methods matter." *Journal of Quantitative Criminology*, 37: 1083–113.

Glaeser, Edward, and Bruce Sacerdote. 1996. "Why is there more crime in cities?" *Journal of Political Economy*, 107(6): S225–58.

Hinton, Elizabeth. 2016. *From the War on Poverty to the War on Crime: The Making of Mass Incarceration in America*. Harvard University Press.

Jackson, Pamela Irving, and Leo Carroll. 1981. "Race and the war on crime: The sociopolitical determinants of municipal police expenditures in 90 non-Southern U.S. cities." *American Sociological Review*, 46(3): 290–305.

Kerrison, Erin, and Alyasah Sewell. 2020. "Negative illness feedbacks: High-frisk policing reduces civilian reliance on ED services." *Health Services Research*, 55(S2): 787–96.

Koper, Christopher, Cynthia Lum, Xiaoyn Wu, and Noah Fritz. 2020. "Proactive policing in the United States: A national survey." *Policing: An International Journal*, 43(5): 861–76.

Liska, Allen, and Paul Bellair. 1995. "Violent-crime rates and racial composition: Convergence over time." *American Journal of Sociology*, 101(3): 578–610.

Lum, Cynthia. 2021. "Perspectives on policing." *Annual Review of Criminology*, 4: 19–25.

Lum, Cynthia, Christopher Koper, Xiaoyun Wu, William Johnson, and Megan Stoltz. 2020. "Examining the empirical realities of proactive policing through systematic observations and computer-aided dispatch data." *Police Quarterly*, 23(3): 283–310.

Makowsky, Michael, and Thomas Stratmann. 2009. "Political economy at any speed: What determines traffic citations?" *American Economic Review*, 99(1): 509–527.

Makowsky, Michael, and Thomas Stratmann. 2011. "More tickets, fewer accidents: How cash-strapped towns make for safer roads." *Journal of Law and Economics*, 54(4): 863–888.

Makowsky, Michael, Thomas Stratmann, and Alex Tabarrok. 2019. "To serve and collect: The fiscal and racial determinants of law enforcement." *Journal of Legal Studies*, 48(1): 189–216.

Manski, Charles, and Daniel Nagin. 2017. "Assessing benefits, costs, and disparate racial impacts of confrontational proactive policing." *Proceedings of the National Academy of Sciences*, 114(35): 9308–9313.

McFarland, Michael, Amanda Geller, and Cheryl McFarland. 2019. "Police contact and health among urban adolescents: The role of perceived injustice." *Social Science & Medicine*, 238: 112487.

McIntosh, Kriston, Emily Moss, Ryan Nunn, and Jay Shambaugh. 2020. "Examining the Black-white wealth gap." *Brookings Institution, Up Front*. https://www.brookings.edu/blog/up-front/2020/02/27/examining-the-black-white-wealth-gap/

National Academies of Sciences, Engineering, and Medicine. 2018. *Proactive Policing: Effects on Crime and Communities*. The National Academies Press.

Owens, Emily, and Bocar Ba. 2021. "The economics of policing and public safety." *Journal of Economic Perspectives*, 35(4): 3–28.

Owens, Emily, David Weisburd, Karen Amendola, and Geoffrey Alpert. 2018. "Can you build a better cop?" *Criminology & Public Policy*, 17(1): 41–87.

Pratt, Travis, and Francis Cullen. 2005. "Assessing macro-level predictors and theories of crime: A meta-analysis." *Crime and Justice*, 32: 373–450.

Rios, Victor. 2011. *Punished: Policing the Lives of Black and Latino Boys*. New York University Press.

San Diego County Sheriff 's Department. 2019. *AB953: Racial and Identity Profiling Act (RIPA) Report 2019*. San Diego County Sheriff's Department.

Sewell, Abigail, Kevin Jefferson, and Hedwig Lee. 2016. "Living under surveillance: Gender, psychological distress, and stop-question-and-frisk policing in New York City." *Social Science & Medicine*, 159: 1–13.

Sharkey, Patrick. 2018. *Uneasy Peace: The Great Crime Decline, the Renewal of City Life, and the Next War on Violence*. W. W. Norton and Company.

Sherman, Lawrence. 2000. "American policing." *The Handbook of Crime and Punishment*, Ed. Michael Tonry, 429–456. Oxford University Press.

Stuart, Henry, Joshua Chanin, Megan Welsh, and Dana Nurge. 2018. "Police noncompliance: Why law enforcers may deviate from laws, rules, and reform mandates." *Contextualizing Compliance in the Public Sector*, 120–137. Routledge.

Stults, Brian, and Eric Baumer. 2007. "Racial context and police force size: Evaluating the empirical validity of the minority threat perspective." *American Journal of Sociology*, 113(2): 507–546.

Vargas, Robert, and Philip McHarris. 2017. "Race and state in city police spending growth: 1980 to 2010." *Sociology of Race and Ethnicity*, 3(1): 96–112.

Voigt, Rob, Nicholas Camp, Vinodkumar Prabhakaran, William Hamilton, Rebecca Hetey, Camilla Griffiths, David Jurgens, Dan Jurafsky, and Jennifer Eberhardt. 2017. "Language from police body camera footage shows racial disparities in officer respect." *Proceedings of the National Academy of Sciences*, 114(25): 6521–6526.

Weisburd, Sarit. 2021. "Police presence, rapid response rates, and crime prevention." *Review of Economics and Statistics*, 103(2): 280–293.

Weisburst, Emily. 2018. "Safety in police numbers: Evidence of police effectiveness from federal COPS grant applications." *American Law and Economics Review*, 21(1): 81–109.

Willis, James, and Stephen Mastrofski. 2016. "Improving policing by integrating craft and science: What can patrol officers teach us about good police work?" *Policing and Society*, 28(1): 27–44.

4. Broken windows policing and crime: Evidence from 80 Colombian cities[1]

Daniel Mejía,[2] Ervyn Norza,[3] Santiago Tobón[4] and Martín Vanegas-Arias[5]

1. INTRODUCTION

Police manpower and deployment strategies are at the core of crime prevention efforts. The idea is simple: Police presence should decrease the probability of crime occurrence by either deterring or incapacitating offenders.[6] Indeed, the consensus in the literature is that increases in police manpower lead to fewer crimes.[7] Moreover, previous studies suggest that deployment strategies—such as hot spots policing—not only reduce crime in high-crime areas but also spill benefits over to surrounding locations.[8] However, we know less about the effects of regular police intensity—or broken windows policing—on crime. This literature usually focuses on the levels of driving under the influence and disorderly conduct arrests as indirect measures of police intensity.[9] As noted by Chalfin and McCrary (2017), however, most studies 'are plagued by problems of simultaneity bias, omitted variables, and the inevitable difficulty involved in finding a credible proxy'.

In this chapter, we benefit from three characteristics of the Colombian context to examine the direct and indirect effects of broken windows policing practices on crime. First, the access to the universe of arrest and crime records for 80 cities for 2019. The effects of police interventions that are not intense in nature, such as broken windows policing, are usually small in magnitude. Hence without a large enough sample, small effects could be undetectable. Crime records include the type of crime, exact coordinates and date of occurrence. Arrest records include the exact coordinates, date of occurrence and information on whether the arrest was conducted following an arrest warrant or rather 'in-the-act', when police patrols happened to observe a crime as they were passing through. These 80 cities account for roughly 44 percent of the population of the country.[10] We restrict our analysis to the urban perimeter of these cities.

The second characteristic is a wide heterogeneity in police activity and local crime patterns both within and across cities. The key empirical challenge when estimating the effects of broken windows policing on crime is that changes in patrolling patterns are not random. We use the coordinates and date of occurrence of all crimes and arrests to build bi-weekly panel data, where we use grids of 200×200 meters within the urban perimeter of the 80 cities as the cross-sectional unit. We use this panel to produce event studies where we look at the effects of shocks in police activity in a given grid and period. We build our direct treatment variable as any grid and period with three or more arrests conducted 'in-the-act'. Two or fewer arrests are common, and we worried this looser definition would not pick up an actual intensification of police presence. We focus on arrests with no arrest warrant as these are more likely to proxy for unplanned police activities. Furthermore, because of the simultaneous determination of crimes and arrests, we expect the treatment period to show a large increase in crime. Hence our outcomes of interest are crimes occurring in the periods following the police activity shock, both where the shock took place as well as in the surrounding areas.

Finally, we leverage the variation within and across cities to look at heterogeneous treatment effects. On the one hand, we examine how the effects change based on the baseline crime levels of the specific locations where the arrests occurred. To some degree, this analysis complements the broad literature on hot spots policing by looking at the effects of policing places with moderate crime levels. On the other hand, we look at how the effects change across cities based on baseline characteristics of the local crime environment. In particular, we study whether the effects are different in cities with a stronger tradition of organized crime. Many criminal organizations plan their actions in advance and strategically adjust to police activity.[11] Hence the effects of broken windows policing may differ depending on how organized criminal activities are in a city.

This chapter offers five sets of results. First, we observe a decrease in total crime in the periods following the shock in police activity. As expected, police activity shocks are associated with an increase in crime in the concurrent period—each arrest necessarily implies at least one crime report. But crimes fall monotonically after the shock, reaching a statistically significant and economically meaningful decrease in the fourth period. Relative to the average number of crimes occurring one period before the shock, the effects in the fourth period are equivalent to a 6 percent decrease. Furthermore, we observe a similar pattern in areas nearby the location of the shock. The coefficients in the third and fourth periods are statistically significant, and their magnitudes are equivalent to a decrease of roughly 3 percent and 5 percent in reported crimes, respectively. This suggests the benefits of police activity that diffuse to the surroundings.[12]

Second, we conduct a back-of-the-envelope estimation of aggregate effects. With many treated locations, and many places exposed to spillovers for each treated grid, the benefits add up to potentially large reductions in crime. We find that the decrease in crimes in the periods after the shock is large enough to offset the observed increase at the shock period. Our estimate of this aggregate reduction in crime is not precise, but it is close to conventional levels of statistical significance.

Third, the direct effects are not circumscribed to a specific type of crime. Rather, we observe similar patterns for both violent and property crimes. For property crimes, however, the direct effects are imprecisely estimated. We do observe differences in spillover patterns. Beneficial spillovers are larger and more precise for property crimes.

Fourth, the direct effects of shocks in police activity seem to be more immediate and precise in low-crime areas. Following the shock, crimes drop between 9 percent and 13 percent in the subsequent periods, relative to the average number of crimes one period before the arrest in low-crime areas. Crimes in high-crime areas seem to fall by period four after the shock, but these effects are imprecisely estimated. Beneficial spillovers are more relevant at crime hot spots.

Fifth, both direct effects and beneficial spillovers seem to be more important in cities with low or moderate presence of organized crime. We proxy for organized crime using the rates of drugs and weapons seizures, as well as the presence of coca crops. Criminal organizations in Colombia are usually associated with local drug markets and widespread use of weapons. Also, criminal organizations are traditionally present in cities with coca crops, both to provide protection and control the supply of coca leaves for the production of cocaine. All results point in the same direction: Direct and spillover effects are larger and more precisely estimated in cities with low or moderate presence of organized crime. The coefficients for direct and indirect effects are imprecise and sometimes positive in places where organized crime is presumably more active, as measured with all these proxies.

This chapter contributes to a few strands of the literature. First, criminologists have long studied the effects of different police deployment strategies on crime. The closest precedent to this chapter are studies focusing on broken windows policing. Sampson and Cohen (1988) use city-level data to study correlates of broken windows policing practices with robbery rates for a sample of 171 cities in the US. Their results suggest a negative association between broken windows policing and crime. MacDonald (2002) and later Kubrin et al. (2010) replicate the Sampson and Cohen (1988) study with variations in the time frame, main outcomes and approach. Their results also point to a negative elasticity of crime with respect to the implementation of broken windows policing practices. Two studies exploit variation within a single city. Harcourt and Ludwig (2006) and Rosenfeld et al. (2007) use precinct-level data from New York and find that misdemeanor arrests lead to very small effects on crime.

Second, also related to this chapter are studies focusing on police deployment strategies such as hot spots policing. Broadly, hot spots policing consists of allocating disproportional police resources in high-crime areas. This has been a frequent subject of study both in criminology and economics.[13] A recent systematic review analyzes 65 studies (Braga et al., 2019). The aggregate analysis suggests crime decreases by a small but precise amount and that most likely benefits diffuse. Studies in the context of Latin America, however, point to the importance of local crime patterns. For instance, two hot spots policing experiments in Colombia show different results. Blattman et al. (2021b) find that hot spots policing led to adverse spillovers of property crime and beneficial spillovers of violent crime in Bogotá. Collazos et al. (2020) find that patrolling hot spots led to beneficial spillovers of property crimes in Medellín. Di Tella and Schargrodsky (2004) study a police re-deployment in Buenos Aires following a terrorist attack. Their results suggest that motor vehicle thefts declined in places that received additional police. Re-analyzing their data, Donohue et al. (2013) find that crime displaced to the surroundings.

Third, this chapter contributes to the literature on the effects of police manpower on crime.[14] This literature generally points to negative elasticities of crime with respect to the number of available police patrols in a city. Notable studies exploiting quasi-experimental variation in city-level police manpower in the US include Levitt (2002), Evans and Owens (2007) and Lin (2009).

Fourth, this chapter relates to a growing literature focusing on how the presence of organized crime might shape the effects of intensifying police and other state resources. For instance, Magaloni et al. (2020) find that police crackdowns in Rio lead to more violence in areas heavily controlled by gangs. Also, Dell (2015) finds that crackdowns in cartel strongholds in Mexico displace violence to other cities. Finally, Blattman et al. (2021a) find that intensifying state presence in gang territories in Medellín does not crowd criminal rule out, probably due to a strategic response by gangs to state actions.

A final contribution of this chapter is to broaden the regional scope of the literature on the relationship between police and crime. The literature on hot spots policing is useful as an example. Of the 65 studies analyzed in the systematic review by Braga et al. (2019), only four are outside developed economies. Indeed, 60 concentrate on only three countries: The US, the UK and Sweden.

This chapter is organized in seven sections including this introduction. Section 2 describes the setting and presents the data. Section 3 describes the empirical strategy. Section 4 presents the baseline results. Section 5 examines the direct effects exploiting within-city variations in baseline crime levels. Section 6 examines both direct and indirect effects exploiting variation between cities in the incidence of organized crime. Section 7 discusses policy implications.

2. SETTING AND DATA

2.1. Setting

Colombia has roughly 48 million people. Per capita income is about $15 000 per year, adjusted for purchasing power parity. The country is divided into 1102 cities or municipalities. Each city has an elected mayor and council. According to the Colombian Constitution, the head of police affairs in the city is the mayor. This role, however, is limited to broad policy decisions and budgeting for specific investments—such as the purchase of technology or motor vehicles. In practice, citizen security in a city is the responsibility of the National Police. The National Police is independent of all municipalities, and a branch of the Ministry of Defense. The Colombian Police is a relatively well-organized and professional force, with roughly 167 000 people—hence there are about 350 police officers per 100 000 residents in the country.

Patrolling activities are organized in multiple layers of jurisdictions. Metropolitan or regional police departments are at the top of the hierarchy.[15] These departments are divided into police districts. In turn, each police district is divided into police stations. Stations are divided into *Comandos de Acción Inmediata* (CAIs). Finally, each CAI is divided into police quadrants—which are equivalent to police beats. The size of each quadrant is usually relatively large. In Medellín, the second largest city, each quadrant covers 50 street blocks on average.

Police quadrants are the basis for police patrolling activities. Each police quadrant has six police officers that patrol in pairs, with each pair covering one of three daily shifts. Police patrols plan their patrolling activities in regular meetings at the police station. In these meetings, the station commander and the police agents in charge of the quadrant decide on routes, times and locations to patrol. Police guidelines include instructions to specifically implement different forms of broken windows policing. Normal duties to signal police presence include running background checks, stopping and frisking people and conducting arrests.[16] Arrests are classified depending on whether there was an arrest warrant for the person, or whether it was conducted 'in-the-act', meaning police patrols happened to observe a crime as they were passing through.

2.2. Data

Crime data was shared by the National Police, this data includes the universe of reported crimes and arrests for 80 Colombian cities in 2019. These are the largest cities by population, excluding the capital Bogotá and a few others where data was not available.

Cities in the sample Figure 4.1 displays the cities in our sample. These cities are distributed throughout all the Colombian territory. The only exception

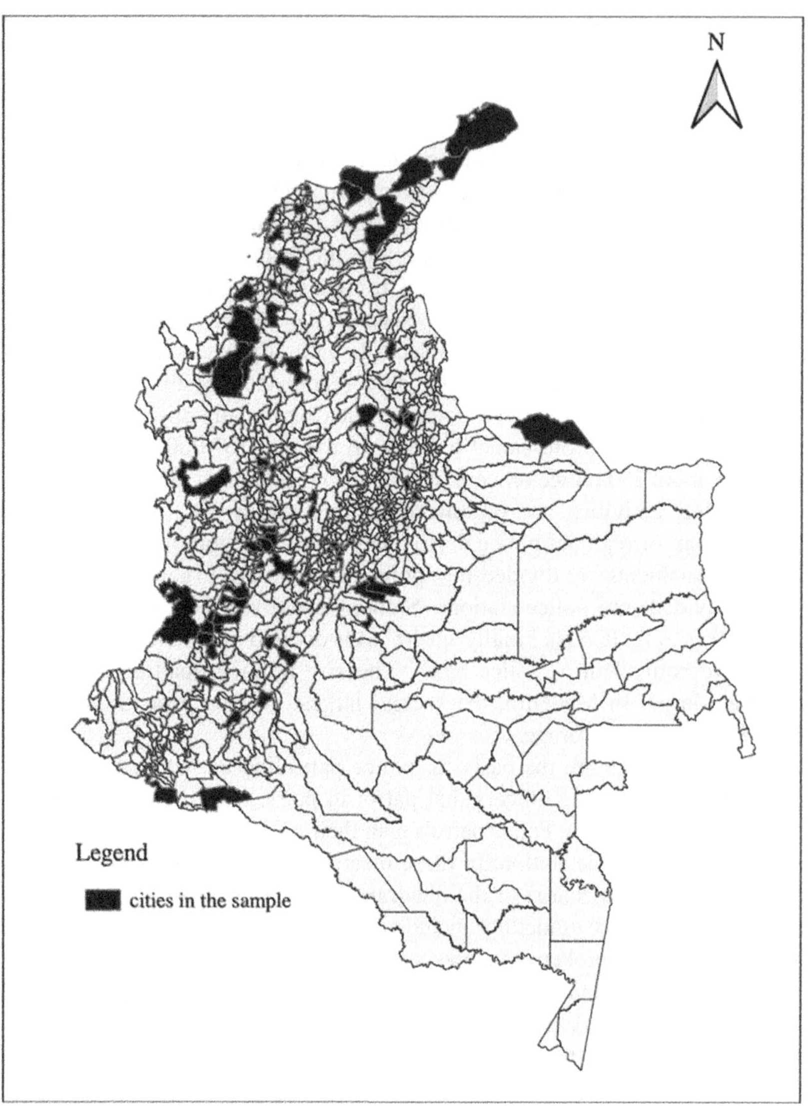

Notes: The map depicts the 80 cities in our analytical sample, in black.

Figure 4.1 Cities in the analytical sample

Table 4.1 *Baseline descriptive statistics for the sample of cities*

Variable	Mean (1)	Std. dev. (2)	Min. (3)	Max. (4)
Population	262 959.9	391 685.7	64 652.0	2 427 129.0
Total crimes rate	485.0	360.5	13.5	1 927.3
Violent crimes rate	123.0	74.8	4.9	341.5
Homicides rate	26.8	23.8	1.6	169.6
Assaults rate	317.8	125.2	22.0	658.2
Property crimes rate	361.9	302.4	6.5	1 625.5
Personal theft rate	410.9	223.5	24.9	977.5
Vehicle theft rate	12.8	14.9	0.0	80.7
Motorcycle theft rate	77.7	59.2	4.9	290.2
Drug seizure rate	140.9	11.3	18.4	498.8
Weapons seizure rate	42.2	24.8	7.1	155.4
Coca presence (ha.)	162.2	840.0	0.0	7 125.3
Number of cities		80		

Notes: The table reports descriptive statistics at the city level for the sample of cities for which data is available. Column (1) reports means, column (2) reports standard deviations, column (3) reports minimum values and column (4) reports maximum values.

is the southeastern region, where the Amazon rainforest lies along with the relatively inhabited eastern plains.

Description of cities Table 4.1 presents summary statistics on baseline data for the cities in our sample. On average, these cities have a population of roughly 260 000 residents. This population ranges from 65 000 to 2.5 million residents. Crime also varies largely along the distribution of cities. For instance, the average homicide rate per 100 000 residents is 27 across all cities. The safest city has a homicide rate of 1.6, and the most insecure has a homicide rate of almost 170, probably placing it among the most murderous cities in the world. These cities also differ in terms of the incidence of organized crime. Drug seizure rates, for instance, vary from 18 to roughly 500 per 1000 residents, with an average of 141. The average city in the sample has 162 hectares of coca crops, but a majority of cities (70) do not have these illegal crops.

Crime and arrest records Criminal records include the exact location coordinates, the type of crime and the time and date. Arrest records include the exact location coordinates, an indicator for whether the arrest followed a warrant or was conducted in-the-act, and the time and date. This data is from *Sistema de Información Estadístico, Delincuencial, Contravencional y Operativo* (SIEDCO). While some coordinates may be imprecise, in urban areas of large cities the extent of imprecision is relatively minor, as most reporting stations have interactive maps to help citizens locate their crime reports. Moreover, while under-reporting is a real concern, the research design accounts for idiosyncratic characteristics of places, which should partly mitigate the problem.

Setup and data structure To study the effects of shocks in police activities, we divide the urban area of all 80 cities into grids of 200 × 200 meters. We build panel data for which the time units are periods of two weeks, and the cross-sectional units are these grids. We use the location coordinates of crimes and arrests to assign each of them to only one grid across all cities.

Treatment conditions We define a shock in broken windows policing as any period of time when three or more arrests were conducted in-the-act in a given grid. Two or fewer arrests are relatively common, and we worried this looser definition of the treatment would not pick up an actual intensification of police activities—i.e., citizens may fail to interpret more common events as actual intensification of police presence. We also define a spillover treatment. Any grid with a shared border—including the corners—with a treated grid is exposed to the spillover condition. For simplicity, we only exploit the extensive margin of both treatments. Finally, grids that are not exposed to either direct treatment or spillovers at a given period are controls. Figure 4.2 illustrates how grids are exposed to these treatment conditions.

Outcomes We use additive crime indexes for total crime, violent crime and property crime. The index for violent crime is the sum of homicides and assaults. The index for property crimes is the sum of personal thefts and motor vehicle thefts. The index for total crime consists of the sum of violent and property crimes. We do not include other types of crimes such as sexual assault or burglary as these are largely under-reported and happen mostly within houses and businesses.[17] We focus on these outcomes in the periods following the shock in broken windows policing.

Descriptive statistics Table 4.2 reports descriptive statistics at the grid-period level for the main analytical sample: Grids that were exposed to either direct or spillover effects at any given period over 2019. Panel A presents information on the exposition of the grids to both treatments. Direct treatment occurs for roughly 0.8 percent of grids and periods. As expected, the spillover treatment occurs more frequently, for about 6.2 percent of grids and periods.[18] Panel B presents data on the main outcomes. On average, a total of 0.44 crimes occurred at any given grid and period. Most of these are property crimes. The average grid and period had 0.36 property crimes and 0.09 violent crimes.

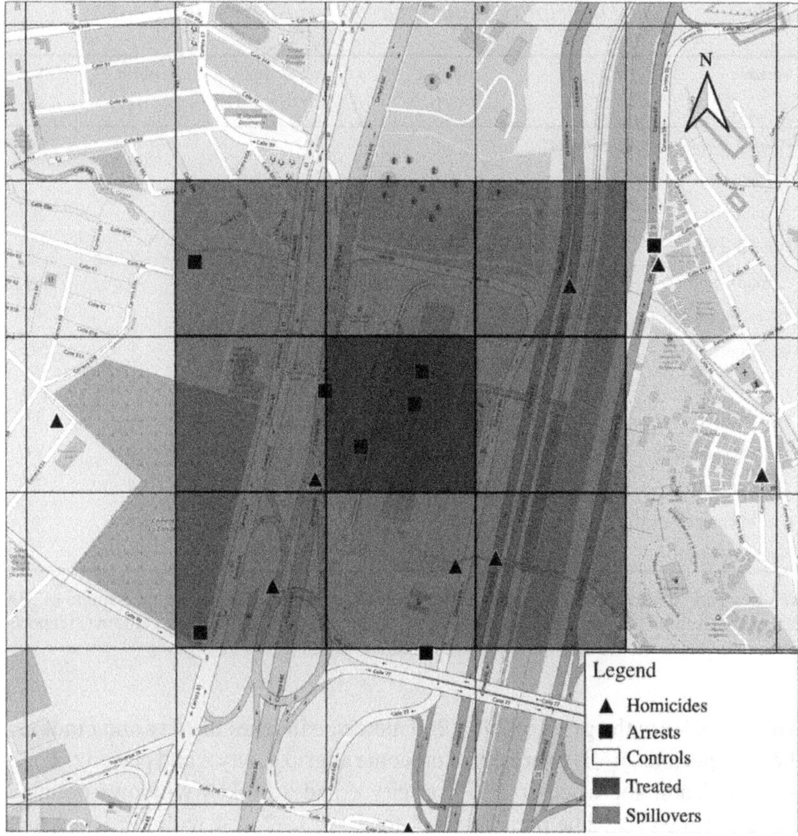

Notes: The figure illustrates how grids are exposed to the direct treatment, spillover or control conditions in a given period.

Figure 4.2 Illustration of treatment and spillover grids

3. EMPIRICAL STRATEGY

We study the effects of broken windows policing on crime by following a difference-in-differences approach with differential treatment timing, including leads and lags to observe pre- and post-trends.[19] In particular, we use ordinary least squares to estimate Equation 4.1:

$$y_{g,c,t} = \sum_{-3<k<4, k\neq 1} \beta_k B_{g,t-k} + \sum_{-3<k<4} \alpha_k S_{g,t-k} + \gamma_g + \eta_c \times \delta_t + \varepsilon_{g,c,t} \tag{4.1}$$

Table 4.2 *Descriptive statistics at the grid-period level*

Variable	Mean	Std. dev.	Min.	Max.
	(1)	(2)	(3)	(4)
Panel A: Exposition to treatments				
Treatment	0.008	0.091	0	1
Spillovers	0.062	0.241	0	1
Panel B: Outcomes				
Total crime	0.444	1.212	0	89
Violent crime	0.088	0.368	0	12
Homicides	0.006	0.084	0	4
Assaults	0.081	0.354	0	12
Property crimes	0.366	1.122	0	89
Personal theft	0.320	1.091	0	89
Car theft	0.006	0.079	0	3
Motorcycle theft	0.029	0.180	0	6
Number of grids		338 208		

Notes: The table reports descriptive statistics at the grid-period level for the sample of 338 208 grids. Column (1) reports means, column (2) reports standard deviations, column (3) reports minimum values and column (4) reports maximum values.

where g indexes the grids of 200×200 meters, c indexes the city and t indexes the time periods. y_{gct} is the relevant outcome at grid g, city c and period t. $B_{g;t-k}$ is an indicator for whether grid g at city c had a broken windows policing shock at time $t-k$. The parameters β_k for $k=-3,-2,\ldots,4$ with $k \neq 1$ measure the direct impact of the broken windows policing shock at each period k, relative to the number of crimes in the period prior to the shock. Furthermore, the parameters α_k for $k=-3,-2,\ldots,4$ measure the spillover impact of the broken windows policing shock at each period k, relative to the number of crimes at grids directly exposed to the shock in the period prior to the shock. γ_g are fixed effects at the grid level and control for unobserved idiosyncratic characteristics of the locations that are invariant over time. $\eta_c \times \delta_t$ control for unobserved temporal shocks fixed for all grids, which we allow to vary across cities. Finally, ε_{gct} is an error term.

This is a relatively standard event study with one difference. In our context, grids can be treated more than once over the study period. Hence, we force early leads and late lags into the α_{-3} and β_{-3} coefficients for direct and spillover effects, respectively.

Inference Assuming that treatment can produce spatial spillovers creates a problem for inference. When one grid is exposed to the direct treatment condition, all the grids around it are exposed to the spillover condition as a cluster. With many grids being treated across each city, this creates a clustering structure that is hard to conform with a standard geographical unit such as a neighborhood. This is a problem of fuzzy clustering (Abadie et al., 2017).[20] To address this problem, we perform two estimations of standard errors and p-values. On the one hand, we use the standard approach in panel data and cluster standard errors at the grid level. On the other hand, we use randomization inference to estimate exact p-values under the sharp null hypothesis of no effect for any unit. While this is more standard in experiments, where treatment can be randomly reassigned across experimental units, we implement it in our context by randomly switching the places that are exposed to the direct treatment and spillover conditions.[21] We estimate treatment effects under 1000 different random scenarios and estimate a p-value comparing our observed effects with the empirical distribution of treatment effects. This procedure is agnostic of the structure of the errors.

4. BASELINE RESULTS

4.1. Direct and Spillover Effects

Table 4.3 presents the baseline results from our estimation of Equation 4.1, and Figure 4.3 plots the conventional figure for event study estimates. In Table 4.3, the relevant independent variables are in panels A and B. Column (1) reports the coefficients for total crime. This is an additive index of all homicides, assaults and personal and motor vehicle thefts at a given grid and period. Columns (3) and (4) report standard errors clustered at the grid level and randomization inference p-values, respectively.

Panel A reports results for direct effects. As expected, we observe a large increase in total crime at the period of the shock. Each arrest necessarily implies at least one crime report (or more, when offenders commit several crimes simultaneously). From this period onward, however, crimes decrease monotonically. Four periods after the shock, the effects are statistically significant at conventional levels when we cluster standard errors at the grid level. Randomization inference p-values suggest the coefficients are rather imprecise, however. The coefficient in the fourth period is –0.067, equivalent to a 6 percent decrease in crimes relative to the average number of crimes at treated grids in the period before the shock.

Panel B reports results for spillover effects. We do not observe a statistically significant increase in crimes at the period of the shock. This suggests crimes were localized where police happened to be present, with no concurrent beneficial or adverse spillovers. In the periods to follow, we also observe a decline in

Table 4.3 *Direct and spillover effects of broken windows policing on crime*

	Coefficient (1)	Standard error (2)	RI p-value (3)
Panel A: Direct effects			
Period –3+ or 5+	–0.011	[0.028]	(0.924)
Period –2	0.008	[0.039]	(0.763)
Period –1	-	-	-
Period 0	0.697	[0.051]***	(0.000)***
Period 1	0.024	[0.040]	(0.741)
Period 2	–0.016	[0.036]	(0.799)
Period 3	–0.036	[0.038]	(0.601)
Period 4	–0.067	[0.038]*	(0.197)
Panel B: Spillover effects			
Period –3+ or 5+	–0.020	[0.017]	(0.446)
Period –2	–0.007	[0.017]	(0.964)
Period –1	–0.013	[0.016]	(0.783)
Period 0	0.005	[0.018]	(0.854)
Period 1	–0.016	[0.019]	(0.630)
Period 2	–0.012	[0.017]	(0.647)
Period 3	–0.033	[0.016]**	(0.337)
Period 4	–0.052	[0.017]**	(0.042)**
Panel C: Tests for pre-trends			
Direct effects: Prob>F		0.795	
Spillover effects: Prob>F		0.426	
Outcome mean in period –1		1.065	
Observations		338 208	
Number of grids		13 008	
Number of cities		80	
R-squared		0.414	
Grid fixed effects		Yes	
Period × city fixed effects		Yes	

Notes: The table reports baseline results for the estimation of Equation 4.1. Column (1) reports coefficients, column (2) reports standard errors clustered at the grid level and column (3) reports randomization inference p-values. We force early leads and late lags into the coefficients denoted as 'Period –3+ or 5+'. ***$p<0.01$; **$p<0.05$; *$p<0.10$.

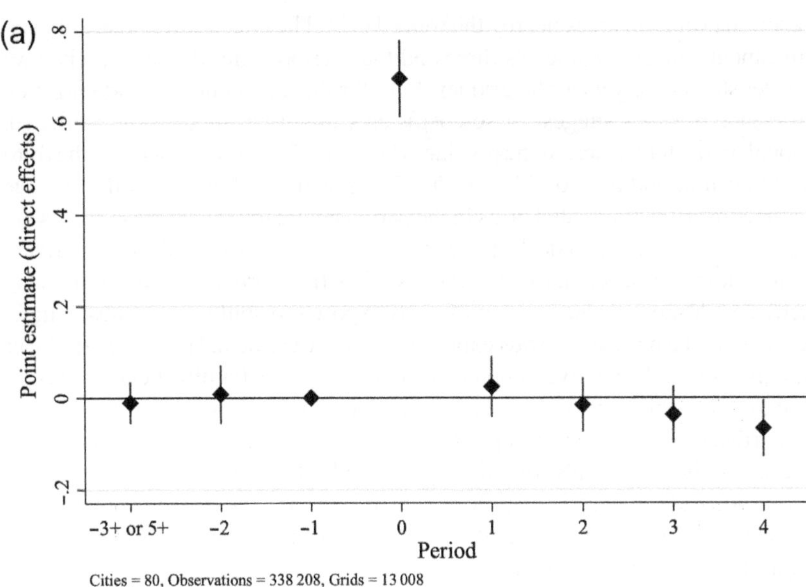

Cities = 80, Observations = 338 208, Grids = 13 008

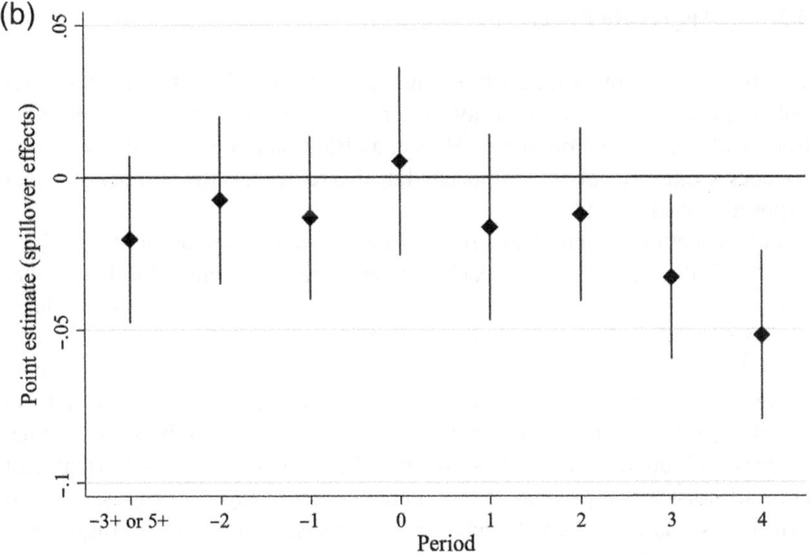

Notes: The figure plots the result of estimating Equation 4.1 for total crimes. The lines denote confidence intervals at the 90 percent level. We force early leads and late lags into the period denoted as '–3+or 5+'.

Figure 4.3 *Direct and spillover effects for the baseline model*

reported crimes in areas nearby the treated grid. The effects are statistically significant at conventional levels three and four periods after the shock, when we cluster standard errors at the grid level. As for the direct effects, randomization inference p-values suggest these coefficients might be imprecisely estimated, though in the fourth period the p-value is below 0.05. The coefficients in the third and fourth period are –0.033 and –0.052, respectively. Relative to the average number of crimes at treated grids in the period before the shock, these effects are equivalent to a 3 percent decline in period three and a 5 percent decline in period four. These are beneficial spillovers resulting from broken windows policing activities. Moreover, the number of grids exposed to spillovers is substantially larger than the number of grids exposed to direct treatment. Hence, the spillover results suggest the relative imprecision of the estimates for direct effects may be due to statistical power rather than to the absence of effects.

Furthermore, the results suggest that crime pre-trends were similar before the shock, both for grids directly exposed to broken windows policing activities and grids exposed to spillovers. Not only are the coefficients not statistically significant individually, but they are also not jointly statistically significant, as reported in panel C.

4.2. Aggregate Effects

Our baseline results suggest the benefits of the shock in broken windows policing materialize several periods after the shock, both in places exposed to treatment and the surroundings. Hence, as Blattman et al. (2021b) point out, the coefficients are not only important but also relevant is the number of places exposed to each condition.

In this section, we conduct a back-of-the-envelope estimation of aggregate effects. To do so, we multiply each estimated treatment effect by the number of grids exposed to each condition. Table 4.4 presents the results. In the shock period, we estimate there is an aggregate increase of 1986 crimes in the grids where police patrols conducted the arrests. After the shock, the aggregate decrease in places exposed to direct treatment and spillover effects adds up to 2503 crimes. Hence we estimate that these policing activities led to a net decrease of roughly 517 crimes. We use the 1000 simulations of treatment effects to produce a p-value of the aggregate net change in crimes. We find that our estimate for the net decrease is imprecise, but borderline significant at conventional levels.

4.3. Effects by Type of Crime

We now turn to examine whether the effects of broken windows policing are different for violent and property crimes. Figure 4.4 plots the event study

Table 4.4 *Aggregate effects of broken windows policing on crime*

	Coefficient (1)	# grids (2)	Total=(1) × (2) (3)
Panel A: Treatment effects, shock			
Direct effects			
Period 0	0.697	2 849	1,985.8
Panel B: Treatment effects, post-shock			
Direct effects			
Period 1	0.024	2 766	6.4
Period 2	–0.016	2 713	–43.4
Period 3	–0.036	2 680	–96.5
Period 4	–0.067	2 651	–177.6
Spillover effects			
Period 1	–0.016	20 572	–329.2
Period 2	–0.012	20 274	–243.3
Period 3	–0.033	19 815	–653.9
Period 4	–0.052	19 718	-1 025.3
Net decrease in crime			–517.0
RI p-value			0.110

Notes: The table reports aggregate effects of preventive policing practices. Column (1) reports coefficients, column (2) reports the number of grids exposed to each condition and column (3) reports the aggregate effect. We estimate RI p-values by simulating 1000 different random scenarios and comparing our estimated aggregate effect with the empirical distribution of aggregate effects.

estimates. Subfigures 4.4a and 4.4b report results for violent crimes. This is an additive index of all homicides and assaults at a given grid and period. Violent crimes are less common and hence entail less variation. The direct effects generally point to a decrease in crimes in the periods following the broken windows policing shock. As with the total crime index, the coefficient turns significant at conventional levels in the fourth period. Spillover effects are far less precise, though the estimates seem to follow a decreasing pattern.

Subfigures 4.4c and 4.4d report results for property crimes. This is an additive index of all personal and motor vehicle thefts at a given grid and period. The direct effects also point to a decrease in crimes in the periods following the broken windows policing shock, though this decrease is imprecisely estimated. Spillover effects are more precise. The coefficients in the periods following the shock are all negative. In periods three and four, the estimates are statistically significant at conventional levels.

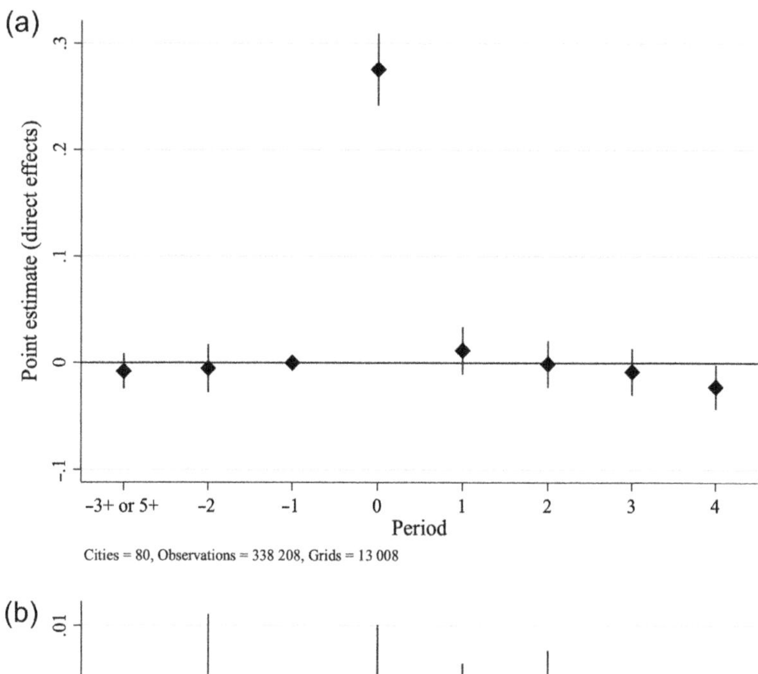

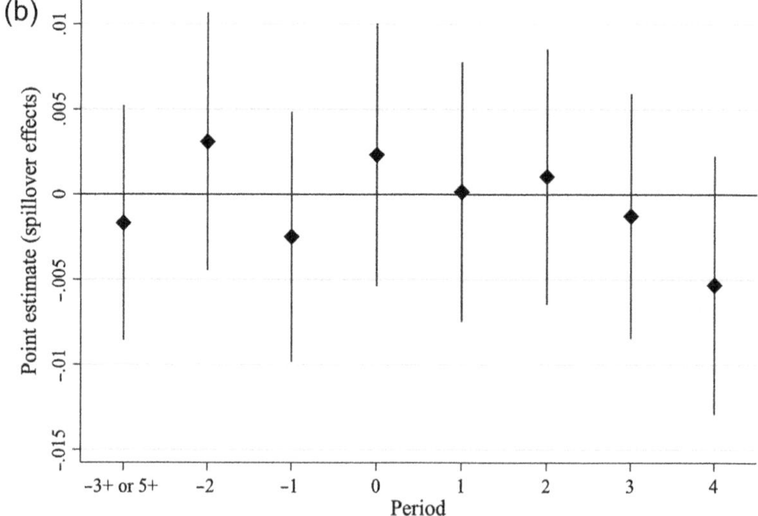

Notes: The figure plots the result of estimating Equation 4.1 for violent and property crimes, separately. Subfigures 4.4a and 4.4b report results for violent crimes, and subfigures 4.4c and 4.4d report results for property crimes. The lines denote confidence intervals at the 90 percent level. We force early leads and late lags into the period denoted as '–3+or 5+'.

Figure 4.4 Direct and spillover effects for violent crime and property crime violent crime

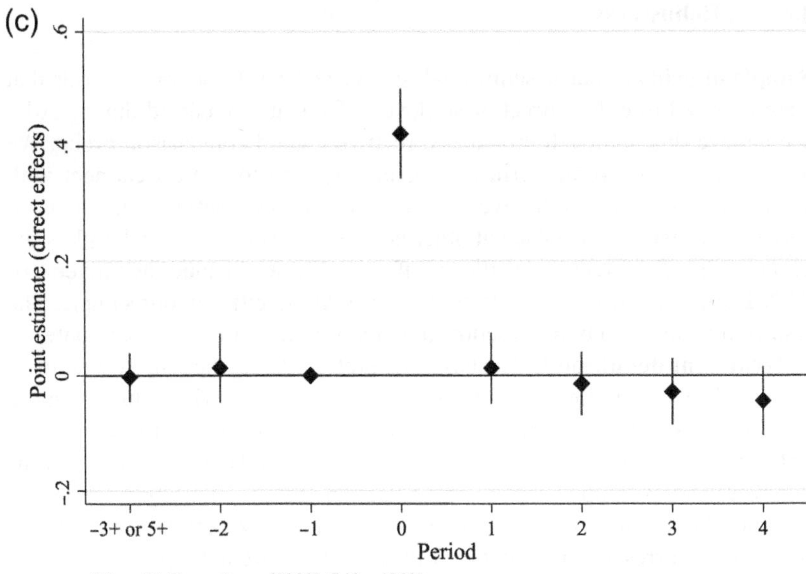

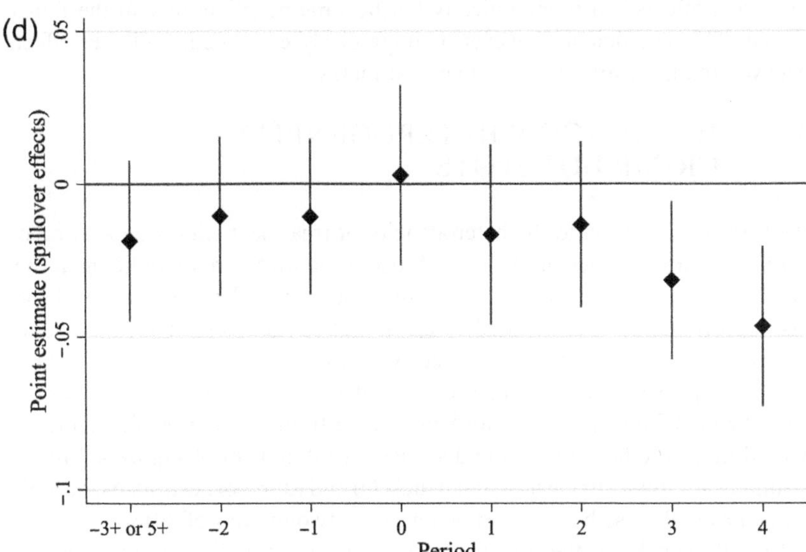

Figure 4.4 *(Continued)*

4.4. Robustness

Sample of grids In our baseline analysis, we restrict the sample to grids that were exposed to either direct or spillover effects at any period during 2019. We believe this approach produces a relatively good comparison group: We directly compare average crimes in grids exposed to some treatment with average crimes in grids that were not exposed to any treatment in that same period, but that were exposed at other period or periods. Figure 4.5 plots the event studies for direct and spillover effects when we include the universe of 73 282 grids covering the urban perimeter of all 80 cities in our sample. The results are similar in both direction and precision to our baseline estimates.

Treatment definition In our baseline, preferred specification, we define a shock in broken windows policing as any period of time where three or more arrests were conducted in-the-act in a given grid. As we mention above, two or fewer arrests are relatively common, and we worried that this looser definition would not pick up an actual intensification of police activities. Figure 4.6 presents the results when we define treatment as any period of time when two or more arrests were conducted in-the-act. As we anticipated, this definition of our treatment leads to more imprecise estimates. The coefficients for direct effects fall monotonically but become negative only in the fourth period. This coefficient, however, is imprecisely estimated. Spillover effects behave broadly similarly to our main estimates.

5. WITHIN-CITY HETEROGENEITY: CRIME HOT SPOTS

We turn our attention to the heterogeneity of treatment effects depending on baseline characteristics of the grids. Most of the literature on policing activities focuses on strategies such as hot spots policing, where police patrols are disproportionately concentrated in crime hot spots. This analysis broadens this scope, looking at effects in places with low or moderate levels of criminal activity. We estimate Equation 4.1 but interact the vector of treatment effects with a dummy variable for being in the 100th percentile of total crimes according to the baseline crime data. Panels (a) and (b) of Figure 4.7 report estimates for low-crime grids, and panels (c) and (d) report estimates for high-crime grids. We use baseline crime levels for two months of 2018.

Broadly speaking, the direct effects of shocks in police activity seem to be more immediate and precise in low-crime areas. Crimes in high-crime areas also seem to fall by period four after the shock, but the corresponding coefficient is imprecisely estimated. Beneficial spillovers are larger and more precise in high-crime grids, as earlier findings from the hot spots policing literature suggest (Braga et al., 2019).

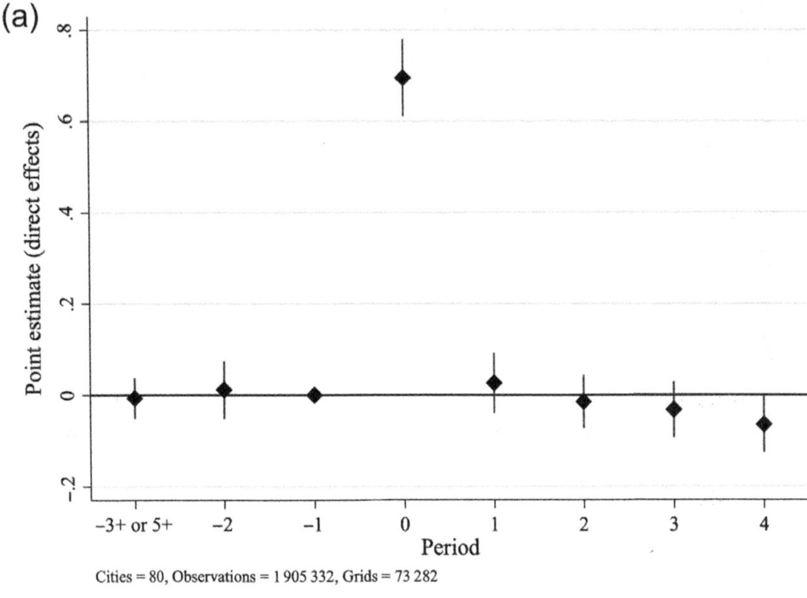

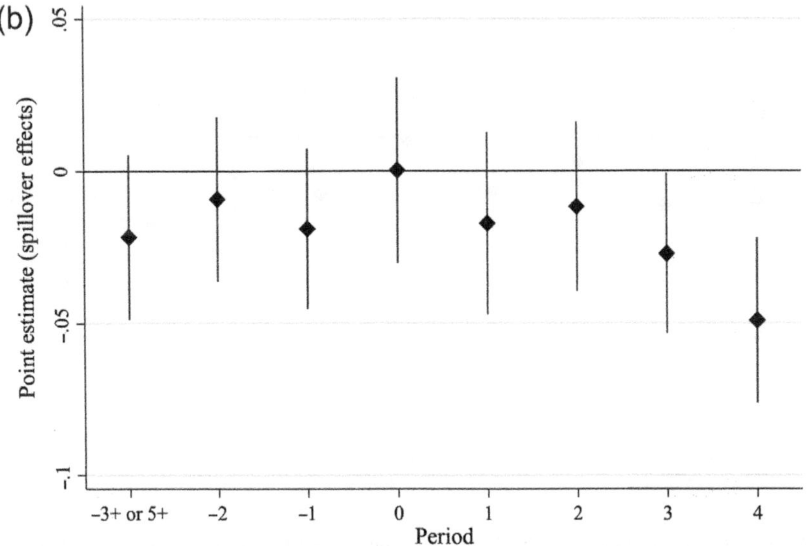

Notes: The figure plots the result of estimating Equation 4.1 for total crimes. The lines denote confidence intervals at the 90 percent level. We force early leads and late lags into the period denoted as '–3+ or 5+'. We include all grids in our sample.

Figure 4.5 *Direct and spillover effects for the universe of grids*

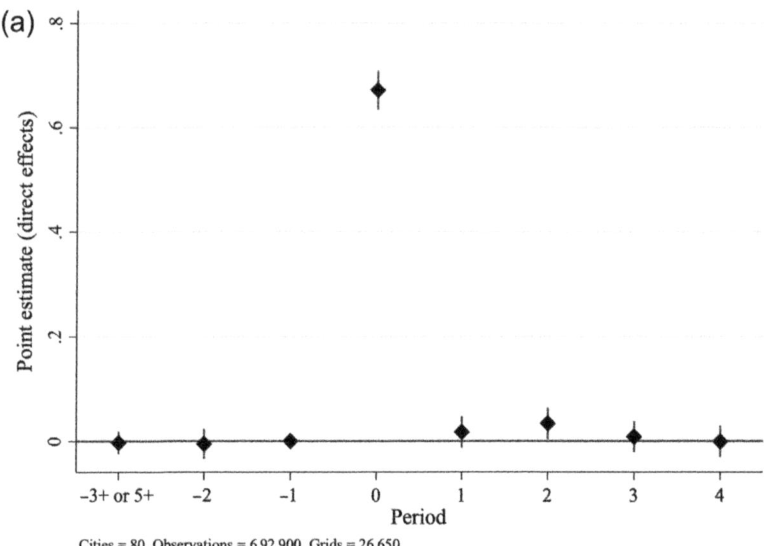

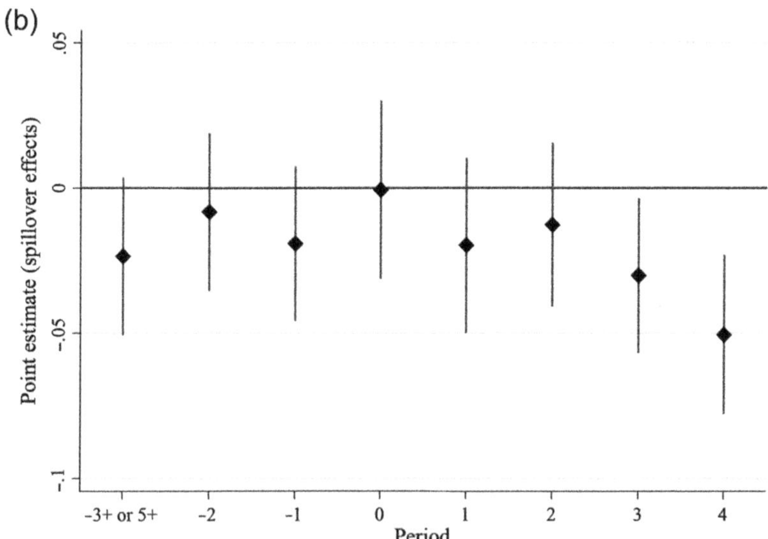

Notes: The figure plots the result of estimating Equation 4.1 for total crimes, using an alternative definition for treatment. We define a shock in broken windows policing as any period of time when two or more arrests were conducted in-the-act in a given grid. The lines denote confidence intervals at the 90 percent level. We force early leads and late lags into the period denoted as '–3+ or 5+'.

Figure 4.6 Direct and spillover effects under a different definition of treatment effects

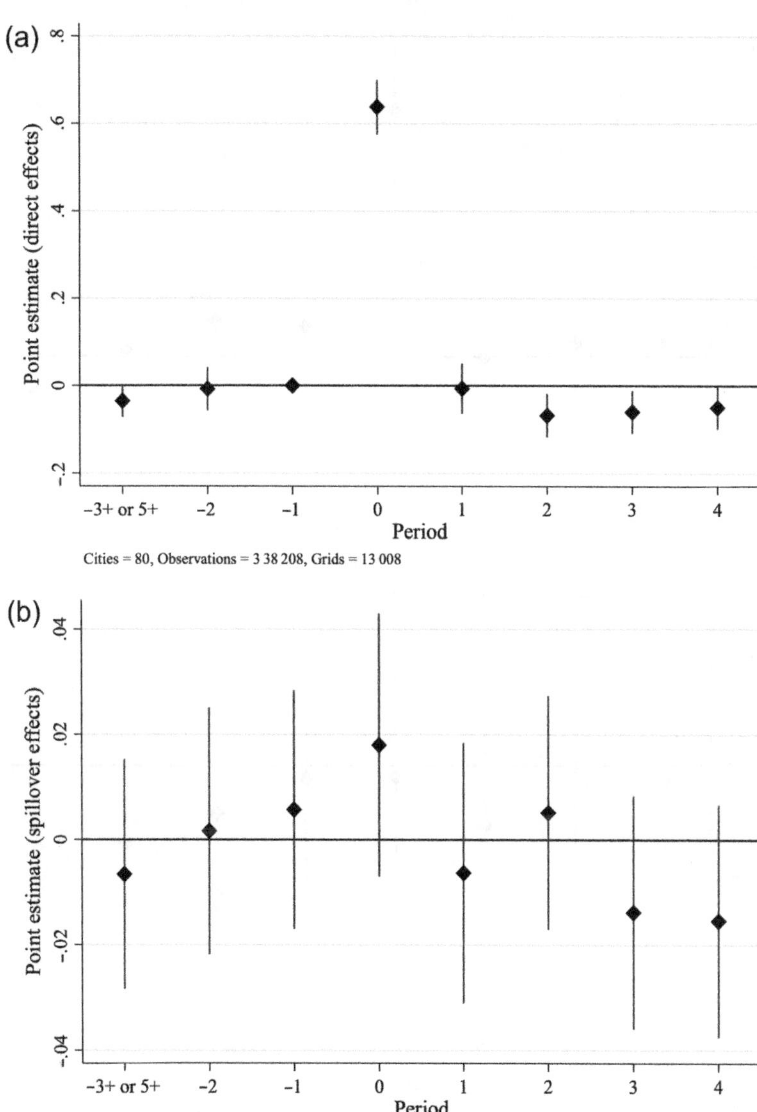

Notes: The figure plots the result of estimating Equation 4.1 for low- and high-crime grids, separately. Subfigures 4.7a and 4.7b report results for low-crime grids, and subfigures 4.7c and 4.7d report results for high-crime grids. The lines denote confidence intervals at the 90 percent level. We force early leads and late lags into the period denoted as '–3+or 5+'.

Figure 4.7 Direct and spillover effects in low- and high-crime grids

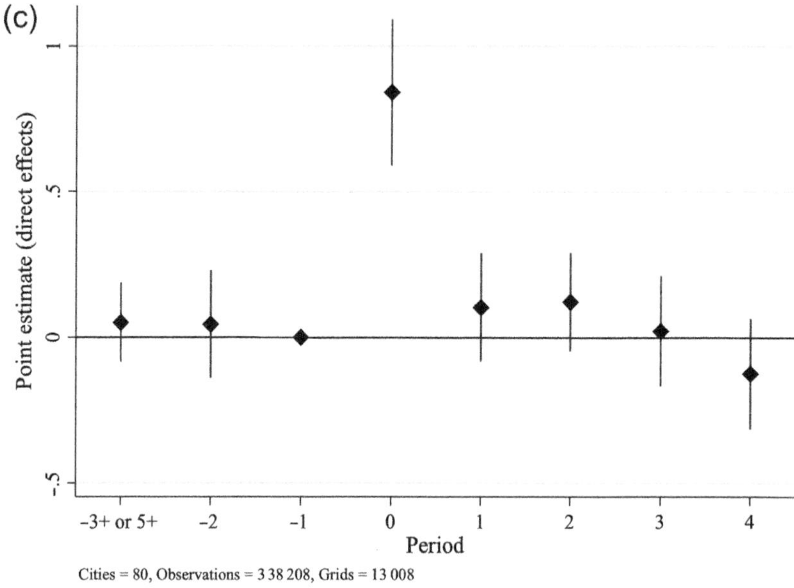

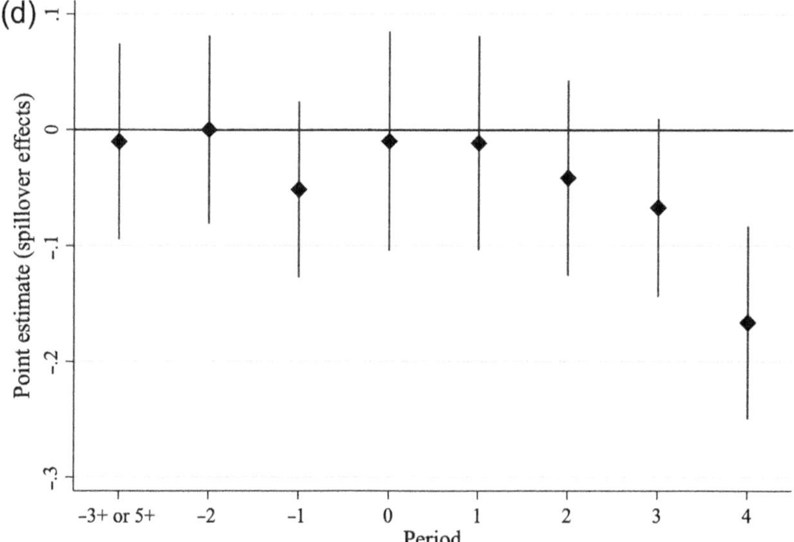

Figure 4.7 *(Continued)*

6. BETWEEN-CITY HETEROGENEITY: ORGANIZED CRIME

In this section, we exploit the wide between-city heterogeneity in the local criminal environment, focusing on proxies for the presence of organized crime. Absent complete data of criminal organizations across the country, we use three alternative proxies: Illegal drug seizure rates, illegal weapon seizure rates and presence of coca crops. Criminal organizations typically engage in illegal drug markets and use illegal weapons to enforce their territorial control, hence our first two proxies. Furthermore, criminal organizations are usually present in cities with coca crops. Their presence serves many purposes, from providing protection to the crops to controlling the supply of coca leaves for the production of cocaine. For the first two proxies, we split the sample of cities at the median. For the third proxy, we split the sample in cities without or with coca crops.

Drug seizures Figure 4.8 reports the results. Subfigures 4.8a and 4.8b present direct and spillover effects for the sub-sample of cities below the median level of the illegal drug seizure rates. Subfigures 4.8c and 4.8d report direct and spillover effects for cities above the median. Broadly, the results suggest the direct effects are similar in both sub-samples, but we only observe evidence of beneficial spillovers in cities with low or moderate levels of organized crime.

Weapon seizures Figure 4.9 reports the results. Subfigures 4.9a and 4.9b present direct and spillover effects for the sub-sample of cities below the median level of the illegal weapon seizure rates. Subfigures 4.9c and 4.9d report direct and spillover effects for cities above the median. We observe direct treatment effects only for the sub-sample of cities below the median. Similarly, we only observe beneficial spillovers in cities with low or moderate levels of organized crime.

Coca presence Figure 4.10 reports the results. Subfigures 4.10a and 4.10b present direct and spillover effects for the sub-sample of cities with no presence of coca crops. Subfigures 4.10c and 4.10d report direct and spillover effects for cities with the presence of coca crops. Most of the cities in our sample have no presence of coca crops (70). We observe direct and spillover effects only for the sub-sample of cities with no coca presence. While we acknowledge that the smaller number of cities in the sub-sample of cities with coca implies more limited statistical power, the coefficients are either positive or close to zero in periods three and four for direct effects and positive for spillover effects across all periods.

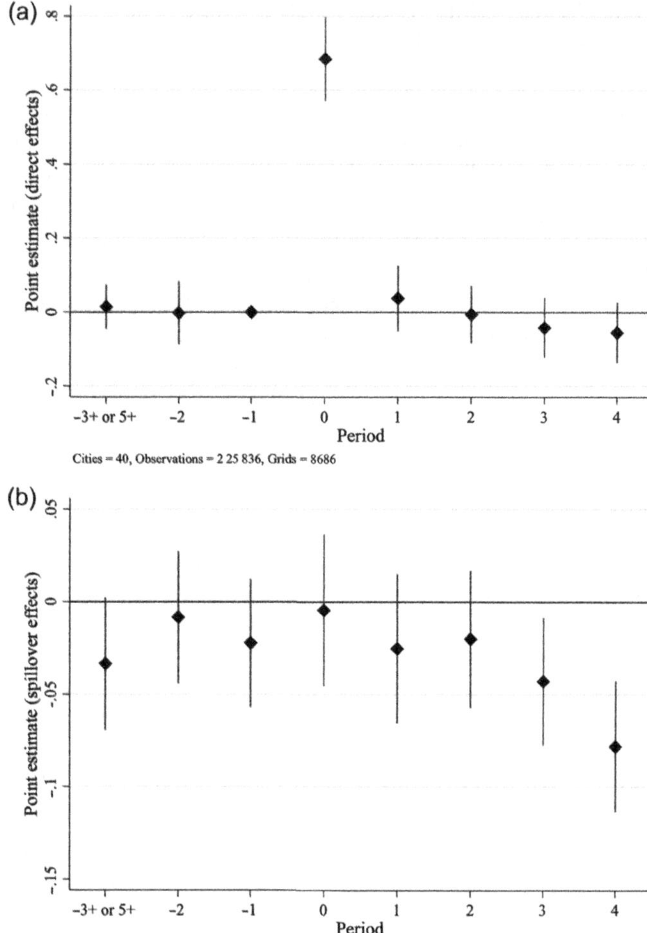

Notes: The figure plots the result of estimating Equation 4.1 for two sub-samples of cities: Those below the median level of the illegal drug seizure rates, and those above the median level. Subfigures 4.8a and 4.8b report results for cities below the median, and subfigures 4.8c and 4.8d report results for cities above the median. The lines denote confidence intervals at the 90 percent level. We force early leads and late lags into the period denoted as '–3+or 5+'.

Figure 4.8 Direct and spillover effects for sub-samples based on the median of the illegal drug seizures rate

(c)

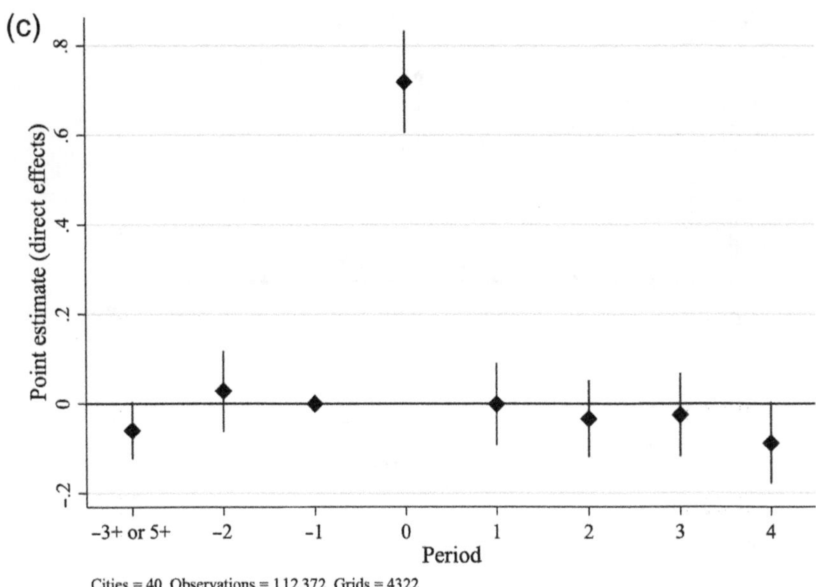

(d)

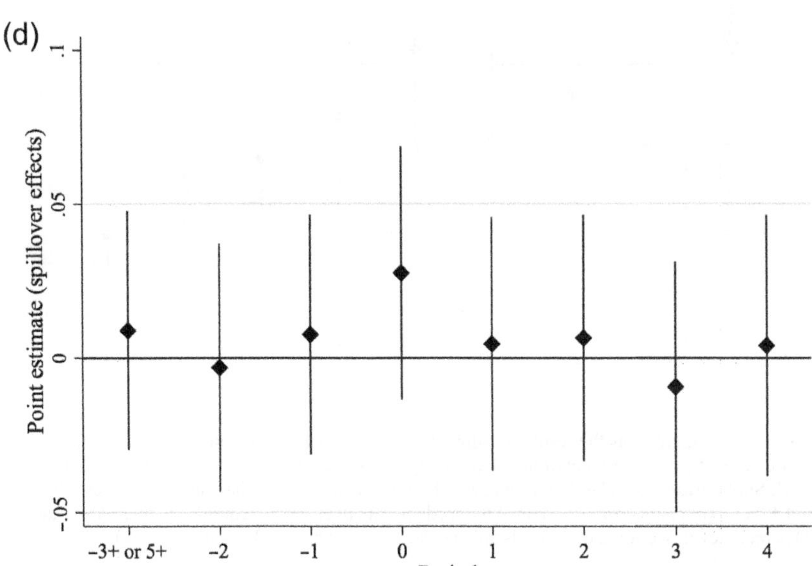

Figure 4.8 *(Continued)*

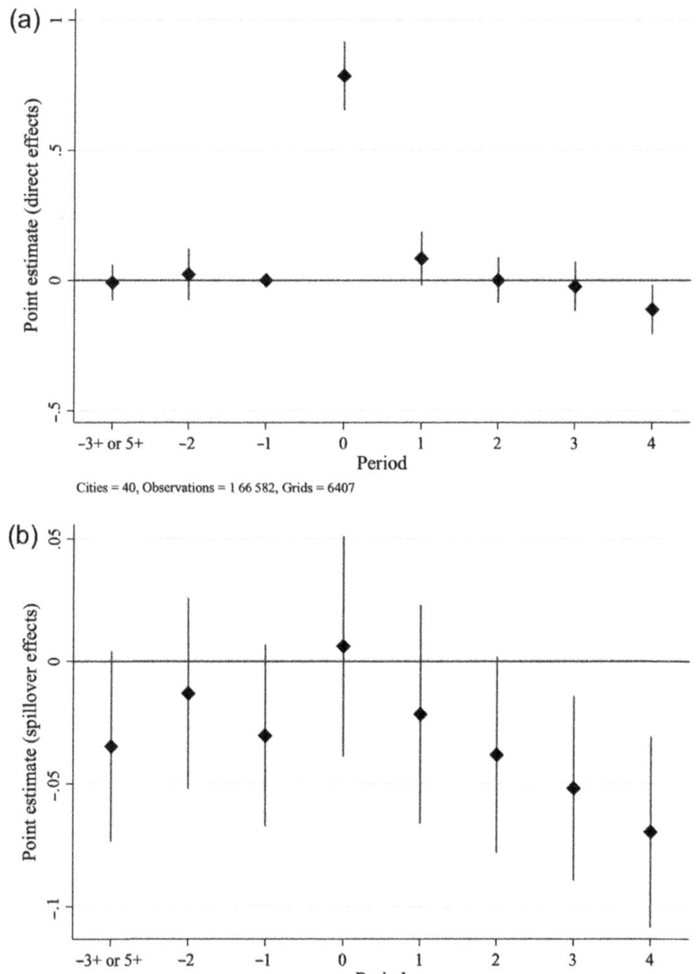

Notes: The figure plots the result of estimating Equation 4.1 for two sub-samples of cities: Those below the median level of the illegal weapon seizure rates, and those above the median level. Subfigures 4.9a and 4.9b report results for cities below the median, and subfigures 4.9c and 4.9d report results for cities above the median. The lines denote confidence intervals at the 90 percent level. We force early leads and late lags into the period denoted as '–3+or 5+'.

Figure 4.9 Direct and spillover effects for sub-samples based on the median of the illegal weapon seizures rate

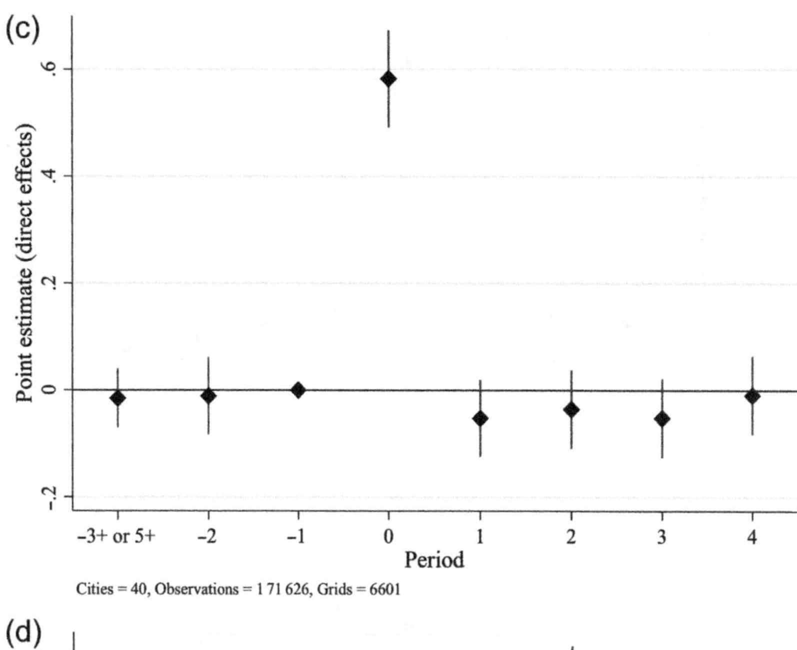

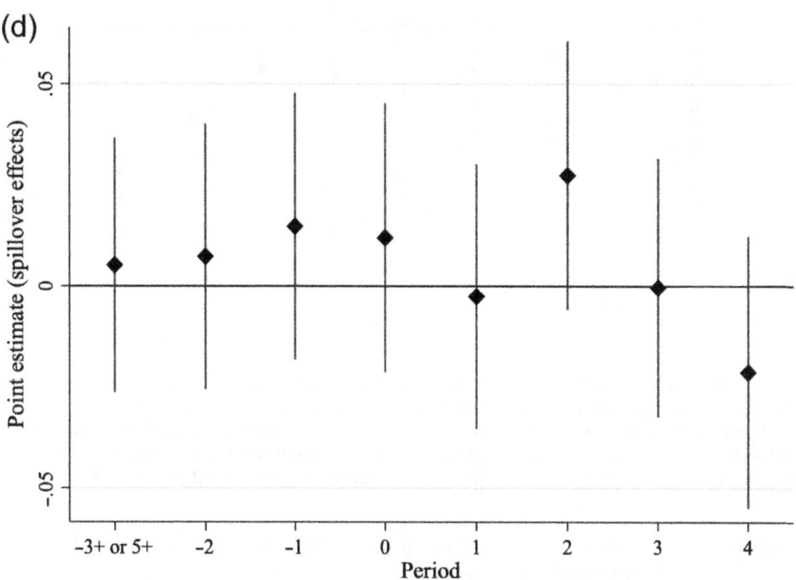

Figure 4.9 *(Continued)*

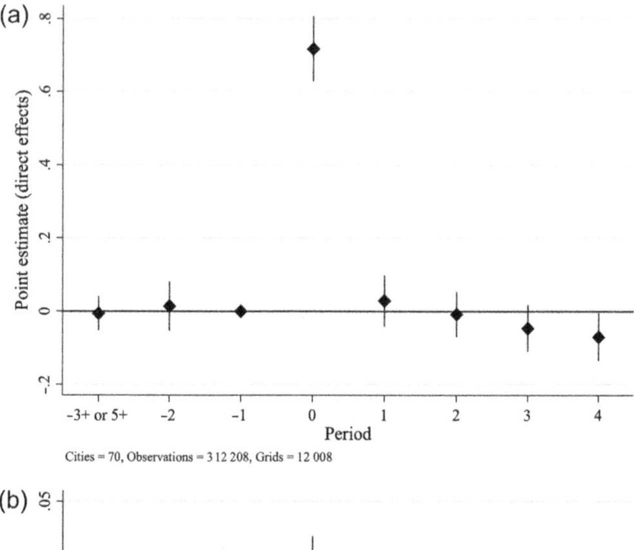

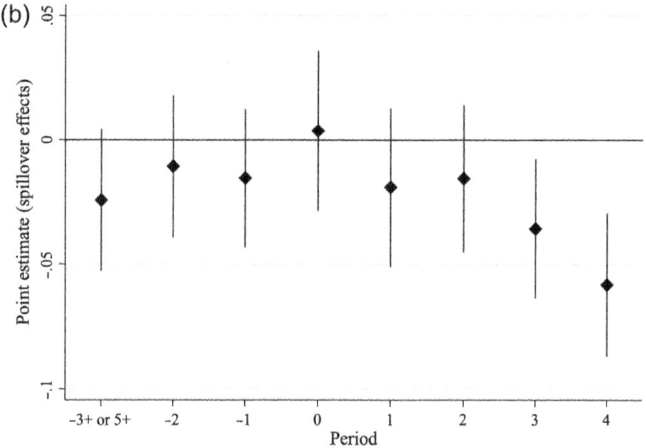

Notes: The figure plots the result of estimating Equation 4.1 for two sub-samples of cities: Those with no presence of coca crops, and those with any presence of coca crops. Subfigures 4.10a and 4.10b report results for cities below with no presence, and subfigures 4.10c and 4.10d report results for cities with presence. The lines denote confidence intervals at the 90 percent level. We force early leads and late lags into the period denoted as '–3+or 5+'.

Figure 4.10 Direct and spillover effects for sub-samples based on the presence of coca crops

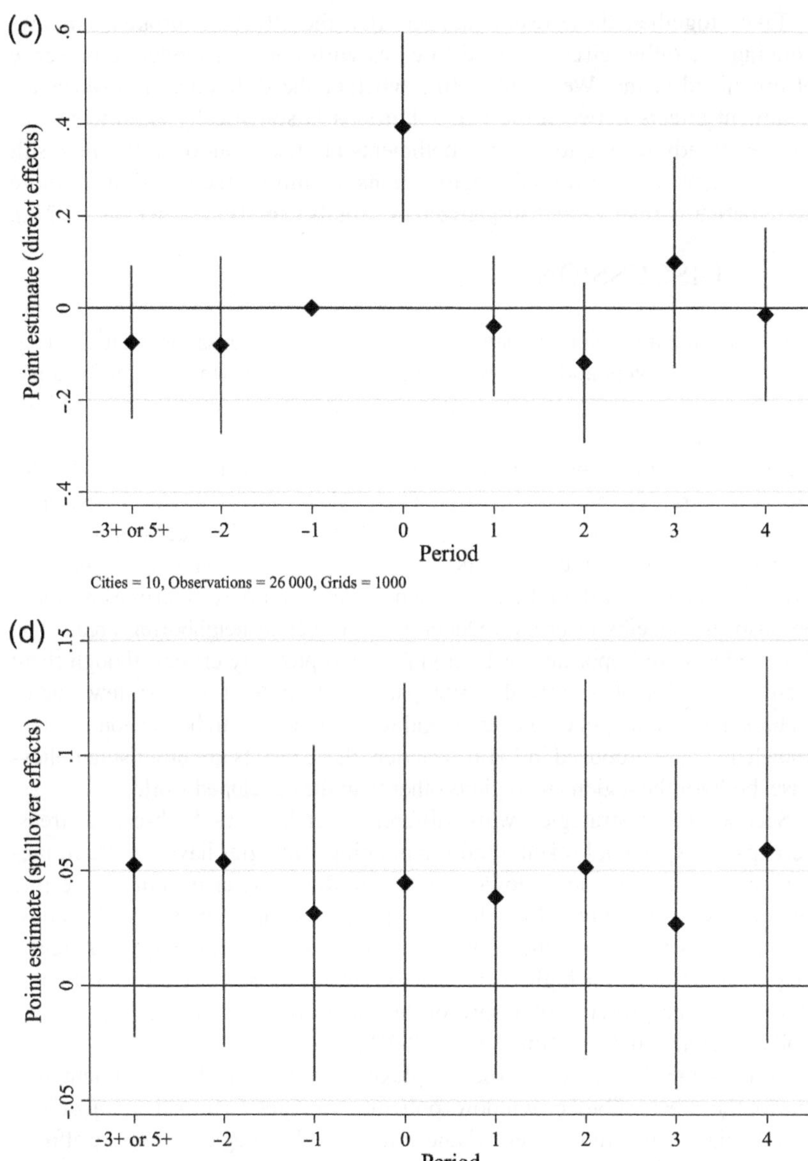

Figure 4.10 *(Continued)*

Taken together, these results suggest that the effects of broken windows policing are rather circumscribed to cities with a low or moderate presence of organized crime. We avoid testing whether the difference in governance treatment effects between the two subgroups is statistically significant—as we are already testing too many coefficients at once—but overall, this result is consistent with criminal organizations planning their activities more systematically relative to disorganized criminals (e.g., Blattman et al., 2021a).

7. DISCUSSION

Crime is a major problem in many parts of the world. Thousands of cities struggle with high violent and property crime rates. In Latin America, for instance, the aggregate homicide rate has remained virtually unchanged for at least three decades—at relatively high levels. Police forces are perhaps the primary policy tool that governments use to control crime. Yet most research in policing strategies concentrates in parts of the world where crime rates are lower, the criminal environment is less diverse and complex and institutional capacity is stronger.

Our work suggests a few insights. First, on average, broken windows policing strategies seem to work in the Colombian context. Not only do crimes decrease but also the benefits in crime reductions spill over to neighboring areas. The direct effects are important for both violent and property crimes, though there seem to be differences in the diffusion patterns. In light of the very few studies on broken windows policing overall, and what we believe to be the non-existent knowledge base produced in Latin America, these results are promising policy-wise, both for the region and regions other than the developed world.

Second, these strategies work differently in low- vs high-crime areas. Perhaps as expected, broken windows policing strategies have a more immediate and precise impact in low-crime areas. Reducing crimes in high-crime hot spots seem to be out of reach for simple patrolling strategies such as broken windows policing. Other deployment tactics, such as hot spots policing, may be a better fit for high-crime places. Hence we see our work as a complement to the growing literature on hot spots policing in the region (e.g., Collazos et al., 2020; Blattman et al., 2021b).

Third, somewhat obviously, the complexity of the criminal environment matters for the effects of broken windows policing strategies. Criminal organizations usually plan their activities beforehand and respond strategically to state efforts. Latin America is a region plagued with criminal organizations controlling retail drug markets, collecting extortion and regulating other forms of crimes such as theft and homicides. Our results are consistent with this idea, as we only see effects in places with low to moderate organized crime (e.g., Blattman et al., 2021a; Dell, 2015; Magaloni et al., 2020). These results suggest policing strategies should follow the local criminal context. A standard approach is probably insufficient to tackle more complex criminal responses.

NOTES

1. This research is thanks to the collaboration of the National Police of Colombia, especially the Director General Jorge Luis Vargas; the Head of Planning, General Luis García; and the Chief of Staff for the Director Colonel Richard Ibáñez. For sharing the data, we thank the Observatorio del Delito from the National Police. Estefany Peña and Hoover Arbeláez provided excellent research assistance. For funding, we thank Universidad EAFIT.
2. Mejía: Universidad de los Andes, Economics.
3. Norza: National Police of Colombia.
4. Tobón: Universidad EAFIT, Economics.
5. Vanegas-Arias: Universidad EAFIT, Economics.
6. See for instance Becker (1968) and Ehrlich (1973).
7. See Chalfin and McCrary (2017) for a complete discussion of the literature on police manpower and other crime prevention strategies.
8. See for instance Braga et al. (2019) for a systematic review of this evidence.
9. Sometimes broken windows policing is described as more aggressive enforcement against minor offenses in order to prevent more serious crime. Hence the focus on arrests for driving under the influence and disorderly conduct. See for instance Kubrin et al. (2010)
10. These are the 80 largest cities of Colombia, excluding the capital Bogotá.
11. Blattman et al. (2021a), for instance, document how street gangs in Medellín are part of an elaborate, hierarchical system. These groups coordinate their responses to state action.
12. Jacob et al. (2007) find that crime shocks could also reduce future crime. Hence, an alternative interpretation of our results is that present crime—rather than police activity—could be driving the effects. However, we believe the most plausible interpretation in our context is that the main treatment is the police activity shock. We reach this conclusion due to the observed patterns of spatial displacement.
13. See also Kennedy et al. (2001) and Raphael and Ludwig (2003) for a related literature on strategies known as 'pulling levers'. Broadly speaking, these strategies intensify police-citizen interactions and are usually implemented at or nearby crime hot spots. Braga and Weisburd (2012) conduct a systematic review of these studies.
14. For summaries of this literature, see Chalfin and McCrary (2017) and Levitt and Miles (2006).
15. Metropolitan departments are for large cities and metropolitan areas, covering a limited number of cities. Regional departments cover a larger number of smaller cities.
16. See the Police Surveillance Guidelines.
17. See Blattman et al. (2021b), who conducted a large survey on crime reporting and other outcomes in Bogotá in 2016.
18. Note for each grid directly treated there are eight grids exposed to spillovers. In some cases, however, one grid is exposed to spillovers resulting from more than one neighbor being treated.
19. See for instance Gómez et al. (2021) for a similar empirical application using grids of 70 × 70 meters over Medellín to study the effects of surveillance cameras on crime.
20. This problem is present in similar crime studies. See for instance Blattman et al. (2021b), Collazos et al. (2020) and Gómez et al. (2021).
21. We randomly change treatment assignment and then assign the spillover condition to the grids that have a common border with a treatment grid.

REFERENCES

Abadie, A., Athey, S., Imbens, G. W., and Wooldridge, J. (2017). *When Should You Adjust Standard Errors for Clustering?* Technical report, National Bureau of Economic Research.

Becker, G. S. (1968). Crime and punishment: An economic approach. *Journal of Political Economy*, 76(2):169–217.

Blattman, C., Duncan, G., Lessing, B., and Tobón, S. (2021a). Gang rule: Understanding and countering criminal governance (No. w28458). National Bureau of Economic Research.

Blattman, C., Green, D., Ortega, D., and Tobon, S. (2021b). Place-based interventions at scale: The direct and spillover effects of policing and city services on crime. *Journal of the European Economic Association*, 19(4):2022–51.

Braga, A. A. and Weisburd, D. L. (2012). The effects of "pulling levers" focused deterrence strategies on crime. *Campbell Systematic Reviews*, 8(1):1–90.

Braga, A. A., Turchan, B., Papachristos, A. V., and Hureau, D. M. (2019). Hot spots policing of small geographic areas effects on crime. *Campbell Systematic Reviews*, 15(3):e1046.

Chalfin, A. and McCrary, J. (2017). Criminal deterrence: A review of the literature. *Journal of Economic Literature*, 55(1):5–48.

Collazos, D., García, E., Mejía, D., Ortega, D., and Tobón, S. (2020). Hot spots policing in a high-crime environment: An experimental evaluation in Medellin. *Journal of Experimental Criminology*, 17:1–34.

Dell, M. (2015). Trafficking networks and the Mexican drug war. *American Economic Review*, 105(6):1738–79.

Di Tella, R. and Schargrodsky, E. (2004). Do police reduce crime? Estimates using the allocation of police forces after a terrorist attack. *American Economic Review*, 94(1):115–33.

Donohue, J. J., Ho, D., and Leahy, P. (2013). Do police reduce crime? A reexamination of a natural experiment. In *Empirical Legal Analysis: Assessing the Performance of Legal Institutions*, 125–43.

Ehrlich, I. (1973). Participation in illegitimate activities: A theoretical and empirical investigation. *Journal of Political Economy*, 81(3):521–65.

Evans, W. N. and Owens, E. G. (2007). Cops and crime. *Journal of Public Economics*, 91(1–2):181–201.

Gómez, S., Mejía, D., and Tobón, S. (2021). The deterrent effect of surveillance cameras on crime. *Journal of Policy Analysis and Management*, 40(2):553–71.

Harcourt, B. E. and Ludwig, J. (2006). Broken windows: New evidence from New York City and a five-city social experiment. *The University of Chicago Law Review*, 73:271–320.

Jacob, B., Lefgren, L., and Moretti, E. (2007). The dynamics of criminal behavior evidence from weather shocks. *Journal of Human Resources*, 42(3):489–527.

Kennedy, D. M., Braga, A. A., and Piehl, A. M. (2001). *Reducing Gun Violence: The Boston Gun Project's Operation Ceasefire*, National Institute of Justice Research Report 188741, US Department of Justice, Office of Justice Programs.

Kubrin, C. E., Messner, S. F., Deane, G., McGeever, K., and Stucky, T. D. (2010). Proactive policing and robbery rates across US cities. *Criminology*, 48(1):57–97.

Levitt, S. D. (2002). Using electoral cycles in police hiring to estimate the effects of police on crime: Reply. *American Economic Review*, 92(4):1244–50.

Levitt, S. D. and Miles, T. J. (2006). Economic contributions to the understanding of crime. *Annual Review Law Social Science*, 2:147–64.

Lin, M.-J. (2009). More police, less crime: Evidence from US state data. *International Review of Law and Economics*, 29(2):73–80.

MacDonald, J. M. (2002). The effectiveness of community policing in reducing urban violence. *Crime & Delinquency*, 48(4):592–618.

Magaloni, B., Franco-Vivanco, E., and Melo, V. (2020). Killing in the slums: Social order, criminal governance, and police violence in Rio de Janeiro. *American Political Science Review*, 114(2):552–72.
Raphael, S. and Ludwig, J. (2003). Prison sentence enhancements: The case of project exile. *Evaluating Gun Policy: Effects on Crime and Violence*, 251:274–77.
Rosenfeld, R., Fornango, R., and Rengifo, A. F. (2007). The impact of order-maintenance policing on New York City homicide and robbery rates: 1988–2001. *Criminology*, 45(2):355–84.
Sampson, R. J. and Cohen, J. (1988). Deterrent effects of the police on crime: A replication and theoretical extension. *Law and Society Review*, 22:163–89.

5. Decarceration and crime: California's experience

Patricio Dominguez, Magnus Lofstrom and Steven Raphael

1. INTRODUCTION

After decades of continuous growth, the US incarceration rate peaked in 2008 at 506 inmates per 100 000 before declining modestly by approximately 10 percent. While several states and the federal prison system have experienced prison population declines, a remarkable and unprecedented series of policy reforms in California contributed disproportionately to the decline in the national incarceration rate.[1] Two reforms in particular generated pronounced and fairly sudden declines in incarceration.

First, under pressure from a federal court order to relieve prison overcrowding, California passed legislation in 2011 that realigned responsibility for punishing and monitoring relatively less serious felony offenses from the state to the counties. These 'realignment' reforms reduced the state prison population by roughly 34 000 inmates (a 20 percent decrease) while generating an offsetting 10 000 person increase in the average daily population of county jails.

Second, in November 2014 California voters passed state proposition 47. The proposition redefined a series of 'wobbler' offenses (offenses that can be charged as either a felony or misdemeanor) as straight misdemeanors. The proposition also included a provision for the filing of resentencing petitions for those under correctional supervision at the time the proposition passed as well as a provision for prior conviction reclassification for those with prior felony convictions that would now be classified as a misdemeanor. The proposition caused a sudden decline in the state's jail population of roughly 7600 inmates (a 9 percent decline), sudden and sharp decreases in arrests for property offenses, a dramatic increase in the proportion of drug arrests that are for misdemeanors and a further reduction in the state prison population of roughly 3.4 percent. Collectively, these reforms reduced the state's prison incarceration rate by roughly one-quarter, from 442 per 100 000 in 2010 to

330 per 100 000 in 2016. California's current incarceration rate has been rolled back to early 1990 levels (a time period that precedes 'Three-Strikes' sentencing reform by several years).[2]

In prior research, we evaluated the effects of the 2011 realignment reform on California crime rates (2016a, b). Our analysis revealed no evidence of an impact on violent crime rates and a relatively small effect on motor vehicle theft. The impact on auto theft and property crime more generally was small relative to the findings from comparable analyses for the US and other nations (Levitt 1996, Liedka, Piehl, and Useem 2006, Johnson and Raphael 2012, Buonanno and Raphael 2013, Vollard 2013, Barbarino and Mastrobuoni 2014). Bartos and Kubrin (2018) provide the sole evaluation of the crime effects of proposition 47. The authors use a synthetic comparison estimator to identify a synthetic comparison group based on crime trends that parallel those for California through 2014. The authors find no effect on violent crime, but suggestive evidence of a modest impact on larceny and motor vehicle theft that are not quite statistically significant.

In this chapter, we present a comprehensive evaluation of the effect on crime rates of California's decade of correctional reforms. Following our earlier realignment research and the methodological strategy pursued in the evaluation of Italy's 2006 Collective Clemency in Buonanno and Raphael (2013), we employ several empirical strategies. First, we use the synthetic cohort estimator presented in Abadi and Gardeazaba (2003) and Abadie, Diamond and Hainmueller (2010) to identify a weighted average of comparison states with crime time series that best match those of California. We use these comparison states to generate a series of difference-in-difference estimates that test for increases in crime rates between California and comparison states for the period spanning the entire reform period as well as for sub-periods that identify the separate impacts of the various reforms implemented in the state.

Beyond the synthetic control analysis, we present additional tests for crime effects of the latter reforms ushered in under proposition 47. Note, this proposition was passed after major reform that drew down the prison population by nearly a quarter. To the extent that there are decreasing returns to scale in incapacitation, one might expect larger crime effects of the latter reform relative to the former. Building on recent work by Bartos and Kubrin (2018), we extend the analysis of proposition 47 in several directions. First, we use higher-frequency monthly data to project counterfactual crime rate trends for California based on pre-intervention momentum in the months leading up to the passage of proposition 47. We then estimate the effect of the proposition by comparing actual monthly crime rates to these projections. We present separate estimates of annualized crime effects based on discontinuous changes in monthly crime coinciding with the implementation of the proposition as well as estimates that use pre-intervention trends to project a counterfactual path for the entire post-intervention period.

Second, we exploit variation across counties in the impact of proposition 47; in particular, the fact that counties with relatively high pre-47 jail incarceration rates experienced the largest relative declines in jail incarceration rates. Using the sharp exogenous shock caused by the policy change we assess whether crime increased more in counties experiencing larger declines in jail incarceration rates, whether changes in county-level crime rates depend on the quantity per capita of resentencing and reclassification petitions filed and whether changes in crime rates depend on county-level changes in arrest activity.

In terms of overall crime trends, crime rates in California following this reform period are no higher than they were in 2010 prior to both policy reforms. While the official violent crime rate is slightly higher, this is due to a change in the definition of rape that mechanically increased the number of incidents and by a change in the process used to classify and record aggravated assaults in the largest police agency in the state beginning in late 2014. The overall property crime rate in 2016 is lower than the level in 2010. In general, crime rates in California remain at historically low levels despite the pronounced declines in incarceration and the downgrading of relatively less serious property and drug offenses.

Regarding actual point estimates, we find little evidence of an impact on violent crime rates in the state. While our proposition 47 analysis of violent crime rates yields a few significant point estimates (a decrease in murder for one method and an increase in robbery for another), these findings are highly sensitive to the method used to generate a counterfactual comparison path. We find more consistent evidence of an impact on property crime. For the earliest major reform, we detect an increase in auto theft, causing a 5 to 7 percent increase in overall property crime. For proposition 47, we detect an impact on larceny theft. The latter estimates are sensitive to the method used to generate the counterfactual, with more than half of the relative increase in property crime (and for some estimates considerably more) driven by a decline in the counterfactual crime rate rather than increases for California for several of the estimators that we employ. Despite these measured increases in specific offenses, California property crime rates remain at historically low levels.

2. THE POTENTIAL CAUSAL PATHWAYS BETWEEN CALIFORNIA POLICY REFORMS AND STATE CRIME RATES

Aggregate indicators of crime and punishment in California have historically moved in lock-step with those of the nation. Figure 5.1 presents the prison

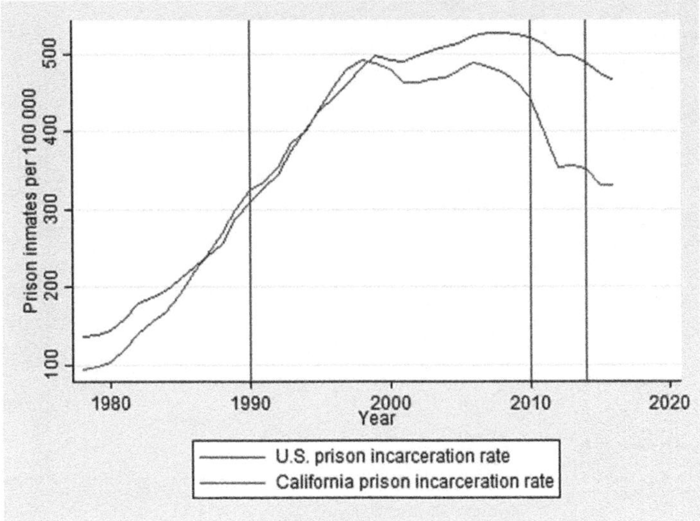

Figure 5.1 *Long-term trends for California and US prison incarceration rates*

incarceration rates for California and for the US from the late 1970s through 2016. Both series exhibit pronounced increases during the last two decades of the twentieth century. From the early 2000s onwards, however, there are notable departures with large relative decreases in California's incarceration rates post-2010. Figure 5.2 presents long-term trends for overall California violent and property crime rates. Similar to national trends, California's violent crime rate peaks in the early 1990s before declining to current historical lows. While the historical peak for property crime occurs in the early 1980s, the largest declines in property crime occur post-1990, with the rate declining by roughly 50 percent over the subsequent 26 years. In both figures, the years 2010 (the last pre-realignment year) and 2014 (a year mostly preceding the implementation of proposition 47) are marked with vertical lines. Notably, these reforms reduced the state's prison incarceration rate to early 1990s levels while crime rates have remained at historical lows.

Two broad factors converged to generate the reduction in the state incarceration rate depicted in Figure 5.1. First, decades of litigation pertaining to conditions of confinement and the availability of health and mental health services in the state prison system culminated in a federal court order to reduce state prison overcrowding. Second, public opinion pertaining to sentencing severity and the use of incarceration in particular softened, resulting in several notable ballot measures aimed at undoing many of the stringent sentencing practices introduced in past decades.

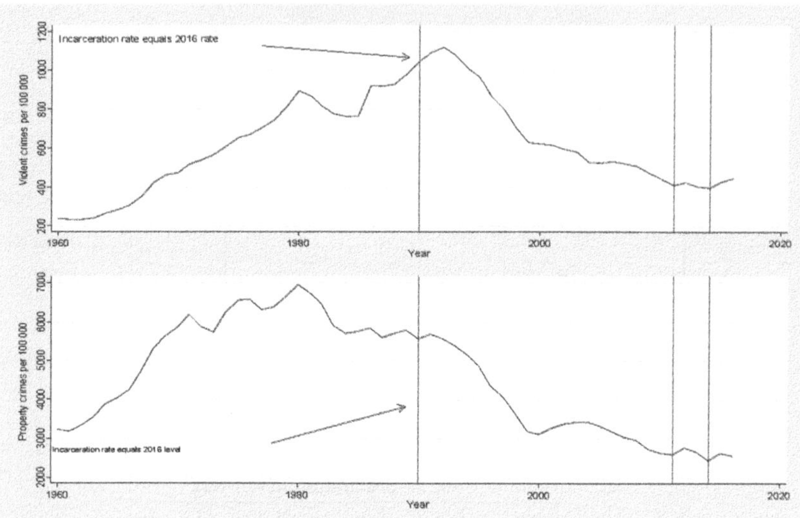

Figure 5.2 *Long-term trends for California violent and property crime rates*

Regarding the response to the federal court order, in 2011 California enacted broad corrections reform legislation under the banner of corrections realignment. The legislation was prompted by pressure from a federal three-judge court overseeing the California prison system, impaneled as a result of legal decisions in two lawsuits against the state filed on behalf of California prison inmates. In one (Coleman v. Brown), it was alleged that California was providing inadequate health care services to its prison population. In the other (Plata v. Brown) it was alleged that the system was providing inadequate mental health services. Both resulted in rulings in favor of the plaintiffs finding that prison overcrowding was the primary cause of the inadequate services and that the poor health and mental health care systems violated the 8th amendment prohibition against cruel and unusual punishment.

Assembly Bill 109 (referred to in the state as 'corrections realignment') was passed and implemented under threat of a federal court order to release up to 35 000 inmates if the state failed to act on its own. The legislation eliminated the practice of returning parolees to state prison custody for technical parole violations for all but a small set of the most serious offenders. The legislation also defined a group of non-serious, non-sexual, non-violent offenders who upon conviction serve their sentences in county jails. The act generated an immediate reduction in weekly prison admissions from roughly 2100 per week to 600 per week and a steady, permanent decline in the prison

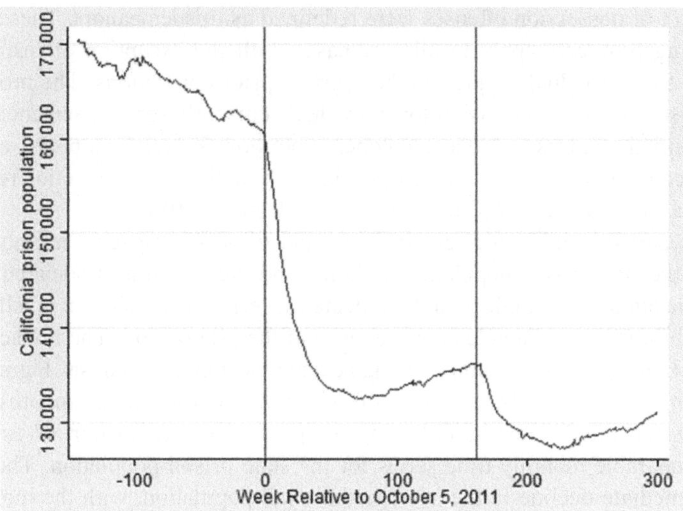

Figure 5.3 *Weekly prison population trends surrounding the implementation of realignment and proposition 47*

population. This resulted in the sharp and sudden reduction in the prison population depicted in Figure 5.3.

Regarding the change in public opinion, in recent years California voters passed several state ballot initiatives aimed at reducing the use of prison along both the intensive and extensive margins. In 2012, voters approved a ballot measure that narrowed the definition of felonies that would qualify for second- and third-strike sentence enhancements, limiting these felonies to serious and violent offenses (proposition 36). More recently, voters passed a proposition that incentivizes prison inmates to engage in rehabilitative programming and refrain from institutional misconduct in exchange for shorter prison terms (proposition 57 passed in November 2016).

The passage of proposition 47 in November 2014 was the most far-reaching sentencing reform passed by way of a ballot initiative and had immediate impacts on the operations and practices of several different arms of the state's criminal justice system. Put simply, the proposition redefined a subset of 'wobbler' offenses (offenses that can be charged as either a misdemeanor or felony) as straight misdemeanor offenses. Regarding property offenses, the proposition redefined shoplifting, forgery, crimes involving insufficient funds, petty theft and receiving stolen property offenses where the value of the property theft falls below $950 as misdemeanors. The proposition also eliminated the offense of petty theft with a prior. Regarding drug offenses, a subset of possession offenses were redefined as misdemeanors. These new charging protocols apply to all new cases with the exception of instances where the individual in question has certain prior convictions. The proposition also included a provision for individuals currently serving sentences for reclassified offenses to file a resentencing petition, as well as a provision for those convicted in the past to file a petition to have the prior conviction reclassified as a misdemeanor (California Judicial Council 2016).

The passage and implementation of proposition 47 impacted jail populations, the state prison population, policing and the sanctions associated with specific offenses. The effect on the expected severity of punishment is self-evident and the direct intended consequence of the proposition. The impacts on correctional populations and policing however bear closer analysis. Figure 5.4 presents the average daily population of county jails for the 26 months preceding and the 26 months following the passage of proposition 47 as well as comparable monthly time series for the state prison population. There is an immediate decline in the average daily jail population, with the monthly average declining by 7717 inmates (a 9.4 percent decrease) between the two periods. We also observe a discrete decrease in the state prison population of 4570 inmates (a 3.4 percent decline). Figure 5.5 reveals a sharp decline in jail bookings, suggesting that the decrease in jail populations is driven by either an increase in the propensity to cite and release for offenses that in the past would have generated a jail booking, an overall reduction in arrests

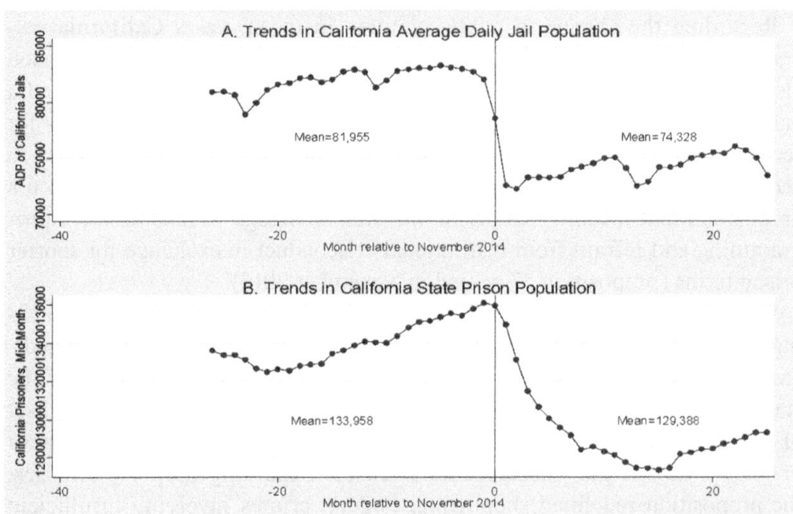

Figure 5.4 Pre-post proposition 47 trends in monthly California jail and prison populations

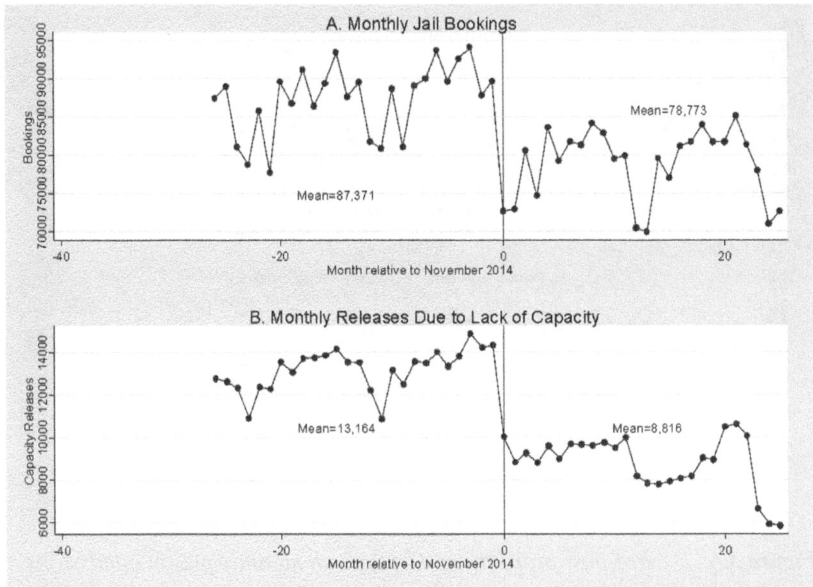

Figure 5.5 *Pre-post proposition 47 trends in monthly jail bookings and releases due to capacity constraints*

or some combination thereof. The figure also reveals a discrete decrease in early releases from jail due to capacity constraints, suggesting that proposition 47 appreciably relieved overcrowding pressure in county jails throughout the state.

One consequence of the 2011 realignment reform was an increase in the average daily population of county jails of approximately 10 000 inmates (essentially undoing one-third of the prison population decline). This increase was driven mostly by the fact that parolees who violated the terms of their supervised release were sanctioned with relatively short local jail spells or some other community sanction rather than prison. Since nearly half of county jail systems in the state were operating under independent court orders to reduce overcrowding, realignment increased emergency releases due to capacity constraints (Lofstrom and Raphael 2013). Proposition 47 relieved many of these pressures on county sheriff departments across the state.

Figure 5.6 reveals the factors driving the decline in the state's prison population associated with the passage of proposition 47. First, we observe a notable decrease in prison admissions overall (displayed in Panel (a)) driven principally by a reduction in admissions for property and drug offenses (displayed in Panel (b)). Second, there is a temporary spike in releases driven by

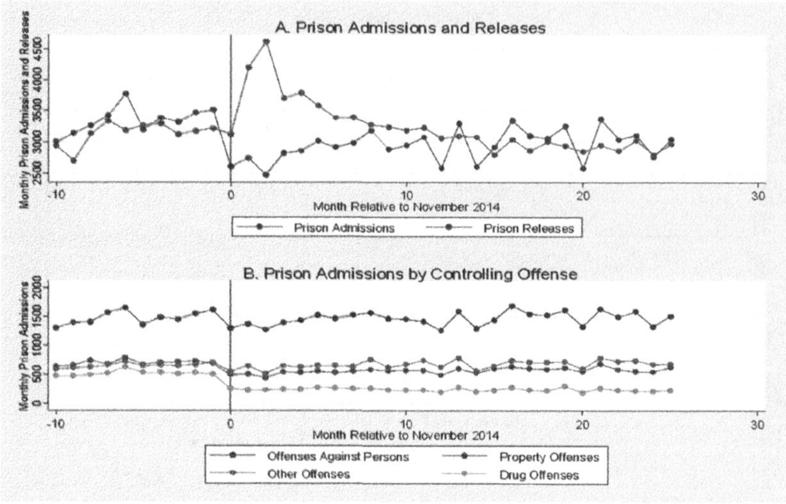

Figure 5.6 *Pre-post proposition 47 trends in monthly prison admissions and releases*

resentencing petitions as well as other population reduction measures coincidentally implemented by the California Department of Corrections and Rehabilitation (CDCR) to comply with the federal court order to reduce prison overcrowding.

Finally, Figure 5.7 displays trends in monthly arrest totals tabulated from the California Monthly Arrest and Citation Register data. The figure displays monthly arrests through the end of 2015 inclusive of booked arrests and arrests that result in citation and release. The figure presents monthly arrest totals by whether the arrest is for a person offense, a property offense, a drug offense or a catch-all 'other arrests' category. Within each arrest category, arrests are further subdivided by whether the offense is classified as a felony or a misdemeanor. There are several notable patterns in Figure 5.7. First, arrests for person offenses and other offenses are essentially stable and not visibly impacted by proposition 47. For drug offenses, however, we observe a sharp decline in felony arrests and a sharp increase in misdemeanor arrests. Comparing the 14 months prior to proposition 47 to the 14 months after, average monthly drug arrests overall (felony and misdemeanors combined) decline by 15 percent. Property arrests also decline discretely. Here, however, there is no apparent increase in misdemeanor arrests. Again, comparing average monthly arrests in the 14 months preceding and following the passage of proposition 47, there is a 20 percent decline in average monthly property crime arrests.

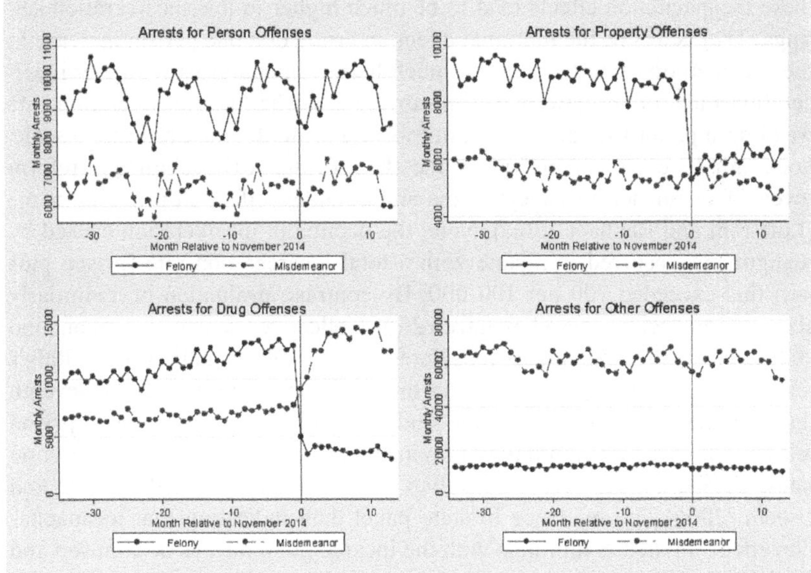

Figure 5.7 *Pre- and post-proposition 47 trends in monthly arrest by offense type*

Given the documented impacts of these reforms on jail populations, prison populations, the likelihood of being arrested and the sanctions one faces in the event of arrest and conviction, there are multiple avenues through which the proposition may impact crime rates. Beginning with incapacitation, there is a sizable body of research estimating the amount of officially recorded crime prevented by a year of detention, with most of the research focusing on prison incarceration. Methodologically, these studies range from surveys of prison inmates regarding past offending (reviewed in Spelman 1994, 2000), state panel data analyses that use various instrumental variable strategies to identify the causal connection from changes in incarceration to crime (Levitt 1996, Liedke, Piehl, and Useem 2006, Johnson and Raphael 2012) and studies that exploit sentencing reforms that either enhance (Vollard 2013) or reduce (Owens 2009) sentences for admittedly criminally active people to studies that evaluate the effects of sudden, discrete and policy-induced changes in correctional populations (Buonanno and Raphael 2013, Barbarino and Mastrobuoni 2014, Lofstrom and Raphael 2016a). While these studies vary greatly methodologically, this corpus of work yields several findings that inform our priors.

First, most careful analyses reveal significant incapacitation effects associated with prison incarceration, and to a lesser extent jail incarceration. Second, these incapacitation effects tend to be much higher in low incarceration settings. That is to say, the marginal effect on crime of a one person increase in the incarceration rate tends to be much higher in countries with low incarceration rates or in periods of time in the US when the incarceration rate was low, a pattern suggestive of diminishing crime-fighting returns to scale. For example, our prior analysis of the effect of the 2011 realignment reform revealed no impact on violent crime and a modest effect on property crime (Lofstrom and Raphael 2016a). Note, the decline in incarceration caused by realignment occurred in a state with a total incarceration rate (prison plus jail) that exceeded 700 per 100 000. By contrast, evaluation of a similarly sized prison decline caused by Italy's 2006 Collective Clemency in Buonanno and Raphael (2013) revealed a considerably larger incapacitation effect. Italy's total incarceration rate on the eve of the clemency was roughly one-seventh that of California. Nonetheless, the study also found smaller effects of prison releases on crime rates in Italian provinces with relatively high incarceration rates, despite the generally low Italian incarceration rate. Liedke, Piehl and Useem (2006) find evidence in state panel data indicating that incapacitation effects in the US diminish with the incarceration rate, as do Johnson and Raphael (2012).

These findings suggest that incapacitation effects are inherently heterogeneous – e.g., likely to be larger for the young than the old, likely to vary with prior criminal history and likely to vary on average with the extensiveness with which a given society deploys incarceration in an attempt to control crime. On the eve of the passage of proposition 47, the California incarceration rate was considerably lower than it was prior to the implementation of realignment, hence we might expect larger effects from proposition 47 than realignment. Nonetheless, prior to both reforms, incarceration rates in the state were high by historical standards in the US and relative to other nations.

Beyond incapacitation, the decline in property and drug arrests caused by proposition 47 as well as the downgrading of several offenses to misdemeanors translates into both a lower likelihood of apprehension conditional on committing one of the reclassified crimes as well as less severe punishment if convicted. Both factors lower the expected value of the sanction one is likely to face for committing a crime impacted by the change in policy, yet may exhibit differential effects on offending to the extent that individuals who criminally offend have high discount rates or are myopic. The results from research on whether changes in sanction severity deter criminal offending tend to be mixed. Among the studies finding evidence of general deterrence, Drago, Galbiati and Vertova (2009) find that individuals released from Italian prisons under the 2006 Italian Collective Clemency who faced larger sentence enhancements for re-offending tended to recidivate at a lower rate. Similarly,

Helland and Tabarrok (2007) find that individuals facing the prospect of a sentence enhancement due to state three-strikes laws recidivate at relatively lower rates. In contrast, research exploiting the discontinuous increase in sentencing severity at the age of majority tends to find little evidence of an impact of the stiffer sentencing on offending (see Hjalmarsson 2009, Lee and McCrary 2009, but Levitt 1998 for a comparable analysis with contrary findings) as does much of the research on the deterrent effects of capital punishment (Blumstein, Cohen, Nagin 1978, Nagin and Pepper 2012). A thorough review of the deterrence effects of sanction severity concludes that general deterrence effects associated with stiffer penalties tend to be small (Nagin 2013, also see the review in Raphael and Stoll 2013, chapter 7).

There is considerably stronger evidence that changes in the likelihood of apprehension, proxied by either changes in police staffing levels or enforcement surges, impact criminal offending. A recent review of experimental research conducted as a part of a National Academies of Sciences consensus panel on proactive policing concluded that hot spots policing, where concentrated enforcement and patrol efforts are targeted toward high-crime city blocks, appreciably reduces crime with little evidence of displacement (National Academies of Sciences 2017). Several quasi-experimental studies of policing and enforcement surges yield similar conclusions. For example, Di Tella and Schargrodsky (2004) analyze an exogenous increase in police presence outside Jewish institutions in Buenos Aires, Argentina. Following a 1994 terrorist attack on an Argentine Jewish center that killed 85 people and wounded 300, Argentina increased police presence to 24 hours per day outside all Jewish and Muslim institutions throughout the country. Comparing monthly auto thefts before and after the terrorist attack, the authors document a sharp decline (on the order of 75 percent) in auto thefts on blocks experiencing increased enforcement, with no measurable effect (negative or positive) in neighboring blocks, or those that are two or more away.

In a similar vein, Klick and Tabarrok (2005) exploit changes in the terror-alert levels under the Homeland Security Advisor System established by the Department of Homeland Security in the wake of the September 11 terrorist attack. Analyzing a 500-day period in 2002 and 2003, the authors exploit the fact that during high-alert time periods, the Washington DC police increase policing resources by roughly 50 percent in key destinations such as the mall. The authors compare average daily crime on days during high-alert periods to other days and find significant reductions in daily crime when the high-alert system was activated.

There is also robust evidence of sizable effects of police staffing levels on crime. Chalfin and McCrary (2018) estimate the effect of changes in city-level police staffing levels on crime rates using panel data for the period 1960 through 2010, with a correction for attenuation bias associated with measurement error in police staffing data. Accounting for attenuation bias leads to quite large (negative) crime-police level elasticities, with sizable and significant effects of the police in reducing homicide, robbery, burglary and motor vehicle theft. Based on these findings and an accompanying cost-benefit analysis, the authors conclude that many cities in the US are under-policed. Evans and Owens (2007) analyze city-level panel data for the period 1990 to 2001 to estimate the effect of changes in police staffing levels caused by the receipt of federal grant funds from the Community-Oriented Policing Services (COPS) program created by the 1994 Violent Crime Control and Law Enforcement Act. The study found that the hiring of new police officers generated statistically significant reductions in robbery, aggravated assault, auto theft and burglary. In accord with Chalfin and McCrary, the authors conclude the dollar value of the crime reduction exceeded budgetary outlays for the new officers.

Finally, Cook and MacDonald (2011) found a causal effect of private security in the context of business improvement districts (BID) created in Los Angeles during the 1990s, with each dollar spent on private security preventing $20 worth of crime and no evidence of displacement to other areas. The creation of a BID had no measurable effect on crime in the absence of security expenditures.

This body of research articulates the possible mechanisms that may link California's correction reforms to changes in crime rates. Both major reforms clearly reduced incarceration rates. Regarding the latter proposition 47 reforms also scaled back the sanctions associated with targeted offenses, eliminating prison time for most. Existing research suggests that such changes have little impact on behavior. However, proposition 47 was well publicized and thus may have impacted the behavior of some. Proposition 47 also caused large decline in arrests for property or drug felonies. To the extent that those who commit or are predisposed to committing the crimes targeted by proposition 47 are short sighted, the realized change in enforcement (as evidenced in the change in the arrest probability) may lead to less overall general deterrence. We now turn to our strategy for estimating the cumulative impact of these three causal channels on state crime rates.

3. METHODOLOGICAL STRATEGY AND DATA DESCRIPTION

Quasi-experimental research investigating the relationship between crime rates and changes in criminal justice policy levers such as incarceration, policing or sentencing severity faces several methodological challenges. First, one must identify exogenous variation in the policy lever to be able to estimate true causal effects from data where both the dependent variable and the explanatory variable are simultaneously determined. Take for example the crime-incarceration relationship. The level of incarceration will certainly depend on the crime rate, with exogenous shocks to crime due to say changes in the economy, changing demographics, changing environmental determinants such as average blood-lead levels or shocks to drug markets, simultaneously generating coincident changes in incarceration and crime. In the other direction, incarceration will incapacitate, may generate a criminogenic or specific deterrence effects on prior inmates in steady-state and may have a general deterrence effect on crime. With causation running in both directions, one must articulate an identification strategy breaking the simultaneity.[3] Similar problems apply to empirical attempts to evaluate the effect of the relationship between policing and enforcement on crime or changes in sentencing severity on crime.

Second, even in the face of an arguably exogenous shock there are many alternative strategies for estimating the counterfactual crime rates that can be used to benchmark realized outcomes and characterize the magnitude of the treatment effect. For example, one could simply use crime levels in the treated area in the pre-period, generate estimates of counterfactual crime rates from pre-intervention trends, look to non-treated areas, such as other states for comparison, or assess whether the dose associated with a policy change varies across sub-geographic units.

The major policy reforms in California are arguably exogenous. Realignment was forced upon the state by the federal courts. In fact, the state Attorney General resisted the initial order to reduce the population-to-capacity ratio, an appeal that was eventually heard and overruled by the US Supreme Court. Similarly, proposition 47 passed against a policy backdrop where the state had not yet met the targeted population-to-capacity ratio ordered by the court. The proposition was opposed by many district attorneys across the state as well as law enforcement. Moreover, as we documented in the previous section, both realignment and proposition 47 generate clear breaks from the pre-intervention trend in prison and jail incarceration and (in the case of proposition 47) arrest activity. Hence, we feel confident that changes to correctional population aggregates as well as arrest totals are attributable to the proposition and that the proposition in turn was not somehow a function of crime rates.

Regarding characterization of the counterfactual path, the raw data on monthly crime rates reveal that estimates of the effect of the proposition are likely to be sensitive to this particular choice. Figure 5.8 displays monthly violent and property crimes per 100 000 for the period from January 2010 through December 2016. Months are indexed along the horizontal axis relative to November 2014. For reference, the annual average for each calendar year is marked with separate horizontal lines. The figure presents separate time series with and without the crime rate for the city of Los Angeles.[4] We present separate series without Los Angeles due to the introduction of a data

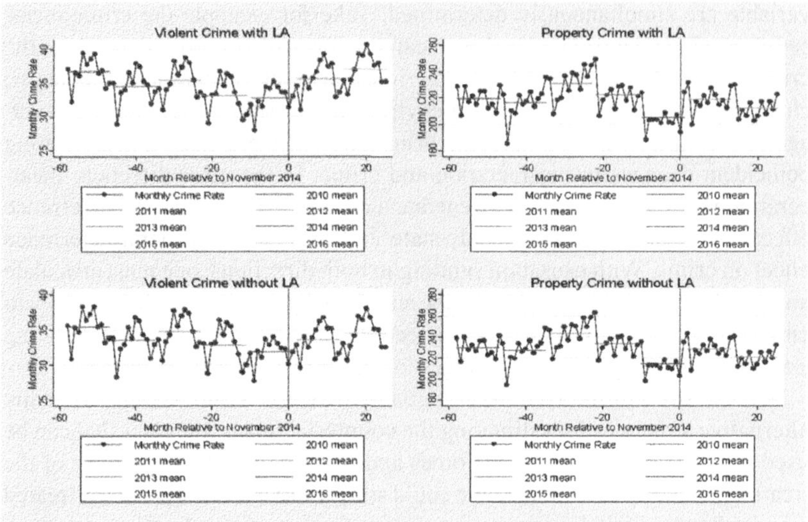

Figure 5.8 *Monthly violent and property crimes per 100 000 with and without crimes reported by the LAPD in the total, January 2010 through December 2016*

integrity unit by the Los Angeles Police Department (LAPD) in November 2014 and a concerted effort in this agency to address a sizable undercounting of aggravated assaults by the department. We discuss this issue in greater detail below.

The figures reveal annual cyclicality in crime rates with what appear to be downward trends in violent and property crime in the two years preceding the passage of the proposition. For violent crime, there is a clear increase when Los Angeles is included but not when Los Angeles is excluded. For property crime, the pre-proposition downward trend is more pronounced and is not sensitive to the inclusion of Los Angeles. However, the year 2014 (the first ten months of which precede the passage of the proposition) appears to be a particularly low crime year (in fact, the year with the lowest recorded crime rates since 1969). The data suggest that a linear trend based on property crimes rates in 2012 and 2013 would project directly through the crime rate outcomes for 2015 and 2016, with 2014 being an outlier year. Alternatively, the low property crime rates in 2014 may be reflective of the true underlying trend that would have continued in the absence of the proposition (suggestive of a visible increase in property crime).

To address these issues, we pursue multiple imperfect, yet complementary strategies for generating counterfactual crime rates for the state to triangulate the impacts of the various reforms on state crime rates. First, we use synthetic cohort analysis to generate comparison annual time series based on other states with pre-reform trends matching those of California. Second, for proportion 47 only we use monthly data for California during the pre-proposition period to project counterfactual crime paths in the post period and then compare actual crime to these projections. Finally, we assess whether cross-county variation in the policy use on local criminal justice practice created by the proposition explains cross-county variation in crime rate changes.

3.1. Difference-in-Difference Estimates from Synthetic Cohort Analysis

Our first strategy analyzes annual state-level crime data from the Federal Bureau of Investigation's Uniform Crime Report for the period 2000–2016. We employ the synthetic control approach of Abadie, Diamond and Hainmueller (2010) to identify a convex combination of states with pre-intervention crime trends that closely match those of California. We then use this synthetic comparison group to chart out the counterfactual path for California, using this as a benchmark against which actual California crime trends can be compared. Given the amount of policy activity in California since 2011 (realignment in 2011, proposition 36 in 2012), we use the period from 2000 to 2010 to identify the synthetic comparison states. We measure the effect of proposition 47 by assessing the degree to which the difference in crime rates relative to the synthetic comparison cohort widens in the latter years of our panel above and beyond differences that emerge in the immediate pre-proposition 47 period due to earlier reforms.

To be specific, let the index $j = (0,1,\ldots,J)$ denote states. The value $j = 0$ corresponds to California and $j = (1,\ldots,J)$ correspond to each of the other J states that are candidate contributors to the control group (or in the language of Abadie et al., the donor pool). Define F_0 as an 11×1 vector with elements equal to the offense-specific crime rates in California in the years 2000 through 2010 (the 11 years we use here as our pre-intervention period). Similarly, define the $11 \times J$ matrix F_1 as the collection of comparable time series for each of the 49 states in the donor pool (with each column corresponding to a separate state-level time series for the period 2000 through 2010).

The synthetic control method identifies a convex combination of the J states in the donor pool that best approximates the pre-intervention time series for the treated state. Define the $J \times 1$ weighting vector $W = (w_1, w_2, \ldots, w_J)'$ such that $\sum_{j=1}^{J} w_j = 1$, and $w_j \geq 0$ for $j = (1,\ldots,J)$. The product F_1W then gives a weighted average of the pre-intervention time series for all states omitting California, with the difference between California and this average given by $F_0 - F_1W$. The synthetic control method essentially chooses a value for the weighting vector, W, that yields a synthetic comparison group (consisting of an average of some subset of donor states) that best approximates the pre-intervention path for California. Specifically, the weighting vector is chosen by solving the constrained quadratic minimization problem

$$W^* = \underset{W}{\arg\min}(F_0 - F_1W)'V(F_0 - F_1W)$$
$$s.t. \tag{5.1}$$
$$W'i = 1, w_j \geq 0, j = (1,\ldots J)$$

where V is an 11 × 11, diagonal positive-definite matrix with diagonal elements providing the relative weights for the contribution of the square of the elements in the vector $F_0 - F_1W$ to the objective function being minimized. Once an optimal weighting vector W^* is chosen, both the pre-intervention path as well as the post-intervention values for the dependent variable in 'synthetic California' can be tabulated by calculating the corresponding weighted average for each year using the donor states with positive weights. The post-intervention values for the synthetic control group serve as our counterfactual outcomes for California.

Our principal estimate of the impacts of realignment and proposition 47 on crime uses the synthetic control group to generate a series of difference-in-difference estimates. Specifically, define $Outcome^{CA}_{2009-2010}$ as the average value of the outcome of interest for California for the pre-intervention years 2009 and 2010, $Outcome^{CA}_{2012-2014}$ as the average value of the outcome during the post-realignment/pre-47 period and $Outcome^{CA}_{2015-2016}$ as the average value for the outcome in the post-47 period. Similarly, define $Outcome^{Synth}_{2009-2010}$, $Outcome^{Synth}_{2012-2014}$ and $Outcome^{Synth}_{2015-2016}$ as the comparable averages for the synthetic control group. With these averages, we define and estimate the following three alternative difference-in-difference estimates:

$$\begin{aligned}
\Delta^2_{realignment} &= \left[Outcome^{CA}_{2012-2014} - Outcome^{Synth}_{2012-2014}\right] \\
&\quad - \left[Outcome^{CA}_{2009-2010} - Outcome^{Synth}_{2009-2010}\right] \\
\Delta^2_{real.+prop47} &= \left[Outcome^{CA}_{2015-2016} - Outcome^{Synth}_{2015-2016}\right] \\
&\quad - \left[Outcome^{CA}_{2009-2010} - Outcome^{Synth}_{2009-2010}\right]
\end{aligned} \tag{5.2}$$

$$\Delta^2_{proposition\ 47} = \left[Outcome^{CA}_{2015-2016} - Outcome^{Synth}_{2015-2016}\right] - \left[Outcome^{CA}_{2012-2014} - Outcome^{Synth}_{2012-2014}\right]$$

The first difference-in-difference estimator identifies the effect of the realignment reforms on crime rates. The second measures the cumulative effects of realignment and proposition 47. The final estimator measured the differential effect of proposition 47 above and beyond the lasting effects of the realignment reforms.

To formally test the significance of any observed relative increase in California's crime rates, we apply the permutation test suggested by Abadie et al. (2010) to the difference-in-difference estimator discussed above.[5] Specifically, for each state in the donor pool, we identify synthetic comparison groups based on the solution to the quadratic minimization problem. We then estimate the three difference-in-difference estimators for each state as if we were testing for comparable policy impacts in these states. The distribution of these 'placebo' difference-in-difference estimates then provides the equivalent of a sampling distribution for the estimates of $\Delta^2_{realignment}$, $\Delta^2_{real.+prop\ 47}$ and $\Delta^2_{proposition\ 47}$. For example, if the cumulative empirical density function of the complete set of estimates of $\Delta^2_{proposition\ 47}$ is given by $F(.)$ the p-value from a one-tailed test of the hypothesis that $\Delta^2_{proposition\ 47} > 0$ is given by $1 - F(\Delta^2_{proposition\ 47})$.

Our principal synthetic cohort analysis uses state-level crime rate data for the period 2000 through 2016 tabulated by the FBI from agency-level data reported through the Uniform Crime Reports program. The main benefit of using the FBI tabulations of state-level crime rates rather than tabulating them directly from agency-level data provided in the annual Offenses Known and Cleared by Arrests computer files concerns the handling of rape. On 1 January 2013, the FBI changed the official definition of rape toward a more inclusive definition that mechanically increased the reported rate for this particular crime. The FBI still collects information on the legacy definition in addition to crime totals using the new definition and reports crime rates by state using both measures. However, the data in the Offenses Known and Cleared by Arrests files are based on the legacy definition prior to adoption of the new definition by each agency and the new definition thereafter. The California Department of Justice officially adopted the new rape definition in 2014, though many police agencies throughout the state including large agencies such as the Los Angeles Police Department (LAPD) did not adopt the new definition until 2015. To avoid a mechanical increase in this crime in 2015 and 2016, we use the state-level rates as tabulated by the FBI where rape is consistently measured with the legacy definition and the total violent crime rate (which includes rape as a component crime) is not impacted by the definitional change.

We also present a parallel series of synthetic control results where we tabulate California crime rates omitting crime reported by the LAPD and the population covered by the LAPD from crime and population totals for the state. The LAPD came under press scrutiny in 2014 for under-reporting aggravated assaults.[6] Aggravated assaults account for nearly 60 percent of all violent crimes and are the largest contributor to the violent crime index, followed robbery (33 percent of the total). A subsequent audit of crime report narratives and arrest charges by the LAPD Office of the Inspector General revealed that between 2008 and 2014 aggravated assaults were under-reported between 30 and 39 percent in each year, with many aggravated assaults involving brandishing a weapon and domestic violence being incorrectly recorded as simple assault (a part II crime not included in official crime rate totals). To address this issue, the LAPD created a data integrity unit in November 2014 (the exact month when proposition 47 went into effect) that closely monitors crime reporting, performs targeted audits and conducts widespread training on crime recording. The data reveal a near 40 percent increase in reported aggravated assaults in Los Angeles between 2014 and 2016.[7] The LAPD has jurisdiction over roughly 10 percent of the state's population. Given the size of the area policed by this agency, the fact that the observed increase in aggravated assaults is likely due to changes in how aggravated assaults are being classified, and the compositional importance of assaults as a contributor to total violent crime, it is important to assess whether results are sensitive to the inclusion of Los Angeles. While the data integrity unit appears to have concentrated their efforts on increasing the accuracy of aggravated assault totals, we adjust all other crimes as well in the event that the enhanced training and monitoring impact the degree of under-reporting of other part I offenses.

To estimate the alternative crime rates for California, we tabulate total crimes in the state using the Offenses Known and Cleared by Arrests files for the years 2000 through 2016 excluding crimes reported by the LAPD from the numerator and the population policed by the LAPD from the denominator. Doing so creates the new issue of the change in the rape definition and the fact that these agency-level data do not include totals for the legacy definition once an agency switches over. Hence, our synthetic cohort estimates using the 'LA-adjusted' California time series omit a separate estimate for rape.[8]

3.2. Projecting a Counterfactual Based on Higher-Frequency California Data

Beyond the synthetic comparison analysis, we provide more in-depth analysis to test for effects of proposition 47.[9] Our second strategy involves a univariate analysis of the monthly crime rate time series for California. We focus on

24 months preceding November 2014 and the first 24 post-proposition months inclusive of November 2014. Figures 5.3 and 5.4 reveal relatively stable prison and jail populations for the 24 months preceding November 2014, while Figure 5.7 shows relatively stable arrest rates. Moreover, the beginning of the period 24 months prior to November 2014 (November 2012) is one full year following the implementation of realignment. Hence, one would expect little effect of realignment on crime rates by that time and little impact of the earlier reform on crime trends during this specified pre-period.

We conduct a univariate analysis of violent and property crime rates overall and for the component part 1 offenses that comprise the aggregate crime indices. Define t as an index measuring month relative to November 2014 (–1 in October 2014, 0 in November 2014, 1 in December 2014 and so on). For each crime rate, we estimate the following model,

$$Crime_t = \alpha_0 + \alpha_1 t + \alpha_2 t^2 + \beta_0 After_t + \beta_1 After_t \cdot t + \beta_2 After_t \cdot t^2 + \varepsilon_t, \quad (5.3)$$

where $After_t$ is a dummy variable indicating $t > -1$, ε_t is an error term and α_0, α_1, α_2, β_0, β_1 and β_2 are parameters to be estimated. Equation 5.3 effectively fits a quadratic trend to the 24 pre-intervention months and a separate quadratic trend to the 24 post-intervention months with a discontinuous break at $t = 0$. The equation is comparable to the model used in Buonanno and Raphael (2013) to test for a discontinuous effect of the Italian Collective Clemency on Italian crime rates. Equation 5.3 can be used to project the counterfactual crime rate based on the estimated pre-intervention quadratic trend and to then measure the difference between the crime predicted by the full equation and the counterfactual. Specifically, for any $t > -1$, the difference in the crime rate predicted by Equation 5.3 and the counterfactual crime rate predicted by the pre-intervention trends is given by

$$Diff\ relative\ to\ cf_t = \beta_0 After_t + \beta_1 After_t \cdot t + \beta_2 After_t \cdot t^2 + \varepsilon_t, \quad (5.4)$$

with the difference in the first post-intervention month simply equal to the coefficient on the variable $After_t$. We use Equation 5.4 to generate several alternative estimates of the annualized effect of proposition 47 on specific crime rates. First, following Buonanno and Raphael (2013), we simply use 12 times the estimate of the discontinuity at November 2014 as an annualized crime effect estimate. Second, we tabulate the difference in Equation 5.4 for each of the first 12 post-intervention months and then sum these estimates. The first estimate is based on the most precise definition of the counterfactual yet may miss impacts of the proposition that occur beyond the first month. On the other hand, the second estimate will be overly sensitive to over-projection of what may be a temporary downward trend in crime during the pre-intervention period, to the extent that property crime levels in California in 2014 were outliers.

We apply the model in Equation 5.3 to the individual part 1 offenses using monthly data tabulated by the California Department of Justice (DOJ). For the major part 1 offenses, again we present analysis with and without crimes reported by LAPD. We pull monthly crime totals from the Offenses Known and Cleared by Arrests file for LAPD and subtract them from the monthly crime totals provided by the California DOJ. We should also note that the monthly data provided by the California DOJ record rape totals based on the definition in use at the time of reporting and do not report a consistent total for the legacy definition.

3.3. Testing whether Cross-County Heterogeneity in the Proposition 47 Dose Predicts Cross-County Heterogeneity in Crime Trends

Two prior analyses of discrete changes in correctional policy tested for changes in aggregate incarceration rates as well as whether variation in the regional impact of the shock explains regional variation in crime rates. Specifically, in our prior work on realignment (Lofstrom and Raphael 2016a), we found that the statewide increase in auto theft coincided with relatively larger increases in auto theft in counties that experienced greater reductions in county-specific prison incarceration rates and no evidence of an impact for other crimes. Buonanno and Raphael (2013) found a discrete increase in Italian crime rates coinciding with a mass prisoner release with larger increases in Italian provinces experiencing larger reductions in local incarceration rates. In both instances, the magnitude of the effects implied by the cross-regional analysis matched the magnitude of the impacts implied by the change in aggregate crime trends.

Our final strategy exploits cross-county variation in the impact of proposition 47 on local incarceration, resentencing and reclassification activity and of arrest rates on local crime rates. Specifically, we calculate the change in average monthly crime rates by county and regress these changes on the change in local jail incarceration rates, the amount of resentencing and case reclassification per capita in the county and changes in arrest rates for property and drug offenses. Monthly data on local jail populations come from the Jail Profile Survey maintained by the California Board of State and Community Corrections. Data on resentencing and reclassification totals by counties come from a survey administered to counties by the Judicial Council of California. Finally, we tabulated average changes in arrest activity by county using data from the California Monthly Arrest and Citation Register files.

3.4. The Relative Strengths and Weaknesses of These Three Approaches

Our three strategies are certainly imperfect, and each individually carries particular weaknesses. The synthetic cohort analysis matches in the years 2000 through 2010. Given the size and scope of realignment reforms, the states that match California from these earlier time periods may no longer be an appropriate gauge of counterfactual crime paths. Our higher-frequency analysis based on monthly data may be overfitting pre-existing trends to an unusual year. The property crime rate in California recorded in 2014 is literally the lowest rate on record since 1969 and notably lower than the immediately preceding years. Hence, estimates based solely on pre-existing trends run the risk of over-projecting the counterfactual crime decline. The cross-county analysis estimates the effects of the proposition based on heterogeneity across counties in the differential impact of the proposition on arrests and jail populations. Any general deterrence effect that impacts state crime levels overall washes out in the analysis.

Nonetheless, the relative strengths of these strategies complement one another. Though problematic, the synthetic cohort and time series strategy will capture statewide general deterrence effects that the cross-county analysis may miss. The clear differences across county permit analysis of the proposition's effect that does not depend on a potentially problematic pre-proposition year. Moreover, whether the projected counterfactuals from the within-state analysis reflect overfitting to an outlier pre-intervention year can be verified by comparison to other states from the synthetic cohort estimator. Our strategy is to present estimation result from all three approaches and to interpret overlapping results that accord with one another as evidence of an effect of the proposition.

4. RESULTS FROM THE STATE-LEVEL SYNTHETIC COHORT ANALYSIS

We begin with a graphical analysis of the total violent crime rate (the sum of the rates of murder, rape, robbery and aggravated assault) and the total property crime rates (the sum of burglary, larceny and motor vehicle theft). Figure 5.9 graphically displays the violent crime rate for California and for the synthetically matched comparison group for the period 2000 through 2016. Recall our synthetic cohort match is based on pre-intervention values for the years 2000 through 2010. The figures on the left display violent crime rates when crime reported by the LAPD is included in the total. The figures on the right display the time series when the LAPD contribution to state crime rates is omitted. In addition to the overall time series, we graphically depict the

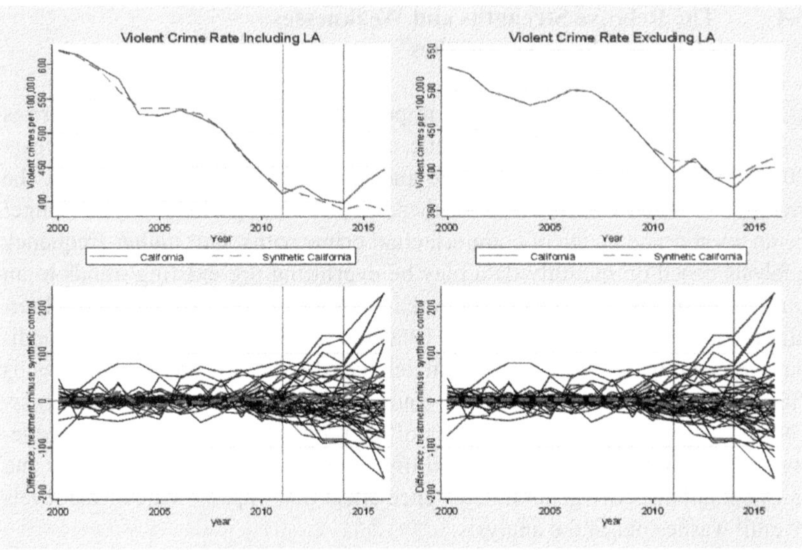

Figure 5.9 *Violent crime rates in California and synthetic California as well as placebo time series of treatment-control differences for two alternative California crime time series (with and without Los Angeles in the tabulation of California violent crime rates)*

difference between the 'treated state' and the synthetic comparison group for all 49 states used to generate the placebo estimates and for California (marked by the thicker dashed line) in the bottom two figures. Vertical lines denote the years 2011 (the year in which realignment goes into effect) and 2014 (the year when proposition 47 passes) in all of the figures. Figure 5.10 presents comparable graphs for property crime.

Beginning with the results for violent crime, there is little evidence of an increase in violent crime following the implementation of realignment, but an increase in violent crime rate in 2015 and 2016 following the implementation of proposition 47. However, the increase (both in terms of the level for California as well as the difference relative to the synthetic comparison group) disappears when the Los Angeles crime rate is excluded from the overall tabulation. In fact, the figure on the right suggests that violent crime in California falls slightly below the value for the comparison group post-proposition 47 when Los Angeles is omitted from the aggregate crime tabulation. The lower figures reveal that the annual differences in violent crime rates between California and synthetic California do not visibly widen after 2011 especially

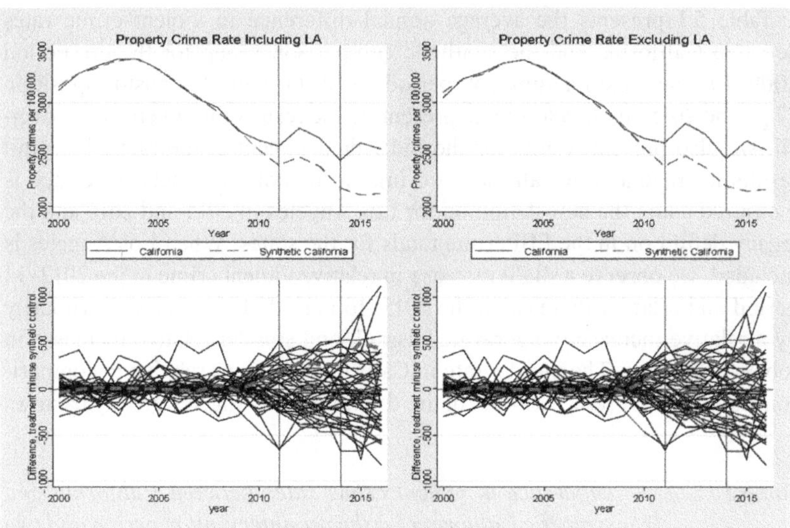

Figure 5.10 *Property crime rates in California and synthetic California as well as placebo time series of treatment-control differences for two alternative California crime time series (with and without Los Angeles in the tabulation of California property crime rates)*

when Los Angeles is dropped from the analysis. Moreover, the plotted time series differences for California lie well within the distribution of placebo estimates.

Figure 5.10 reveals stronger evidence of a departure from trends for property crime. Moreover, the results are not sensitive to the inclusion of Los Angeles in the total property crime rate. California property crime rates increase relative to the synthetic comparison groups in 2012, remain above the trend for other states in 2013, and 2014, and widen again in 2015 and 2016. The later widening is due in part to a decline in property crime in the comparison states and in part due to an increase in property crime levels in 2015. The time series of the difference between California and its synthetic comparison group visibly widens after 2011 and appears large relative to the distribution of placebo differentials. Interestingly, we do observe comparable proportionate declines of roughly 8 percent in the property crime rate for both California and the synthetic comparison group between 2013 and 2014. In the years following, however (between 2014 and 2016), property crime in the synthetic comparison group declines by only 2 percent. That is to say, the sharp decline between 2013 and 2014 does not continue in the comparison states.

Table 5.1 presents the average annual difference in violent crime rates between California and the synthetic comparison group for the pre-period 2009–10, the post-realignment period 2012–14 and the post-proposition 47 period 2015–16. In addition to presenting the results for violent crime overall, we also present results for the individual violent crime rates. We omit results for rape and overall violent crime in the bottom panels since rape is measured using the new definition for Los Angeles in 2015 and 2016 and the legacy definition in the FBI crime totals for the states. When Los Angeles is included, we observe a slight increase in relative violent crime in the 2012–14 period and a larger increase in the 2015–16 period. This is driven primarily by a relative increase in aggravated assault and smaller relative increases in robbery and rape. The murder rate in California declines relative to comparison states in both post periods. Again, dropping Los Angeles greatly narrows

Table 5.1 *Difference in violent crime rates between California and synthetic California for the pre-intervention period and two post-intervention periods*

	Difference, CA-synthetic CA 2009–10	Difference, CA-synthetic CA 2012–14	Difference, CA-synthetic CA 2015–15
With LA			
Total violent crime	2.40	8.37	45.45
Murder	–0.17	–0.15	–1.13
Rape	–0.09	–0.87	1.66
Robbery	2.55	1.19	4.64
Aggravated assault	–12.65	–6.59	18.46
Without LA			
Total violent crime	–0.73	–3.10	–8.38
Murder	–0.16	–0.26	–0.98
Rape[a]	-	-	-
Robbery	1.58	4.61	4.09
Aggravated assault	–0.14	7.04	9.88

Notes: The figures in the table are the average of the difference in annual crime rates between California and the synthetic comparison group for the noted time period. Actual values for the violent crime rate levels are provided in appendix Table A1.

a. We omit tabulations for rape without Los Angeles due to the fact that the FBI UCR agency-level data do not include rape tabulation for recent years using the legacy definition. Our state-level panel data set produced by the FBI uses the legacy definition for rape through 2016. Tabulating the rate of rape per 100 000 for California from agency-level data yields a mechanical increase in rape in 2015 and 2016 due to the adoption of the new rape definition in several large agencies in California.

the increase in aggravated assault especially between the years 2012–14 and 2015–16.

Table 5.2 presents estimates of the difference-in-difference equations specified in Equation 5.4 from the previous section for violent crime. The first column presents the estimate for the period 2012–14 relative to 2009–10 and is akin to the estimated impact of realignment. The second column presents estimates for the period 2015–16 relative to 2009–10 and amounts to our estimates of the cumulative effects of both reforms on crime. The final column

Table 5.2 *Difference-in-difference estimates of the effects of the estimates of sentencing reforms on violent crime rates along with statistical inference from the distribution of placebo estimates*

	Diff-in-diff, 2012–14 minus 2009–10		Diff-in-diff, 2015–16 minus 2009–10		Diff-in-diff, 2015–16 minus 2012–14	
	Δ^2	Rank ($P[\Delta^2 > \Delta^2_{CA}]$)	Δ^2	Rank ($P[\Delta^2 > \Delta^2_{CA}]$)	Δ^2	Rank ($P[\Delta^2 > \Delta^2_{CA}]$)
With LA						
Violent	5.97	34/50 (0.32)	43.05	44/50 (0.12)	37.09	44/50 (0.12)
Murder	0.02	30/50 (0.40)	–0.96	10/50 (0.80)	–0.98	4/50 (0.92)
Rape	–0.78	23/50 (0.54)	1.74	36/50 (0.28)	2.53	43/50 (0.14)
Robbery	–1.35	25/50 (0.50)	2.08	31/50 (0.38)	3.44	32/50 (0.36)
Assault	6.07	37/50 (0.26)	31.11	44/50 (0.12)	25.05	42/50 (0.16)
Without LA						
Violent	–2.37	33/50 (0.34)	–7.66	26/50 (0.48)	–5.92	23/50 (0.54)
Murder	–0.10	27/50 (0.46)	–0.82	10/50 (0.80)	–0.72	8/50 (0.84)
Rape[a]	-	-	-	-	-	-
Robbery	3.02	33/50 (0.34)	2.50	32/50 (0.36)	–0.51	27/50 (0.46)
Assault	7.17	37/50 (0.26)	10.02	34/50 (0.32)	2.84	33/50 (0.34)

Notes: Δ^2 statistics present the difference-in-difference between California and synthetic California in the given crime rate for the two noted time periods. The rank indicates where California's estimate sits within the distribution of placebo estimates for all 50 states. The probability value estimate provides the empirical probability that a placebo difference-in-difference crime rate effect exceeds the estimate for California. We interpret this figure as the p-value from a one-tailed test of the significance of the California crime effect.

a. We omit tabulations for rape without Los Angeles due to the fact that the FBI UCR agency-level data do not include rape tabulation for recent years using the legacy definition. Our state-level panel data set produced by the FBI uses the legacy definition for rape through 2016. Tabulating the rate of rape per 100 000 for California from agency-level data yields a mechanical increase in rape in 2015 and 2016 due to the adoption of the new rape definition in several large agencies in California.

presents the difference-in-difference estimates for the period 2015–16 relative to 2012–14. These are our principal estimates of the effect of proposition 47 on violent crime from the synthetic cohort analysis. For each estimate, we also display California's rank in the distribution of estimates for all states (California plus the estimates for the remaining 49 placebo estimates). We also present the proportion of states with a higher value than that for California (in essence, the p-value for a one-tailed test of whether California's violent crime rate increases in the post-proposition period). When Los Angles is included, we observe a relative increase in overall violent crime in the post-proposition period driven primarily by the increase in aggravated assault. While the p-values do not fall below 0.10, California's relative increase in violent crime is in the right tail of the distribution of placebo estimates. Interestingly, we observe a statistically significant relative decline in the murder rate for California post-proposition 47 when Los Angeles is included, with the probability of experiencing a decline larger than California's equal to 0.06 (which our method would indicate is a statistically significant relative decline in homicide).

Omitting Los Angeles from the overall violent crime rate tabulation eliminates any evidence of an effect of the proposition on violent crime. The relative changes in violent crime in 2015–16 are negative for murder, and robbery, and relatively small for aggravated assault. All of the estimates lie either close to the placebo estimate for the median state or well within the left tail of the placebo distribution (for murder in particular). Our reading of the results in Figure 5.9 and Tables 5.1 and 5.2 is that proposition 47 had no measurable adverse impact on violent crime rates in the state.

Tables 5.3 and 5.4 present a comparable analysis for overall property crime and the individual components that constitute property crime. Beginning with the results for overall property crime in Table 5.3, we observe an increase in the difference between California and synthetic California in 2012–14, and a further increase in 2015–16. Interestingly, this is driven mostly by declining crime in the synthetic comparison states. Specifically, between 2009–10 and 2012–14, average annual property crime rates in California decline by 64 incidents per 100 000. The comparable decline in synthetic comparison states is 234 per 100 000. Between 2012–14 and 2015–16, average annual property crime in California declines by 34 per 100 000. The comparable decline in the comparison states is 194 per 100 000. In terms of the specific crime categories, we observe a sizable increase in the relative rate of auto theft in the post-realignment period but no further widening of this differential in 2015–16. The relative larceny theft rate, however, increases in 2015–16. The exclusion of Los Angeles does not impact the basic patterns in Table 5.3.

Table 5.4 presents our difference-in-difference estimates for property crime along with our test for statistical significance using the placebo

Table 5.3 Difference in property crime rates between California and synthetic California for the pre-intervention period and two post-intervention periods

	Difference, CA-synthetic CA 2009–10	Difference, CA-synthetic CA 2012–14	Difference, CA-synthetic CA 2015–15
With LA			
Total property crime	37.02	270.83	464.68
Burglary	2.16	41.91	42.65
Larceny	12.89	20.75	157.51
Motor vehicle theft	76.88	141.32	128.33
Without LA			
Total property crime	31.68	297.13	431.27
Burglary	11.47	63.12	58.46
Larceny	15.33	43.51	168.48
Motor vehicle theft	69.51	129.17	110.79

Notes: The figures in the table are the average of the difference in annual crime rates between California and the synthetic comparison group for the noted time period. Actual values for the violent crime rate levels are provided in appendix Table A2.

distributions of estimates for the other 49 states. The structure of the table is comparable to that of Table 5.2 for violent crime. Again our principal estimates of the effect of proposition 47 on property crime are in the final column of the table. For property crime overall, we observe a statistically significant increase in property crime in the post-proposition 47 period of roughly 194 incidents per 100 000 in the estimates excluding Los Angeles. Relative to property crime rates for the state during the period 2012–14, this represents a 7.5 percent increase. Most of this effect (83 percent) is driven by the decline in average crime rates in the comparison states rather than an actual increase in property crime in California. When Los Angeles is omitted from the analysis, relative property crime rates increase by 134 incidents per 100 000. Here, however, California ranks 41/50 and thus the increase is no longer statistically significant. Again, the lion's share of this effect is generated by the decline in crime rates in comparison states. At face value, an increase of 134 incidents per 100 000 represents a 5 percent increase in property crime relative to property crime levels during the period 2012–14. Regardless of whether Los Angeles is included in the analysis, the post-proposition 47 effect is driven compositionally by increases in larceny theft relative to comparison states.

Table 5.4 *Difference-in-difference estimates of the effects of the estimates of sentencing reforms on property crime rates along with statistical inference from the distribution of placebo estimates*

	Diff-in-diff, 2012–14 minus 2009–10		Diff-in-diff, 2015–16 minus 2009–10		Diff-in-diff, 2015–16 minus 2012–14	
	Δ^2	Rank ($P[\Delta^2 > \Delta^2_{CA}]$)	Δ^2	Rank ($P[\Delta^2 > \Delta^2_{CA}]$)	Δ^2	Rank ($P[\Delta^2 > \Delta^2_{CA}]$)
With LA						
Property	233.79	46/50 (0.08)	427.63	46/50 (0.08)	193.85	42/50 (0.16)
Burglary	39.75	37/50 (0.26)	40.49	36/50 (0.28)	0.74	28/50 (0.44)
Larceny	7.86	29/50 (0.42)	144.62	38/50 (0.24)	136.76	45/50 (0.10)
MVT	64.43	49/50 (0.02)	51.45	40/50 (0.20)	–12.98	20/50 (0.60)
Without LA						
Property	256.46	47/50 (0.06)	399.60	45/50 (0.10)	134.13	41/50 (0.18)
Burglary	51.65	42/50 (0.16)	46.98	36/50 (0.28)	–4.67	26/50 (0.48)
Larceny	28.18	33/50 (0.34)	153.16	38/50 (0.24)	124.98	43/50 (0.14)
MVT	59.76	48/50 (0.04)	41.28	38/50 (0.24)	–18.48	18/50 (0.64)

Notes: Δ^2 statistics present the difference-in-difference between California and synthetic California in the given crime rate for the two noted time periods. The rank indicates where California's estimate sits within the distribution of placebo estimates for all 50 states. The probability value estimate provides the empirical probability that a placebo difference-in-difference crime rate effect exceeds the estimate for California. We interpret this figure as the p-value from a one-tailed test of the significance of the California crime effect.

To summarize the results of this section, the synthetic comparison analysis of state-level data yields little evidence of an impact of proposition 47 on violent crime. The results for violent crime are particularly sensitive to the inclusion of crimes reported by the LAPD, where we know a priori that changes in reporting have mechanically increased the rate of aggravated assault. Even when Los Angeles is included in the tabulation of crime rates, we fail to find a statistically significant increase in violent crime.

For property crime, however, we observe relative increases in California in the post-proposition 47 period. The magnitude of the estimates suggests increases in property crime ranging from 5 to 7.5 percent of pre-proposition 47 levels, with the effect driven mostly by a relative increase in larceny. The relative increase in property crime actually reflects declines in average annual property crime in California that are considerably smaller than the coinciding decline in comparison states. Hence, most of the 5 to 7.5 percent relative increase reflects crime trends in the comparison states rather than absolute increase in California.

5. RESULTS FROM THE WITHIN-STATE TRENDS ANALYSIS

Figure 5.11 graphically depicts the estimation procedure we deploy to use within-state time trends to project counterfactual crime rates. Specifically, for 24 pre-47 and 24 post-47 months, we fit a simple regression model of crime rates on time measured relative to November 2014, time squared, an indicator variable for time > –1 and interactions between the quadratic function and the indicator variable (Equation 5.3 above). The models allow for first-order serial correlation in the residuals.[10] Figure 5.11 plots the actual monthly crime rate against time (denoted with dots), the fitted values from the interacted quadratic function in time and the projected counterfactual values for the post-period (the predicted value less the post-period differential given by Equation 5.4 above). Our estimates of the effect of the proposition are based on either 12 times the discontinuous break in the crime rate time series in November 2011 or the difference between the predicted value and the counterfactual value over the first post-proposition 47 year. While we are also able to

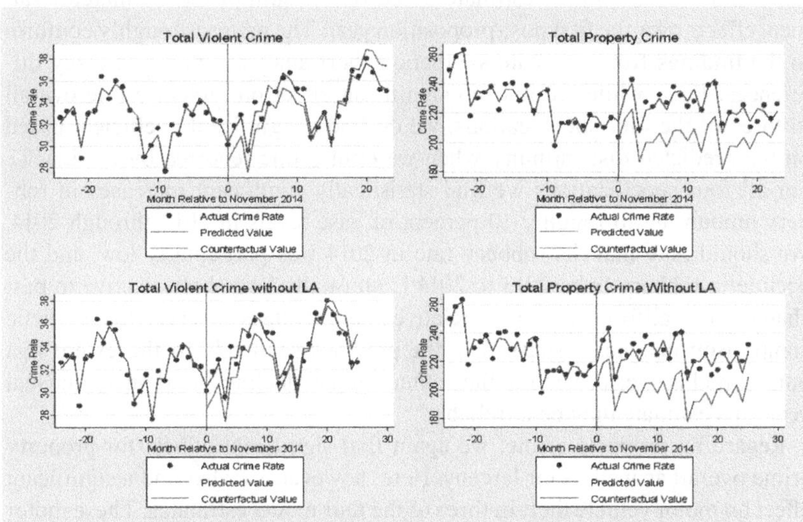

Figure 5.11 *Actual and projected monthly violent and property crime rates for the two pre-47 years and two post-47 years, rates tabulated with and without Los Angeles County*

generate estimates for the second post-proposition 47 year, these estimates are quite imprecise (with standard errors larger than the point estimates in each case), and thus we focus on various estimates of the annualized crime effect over the first year.

For violent crime, the predicted and counterfactual values are visibly similar regardless of whether crime reported by the LAPD is included in the state monthly crime totals. For property crime, however, there is a visible difference between the projected counterfactual and predicted crime rate, with the pre-intervention trends predicting substantial subsequent declines in crime in 2015 and 2016. In fact, the difference between the two series increases with time. The average monthly counterfactual crime rate declines by approximately 6 percent when comparing the first 12 post-proposition months to the 12 preceding months and declines by another 2 percent between the first and second post-proposition years. Similar to the results for violent crime, these estimates are not sensitive to the exclusion of offenses reported by the LAPD.

Table 5.5 presents annualized estimates for total violent crime, total property crime and for each part 1 offense making up the violent and property crime indices. For each crime rate, we present estimates including and excluding crime reported by the LAPD in the aggregate crime series. Within each of these groups, we first present annualized estimates based on the discontinuity and then an annual estimate based on the sum of the estimated treatment effects over the first post-proposition year. The patterns roughly conform to the findings from the state synthetic cohort analysis, with a few key differences. First, while we find no significant effect on violent crime overall in three of the four specifications, we do find a significant coefficient based on the predicted discontinuity when we omit crime reported by the LAPD. For all four specifications we find statistically significant increases in robbery amounting to roughly 10 percent of base levels in 2012 through 2014. We should note that the robbery rate in 2014 was particularly low, and the decline in robbery from 2013 to 2014 is unusually large both relative to past changes for California as well as relative to the changes observed for synthetic comparison matches discussed in the previous section.[11] To the extent that our method is over-projecting the counterfactual decline based on an unusual year, this estimate may be unreliable.

Regarding property crime, we again find significant effects for property crime overall as well as for larceny. Here, however, we also find a significant effect on motor vehicle theft in three of the four model estimates. These motor vehicle theft results contrast sharply with the results from the synthetic comparison group analysis, and thus we should identify the source of the contrast in results. Our time series projections generate a counterfactual decrease in motor vehicle theft between the last pre-proposition year and the first post-proposition year of 7.4 percent and a further decrease of 2.9 percent between

Table 5.5 *Estimates of the effect of proposition 47 on crime rates based on the discontinuous change in crime as well as the difference between the model predicted value and the counterfactual values over the first post-47 year*

	Including LAPD crime reports		Excluding LAPD crime reports	
	Annualized estimates based on discontinuous break at t = 0	Difference between prediction and counterfactual over first 12 months	Annualized estimates based on discontinuous break at t = 0	Difference between prediction and counterfactual over first 12 months
Violent	19.81	11.01	21.07[c]	17.43
	(13.70)	(22.94)	(10.88)	(17.69)
Murder	0.24	0.34	0.15	0.43
	(0.57)	(0.79)	(0.40)	(0.50)
Rape	0.07	–2.81	0.05	–2.84
	(1.48)	(3.49)	(1.31)	(2.64)
Robbery	14.29[a]	14.79[a]	14.74[a]	17.14[a]
	(2.77)	(4.14)	(2.60)	(3.64)
Assault	6.05	–0.62	7.89	4.48
	(12.12)	(20.75)	(10.86)	(16.33)
Property	152.14[a]	266.43[b]	155.41[a]	267.23[b]
	(56.72)	(104.75)	(61.18)	(113.55)
Burglary	–9.30	–1.27	–10.79	6.88
	(10.08)	(18.28)	(9.92)	(17.09)
Larceny	128.94[a]	193.85[b]	129.33[a]	186.44[b]
	(43.27)	(66.84)	(46.43)	(86.90)
Motor vehicle theft	24.86[c]	63.10[a]	21.78	61.99[b]
	(13.13)	(23.30)	(14.35)	(25.34)

Notes: Standard errors are in parentheses. Estimates are based on estimation of Equations 5.3 and 5.4 from the main text inclusive of calendar month fixed effects. Regression models allow for an AR(1) error structure.

a. Statistically significant at the 1 percent level of confidence.

b. Statistically significant at the 5 percent level of confidence.

c. Statistically significant at the 10 percent level of confidence.

the first and second post years. Moreover, the predicted value from the full model projects an 8.5 percent increase in motor vehicle theft which, when combined with the decline in the counterfactual crime rate, generates the statistically significant relative increases in motor vehicle theft presented in the table. The difference here relative to the synthetic comparison analysis is due entirely to the behavior of the counterfactual crime rate from these two estimators. For our synthetic comparison states for California, motor vehicle theft increases by 9 percent between 2014 and 2015 (an increase larger than the 8.5 percent predicted absolute increase for this period generated by our full time series model) and increases by another 10 percent between 2015 and 2016. Hence, the difference in results is due in its entirety to the different counterfactual predictions generated by the two estimators.

More generally, when we estimate based on the discontinuity the magnitudes better align with the results from the synthetic cohort analysis. For example, the estimated effect on overall property crime from the synthetic cohort analysis was an increase in property crimes per 100 000 of between 134 and 193 incidents. The results based on the discontinuous change in property crime are increases of 152 to 155, lying within the range of these estimates. Similarly, the synthetic cohort analysis yielded estimated increases in the larceny theft rate of between 124 and 136 incidents per 100 000. The annualized estimates based on the discontinuous change are comparable (roughly 129 whether or not LAPD crimes are included). In contrast, when we estimate the effect based on the sum of the first 12 treatment effects, the effect size grows considerably, with the overall property crime effect 72 percent larger and the overall larceny effect roughly 50 percent larger. This disparity is driven by the fact that the pre-existing trends predict continuous declines in crime over the subsequent two years largely due to the very low property crime rate in 2014.

6. CROSS-COUNTY ANALYSIS

Thus far we have tested for breaks in trends and deviation of California's crime rate from those of comparison states. While the results from these two exercises do not entirely line up, we find consistent evidence of an impact on property crime, larceny theft in particular, on the order of 5 to 7 percent relative to pre-proposition 47 levels. In this section, we exploit a different source of variation. Specifically, we assess whether crime rates increased by more in counties that experienced larger proportional declines in their average daily jail population, larger declines in arrest rates for drug and property offenses and larger volumes of resentencing and reclassification petitions. In our prior research on realignment (Lofstrom and Raphael 2016), we found comparable results from analysis that exploited cross-county variation in the policy dose and a state-level synthetic cohort analysis. Similarly, Buonanno and Raphael (2013) found larger increases in crime in Italian provinces that received more reentering inmates per capita as a result of the Collective Clemency. Moreover, the magnitude of the effect implied by the cross-province relationship was similar to the estimates based on the discontinuous breaks in crime trends. Here, we assess whether the cross-county relationship accords with the findings thus far.

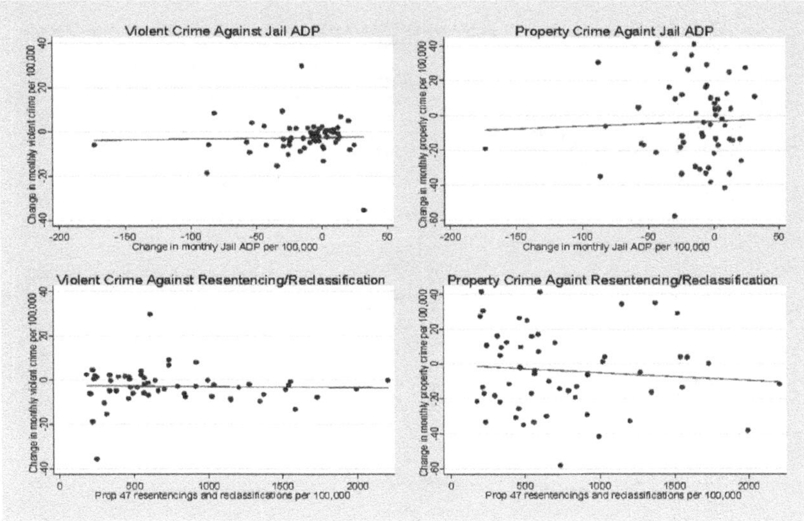

Figure 5.12 *Scatter plots of county-level pre-post 47 changes in average monthly crime rates against change in average monthly jail Average Daily Population (ADP) per 100 000 and the level of proposition 47 resentencing/reclassification activity per 100 000*

Figure 5.12 presents scatter plots of the pre-post change in the average monthly crime rate for the 52-month period surrounding the implementation of proposition 47 against county-level changes in the jail incarceration rate and the quantity per 100 000 of resentencing and reclassification petitions filed between November 2014 and June 2017.[12] Separate scatter plots are presented for overall violent crime and overall property crime. There is quite a bit of variance across counties in the change in jail incarceration rates. The mean change is a decline of 15 per 100 000 with an inter-quartile range of approximately 28 per 100 000. This is relative to an unweighted pre-intervention average of 239 per 100 000. The figure also reveals substantial variation across counties in the volume per capita of resentencing and reclassification petitions, a factor likely correlated with prison releases to the county and the extent to which the county aggressively prosecuted proposition 47 crimes in the past.[13] There is little evidence in the scatter plots that counties that experienced larger declines in the jail population or larger quantities of resentencing and reclassification proceedings experience larger increases in crime for either violent or property crime.

Figure 5.13 presents comparable scatter plots of changes in county-level average crime rates against change in combined property and drug arrests

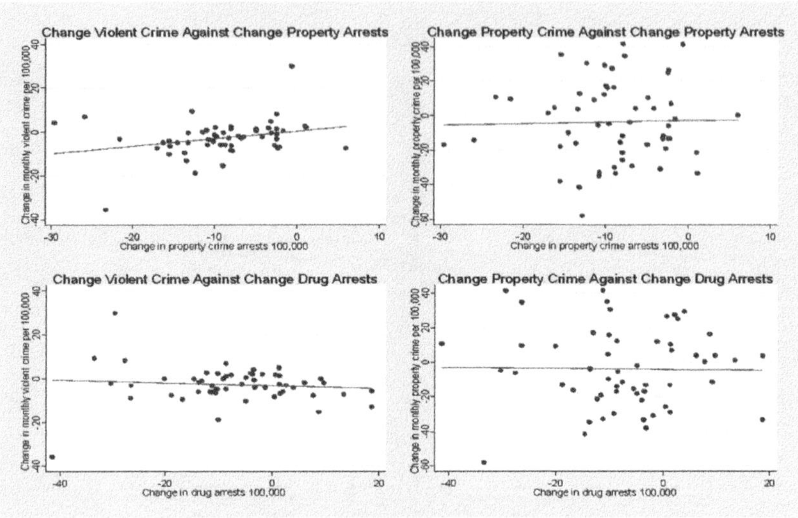

Figure 5.13 *Scatter plots of county-level pre-post 47 changes in average monthly crime rates against change in average monthly property and drug crime arrests per 100 000*

per 100 000.[14] Again we observe substantial cross-county heterogeneity in the change in arrest rates. The unweighted average decline in combined property and drug arrests is 16 per 100 000 relative to a pre-intervention level of 99. The standard deviation or the change is 15.4. There is no evidence in the scatter plots that counties that experienced greater declines in arrest experienced relative increases in either property crime rates or violent crime rates.

Table 5.6 presents the results from county-level regressions of changes in monthly crime rates on changes in the jail average daily population per 100 000, the number of resentencing/reclassification petitions per 100 000 and the change in drug and property arrests per 100 000. Each row corresponds to a separate regression model. For each crime we present separate estimates for unweighted models and regression models that are weighted by county-level population. We interpret a significant negative coefficient on the change in jail incarceration rates, a significant positive coefficient on petition rates and a significant negative coefficient on the change in arrest rates as evidence of an adverse effect of the proposition 47 shock to these variables on crime rates. The models in Table 5.7 are based on changes for the 24 months preceding and following the passage of proposition 47. In appendix Table A3, we present comparable model estimates where the changes are calculated using the 12 months preceding and 12 months following the passage of the proposition.

Table 5.6 *Regression pre-post changes in average county-level monthly crime rates on corresponding changes in average jail ADP per 100 000, average arrests for drug and property offenses per 100 000 and the number of proposition 47 resentencing and reclassification petitions per 100 000 using 26 pre- and post-proposition 47 months*

	Change in jail ADP rate	Resentencing/reclassification petitions per 100 000	Change in drug and property arrests per 100 000
Violent			
Unweighted	0.005 (0.034)	–0.001 (0.002)	0.027 (0.076)
Weighted	0.051[c] (0.030)	–0.003[a] (0.001)	–0.030 (0.038)
Murder			
Unweighted	0.002 (0.002)	0.0000 (0.0001)	0.0005 (0.003)
Weighted	–0.002 (0.002)	–0.0000 (0.0001)	0.004[b] (0.002)
Rape			
Unweighted	0.009 (0.007)	–0.0002 (0.0004)	0.026[c] (0.015)
Weighted	0.008 (0.006)	–0.0004[b] (0.0002)	0.008 (0.007)
Robbery			
Unweighted	0.006 (0.008)	–0.0005 (0.0006)	–0.023 (0.018)
Weighted	0.009 (0.011)	–0.0009[b] (0.0003)	–0.030[b] (0.025)
Assault			
Unweighted	–0.011 (0.032)	0.000 (0.002)	0.023 (0.072)
Weighted	0.036 (0.025)	–0.001[c] (0.0007)	–0.009 (0.032)
Property			
Unweighted	0.032 (0.093)	–0.005 (0.006)	0.015 (0.211)
Weighted	–0.284 (0.172)	–0.011 (0.004)	–0.015 (0.221)
Burglary			
Unweighted	–0.003 (0.035)	–0.003 (0.002)	0.083 (0.079)
Weighted	0.012 (0.045)	–0.002[c] (0.001)	–0.090 (0.059)
Larceny			
Unweighted	0.051 (0.069)	–0.003 (0.005)	–0.183 (0.154)
Weighted	–0.194[c] (0.119)	–0.005 (0.003)	–0.061 (0.143)
Motor veh. theft			
Unweighted	–0.015 (0.024)	0.001 (0.002)	0.115 (0.055)[b]
Weighted	–0.102[c] (0.053)	–0.003[b] (0.001)	0.136[c] (0.068)

Notes: Standard errors are in parentheses. Each row presents the results from a separate regression of the change in monthly crime rates pre-post proposition 47 on the change in the jail incarceration rate, the quantity of resentencing/reclassification petitions filed per capita and the change in property and drug crime arrests per 100 000. Each regression has 56 observations. We omit observations for Alpine and Sierra counties since they do not operate independent jail systems for the entire period analyzed.

a. Statistically significant at the 1 percent level of confidence.

b. Statistically significant at the 5 percent level of confidence.

c. Statistically significant at the 10 percent level of confidence.

Beginning with the results for violent crime rates, we find no evidence of a relative increase in violent crime overall or on any of the individual violent crime rates of prop-47 induced changes in jail incarceration, resentencing/reclassification petitions or changes in arrests activity. All of the coefficient estimates on the change in the jail population are all small and statistically insignificant and often the wrong sign. We do see significant negative coefficients in several models on the number of resentencing/reclassification petitions per 100 000 residents. However, the estimates suggest that crime fell by more in counties with more petition activity, suggestive of a crime-abating effect of the proposition. Regarding the estimates for change in arrest activity on violent crime, there is one significant negative coefficient on robbery when the model is weighted by county populations. Statewide the arrest rate declined by roughly 16 per 100 000. Taking the one significant coefficient estimate for robbery at face value (–0.03) suggests an annualized effect of the decline in arrest activity of 5.76 incidents per 100 000 (0.03 × 16 × 12). When we estimate these models using the year-over-year changes in crime to construct the dependent variable for the regression rather than the average change over two pre and two post years (presented in Table A3), again we find little evidence of any effects on violent crime. The negative effect of the change in arrests on robbery does not appear in these models.

Turning to the results for property crime, there are notable differences between the models that weight the regressions by county population and those that do not. None of the unweighted models yield evidence of a proposition 47 effect on property crime overall or the individual property crime rates. In the weighted models, however, we find a nearly significant negative coefficient on the change in jail incarceration rates for property crime overall (with a p-value of 0.105) and marginally significant coefficients on the jail incarceration rate for larceny and motor vehicle theft. The coefficient estimate for property crime overall in the weighted model is consistent with an annualized effect of 71.6 additional property crimes per 100 000 (calculated by multiplying the coefficient estimate (0.284) by the statewide decline in the jail incarceration rate (21) by the number of months in a year). The comparable implied annualized estimates for larceny theft and motor vehicle theft are 48.9 and 25.7, respectively. These estimates are considerably smaller than the results from the within-state time series analysis as well as the results from the synthetic cohort analysis. These estimates suggest a 2.8 percent increase in property crime rates overall, a 3.1 percent increase in larceny theft and a 7 percent increase in auto theft. We find no evidence of an effect of resentencing/reclassification petitions activity nor of the change in arrest rates in any of the models.

The results for property crime using year-over-year changes presented in appendix Table A3 are roughly consistent with the findings in Table 5.7, though the point estimates on the change in the jail incarceration rate imply much smaller effects on property crime overall and larceny theft and little effect on motor vehicle theft. None of the coefficients on the change in the jail incarceration rate are statistically significant in these models.

To summarize the results in this section, we find very little evidence that cross-county variation in the effect of proposition 47 on jail populations, resentencing and reclassification petitions and on arrest activity predicts inter-county variation in the pre-post 47 change in violent crime rates in a manner consistent with an adverse effect of the proposition. There is some evidence of an impact on property crime overall and on larceny and motor vehicle theft, though the estimates are sensitive to whether the models are weighted by population and by the time periods used to calculate the changes in crime and jail incarceration rates. Moreover, the largest estimates from this analysis imply property crime effects that are considerably smaller than those implied by the synthetic cohort analysis and the within-state time series results.

7. DISCUSSION

To summarize the results of our empirical analysis, we find little evidence that the changes in correctional populations, arrests and convictions reclassifications ushered in by recent California reforms have impacted violent crime rates in the state. Once changes in offense definitions and reporting practices in key agencies are accounted for, violent crime rates in California are lower than the levels that existed in 2010 prior to major reforms to the state's criminal justice system, and did not rise relative to comparison states. While our analysis of proposition 47's effect on violent crime rates yields a few significant point estimates (a decrease in murder for one method and an increase in robbery for another), these findings are highly sensitive to the method used to generate a counterfactual comparison path.

We find more consistent evidence of an impact on property crime. The earlier reform that primarily impacted prison populations led to a significant increase in auto theft. The latter reform which primarily impacted the likelihood of arrest for drug offense and low-level property offenses and jail populations caused a measurable increase in larceny theft. The magnitudes of the property crime effect range from an increase of 0 to 3 percent when we analyze cross-county crime patterns which suggests an increase in the overall property crime rate on the order of 5 percent.

We are able to say very little about specific mechanisms that may be driving these results, since these reforms are impacting several different correctional and law enforcement levels. That being said, it is notable that the state has pulled back from the use of incarceration more than any other in the country, yet is still experiencing historically low crime rates.

Table A1 *Violent crime rate levels in California and synthetic California from 2000 to 2016 with and without Los Angeles in the tabulation of California's state-level crime rates*

Year	Violent, CA	Violent, synth. CA	Murder, CA	Murder, synth. CA	Rape, CA	Rape, synth. CA	Robbery, CA	Robbery, synth. CA	Assault, CA	Assault, synth. CA
Panel A: Including Los Angeles in the tabulation of state-level crime rates										
2000	621.60	620.68	6.1	6.1	28.90	28.87	177.90	178.05	408.70	395.85
2001	615.20	611.68	6.4	6.4	28.80	28.75	186.70	185.80	393.30	389.87
2002	595.40	592.49	6.8	6.8	29.10	29.02	185.60	185.69	373.80	379.23
2003	579.60	561.88	6.8	6.8	28.20	28.19	179.80	179.73	364.80	338.62
2004	527.80	536.76	6.7	6.6	26.80	26.78	172.30	172.34	322.00	335.00
2005	526.00	536.68	6.9	6.8	26.00	26.00	176.00	175.48	317.10	320.66
2006	533.30	535.94	6.8	6.8	25.30	25.27	195.00	195.43	306.20	312.27
2007	522.60	527.11	6.2	6.3	24.70	24.68	193.00	192.54	298.80	302.81
2008	506.20	506.86	5.9	5.9	24.30	24.28	189.70	189.34	286.30	287.49
2009	472.00	468.51	5.3	5.4	23.60	23.58	173.40	172.28	269.70	281.15
2010	440.60	439.29	4.9	5.1	22.40	22.59	156.00	152.02	257.40	271.27
2011	411.20	419.99	4.8	4.8	20.30	22.44	144.10	141.39	242.00	255.43
2012	423.10	409.83	5.0	4.7	20.60	21.87	148.60	140.71	248.90	252.75
2013	402.10	399.45	4.6	4.9	19.50	20.53	139.90	137.37	232.30	246.48
2014	396.40	387.23	4.4	4.8	21.60	21.91	125.50	132.35	236.70	238.44
2015	426.30	394.75	4.8	5.8	24.00	22.81	135.00	131.56	253.80	238.72
2016	445.30	385.95	4.9	6.1	25.90	23.78	139.60	133.77	265.90	244.06

Panel B: Excluding Los Angeles in the tabulation of state-level crime rates										
2000	529.14	529.07	5.0	5.0	27.50	-	147.68	147.89	348.91	349.02
2001	520.68	520.57	5.2	5.2	27.72	-	153.83	152.86	333.89	333.95
2002	498.41	498.28	5.5	5.6	27.92	-	152.06	152.43	312.88	313.75
2003	490.56	490.38	6.0	6.0	27.37	-	148.08	150.84	309.15	308.66
2004	481.14	481.04	5.8	5.8	26.33	-	147.44	147.08	301.54	302.27
2005	487.54	487.42	6.2	6.2	25.45	-	153.30	152.14	302.56	302.49
2006	500.38	500.13	6.1	6.1	24.94	-	173.17	173.91	296.15	296.21
2007	497.55	497.30	5.7	5.7	24.42	-	173.94	171.95	293.51	294.13
2008	480.29	480.05	5.3	5.3	24.08	-	169.45	168.80	281.43	281.84
2009	453.30	453.06	5.0	5.0	23.47	-	155.93	154.87	268.90	269.20
2010	424.93	426.64	4.5	4.8	22.06	-	140.60	138.49	257.75	257.73
2011	396.75	411.84	4.4	4.7	20.10	-	130.04	131.21	242.20	244.88
2012	414.64	411.00	4.6	4.5	20.09	-	138.42	129.10	251.51	243.60
2013	390.90	390.74	4.3	4.6	19.35	-	132.14	123.64	235.09	227.43
2014	377.57	390.66	4.1	4.7	23.59	-	116.14	120.13	233.73	228.18
2015	400.35	404.87	4.5	5.3	29.94	-	124.04	119.96	241.90	237.27
2016	403.52	415.77	4.6	5.7	31.59	-	125.45	121.35	249.41	234.27

Notes: Crime rates for California in panel A are official UCR crime rates for California tabulated by the FBI. The crime rates in panel A for synthetic California are the comparison crime rates for the weighted average of control states matching California crime rates from 2000 through 2010. The California crime rates for panel B are tabulated from the agency-level UCR Offenses Known and Cleared by Arrests files for 2000 through 2016. These tabulations drop crimes reported by the Los Angeles Police Department from the state total. Rates are tabulated adjusting the population for the omission of the city of Los Angeles. The synthetic California crime rates in panel B are based on a synthetic control match to these alternative time series.

Table A2 *Property crime rate levels in California and synthetic California from 2000 to 2016 with and without Los Angeles in the tabulation of California's state-level crime rates*

Year	Property, CA	Property, synth. CA	Burglary, CA	Burglary, synth. CA	Larceny, CA	Larceny, synth. CA	MVT, CA	MVT, synth. CA
Panel A: Including Los Angeles in the tabulation of state-level crime rates								
2000	3 118.20	3 155.00	656.30	655.95	1 924.50	1 997.44	537.40	549.80
2001	3 278.00	3 284.32	671.30	670.98	2 016.60	2 009.52	590.10	585.58
2002	3 361.20	3 342.86	681.20	680.89	2 044.70	2 013.07	635.30	632.81
2003	3 426.40	3 414.20	683.20	682.82	2 062.70	2 046.29	680.50	687.47
2004	3 423.90	3 420.11	686.10	685.90	2 033.10	1 985.34	704.80	696.15
2005	3 321.00	3 319.00	692.90	692.82	1 915.00	1 929.44	712.00	720.23
2006	3 175.20	3 185.25	676.90	676.88	1 831.50	1 835.26	666.80	686.22
2007	3 032.60	3 047.74	648.40	648.27	1 784.10	1 785.46	600.20	600.82
2008	2 954.50	2 912.40	649.90	649.83	1 778.30	1 779.62	526.30	485.56
2009	2 731.50	2 746.67	622.60	622.45	1 665.10	1 683.80	443.80	376.71
2010	2 635.80	2 546.55	614.30	610.13	1 612.10	1 567.61	409.40	322.72
2011	2 584.20	2 398.57	610.50	621.69	1 584.00	1 520.06	389.70	297.02
2012	2 758.70	2 478.74	646.10	601.95	1 669.50	1 648.63	443.20	289.78
2013	2 658.10	2 388.14	605.40	553.40	1 621.50	1 596.34	431.20	276.05
2014	2 441.70	2 179.13	522.40	492.82	1 527.80	1 511.57	391.40	276.01
2015	2 618.30	2 114.31	504.30	459.26	1 677.10	1 488.08	436.80	300.84
2016	2 553.00	2 127.64	479.80	439.55	1 623.00	1 497.00	450.30	329.59

Panel B: Excluding Los Angeles in the tabulation of state-level crime rates								
2000	3 050.74	3 101.59	653.41	652.81	1 900.64	1 978.34	496.68	531.89
2001	3 228.36	3 228.19	669.60	668.53	2 002.99	1 991.59	555.77	555.86
2002	3 298.23	3 276.34	676.88	676.11	2 022.07	1 996.42	599.28	600.72
2003	3 379.85	3 378.59	678.90	678.51	2 048.34	2 033.93	652.60	654.39
2004	3 416.45	3 415.17	689.92	689.08	2 036.47	1 988.42	690.06	666.60
2005	3 330.31	3 341.89	701.13	699.81	1 924.02	1 942.43	705.16	709.65
2006	3 213.21	3 214.94	691.54	690.82	1 857.01	1 861.81	664.66	687.67
2007	3 070.37	3 075.19	662.72	661.63	1 810.56	1 810.92	597.08	598.75
2008	2 967.18	2 923.81	660.07	659.07	1 792.65	1 793.78	514.47	483.51
2009	2 747.64	2 777.86	635.71	634.89	1 674.85	1 701.39	437.08	376.81
2010	2 658.39	2 564.82	629.89	607.76	1 624.81	1 567.61	403.70	324.93
2011	2 610.21	2 395.82	625.89	620.13	1 598.31	1 511.67	386.01	307.76
2012	2 800.92	2 491.03	667.84	601.50	1 686.05	1 639.20	447.03	302.88
2013	2 694.59	2 378.10	624.73	551.38	1 634.03	1 583.81	435.82	291.47
2014	2 463.76	2 198.74	534.92	485.25	1 535.16	1 501.72	393.68	294.36
2015	2 632.04	2 152.46	512.19	453.44	1 682.36	1 473.31	437.50	314.31
2016	2 547.49	2 164.54	486.75	428.59	1 615.03	1 487.10	446.41	348.00

Notes: Crime rates for California in panel A are official UCR crime rates for California tabulated by the FBI. The crime rates in panel A for synthetic California are the comparison crime rates for the weighted average of control states matching California crime rates from 2000 through 2010. The California crime rates for panel B are tabulated from the agency-level UCR Offenses Known and Cleared by Arrests files for 2000 through 2016. These tabulations drop crimes reported by the Los Angeles Police Department from the state total. Rates are tabulated adjusting the population for the omission of the city of Los Angeles. The synthetic California crime rates in panel B are based on a synthetic control match to these alternative time series.

Table A3 *Regression pre-post changes in average county-level monthly crime rates on corresponding changes in average jail ADP per 100 000, average arrests for drug and property offenses per 100 000, and the number of proposition 47 resentencing and reclassification petitions per 100 000 using 12 pre- and post-proposition 47 months*

	Change in jail ADP rate	Resentencing/ reclassification petitions per 100 000	Change in drug and property arrests per 100 000
Violent			
Unweighted	–0.020 (0.031)	–0.001 (0.002)	0.066 (0.070)
Weighted	0.041 (0.036)	–0.003[a] (0.001)	0.082[b] (0.036)
Murder			
Unweighted	0.003[c] (0.001)	0.0000 (0.0001)	0.002 (0.004)
Weighted	–0.001 (0.003)	–0.00002 (0.00006)	0.005[c] (0.003)
Rape			
Unweighted	0.008 (0.006)	–0.0004 (0.0004)	0.024 (0.014)
Weighted	0.008 (0.007)	–0.004[b] (0.002)	0.009 (0.007)
Robbery			
Unweighted	0.013 (0.009)	–0.001 (0.001)	–0.013 (0.020)
Weighted	0.014 (0.015)	–0.001[a] (0.0003)	–0.0007 (0.015)
Assault			
Unweighted	–0.044 (0.030)	0.0003 (0.002)	0.054 (0.067)
Weighted	0.019 (0.031)	–0.001[b] (0.0007)	0.069[b] (0.031)
Property			
Unweighted	0.042 (0.085)	–0.006 (0.006)	0.120 (0.188)
Weighted	–0.158 (0.181)	–0.014[a] (0.005)	0.133 (0.182)
Burglary			
Unweighted	0.010 (0.036)	–0.003 (0.002)	0.139[c] (0.081)
Weighted	0.019 (0.052)	–0.003[b] (0.001)	–0.077 (0.052)
Larceny			
Unweighted	0.036 (0.061)	–0.003 (0.004)	–0.195 (0.137)
Weighted	–0.143 (0.123)	–0.007[b] (0.003)	0.021 (0.125)

(Continued)

Table A3 *(Continued)*

	Change in jail ADP rate	Resentencing/ reclassification petitions per 100 000	Change in drug and property arrests per 100 000
Motor veh. theft			
Unweighted	−0.005 (0.025)	0.0002 (0.002)	0.175[a] (0.056)
Weighted	−0.034 (0.065)	−0.004[a] (0.001)	0.189[a] (0.065)

Notes: Standard errors are in parentheses. Each row presents the results from a separate regression of the change in monthly crime rates pre-post proposition 47 on the change in the jail incarceration rate, the quantity of resentencing/reclassification petitions filed per capita and the change in property and drug crime arrests per 100 000. Each regression has 56 observations. We omit observations for Alpine and Sierras counties since they do not operate independent jail systems for the entire period analyzed.

a. Statistically significant at the 1 percent level of confidence.

b. Statistically significant at the 5 percent level of confidence.

c. Statistically significant at the 10 percent level of confidence.

NOTES

1. Between 2008 and 2016, the US prison population declined by 102 885 inmates. Comparing totals for the federal prison population and state prison populations published in Carson (2018) and West and Sabol (2010) reveals that 12 percent of this decline is attributable to a decline in the federal prison population, 40 percent is attributable to the decline in California's prison population and 48 percent is attributable to declines in the remaining 49 state prison populations.
2. Relative to other states, California's incarceration rate ranked 31 out of 50 in 2010 and 18 out of 50 in 2016.
3. See Johnson and Raphael (2012) and Buonanno and Raphael (2013) for a formal model of the determination of crime and incarceration rates.
4. The series without Los Angeles adjusts both the numerator (reported crimes) and the denominator (population) for the omission of the city of Los Angeles.
5. Buchmueller, DiNardo and Valletta (2009) use a similar permutation test to that described here to test for an impact of Hawaii's employer-mandate to provide health insurance benefits to employees on benefits coverage, health care costs, wages and employment.
6. See Poston, Ben and Joel Rubin "LAPD Misclassified Nearly 1,200 Violent Crimes as Minor Offenses," *Los Angeles Times*, August 9, 2014.
7. For 2010 through 2016, the numbers of aggravated assaults reported by the LAPD are 9344, 8843, 8329, 7624, 9836, 13 713 and 15 874, respectively.
8. We do however present an estimate for overall violent crime which is inclusive of rape. As the California rape rate for some agencies in 2014 and most if not all agencies in 2015 and 2016 will be based on the new more inclusive definition, the estimate of proposition 47 on violent crime will be upwardly biased. This bias, however, is likely to be negligible as rape accounts for only 6 percent of violent crime in California.
9. We have analyzed realignment thoroughly in prior research (see Lofstrom and Raphael 2013, 2016a and 2016b).

10. Model estimates using OLS with Newey-West standard errors specifying one, two or three lags yield similar results.
11. The robbery rate increased by 3 percent from 2011 to 2012, declined by 5.8 percent from 2012 to 2013, declined by 10.2 percent from 2013 to 2014 and then increased by 7.6 percent from 2014 to 2015. For comparison, the robbery rate in our synthetic comparison group inclusive of Los Angeles declined by half a percent between 2011 and 2012, declined by 2.3 percent between 2012 and 2013, declined by 3.7 percent between 2013 and 2014, declined by 0.6 percent between 2014 and 2015 and then increased by 1.7 percent between 2015 and 2016.
12. The period for resentencing and reclassification petitions is based on survey results of county courts conducted by the California Judicial Council. According to Judicial Council tabs, most of the petitions are filed within the first year and half of November 2014. While several counties report separate totals for resentencing and reclassification petitions, a handful of key California counties (inclusive of San Diego and Alameda) only report the total. Hence, we do not break up petitions by type. The scatter plots in Figures 5.12 and 5.13 are based on 56 of California's 58 counties. We omit Alpine and Sierra counties as these two counties do not operate independent county jail systems for the entire period that we analyze (Alpine does not at all and Sierra for only the beginning of the period).
13. We have requested high-frequency admissions and releases data from the California Department of Corrections and Rehabilitation (CDCR). In future work, we will add the change in prison releases by county caused by proposition 47 to the list of covariates analyzed.
14. Separate analysis for drug and property arrests yields similar results. Here we calculate the change in average arrest rates using the 26 pre-proposition months and 14 post-proposition months. This difference is due to the fact that our arrest data end in 2015.

REFERENCES

Abadie, Alberto and Javier Gardeazabal (2003), "The Economic Costs of Conflict: A Case Study of the Basque Country," *American Economic Review*, 93(1): 113–32.

Abadie, Alberto, Diamond, Alexis and Jens Hainmueller (2010), "Synthetic Control Methods for Comparative Case Studies: Estimating the Effect of California's Tobacco Control Program," *Journal of the American Statistical Association*, 105(490): 493–505.

Barbarino, Alessandro and Giovanni Mastrobuoni (2014), "The Incapacitation Effect of Incarceration: Evidence from Several Italian Collective Pardons," *Economic Journal: Economic Policy*, 6(1): 1–37.

Bartos, Bradley J. and Charis Kubrin (2018), "Can We Downsize Our Prisons and Jails Without Compromising Public Safety: Findings From California's Proposition 47," *Criminology & Public Policy*, 17(3): 1–23.

Blumstein, Alfred, Cohen, Jacqueline and Daniel Nagin (1978), *Deterrence and Incapacitation: Estimating the Effects of Criminal Sanctions on Crime Rates*, National Academy of Sciences, Washington, DC.

Buchmueller, Thomas C, DiNardo, John and Robert G. Valleta (2009), *The Effect of An Employer Health Insurance Mandate on Health Insurance Coverage and the Demand for Labor: Evidence from Hawaii*, Federal Reserve Bank of San Francisco Working Paper #2009-08.

Buonanno, Paolo and Steven Raphael (2013), "Incarceration and Incapacitation: Evidence from the 2006 Italian Collective Pardon," *American Economic Review*, 103(6): 2437–65.

California Judicial Council (2016), *Proposition 47 Frequently Asked Question*, Updated November 2016, San Francisco, CA.

Carson, E. Ann (2018), *Prisoners in 2016*, U.S. Department of Justice, Office of Justice Programs, Bureau of Justice Statistics, NCJ 251149.

Chalfin, Aaron and Justin McCrary (2018), "Are U.S. Cities Underpoliced? Theory and Evidence," *Review of Economics and Statistics*, 100(1): 167–86.

Cook, Philip J. and John MacDonald (2011), "Public Safety through Private Action: An Economic Assessment of BIDs," *The Economic Journal*, 121: 445–62.

Di Tella, Rafael and Ernesto Schargrodsky (2004), "Do Police Reduce Crime? Estimates Using the Allocation of Police Forces after a Terrorist Attack," *American Economic Review*, 94, 115–33.

Drago, Francesco, Galbiati, Roberto and Pietro Vertova (2009), "The Deterrent Effects of Prison: Evidence from a Natural Experiment," *Journal of Political Economy*, 117(2): 257–80.

Evans, William N. and Emily G. Owens (2007), "COPS and Crime," *Journal of Public Economics*, 91, 181–201.

Helland, Eric and Alexander Tabarrok (2007), "Does Three-Strikes Deter? A Non-Parametric Estimation," *Journal of Human Resources*, 42(2): 309–30.

Hjalmarsson, Randi (2009), "Juvenile Jails: A Path to the Straight and Narrow or Hardened Criminality?" *Journal of Law and Economics*, 52(4): 779–809.

Johnson, Rucker and Steven Raphael (2012), "How Much Crime Reduction Does the Marginal Prisoner Buy?"*Journal of Law and Economics*, 55(2): 275–310.

Klick, Jonathan and Alexander Tabarrok (2005), "Using Terror Alert Levels to Estimate the Effect of Police on Crime," *Journal of Law & Economics*, 48, 267–79.

Lee, David S. and Justin McCrary (2009), "*The Deterrent Effect of Prison: Dynamic Theory and Evidence*," Industrial Relations Section Working Paper, Princeton University.

Levitt, Steven D. (1996), "The Effect of Prison Population Size on Crime Rates: Evidence from Prison Overcrowding Legislation," *Quarterly Journal of Economics*, 111(2): 319–51.

Levitt, Steven D. (1998), "Juvenile Crime and Punishment," *Journal of Political Economy*, 106(6): 1156–85.

Liedke, Raymond, Piehl, Anne Morrison and Bert Useem (2006), "The Crime Control Effect of Incarceration: Does Scale Matter?" *Criminology and Public Policy*, 5: 245–75.

Lofstrom, Magnus and Steven Raphael (2013), *Impact of Realignment on County Jail Populations*, Public Policy Institute of California, San Francisco.

Lofstrom, Magnus and Steven Raphael (2016a), "Incarceration and Crime: Evidence from California's Public Safety Realignment," *The Annals of the American Academy of Political and Social Science*, 664(1): 196–220.

Lofstrom, Magnus and Steven Raphael (2016b), "Prison Downsizing and Public Safety," *Criminology and Public Policy*, 15(2): 349–65.

Nagin, Daniel S. (2013), "Deterrence: A Review of the Evidence by a Criminologist for Economists," *Annual Review of Economics*, 5: 83–105.

Nagin, Daniel S. and John V. Pepper (2012), *Deterrence and the Death Penalty*, National Academy of Sciences, Washington, DC. National Academy of Sciences 2017.

National Academies of Sciences, Engineering, and Medicine (2017), *Proactive Policing: Effects on Crime and Communities*. The National Academies Press, Washington, DC. https://doi.org/10.17226/24928.

Owens, Emily (2009), "More Time, Less Crime? Estimating the Incapacitative Effects of Sentence Enhancements," *Journal of Law and Economics*, 52(3): 551–79.
Raphael, Steven and Michael A. Stoll (2013), *Why Are So Many Americans in Prison?*, Russell Sage Foundation, New York.
Spelman, William (1994), *Criminal Incapacitation*, Plenum Press, New York.
Spelman, William (2000), "What Recent Studies Do (and Don't) Tell Us About Imprisonment and Crime," in Michael Tonry (ed.) *Crime and Justice: A Review of the Research*, University of Chicago Press, Chicago, 27: 419–94.
Vollard, Ben (2013), "Preventing Crime through Selective Incapacitation," *Economic Journal*, 123: 262–84.
West, Heather C. and William J. Sabol (2010), *Prisoners in 2009*, U.S. Department of Justice, Office of Justice Programs, Bureau of Justice Statistics, NCJ 23167.

6. A note on electronic monitoring and some challenges to its implementation[1]

Rafael Di Tella and Ernesto Schargrodsky

1. MOTIVATION

There are many instances in which policies that could raise overall welfare are not implemented. Economists emphasize one type of challenge arising from redistributive conflicts: sometimes a policy raises total welfare, but some groups affected negatively by the intervention are able to veto it. Coordination failures regarding the policy implementation or its financing may also be an impediment. Moreover, the optimality of some policies is hard to prove beyond doubt. In addition to prejudice or ideological reasons, there could be genuine hesitation about its benefits.

In this chapter, we analyze the interruption of a policy in which the above-mentioned reasons played a minor role. Instead, this policy suffers from a different drawback: its benefits are difficult to observe, but its costs are very salient. And, although the cost-benefit analysis suggests a large positive net effect, benevolent policy-makers may find it hard to convince citizens, or the media, of the virtues of this policy.

The policy in question is the use of electronic monitoring (EM) as an alternative to incarceration. In particular, we analyze the experience of using EM for pre-trial detention in the Province of Buenos Aires, Argentina, that we previously studied in Di Tella and Schargrodsky (2013). After this motivation, in Section 2 we describe the policy, its implementation and its estimated casual effect on recidivism. In Section 3, we relate the events that led to the policy interruption. Section 4 concludes with a discussion on the welfare calculation and the political challenges of EM implementation.

2. ELECTRONIC MONITORING IN ARGENTINA

For centuries, incarceration has been one of the main technologies to deal with criminals. However, prisons may have criminogenic effects, possibly contributing to the conversion of inmates into 'hardened' criminals. In addition, they are expensive to build and run. Naturally, alternatives to imprisonment have been tried out. A modern strategy is the substitution of incarceration for EM.[2]

EM consists of fitting offenders with an electronic device (on the ankle or wrist) that can be monitored remotely by employees of a correctional facility to verify whether the individual is fulfilling a set of pre-established conditions like, for example, staying at home or keeping away from a former victim. Technological progress has fostered the use of these devices, making them cheaper and safer (e.g., recent versions can include GPS, voice recognition and transdermal measurement of alcohol and drug consumption).

In late 1997, the Province of Buenos Aires pioneered in Latin America the use of EM for the custody of inmates.[3] In Di Tella and Schargrodsky (2013), we study the impact of EM – relative to incarceration – on recidivism rates. In addition to fiscal savings, EM can reduce the criminogenic effect of overcrowding, harsh conditions and negative peer effects in prisons, mitigate stigmatization and inmates' perception that society is 'evil' and improve the offenders' social skills and labor market prospects. It can reduce, however, the incapacitation and deterrence effects that imprisonment has.

Under the EM program, offenders must stay at home wearing a bracelet on their ankle. The bracelet transmits a signal to a receptor installed in the offender's house. If the signal is interrupted, manipulation is detected or the vital signs of the individual are not received, the receptor sends a signal to the service provider. The provider investigates the reason for the signal and, when necessary, reports to the EM office of the Buenos Aires Penitentiary Service, which sends a patrol unit to the inmate's house.

The EM program of the Province of Buenos Aires was relatively small, with the capacity to handle a maximum of 300 detainees simultaneously. From January 1998 through October 2007, more than 910 alleged offenders were at some point under electronic surveillance.

At its inception, EM was granted to the old and terminally ill, with the objective of allowing them to spend their final days with their families under house arrest. But Buenos Aires' legislation also allowed the use of EM as a way of improving the conditions of the individuals awaiting trial which, given the very slow functioning of the legal system, represented a large fraction of detainees in the Province of Buenos Aires during the period studied. Eventually, all new entries to the EM program were individuals on pre-trial detention. Thus, the coverage shifted over time toward individuals under criminal indictment awaiting final sentence. In practice, there were few restrictions on its allocation. As the first two columns of Table 6.1 show, individuals accused of any type of crime, including rape or murder, still qualified for the use of EM. A previous criminal history was not a reason for exclusion either.

Table 6.1 Type of crime for the electronic monitoring and prison population, 1998–2007

Type of crime	Offenders released from EM		Offenders released from prison		Difference
	Freq.	Percent	Freq.	Percent	Percent
Homicide	30	7.77	1 399	5.84	1.93
Attempted homicide	8	2.07	398	1.66	0.41
Sexual offenses	10	2.59	448	1.87	0.72
Other serious crimes	10	2.59	482	2.01	0.58
Aggravated robbery	224	58.03	11 647	48.58	9.45
Attempted aggravated robbery	12	3.11	1 814	7.57	–4.46
Robbery	25	6.48	2 930	12.22	–5.74
Attempted robbery	22	5.7	1 922	8.02	–2.32
Possession of firearms	18	4.66	1 102	4.6	0.06
Larceny/attempted larceny	4	1.04	889	3.71	–2.67
Other minor crimes	23	5.96	945	3.94	2.02
Total	386	100	23 976	100	

Notes: Distribution by type of crime of all male alleged offenders below 40 years of age with complete data released from the Buenos Aires penal system before reaching a final sentence from 1 January 1998 until 23 October 2007.

Source: Table 1 from Di Tella and Schargrodsky (2013).

In order to study the effect of EM on recidivism, a simple comparison across the prison and EM population is not informative. Selection bias is, of course, a main concern: a potential criterion for the granting of EM to an offender could be her/his risk of recidivism. Thus, low post-release recidivism of a group of offenders treated with EM could simply reflect the success of the legal system at the selection stage if the objective was to target low-risk offenders. To address this selection concern, we exploited a source of exogeneity in the allocation of cases to judges with heterogeneous preferences.

When a person is arrested by the police, the case is assigned to the judge who is on duty on that day in that judicial district. Judicial duty turns last for one or two weeks and are assigned by a lottery at the judicial district (the Province of Buenos Aires is divided into 18 judicial districts). If the judge, upon the request of the prosecutor, decides that the detainee will be incarcerated until trial, she/he can decide, at her/his discretion, to 'attenuate' this preventive imprisonment (the term in Spanish is *prisión preventiva*) by granting EM.[4] Thus, the allocation of alleged offenders to the judges who decide on EM assignment was exogenous to the felon's characteristics.

Once the EM office received the formal requests from the judges, it allocated the bracelets on a first come, first serve basis. Frequently, the EM equipment was not available when requested; in this case, the detainee was added to a waiting list.[5] During the waiting time, the offender could be in prison. But, as overcrowding is a recurrent problem in Province of Buenos Aires prisons, it was also common for that pre-trial detention to take place in jails or police stations. This means that some alleged offenders on EM previously stayed in prisons while others went directly to EM. In the sample under study, almost 40 percent of alleged offenders on EM spent no time in prison.

Not only was the assignment of alleged offenders to judges exogenous to detainees' characteristics and judges had discretion in the allocation of EM, but also judges showed heterogeneity in their EM allocation decisions. This heterogeneity comes from a combination of differences in ideological views and practical considerations.

Two extreme judicial positions have been widely reported in the media: liberal (*garantistas*) vs conservative (*mano dura*) judges. Liberal judges in Argentina (i.e., *garantistas*) often take the position that long periods of pre-trial imprisonment, particularly when prisons are in poor shape, violate basic human rights and, thus, should be rarely used. Therefore, individuals who do not have a final sentence, and hence are still formally innocent, should be either free or under minimum supervision.

On the other hand, conservative judges in Argentina (i.e., '*mano dura*') typically emphasize in their rulings the rights of the victims and their families. They certainly consider prisons to be in bad shape but not out of line with other problems in the country and largely out of their sphere of influence. Moreover, they take the position that individuals coming before them are already likely to be guilty: given that the police do not cast a very wide net, the only cases which reach the legal system are those where there is flagrancy or other clear evidence against the alleged offender.

Interestingly, while in other countries there has been an attempt to harmonize treatment through sentencing guidelines so as to remove the arbitrary component of the judge's identity, these are absent in Argentina. The result is an institutional setting where judges have very different criteria when it comes to assigning EM. Liberal judges regularly assign it, while conservative judges never do so.

These judges' preferences are observable in the data. Some judges in the sample tend to assign EM more frequently than others. From a total of 293 judges acting on the cases in our sample, only a third of them (100) have ever used EM, while two-thirds of judges never used it. Hence, for each detainee, we constructed a measure of the intervening judge's liberal ideology, namely the proportion of all alleged offenders who stood before the intervening judge who were assigned to EM – excluding the individual in question.

Hereafter we refer to this variable as *% Judge sent to EM*. The exogeneity in the assignment of detainees to judges, together with this heterogeneity in judges' decisions, makes this measure a valid instrument to identify the causal effect of EM on recidivism.

In order to compare the effect of EM with the effect of imprisonment on criminal recidivism, we used administrative data from the Penitentiary Service of the Province of Buenos Aires on all offenders released from 1 January 1998 until 23 October 2007. From this database we obtained two groups. The first group (the EM group) is made up of individuals whose last period under the supervision of the penal system was spent under EM. Given that the involvement in criminal activity is mainly a male phenomenon and declines with age, we focused on men below 40 years of age. We also excluded from the sample offenders who died while under EM, those who were sick or characterized as dangerous and those with missing data on the specific type of crime, the intervening judge, their birth date, their detention date or their release date. This gave us an EM final sample of 386 individuals, with an average spell on EM of 420 days.

The comparison group was constructed starting with the group whose last period under the Buenos Aires penal system's supervision was spent in prison. Using the same sample criteria as for the EM sample, we obtained a sample of 23 976 alleged offenders who were released from prisons before reaching a final sentence. Table 6.1 shows the pattern of crimes for these two populations, which totalize 24 362 individuals. A unique feature of the Argentine system is immediately apparent: many of the offenders under EM are being prosecuted for serious offenses, and the distributions of alleged offenses for the EM and prison groups are similar.

Using this sample, we explored formally if the evidence is consistent with the assumption of random assignment to judges, by comparing whether the observable characteristics of the alleged offenders standing in front of conservative judges differed from those of alleged offenders standing in front of liberal judges. Accordingly, Table 6.2 presents the observable characteristics of alleged offenders in our sample across liberal and conservative judges, where 'liberal' is defined as having *% Judge sent to EM* above the median in the sample. Consistent with random assignment of alleged offenders to judges on duty within each district, the means of the demographic, judicial and criminal characteristics of the cases standing in front of liberal and conservative judges are remarkably similar.

From this sample, and due to data recollection constraints for the recidivism information, we then performed the following matching procedure. For each prisoner released from EM, we identified all those prison-released prisoners with similar age (+/– 6 months), similar imprisonment date (+/– 6 months), similar imprisonment length (+/– 20 percent), same type of crime, similar

Table 6.2 *Comparison of means of pre-treatment characteristics*

Pre-treatment characteristic	(1) Cases before judges w/ low EM rate	(2) Cases before judges w/ high EM rate	(3) p-value	(4) N
% Judge sent to EM	7.56E-04	0.021	0.000***	24 003
Argentine = 1	0.976	0.976	0.990	24 003
Age (in days)	9 257.96	9 219.30	0.276	23 928
Entry date	15 303.89	15 353.07	0.711	23 997
Court size	207.774	203.854	0.839	24 003
Ever imprisoned = 1	0.265	0.265	0.963	24 003
# of previous imprisonments	0.404	0.408	0.848	24 003
Income-profession	1 003.23	1 008.83	0.424	14 635
Spouse = 1	0.612	0.605	0.528	19 697
Homicide = 1	0.055	0.055	0.981	24 003
Attempted homicide = 1	0.018	0.017	0.796	24 003
Sexual offenses = 1	0.021	0.021	0.997	24 003
Other serious crimes = 1	0.026	0.020	0.006***	24 003
Aggravated robbery = 1	0.480	0.509	0.117	24 003
Attempted aggravated robbery = 1	0.073	0.070	0.584	24 003
Robbery = 1	0.122	0.120	0.742	24 003
Attempted robbery = 1	0.078	0.071	0.170	24 003
Possession of firearms = 1	0.037	0.036	0.791	24 003
Larceny/attempted larceny = 1	0.045	0.038	0.230	24 003
Other minor crimes = 1	0.045	0.043	0.643	24 003
Serious crimes	0.600	0.623	0.230	24 003
Middle crimes	0.311	0.297	0.310	24 003
Minor crimes	0.090	0.081	0.294	24 003

Notes: categories in columns 1 and 2 defined by the median of the instrument: *% Judge sent to EM.* Column 1 is the unconditional mean. Column 2 is the predicted value from an OLS regression of the characteristic on the indicator that the judge's incarceration rate is higher than this median, controlling for district fixed effects. The p-values are for the significance of the indicator variable, calculated using standard errors clustered at judicial district level. The sample is limited to judges with at least ten offenders in the full sample. *Argentine* is an indicator variable for nationality. *Age* is the age in days at the time of entry. *Entry date* is the date at the time of entry into the Buenos Aires Penitentiary Service. *Court size* is the number of offenders under the judge in the sample. *Ever imprisoned* is an indicator variable for previous imprisonment. *# of previous imprisonments* is the number of times that a prisoner has been imprisoned before. *Income-profession* is an income estimate based on reported profession, using the General Household Survey. *Spouse* is an indicator if the alleged offender has a wife or partner. *Serious crimes* is a dummy that equals 1 for prisoners whose most serious crime is homicide, attempted homicide, sexual offenses, other serious crimes or aggravated robbery, and 0 for any other crime. *Middle crimes* is a dummy that equals 1 for prisoners whose most serious crime is attempted aggravated robbery, robbery, attempted robbery or possession of firearms, and 0 for any other crime. *Minor crimes* is a dummy that equals 1 for prisoners whose most serious crime is larceny, attempted larceny or other minor crimes, and 0 for any other crime. ***Significant at 1 percent.

Source: Table 3 from Di Tella and Schargrodsky (2013).

judicial status and same number of episodes of previous imprisonment, and we randomly selected 3 individuals with these same conditions for each individual released from EM. This procedure gave us complete information for a total database of 1526 individuals (1140 formerly in prison and 386 formerly under EM).

In the raw data, the recidivism rates (i.e., the proportion of released individuals who returned to the custody of the Buenos Aires Penitentiary Service for another crime) are 13.21 percent (51/386) for the alleged offenders released from EM and 22.37 percent (255/1140) for the individuals released from prison.

Using this sample, we estimate the causal effect of EM assignment (relative to imprisonment) on recidivism running the following 2SLS regression model:

$$R_i = a + b\,EM_i + c\,X_i + \varepsilon_i,$$

where R_i is a dummy variable that indicates whether individual i went back to detention in the Province of Buenos Aires after his release; EM_i is a dummy variable that indicates whether individual i was in the electronic monitoring group; and *% Judge sent to* EM_i instruments for EM allocation exploiting the random assignment of alleged offenders to judges within each judicial district.[6] We also introduced *Judge already used* EM_i, a dummy variable for whether the judge had previously sent an alleged offender to EM (prior to facing offender *i*), as an instrument to capture a time dimension of judges' ideology. The regressions include control variables X_i: type of crime dummies, age, age squared, an Argentine nationality dummy, number of previous imprisonments, judicial district dummies and year dummies.

The 2SLS results using the proxies for judge ideology as an instrument to estimate the effect of EM on recidivism are presented in Table 6.3. Column (1) in Table 6.3 first uses as instrument *% Judge sent to EM.* The instrument is highly significant in the first stage, and the EM coefficient is negative and significant in the second stage. Column (2) adds an additional instrument measuring how early the judge started using EM. Both instruments are statistically significant in the first stage, and the second stage again shows a negative and significant effect of EM on recidivism. Finally, in column (3), we run the same first-stage regression of column (1) not in the sample with complete recidivism data, but in the full sample of alleged offenders of the Buenos Aires penitentiary system where EM bracelets were actually assigned, and then used the predicted EM assignment from this full sample regression as an instrument for actual EM usage. Again, the 2SLS estimate shows a negative and significant effect of EM on recidivism.

Exploiting random assignment to judges with differing inclinations to allocate EM, our 2SLS estimates suggest that treating alleged offenders with EM instead of prison induces a significant reduction in recidivism of between

Table 6.3 *Recidivism and electronic monitoring – 2SLS regressions*

	1	2	3
Second stage:			
Electronic monitoring = 1	−0.13**	−0.16**	−0.15**
	(2.33)	(2.29)	(2.33)
Adjusted R^2 (second stage)	0.16	0.16	0.16
First stage:			
% Judge sent to EM	3.09***	2.94***	
	(9.91)	(9.18)	
Judge already used EM		0.05**	
		(2.09)	
Large-sample estimated EM			4.73***
			(10.10)
Adjusted R^2 (first stage)	0.26	0.26	0.26
Observations	1 503	1 503	1 503

Notes: 2SLS regressions. The dependent variable is a dummy that equals 1 if the offender went back to prison for a new crime at the Province of Buenos Aires, and 0 otherwise. All the regressions include as controls type of crime dummies, age, age squared, Argentine dummy, number of previous imprisonments, judicial district dummies and year dummies. The sample is limited to judges with at least ten offenders in the full sample. In column 1, the instrument is *% Judge sent to EM*, the percentage of alleged offenders the judge sent to EM, excluding him. In column 2, we add *Judge already used EM*, a dummy that equals 1 if, before the alleged offender, the judge has previously used EM and equals 0 otherwise. Both instruments are calculated in the original database of 24 362 alleged offenders. In column 3, the same first-stage regression of column 2 is run in the full sample of 24 362 individuals and the predicted EM assignment is used as instrument. Absolute values of robust t statistics are in parentheses. Standard errors clustered at judicial district level. *Significant at 10 percent; **significant at 5 percent; ***significant at 1 percent.

Source: Table 5 from Di Tella and Schargrodsky (2013).

13 and 16 percentage points. The effect is large: 13 percentage points represent a drop of approximately 58 percent of the base recidivism rate of the prison sample. It translates into a difference of 4.55 percentage points in the average yearly recidivism rate.

Previous work on EM had been inconclusive on its effect on recidivism, as summarized in the reviews by Renzema and Mayo-Wilson (2005) and Aos et al. (2006).[7] The failure to detect significant effects is probably explained because, in most of those studies, EM programs were restricted to low-risk populations. Instead, Di Tella and Schargrodsky (2013) considered (alleged) offenders who were accused of crimes comparable to those of the prison population, including severe felonies. The recent literature is more systematic in finding beneficial effects of EM on recidivism (see Henneguelle et al. 2016,

Williams and Weatherburn 2022 and the meta-studies by Bouchard and Wong 2017 and Belur et al. 2020). Moreover, in agreement with our previous results, Andersen and Andersen (2014) find stronger benign effects for younger offenders, and Andersen and Telle (2022) for offenders without a previous prison record. Instead, Avdija and Lee (2014) and Meuer and Woessner (2020) find no statistically significant difference between the recidivism rates of the EM and control group subjects.

3. THE SUSPENSION OF ELECTRONIC MONITORING IN ARGENTINA

By late 2007, the EM system in the Province of Buenos Aires was up and running. Given the satisfaction with the system, the Province of Buenos Aires was planning an expansion in the number of bracelets, from 300 to 800, and had already started the corresponding procurement process.[8]

However, a violent episode shook the Buenos Aires EM system. In July 2008, Angel Fernandez, who had been detained accused of illegal possession of a handgun and was under EM, escaped from his house and killed a family of four (including children aged eight and ten) in an episode known as the 'Campana massacre'.[9] Fernandez had been assigned EM although he had a prior entry into the penal system: in 1987 he had been sentenced to 25 years in prison for robbery and rape, followed by triple murder, but had been released after only 15 years.

This was the most salient, but actually not the only episode of evasion from EM in our sample: 66 out of 386 (17 percent) individuals in our EM sample fled from the supervision of the penal system by breaking their electronic bracelets. Eighteen of these 66 escapees were re-apprehended for new crimes: a recidivism rate of over 27 percent. Escape from EM occurred at a lower rate for the group that never went to prison (13 percent) compared to the group that had already spent some time in prison (20 percent). In addition, Di Tella and Schargrodsky (2013) show that offenders with a previous criminal record were more likely to both escape and commit new crimes, suggesting that a reasonable assignment rule should have excluded offenders with a previous criminal record from the small EM program.

In other countries, there were also episodes of offenders who escaped EM supervision and committed new crimes. A salient episode (the Peter Williams case) jeopardized the UK system when a young offender under EM was part of a murder in Nottingham, UK, in 2005.[10] Also, several cases of recidivism by offenders under EM occurred in Bogotá when the system was implemented.[11]

In spite of these episodes, in these countries, the system continued as planned. Instead, after the 'Campana massacre', the planned expansion of the EM system in the Province of Buenos Aires was suspended. And the existing EM system was limited to a smaller scale, restricted to pregnant women, HIV infected and detainees above 65 years old.[12] The EM system expansion remained on hold until 2013, when it was restored (see Crisconio and Solano, 2017).

Nicolas Schiavo, the judge who had assigned EM to Angel Fernandez despite his prior record of conviction for robbery, rape and triple murder, was harshly questioned in the media after the 'Campana massacre'. During the media scandal triggered by this episode, he defended his decision arguing that 'denying EM because a person is "dangerous" would violate the law and the Constitution', as EM was used in the Province of Buenos Aires at a pre-conviction stage. Judge Schiavo had to stand trial for his decision but was eventually acquitted.[13]

4. THE POLITICAL CHALLENGES OF THE IMPLEMENTATION OF ELECTRONIC MONITORING

Di Tella and Schargrodsky (2013) used the estimated difference in recidivism rates of offenders treated with EM relative to incarcerated offenders to provide a cost-benefit analysis of the EM system.

The analysis highlighted three main components of the change in social welfare (W), when an alleged offender is assigned to EM instead of prison:

$$\Delta W = Current\ fiscal\ gain + Gain\ in\ lower\ future\ victimization$$
$$-Loss\ in\ lower\ current\ incapacitation$$

The first component is the fiscal savings, as the daily cost of EM per inmate per day in the Province of Buenos Aires during the period of analysis was below one-third of the cost of imprisonment. The second component is the gain in lower future victimization after release, which is calculated by combining the estimated reduction in recidivism of Table 6.3 with estimates of the dollar cost to crime victims in Argentina at the time. Finally, the last term considers the estimated costs of crimes originating from the escapees under EM (there were no registered escapes from prison in our sample). Using these estimates, Di Tella and Schargrodsky (2013) calculate that the net welfare benefit of sending one alleged offender to EM, instead of prison, amounts to 2.4 times the average Argentine GDP per capita.

This cost-benefit analysis obviously simplifies the complexity of this welfare calculation. Many relevant issues are ignored such as the loss to society of having imprisoned a person who is eventually declared innocent (Judge Schiavo's concern), the loss for victims and their families of knowing that their alleged aggressor is not incarcerated, the value of future differences in labor income under both systems, the police and judicial costs originating from differences in criminal activity, the public and private prevention costs triggered by these crime variations and the possibility that substitution of prison for EM might lead to reduced general deterrence, *inter alia*.

Beyond these limitations, in this chapter we aim to highlight a different challenge for the sustainability of this intervention. Assuming our previous estimates on the reduced recidivism under EM and the subsequent cost-benefit analysis are correct, a benevolent government who observes this positive net welfare gain would certainly sustain and expand the use of EM devices.

However, policy-making in the real world, under media scrutiny, can be more challenging. In particular, the welfare effects of EM suffer an asymmetry: the costs are very salient, but the benefits are difficult to observe.

When an alleged offender under EM escapes and commits a new crime there is, appropriately, a media scandal.[14,15] And public opinion becomes, justifiably, even more horrified if, like in the Campana episode, children are murdered and if the person benefited with EM already had an atrocious (and observable) previous criminal record. Even if, as mentioned above, an assignment rule based on expected escape and recidivism using observable – to the judge – data should have excluded Angel Fernandez from the EM program, there is no guarantee that these cases will never occur. Thus, the negative term in the welfare equation, the reduction in incapacitation power under EM, is salient and observable.

Instead, the reduction in future crimes from lower recidivism is, by definition, unobservable. We will never read on the front page of a newspaper that a crime did not happen the day before. Thus, the welfare gain from avoiding the criminogenic effects of prison is not observable in the public debate. The fiscal gain, in turn, can be publicly shown but it is perhaps too abstract for the general population.

This asymmetry weakened the sustainability of a modern penitentiary policy which, according to our estimates, had a net positive (and rather large) welfare effect. The horrendous Campana episode and the subsequent media scandal, combined with a weak institutional environment, led to the reduction of the scope and the deferment of the planned expansion of the EM system in the Province of Buenos Aires.

How could a benevolent government, under the media and public opinion pressure, defend the continuation of the EM program? Perhaps timely impact evaluations, performed by independent researchers, could be used in the public debate to demonstrate the (hidden) advantages of the EM system and convince citizens and the media of the virtues of this policy. This episode highlights the importance of independent and rigorous impact evaluation for the design and sustainability of public policy.

NOTES

1. Rafael Di Tella, Harvard Business School, CIfAR and NBER. Ernesto Schargrodsky, CAF, UTDT and CONICET. Several parts of this chapter are summarized from our article "Criminal Recidivism after Prison and Electronic Monitoring", *Journal of Political Economy* (2013), Vol. 121 (1), pp. 28–73. See the original article for further details. We thank Layla Such Nachtrieb for thorough literature revision.
2. On the origins of electronic monitoring, see Gomme (1995). For early discussions see Schwitzgebel (1969), Petersilia (1987), Schmidt and Curtis (1987), Morris and Tonry (1990) and Tonry (1998). On the impact of prisons on crime and recidivism, see Gendreau et al. (1999), Bushway and Paternoster (2009), Nagin et al. (2009), Chen and Shapiro (2007) and Kuziemko (2013), *inter alia*.
3. Several Latin American countries followed. Mexico implemented EM in 2008. A GPS monitoring system was launched in Bogotá, Colombia, in 2009. The Peruvian Congress approved the use of EM in 2010, but it was not regulated until 2020. In Brazil, an EM law was sanctioned in 2010. After enacting a law in 2012, Chile started the use of EM for minor offences in 2014, and it is expected to expand it for cases of domestic violence by late 2021. Uruguay launched a pilot plan to implement EM in 2013. Ecuador included EM in the penal code in 2014, implemented a pilot plan in 2016 and started its use in 2017. Finally, Paraguay sanctioned a law in 2017 and launched a pilot plan in 2021.
4. There were three legal requirements at this stage: a 'technical' report on the availability of a telephone line and the suitability of the house to install EM, a 'social-environmental' report on the family and neighborhood and a declaration of a family member accepting to take care of the alleged offender. Early in the program the system required a fixed line, although later cellular phones (with GPS incorporated to guarantee that they are physically 'fixed') were also allowed.
5. The waiting list was unique (for the whole province), with no quotas per judicial district, judge or type of crime. The judge typically did not request information on its length at the time of deciding on EM assignment.
6. On the use of instrumental variables calculated from the random assignment of judges or investigators see, for example, Kling (2006), Doyle (2008), Aizer and Doyle (2015) and Dobbie et al. (2018).
7. See also Petersilia and Turner (1990), Courtright et al. (1997), Gainey et al. (2000), Finn and Muirhead-Steves (2002), Padgett et al. (2006), Marie (2009) and Marklund and Holmberg (2009).
8. See "La eficacia del control satelital, cuestionada", *La Nación*, August 2, 2008, https://www.lanacion.com.ar/sociedad/la-eficacia-del-control-satelital-cuestionada-nid1035876/.
9. Campana is a mid-size city in the northeast of the Province of Buenos Aires.
10. See Nellis (2006); "Criminal removed tag before horrific murder," *Rochdale Observer*, March 22, 2005; and "Mistakes' admission over killer", *BBC News*, September 19, 2005, http://news.bbc.co.uk/2/hi/uk_news/england/nottinghamshire/4257884.stm.
11. See "Police caught a man who violated detention under electronic monitoring," Elespectador.com, Colombia, March 24, 2010; "Preso con manilla de vigilancia hacia parte de banda de apartamenteros" ElTiempo.com, July 6, 2009; "Policía sorprendió a un hombre que violó detención monitoreada con manilla del Inpec" ElTiempo.com; March 24, 2010. "Ordenan investigar asignaciones de brazaletes electrónicos" Elespectador.com, March 10, 2010; and "Los brazaletes de la impunidad" Elespectador.com, November 23, 2010.
12. See "Scioli limitará las excarcelaciones", *La Nación*, August 6, 2008, https://www.lanacion.com.ar/sociedad/scioli-limitara-las-excarcelaciones-nid1036944/
13. See "Should Judge Schiavo stand trial?" in *Critica*, October 5, 2008, and "ADN del crimen: nadie se hace cargo de los presos liberados", *La Nación*, March 26, 2021, https://www.lanacion.com.ar/seguridad/adn-del-crimen-nadie-se-hace-cargo-de-los-presos-liberados-nid27032021/.

14. In addition to the media articles on the Massacre of Campana already mentioned, see, for example: "Un preso que usó la tobillera cuenta cómo hizo para burlar ese control", *Clarín*, August 4, 2008; "Masacre de Campana: al acusado le desconectaban la pulsera por horas", *UNO Diario de Santa Fe*, August 5, 2008; "Tras la masacre de Campana, Scioli quiere reformar el Código de Procedimiento Penal", *Clarín*, August 5, 2008; and "Lecciones que deja el crimen", *Clarín*, August 8, 2008.
15. On examples of media influence affecting security policies (particularly policing behavior) see, for example, Premkumar (2019) and Mastrorocco and Ornaghi (2021). On penal populism, see Roberts et al. (2002).

REFERENCES

Aizer, Anna, and Joseph J. Doyle, Jr. 2015. "Juvenile Incarceration, Human Capital, and Future Crime: Evidence from Randomly Assigned Judges", *The Quarterly Journal of Economics*, 130(2, May): 759–803.

Andersen, Lars H., and Signe H. Andersen. 2014. "Effect of Electronic Monitoring on Social Welfare Dependance", *Criminology & Public Policy* 13(3): 349–79.

Andersen, Synøve N., and Kjetil Telle. 2022. "Better out than in? The Effect on Recidivism of Replacing Incarceration with Electronic Monitoring in Norway", *European Journal of Criminology* 19(1): 55–76.

Aos, Steve, Marna Miller, and Elizabeth Drake. 2006. *Evidence-Based Public Policy Options to Reduce Future Prison Construction, Criminal Justice Costs, and Crime Rates*, Olympia: Washington State Institute for Public Policy.

Avdija, Avdi S., and JiHee Lee. 2014. "Does Electronic Monitoring Home Detention Program Work? Evaluating Program Suitability Based on Offenders' Post-Program Recidivism Status", *Justice Policy Journal* 11(1): 1–15.

Belur, Jyoti, Amy Thornton, Lisa Tompson, Matthew Manning, Aiden Sidebottom, and Kate Bowers. 2020. "A Systematic Review of the Effectiveness of the Electronic Monitoring of Offenders", *Journal of Criminal Justice* 68. https://doi.org/10.1016/j.jcrimjus.2020.101686.

Bouchard, Jessica, and Jeniffer S. Wong. 2017. "The New Panopticon? Examining the Effect of Home Confinement on Criminal Recidivism", *Victims & Offenders* 13(5): 589–608.

Bushway, Shawn D., and Raymond Paternoster. 2009. "The Impact of Prison on Crime", in *Do Prisons Make us Safer? The Benefits and Costs of the Prison Boom*, Raphael, Steven, and Stoll, Michael A. (editors), New York: Russell Sage Foundation.

Chen, Keith, and Jesse Shapiro. 2007. "Do Harsher Prison Conditions Reduce Recidivism? A Discontinuity-based Approach", *American Law and Economics Review* 9(Spring): 1–29.

Courtright, K. E., B. L. Berg, and R. J. Mutchnick. 1997. "Effects of House Arrest with Electronic Monitoring on DUI Offenders", *Journal of Offender Rehabilitation* 24: 35–51.

Crisconio, María Magdalena, and Mauro Solano, 2017. "La política penitenciaria en la provincia de Buenos Aires 1983–2017: marchas y contramarchas de una política anclada en el corto plazo", in mimeo, 9° Congreso Latinoamericano de Ciencia Política, ALACIP, Montevideo (Uruguay).

Di Tella, Rafael, and Ernesto Schargrodsky. 2013. "Criminal Recidivism after Prison and Electronic Monitoring", *Journal of Political Economy* 121(1): 28–73.

Dobbie, Will, Jacob Goldin, and Crystal S. Yang. 2018. "The Effects of Pretrial Detention on Conviction, Future Crime, and Employment: Evidence from Randomly Assigned Judges", *American Economic Association* 108(2): 201–40.

Doyle, Joseph J. Jr. 2008. "Child Protection and Adult Crime: Using Investigator Assignment to Estimate Causal Effects of Foster Care", *Journal of Political Economy* 116(4): 746–70.

Finn, M. A., and S. Muirhead-Steves. 2002. "The Effectiveness of Electronic Monitoring with Violent Male Parolees", *Justice Quarterly* 19(2, June): 293–312.

Gainey, Randy, Brian Payne, and Mike O'Toole. 2000. "The Relationship between Time in Jail, Time on Electronic Monitoring, and Recidivism: An Event History Analysis of a Jail-based Program", *Justice Quarterly* 17(4, December): 733–52.

Gendreau, Paul, Claire Goggin, and Francis Cullen. 1999. *The Effect of Prison Sentences on Recidivism, User Report 1999–3, Corrections Research*, Canada: Department of Solicitor General.

Gomme, I. M. 1995. "From Big House to Big Brother: Confinement in the Future", in *The Canadian Criminal Justice System* N. Larsen (editors), Toronto: Canadian Scholars' Press, 489–516.

Henneguelle, Anaïs, Benjamin Monnery, and Annie Kensey. 2016. "Better at Home than in Prison? The Effects of Electronic Monitoring on Recidivism in France". *The Journal of Law and Economics* 49(3): 629–68.

Kling, Jeffrey R. 2006. "Incarceration Length, Employment, and Earnings," *American Economic Review* 96(3, June): 863–76.

Kuziemko, Ilyana. 2013. "Going Off Parole: How the Elimination of Discretionary Prison Release Affects the Social Cost of Crime", *Quarterly Journal of Economics* 128(1): 371–424.

Marie, Oliver. 2009. *Early Release from Prison and Recidivism: A Regression Discontinuity Approach*, manuscript, London: London School of Economics.

Marklund, Fredrik, and Stina Holmberg. 2009. "Effects of Early Release from Prison using Electronic Tagging in Sweden", *Journal of Experimental Criminology* 5 (March): 41–61.

Mastrorocco, Nicola, and Arianna Ornaghi. 2021. *Who Watches the Watchmen? Local News and Police Behavior in the United States*. Working Papermimeo, NBER, Summer Institute, Political Economy.

Meuer, Katharian, and Gunda Woessner. 2020. "Does Electronic Monitoring as a Means of Release Preparation Reduce Subsequent Recidivism? A Randomized Controlled Trial In Germany", *European Journal of Criminology* 17(5): 563–84.

Morris, Norval, and Michael Tonry. 1990. *Between Prison and Probation: Intermediate Punishments and a Rational Sentencing System*, New York: Oxford University Press.

Nagin, Daniel S., Francis Cullen, and Cheryl Jonson. 2009. "Imprisonment and Reoffending", *Crime and Justice* 38(1): 115–200.

Nellis, Mike. 2006. "The Limitations of Electronic Monitoring: Reflections on the Tagging of Peter Williams," *Prison Service Journal* 164(March): 3–12.

Padgett, Kathy G., William D. Bales, and Thomas G. Bloomberg. 2006. "Under Surveillance: An Empirical Test of the Effectiveness and Consequences of Electronic Monitoring." *Criminology & Public Policy* 5(1, February): 61–91.

Petersilia, Joan. 1987. *Expanding Options for Criminal Sentencing*, Santa Monica: The Rand Corporation.

Petersilia, Joan, and Susan Turner. 1990. "Comparing Intensive and Regular Supervision for High-Risk Probationers: Early Results from an Experiment in California", *Crime and Delinquency* 36 (1, January): 87–111.

Premkumar, Deepak. 2019. "Public Scrutiny and Police Effort: Evidence from Arrests and Crime After High-Profile Police Killings". Available at SSRN: https://ssrn.com/abstract=3715223.

Renzema, Marc, and Evan Mayo-Wilson. 2005. "Can Electronic Monitoring Reduce Crime for Moderate to High-risk Offenders?", *Journal of Experimental Criminology*, 1(Summer): 215–37.

Roberts, Julian V., Loretta J. Stalans, David Indermaur, and Mike Hough (2002). *Penal Populism and Public Opinion: Lessons from Five Countries*, Oxford: University of Oxford Press.

Schmidt, Annesley, and Christine E. Curtis. 1987. "Electronic Monitoring", in *Intermediate Punishments: Intensive Supervision, Home Confinement and Electronic Supervision*, Belinda McCarthy (editor), Monsey: Willow Tree Press.

Schwitzgebel, Ralph K. 1969. "Issues in the Use of an Electronic Rehabilitation System with Chronic Recidivists", *Law and Society Review* 3: 597–615.

Tonry, Michael. 1998. "Intermediate Sanctions", Chapter 25 in *The Handbook of Crime and Punishment*, Michael Tonry (editor), New York: Oxford University Press.

Williams, Jenny, and Don Weatherburn. 2022. "Can Electronic Monitoring Reduce Reoffending?", *The Review of Economics and Statistics* 104(2): 232–45.

7. Education and crime: What we know and where do we go?

Joel Carr, Olivier Marie and Sunčica Vujić

1. INTRODUCTION

There is a growing strand of literature in the economics of crime advocating that improvement in education quantity and quality and early intervention education programmes will result in lower criminal activity (see for example Lochner and Moretti, 2004; Jacob and Lefgren, 2003). In fact, researchers argue that education may be a more cost-effective crime deterrent than traditional methods such as smarter policing or harsher punishment so long as the education expansion targets the most high-risk individuals (Donohue and Siegelman, 1998; Bell et al., 2018). However, due to empirical challenges, evidence remains limited and sometimes contradictory (Lualien, 2006; Jacob and Lefgren, 2003). In this chapter, we will discuss the research developments on the causal relationship between education and crime over the past two decades, as well as the future of this research topic. Moreover, we will discuss the heterogeneous effect of education on crime across race and gender.

The US high-school diploma is one of the most important qualifications in the US labour market, with major differences in earnings, employment and life-chances associated with holding, or not holding, the diploma (Hungerford and Solon 1987; Jaeger and Page 1996). To illustrate further the most high-risk population of low education levels, in the 1990s, prison inmates in the US were more than twice as likely to not have a high school diploma or a General Education Development (GED) test[1] compared to the general population (41.3 per cent vs 18.4 per cent) and were much less likely to have a postsecondary education (Harlow, 2003). The number of prisoners in state prisons without a high school diploma increased from 1991 to 1997 (from 293 000 to 420 600) while the number with a high school diploma remained the same. Moreover, comparisons between whites, blacks and Hispanics show that minority inmates are much more likely to not have either the GED or the high school diploma (Hetland et al., 2007).

Hetland et al. (2007) also found that the education levels of Norwegian prison inmates in 2006 were similar to education levels of the general Norwegian population in the 1980s and 1990s, while the education levels of the general population have increased significantly since the 1980s. Compared to the education levels of Norwegian inhabitants in 2004, prison inmates were twice as likely to only have a primary and lower secondary education and about half as likely to have a higher education.

This negative relationship between education and incarceration is also found in a variety of countries such as Australia (Butler and Milner, 2003), Germany (Entorf, 2009), Greece (Vergidis et al., 2007) and Mexico (Bautista-Arredondo et al., 2015) to list a few. These studies use incarcerated individuals to estimate the correlation between education and crime due to the fact that it is possible to observe or record the education levels of prisoners. However, to identify a causal effect of education on crime rather than correlations, additional econometric techniques must be applied. Compared to correlation studies, causal evidence is less widespread and will be the focus of the chapter.

In the US, the most vulnerable youth populations (high-poverty or high-minority areas) had an average funding gap of over $1000 per student compared to low-poverty or low-minority areas. Research has shown that parental income and poverty significantly impact the educational attainment of children (see Dahl and Lochner, 2012) and that raising the permanent income of the poorest households by $4000 per year significantly reduces youth crime (Akee et al., 2010). The positive relationship between parental income and a child's educational attainment has also been observed in the United Kingdom (Chevalier et al., 2013), Brazil (Torche and Costa-Ribeiro, 2012), France (Maurin, 2002), Nigeria (Kainuwa et al., 2013) and Japan (Machebe et al., 2017). Findings on the importance of socio-economic status and the educational attainment of prisoners suggest that individuals most at risk for having a low educational attainment are also most at risk for committing a crime and ending in a criminal career. This raises an important question for researchers and policy makers: can crime be reduced by increasing the educational attainment of at-risk youths?

In Section 2, we first discuss the theoretical relationship between schooling and crime and the mechanisms behind it. In the crime model which we adopt in this chapter, rational individuals choose to commit a crime based on expected costs and benefits associated with criminal activity. By influencing the costs and benefits from these activities, schooling can have a profound effect on criminal activity.

In Section 3, we discuss the data used to find a causal relationship between education and crime as well as the limitations and future possibilities of crime data and thus research. Section 4 explores the identification methods and results found in past research. We then discuss cost-benefit analyses of education expansion and crime reduction in Section 5. In Section 6, we conclude with a discussion on the future of research on the relationship between education and crime.

2. MECHANISMS: HOW WOULD EDUCATION (THEORETICALLY) AFFECT CRIME?

We rely on the traditional economics of crime models beginning with the seminal work of Becker (1968) to focus on the multifaceted relationship between education and crime using a human capital approach (see also Ehrlich, 1973, and Witte, 1980). The model assumes that individuals are rational, investment in education results in improvement in the legitimate labour market and crime is time-consuming. This expected crime time consumption includes not only the planning and execution of the crime but also expected time spent in custody, courts and possible imprisonment. Our model follows the Becker model by modelling the choice to commit crime as a rational choice based on the estimated costs and benefits of crime but is somewhat expanded (or specified) in order to take into account the many mechanisms through which education can impact crime. The model predicts that an individual will choose to participate in criminal activity when the perceived benefits outweigh the expected costs, or:

$$E\left[\text{Benefit}_{\text{crime}}\left(R\left(CC(S)\right),P(S)\right)\right]$$
$$>E\left[\text{Cost}_{\text{crime}}\left(T(S),W\left(HC(S,A)\right),C(S,F),P(S)\right)\right],$$

where the (expected) benefit of crime is determined by the returns to crime (R) which depend on the criminal capital (CC) of the individual, which is in turn affected by schooling (S). Criminal capital is analogous to human capital and refers to the stock of skills, experiences and network which are conducive to criminal activity. Personal characteristics or preferences (P) such as time discounting and risk preferences also affect the non-pecuniary benefits of crime but are in turn influenced by schooling, particularly early childhood education. In the model we assume that P is increasing with crime preferences, with higher levels of P representing individuals with high future discounting (myopic) or risk-loving while lower levels of P refer to individuals with the opposite preferences.

In the case of crime, the expected benefits or costs could be expressed in monetary terms: returns from crime or lost wages, or in terms of utility and non-pecuniary gains of crime or time costs if captured and imprisoned.

Expected costs of committing a crime include time costs (T) from planning and executing a crime as well as time lost due to arrest, possible court appearances and, finally, imprisonment. In a similar vein, the costs of committing a crime include the opportunity cost of lost wages due to capture and imprisonment or termination from job due to suspected criminal activity. Lost wages in the legal sector are partially determined by the human capital (HC) of the individual, which is in turn strongly affected by education (S) and ability (A). These two channels are mediated by the perceived probability of capture as there are lower time costs and no lost wages due to imprisonment if they are not detected or captured. The probability of capture is determined by schooling and external factors such as police staffing and funding, which are assumed to be unaffected by changes in education. Finally, personal characteristics such as time preferences may impact the evaluation of expected long-term costs of crime, particularly myopia toward expected imprisonment.

2.1. Income Channel

Research has shown that education expansion leads to both an increase in productivity (wages) and a decrease in crime (Lochner, 2004; Lochner and Moretti, 2004; Hjalmarsson, 2008) suggesting that income explains at least part of the crime deterrent effect of education. This mechanism is referred to as the income channel. We expect education to have a deterrent effect on future crime given that the returns to schooling in terms of legitimate wages are greater than the returns from crime. In this case, wages from legitimate labour are an opportunity cost of criminal activity and therefore should be negatively correlated with time allotted to crime. This opportunity cost is present in the planning and execution of a crime since that is time that could be spent earning a wage as well as in the potential punishment for the crime due to earned wages missed out on while in court and/or prison.

Returns to schooling are dependent on two endowments: previous human capital and productivity predisposition. Returns to education are greater for individuals with low baseline human capital and benefit more from learning (high A). Therefore, we expect the low education attainment population to have the highest marginal returns from learning. For individuals who do not gain any human capital from an extra year of education we do not expect any changes in crime via the income channel as wages are not expected to change:

$$\text{Income channel: Education reduces crime if } \frac{\partial W}{\partial HC} \times \frac{\partial HC}{\partial S} > 0.$$

There are, however, exceptions to this. Some forms of crime such as tax fraud will increase with income since the benefit of committing the crime increases with wages. To take into account the possible multiple effects of schooling on returns to crime and wages in the legal sector, the previous inequality becomes:

$$\text{Education reduces crime if: } \frac{\partial W}{\partial HC} \times \frac{\partial HC}{\partial S} > \frac{\partial R}{\partial CC} \times \frac{\partial CC}{\partial S}.$$

Given a rational individual we expect crime to decrease if, all else equal, the returns to legal wages from additional schooling are greater than the returns to crime. This raises the question of whether human capital and crime capital are substitutes or complements. Does some education increase expected payoffs of crime? This can be linked to Levitt and Lochner (2001) who find that males with higher scores on mechanical tests had higher offence rates.

Moreover, rates of other forms of white-collar crime such as forgery, fraud, insider trading etc. have been found to be positively correlated with education levels as the skills acquired in school may be complementary to skills required to commit these crimes (Lochner, 2004). For example, accountants may be more able to commit tax fraud and locksmiths could more easily commit burglaries. In other words, the human capital acquired in school may also act as criminal capital that will increase the payoff from white-collar crime. Therefore, when examining the effects of schooling on crime, quality and substance can be as relevant as quantity.

2.2. Non-Cognitive Effects

Education may have non-cognitive effects, by making people more risk-averse and future oriented (Becker and Mulligan, 1997; Oreopoulos, 2006). In addition to building human capital that then reduces crime by increasing the opportunity costs, education can have a deterrent effect by changing the non-cognitive behaviours or preferences of individuals. For example, critical thinking and social skills are both positively correlated with education (Soskice, 1993; Heckman, 2006). Another behaviour learnt in school is *time discounting* (Frederick et al., 2002). Education can shape individuals to be more forward-looking and therefore place more equal weight on their future utility, including future wages. Consequentially, any future punishment or lost wages due to criminal activity will bear more weight in their expected utility and they will commit fewer crimes. Moreover, future gains from investment in schooling will bear greater weight on their schooling decision. Becker and Mulligan (1997, p. 735) state that

> schooling focuses students' attention on the future. . . . In addition, through repeated practice at problem solving, schooling helps children learn the art of scenario simulation. Thus, educated people should be more productive at reducing the remoteness of future pleasures.

Oreopoulos (2006) provides evidence that adolescents who do not complete secondary education are more myopic and place greater weight on present costs of education and less on future gains from additional schooling.

Education may also influence the *risk aversion* of an individual, leading them to place greater weight on negative outcomes (detection) relative to positive outcomes (non-detection) and as such commit fewer crimes. For example, Chevalier and Marie (2022) find that children of riskier mothers have a higher criminal propensity perhaps due to a transmission of risk preference from mother to child. One final non-cognitive effect of education is patience which may lead to less impulsive and negative actions (see Heller et al., 2017). Meanwhile Bell et al. (2018) found no significant changes in labour market outcomes (employment and wages) due to education expansion policies but negative effects on crimes suggesting a notable non-cognitive effect:

$$\text{Non-cognitive effects: Education reduces crime if } \frac{\partial P}{\partial S} < 0.$$

Therefore, we expect crime to decrease if additional schooling reduces the individual preferences and tastes that facilitate more crime, such as myopia and risk-loving preferences.

2.3. Incapacitation and Concentration Effects

Finally, education can have a contemporaneous impact on crime through the incapacitation and concentration effects. By forcing students into schooling (via mandatory schooling laws, parental control etc.) less time can be allotted to criminal activity outside of school. Therefore, one would anticipate a contemporaneous reduction in juvenile crimes for an individual during the course of their education. A displacement effect is possible, meaning that students commit more crimes outside of schooling hours which causes the net effect to be negligible. The incapacitation effect is particularly strong for adolescents, as those are the peak years in the crime-age profile (see Hirschi and Gottfredson, 1983). Moreover, forcing students into additional school by education policy in the current period may lead to a voluntary increase in future schooling (via an increase in *HC* and *A*), further incapacitating students. This is known as a dynamic incapacitation effect:

$$\text{Incapacitation effect: Education reduces crime if } \frac{\partial T_t}{\partial S_t} > 0$$

$$\text{Dynamic incapacitation effect: Education reduces crime if } \frac{\partial S_{t+1}}{\partial A_{t+1}} \times \frac{\partial A_{t+1}}{\partial S_t} > 0.$$

We therefore expect that (juvenile) crime will decrease if contemporaneous schooling increases the time costs of committing a crime by crowding out available time to commit a crime. In the case of the dynamic incapacitation effect, we include a time subscript to make clear that inducing individuals into additional schooling today (S_t) could lead to additional schooling in the next period (S_{t+1}), if the schooling today has increased the ability of the individual (A_{t+1}), and makes obtaining additional schooling in the next period optimal due to returns to legal wages.

We expect the incapacitation effect to hold given individual time constraints. Adolescents who would have previously dropped out of school to work in the legitimate sector are now induced to spend more time on education and have no reason to increase time allotted to crime as contemporaneous returns to legitimate and criminal labour have not changed. However, individuals who otherwise would have committed crimes are now forced to increase time allotted to schooling which will mechanically decrease criminal activity. The dynamic concentration effect is less certain to be observed as the individuals forcefully incapacitated by education policy have relatively low levels of human capital and A. As such, it may not be utility maximising for the adolescent to continue schooling beyond the level mandated.

Inducing adolescents into additional schooling rather than employment may also have a positive impact on adolescent criminal activity as research has found that teenage employment results in negative educational outcomes and antisocial behaviour (Paternoster et al., 2003; Brame et al., 2004; Apel et al., 2006; Apel et al., 2007):

$$\text{Concentration effect: Education increases crime if } \frac{\partial P_t}{\partial S_t} > 0 \text{ or } \frac{\partial T_t}{\partial S_t} < 0.$$

On the other hand, by constraining many adolescents into one dense area, there is a concentration effect which increases crime by reducing costs of criminal activity (i.e., reduction in planning costs as partners and victims are in close proximity) (Jacob and Lefgren, 2003; Luallen, 2006). Violent and emotional crimes will likely increase as negative interactions between high-risk adolescents increase due to schooling. These two taken together may also impact the preferences of individuals via their peer network. A similar phenomenon has been found to exist between football stadiums and crime rates (Marie, 2016).

2.4. Early Education, Peer Effects, Knowledge Effects, Modernisation Hypothesis

Similarly, early childhood programmes could have a potential impact on returns from learning, information channel of education, positive peer-effects, teacher role-models etc. (Henry and Rickman, 2007; Walters, 2015). By investing in early childhood education, the future returns from schooling are expected to increase. Therefore, these programmes will have a deterrent effect if ability or skills needed to gain human capital from schooling increase with early childhood education. An increase in learning productivity will lead to an increase in expected wages and prolong schooling beyond the required amount. Therefore, we expect that early childhood education to have a reducing effect on future criminal activity through both the income channel and non-cognitive effects:

Learning capacity effect: Education reduces crime if $\frac{\partial A}{\partial S} > 0$.

3. DATA ISSUES: MEASURING CRIME AND (SIMULTANEOUSLY) EDUCATION

The greatest limitation to *causal* empirical research on the effect of education on crime – and the identification of the underlying mechanisms – is the availability of sufficiently detailed data. Researchers can match aggregate data on crime and education, but matching micro-data containing education levels and criminal justice records is more difficult, thus limiting research opportunities.

Crime data have different components and definitions depending on the source and timing. First, crime data can come from official (police) sources, victimisation surveys and self-reported crime. Second, official data contain different measures of crime or criminal activity including incident counts, arrest data and conviction data.

3.1. Police Recorded Data

The most common source of crime data is from law enforcement agencies which provide detail on crime observed and reported to the police. At a more fundamental level, crime data are limited by the fact that only observed crime is recorded leading to a 'dark figure of crime' (Coleman and Moynihan, 1996). The dark figure of crime means that the official crime statistics provide an underestimated figure, only capturing observed and recorded crime and therefore suffering from measurement error. As such, if education is negatively correlated with the probability of a crime being observed and recorded, the estimated relationship between schooling and crime would be overestimated. In this estimate, the coefficient for schooling will capture not just any decrease in committed crimes but also a substitution of observed crime for unobserved crime. Both will reduce the official crime rate, causing the deterrent effect to be overestimated as it does not consider the increase in unobserved crime. An increase in education could increase the dark figure of crime if educated individuals are more successful in having their crimes go unreported. In this case, any measured correlation between education and crime would be overestimated.

3.2. Victimisation Surveys

One way to remedy the dark figure of crime is to use the victimisation surveys such as the Crime Survey of England and Wales (CSEW) or the National Crime Victimization Survey (NCVS) by the Federal Bureau of Investigation (FBI) (Maguire and McVie, 2017). In these surveys, households disclose if they were victims of different crime types as well as if the crime was reported to the police, providing information on the percentage of crimes the police became aware of. By combining the data from the victimisation surveys and the police records, one finds perhaps a more accurate count of criminal activity as there are data on both reported crimes and reporting probabilities by the victim (recorded crime = true crime * reporting probability ⊛ true crime = recorded crime / reporting probability). Even with victimisation surveys, it is still impossible to ensure a representative sample of criminals to measure the relationship between education and crime as the detection of crime by the police and reporting probability by the victim are dependent on the education of the offender and victim, respectively (Maguire and McVie, 2017).

3.3. Self-Reported Crime Surveys

Self-reported crime surveys such as the National Longitudinal Survey of Youth (NLSY) provide complementary information on criminal activity which are highly correlated with official arrest data (Lochner, 2011). One potential benefit to self-reported crime surveys is the inclusion of questions regarding returns from illegitimate activity. Otherwise, this information is unobserved preventing researchers from looking into the effect of education on crime vis-à-vis changes in returns to crime. This highlights the importance of being able to match survey data on self-reported crimes with official criminal data to allow researchers to estimate the mechanisms through which education decreases – or even increases – crime.

3.4. Arrest and Conviction Data

Arrest and conviction data provide individual-level information on criminal justice history. Researchers are interested in individual-level data as it may contain information on the education level of the criminal which is otherwise not available from aggregated police recorded data. Similar to area crime counts, arrest data will be unreliable if the probability of capture given that a crime was committed is (negatively) correlated with schooling. This may be true for two reasons. First, if schooling is complementary with criminal capital, schooling may provide skills which allow an individual to evade capture. Second, police may be biased against those with lower education levels and have a higher propensity to arrest low-educated suspects.

Even given that a highly educated individual is captured and prosecuted, there is a possibility that more educated defendants are better able to avoid conviction due to more knowledge of the legal system and their rights and are more able to hire a personal lawyer rather than a public defender. Finally, the court system may sentence the higher-educated individuals more favourably, leading prison data to be biased against the lower-educated individuals at the intensive margin. Therefore, we could expect that the estimated relationship between education and crime is greater the further along the criminal event timeline the dependent variable is as the effect is cumulative across the event timeline (the negative effect at each step contains the negative relationship at that step plus the negative relationship of the previous steps). Webbink et al. (2013) find evidence against this and conclude that their estimated relationship between education and crime was not biased by a measurement error in the crime data.

3.5. Administrative Data

More recently, administrative data have increased the availability of large datasets with individual criminal records, education levels, income etc. Administrative data contain official crime data for crimes that are observed by the police, as well as arrest and imprisonment statistics (Lochner, 2011). Therefore, they do not contain unobserved crimes which could lead to biased estimations of the relationship between education and crime. However, administrative data are not a panacea due to difficulties in merging individual-level data across different datasets. This requires unique individual identifiers which have mostly been used in the past in the Netherlands and Scandinavian countries (see for example Oreopoulos and Salvanes, 2011; Marie et al., 2013; Hjalmarsson et al., 2015). Even larger more contemporary administrative datasets, as those becoming ever-more available in the US for example, may not be able to be matched with survey or experimental data.

3.6. Freedom of Information (FOI) Requests

A final and up-and-coming source of crime data is the Freedom of Information (FOI) requests or Right to Information (RTI) requests. The FOI requests can be used to acquire publicly held data that are otherwise not easily accessible (Clifton-Sprigg et al., 2020) but are limited to countries that have passed an FOI act. These are restricted to developed Anglophone countries such as the US, United Kingdom, Australia, Canada and New Zealand (Hazell and Worthy, 2010). Compared to publicly available crime data, crime data obtained through the FOI requests can provide more detailed and concise information at the level of the individual crime, including localised geographical areas, precise timing of the incident and victim and perpetrator information when available and applicable. The papers which used the FOI requests to obtain data for empirical crime research are Bell et al. (2014) and Hanes and Machin (2014), and more recently Mello (2019) and Carr et al. (2020).

3.7. Summary of Data Issues When Measuring Crime

Merged with the survey data containing individual behavioural information, researchers will be able to identify the relationship between education and crime and determine the mechanisms. However, this requires a national identification number in order to match individuals across different datasets. While administrative data provide information regarding arrests, convictions, imprisonments, educational levels and other characteristics, survey and experimental data provide more insights into individual behaviour such as risk and time preferences, victimisation and beliefs. Moreover, survey data can provide information on the criminal earnings and behaviour of individuals which is not always observed by the police. Possessing information on earnings from criminal activity allows researchers to more clearly define the income channel, as earnings from crime are an opportunity cost of legal labour and should be included in the analysis (see Section 2.1). Currently, only a few papers have been able to identify earnings from criminal activity (Grogger, 1998; Levitt and Venkatesh, 2000). Combining these types of datasets would allow for the identification of the mechanisms – cognitive and non-cognitive – filling a crucial gap in the literature. However, for such a feature to be achieved, countries must first create a unique ID number to accurately merge individuals across datasets.

Large administrative data will also help isolate the heterogeneous effects of education on specific demographic groups due to less sample size restrictions. Heterogeneity analysis will allow researchers to offer important insight into groups most affected by education policies so policy makers can make more accurate cost-benefit analyses and invest more efficiently in education.

Finally, there is evidence that the significance of the schooling effect depends on the measurement of crime. For example, Hjalmarsson et al. (2015) find a significant effect on the crime extensive margin, the probability an individual commits any crime and arrest rates, but no effect on the intensive margin, or the number of crimes committed. This suggests that school has a greater effect on crime at the extensive margin rather than the intensive margin and demonstrates the importance of individual-level data which, compared to police recorded data, allow researchers to look at the extension margin.

While an ideal dataset will go a long way for research in economics and crime, researchers still need a quasi-experimental setting to find exogenous sources of schooling variation in order to identify a causal relationship between education and crime. Finding ideal policies and events to use as natural experiments is still crucial. In the next section, we will review the most common methods used to identify a causal relationship between education and crime.

4. METHODS AND ESTIMATES OF THE (CAUSAL) IMPACT OF EDUCATION ON CRIME

Early research used naïve estimators – estimators which capture correlations between education and schooling – to find a relationship between human capital (wages and education levels) and crime. Grogger (1998) used the National Longitudinal Survey of Youth (NLSY) from 1980 to estimate the correlation between wages and criminal activity of males ages 17–23 not in school or the military. He found that, on average, a 10 per cent increase in wages is correlated with a reduction in the criminal participation rate by 1.8 percentage points. Education is not significantly correlated with crime in the model including wages but education is a significant determinant of wages in the model. While a causal interpretation cannot be applied, this suggests a possible income channel as a source of crime deterrent.

Identifying the causal relationship between education and crime is difficult as the traditional ordinary least-squares (OLS) estimator is biased, due to endogeneity caused by the omitted variables bias, reverse causality and/or the selection bias (Lochner, 2004; Lochner and Moretti, 2004). The OLS estimator suffers from omitted variable bias due to the exclusion of unobservable individual characteristics such as intelligence, ability and propensity to criminality (Machin et al., 2011). These characteristics are in turn likely correlated with education levels, as those with higher intelligence and ability are more likely to have more education while those with high propensity to commit crime will have low education due to their taste in crime. At the aggregate levels, there may be time-variant characteristics that cannot be measured which are correlated with education and crime levels of an area, especially due to budget constraints of governments.

Further, the OLS estimator suffers from reverse causality as crime could also have an effect on education (see for example Webbink et al., 2013). Those who previously committed crimes are less likely to gain further education due to a possible interruption in schooling during the criminal justice process which would in turn make them more likely to commit additional crimes (Hjalmarsson, 2008; Koppensteiner and Menezes, 2021). The OLS estimator of the effect of education on crime would capture this relationship as a deterrent effect of education on crime, overestimating the true relationship.

Finally, there is concern of a selection bias as individuals with low expected returns to education relative to crime will self-select into a criminal career rather than continue education. This will bias the returns to education vis-à-vis crime upwards (more negative coefficient) since the coefficient will also capture the selection bias. Moreover, youths who plan to commit crime as adults due to higher expected returns or crime propensity will self-select into the school dropout group.

In an ideal setting, researchers would be able to randomly select adolescents to continue schooling or to drop out with full compliance. This would create an exogenous source of schooling levels which can be exploited to measure the relationship between education and crime. Since such experiments are unlikely to occur, researchers have used natural or quasi-experiments to exploit exogenous variations in education levels. To argue causality, researchers must use exogenous changes in education levels to instrument the education levels of individuals. Examples of quasi-experiments include compulsory school leaving age laws (Lochner and Moretti, 2004; Machin et al., 2011; Hjalmarsson et al., 2015; Anderson, 2014; Bell et al., 2016), school starting age (McAdams, 2016), twin fixed effects (Webbink et al., 2013; Bennett, 2018), teacher training days (Jacob and Lefgren, 2003) and teacher strikes (Luallen, 2006) which created a variation in schooling that is not correlated with omitted factors such as ability and taste for crime. In what follows, we will describe in turn each of the main methods used to overcome the deficiencies of the OLS estimator, obtain causal estimates of the education-crime relationship and discuss the (heterogeneous) results they yield.

4.1. Raising of the School Leaving Age (RoSLA)

One prominent identification strategy used by researchers to estimate the effects of education is raising of the school leaving age (RoSLA). These laws can include policies that dictate the minimum number of schooling years or minimum age that adolescents can leave school. This identification strategy is valid because the policy change induces extra years of schooling and does not have a direct influence on crime rates except through changes in education attainment.

A two-stage least-squares (2SLS) estimator or instrumental variables (IV) (Lochner and Moretti, 2004; Machin et al., 2011) is the most common estimation approach used to overcome the deficiencies of the OLS estimator and obtain causal estimates of the education-crime relationship. The first stage estimates the effect of RoSLA laws on education levels, capturing an exogenous change in education. This exogenous change is then used to estimate the effect of education on crime in the second stage. However, for a causal relationship to be measured, RoSLA must have a significant effect on education levels in the first stage. Moreover, the effect measured in the second stage is a local average treatment effect (LATE), measuring only the effect for those induced into additional schooling by the RoSLA (Imbens and Angrist, 1994). These individuals also have the lowest marginal gains from education in terms of human capital and future wage increases suggesting that this group would have the lowest returns from education vis-à-vis crime reduction (Lochner, 2004). Therefore, positive returns to education may be due in part to non-cognitive benefits of education in addition to improved expected income with additional schooling. The former can be addressed by the IV estimation (which assumes the effect of the policy is through the schooling variable), and the latter will be discussed at length in this section.

In addition to a two-stage least squares (2SLS) approach where increases of the school-leaving age laws are used to instrument years of schooling, researchers have also used the reduced form equation, such that the laws are permitted to have a direct effect on crime instead of the effect being through a measure for the educational attainment of an individual or cohort (years of schooling or qualification/diploma level). The model includes RoSLA changes as a regime change binary variable and estimates an average treatment effect (ATE) using OLS. One prominent reason for this approach is that education policies such as minimum schooling laws are usually multifaceted and can have influences on education and adolescent human capital through mechanisms other than additional schooling. For example, education reform could also include additional funding to improve the quality of schooling.[2]

Lochner and Moretti (2004) applied the 2SLS estimator to identify the causal relationship between education and crime. Using US Census data from 1960–80, the authors use variations in RoSLA (and timing) across different US states. They found that an extra year of education reduces the probability of imprisonment by slightly more than 0.1 percentage point for whites and by about 0.4 percentage points for blacks. Moreover, blacks were more treated by the education expansion than their white counterparts. Incarceration rates among black graduates were 7 percentage points lower than among dropouts, and high school graduates had a 0.76 percentage point lower probability of incarceration than did dropouts. They calculated that if high school graduation rates had been 1 percentage point higher in 1990, 400 fewer murders and 8000 fewer assaults would be realised. Furthermore, the effect they found is similar to the product of the effect of schooling on wages and effect of wages on crime (Gould et al., 2002), suggesting that the effect of extra schooling is driven by the income channel.

Machin et al. (2011) used RoSLA from 15 to 16 in England and Wales in 1972 to instrument education achievement in a regression discontinuity design in time (RDiT) setting. RDiT is used to identify changes that occur following the implementation of a policy (see for example Davis 2008; Auffhammer and Kellogg, 2011). It assumes that given the temporal proximity of those impacted by the policy change, such as an education reform, and the cohorts not affected by the policy change that any observed difference in outcomes between these groups is due to the reform itself. The authors found that a 1 per cent reduction in the population with no educational qualifications and a 1-year increase in the average age men leave school led to a 0.851–0.999 per cent and 0.26–0.30 per cent fall in property crime convictions, respectively.

A summary of the main estimated impact uncovered by research exploiting RoSLA to identify the effect of schooling on crime can be found in Figure 7.1. Across the studies the relative effect of schooling – no matter how measured – on crime rates is similar between property and violent crimes, with perhaps a slightly larger and more often statistically significant effect observed for property crimes. As property crimes are likely to be financially motivated, we expect property crimes to be significantly affected if the instrument has a significant influence on education attainment which then changes expected legitimate wages. Significant findings suggest the existence of an income channel. Violent crime on the other hand is typically not financially motivated, suggesting that there are other mechanisms at work other than the income channel. It is likely given the significant coefficients for violent crime that additional schooling has positive non-cognitive effects, such as patience, which reduces violent crime rates as violent crimes should not respond to changes in the income channel.

While the use of RoSLA as an instrument attempts to address the problem of endogeneity, there are some weaknesses worth discussing. First, 2SLS or IV estimate a local treatment effect, therefore only measuring the effect of additional education for those induced by the policy. These individuals do not reflect the general population so the results cannot necessarily be extrapolated across all groups. Furthermore, the induced population will have low marginal returns to education and therefore the effects on wages (and thus indirect effect on crime) will be minimal, potentially minimising the effect of education and wages for the entire population. Low marginal returns for compliers could explain the results of Pischke and von Wachter (2008) who found no effect of compulsory schooling changes on labour market outcomes in Germany. They attributed this to the role of apprenticeships and the possibility that compliers who drop out after ninth grade are no more productive than those who finished after eighth grade. Meanwhile, the effect size

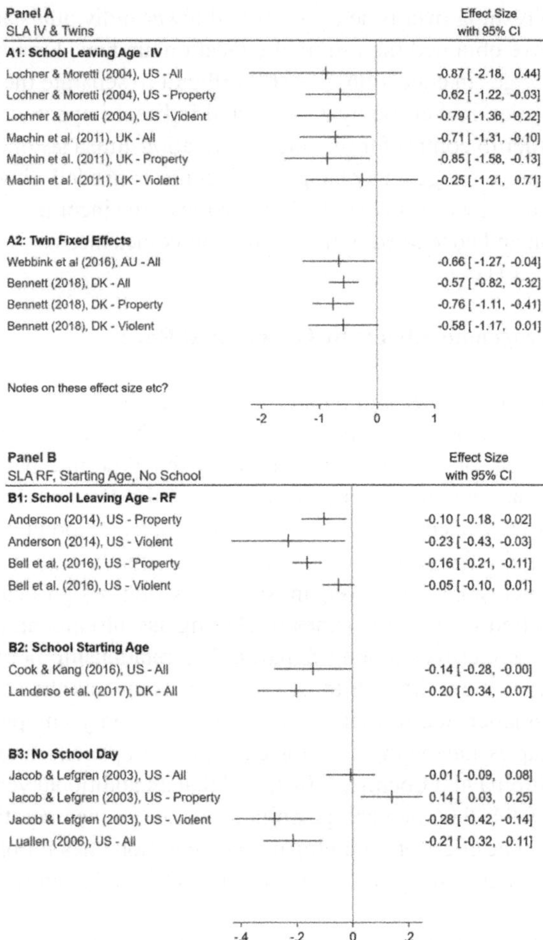

Notes: Panel A provides estimates of the effect of schooling on criminal activity where the identification relies on raising of the school leaving age (RoSLA) policies as instruments (A1) or twin fixed effects (A2). Panel B provides estimates of the effect of schooling on criminal activity using RoSLA policies in a reduced form (B1), school starting age (B2) and no school days (B3) to identify the relationship between education and crime. The first two groups show the effect of an additional year of education. The third group shows the effect of mandatory schooling policy changes. The last identification method finds contemporaneous effects, and the coefficient can be interpreted as the effect of not having school on juvenile crime that day. The treatment effect can be interpreted as the per cent change in aggregate crime (rate) for either a one unit change in education (A1 and A2), a change in RoSLA policy (B1), a change at the discontinuity for school cohort cut-off birthday (B2) or a dummy equal to 1 for exogenous no-school days (B3).

Figure 7.1 *Summary of estimates of the causal impact of education on crime (expressed in % change of not dropping out of school or being in school)*

has been diminishing over time as fewer and fewer individuals are treated as they would have obtained the minimal education anyhow. Finally, even with exogenous changes in education, it is still difficult to separate the relationship between education and crime by a direct and indirect impact via the income channel. In order to control for this indirect relationship, a second instrument or identification of exogenous changes in income is needed, though controlling for individual income may still help if some of the income is uncorrelated with education and correlated with criminal outcomes measures (Oreopoulos and Salvanes, 2011).

4.2. Heterogenous Effects by Gender and Race

Differences between males and females can be clearly seen as coefficients for female crime which are insignificant for most of the studies. While we find a significant effect of additional education on female crime participation in some studies for some crime types (Anderson, 2014; Bennett, 2018), each of the magnitudes of the coefficients is lower than the corresponding male coefficient. Results for females by crime type differ greatly across studies with conflicting conclusions. However, most studies find a significant deterrent effect of education for violent crimes (including assault) and an insignificant effect for property crimes among females. The relationship between education and crime is more difficult to estimate for women as the sample size is significantly smaller due to their lower criminal activity compared to men, though this gap is narrowing (see for example Campanello and Gavrilova, 2018). Cano-Urbina and Lochner (2019) find that an additional year of schooling leads to a 0.04–0.06 percentage point reduction in incarceration rates for white females. The effect of schooling on incarceration rates for black females was slightly greater in magnitude but was not statistically significant due to a smaller sample size.

Among males we find more significant and larger effects across different crime types and aggregate crime. Overall, education has a similar (relative) long-term deterrent effect on property crime and violent crime (Figure A1, studies 1, 6, 7, 9, 10, 11). From this we can postulate that the significant effects measured in total crime rates (rather than individual arrests) are largely driven by effects on males, who are both more affected by additional schooling and commit a large majority of crimes.

In addition to a significant difference between the effects on males and females, there is evidence of a difference between races. Most research finds that the effect of education on crime reduction is stronger for blacks than whites in the US (the research of Bell et al. (2016) is an exception to this). One explanation for this is that whites are less induced by the reforms as more (especially relative to blacks) are always compliers, causing the instruments to be weak. Moreover, the coefficient could be *greater* for blacks who as a group are under-investing and therefore have the highest marginal gains from additional schooling with respect to human capital and wage gains.

4.3. The Vicissitudes of Birth

Another strain of literature in crime and education uses the vicissitudes of birth to quantify the causal relationship between education and crime. These identification methods include twin comparisons and birth timing relative to school starting age.

Data using same-gendered twins would control for the unobserved genetic and environmental factors that cause endogeneity of the model. This is because twins share the same household and general social environment and are in the same cohort and share much (dizygotic twins) or all (monozygotic twins) genetic information (have same 'genetic make-up'). Therefore, any differences in education attainment between the two twins are argued to be exogenous to these forces (Ashenfelter and Krueger, 1994), though the use of twins to identify causal effects of education has been criticised (see for example Bound and Solon, 1999).

Comparing same-gendered twins born in Denmark in 1965–82, Bennett (2018) finds that completion of upper secondary education reduces total crimes for men by 57 per cent, property crimes by 76 per cent and violent crimes by 59 per cent. Men are more impacted by changes in education levels compared to women, and adolescents from low-income families are more impacted at a young age, but the gap narrows with time. Webbink et al. (2013) estimate that completing high school reduces the probability of incarceration by 2.6 percentage points using Australian twin data. The authors also found that early arrests had a negative impact on education attainment.

Finally, Marie et al. (2013) and Landersø et al. (2017) use timing of birth as an exogenous source of variation in education levels. Previous research has shown a relationship between education outcomes and timing of birth (Angrist and Krueger 1991, 1992; Bedard and Dhuey 2006; Crawford et al., 2010; and Grenet, 2013). Marie et al. (2013) find that students in the Netherlands who were 11 months older than their peers in the first year of primary school are 7–9 per cent more likely to leave schooling without qualifications. In turn, they estimated a 34 per cent lower probability of arrest resulting from completing a high-school degree. Landersø et al. (2017) on the other hand find that being old for their school grade (cohort) reduces propensity to commit a crime at each age until 19 (boys) or 15 (girls).

> The fading effect suggests that crime at the extensive margin is aligned to key life events rather than age. If criminal behaviour instead was fixed to age, any effects of

> school starting age on crime should shift the crime-age profile in a vertical direction . . . the fact that the effects only approach zero from below suggests that the crime-age profile is shifted in both vertical and horizontal directions.
>
> (Landersø et al., 2017)

For girls, higher school starting age initially reduces crime (no late catch up). For boys this lasts until 22 (reduction in propensity to commit crime up to the age of 22).

Together the two studies show that there is a trade-off to education expansion. Starting school at an older age will cause adolescents to remain in schooling (due to RoSLA) until a relatively later age but, on average, the students are more likely to have no qualifications. The former will lead to a contemporaneous decrease in (property) crime due to the incapacitation effect, while the latter will lead to an increase in future crime due to lower human capital.[3] Moreover, other research finds that, conditional on school grade, educational attainment measures such as grade point average (GPA) and standardised test scores increase with age and could mitigate some of the negative effect vis-à-vis a higher propensity of dropping out.

Among the strain of literature using timing of birth as an identification tool, there is an argument over whether timing of birth is truly exogenous (Buckles and Hungerman, 2013). In the US, there is a significant correlation between mother, family characteristics and birth timing including a decrease in children born to non-teenagers during winter months. With respect to education, parents may plan the timing of birth in order to maximise the future human capital of the child. Buckles and Hungerman (2013) conclude that including family background characteristics could explain 25–50 per cent of the relationship between timing of birth and later outcomes.

4.4. Contemporaneous Effects

To estimate contemporaneous effects of schooling on crime researchers use exogenous days off during the school year to test for the presence of any concentration or incapacitation effects. These studies look at the effect of exogenous free days during the academic year on contemporaneous juvenile crime during the school week. Examples of exogenous free days include teacher strikes (Luallen, 2006) and teacher training days (Jacob and Lefgren, 2003). The use of exogenous free days is important as planned free days such as holidays, weekends and summers are anticipated and criminal activity can be planned with this in mind. This technique uses a dummy variable for exogenous free days, controlling for other free days, to capture any contemporaneous effects of not being incapacitated by school on juvenile crime. While in the previous examples, researchers were interested in the effect of education policies in the past on future crime rates, this method looks at juvenile crime rates on the day of the exogenous change in schooling to evaluate the contemporaneous effects.

Teacher training days are considered to be exogenous as they occur on days with similar expected payoffs to crime as scheduled school days. Jacob and Lefgren (2003) find that during teacher training days, juvenile property crime rates are 15 per cent higher while juvenile violent crime rates are 30 per cent lower – additional evidence in favour of the incapacitation and concentration effects. The authors rule out the mechanism of a reduction in crime costs due to facilitated coordination among criminally active students. Therefore, they conclude that a concentration effect may increase crimes by increasing negative interactions between high-risk students.

Luallen (2006) uses unexpected school closings driven by teacher strikes as an instrument for student absence from school. Teacher strikes are used as exogenous shocks to school attendance as they are unanticipated changes of time spent in education. Expected free days such as weekends, holidays and summer breaks are not considered exogenous as the benefits to crime are different during the weekends (more people out shopping) and summers (high temperatures). Luallen (2006) finds that during school days, property crime decreases by up to 29 per cent while violent crime increases by up to 36 per cent. The former can be attributed to an anticipation effect, and the latter can be attributed to a concentration effect. Furthermore, no displacement effect was found.

Akee et al. (2014) use the furloughing of school teachers in Hawaii in the 2009–2010 academic year to estimate contemporaneous effects of education. On days of furlough, the number of juvenile arrests significantly decreased for assault and drug offences, with no changes in burglaries. A decrease in violent crime and drug offences provides evidence of a significant concentration effect of school. The effects of the furlough are also heterogeneous, with males and low-income areas being more affected. Bell et al. (2018) estimate the contemporaneous effects of education expansion and estimate that the changes in compulsory schooling not only reduce crime during the additional schooling, but have medium-run effects as well. The authors argue that this is evidence in favour of a dynamic incapacitation effect which changes the age-crime profile. It could be, they argue, that completing schooling without a criminal record due to incapacitation prevents individuals from later beginning criminal participation.

Meanwhile, Huttunen et al. (2018) exploit a discontinuity in eligibility for upper-secondary schools in Finland based on grade point average up to year nine to identify the effect of education on crime and the mechanisms. Following admission to higher quality upper-secondary school tracks, male crime participation in property, traffic and drug-related offences is reduced up to five years later while there are no significant labour market impacts or long-term reduction in crime to indicate the income channel. They attribute their findings to the incapacitation and dynamic incapacitation effects and conclude that in addition to these two mechanisms schooling can deter crime by 'offering different peer groups and future prospects that may all have an impact on criminal behaviour'.

4.5. Early Childhood Education and Interventions

The effect of early childhood education programmes and interventions is also of importance in the discussion of the crime-education relationship. The four most prominent programmes found in the literature are the Abecedarian Project, Chicago Child Parent Centers (CPC), High/Scope Perry Preschool Program (PPP) and the Infant Health and Development Program (IHDP). These programmes all took place in the US and targeted low socio-economic students by providing access to early childhood education (three to five years of age) which is otherwise not universally provided in the US.

Research on CPC and PPP found significant improvements in educational attainment and participation in crime (Reynolds et al., 2001; Nores et al., 2005). The Chicago project led to a 30 per cent decrease in probability of having been arrested by the age of 18 while the Perry project reduced the percentage of individuals arrested five or more times by 30 per cent for males and females. Moreover, Donohue and Siegelman (1998) found that 40 per cent fewer treated individuals were arrested at least once by the age of 19. Meanwhile, the IHDP had no significant effects on schooling or future crime outcomes (McCormick et al., 2006). Finally, the Abecedarian Project increased enrolment in four-year colleges but had no significant effect on future crime outcomes (Clarke and Campbell, 1998).

While the differences in the programmes allow there to exist many explanations for the differences in the results, the most plausible reason is differences in pre-treatment and control group graduation rates. Abecedarian and IHDP had higher education attainment relative to Perry and CPC which had graduation rates under 50 per cent. As such, we expect greater effects in lower-achieving areas as they have the greatest marginal benefit of investment into early human capital and learning capacity.

Compared to the previous four studies, we now look at the impact of a larger programme, Head Start. Research into the effects of Head Start has been conducted by Garces et al. (2002), Carneiro and Ginja (2009) and Deming (2009). Garces et al. (2002) and Deming (2009) find contradicting results despite using similar methods. The former finds a 12 percentage point decrease in probability of being booked or charged with a crime for blacks only, and the latter found no significant effects. Both however find a significant increase in both high school graduation rates and university enrolment of 11–20 percentage points and 14–28 percentage points, respectively. Carneiro and Ginja use a regression discontinuity design (RDD) to exploit the programme eligibility cut-off at the poverty line. The authors only find a 47 per cent decrease in the expected number of arrests for more severe infractions by individuals with risk levels at or above the 13th percentile, suggesting the programme had a significant impact only on the most high-risk adolescents. The coefficient can be interpreted as a local effect at the programme eligibility cut-off and therefore captures the expected effect if the eligibility cut-off is shifted marginally. Internal validity becomes less clear as we move away from the cut-off so we cannot assume a 47 per cent decrease in the general population.

A more recent programme, Fast Track, followed students in grades 1–10 in four cities in the US. The programme targeted high-risk children who exhibited conduct problems from high crime and poverty neighbourhoods. Moving away from crime, research has found a significant positive effect on preventing childhood and adolescent externalising psychiatric disorders and antisocial behaviour among the most at-risk kindergartners. They concluded that 'long-term, developmentally appropriate services that target child social-cognitive and cognitive skills, peer relationships, and parenting improved antisocial outcomes for highest risk youth' (Conduct Problems Prevention Research Group, 2010).

Research on the effect of early childhood education on adult criminal participation provides two main takeaways. First, the crime reducing effect of early childhood education may be very large in magnitude and have significant fiscal benefits to society. Second, additional research is needed, particularly for large universal programmes, in order to understand better the mechanisms behind the effect and heterogenous effects across different populations. Current research is limited by the small sample number of programme participants and is limited to the US, raising concerns of the external validity of the findings. While research on early childhood education programmes outside of the US exists, none has connected it with later criminal activity of the programme participants.

4.6. School Quality

Researchers have also exploited school lotteries as a source of exogenous variety in school quality. Cullen et al. (2006) researched the effects of winning a high school lottery in Chicago and found that winning the lottery significantly increased enrolment in high-quality schools. However, no evidence was found that lottery winners perform better in academic measures including test scores, enrolment, attendance etc. Instead, lottery winners had higher dropout rates potentially due to a mismatch between schools' abilities and students' needs. Despite little improvement in education attainment, winners reported 60 per cent fewer arrests on a ninth-grade (ages 14/15) student survey. This could be due to a difference in etiquette and criminal procedures between high- and low-quality schools as high-quality schools may report less delinquent behaviour to the police and instead keep the punishment within the school and not involve the criminal justice system in addition to a more structured discipline system.

Deming (2011) looked at effects of open-enrolment in a North Carolina school district to find any long-term impact on crime. Deming finds that winning the lottery significantly increased the quality of the school attended but had no effects on academic achievements. High-risk – defined by demographics and previous test scores – lottery winners had 45 per cent fewer adult felony arrests.

Desegregation also provides an opportunity to study the relationship between school quality and crime. Following the ruling of *Brown v. Board of Education of Topeka*, the quality of schools attended by black Americans improved as previously segregated schools had a great racial disparity in investment of public funds. First, Guryan (2004) found that after desegregation high school graduation rates among blacks increased by 2–3 percentage points while high school graduation rates among whites remained constant. Next, Weiner et al. (2009) found that in the five years following *Brown v. Board of Education of Topeka* while homicide deaths among 16- to 19-year-old blacks and whites decreased, arrest rates for the same age group only decreased among blacks. This suggests that acts of homicides by blacks declined due to an increase in schooling after desegregation.

Taking all of this into account, research has shown that school quality can be a significant crime deterrent. Policy makers could find it more cost-effective to invest in improving school quality or increasing access to high-quality schools for high-risk students versus traditional crime deterrent measures. Robust results show no significant improvement in test scores and weaker evidence of no effect on quantity of education. From this we draw two conclusions. First, quality of education, even without human capital improvements, plays a role in the crime reducing effect of education. Second, by finding no improvement on test scores, it is likely that the reduction in crime can be attributed to non-cognitive benefits from a higher quality education. For example, higher quality schools may have a more structured and disciplined approach that is beneficial for preventing future criminal behaviour of high-risk students.

4.7. Summary of Estimates of the Causal Impact of Education on Crime

We present summaries of the findings from this literature in Figures 7.1 and A1, respectively. Figure A1 in the Appendix covers most papers we survey in this chapter and summarises the methods they exploit, the data they use and their findings. Figure 7.1 is more limited in scope as it only presents more directly comparable estimates across a number of methods and papers of the impact on crime of, in most cases, dropping out of school or of not being in school on a specific day (i.e., contemporaneous effects).

The causal impact of education on crime is presented in percentage change for all studies and by broad offence type (when available), by dividing the estimated coefficient by the crime baseline it relates to. The figure is split into two panels because of the large difference in the size of estimates between the methods. However, these show that across papers within the same method there is a lot of similarity in the magnitude expressed in percentage change. The main conclusion is that finishing high school or being in school has a significant (large) negative causal effect on the amount of crime observed at the cohort or individual level.

5. COST-BENEFIT ANALYSIS

The consensus of education and crime research suggests great crime-reduction benefits can be achieved through investment in education. While policing and criminal justice are traditional tools used to reduce crime, evidence suggests that education may perhaps be the most efficient crime fighting tool! Calculations by Lochner and Moretti (2004), Machin et al. (2011) and Donohue and Siegelman (1998) even suggest that human capital-oriented policies are competitive with more traditional law enforcement and incarceration efforts when all benefits are considered.

Lochner and Moretti (2004) estimate that the total savings from increasing high school completion rates by 1 per cent is 1.4 billion 1993 USD per year. This is largely driven by the social benefits of a reduction in murders (by 373). There is a saving of $1170–2100 per additional high school graduate (per year), or 14–26 per cent of the private return to schooling. Meanwhile, the cost of an additional year of schooling is $6000 per student in 1990, suggesting that the monetary benefit of crime reduction covers one-quarter of the costs if the programme is well-targeted.

Anderson (2014) found that benefits can be calculated as ranging between £54.1 and £62.7 million. The cost of making 1 per cent of those with no qualifications stay on and get some qualification as a result of raising the school leaving age would be a little over £20 million each year, presuming that the 1 per cent who could benefit from staying on and getting some qualifications can be well targeted.

Machin et al. (2011) estimated a net crime reduction of between 39 325 and 45 836 offences following the education reform in England and Wales in 1972 using the RoSLA to identify an exogenous variation in schooling. The average social benefits due to the crime reduction range between £54.1 and £62.7 million. This is modest relative to Lochner and Moretti (2004) who found a significant impact on violent crime which carries greater societal costs when looking at the effects of RoSLA in the US. With a cost of £20 million each year to make 1 per cent of those with no qualifications stay on and get any qualifications, education expansion policies can be cost-effective through crime reduction alone assuming that the 1 per cent induced into education can be well targeted. They furthermore argue that increasing high school graduation rates is a more effective crime deterrent than additional policing.

Groot and van den Brink (2010) compare the costs of additional white-collar crime and the benefits of a reduction in other crimes in the Netherlands using parental characteristics as instruments for an individual's education. They find that an increase in the average level of schooling of the population by one year would save society €623 million per year in cost of criminality while the cost of the increase of tax fraud is €45 million per year.

Comparing the effects of minimum dropout age and grade requirement policies, Bell et al. (2018), who look at the effect of RoSLA in the US, similarly find education expansion to be extremely cost-effective with respect to crime reduction. Following the methodology of Lochner and Moretti (2004), they find that for every dollar spent on additional education, $0.94 is saved on crime (and imprisonment) reduction. When considering the effects of dynamic incapacitation, the crime benefits are nearly double the education costs.

Contemporaneously, the benefits of education are less significant due to an increase in violent crimes. While there is a reduction in property crimes, the cost associated with violent crime is far greater than that of property crimes. Jacob and Lefgren (2003), who used exogenous teacher training days to evaluate contemporaneous effects, found that lengthening the school year by 1 day will lead to a decrease of 0.29 property crimes and an increase of 0.25 violent crimes in a city with a population of about 120 000. The reduction of property crime would result in a saving of approximately $318 while additional violence associated with having school in session another day costs about $2170.

Early childhood programmes are perhaps where the greatest benefits can be found. Given the estimated $1.2 to 2 million cost to society to rehabilitate high-risk youth (Cohen, 1998) and a cost of $58 000 per youth over ten years, the Fast Track programme would be cost-effective if only 4 per cent of the individuals are *impacted* high-risk youths. Conduct Problems Prevention Research Group (2007) estimates that 16–20 per cent of the treated sample fell into this category, making the programme extremely cost-effective. The Perry Preschool Program was also extreme cost-effective even when only considering the benefits from a reduction in criminal activity. Donohue and Siegelman (1998) hypothesise that a nationwide Perry Preschool Program targeting the

6 per cent most high-risk would be as cost-effective as using incarceration as a crime deterrent if the nationwide programme is half as effective as the 40 percent estimated for the PPP.

Taken all together, the cost-benefit analysis performed in the research suggests that education can be extremely cost-effective when just considering the reduction in crime, critically assuming education policies can effectively target high-risk youths.

6. DISCUSSION AND CONCLUSIONS: WHERE DO WE GO FROM HERE?

While great steps have been taken to identify the causal relationship between education and crime in the past two decades, there are still many questions left unanswered. Researchers need to disentangle the main underlying mechanisms of the relationship between education and crime. Does education reduce crime due to the income channel or does the effect of education lie in the non-cognitive benefits of education such as changes in risk and time preferences? Empirical estimations of the mechanisms will allow policy makers and educators to identify ways to best reduce crime through education policy. This could include subsidies to lower the costs of education as well as focussing curriculum best adapted to change the non-cognitive behaviour of adolescents.

While evidence largely suggests that education reduces crime, there is also evidence that some education fields are complementary to criminal capital. For this reason, white-collar crime is often committed by the highly educated, suggesting a positive relationship. Future research could use administrative data matched with large self-reported crime data to identify education fields with positive effects of education on crime. Moreover, educated individuals may be more attracted to more ideological crime such as terrorism and hate crimes. Krueger and Malečková (2003) found that Hezbollah operatives and Israeli settlers who attacked Palestinians did not come from especially impoverished backgrounds and the later were overwhelmingly from high-paying occupations.

Education quality might matter more than quantity and for the design of optimal policies. The importance of education quality could explain why instrumental variables (IV) estimates are not significant. Changes in education policy, the instrument, may not affect (average) educational achievement but may impact the overall school quality. This can have potential non-cognitive benefits for the pupils and reduce crime through this channel rather than an income channel. It is also possible that education quality – and its influence on non-cognitive abilities – is not an important factor but rather perception of the school's quality has an impact on labour market outcomes for the students and higher education opportunities.

As discussed in Section 3, there is likely an effect of crime on education. At micro and macro levels, it seems that the inverse relationship is significant. Researchers find, depending on the timing of events, that past juvenile crimes and exposure to crime impact education attainment and academic performance (see Hjalmarsson, 2008; Webbink et al., 2013; Ward and Williams, 2015; Koppensteiner and Menezes, 2021).

Of the previously discussed research, the vast majority originates from highly developed countries. Future researchers could turn their attention to developing nations. Researching the effects of education in developing countries would be interesting as research on developed countries finds that it is those on the lower bounds of the socio-economic ladder that are most impacted by education expansion.

Furthermore, as education levels increase, it is possible that the age-crime curve is shifting to the right, so that peak years now occur later due to changes in average schooling. Previously, criminal activity was estimated to peak at the ages of 16–18 and decrease in the late teens and early twenties. It is possible that as the average schooling age has increased, there has been a similar shift in the peak crime age so that it occurs when most of the population finishes schooling. This would suggest that the incapacitation effect is limited and only displaces crime to a later point in time.

Finally, a general equilibrium effect could exist where an increase in the education levels of the individuals around you may decrease your own likelihood of participating in criminal activity. As others' education attainment increases, their criminality should also decrease, reducing the local criminal network and thereby decreasing your own expected benefits of crime.

NOTES

1. The General Educational Development (GED) tests measure proficiency in science, mathematics, social studies, reading and writing. The GED test in the US was introduced in 1942 to provide a way for veterans without a high school diploma to earn a secondary school credential. The GED programme has evolved so that today the credential is the 'secondary chance' route to a high school diploma for school dropouts in the US.
2. Acemoglu and Angrist (2001) first used raising of the school-leaving age laws as instruments to estimate the social returns of education (the increase in total earnings resulting from a one-year increase in average schooling) as 'individual education and average schooling levels are correlated with wages for a variety of reasons, so the observed association between schooling variables and wages is not necessarily causal'. They found that compulsory attendance laws had a statistically significant influence on individuals' schooling in the US for the years 1950–80.
3. Bell et al. (2018) also found that RoSLA have a comparably large effect on high-risk adolescents who committed a crime as adolescents. Together this provides additional evidence that education expansion programmes will be more cost-effective with respect to crime if they are able to precisely target high-risk and under-invested groups.

REFERENCES

Acemoglu, D. and Autor, D. (2011). "Skills, Tasks and Technologies: Implications for Employment and Earnings". In Ashenfelter, O. and Card, D. (eds.) *Handbook of Labor Economics*, Volume 4, pp. 1043–171, Amsterdam: Elsevier.

Acemoglu, D. and Angrist, J. (2001). "How Large are Human Capital Externalities? Evidence from Compulsory Schooling Laws". In Bernanke, B. and Rogoff, K. (eds.) *NBER Macroeconomics Annual 2000*, Cambridge MA: MIT Press.

Auffhammer, M. and Kellogg, R. (2011). "Clearing the Air? The Effects of Gasoline Content Regulation on Air Quality". *American Economic Review*, 101(6): 2687–722.

Akee, R. K., Copeland, W. E., Keeler, G., Angold, A., and Costello, E. J. (2010). "Parents' Incomes and Children's Outcomes: A Quasi-Experiment". *American Economic Journal: Applied Economics*, 2(1): 86–115.

Akee, R. Q., Halliday, T. J., and Kwak, S. (2014). "Investigating the Effects of Furloughing Public School Teachers on Juvenile Crime in Hawaii". *Economics of Education Review*, 42: 1–11.

Anderson, D. (2014). "In School and Out of Trouble? The Minimum Dropout Age and Juvenile Crime". *Review of Economics and Statistics*, 96(2): 318–31.

Angrist, J. D. and Krueger, A. B. (1991). "Does Compulsory School Attendance Affect Schooling and Earnings?". *The Quarterly Journal of Economics*, 106(4): 979–1014.

Angrist, J. D. and Krueger, A. B. (1992). *Estimating the Payoff to Schooling Using the Vietnam-era Draft Lottery.* National Bureau of Economic Research (NBER) working paper series, number 4067. https://back.nber.org/bibliographic/w4067.bib

Apel, R., Paternoster, R., Bushway, S. D., and Brame. R. (2006). "A Job Isn't Just a Job: The Differential Impact of Formal versus Informal Work on Adolescent Problem Behavior". *Crime and Delinquency*, 52: 333–69.

Apel, R., Bushway, S., Brame, R., Haviland, A. M., Nagin, D. S., and Paternoster, R. (2007). "Unpacking the Relationship between Adolescent Employment and Antisocial Behavior: A Matched Samples Comparison". *Criminology*, 45(1): 67–97.

Ashenfelter, O. and Krueger, A. (1994). "Estimates of the Economic Return to Schooling from a New Sample of Twins". *The American Economic Review*, 84(5): 1157–73.

Bautista-Arredondo, S., González, A., Servan-Mori, E., Beynon, F., Juarez-Figueroa, L., Conde-Glez, C. J., Gras, N., Sierra-Madero, J., Lopez-Ridaura, R., Volkow, P., and Bertossi, S. M. (2015). "A Cross-Sectional Study of Prisoners in Mexico City Comparing Prevalence of Transmissible Infections and Chronic Diseases with that in the General Population". *PLoS ONE*, 10(7): e0131718.

Beatton, T., Kidd, M., Machin, S., and Sarkar, D. (2018). "Larrikin Youth: New Evidence on Crime and Schooling". *Labour Economics*, 52: 149–59.

Becker, G. S. (1968). "Crime and Punishment: An Economic Approach". *Journal of Political Economy*, 76(2): 169–217.

Becker, G. S. and Mulligan, C. B. (1997). "The Endogenous Determination of Time Preference". *The Quarterly Journal of Economics*, 112(3): 729–58.

Bedard, K. and Dhuey, E. (2006). "The Persistence of Early Childhood Maturity: International Evidence of Long-run Age Effects". *The Quarterly Journal of Economics*, 121(4): 1437–72.

Bell, B., Jaitman, L., and Machin, S. (2014). "Crime Deterrence: Evidence from the London 2011 Riots". *The Economic Journal*, 124(576): 480–506.

Bell, B., Costa, R., and Machin, S. (2016). "Crime, Compulsory Schooling Laws and Education". *Economics of Education Review*, 54: 214–26.
Bell, B., Bindler, A., and Machin, S. (2018). "Crime Scars: Recessions and the Making of Career Criminals". *Review of Economics and Statistics*, 100(3): 392–404.
Bennett, P. (2018). "The Heterogeneous Effects of Education on Crime: Evidence from Danish Administrative Twin Data". *Labour Economics*, 52: 160–77.
Bound, J. and Solon, G. (1999). "Double Trouble: On the Value of Twins-based Estimation of the Return to Schooling": *Economics of Education Review,* 18(2): 169–82.
Brame, R., Bushway, S. D., Paternoster, R., and Apel, R. (2004). "Assessing the Effect of Adolescent Employment on Involvement in Criminal Activity". *Journal of Contemporary Criminal Justice*, 20(3): 236–56.
Buckles, K. S. and Hungerman, D. M. (2013). "Season of Birth and Later Outcomes: Old Questions, New Answers". *Review of Economics and Statistics*, 95(3): 711–24.
Butler, T. and Milner, L. (2003). *The 2001 New South Wales Inmate Health Survey.* Sydney: Corrections Health Service.
Campaniello, N. and Gavrilova, E. (2018). "Uncovering the Gender Participation Gap in Crime", *European Economic Review*, Elsevier, 109: 289–304.
Cano-Urbina, J., and Lochner, L. (2019). "The Effect of Education and School Quality on Female Crime". *Journal of Human Capital*, 13(2): 188–235.
Carneiro, P., and Ginja, R. (2009). *Preventing Behavior Problems in Childhood and Adolescence: Evidence from Head Start.* London: Department of Economics, University College London, Working Paper.
Carr, J., Clifton-Sprigg, J., James, J., and Vujić, S. (2020). "Love Thy Neighbour? Brexit and Hate Crime (No. 13902)". *IZA Discussion Papers.*
Chevalier, A., Harmon, C., O' Sullivan, V., and Walker, I. et al. (2013). "The Impact of Parental Income and Education on the Schooling of Their Children". *Journal of Economics*, 2(1): 1–22.
Chevalier, A. and Marie, O. (2022). "Risky Moms, Risky Kids? Fertility and Crime after the Fall of the Wall". CESifo Working Paper No. 9683, Available at SSRN: https://ssrn.com/abstract=4082588.
Clarke, S. H., and Campbell, F. A. (1998). "Can Intervention Early Prevent Crime Later? The Abecedarian Project Compared with Other Programs", *Early Childhood Research Quarterly*, 13(2): 319–43.
Clifton-Sprigg, J., James, J., and Vujić, S. (2020). "Freedom of Information (FOI) as a data collection tool for social scientists". *PloS ONE*, 15(2): e0228392.
Cohen, M. A. (1998). "The Monetary Value of Saving a High-risk Youth". *Journal of Quantitative Criminology*, 14(1): 5–33.
Coleman, C. and Moynihan, J. (1996). *Understanding Crime Data: Haunted by the Dark Figure*, Volume 120. Buckingham: Open University Press.
Conduct Problems Prevention Research Group. (2007). "The Fast Track Randomized Controlled Trial to Prevent Externalizing Psychiatric Disorders: Findings from Grades 3 to 9". *Journal of the American Academy of Child and Adolescent Psychiatry,* 46(10): 1250–62.
Conduct Problems Prevention Research Group. (2010). "Fast Track Intervention Effects on Youth Arrests and Delinquency", *Journal of Experimental Criminology*, 6: 131–57.
Crawford, C., Dearden, L., and Meghir, C. (2010). *When You Are Born Matters: The Impact of Date of Birth on Educational Outcomes in England.* Institute for Fiscal Studies, IFS Working Papers W10/06.

Cullen, J. B., Jacob, B. A., and Levitt, S. (2006). "The Effect of School Choice on Participants: Evidence from Randomized Lotteries". *Econometrica*, 74(5): 1191–230.

Dahl, G. B. and Lochner, L. (2012). "The Impact of Family Income on Child Achievement: Evidence from the Earned Income Tax Credit". *American Economic Review*, 102(5): 1927–56.

Davis, L. (2008). "The Effect of Driving Restrictions on Air Quality in Mexico City". *Journal of Political Economy*, 116(1): 38–81.

Deming, J. (2009). "Early Childhood Intervention and Life-cycle Skill Development: Evidence from Head Start". *American Economic Journal: Applied Economics*, 1(3): 111–34.

Deming, D. J. (2011). "Better Schools, Less Crime?". *The Quarterly Journal of Economics*, 126(4): 2063–115.

Donohue III, J. J. and Siegelman, P. (1998). "Allocating Resources Among Prisons and Social Programs in the Battle Against Crime". *The Journal of Legal Studies*, 27(1): 1–43.

Ehrlich, I. (1973). "Participation in Illegitimate Activities: A Theoretical and Empirical Investigation". *Journal of Political Economy*, 81(3): 521–65.

Entorf, H. (2009). *Crime and the Labour Market: Evidence from a Survey of Inmates.* Frankfurt: Goethe University.

Frederick, S., Loewenstein, G., and Donoghue, T. O. (2002). "Time Discounting and Time Preference: A Critical Review". *Journal of Economic Literature*, 40(2): 351–401.

Garces, E., Thomas, D., and Currie, J. (2002). "Longer-term Effects of Head Start". *American Economic Review*, 92(4): 999–1012.

Gould, E. D., Weinberg, B. A., and Mustard, D. B. (2002). "Crime Rates and Local Labor Market Opportunities in the United States: 1979–1997". *Review of Economics and Statistics*, 84(1): 45–61.

Grenet, J. (2013). Is Extending Compulsory Schooling Alone Enough to Raise Earnings? Evidence from French and British Compulsory Schooling Laws. *The Scandinavian Journal of Economics*, 115(1): 176–210.

Grogger, J. (1998). "Market Wages and Youth Crime". *Journal of Labor Economics*, 16(4): 756–91.

Groot, W. and van den Brink, H. M. (2010). "The Effects of Education on Crime". *Applied Economics*, 42(3): 279–89.

Guryan, J. (2004). "Desegregation and Black Dropout Rates". *American Economic Review*, 94(4): 919–43.

Hanes, E. and Machin, S. (2014). "Hate Crime in the Wake of Terror Attacks: Evidence from 7/7 and 9/11". *Journal of Contemporary Criminal Justice*, 30(3): 247–67.

Harlow, C. W. (2003). "Education and Correctional Populations". *Bureau of Justice Statistics Special Report*, U.S. Department of Justice. NCJ 195670.

Hazell, R. and Worthy, B. (2010). "Assessing the Performance of Freedom of Information". *Government Information Quarterly*, 27(4): 352–59.

Heckman, J. (2006). "Skill Formation and the Economics of Investing in Disadvantaged Children". *Science*, 312(5782): 1900–902.

Heller, S., Anuj K. Shah, A. K., Guryan, J., Ludwig, J., Mullainathan, S., and Pollack, H. A. (2017). "Thinking, Fast and Slow? Some Field Experiments to Reduce Crime and Dropout in Chicago". *The Quarterly Journal of Economics*, 132(1): 1–54.

Henry, G. T. and Rickman, D. K. (2007). "Do peers Influence Children's Skill Development in Preschool? " *Economics of Education Review*, 26(1): 100–12.

Hetland, H., Eikeland, O. J., Manger, T., Diseth, A., and Asbjørnsen, A. (2007). "Educational Background in a Prison Population". *Journal of Correctional Education*, 58(2): 145–56.
Hirschi, T. and Gottfredson, M. (1983). "Age and the Explanation of Crime". *American Journal of Sociology*, 89(3): 552–84.
Hjalmarsson, R. (2008). "Criminal Justice Involvement and High School Completion". *Journal of Urban Economics*, 63(2): 613–30.
Hjalmarsson, R., Holmlund, H. and Lindquist, M. (2015). "The Effect of Education on Criminal Convictions and Incarceration: Causal Evidence from Micro-data". *The Economic Journal*, 125(187): 1290–326.
Hungerford, T. and Solon, G. (1987). "Sheepskin Effects in the Returns to Education". *The Review of Economics and Statistics*, 69(1): 175–77.
Huttunen, K., Pekkarinen, T., Uusitalo, R., and Virtanen, H. (2018). "Lost Boys: Access to Secondary Education and Crime". 12084.
Imbens, G., and Angrist, J. (1994). "Identification and Estimation of Local Average Treatment Effects". *Econometrica*, 62(2): 467–75. https://doi.org/10.2307/2951620
Jacob, B. and Lefgren, L. (2003). "Are Idle Hands the Devil's Workshop? Incapacitation, Concentration and Juvenile Crime". *American Economic Review*, 93(5): 1560–77.
Jaeger, D. A. and Page, M. E. (1996). "Degrees Matter: New Evidence on Sheepskin Effects in the Returns to Education". *The Review of Economics and Statistics*, 78(4): 733–40.
Kainuwa, A., Binti, N., and Yusuf, M. (2013). "Influence of Socio-economic and Educational Background of Parents on Their Children's Education in Nigeria". *International Journal of Scientific and Research Publications*, 3(10): 2250–3153.
Koppensteiner, M. and Menezes, L. (2021). "Violence and Human Capital Investments". *Journal of Labor Economics*, 39(3): 787–823.
Krueger, A. B., and Malečková, J. (2003). "Education, Poverty and Terrorism: Is There a Causal Connection?". *Journal of Economic Perspectives*, 17(4): 119–44.
Landersø, R., Nielsen, H., and Simonsen, M. (2017). "School Starting Age and the Crime-Age Profile". *Economic Journal*, 127(602): 1096–118.
Levitt, D. and Lochner, L. (2001). "The Determinants of Juvenile Crime". NBER chapters. In: *Risky Behavior among Youths: An Economic Analysis. National Bureau of Economic Research, Inc.* (327–74). University of Chicago Press.
Levitt, S. and Venkatesh, S. (2000). "An Economic Analysis of a Drug-selling Gang's Finances". *The Quarterly Journal of Economics,* 115(3): 755–89.
Lochner, L. (2004). "Education, Work and Crime: A Human Capital Approach". *International Economic Review*, 45(3): 811–43.
Lochner, L. (2011). "Non-Production Benefits of Education: Crime, Health, and Good Citizenship", In Hanushek, E., Machin, S. and Woessmann, L. (eds.), *Handbook of the Economics of Education*, Volume 4, pp. 183–282. Amsterdam: Elsevier.
Lochner, L. and Moretti, E. (2004). "The Effect of Education on Crime: Evidence from Prison Inmates, Arrests and Self-reports". *American Economic Review*, 94(1): 155–89.
Luallen, J. (2006). "School's Out… Forever: A Study of Juvenile Crime, At-Risk Youths and Teacher Strikes". *Journal of Urban Economics*, 59(1): 75–103.
Machebe, C. H., Ezegbe, B. N., and Onuoha, J. (2017). "The Impact of Parental Level of Income on Students' Academic Performance in High School in Japan". *Universal Journal of Educational Research*, 5(9): 1614–20.
Machin, S., Marie, O., and Vujić, S. (2011). "The Crime Reducing Effect of Education". *Economic Journal*, 121(552): 463–84.

Maguire, M. and McVie, S. (2017). Crime data and criminal statistics: A critical reflection. *The Oxford Handbook of Criminology* (Vol. 1, pp. 163–89). Oxford: Oxford University Press.

Marie, O. (2016). "Police and Thieves in the Stadium: Measuring the (multiple) Effects of Football Matches on Crime". *Journal of the Royal Statistical Society: Series A (Statistics in Society)*, 179(1): 273–92.

Marie, O., Traag, T., and van der Velden, R. (2013). "The Relationship between School Performance, Delinquency, and Early School Leaving". In Weerman, F. and Bijleveld, C. C. J. H. (eds.) *Criminal Behaviour from School to the Workplace*. London: NSCR/Routledge.

Maurin, E. (2002). "The Impact of Parental Income on Early Schooling Transitions: A Re-examination Using Data over Three Generations". *Journal of Public Economics*, 85(3): 301–32.

McAdams, J. (2016). "The Effect of School Starting Age Policy on Crime: Evidence from U.S. Microdata". *Economics of Education Review*, 54: 227–41.

McCormick, M. C., Brooks-Gunn, J., Buka, S. L., Goldman, J., Yu, J., Salganik, M., Scott, D. T., Bennett, F. C., Kay, L. L., Bernbaum, J. C., Bauer, C. R., Martin, C., Woods, E. R., Martin, A., and Casey, P. H. (2006). "Early Intervention in Low Birth Weight Premature Infants: Results at 18 Years of Age for the Infant Health and Development Program". *Pediatrics*, 117(3): 771–80.

Mello, S. (2019). "More COPS, Less Crime". *Journal of Public Economics*, 172: 174–200.

Merlo, A., and Wolpin, K. I. (2015). "The Transition from School to Jail: Youth Crime and High School Completion among Black Males". *The European Economic Review*, 79: 234–51.

Nores, M., Belfield, C. R., Barnett, W. S., and Schweinhart, L. (2005). "Updating the Economic Impacts of the High/Scope Perry Preschool Program". *Educational Evaluation and Policy Analysis*, 27(3): 245–61.

Oreopoulos, P. (2006). "Estimating Average and Local Average Treatment Effects of Education when Compulsory Schooling Laws Really Matter". *American Economic Review*, 96(1): 152–75.

Oreopoulos, P. and Salvanes, K. (2011). "Priceless: The Nonpecuniary Benefits of Schooling". *Journal of Economic Perspectives*, 25(1): 159–84.

Paternoster, R., Bushway, S., Brame, R., and Apel, R. (2003). "The Effect of Teenage Employment on Delinquency and Problem Behaviors". *Social Forces*, 82(1): 297–335.

Pischke, J-S. and von Wachter, T. (2008). "Zero Returns to Compulsory Schooling in Germany: Evidence and Interpretation". *Review of Economics and Statistics*, 90(3): 592–98.

Reynolds, A. J., Temple, J. A., Robertson, D. L., and Mann, E. A. (2001). "Long-term Effects of an Early Childhood Intervention on Educational Achievement and Juvenile Arrest: A 15-year Follow-up of Low-income Children in Public Schools". *JAMA*, 285(18): 2339–46.

Soskice, D. (1993). "Social Skills from Mass Higher Education: Rethinking the Company-Based Initial Training Paradigm". *Oxford Review of Economic Policy*, 9(3): 101–13.

Torche, F. and Costa-Ribeiro, C. (2012). "Parental Wealth and Children's Outcomes over the Life-course in Brazil: A Propensity Score Matching Analysis". *Research in Social Stratification and Mobility*, 30(1): 79–96.

Vergidis, D., Asimaki, A., and Tzintzidis, A. (2007). "Correctional Education. The Second Chance School of Korydallos Prison". *Arethas Scientific Yearbook*, 4(1): 61–93.

Walters, C. R. (2015). "Inputs in the Production of Early Childhood Human Capital: Evidence from Head Start". *American Economic Journal: Applied Economics*, 7(4): 76–102.

Ward, S. and Williams, J. (2015). "Does Juvenile Delinquency Reduce Educational Attainment?". *Journal of Empirical Legal Studies*, 12(4), 716–56.

Webbink, D., Koning, P., Vujić, S., and Martin, N. G. (2013). "Why Are Criminals Less Educated than Non-criminals? Evidence from a Cohort of Young Australian Twins", *The Journal of Law, Economics, & Organization*, 29(1): 115–44.

Weiner, D. A., Lutz, B. F., and Ludwig, J. (2009). *The Effects of School Desegregation on Crime* (No. w15380). National Bureau of Economic Research. https://back.nber.org/bibliographic/w15380.bib.

Witte, D. (1980). "Estimating the Economic Model of Crime with Individual Data". *Quarterly Journal of Economics*, 94(1): 57–84.

APPENDIX

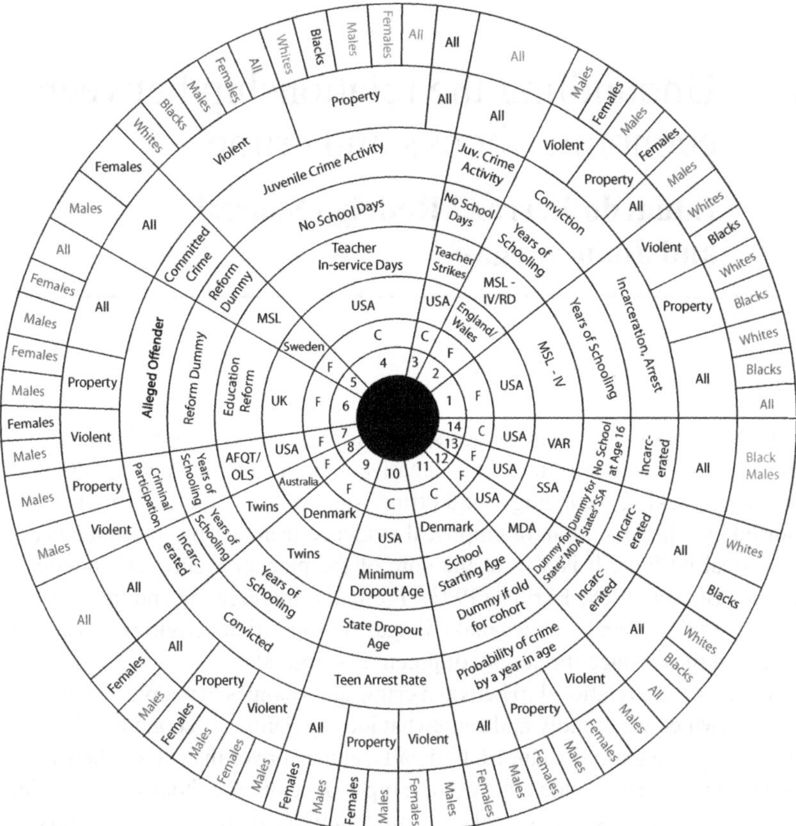

Notes: Content of rings from inside, out: paper number (1), contemporaneous versus future effect (2), country (3), identification strategy (4), schooling measure (5), crime measure (6), crime type (7), subpopulation group and effect (8). Important abbreviations: MSL = mandatory schooling laws, SSA = school starting age, MDA = minimum dropout age, VAR = vector autoregression, AFQT = armed forces qualification test, OLS = ordinary least-squares, IV = instrumental variables, RD = regression discontinuity, C = contemporaneous (effect), F = future (effect). Black bold font means that for the subpopulation and crime type there is a significant positive relationship between the schooling and crime measures, black signifies a negative relationship, and grey signifies a statistically insignificant relationship. Paper numbering: (1) Lochner and Moretti (2004), (2) Machin et al. (2011), (3) Luallen (2006), (4) Jacob and Lefgren (2003), (5) Hjalmarsson et al. (2015), (6) Beatton et al. (2018), (7) Lochner (2004), (8) Webbink et al. (2013), (9) Bennett (2018), (10) Anderson (2014), (11) Landersø et al. (2017), (12) Bell et al. (2016), (13) McAdams (2016), (14) Merlo and Wolpin (2015).

Figure A1 *Summary of method exploited, data used and findings of selected published economic papers estimating the causal relationship between education and crime*

8. Unbundling the relationship between economic shocks and crime

Eduardo Ferraz,[1] Rodrigo Soares[2] and Juan Vargas[3]

1. INTRODUCTION

The most basic intuition suggests that improvements in employment and wages should reduce crime. This negative relationship between income – or broadly speaking wellbeing – and crime is not only instinctual but also supported by a large amount of empirical evidence from a range of contexts and historical periods. It is also at the core of the pioneer theoretical models of crime (Becker, 1968; Ehrlich, 1973). Formally, increases in the income that is derived from legal sources make illegal appropriation activities less attractive, and thus reduce the supply of potential criminals.

However, the relationship between crime and changes in people's income or wealth (which we broadly and somewhat loosely define as 'economic shocks') is actually much more nuanced. Crucially, at the core of the classic theories of crime there is also the idea that certain types of economic shocks, even within the realm of legal sources, make criminal activity *more* attractive. Thus, in addition to the afore-explained 'opportunity cost effect', whereby increases in income make criminal enterprises less attractive, there is also a potential 'rapacity effect', by which income surges increase the value of the booty and thus promote crime (Tornell and Lane, 1999; Dube and Vargas, 2013).

The extent to which one such channel dominates the other – thus making income and crime either positively or negatively related – depends on at least three key factors. The first one is the legality of the income source. Because property rights over illegal goods and services cannot be enforced by legal institutions (such as courts), property disputes that arise in illegal markets tend to be resolved by violent means.

The second is the source of the economic shock. Goods that are easily lootable because their production is concentrated in just a few geographical areas (such as oil), because they concentrate very high values in small volumes (such as gold, diamonds or emeralds) or because they are capital intensive so that their associated revenue disproportionally benefits capital owners (like most natural resources) are likely to attract plunder and crime especially during periods when their price is high. Instead, goods that are produced over a much more widespread space that have a lower value per unit of volume or that are labor intensive so that their associated revenue disproportionately benefits workers are more likely to discourage criminal activities when their price is higher.

The third is the contextual factors that shape the relative importance of the opportunity cost and the rapacity effect. Salient examples of such factors include the level of inequality and the strength of the institutional environment. In highly unequal societies, positive economic shocks that increase the income of the rich make them more vulnerable to becoming targets of (property) crime. Alternatively, to the extent that income shocks do not affect everybody in the same way, they may also have distributional consequences that in turn exacerbate crime. Moreover, institutional environments characterized by weak property rights and a fragile rule of law tend to promote criminal behaviors insofar as positive economic shocks translate more easily into plunder and appropriation. Relatedly, instances of accelerated and disorganized growth, such as those driven by unexpected favorable changes in the terms of trade, commodity booms or the discovery of natural resources, make the rapacity effect more likely to dominate. This is because such economic shocks may create social disorganization and take place at a pace that can rarely be followed by institutional adjustments to obtain revenue out of booms and to provide public goods that benefit a broad base of society.

This discussion implies that, while the relationship between economic shocks and crime is theoretically complex (and thus empirically elusive), a comprehensive taxonomy of it must include the three mentioned factors. Such taxonomy determines the structure of this chapter. Specifically, in Section 2, we lay down a simple and stylized theoretical model of economic shocks and crime, and show that the nuanced relationship between these variables can be easily derived from very few assumptions that speak to the three determinants described above. This implies that, far from discouraging researchers, the wide variability of the empirical estimates of the relationship between economic shocks and crime can well be accounted for by a simple modified Beckerian framework. The subsequent sections of the chapter review the existing empirical evidence in the light of the suggested taxonomy, thus distinguishing between economic shocks that pertain to legal versus illegal markets and between different income sources, as well as accounting for the contextual factors that push the relationship in one direction or the other. We conclude the chapter highlighting persisting puzzles such as why violent crime is often related to economic shocks the way property crime is, as well as areas that need additional research to complement our current understanding of the relationship between economic shocks and crime.

2. A SIMPLE MODEL OF CRIMINAL PARTICIPATION

We develop a bare-bones version of a criminal participation model. The objective of the model is simply to provide a conceptual background for our discussion on the potential effects of economic shocks on crime. The model helps structure this discussion and put in concrete terms the different competing mechanisms that we want to highlight in our ensuing discussion of the empirical literature.

Consider a simple framework inspired by the original contributions of Becker (1968) and Ehrlich (1973). Potential criminals decide on whether to take part in illegal activities by comparing the expected utility from crime, C, with the expected utility from leading an honest life, V.

The expected utility from crime is given by

$$C = g + \Phi(-s)$$

where g represents the monetary gain from crime, Φ is the probability that a criminal is caught and convicted once he commits a crime and $-s$ is the welfare loss associated with punishment (sentence length or some other form of punishment) in case the criminal is caught and convicted. One could also consider the psychological or moral cost of committing a crime, but we abstract from this dimension here to keep the framework as simple as possible.

Individuals who choose not to commit crimes become potential victims. The expected utility of potential victims is given by

$$V = (1-\pi)u(y) + \pi\left[u(y-g) - p\right]$$

where π is the probability that the individual is a victim of a crime, $u(.)$ indicates the instantaneous utility function from consumption, y is legal income (and consumption) and p is a psychological or physical cost of victimization, associated with the trauma from the event and the possibility of physical injury. The gain g from crime to criminals corresponds to the amount g of the good stolen when an honest individual is victimized.

Individuals decide to commit crimes if $C > V$. The framework assumes, for simplicity, that crime and legal work are mutually exclusive alternatives and, therefore, there is only an extensive-margin choice to engage in crime. Also, we abstract from criminal effort – either to better target potential victims or to evade police capture – and consider a single type of crime.

Finally, it is worth highlighting, for later reference, that both the probability of apprehending a criminal θ and the probability of victimization π are endogenous equilibrium objects. These are functions of the number of individuals who decide to engage in crime, the number of potential victims and the size and effectiveness of the police force. We believe this basic framework is enough to shed light on the main channels that we have in mind.

The model is framed with common economic crimes – such as robbery and thefts – in mind. It could be easily adapted to the case of trade in illegal goods, such as illegal drugs for example. In this case, we would not have victims and, instead, would have two sides of a market, both subject to punishment from the state, though potentially at different levels. Gains from crime g from the perspective of sellers in this scenario would reflect the market price of the illegal good net of its retail cost. A similar framing would apply as well to sellers along the supply chain of illegal goods or to exporters, such as international drug traffickers. For consumers of illegal goods in the domestic market, in turn, utility would simply be the consumer surplus from engaging in the transaction, netted out from the expected punishment (probability of being caught times the punishment) and potential psychological costs of being involved in an illegal trade.

We use this framework to illustrate conceptually how different types of economic shocks may affect individual decisions to engage in crime and, therefore, the equilibrium crime rate in the economy. Any effect on the crime rate in this simple setting must work through relative changes in the net benefits and opportunity cost of crime, C and V respectively.

As mentioned in Section 1, the most traditional perspective considers the effect of changes in legal labor market opportunities, through changes in wages and unemployment, on crime. This view posits that increased economic activity is associated with better labor market opportunities for individuals, therefore increasing the opportunity cost of crime and reducing criminal participation. It can be interpreted in our setting through relative changes in y and g. The key requirement in this scenario is that the effect of increased economic activity through y is greater than that through g. One justification for this, not incorporated explicitly in our model, is that y is directly linked to ongoing wages and unemployment, while g, the booty from crime, depends also to a great extent on the stock of wealth, which does not respond so much to short-term economic fluctuations in economic activity. So cyclical changes in economic activity would tend to increase the opportunity cost of crime more than proportionally to its benefits, therefore reducing equilibrium crime rates.

The discussion from the previous paragraph already anticipates part of the limitations of the view that associates positive economic shocks unequivocally to reductions in crime. In general, different economic shocks may have different compositions in terms of their effects on y and g and, therefore, may have different implications for equilibrium crime rates. From a market perspective, for example, increases in the price of illegal goods are completely analogous to increases in the price of legal goods, so they can both be seen as representing positive economic shocks from the perspective of production. But their implications for crime rates can be vastly different. Increases in the price of illegal goods should increase the value of g with only minor equilibrium effects, if any, on y. More generally, economic shocks concentrated on what Dube and Vargas (2013) call contestable income, or rents subject to poorly enforced property rights, should affect mostly the gains from criminal activity g, leading to increases in crime through what they call the *rapacity effect*.

The discussion in the previous two paragraphs, however, assumes the perspective of individual agents considering whether to engage in crime, taking as given equilibrium variables at the economy level. But, in reality, several of the economic shocks explored in the empirical literature are aggregate shocks affecting not only individual incomes but also other variables that may interfere with the individual decision to engage in crime. This point is discussed extensively by Dix Carneiro et al. (2018) in the context of shocks to local labor markets. Local shocks that reduce employment and wages, for example, typically also reduce local government revenues, potentially disrupting the provision of local public goods. Reductions in the provision of public security might change the probability θ of punishment, making crime relatively more attractive at the margin. Reductions in the provision of schooling for teenagers could reduce the incapacitation effect of schooling in the short term and reduce long-term earnings of affected cohorts. Both these effects would tend to increase crime through channels that are different from the immediate short-term effect of the economic shock on legal employment opportunities. Aggregate shocks can also affect different parts of the income distribution in different ways. Shocks that increase inequality, for instance, tend to increase the share of the population for which y is relatively small in comparison to g and, therefore, for which crime becomes relatively more attractive. In summary, potential aggregate effects of economic shocks on crime are also relevant dimensions that should be kept in mind when discussing this relationship.

Finally, these aggregate – or contextual – factors do not necessarily work in the same direction as the original income shock. A long tradition in criminology is concerned about the role of social disorganization in determining crime rates (see, for example, Wilson and Kelling, 1982). Positive economic shocks that lead to very accelerated and disorganized urban growth in the short-term can be interpreted as representing settings where public good provision does not respond fast enough. In these contexts, reductions in θ and in other mechanisms of social control, coupled with increases in g due to increased local demand for illegal goods, can lead to increases in crime amid positive shocks to legal economic activities (y). These settings can generate the somewhat surprising result that increases in local incomes and, by all measures, economic development are accompanied by short-term increases in crime.

In the next sections of this chapter, we review the literature on economic shocks and crime. We argue that the different mechanisms discussed in this section are not only theoretical curiosities but in fact are essential for us to understand the wealth of evidence currently available on the response of crime and violence to different types of economic shocks.

3. ECONOMIC SHOCKS IN LEGAL AND ILLEGAL MARKETS

The relationship between labor market opportunities and crime is one of the most traditional topics in the research on socio-economic determinants of criminal participation (see, for example, Jones, 1932; Simpson, 1932; a review of this topic from the criminology perspective is available from Bushway and Reuter, 2001; Mustard, 2010, provides a more recent review from the economics of crime perspective). Public policy concerns related to the potential criminogenic effect of economic downturns are at least as old. Fishback et al. (2010), for example, document that the work relief efforts of US President Roosevelt during the Great Depression of the 1930s were partly motivated by concerns related to potential increases in crime, and that they indeed seem to have contributed to reducing property crime during the ensuing period.

Most of the contemporaneous literature on the topic has focused on the relationship between aggregate local labor market conditions and local crime rates. Some of the older papers in this literature rely on time-series or panel correlations, without explicit sources of exogenous identification. These include, for example, Cook and Zarkin (1985), who analyze the cyclical patterns for different types of crimes in the US for a period of over 50 years (1930 to 1982), Machin and Meghir (2004), who look at panel data and analyze the correlation between changes in wages at the bottom of the distribution and crime rates, focusing on police force areas of England and Wales, and Edmark (2005), who looks at unemployment rates and property crime across Swedish counties. The main concerns in this correlational evidence are the endogeneity of labor market conditions to crime – as when a region experiences economic decay because of increased violence – and the presence of unobserved factors determining simultaneously local labor market prospects and criminal dynamics.

More recent work has typically relied on Bartik instruments or on some type of natural experiment based on sectoral shocks to try to improve the identification of causal effects. Raphael and Winter-Ebmer (2001) and Gould et al. (2002) are early examples of these efforts. Raphael and Winter-Ebmer (2001) look at US state-level data and use defense contracts and exposure to oil shocks to identify the effects of unemployment on crime, while Gould et al. (2002) look at state- and county-level US data and build a Bartik instrument based on the initial industrial composition of the different areas to analyze the effect of both wages and unemployment on crime. Fougère et al. (2009) adopt an empirical strategy very similar to the latter to analyze the case of 95 départements of metropolitan France. Lin (2008), in turn, builds an instrument inspired by Raphael and Winter-Ebmer, in his case based on real exchange rate movements and union membership, and explores state-level US data. Finally, Axbard et al. (2019) show that increases in international mineral prices are associated with increases in employment opportunities and reductions in crime in mining areas of South Africa (mostly property crime). They also show that the crime response to mineral price fluctuations was minimized once an employment guarantee program was introduced by the government. Most of this evidence, dominantly from developed countries, indicates a robust relationship between local labor market conditions and property crime, with less consistent results for violent crime, and particularly, no effect for homicides.

Dix-Carneiro et al. (2018) follow a similar strategy for the case of Brazil, but rely on the unilateral Brazilian trade liberalization from the early 1990s for identification. This shock is arguably more exogenous than some of those used before in the literature, and it is also a one-time policy change, which allows the authors to characterize its dynamic implications more clearly. They document a significant effect on homicides, differently from the previous literature from developed countries. But, in addition, they argue (and show empirically) that the types of aggregate shocks explored in this literature may affect many relevant dimensions of local economies: local government spending and revenue, public good provision and inequality, among others. So, in principle, it is difficult to attribute their criminogenic effects particularly to the labor market. This conclusion calls into question the labor market interpretation present in most of the previous literature and calls for a cleaner identification of the labor market channel. Dix-Carneiro et al. (2018) follow on in this direction and propose a partial identification strategy that imposes theoretical restrictions on the criminogenic effect of the different potential mechanisms. They conclude that, in their context, most of the effect on crime seems indeed to work through the labor market.

As surprising as it may sound, truly clean identification of the individual-level response of criminal involvement to labor market opportunities was achieved only recently by a set of papers exploring administrative employment records and courts data. Grogger (1998) had already explored the individual-level correlation between wages and criminal involvement among youth in the context of the US using the National Longitudinal Survey of Youth (NLSY) survey, but without using a clear source of causal identification for variations in wages. More recently, Bennett and Ouazad (2020) use individual-level data from Norway to analyze the relationship between unemployment and crime. Linking labor market data with individual crime records and unemployment benefits, they show that workers fired during mass layoffs display permanently higher levels of involvement in crime (as proxied by convictions) during several years following the layoff, and that these effects are not driven by aggregate shocks to local economies. They also show that the peaks in the later involvement in crime match closely the timing of termination of (or reduction in) unemployment benefits. Along the same lines, Britto et al. (2020) look at plant closures in Brazil and document analogous patterns, showing in addition that the effects are driven mostly by young and low-tenured workers. They also show a similar minimizing effect of eligibility for unemployment insurance. Relative increases in crime following termination of employment, when compared to baseline crime rates, are of similar magnitude across these two studies (of the order of 20–30 percent). Though focused mostly on migration, Pinotti (2017) also provides individual-level evidence of this same effect but considering improvements in legal labor market prospects. Relying on a regression discontinuity design based on the timing of applications for legalization of residence status in Italy, he shows that access to the legal labor market reduces immigrants' probability of criminal involvement (based on criminal records) by more than 50 percent of the baseline value. This set of papers provides what is possibly the cleanest evidence on the direct relationship between individual-level legal labor market opportunities and crime.[4]

But positive shocks to local economic activity and labor markets do not always come from legal sources. Increased international demand for illegal goods or regulatory changes coupled with poor enforcement can generate local economic booms driven by increased rents from illegal goods. A traditional literature in criminology associates illegal markets intrinsically with violence (Reuter, 2009). Without access to the legal justice system, agents operating in illegal markets tend to resort to violence to enforce contracts, settle labor and competition disputes and enforce property rights. In these contexts, expanded illegal activities not only increase crime through the illegal activity itself but also bring with them increased violence. This highlights that, as discussed in the context of the model from the previous section, the impact of economic shocks on crime rates should depend crucially on the legal or illegal status of the relevant market. Recent research has repeatedly documented that increased demand for illegal goods tends to increase violence in areas associated with production, most of the time focusing on the illegal drugs market.

Angrist and Kugler (2008), for example, document how the reallocation of coca production from Bolivia and Peru to Colombia in the 1990s was followed by increased violence in cultivating areas. Similarly, Mejía and Restrepo (2014) show that coca production booms in Colombia due to changes in repressive policies in other countries were associated with relative increases in violence in areas adequate for cultivation. Dube et al. (2016) document how increases in the cultivation of marijuana and opium poppies driven by exogenous variation in the price of alternative crops are associated with increases in killings by drug-trafficking organizations in Mexico. Also in the Mexican context, Castillo et al. (2020) present evidence that increased rents in the cocaine market driven by seizures in Colombia (Mexico's main supplier) increased violence in municipalities closer to the US border, which are likely to be involved in the international drug-trafficking routes and also in municipalities that were contested by different drug-trafficking organizations.

Evidence on the interaction between illegal booms and violence is not restricted to the drugs market. Poorly enforced environmental regulations can also lead to increased illegal activity and violence. Idrobo et al. (2014), for example, show that, when the international price of gold increases, violence also tends to increase in reservations and environmental protection areas of Colombia that contain gold deposits (it is very difficult to obtain permits to mine gold legally in these areas). In a similar vein, Pereira and Pucci (2021) show that a relatively modest change in the regulation for raw gold purchases in Brazil – which effectively reduced the incentives for private monitoring of the gold's origin – ended up increasing the demand for illegally extracted gold. They then show that this increased demand generated violence in reservations and environmental protection areas (where the mineral could not be mined legally) but not in areas with legal gold mines. Finally, Chimeli and Soares (2017) show that the transition of the mahogany market in Brazil from legal to illegal in the late 1990s and early 2000s – followed by what seemed to be an increase in extraction – led to an explosion in violence in areas of natural occurrence of mahogany. They also show that, later on, once the illegal market shrank because of increased monitoring capabilities on the part of the Brazilian government, so did the violence.

The discussion in this section suggests that one should not expect economic booms to have unequivocal effects on crime and violence. We highlighted that the nature of the market experiencing the boom – whether legal or illegal – should be key in determining the expected effects on crime and violence. From the perspective of the model discussed previously, the key aspect is the relative effect of the shock on the opportunities in legal and illegal activities. More generally, this depends not only on the legal and illegal nature of the market, but also on other aspects that we discuss in the next sections of this chapter.

4. THE OPPORTUNITY COST AND THE RAPACITY EFFECT

While in the previous chapter we discussed the importance of the legal or illegal nature of economic shocks regarding their relationship with the incidence of crime, in this section we focus on a different – but complementary – taxonomy of economic shocks: irrespective of whether they pertain to legal or to illegal markets, positive shocks may reduce crime by improving the opportunities that potential criminal face in the legal sector, or they may make the profits of crime more attractive. If the first mechanism dominates, positive shocks will be crime-reducing, but if the second is more salient, they will be criminogenic.

In terms of the model of Section 2, positive economic shocks may change either y or g, or both, but if the crime-reducing incentive that comes from an increase in y more than compensates the criminal incentive associated with an increase in g then the shock will end up reducing crime. The opposite holds if the criminogenic incentive associated with a higher g more than compensates the crime attenuation that stems from a larger y. Following Dube and Vargas (2013), we call the first mechanism the *opportunity cost* effect and the second the *rapacity* effect.

Dube and Vargas (2013) study how the dynamics of the Colombian internal armed conflict responded to economic shocks during the period 1988–2005.[5] In particular, they study the relationship between commodity-driven economic shocks and the intensity of the Colombian conflict across municipalities. Their findings suggest that the direction of this relationship critically depends on the type of commodity. While exogenous increases in the value of agricultural products such as coffee decreased the activity of illegal armed groups as well as the number of conflict-related casualties, positive shocks to the value of natural resources such as oil increased conflict-related activity. Dube and Vargas (2013) argue that this heterogeneity is a function of the relative labor intensity of different commodities. Growing and harvesting agricultural products, especially in developing countries – which are also most likely to be affected by internal conflicts – tend to be labor intensive activities. On the other hand, the exploitation of natural resources tends to be more capital intensive. As suggested by the Stolper-Samuelson trade theorem, this implies that, for the first type of commodities, exogenous price surges tend to translate into higher wages more than proportionally than in higher capital rates of return. On the contrary, for the latter, price increases translate more than proportionally in higher capital rates of return. In turn, this implies that the effects of economic shocks that affect agricultural products are much more likely to be mediated by the opportunity cost effect, because they affect the legal wages of agricultural workers (y).[6] By the same token, the effects of economic shocks that affect natural resources are potentially driven by the rapacity effect, as they influence the size of vulnerable rents (g).[7]

More generally, the *opportunity cost* effect is determined by the extent to which economic shocks affect the opportunity cost of committing a crime. Thus, all else equal, economic shocks that translate into higher wages or better employment prospects in the legal sector should discourage individuals from engaging in criminal activities (or from joining criminal organizations for that matter). This occurs because such shocks increase the opportunity cost of crime. The opportunity cost effect is thus the main mechanism that explains the evidence discussed in the previous section on how higher wages and better employment prospects are negatively associated with crime.

On the other hand, the *rapacity* effect is the extent to which economic shocks increase the value of a potential booty or target and thus the incentive to engage in criminal efforts to appropriate at least part of those additional rents. To put it differently, more income also means there is more to fight for and thus more economic opportunities may also attract more looting.[8] The rapacity effect is thus the main mechanism that explains the evidence presented in the previous section on how economic shocks in illegal markets tend to be criminogenic. This is especially salient for the case of illegal substances that create addiction, such as cocaine or heroin. The interplay between illegality (and thus prohibition which comes hand in hand with supply suppression efforts) and an inelastic demand curve makes these types of products extremely profitable, especially in the wake of government interdictions and crackdowns that create scarcity and make the business even more attractive.[9]

But the rapacity effect is not a concomitant of illegal markets. Economic shocks on legal commodities may also funnel appropriation incentives. One key example is given by the observation that the income generated by large government investments in transport infrastructure may have the unintended consequence of increasing crime. Such investments have been shown to improve the material conditions and economic opportunities of neighboring communities insofar as new roads expand market access and reduce the cost of accessing better jobs, health services and education (Berg et al., 2015). Thus, at least theoretically, this should increase the opportunity cost of vulnerable populations to engage in criminal activities. However, by improving living conditions and increasing people's income, large infrastructure projects may also exacerbate the predatory incentives of criminals and illegal organized groups seeking to reap part of the economic surplus and may also increase the demand for illegal goods. This has been shown for El Salvador by Baires et al. (2020). The authors study the effects of the construction of a highway in the north of the country and find short-term increases in the economic activity of newly connected regions. However, prosperity attracted gangs, who engaged in crime and extortion, and recruited local minors thus increasing school dropout in the affected areas.[10]

The above example illustrates an important point, namely that the extent to which the opportunity cost is more salient than the rapacity effect or vice versa is not necessarily associated with the realization of different types of shocks (as in Dube and Vargas, 2013). Rather, the temporal dynamics of the effect of a single shock may imply that, while in the short run the opportunity cost effect dominates, in the long run the newly available rents attract sufficient criminals and the rapacity effect offsets the former. In El Salvador, the new highway generated short-term beneficial economic opportunities but ultimately attracted enough criminals so that the net effect of the highway on crime was positive. A similar pattern was apparent in US counties that introduced large casinos. Grinols and Mustard (2006) compare crime rates in US counties before and after the introduction of the first large operating casinos. As these establishments created many low-skilled jobs in the short run, employment rose and a large fraction of society obtained additional income. Thus, crime rates went down. However, the casinos ultimately attracted criminal structures such as loan-sharking gangs or money laundering organizations and the rapacity effect ultimately dominated, making property crime rise over time.

Clearly, the extent to which economic shocks are able to create criminal incentives through a rapacity effect depends on key contextual factors such as the degree of inequality or the overall level of law enforcement and property rights protection. On the one hand, for a given level of law enforcement (θ in our model) in more unequal societies, the more disadvantaged have more to gain from engaging in property crime. Conversely, positive economic shocks are more likely to induce decreasing crime rates if they benefit individuals at the bottom of the income distribution. On the other hand, the very existence of a rapacity effect largely depends on society's underlying law enforcement (θ) and more generally on its degree of state capacity (Besley and Persson, 2009; Acemoglu and Robinson, 2012). In weakly institutionalized environments in which the state lacks the basic function of its monopoly of violence, more income also means a more attractive booty. In the next section, we discuss in more detail how these and other contextual factors shape the relationship between economic shocks and crime.

5. THE ROLE OF CONTEXTUAL FACTORS

Independently of whether economic shocks take place in legal or illegal markets and of whether the incentives created by them are more likely to manifest in a higher opportunity cost or a higher rapacity effect, there are several predetermined contextual conditions that can shape the way in which such shocks affect criminal behaviors. In this section, we discuss some of these conditions. First, we examine the role of both poverty and income inequality, which are two of the most studied potential drivers of crime. Second, we discuss jointly how instances of accelerated economic growth can create social disorganization and demographic changes which in turn may condition the relationship between economic shocks and crime. And third, we turn our attention to the potential mitigating effect of institutional factors such as state capacity and the underlying level of property rights protection.

When thinking about the effect of economic shocks on crime, poverty and inequality are hard to study in isolation. In part, this is because the poor are generally more vulnerable to negative economic shocks (for instance due to the lack of protection or insurance mechanisms), so in the context of high poverty rates, negative shocks tend to increase both poverty and inequality, as well as reduce the opportunity cost of becoming a criminal.[11] This is exactly what Foley (2011) finds (looking at a positive economic shock): exploiting the staggered timing of welfare payments to poor households across US jurisdictions, the author shows that property crime drops just after the payments are made. The implication of this theoretical discussion – as well as of the related empirical evidence – is that poverty amplifies the effect of economic shocks on crime, but this occurs if and only if there is inequality and such shocks affect the most vulnerable individuals. Indeed, Bourguignon et al. (2003) argue that only economic shocks to a specific part of the income distribution affect the property crime rate.

In general, the role of poverty in shaping the relationship between economic shocks and crime is more nuanced. To see why, imagine a community of potential criminals and crime targets in which all individuals have the same income, and suppose that an economic shock takes place reducing everybody's income by the same amount, making all of them equally poorer. Such a shock would reduce the expected pecuniary gain from property crime, thus likely reducing crime. In contrast, a shock that hit the same type of society, but that represented a transfer of income from half of it to the other half, would unambiguously increase crime.

The above discussion implies that inequality is probably much more important than poverty in shaping the relationship between economic shocks and criminal behavior. In fact, inequality is certainly the contextual factor that has received the most attention in the empirical literature. In addition, and consistent with the observation that negative economic shocks tend to affect the poor more than proportionally, by and large the literature suggests that inequality is criminogenic (see, for example, Fajnzybler et al. 2002; Bourguignon et al. 2003; Soares 2004; Choe 2008; Enamorado et al. 2016). This result generally holds for different metrics of inequality, using different units of observation (county, state or country level), controlling for past levels of crime and controlling for poverty, and applies to different types of crime (violent, property and drug-related).[12]

It remains true, nevertheless, that the evidence mentioned in the previous paragraph is dominantly based on correlations, without clear sources of causal identification. The causal effect of inequality on crime is still elusive. The identification concerns in this context are related to the possibility of omitted variable bias – as when shocks increasing inequality also affect other determinants of crime – and to the specific measurement of inequality. Inequality metrics such as the Gini coefficient, which are mute about what part of the income distribution is affected, may lead to problems analogous to measurement error when used to assess the relationship between inequality and crime. Recently, Buonanno and Vargas (2019) overcame several of the identification challenges by using the municipal share of slaves before the abolition of slavery in the mid-nineteenth century in Colombia as a source of plausibly exogenous variation in current inequality levels. Consistent with the previous literature, the authors find that inequality does cause (both property and violent) crime.

While Becker (1968)'s model offers a theoretical explanation compatible with the empirical findings of the link between inequality and property crime, at first glance it cannot account in a satisfactory way for the relationship between inequality and violent crime. In fact, violent crime can be, to some extent, a by-product of property crime, and this could help explain the observed patterns. However, inequality also impacts certain crimes that seem to lack any connection with clear pecuniary motivation. For example, Sanz-Barbero et al. (2015) find that inequality is positively associated with the incidence of intimate partner violence, even after controlling for income. This illustrates the limitations of the Beckerian framework to account for the relationship between inequality and violent crime more generally.

The social disorganization theory offers an alternative that complements the basic rational choice framework in explaining the effect of inequality on violent crime. It is beyond the scope of this chapter to describe all the nuances and implications of this theory (for a comprehensive review, see Kubrin and Weitzer, 2003). But the core idea is that communities establish enduring relationships that function as an extra layer of social control beyond the control exerted by the state. Social disorganization is associated with factors that weaken such relationships. Thus, a shock that increases inequality may also increase segregation and isolation, disrupting social networks, community cohesion and ultimately social control. In turn, this may increase the level of violence observed in society.

Social disorganization can also explain another puzzle from the crime literature. The empirical evidence has documented various contexts where short-term accelerations in economic growth are accompanied by increases in crime. For instance, Freedman and Owens (2016) study the impact on crime of a governmental program of renovation and construction of military bases in San Antonio that benefited federally contracted construction workers. The authors find that neighborhoods in which more construction workers were hired saw an increase in both property and violent crimes. A higher degree of inequality seems to be associated with these results, but through different channels. The increased gain from stealing might be the main driver for the increase of larceny, auto theft and burglary – which could be, qualitatively, fully explained by Becker's model. By contrast, a stronger social disorganization can better describe the rise of assaults and rapes.

James and Smith (2017) reach similar conclusions when analyzing the boom of shale oil and gas in the US. A sudden technological innovation in the extraction of fossil fuel made the extraction of shale gas and tight oil a very profitable business almost overnight. The authors find that countries that benefited from the extraction boom experienced a differential increase in the rates of rape, aggravated assault, robbery, larceny and murder. In addition to the channels highlighted by Freedman and Owens (2016) regarding social disorganization, James and Smith (2017) also highlight the role of sudden demographic changes driven by the migration patterns into boom counties. Oil and gas drilling disproportionately attracts young men. In turn, this demographic group commits more crimes (of all types) than any other demographic group.[13] Soares and Souza (2021) document similar effects for homicides in oil-producing areas of Brazil that benefited from the 2000s increase in oil prices but identify a potentially different channel. They do not find changes in demographic composition in these areas – possibly because in this context extraction was mostly offshore and very capital intensive – but document increased local economic and population growth not accompanied by proportional expansions in the provision of public goods. The evidence on road constructions in El Salvador presented by Baires et al. (2020), discussed in the previous section, represents also another setting where local accelerated growth seemed to have been associated with increased crime.

The last contextual factor we discuss is the role of a strong state and institutional environment. Clearly, better law enforcement institutions and property rights protection are likely correlated with lower crime *levels* (via a higher θ parameter in the model presented in Section 2). But remember that we are primarily interested in the effects on *variations* in crime due to economic shocks. Although the concept of a 'better institutional environment' encompasses many distinct aspects of state capacity, the main prediction of our theoretical model is that good institutions mitigate crime changes whenever they can offer quick and efficient countercyclical policies. For instance, Cortés et al. (2016) show how the crash of a large network of Ponzi schemes in Colombia affected thousands of investors and increased property crime. But the authors also show that the Ponzi-driven crime surge was only present in places with weak judicial and law enforcement institutions and with less access to consumption smoothing opportunities. This implies that governments can reduce crime if they can provide safety nets and compensate losers from negative economic shocks, which is also in line with the evidence from welfare payments and crime discussed before.

Acemoglu et al. (2020) provide a related, but different, example, associated with organized crime: after Sicily was hit by a large drought at the end of the nineteenth century, mafia organizations became stronger in provinces with weaker state capacity. This is because affected areas sought help and relief from either the state or its closest substitute, depending on the varying levels of state presence. As a result, the drought strengthened criminal organizations in various parts of the island. This illustrates a more general (and policy relevant) point: if the state is not strong enough to retain the monopoly of violence (or does not have the capacity to provide additional public goods other than security), unexpected economic shocks that generate scarcity can consolidate organized criminal organizations.

6. DISCUSSION AND AREAS OF FUTURE RESEARCH

In this chapter, we have discussed that the relationship between economic shocks and crime is complex and definitely not unidirectional. This is because economic shocks can be manifold and may affect the equilibrium level of crime through a variety of channels. Guided by a simple theoretical framework, the chapter discusses these channels as well as the empirical evidence, distinguishing between shocks that take place in legal or illegal markets, that make either the opportunity cost or the rapacity effect more salient and that are shaped by key contextual factors such as inequality and institutional strength.

Understanding the main drivers of crime and disentangling these channels is essential, among other reasons, for policy purposes. For example, consider two equally costly projects to reduce crime after an economic shock: a welfare program and an increase in the size of the police. The most effective policy depends on how the shock may induce increases in crime. Offering income relief may be more effective if the shock is poverty-augmenting. By contrast, reinforcing the police is likely to be the best policy to respond if the cause is social disorganization induced by accelerated urban growth.

While we have tried to rationalize the proposed channels as well as the empirical evidence using a Beckerian framework complemented with insights from the social disorganization theory, it is important to acknowledge that there are other influential ecological theories of crime that can account for some of the empirical findings. For example, Merton (1938)'s *strain theory* argues that inequality increases violent crime by exacerbating the frustration of unsuccessful individuals who witness the relative success of others. Whether the increases in violent crime that result from changes in inequality are a byproduct of the dynamics of property crime (à la Becker), or can be explained by social disorganization theory or else by strain theory, implies quite different policy prescriptions. It is therefore extremely important to engage in more research about the mechanisms that link each type of economic shock to crime in general and to violent crime in particular.

There are other dimensions that also need further research. While the literature has primarily focused on who commits crimes and the context under which criminal decisions are taken, less attention has been given, for example, to the identity of victims. Understanding how economic shocks may affect the vulnerability of different populations to crime is a largely understudied topic. Indeed, victimization surveys worldwide suggest that the likelihood of being a victim of a crime is strongly associated with the victim's income and also depends on the type of crime. However, while in the US low-income individuals are disproportionately more likely to be victims of both property and violent crime (see the US National Crime Victimization Survey), in Latin America and the Caribbean the rich are more vulnerable to property crime (Schargrodsky and Freira, 2021). How different types of economic shocks may exacerbate or mitigate these striking heterogeneities in victimization is a potentially interesting area for further research.

NOTES

1. School of Economics, Universidad del Rosario.
2. Insper and Columbia University.
3. School of Economics, Universidad del Rosario.
4. Additional recent causal evidence on how better labor market opportunities reduce crime includes Gelber et al. (2016), Freedman et al. (2018), Schnepel (2018), Modestino (2019), Khanna et al. (2021) and Galbiati et al. (2021).
5. Even if civil conflict is in principle a different social phenomenon than the type of small-scale crime that we conceptualize in Section 2, we argue that such a simple theoretical framework can account for some of the stylized facts of civil conflict. In that respect, while conflict may be conceptually closer to large-scale organized crime and more valid theoretical frameworks should complement the individual-level determinants of the decision of potential fighters with the industrial organization of insurgencies, some of the claims that we make in the chapter about the relationship between economic shocks and crime also apply to civil conflicts.
6. These are precisely the people who could potentially join the ranks of illegal organizations when facing limited alternatives in the legal sector, thus the similarity to the model presented in Section 2.
7. There is a large empirical literature that has documented a positive association between valuable resources and civil conflict. This association is so pervasive and robust that scholars refer to it with the concept of 'conflict resource curse'. Ross (2012) and Le Billon (2013) are two recent reviews of this literature.

8. This idea is at the heart of the classic theories of conflict as a result of greed. See, e.g. Hirshleifer (1991) and Grossman (1991).
9. Incidentally, this is one key reason (but by and large not the only one) why drug prohibition policies are largely ineffective and often backfire (see, e.g. Baum, 1996 and Gray, 2013).
10. Moreno et al. (2020), in turn, show that Colombia's large investment in rural road infrastructure projects also increased local economic activity along with the intensity of the internal conflict.
11. In terms of our theoretical framework, such a shock would decrease y and thus V, whilst C remains approximately constant.
12. The empirical literature, however, has also identified interesting heterogeneities related to the specific types of crime. For instance, different property crimes are affected in different ways by inequality. To give a simple example, an increase in inequality might make pick-pocketing more attractive, but auto thefts might become more costly (since more expensive cars might be better protected). In other words, using our theoretical model, the g in the expected utility from committing an offense C is specific to each type of crime.
13. Street (2020) investigates the same oil boom episode but focuses on the crimes committed by the individuals who lived in the booming counties before the shock (the non-migrants). She finds null effects, which supports the idea that the crime surge was driven by the incoming migrants.

REFERENCES

Acemoglu, D., De Feo, G., and De Luca, G. (2020). Weak States: causes and consequences of the Sicilian Mafia. *Review of Economic Studies*, 87(2), 537–81.

Acemoglu, D. and J. A. Robinson (2012). *Why Nations Fail: The Origins of Power, Prosperity, and Poverty.* Crown Books.

Angrist, Joshua D., and Adriana D. Kugler. (2008). Rural Windfall or a New Resource Curse? Coca, Income, and Civil Conflict in Colombia. *Review of Economics and Statistics* 90(2), 191–215.

Axbard, S., Poulsen,J., and Tolonen, A. (2019). Extractive Industries, Price Shocks and Criminality. CDEP-CGEG WP No. 30.

Baires, Wilber, Lelys Dinarte and Carlos Schmidt-Padilla (2020). *Unintended Effects of Public Infrastructure: Labor, Education, and Crime Outcomes in El Salvador*, unpublished manuscript.

Baum, D. (1996): *Smoke and Mirrors: The War on Drugs and the Politics of Failure.* Little, Brown.

Becker, G.S. (1968). Crime and Punishment: An Economic Approach. In *The Economic Dimensions of Crime.* Palgrave Macmillan, pp. 13–68.

Bennett, Patrick, Amine, Ouazad (2020). Job Displacement, Unemployment, and Crime: Evidence from Danish Microdata and Reforms. *Journal of the European Economic Association*, 18(5), 2182–220.

Berg, C., U. Deichman, and H. Selod. *Transport Policies and Development.* Policy research working paper 7366, World Bank.

Besley, T. and T. Persson. (2009, September). The origins of state capacity: Property rights, taxation, and politics. *American Economic Review*, 99(4), 1218–44.

Bourguignon, F., Sanchez, F. and Nuñez, J. (2003) A structural Model of Crime and Inequality in Colombia. *Journal of the European Economic Association* 1(2–3), 440–49.

Britto, D., Pinotti, P. and Sampaio, B. (2020.). The Effect of Job Loss and Unemployment Insurance on Crime in Brazil. Unpublished manuscript.

Buonanno, P. and Vargas, J.F. (2019) Inequality, crime, and the long run legacy of slavery. *Journal of Economic Behavior & Organization*, 159, 539–52.

Bushway, S. and P. Reuter (2001). Labor Markets & Crime in Wilson, J. and J. Petersilia (eds.) *Crime and Public Policy*. Oxford University Press, pp.191–224.
Castillo, J.C., Mejía, D. and Restrepo, P. (2020). Scarcity without leviathan: The violent effects of cocaine supply shortages in the Mexican drug war. *Review of Economics and Statistics*, 102(2), 269–86.
Chimeli, A. and Soares, R. R. (2017). The Use of Violence in Illegal Markets: Evidence from Mahogany Trade in the Brazilian Amazon. *American Economic Journal: Applied Economics*, 9(4), 30–57.
Choe, J. (2008). Income inequality and crime in the United States. *Economic Letters*, 101, 31–33.
Cook, Philip J., and Gary A. Zarkin. (1985). Crime and the Business Cycle. *Journal of Legal Studies* 14(1), 115–28.
Cortés, D., Santamaría, J. and Vargas, J.F. (2016). Economic shocks and crime: Evidence from the crash of Ponzi schemes. *Journal of Economic Behavior & Organization*, 131, 263–75.
Dix-Carneiro, Rafael, Rodrigo R. Soares, and Gabriel Ulyssea (2018). Economic Shocks and Crime: Evidence from the Brazilian Trade Liberalization. *American Economic Journal: Applied Economics*, 10(4), 158–95.
Dube, O. and Vargas, J.F. (2013). Commodity price shocks and civil conflict: Evidence from Colombia. *The Review of Economic Studies*, 80(4), 1384–421.
Dube, Oeindrila, Omar García-Ponce, and Kevin Thom. (2016). From Maize to Haze: Agricultural Shocks and the Growth of the Mexican Drug Sector. *Journal of the European Economic Association* 14(5), 1181–224.
Edmark, K. (2005). Unemployment and Crime: Is There a Connection? *Scandinavian Journal of Economics*, 107, 353–73.
Ehrlich, I. (1973). Participation in illegitimate activities: A theoretical and empirical investigation. *Journal of Political Economy*, 81(3), 521–65.
Enamorado, T., López-Calva, L., Rodríguez-Castelán, C. and Winkler, H. (2016). Income inequality and violent crime: Evidence from Mexico's drug war. *Journal of Development Economics*, 120(C), 128–43.
Fajnzybler, P., Lederman, D. and Loayza, N. (2002). Inequality and Violent Crime. *The Journal of Law and Economics*, 45(1), 1–39.
Fougère, Denis, Francis Kramarz, and Julien Pouget. (2009). Youth Unemployment and Crime in France. *Journal of the European Economic Association*, 7(5), 909–38.
Fishback, Price V., Ryan S. Johnson, and Shawn Kantor. (2010). Striking at the Roots of Crime: The Impact of Welfare Spending on Crime during the Great Depression. *Journal of Law and Economics* 53(4), 715–40.
Foley, C.F. (2011). Welfare payments and crime. *Review of Economics and Statistics*, 93(1), 97–112.
Freedman, M. and Owens, E. (2016). Your Friends and Neighbors: Localized Economic Development and Criminal Activity. *The Review of Economics and Statistics*, 98(2), 233–53.
Freedman, Matthew, Emily Owens, and Sarah Bohn. (2018). Immigration, Employment Opportunities, and Criminal Behavior. *American Economic Journal: Economic Policy*, 10(2), 117–51.
Galbiati, Roberto, Aurélie Ouss, Arnaud Philippe. (2021). Jobs, News and Reoffending after Incarceration. *The Economic Journal*, 131(633), 247–70.
Gelber, Alexander, Adam Isen, Judd B. Kessler (2016). The Effects of Youth Employment: Evidence from New York City Lotteries. *The Quarterly Journal of Economics*, 131(1), 423–60.

Gould, Eric D., Bruce A. Weinberg, and David B. Mustard. (2002). Crime Rates and Local Labor Market Opportunities in the United States: 1979–1997. *Review of Economics and Statistics* 84(1): 45–61.

Gray, M. (2013). *Drug Crazy: How We Got into this Mess and How We Can Get Out.* London: Routledge.

Grinols, Earl L. and Mustard, David (2006). Casinos, Crime, and Community Costs. *The Review of Economics and Statistics*, 88(1), 28–45.

Grogger, J. (1998). Market Wages and Youth Crime. *Journal of Labor Economics*, 16(4), 756–91.

Grossman, Herschel. (1991). A General Equilibrium Model of Insurrections, *American Economic Review*, 81(4): 912–21.

Hirshleifer, J. (1991). The technology of conflict as an economic activity. *American Economic Review*, 81(2), 130–34.

Idrobo, N., D. Mejía, and A. M. Tribin (2014). Illegal Gold Mining and Violence in Colombia. *Peace Economics, Peace Science and Public Policy*, 20(1), 83–111.

James, A. and Smith, B. (2017). There Will Be Blood: Crime Rates in shale-rich U.S. Counties. *Journal of Environmental Economics and Management*, 84(C), 125–52.

Jones, Vernon. (1932). Relation of Economic Depression to Delinquency, Crime, and Drunkenness in Massachusetts. *The Journal of Social Psychology*, 3(3), 259–82.

Khanna, Gaurav, Carlos Medina, Anant Nyshadham, Christian Posso, and Jorge Tamayo. (2021). Job Loss, Credit, and Crime in Colombia. *American Economic Review: Insights*, 3(1): 97–114.

Kubrin, C.E. and Weitzer, R. (2003). New Directions in Social Disorganization Theory. *Journal of Research in Crime and Delinquency*, 40(4), pp.374–402.

Le Billon, P. (2013). *Wars of Plunder: Conflicts, Profits and the Politics of Resources.* London, New York: Hurst and Oxford University Press.

Lin, Ming-Jen. (2008). Does Unemployment Increase Crime? Evidence from U.S. Data 1974–2000. *Journal of Human Resources* 43(2), 413–36.

Machin, Stephen and Costas Meghir (2004). Crime and Economic Incentives 47. *Journal of Human Resources*, October 2, XXXIX, 958–79.

Mejía, Daniel, and Pascual Restrepo. (2014). Bushes and Bullets: Illegal Cocaine Markets and Violence In Colombia? Unpublished.

Merton, R. (1938). Social Structure and Anomie. *American Sociological Review* 3, 672–82.

Modestino, A.S. (2019). How Do Summer Youth Employment Programs Improve Criminal Justice Outcomes, and for Whom?. *Journal of Policy Analysis and Management*, 38, 600–28.

Moreno, L.E., Gallego, J.A. and Vargas, J.F. (2020). The Effect of Rural Roads on Armed Conflict and Illegal Economies in Colombia. In *Documentos de Trabajo No. 018154,* Universidad del Rosario.

Mustard, David B. (2010). Labor Markets and Crime: New Evidence on an Old Puzzle. In *Handbook on the Economics of Crime*, edited by Bruce L. Benson and Paul R. Zimmerman, 342–58. Cheltenham: Edward Elgar Publishing.

Pereira, L. and Pucci, R. (2021). A Tale of Gold and Blood: The Unintended Consequences of Market Regulation on Local. PUC-Rio Climate Policy Initiative Working Paper No. 005.

Pinotti, P. (2017). Clicking on Heaven's Door: The Effect of Immigrant Legalization on Crime. *American Economic Review*, 107(1), 138–68.

Raphael, Steven, and Rudolf Winter-Ebmer. (2001). Identifying the Effect of Unemployment on *Crime. Journal of Law and Economics*, 44(1), 259–83.

Reuter, Peter. (2009). Systemic violence in drug markets. *Crime, Law and Social Change*, 52(3), 275–84.

Ross, M.L. (2012). *The Oil Curse*. Princeton University Press.

Sanz-Barbero, B., Vives-Cases, C., Otero-García, L., Muntaner, C., Torrubiano-Domínguez, J. and O'Campo, P. (2015). Intimate Partner Violence Among Women in Spain: The Impact of Regional-level Male Unemployment and Income Inequality. *European Journal of Public Health*, 25(6), 1105–11.

Schargrodsky, Ernesto and Lucía Freira (2021). *Inequality and Crime in Latin America and the Caribbean: New Data for an Old Question*, forthcoming in Economia: *Journal of the Latin America and the Caribbean Economics Association.*

Schnepel, K.T. (2018). Good Jobs and Recidivism. *Economic Journal*, 128, 447–69.

Simpson, R. (1932). Unemployment and Prison Commitments. *Journal of Criminal Law and Criminology*, 23(3), 404–14.

Soares, R.R. (2004). Development, Crime and Punishment: Accounting for the International Differences in Crime Rates. *Journal of Development Economics*, 73, 155–84.

Soares, R.R. and Souza, D. (2021). *Income Shocks, Social Disorganization, and Crime*. Unpublished manuscript.

Street, B. (2020). *The Impact of Economic Opportunity on Criminal Behavior: Evidence from the Fracking Boom*. Working Paper.

Tornell, Aaron, and Philip R. Lane. (1999). The Voracity Effect. *American Economic Review*, 89 (1): 22–46.

Wilson, James, Q. and Kelling, G. L. (1982). Broken Windows: The Police and Neighborhood Safety. *The Atlantic*. https://www.theatlantic.com/magazine/archive/1982/03/broken-windows/304465/

9. Social prevention of crime: Alternatives to policing measures in an urban context

Magdalena Domínguez[1] and Daniel Montolio[2]

1. INTRODUCTION

Crime is a salient social problem that affects well-being as a large-scale disruptive activity and is also a critical welfare determinant. In the European Union, for example, crime remains a threat to society: in 2018, 11.5 percent of the population reported crime, violence or vandalism in their local area.[3] Meanwhile, crime prevention has become a substantial economic activity worldwide. In 2018, government expenditure for public order and safety was 1.7 percent of gross domestic product in the European Union and 2.0 percent in the United States.[4] In the European Union specifically, 53 percent of total expenditure under this heading was spent on police services, 18 percent on law courts and 24 percent on fire protection services and prisons. For most OECD countries, these values have remained stable over the last decade, in line with recent global crime trends. To understand such a relevant and persistent issue, the economics of crime 'focuses on the effect of incentives on criminal behavior . . . and the use of a benefit-cost framework to assess alternative strategies to reduce crime' (Freeman 1999).

The pioneer model by Becker (1968) frames crime as a rational act with costs and benefits, concluding that individuals might turn to crime if the latter outweigh the former. Two of the model's main contributions are the demonstration that optimal crime-fighting policies derive from optimal resource allocation and the introduction of uncertainty as a decision variable. After this seminal work, a rich strand in the economic literature sought to prove the model's theoretical predictions. Since then, research has focused on explaining criminal behavior through individual, regional and macroeconomic determinants. The causal effects of education, the labor market, healthcare, criminal justice, policing and public policies on crime have all been studied. Some of the most notable contributions to date have been previously summarized in Di Tella et al. (2010), Cook et al. (2013) and Draca and Machin (2015).

Crime economics is a field with room for many voices, programs and interdisciplinary contributions. In terms of policy, there is still considerable debate over the approaches to follow for crime prevention. Measures to fight crime are broadly split into 'hard' policies, with an emphasis on heavy policing and sturdy prosecution measures, and 'soft' policies, which focus on reducing crime-triggering disparities. As far as hard measures are concerned, Becker (1968) indicates that public policies can straightforwardly fight crime through expenditure on police and courts, which can affect the probability that an offender is apprehended and the severity of the punishment. Another early example is Ehrlich (1973), which shows how deterrence variables are good crime predictors. Public order expenditure worldwide shows that police-based measures are still the most widespread.

Still, contributions to the literature have also shown that tough-on-crime measures can sometimes lead to a worsening of initial conditions. This kind of policies can entail a high cost to society, in terms of both monetary and welfare costs. Kovandzic et al. (2004) outline as important not only the financial costs of trials and prisons but also the personal costs derived from discrimination and stigmatization. As an alternative, innovative strategies to prevent crime have been implemented, in which new societal agents play a key role. For example, Rose and Clear (1998) explore the effectiveness of deployed crime prevention measures related to self-protection, situational crime prevention and community organization, looking at community awareness and participation, social prevention and environmental modifications among others. Moreover, Weisburd (2012) states that interventions that emphasize the social features of a place should be an important part of the crime prevention toolbox.

In this chapter, we review the literature on crime prevention policies beyond policing. We mainly focus on examples of policies that target a specific location and have a significant community component. With a novel analysis of a community-based initiative, we also provide convincing evidence that there are simple, effective and efficient crime-fighting measures beyond tough policing.

2. HARD VS. SOFT POLICIES: A SIMPLIFIED FRAMEWORK

Starting in the 1970s in the United States and spreading worldwide from there, typical public safety policies have tended to follow a 'tough-on-crime' approach. Such policies include police search and seizure powers, strict criminal codes and severe sentences. The economics literature has long emphasized the potential deterrence value of police action and the criminal justice system (Becker 1968; Ehrlich 1973; Levitt 1997; Di Tella and Schargrodsky 2004; Machin and Marie 2011; Draca et al. 2011; Bindler and Hjalmarsson 2021). Still, contributions to the literature have also shown that, in many circumstances, tough measures do not lead to improvements in criminal outcomes. Research has shown that, in many scenarios, tough policies can be expensive, ineffective and discriminatory (Lynch 1997; Kovandzic et al. 2004; Evans and Owens 2007; Arora 2018).

Alternatives have been deployed and studied. Lewis and Salem (1981) indicate that programs with a social control perspective strengthen the local community's capacity to exert social control. So-called 'soft' approaches are of particular importance in deprived areas, where social interventions are most needed and strong police presence may be disruptive (Geller et al. 2014; Brayne 2014). Lawless (2006) analyzes the New Deal for Communities program, an English area-based initiative that aims to transform deprived neighborhoods. While outcomes indicate modest changes against benchmarks, the author concludes that working with non-law enforcement agencies helps change, and having the community at the heart of the initiative enhances outcomes. Cozens (2008) argues that crime prevention through environmental design has potential benefits for public health and in delivering safer environments.

Within the 'soft' strand of the economics of crime literature, Machin et al. (2011) analyze a law that changed the compulsory school-leaving age in England and Wales and show significant decreases in property crime. In this way, the authors find that improving education can enhance social benefits and reduce crime. Dinarte Diaz and Egaña-delSol (2019) provide experimental evidence of the offense-reducing impact of an after-school leisure program for vulnerable public-school students in El Salvador. Crowley (2013) states that policymakers wishing to install effective and efficient developmental measures against crime should invest in interventions that deliver prevention programs as well as engage innovative mechanisms for investing in crime prevention efforts. Although these 'soft' interventions are usually less expensive than 'hard' ones, their outcomes unfold over longer time frames (Lawless et al. 2010), and interdisciplinary approaches are greatly needed as new societal agents play a crucial role. As Owens (2019) explains, acknowledging both the costs and the benefits of aggressive policing is a first step to identifying policies that provide social benefits with minimal social costs. Questions remain on the implementation of the approaches mentioned above and if they can serve different purposes.

Note that soft policies to tackle crime may also stem from the courts and the police. Judges and prosecutors can avoid sending low-level, non-violent offenders to prison, divert them into treatment programs, work to eradicate the death penalty or reverse wrongful convictions. Police forces, too, can be organized in different ways to fight crime and guarantee law enforcement. Indeed, the organization of police forces varies hugely across countries and over time, with organizational forms ranging from neighborhood patrols to special forces such as anti-terrorist or narcotics units. Community policing is one option that can be framed as a soft approach to fighting crime and lessening citizens' perceptions of insecurity (see for instance Kenney et al. 2010; Wells et al. 2005). However, two types of 'soft' intervention have attracted the most attention, at least in the economic literature: place-based policies and social capital interventions. We now turn our attention to these.

2.1. Place-Based Policies

As stated in Neumark and Simpson (2015), place-based policies consist of government efforts to enhance the economic performance of an area. The best-studied cases are policies targeting areas that are underperforming in terms of specific socioeconomic indicators. Common examples include enterprise zone programs, real-estate development, welfare credits or regional development aid. Still, there is some evidence as to the role of place-based policies in crime deterrence. According to Eck and Guerette (2012), place-based crime prevention might hinder opportunities for crime by making offending riskier, more difficult, more salient, less rewarding, less excusable or less likely to be triggered.

Some kinds of police interventions may also be considered a type of place-based policy. For example, Di Tella and Schargrodsky (2004) show how an exogenous geographical allocation of police forces has large deterrent effect on crime, and Draca et al. (2011) show how 'Operation Theseus' in London reduced crime significantly while in place. Moreover, Blattman et al. (2017) study the effects of randomly assigned place-based interventions and find that more intense government presence deters more crime. More broadly, the review by Chalfin and McCrary (2017) on deterrence effects shows that crime is responsive to police presence.

Many examples of 'soft' policies are based on community approaches. A first example is the New Deal for Communities, which was implemented in England. The aim was to improve living standards in the country's most deprived neighborhoods, and it involved local committees implementing policies to improve living standards in five outcome areas: education, health, unemployment, housing and the physical environment, and crime. A total budget of £2 billion was allocated to 39 targeted neighborhoods over a 10-year period. Lawless (2006) shows that there was a statistically significant reduction in fear of crime in participating neighborhoods, while actual experience of crime declined to a lesser extent. Another example is Chicago's Safe Passage program, which aims to ensure the safety of students traveling to and from schools (140 schools by 2016) by placing civilian monitors along specified routes. Evidence shows significant effects in terms of crime reduction: McMillen et al. (2019), Sanfelice (2019) and Gonzalez and Komisarow (2020) all find lower levels of crime, particularly violent crime. Moreover, all three studies suggest that this program is more cost-effective and efficient than deploying police officers.

The above review of place-based crime prevention policies largely supports this type of approach, thus showing the applicability of alternative crime-fighting approaches beyond policing measures. Results show that place-based crime prevention works, and that it does so for different types of crime and contexts. Efficiency analysis also highlights some positive points of this set of initiatives. According to the review by Eck and Guerette (2012), research on place-based crime prevention shows how crime can be productively reduced by targeting high-crime areas when deploying prevention measures, how using situational approaches can often reduce crime rates and how tailor-made place-based prevention may be more effective than one-size-fits-all approaches.

Still, one of the key issues in place-based policy research is identifying which sets of individuals are affected by the policy and whether the policy is reaching the target groups. Moreover, when such policies comprise a variety of objectives or initiatives, actually understanding which components are driving the effects achieved is crucial. When policies are unsuccessful, it is good to determine whether they did not work because they failed to reach their target population or because funding was insufficient to make significant changes. Other issues that need improved research efforts include the analysis of long-run effects and of their interplay with broader policies, policies taking place in other jurisdictions or policies carried out by other agents.

Regarding this last point, the literature has also emphasized the role of networks with respect to place-based policies. Early on, Ladd (1994) pointed out how place-based policies should recognize the potential lack of social networks in deprived areas and the social isolation of their inhabitants. Neumark and Simpson (2015) outline how network effects may correct the underprovision of other public goods in deprived areas by providing opportunities or information to some local residents who then cause positive externalities for other agents in their networks. In this way, network effects can lead to more cost-effective policies. In either scenario, place-based policies to fight crime should consider the existence or absence of social interactions in the area when assessing their results.

2.2. (Local) Social Capital

Crime and social interactions have been studied in economics for quite some time. Early on, Glaeser et al. (1996) detected a large number of social interactions in criminal behavior. These authors present an index of social interactions that suggests that the number of social interactions is highest in petty crimes, moderate in more serious crimes and almost negligible in murder and rape.

More recent work emphasizes that more tightly knit social networks can raise aggregate crime levels due to the sharing of know-how among criminals (Calvó-Armengol and Zenou 2004) or imitation of peer behavior (Glaeser et al. 1996; Calvó-Armengol et al. 2005). However, they also increase the opportunity cost of committing a crime. This possibility is closely related to the concept of social capital, defined by Guiso et al. (2011) as 'a set of values and beliefs that help cooperation within a community'.[5] Very recently, Jackson (2020) provide a typology of social capital and considers seven forms: information capital, brokerage capital, coordination and leadership capital, bridging capital, favors capital, reputation capital and community capital. Jackson (2020) defines community capital as 'the ability to sustain cooperative behavior in transacting, the running of institutions, the provision of public goods, the handling of commons and externalities, and/or collective action, within a community'. Previously, Coleman (1988) had already related the strength of social sanction to social network closure. Additionally, systemic models of community organization are built on the notion that well-developed local network structures reduce crime (Flaherty and Brown 2010). This reduction is related to the fact that networks may increase returns on non-criminal activities and raise detection probabilities. Community-based interventions and initiatives can play a crucial role in this regard, particularly in deprived areas.

Undoubtedly, community capital can make a difference in many economic spheres. Among these, economics of crime is highly salient, and a number of papers have focused on social capital as a driver of crime at a low geographical level (Hirschfield and Bowers 1997; Lederman et al. 2002; Buonanno et al. 2009; Akçomak and Ter Weel 2012). For example, Buonanno et al. (2009) find a negative effect of social capital on property crimes. Lederman et al. (2002) state that trust has a significant and negative effect on violent crime. Moreover, Akçomak and Ter Weel (2012) use both historical and present data for Dutch municipalities and find a negative correlation between social capital levels and crime rates. Additionally, they find that current levels of social capital are affected by historical data on sociodemographic characteristics. This last finding is also shared by Lederman et al. (2002). Hirschfield and Bowers (1997) state that there is a significant relationship between social cohesion (measured by a social control component and another component of ethnic heterogeneity) and crime levels in disadvantaged areas. They also indicate that where levels of social cohesion are high, crime is significantly lower than expected.

More recently, and regarding the causal impact of social capital on crime, Damm and Dustmann (2014) state that social interactions are an important channel through which neighborhood crime affects individual criminal behavior, particularly in violent crimes for young males. Additionally, Sharkey et al. (2017) incorporate the so-called systemic model of community life and estimate the causal effect on violent crime of non-profits focused on reducing violence and building stronger communities. The authors estimate that a higher presence of organizations focusing on crime and community life achieves significant reductions in violent and property crime. In one specific instance, García-Hombrados (2020) investigates the 2010 earthquake in Chile and finds that it had a positive effect on the strength of community life and ultimately led to a decrease in crime in the affected neighborhoods. The author presents robust estimates consistent with an informal guardianship mechanism reported after natural disasters. The improvement in social capital at the community level facilitated cooperation among neighbors and boosted the adoption of community-based measures to prevent crime.

Sociologists have also devoted efforts to understanding such a link. Over the last two decades, researchers have explored social capital as a local factor in crime prevention. Here, efforts in understanding the social pattern of crime rely on social disorganization theory and systemic models of community attachment. Social disorganization is defined as the inability of a community structure to realize the common values of its residents and maintain effective social controls (Sampson 1988; Sampson and Groves 1989). This theory has recently been linked to the concept of social capital, defined as those features of social organization that facilitate cooperation between citizens for mutual benefits (Putnam et al. 1994). On that note, a growing number of studies support the link between low social capital and high crime (Rose and Clear 1998; Kennedy et al. 1998). Moreover, the systemic model of community attachment (Flaherty and Brown 2010) emphasizes the effect of community structural characteristics on neighborhood friendship and associational ties, and their effect on informal social control and crime levels. The systemic model hypothesis is that more extensive social ties will decrease crime rates since communities with wider friendship and associational ties should have greater potential for informal social control due to social cohesion. In this line of work, Warner and Rountree (1997) analyze the role of local social ties as a mediator between structural conditions and crime rates, conditional upon neighborhood characteristics. Using data for 100 Seattle census tracts, authors find that the extent to which friendship networks decrease crime depends in part on the racial makeup of the neighborhood. Kawachi et al. (1999) present a conceptual framework for analyzing the influence of the social context on community health, using crime as the indicator of collective well-being. Authors argue that two sets of societal characteristics influence the level of crime: the degree of relative deprivation and the degree of cohesiveness in social relations among citizens. Unlike Warner and Rountree (1997), Kawachi et al. (1999) find evidence consistent with social disorganization theory, as the strongest correlates of violent crime in their sample turn out to be social capital indicators. Additionally, Takagi et al. (2012) find that neighborhood generalized trust, reciprocity, supportive networks and social capital are inversely associated with crime victimization. Social capital may influence not only crime levels in a neighborhood but also fear of crime among its residents. Ferguson and Mindel (2007) report reductions in individual levels of fear due to factors related to social capital, such as social support networks or collective efficacy.[6]

In this way, the existing literature also indicates that local social capital can deter certain types of crime in certain circumstances. Moreover, there seems to be an interplay between place-based policies and social capital when it comes to fighting crime. Taking these points into consideration, in the following section we provide a new set of evidence that shows how a place-based policy that emphasizes the role of community ties can reduce crime.

3. NEW EVIDENCE IN AN URBAN CONTEXT: LOCAL COMMUNITY TIES AND CRIME

The previous section reviewed how 'soft' or non-traditional policies can deter crime. We now move to enrich such evidence. The results we present in this section support approaches that bolster community ties to reduce crime in an urban context.

We analyze the deployment of a community health policy in the city of Barcelona, Spain. The program, called 'Health in the Neighborhoods' (*Barcelona Salut als Barris*, BSaB), aimed to improve health outcomes and reduce inequality between the disadvantaged neighborhoods and the rest of the city. It is thus both a place-based policy and focused on the community component. The program is managed and run in each neighborhood by the local health center, and it was deployed in a quasi-random order across the city. Due to the high degree of involvement that BSaB requires from neighbors, we expect the building of closer ties within the neighborhood, which in turn might have the effect of reducing criminal outcomes.[7]

3.1. Description of the Program

The city of Barcelona states that community action becomes meaningful when it arises from within a human community that shares the same physical space and a sense of belonging that both gives rise to reciprocal ties and support and drives its members to engage actively in improving their situation

(Ajuntament de Barcelona 2005). The purpose of community action is thus to improve social well-being by promoting active participation. Community action requires the empowerment of citizens to drive change and improvements beyond the individual spheres.

In 2005, local health authorities in the city of Barcelona started to develop the BSaB community health program. Its aim was to improve health outcomes and reduce inequality between the disadvantaged neighborhoods and the rest of the city through community-based interventions. BSaB was rolled out between 2008 and 2014 in 12 of the 49 candidate neighborhoods potentially participating, out of the total of 73 neighborhoods in Barcelona city. The 49 potential candidate neighborhoods were the ones where per capita income was below 90 percent of the city median and were considered deprived.[8] The 12 neighborhoods finally reached by the program comprise 15 percent of the total city population and 25 percent of the potentially participating population. The interventions were intended to facilitate non-competitive physical activity, social relationships, healthy recreation, health literacy and sexual health. Interventions included the treatment and prevention of substance abuse, training and job placement, sexual and reproductive health advice, parenting skills programs, mental healthcare and healthy leisure activities (Díez et al. 2012; Generalitat de Catalunya 2014; Comissionat de Salut 2016). The roll-out schedule by neighborhood is shown in Table 9.1.

Table 9.1 *BSaB deployment by neighborhood*

Neighborhood	Start date
Roquetes	Jun-2008
Poble Sec	Jun-2008
St. Pere, Santa Caterina i la Ribera	Jun-2009
Torre Baró	Jun-2009
Ciutat Meridiana	Jun-2009
Vallbona	Jun-2009
Barceloneta	Jul-2010
Baró de Viver	Mar-2011
Bon Pastor	Mar-2011
Raval	Oct-2011
El Besós i el Maresme	Oct-2013
Verneda i La Pau	Nov-2014

Notes: The table lists the 12 neighborhoods that benefited from the BSaB policy in the city of Barcelona from 2008 to 2014, ordered chronologically. It also lists the start date of the program in each neighborhood.

Source: Barcelona Public Health Agency (ASPB).

A key identification point is that the gradual roll out of BSaB in the territory did not follow any specific pattern concerning socioeconomic or demographic characteristics. The authorities in charge of BSaB shared knowledge on the design and running of the program and confirmed to us that neighborhoods were not assigned to the intervention according to any rule-based procedure or any objectifiable variables.[9] This roll-out approach allows the program to be regarded as a quasi-random experiment. Another critical factor is that the interventions were mainly managed in each neighborhood by the local health center. There are 70 local health centers citywide, and their catchment areas mostly correspond to neighborhood demarcations. Because each local health center has a specific area and population under its responsibility set by the administration, the outlined identification strategy is strengthened, as spillovers from one neighborhood to another are highly unlikely. Another important point is that all interventions were run from the outset on a community basis, involving a steering group, the local community and the authorities. This communal component of BSaB is what leads us to hypothesize that the program boosted community ties and thereby reduced local crime rates.

3.2. How Community Ties Can Affect Crime

Theoretically, criminal activity could be influenced by the BSaB policy through different pathways. Health might have seemed the most obvious candidate: an improved health status among the target population might reduce criminal activity. However, due to the strong community component of BSaB, we claim that a stronger mechanism of community ties operates here. As previously mentioned, a body of research documents the association between community capital and becoming a victim of crime. The theoretical pathways whereby community capital can lead to crime prevention include both formal and informal mechanisms. Sampson and Laub (1995) state that communities with substantial social capital can exert informal social control and bolster the capacity to obtain services from public agencies and formal institutions. Because of the high degree of involvement that BSaB requires from neighborhood residents, the development of closer links within the neighborhood is to be expected. Informal social control may also arise as a result, increasing the probability of getting caught, and thus potentially leading to a fall in the neighborhood's crime rate. Following Putnam et al. (1994), Buonanno et al. (2009) and Guiso et al. (2011), we use the number of associations per capita, or association density, as a measure of community ties at the neighborhood level. Several points can help elucidate the mechanisms that lead to the effects found. First, we assess whether BSaB impacts the association density. Second, we examine whether there have been any changes in the health status of participants and non-participants. Third, we analyze whether there have been any changes in unemployment after the policy implementation, as this was the aim of some interventions and employment status can affect engagement in criminal behavior. In this way, we aim to identify the effects that operate through association density while addressing the potential effects of other mechanisms such as improved health or lower unemployment.

3.3. Empirical Strategy and Data

Our central hypothesis is that the BSaB policy reduces criminal activity at the local level through its community component. One way to test this hypothesis is to link association density to crime via BSaB. Specifically, we assess whether BSaB increased association density and then whether this increase further translated into lower crime rates. Local community capital in the form of local associations that invigorate neighborhood ties may be reduced or increased as a result of criminal activity in the neighborhood. Local criminality levels or residents' perceptions of (in)security may influence their willingness to be involved in activities that often extend beyond the private sphere and require interactions and relationships with other members of the community.

For this reason, we perform a two-stage least square (2SLS) regression where we use the exogenous deployment of BSaB as an instrument for association density which, as we just explained, can be endogenous to local crime rates:

$$
\begin{aligned}
Crime_{it} &= \alpha_2 + \beta_2 \cdot \widehat{Assoc_{it}} + \theta_2 \cdot X_{it} + \gamma_t + \delta_i + \varepsilon_{it} \\
Assoc_{it} &= \alpha_1 + \sum_{d \neq -1} \beta_t \cdot \left(BSaB_i \cdot Time_t\right)_{it} + \theta_1 \cdot X_{it} + \gamma_t + \delta_i + \varepsilon_{it}
\end{aligned}
\tag{9.1}
$$

where the observational unit is a 'neighborhood–year–month' pair, i is the neighborhood, t is the time period (year–month), the dependent variable is the crime rate per 1000 inhabitants, $Assoc_{it}$ is the association density (number of per capita associations per 1000 inhabitants), $BSaB_i = 1$ for participant neighborhoods, $Time_{it} = 1$ is the distance to BSaB start (different for each unit), δ_i and γ_t are neighborhood and year–month fixed effects and ε_{it} are the error terms.

For the instrument to be valid, it must hold that (1) BSaB highly correlates with association density (relevance) and (2) BSaB is exogenous to local crime rates (exogeneity). The first requirement is tested by regressing of BSaB on association density. The second is backed up by a logit regressing the probability of a neighborhood's receiving the intervention on several sociodemographic variables, including crime (Table 9.4, run for all 49 potential candidate neighborhoods), all of which turn out not to be significant determinants of policy deployment. As in many instrumental variables, this condition is more difficult to pin down regarding the exclusion restriction. We argue that if BSaB affects crime, it mostly does so through association density. This argument is based on the program's design, in which local associations were an important catalyst and mediator at the local level and a key ally in achieving its goals. Other potential main influences are tested using the same 2SLS exercise (see results reported in Table 9.5).

Regarding data, we start with a geocoded administrative dataset of all crimes reported in the city of Barcelona from 2008 to 2014. This data is provided by the police. With over one million entries, the dataset comprises all reported crimes with information on the exact time and place where they occurred and the crime type. Second, information on the BSaB program (targeted and treated neighborhoods, timing and activities in each intervention) is provided by the local health authority. Finally, Barcelona city council provided the information for a set of socioeconomic variables that include registered local associations, registered unemployment rates, housing prices per square meter and a proxy for tourist pressure. With these datasets we construct a panel at the neighborhood–year–month level. A description of the variables used for this analysis and our crime categorization are shown in Tables 9.2 and 9.3, respectively.

3.4. Results

Table 9.5 presents results on the impact of BSaB on association density, registered unemployment, health status and mental health. First, results reported in Table 9.5 show a positive and statistically significant effect of BSaB on

Table 9.2 Description of main variables

Variable	Description	Source	Frequency availability
Crime counts	Registered crime counts	Police	Geocoded; exact time
Population	Registered inhabitants	City council	Neighborhood; year
Crime rates	Crime counts per 1000 inh.	Police and city council	Neighborhood-month
Associations	Per capita local associations	Regional government	Neighborhood-month
Health status	Self-reported from 1 to 5	Health survey	Neighborhood-year
Mental health	Self-reported from 1 to 12	Health survey	Neighborhood-year
Unemployment	Registered unemployment rate	City council	Neighborhood-month
Housing prices	House prices per square meter	City council	Neighborhood-month
Tourism	Per capita visitors to tourist sites	City council	Neighborhood-month

Notes: This table presents a description of the main variables under analysis. It contains a brief description of how each is constructed, its sources and the frequency with which they are available.

Source: Own construction from local police, local government and Barcelona city council data.

Table 9.3 *Broad and detailed crime categories*

Broad	Share %	Detailed	Share %
Against property	86.6	Damage to property	8.5
		Fraud	5.2
		Car theft	11.4
		Robbery	14.5
		Theft	47.1
Against persons	8.9	Family	0.7
		Gender violence	2.0
		Bodily harm	3.0
		Murder	0.1
		Sexual	0.3
		Threat	2.5
		Other	0.3
Other	4.5	Arson	0.0
		Drugs	0.7
		Environmental crime	0.2
		Disobeying authority	1.8
		Criminal traffic violations	1.8
Total	100		100

Notes: This table presents a categorization of all crime types available in our administrative database obtained from the local police. We present both a broad categorization (left panel, 3 categories) and a detailed one (right panel, 17 categories).

Source: own construction from local police data.

association density. Second, results indicate no statistically significant impact on unemployment. Third, there is no evidence of significant differences in mean health and mental health scores between treated and control neighborhoods before and after BSaB implementation. In line with this last result, Palencia et al. (2018) find no changes in self-rated health for men and women in treatment and control neighborhoods. The evidence in Table 9.5 supports the relevance of BSaB as an instrument for association density, our proxy for community ties. Moreover, to a certain extent, Table 9.5 also provides a degree of evidence that BSaB could affect crime only through association density, as it does not affect any of the other primary drivers.

Additionally, Figure 9.1 shows an event study exercise for the impact of BSaB on association density. It evidences that after the implementation of the policy, association density increased in the neighborhoods benefiting from the policy. Even if the monthly point estimates evidence a certain lack of precision, the point estimates of the effect increase early on. Specifically, two

Table 9.4 *Panel logit regression for intervention timing*

P(BSaB) = 1	Coef.	Std. err.	z	P > z
Income	0.03	0.29	0.090	0.925
Population	0.00	0.00	–0.880	0.377
Mortality	0.02	0.02	1.350	0.178
Teenage birth rate	0.40	0.34	1.180	0.239
Non-Spanish population	0.00	0.00	0.880	0.378
Pensions	–0.04	0.04	–1.200	0.230
Housing prices	–0.51	0.19	–2.730	0.006
Overall crime	0.00	0.00	1.140	0.253
Associations	0.42	0.55	0.770	0.440
Tourism	0.04	0.13	–0.06	0.956
ln(sigma² u)	5.26	0.53		
sigma u	13.89	3.66		
rho	0.98	0.009		
Prob W > chi² = 0.01056; Prob LR (rho = 0) > chi² = 0				

Notes: This table presents the results of a panel logistic regression of the probability of a neighborhood receiving intervention on several sociodemographic characteristics, for the 2007–14 period and for the 49 potential candidate neighborhoods. Robust standard errors.

Source: own construction from Barcelona city council data.

Table 9.5 *Effect of BSaB on socioeconomic variables: potential mechanisms*

	Association density	Registered unemployment	Health status	Mental health
BSaB	0.504***	–0.003	–0.087	–0.064
	(0.171)	(0.003)	(0.081)	(0.157)
Observations	3264	3264	3716	3653
Neighborhood FE	Y	Y	Y	Y
Year-month FE	Y	Y	Y	Y
Neighborhood-time trends	Y	Y	Y	Y

Notes: This table presents difference-in-differences estimates of the BSaB policy on outcomes other than crime, each presented in a different column. The observational unit is a neighborhood–year–month pair. Treated units are those in which the BSaB policy took place, while those in which it did not are controls. Treatment timing differs across units, and the specification is the same as in our baseline specification for crime. Confidence intervals are based on standard errors clustered at the neighborhood level.

***p < 0.01, **p < 0.05, *p < 0.1.

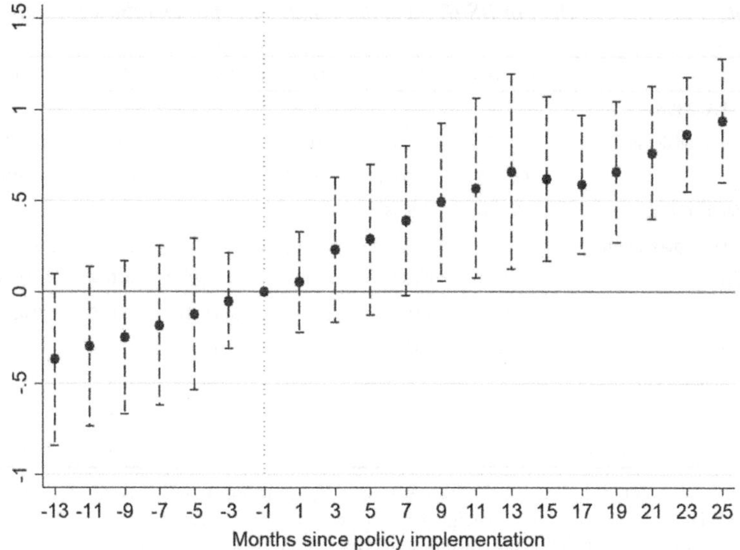

Notes: This graph reports the results of an event study exercise derived from the first stage estimation for the 2008–14 period for association density on BSaB. The observational unit is a neighborhood–year–month pair, binned by two-month periods. Treated units are those in which the BSaB policy took place, while those in which it did not but were eligible are controls. BSaB timing differs across units. Confidence intervals are based on standard errors clustered at the neighborhood level.

Figure 9.1 Effect of BSaB on association density. Event study exercise, 95 percent confidence intervals

months after the policy implementation there is a jump in the estimated coefficient, and this effect seems to be persistent over time.

Given that BSaB positively affects association density, we perform an instrumental variables exercise. We use BSaB as an instrument for association density to study its impact on local crime rates. Results, shown in Table 9.6, indicate a negative and significant impact of BSaB on local crime rates. Specifically, we find that it reduces crimes against persons and other crime, while no effect is found for crimes against property. The coefficients translate into a 23 percent reduction with respect to the mean in crimes against persons, and a 35 percent reduction in other crime. Additionally, we find a significant reduction in crimes involving a very close personal link between offender and victim, which we label as 'intimate crimes', and also in crimes in which emotion management skills play a role, which we label as 'crimes of anger'.[10] Evidence indicates that BSaB reduces intimate crimes by 55 percent

Table 9.6 *Effect of BSaB on crime: instrumental variables estimates*

	Property	Person	Other	Intimate	Anger	Drugs
Panel A: 2SLS						
Association density	–0.672	–0.118***	–0.076**	–0.094***	–0.117*	–0.038**
	(0.487)	(0.035)	(0.035)	(0.018)	(0.064)	(0.019)
F-stat first stage	16.88	16.88	16.88	16.88	16.88	16.88
Panel B: reduced form						
BSaB	0.186	–0.088***	–0.095**	–0.066***	–0.098*	–0.018
	(0.626)	(0.027)	(0.040)	(0.013)	(0.055)	(0.020)
Observations	3264	3264	3264	3264	3264	3264
Neighborhood FE	Y	Y	Y	Y	Y	Y
Year–month FE	Y	Y	Y	Y	Y	Y
Neighborhood-time trends	Y	Y	Y	Y	Y	Y

Notes: This table lists estimates of the effect of association density on crime for the 2008–14 period. The observational unit is a neighborhood–year–month pair. Panel A presents 2SLS estimates, in which association density is instrumented with the deployment of the BSaB. The coefficient shown is that of $Assoc_{it}$ as in equation (9.1). Panel B presents reduced-form estimates, in which we directly estimate the effect of the BSaB policy on crime. The coefficient shown is that of $BSaB_{it}$. This variable takes value one for neighborhoods where BSaB was deployed, after the deployment. Each column presents results for a different type of crime. Confidence intervals are based on standard errors clustered at the neighborhood level. ***$p < 0.01$, **$p < 0.05$, *$p < 0.1$.

and crimes of anger by 13 percent. Lastly, it must be noted that the instrumental variables exercise provides evidence in the same direction as reduced-form estimates and that the F-stat reported for the first stage of this exercise shows that this is a strong instrument.

Our results therefore show that BSaB reduces crimes against the person and that this effect is specifically linked to a short-term 55 percent reduction in intimate crime. Drug crimes also decline, but over a longer period. Turning to offense rates, we find a decline among younger individuals. In sum, we take the results in Tables 9.5 and 9.6 as suggestive evidence that (1) BSaB significantly reduces crime in neighborhoods benefiting from the program and that (2) the key mechanism behind the effectiveness of BSaB against crime is related to the bolstering of community ties.

Overall, the above results are in line with those of previous studies. For instance, Takagi et al. (2012) establish that support networks and social capital are inversely associated with crime. Buonanno et al. (2009) find a clear effect of social capital on crime, although their focus, unlike ours, is property crime, and we do not find a significant effect on all property crime. Lederman et al. (2002) state that trust (seen as a proxy for social capital) has a significant and robust effect on violent crime, proxied by homicide rates. In a line similar to ours, the theoretical model proposed by Buonanno et al. (2012) predicts that the effectiveness of social sanction increases with the density of social interaction. Lastly, our results also embrace an interpretation related to the strengthening of cooperation and social control among individuals at the local level, so that that community ties within the neighborhood are strengthened (Buonanno and Vanin 2017).

4. CONCLUDING REMARKS

Crime is one of the most salient phenomena with a detrimental effect on individual and societal welfare. The economics of crime focuses on the effect of incentives on criminal behavior and on the use of a cost-benefit framework to assess alternative crime-reduction strategies (Freeman 1999). It is a relevant field of study, as crime is a high-profile issue in current societies.

This chapter evidenced that non-traditional policies work against crime and that less disruptive means of reducing criminal activity in disadvantaged areas can be effective. Even if building community ties can be more challenging than deploying traditional policing, this type of alternative policy may work better in several contexts. Buonanno et al. (2009) conclude that a policy of promoting associational life may usefully complement traditional anti-crime policies. Moreover, Takagi et al. (2012) argue that policymakers should not overlook policies aimed at reducing inequalities to promote social cohesion, social stability and safer neighborhoods. A better understanding of the interactions between social cohesion and public policy is essential to reduce criminal activity induced by the lack of integration of some citizens facing disadvantaged social and economic conditions.

Our findings from the empirical exercise presented in this chapter are of value in the context of the policy evaluation, especially when highlighting the potential effects of 'soft' policies to prevent and reduce crime. Moreover, the type of crime that BSaB reduced most is intimate crime, the type where women are the most likely to be victimized. Even though intimate crimes may not seem to be a salient share of overall crime, they inflict a much higher disutility on their victims than more frequent types of crime. In fact, Dolan et al. (2005) point out that discounted quality-adjusted life years (QALY) losses resulting from rape and sexual assault are 0.561 and 0.160, compared to only 0.007 for common assault. These figures demonstrate the importance of addressing such offenses. Our findings are highly relevant for another reason. Many BSaB interventions aimed to empower women and raise awareness about sexual health and education. This is relevant as findings indicate that progress was achieved on such an essential issue as violence against women.

According to Spain's National Statistics Institute, in 2018 there were over 30000 registered cases of gender violence in Spain.[11]

Although crime was not one of the policy's specific targets, it is indirectly linked to them, as they reflect local disparities. We therefore consider the policy to have been successful in achieving one of its goals. However, we also understand that policy design improvements are needed, as some key crime categories are not affected by the program. In light of the results on the underlying mechanisms, cooperation with existing local associations and other institutions is crucial if any new initiatives are to be carried out.

Our results indicate that traditional policies against crime are not the only ones that work and that new ways of reducing criminal activity in disadvantaged neighborhoods can be effective. Additionally, these policies speak to efficiency. BSaB had an annual cost of € 500000 in 2015, which means a cost of € 5000 per annual activity, € 70 per active participant or € 2 per potential participant. Hence, the policy can also be seen as advantageous from a cost-effectiveness perspective.

Still, we believe that traditional and non-traditional crime prevention policies are not perfect substitutes for one another but should complement each other to fight crime. An interesting research avenue would be to seek evidence as to how both approaches can be optimally combined when putting together a crime-fighting strategy. Even in contexts where a 'tough-on-crime' approach might be suitable, other, less visible issues might require policies based on community approaches. Policy design should incorporate hard and soft approaches into a unified strategy, combining and coordinating efforts that tackle crime.

NOTES

1. Department of Economics – Uppsala University.
2. Department of Economics and IEB – Universitat de Barcelona.
3. EU Statistics of Income and Living Conditions Survey (EU-SILC): https://ec.europa.eu/eurostat/Population-reporting-crime, https://ec.europa.eu/eurostat/statistics-explained/index.php?title=Government_expenditure_on_public_order_and_safety
4. https://data.oecd.org/gga/general-government-spending
5. There has been an extensive debate in the literature regarding social capital, what it actually is and how it can be measured. Putnam et al. (1994) set up the basis for such considerations when analyzing the effects of social engagement. Ever since, social capital has been defined and measured in several ways by economic researchers. For example, Tabellini (2010) measured culture according to indicators of individual values and beliefs (such as trust and respect for others) in order to explore whether it has a causal effect on economic development, and he finds that the exogenous component of culture due to history is strongly correlated with current regional economic development. Taking a different approach, Nannicini et al. (2013) investigate political accountability as a channel through which social capital may improve economic well-being. The authors find that punishment for political misbehavior is greater in districts with higher social capital, proxied by blood donations. Finally, Guiso et al. (2011) take a more theoretical perspective on social capital. They review previous research on its role, as they understand previous definitions were

too vague or broad, leading to mixed results and interpretations. To solve such discrepancies, authors restrict their definition of social capital to one of civic capital, seen as a set of values and beliefs that help cooperation in a community.

6. As stated in Sampson (2001), the notion of collective efficacy refers to shared expectations and mutual civic engagement by community members in local social control, with an emphasis on residents' joint capacity to act together to generate solutions to local problems.
7. The empirical results we present in this section stem from the analysis in Domínguez and Montolio (2021). In Domínguez and Montolio (2021) we analyze the effects of the BSaB program on crime, offense and victimization rates. Taking advantage of the staggered and quasi-random roll out of the program across neighborhoods, we follow a difference-in-differences approach comparing treated neighborhoods to those eligible but not treated, before and after the program implementation. The results and conclusions presented in this section point in the same direction as Domínguez and Montolio (2021).
8. The city median referred to is the median among neighborhoods, not individuals.
9. Further formal testing is developed in later sections.
10. We create a crime category, termed 'intimate crimes', which includes the detailed categories of family, sexual and gender violence. The rationale behind this aggregation is that it summarizes all crimes related to very close personal interactions. Second, we define a crime category termed 'crimes of anger' that comprises the detailed categories of damage to property, bodily harm, disobeying authority and threat. These are crimes that are not motivated by money or close links but still have some behavioral or personal component, see Currie and Almond (2011).
11. https://www.ine.es/prensa/evdvg_2019.pdf

REFERENCES

Ajuntament de Barcelona (2005). *Marc municipal per a l'accio comunitaria. bases conceptuals i metodologiques.* Technical report, Ajuntament de Barcelona, Benestar Social.

Akçomak, I. S. and Ter Weel, B. (2012). The impact of social capital on crime: Evidence from the Netherlands. *Regional Science and Urban Economics*, 42(1–2):323–40.

Arora, A. (2018). Too tough on crime? The impact of prosecutor politics on incarceration. American Economic Association Conference Presentation.

Becker, G. S. (1968). Crime and punishment: An economic approach. *Journal of Political Economy*, 76(2):169–217.

Bindler, A. and Hjalmarsson, R. (2021). The impact of the first professional police forces on crime. *Journal of the European Economic Association*, 19(6):3063–103.

Blattman, C., Green, D., Ortega, D., and Tobon, S. (2017). *Place-based Interventions at Scale: The Direct and Spillover Effects of Policing and City Services on Crime.* Technical report, National Bureau of Economic Research.

Brayne, S. (2014). Surveillance and system avoidance: Criminal justice contact and institutional attachment. *American Sociological Review*, 79(3):367–91.

Buonanno, P. and Vanin, P. (2017). Social closure, surnames and crime. *Journal of Economic Behavior & Organization*, 137:160–75.

Buonanno, P., Montolio, D., and Vanin, P. (2009). Does social capital reduce crime? *The Journal of Law and Economics*, 52(1):145–70.

Buonanno, P., Pasini, G., and Vanin, P. (2012). Crime and social sanction. *Papers in Regional Science*, 91(1):193–218.

Calvó-Armengol, A. and Zenou, Y. (2004). Social networks and crime decisions: The role of social structure in facilitating delinquent behavior. *International Economic Review*, 45(3):939–58.

Calvó-Armengol, A., Patacchini, E., and Zenou, Y. (2005). *Peer Effects and Social Networks in Education and Crime.* Technical report, CEPR Discussion Paper.

Chalfin, A. and McCrary, J. (2017). Criminal deterrence: A review of the literature. *Journal of Economic Literature*, 55(1):5–48.

Coleman, J. S. (1988). Social capital in the creation of human capital. *American Journal of Sociology*, 94:S95–S120.

Comissionat de Salut (2016). *Impuls de la salut comunitaria a barcelona*. Technical report, Ajuntament de Barcelona.

Cook, P. J., Machin, S. J., Marie, O., and Mastrobuoni, G. (2013). Lessons from the economics of crime. In Cook, P. J., Machin, S. J., Marie, O., and Mastrobuoni, G., editors, *Lessons from the Economics of Crime*. MIT Press.

Cozens, P. (2008). Public health and the potential benefits of crime prevention through environmental design. *New South Wales Public Health Bulletin*, 18(12):232–37.

Crowley, D. M. (2013). Building efficient crime prevention strategies: Considering the economics of investing in human development. *Criminology & Public Policy*, 12(2):353.

Currie, J. and Almond, D. (2011). Human capital development before age five. In Ashenfelter, O. C. and Card, D., editors, *Handbook of Labor Economics*, volume 4, pages 1315–486. Elsevier.

Damm, A. P. and Dustmann, C. (2014). Does growing up in a high crime neighborhood affect youth criminal behavior? *American Economic Review*, 104(6):1806–32.

Di Tella, R. and Schargrodsky, E. (2004). Do police reduce crime? Estimates using the allocation of police forces after a terrorist attack. *American Economic Review*, 94(1):115–33.

Di Tella, R., Edwards, S., and Schargrodsky, E. (2010). *The Economics of Crime: Lessons for and from Latin America*. University of Chicago Press.

Díez, E., Pasarín, M., Daban, F., Calzada, N., Fuertes, C., Artazcoz, L., and Borrell, C. (2012). Salut als barris en Barcelona, una intervenci´on comunitaria para reducir las desigualdades sociales en salud. *Comunidad*, 14:121–26.

Diaz, I. and Egaña-delSol, P. (2019). *Preventing Violence in the Most Violent Contexts: Behavioral and Neurophysiological Evidence*. The World Bank Policy Research Working Paper No. 8862.

Dolan, P., Loomes, G., Peasgood, T., and Tsuchiya, A. (2005). Estimating the intangible victim costs of violent crime. *British Journal of Criminology*, 45(6):958–76.

Domínguez, M. and Montolio, D. (2021). Bolstering community ties as a mean of reducing crime. *Journal of Economic Behavior & Organization*, 191:916–45.

Draca, M. and Machin, S. (2015). Crime and economic incentives. *Annual Review of Economics*, 7(1):389–408.

Draca, M., Machin, S., and Witt, R. (2011). Panic on the streets of London: Police, crime, and the July 2005 terror attacks. *American Economic Review*, 101(5):2157–81.

Eck, J. E. and Guerette, R. T. (2012). Place-based crime prevention: Theory, evidence, and policy. *The Oxford Handbook of Crime Prevention*, pages 354–83. Oxford University Press.

Ehrlich, I. (1973). *The Deterrent Effect of Capital Punishment: A Question of Life and Death*. Technical report, National Bureau of Economic Research.

Evans, W. N. and Owens, E. G. (2007). Cops and crime. *Journal of Public Economics*, 91(1–2):181–201.

Ferguson, K. M. and Mindel, C. H. (2007). Modeling fear of crime in Dallas neighborhoods: A test of social capital theory. *Crime & Delinquency*, 53(2):322–49.

Flaherty, J. and Brown, R. B. (2010). A multilevel systemic model of community attachment: Assessing the relative importance of the community and individual levels. *American Journal of Sociology*, 116(2):503–42.

Freeman, R. B. (1999). The economics of crime. In Ashenfelter, O. C. and Card, D., editors, *Handbook of Labor Economics*, volume 3, pages 3529–71. Elsevier.

García-Hombrados, J. (2020). The lasting effects of natural disasters on property crime: Evidence from the 2010 Chilean earthquake. *Journal of Economic Behavior & Organization*, 175:114–54.

Geller, A., Fagan, J., Tyler, T., and Link, B. G. (2014). Aggressive policing and the mental health of young urban men. *American Journal of Public Health*, 104(12):2321–27.

Generalitat de Catalunya (2014). *Salut als barris*. Technical report, Departament de Salut, Generalitat de Catalunya.

Glaeser, E. L., Sacerdote, B., and Scheinkman, J. A. (1996). Crime and social interactions. *The Quarterly Journal of Economics*, 111(2):507–48.

Gonzalez, R. and Komisarow, S. (2020). Community monitoring and crime: Evidence from Chicago's safe passage program. *Journal of Public Economics*, 191:104250.

Guiso, L., Sapienza, P., and Zingales, L. (2011). Civic capital as the missing link. In Benhabib, J., Bisin, A., and Jackson, M. O., editors, *Handbook of Social Economics*, volume 1, pages 417–80. Elsevier.

Hirschfield, A. and Bowers, K. J. (1997). The effect of social cohesion on levels of recorded crime in disadvantaged areas. *Urban Studies*, 34(8):1275–95.

Jackson, M. O. (2020). A typology of social capital and associated network measures. *Social Choice and Welfare*, 54(2):311–36.

Kawachi, I., Kennedy, B. P., and Wilkinson, R. G. (1999). Crime: Social disorganization and relative deprivation. *Social Science & Medicine*, 48(6):719–31.

Kennedy, B. P., Kawachi, I., Prothrow-Stith, D., Lochner, K., and Gupta, V. (1998). Social capital, income inequality, and firearm violent crime. *Social Science & Medicine*, 47(1):7–17.

Kenney, D. J., White, M. D., and Ruffinengo, M. A. (2010). Expanding the role of patrol in criminal investigations: Houston's investigative first responder project. *Police Quarterly*, 13(2):136–60.

Kovandzic, T. V., Sloan III, J. J., and Vieraitis, L. M. (2004). "Striking out" as crime reduction policy: The impact of "three strikes" laws on crime rates in US cities. *Justice Quarterly*, 21(2):207–39.

Ladd, H. F. (1994). Spatially targeted economic development strategies: Do they work? *Cityscape*, 1(1):193–218.

Lawless, P. (2006). Area-based urban interventions: Rationale and outcomes: The new deal for communities programme in England. *Urban Studies*, 43(11):1991–2011.

Lawless, P., Foden, M., Wilson, I., and Beatty, C. (2010). Understanding area-based regeneration: The new deal for communities programme in England. *Urban Studies*, 47(2):257–75.

Lederman, D., Loayza, N., and Menendez, A. M. (2002). Violent crime: Does social capital matter? *Economic Development and Cultural Change*, 50(3):509–39.

Levitt, S. D. (1997). Using electoral cycles in police hiring to estimate the effects of police on crime. *American Economic Review*, 87(3):270–90.

Lewis, D. A. and Salem, G. (1981). Community crime prevention: An analysis of a developing strategy. *Crime & Delinquency*, 27(3):405–21.

Lynch, J. P. (1997). *Did Getting Tough on Crime Pay?: Crime Policy Report no. 1.* Technical report, The Urban Institute.

Machin, S. and Marie, O. (2011). Crime and police resources: The street crime initiative. *Journal of the European Economic Association*, 9(4):678–701.

Machin, S., Marie, O., and Vuji´c, S. (2011). The crime reducing effect of education. *The Economic Journal*, 121(552):463–84.

McMillen, D., Sarmiento-Barbieri, I., and Singh, R. (2019). Do more eyes on the street reduce crime? evidence from Chicago's safe passage program. *Journal of Urban Economics*, 110:1–25.

Nannicini, T., Stella, A., Tabellini, G., and Troiano, U. (2013). Social capital and political accountability. *American Economic Journal: Economic Policy*, 5(2):222–50.

Neumark, D. and Simpson, H. (2015). Place-based policies. In *Handbook of Regional and Urban Economics*, volume 5, pages 1197–287. Elsevier.

Owens, E. (2019). Economic approach to "de-policing". *Criminology and Public Policy*, 18(1):77–80.

Palencia, L., Rodriguez-Sanz, M., L´opez, M. J., Calzada, N., Gallego, R., Morales, E., Barbieri, N., Blancafort, X., Bartroli, M., and Pasarĺn, M. I. (2018). Community action for health in socioeconomically deprived neighbourhoods in Barcelona: Evaluating its effects on health and social class health inequalities. *Health Policy*, 122(12):1384–91.

Putnam, R. D., Leonardi, R., and Nanetti, R. Y. (1994). *Making Democracy Work: Civic Traditions in Modern Italy*. Princeton University Press.

Rose, D. R. and Clear, T. R. (1998). Incarceration, social capital, and crime: Implications for social disorganization theory. *Criminology*, 36(3):441–80.

Sampson, R. J. (1988). Local friendship ties and community attachment in mass society: A multilevel systemic model. *American Sociological Review* 53(5):766–79.

Sampson, R. J. (2001). Crime and public safety: Insights from community-level perspectives on social capital. In S. Saegert, P. J. Thompson and M. Warren (eds.), *Social capital and poor communities: Building and using social assets to combat poverty*. New York: Russell Sage.

Sampson, R. J. and Groves, W. B. (1989). Community structure and crime: Testing social-disorganization theory. *American Journal of Sociology*, 94(4):774–802.

Sampson, R. J. and Laub, J. H. (1995). *Crime in the Making: Pathways and Turning Points through Life*. Harvard University Press.

Sanfelice, V. (2019). Are safe routes effective? assessing the effects of Chicago's safe passage program on local crimes. *Journal of Economic Behavior & Organization*, 164:357–73.

Sharkey, P., Torrats-Espinosa, G., and Takyar, D. (2017). Community and the crime decline: The causal effect of local nonprofits on violent crime. *American Sociological Review*, 82(6):1214–40.

Tabellini, G. (2010). Culture and institutions: Economic development in the regions of Europe. *Journal of the European Economic Association*, 8(4):677–716.

Takagi, D., Ikeda, K., and Kawachi, I. (2012). Neighborhood social capital and crime victimization: Comparison of spatial regression analysis and hierarchical regression analysis. *Social Science & Medicine*, 75(10):1895–902.

Warner, B. D. and Rountree, P. W. (1997). Local social ties in a community and crime model: Questioning the systemic nature of informal social control. *Social Problems*, 44(4):520–36.

Weisburd, D. (2012). Bringing social context back into the equation: The importance of social characteristics of places in the prevention of crime. *Criminology & Public Policy*, 11:317.

Wells, W., Horney, J., and Maguire, E. R. (2005). Patrol officer responses to citizen feedback: An experimental analysis. *Police Quarterly*, 8(2):171–205.

10. Peer effects in crime

Evelina Gavrilova[1] and Marcello Puca[2]

1. INTRODUCTION

In a seminal study, Glaeser et al. (1996) find that after controlling for observable characteristics, there remains a large unexplained part in what generates crime rates in different cities. Glaeser et al. (1996) put forth the theory that positive correlation in the decision to commit crimes among individuals could account for this unexplained variation. In other words, the personal exchanges between peers could be important to the individual decision to commit a crime. On the one hand, these exchanges can be rich on criminal knowledge, if the two peers are in prison. On the other hand, these meetings can serve to update perceived probabilities of detection, if the two peers are neighbors discussing the probability of a tax audit. Overall, based on such peer effects, potential criminals revise their expected utility from crime and make the decision whether or not to commit the crime. These individual decisions contribute to the aggregate crime rate, observed by the policymaker.

From the perspective of the policymaker, there is an interest in finding an efficient mix of deterrence policies. Such policies impact a potential criminal both directly, in the decision to commit a crime, and indirectly, through an information exchange with his or her peers. These indirect effects can be summarized by a social multiplier and contribute to more effective deterrence policies. By specifying and quantifying the individual channels of peer effects, economists can disentangle the mechanisms of influence of aggregate deterrence policies. This would allow policymakers to maximize deterrence by choosing the most appropriate policies.

With this objective in mind, this chapter provides a summary of the findings in the literature on peer effects in crime. We present the linear-in-means model in the context of crime and illustrate some of the mechanisms of interest. We review studies that focus on estimating peer effects behind bars and in social networks. We link these findings to complementary findings in criminology and chart the way forward for the discipline.

Rather than repeating previous contributions, this chapter builds on the survey on reduced-form peer effects by Sacerdote (2014). Furthermore, the analysis of social networks is complementary to the estimation of peer effects. Two recent reviews, Topa and Zenou (2015) and Lindquist and Zenou (2019), provide a recent review on contributions in the economics of neighborhoods and crime with a focus on network analysis.

We find that the intuition of Glaeser et al. (1996) is correct. There seems to be a significant influence of criminal peers on the individual decision to commit a crime (e.g. Drago and Galbiati, 2012; Stevenson, 2017; Corno, 2017; Billings and Schnepel, 2020; Dimmock et al., 2018). Peers behind bars seem to reinforce the development of a criminal career in a given crime category (e.g. Bayer et al., 2009; Damm and Gorinas, 2020). Consistent with these significant effects, Drago and Galbiati (2012) estimate a social multiplier of two – i.e. an exogeneous policy decreasing the individual propensity for crime by 1 percent would reduce aggregate propensity for crime by 2 percent. However, these effects are not across the board – usually, the estimated effects are strongest within a narrow subset of homophilic peer groups.[3] These findings are in line with criminology studies on the composition of delinquent peer groups and with economic studies on shared identities (Akerlof and Kranton, 2000). Overall, potential criminals seem to be mostly influenced by peers of similar age, gender and socioeconomic background.

All of the studies mentioned herein identify a different piece of the puzzle of how peers interact and contribute to the crime rate, yet there are still many pieces missing. For example, it could be important to understand whether behavioral aspects, such as shame or fear, can amplify (or reduce) the influence of peers. In this respect, we report very recent experimental research on non-violent forms of crime such as tax evasion showing that, indeed, emotions may have a role in increasing the size of the peer effect. Understanding whether other behavioral components may affect the size of peer influence, therefore, constitutes a promising path for future research.

The rest of the chapter is organized as follows. Section 2 presents the intuition underlying peer effects and illustrates the channels through which peer effects materialize. We then review the relevant papers that estimate a causal effect of peers in studies on prisoners, in Section 3. We follow up by examining the effect of peers in the social environment in Section 4 and on the use of the experimental approach, in Section 5. Section 6 outlines some of the open research questions.

2. INTUITION

How should we model peer effects? The answer is not trivial, as their estimation poses several empirical challenges. Because individuals sort into different groups (e.g. schools, neighborhoods and workplaces), it is difficult to disentangle the effect of self-selection from the causal effect of peers' influence

(Manski, 1993; Sacerdote, 2014). More specifically, the influence of peers may be the result of self-selection in the same group, the exogenous influence of a peer's background or the endogenous effect of a peer's outcome. As a baseline approach, researchers estimate the following general linear-in-means model:

$$Y_i = \alpha + \beta_1 \hat{Y}_{-i} + \gamma_1 X_i + \gamma_2 \hat{X}_{-i} + \varepsilon_i \tag{10.1}$$

where Y_i represents the outcome of an individual i, $\hat{Y}_{-i}$ is the average outcome of the individual's peers, X_i is a vector of i's background characteristics and $\hat{X}_{-i}$ is the vector of average peers' characteristics. Using Manski (1993)'s terminology, γ_2 represents the exogenous effects from the peers' background, while β_1 is the endogenous effect from peers' outcomes. The tendency of peers to self-select into a given group means that a naive estimation of Equation 10.1 would not result in the identification of a causal effect.

Most of the studies considered in this review use as dependent variable Y_i the decision to re-offend for an individual i who has served time in prison. The peer group $\{-i\}$ is usually composed of other prisoners within the same crime category, neighbors or friends. Most of the studies assume that the simultaneously determined β_1 is zero and focus on identifying the impact γ_2 of background characteristics of the peers on the decision to commit a crime. This assumption precludes the estimation of a social multiplier effect, where the criminal decision of an individual impacts his/her peers. Unlike reduced-form studies, experimental research (see Section 4) focuses on the estimation of the effect contemporaneous peers' outcomes β_1 of Equation 10.1.

The linear-in-means model implicitly assumes that the effect attributable to each peer is constant across peers. One emerging argument that this assumption is faulty is the possible presence of a peer who might exert disproportionally large influence on the decision to commit a crime. For example, Stevenson (2017) finds that there are such key peers in juvenile prisons. A second emerging argument is the use of variable peer groups in recent studies that point toward the existence of different influences of wider peer groups (e.g. Corno, 2017; Billings and Schnepel, 2020).

There are several mechanisms underlying the estimation of peer effects in the economics of crime. First, we will start with defining the peer group and the processes that occur in a social network before we arrive at the estimation of Equation 10.1. Criminologists have noticed that the background characteristics of peers tend to be positively correlated. Research on delinquent groups in criminology focuses on co-offending groups, which are a narrow subsection of the general peer group. In a review of the literature, Van Mastrigt and Carrington (2013) show that criminal co-offending groups tend to be homophilic in characteristics such as age, sex, ethnicity, residence and criminal experience. This implies that peers tend to have similar or overlapping identities (Akerlof and Kranton, 2000). These identities allow peers to establish a social contact and gain reciprocal trust by sharing sensitive information about crime with one another. Because of these shared identities, likely the peer group with the highest impact will tend to be homophilic, which is the implicit finding of recent studies (Billings and Schnepel, 2020; Damm and Gorinas, 2020; Mastrobuoni and Rialland, 2020).

Once a social connection is established, peers can exchange several types of knowledge. First, a given peer has experience-based knowledge on the crime categories in which he/she specializes on how to identify potential targets, an estimate on the probability of arrest and on the probability and magnitude of punishment, and on how to impact these probabilities. Bayer et al. (2009) introduce a useful terminology. They investigate two types of peer effect: (i) a *reinforcing effect*, where a peer reinforces existing criminal tendencies and essentially leads a criminal to commit and specialize in the same type of crime; and (ii) a *branching-out effect*, occurring when criminals learn and branch out into new areas of criminal activity. This terminology can be also translated into intensive margin – when a criminal learns more about a given crime type – and extensive margin – when criminals learn a new crime type.

In this respect, consider the following example. Suppose an experienced burglar knows how to gain access to a building and has knowledge on how to fence the stolen items. The burglar has an estimate about what contributes to higher arrest and punishment likelihoods. If this burglar were to enter prison, he could provide a reinforcing peer effect to other burglars. By imparting his knowledge, he gives the tools to other burglars to successfully re-offend after prison. The burglar could also provide a branching out peer effect, if he recruits a thief and teaches him how to gain access to a building.

A second mechanism of peer effects involves the acquisition of criminal attitudes from the peer group. In this case, the decision to commit a crime is not based on the explicit criminal history of the peers but rather on the incentives and expectations of the peer group. An individual may decide to commit a crime just to show to other members of the relevant group, or even to his/her self, that he/she is capable of committing a criminal action. Put differently, such a decision is aimed at adhering to the social norm of the reference group. In contrast, emotions such as shame or fear of being caught, triggered by the observed experience of peers, can reduce the likelihood of committing crime and can therefore be used by policymakers for deterrence. Some studies have found that peer groups exert such influence (see below example in Drago and Galbiati, 2012; Stevenson, 2017), while other studies find no effect (Perez-Truglia and Troiano, 2018).

A third mechanism of peer effects could be the establishment of a more rigid peer structure, such as co-offending or organized crime. In this case, criminals would have a correlation in the outcomes, such that the coefficient $\beta_1 \neq 0$ in Equation 10.1. On the one hand, the expectation is that co-offending groups will be homophilic (Van Mastrigt and Carrington, 2013; Weerman, 2014). On the other hand, likely co-offenders require a complementarity in criminal skills to pull off a crime (Gavrilova, 2019). For example, a bank robbery requires at least a robber and an escape driver. This production complementarity is an argument against the assumption that the optimal peer group is defined along the same crime category, which underpins several studies described below.

To identify the impact of any of these mechanisms, studies in this literature rely on several types of (quasi-) exogenous variation. In the next section, we consider reduced-form studies, which rely mainly on the number of days on which imprisoned peers are exposed to one another (e.g. Bayer et al., 2009). A second source of variation is exogenous shifts in the availability of criminal peers in the social network (e.g. Billings et al., 2014; Corno, 2017; Dimmock et al., 2018; Billings and Schnepel, 2020). Finally, for a class of non-violent crimes such as tax evasion, studies use randomized controlled experiments with letters to induce an explicit variation of the treatment (e.g. Boning et al., 2018; Perez-Truglia and Troiano, 2018; Drago et al., 2020).

3. LEARNING IN PRISON

The first strand of the literature focuses on examining the peer effects of prisoners. The dependent variable is the re-offense after the expiration of the prison sentence. The main identification problem lies in the self-selection into a prison environment. Criminals who land in prison are potentially more likely to re-offend than criminals who avoid the prison sentence. This would imply that they would recidivate regardless of the peer environment, which attenuates the peer effects. One way to overcome this and other endogeneity issues is to explore the effects of a quasi-random shock on the exposure to the peer group.

The most cited study in this strand is the contribution by Bayer et al. (2009). It is important to consider here their identification strategy, as their intuition has been used in several subsequent studies. Bayer et al. (2009) analyze peer effects between juvenile offenders in Florida, who are assigned to a facility based on their risk levels, and focus on evaluating whether there is a transfer of knowledge between criminals from different crime categories. To do so, Bayer et al. (2009) estimate an equation similar to Equation 10.1, with a dependent variable re-offending within a given offense type, e.g. auto theft. The outcome of an individual is not influenced by the simultaneous outcome of his/her peer, implying that the coefficient β_1 is set to zero. The background characteristics of the peer group are used to estimate separate peer effects for exposure to known or new offenses, and thus serve to identify reinforcing and branching out effects. The exposure is estimated based on the number of days for which two criminals' stays in prison overlap. The identifying assumption in Bayer et al. (2009) is that the number of overlap days is random, conditional on facility fixed effects and facility-by-prior-offense fixed effects. The former remove the difference in re-offending levels between different facilities. The latter account for unobserved differences between crime categories within a given facility. Therefore, the remaining variation is the differences between peers in a given crime category, over time. For the identification of a causal effect, the timing of imprisonment has to be as good as random relative to the existing pool of prisoners at the facility. Therefore, criminals are compared based on the exposure to peers in the same crime category and based on their own recidivism behavior. In terms of mechanism, this implies that any two individuals whose imprisonment happens to overlap are exposed to one another and can influence one another.

Note that the equation in Bayer et al. (2009) is estimated by crime type. Thus, the probability of re-offending in a given crime type is a function of: (i) an individual's own criminal history in the same crime type interacted with the exposure to similar peers; and (ii) the average effect of the exposure to peers with different crime type histories. For example, in the case of the equation for larceny, burglars and robbers, each peer enters this equation in the same way, allowing the researcher to identify the branching out peer effect. Therefore, the branching out peer effect is averaged over all residual crime types. This implies that when there is a scope for burglars to branch out into larceny, this effect is attenuated for robbers who would rather branch out into more violent crimes. These different influences cancel each other out and lead to an average peer effect close to zero in expectation. This finding is consistent with Harris et al. (2018), described later, who average over all crime types and also find a null peer effect from cellmate peers.

Bayer et al. (2009) find strong evidence for reinforcing peer effects and null branching out peer effects. In terms of explanation, they suggest that learning a new offense type involves start-up costs, while continued specialization is less costly. In other words, being exposed to criminal peers means that an individual can exchange information on results within a given field like new type of locks for burglars, similar to academics at a conference, while it is more difficult to branch out into a new field and learn how to jump-start a car.

As a follow-up, Stevenson (2017) uses a similar research design and a more comprehensive data set than Bayer et al. (2009), in order to delve into the possible mechanisms of peer effects. In particular, Stevenson (2017) considers three possible mechanisms of peer influence: criminal skill transfer, persistent network formation and social contagion of crime-oriented attitudes and behavioral traits. She finds strong evidence for a social contagion mechanism, in which the most influential peers come from unstable homes and exhibit emotional and behavioral problems. Exposure to such peers leads to increases in crime, aggression and antisocial attitudes. Given that the subjects are juvenile criminals, it is likely that exposure to such peers positively impacts the formation of a criminal identity.

In both studies by Bayer et al. (2009) and Stevenson (2017), the analyzed population is juvenile criminals. This feature makes it difficult to vary the peer group of the individual. Indeed, juvenile criminals are in a narrow age range, in which it is natural to assume that all possible inmates serve as a peer group. However, very likely this would not be the case in a normal prison, where two adults from different age groups might not find common ground despite similar offenses.[4]

This gap is addressed by Damm and Gorinas (2020), who focus on Danish prisoners between 18 and 21 years old. Damm and Gorinas (2020) use a similar identification strategy as Bayer et al. (2009), however extending the estimating equation by accounting for exposure to general and narrower peer groups. The intuition behind the narrower peer groups follows from the finding of homophily in the criminology literature. In that way, the narrow peer groups for the young offenders are defined along dimensions of ethnic origin and age category, where age is lower than 26. In addition, Damm and Gorinas (2020) explore the impact of peer groups that are different than the analyzed individuals: older inmates and criminals with prior convictions. The purpose of the latter is to determine whether the reinforcing peer effects are transmitted within a network structure, in which, for example, experienced burglars impart knowledge to young criminals. Consistent with the homophily expectation, Damm and Gorinas (2020) find a strong impact from the peer groups defined by young age and ethnic origin, and no impact from the dissimilar groups.

Overall, in this literature, there seems to be a common finding of reinforcing peer effects and no branching out peer effects. Bayer et al. (2009) find evidence for peer effects for crime categories such as burglary, drug crimes, assault and sex offenses. They find null effects in auto theft, larceny, robbery and weapon offenses. Damm and Gorinas (2020) find an effect for drug crimes, threats, vandalism and arson. They also find negative peer effects for violent crimes, consistent with a deterrence mechanism. The findings in the two studies coincide for drug crimes. In the American context, Bayer et al. (2009) find that one standard deviation increase in exposure to peers who have committed felony drug crimes increases the likelihood of re-offending from a mean at 28.5 percent to 31.6 percent. On the other hand, in the Danish context, one standard deviation increase of exposure increases the likelihood for re-offending by 1 percent. The peer groups in both studies are similar in size, that is 40 to 60 peers, meaning that this difference in effect could be driven by social norms or prison population composition.

One of the main issues with the studies examined so far is that there is still little evidence on how much individuals actually interact with their peer group. The exposure in terms of days together, indeed, is just an approximation for the possibility to establish a social contact, which obviously may never take place. In this respect, Harris et al. (2018) take a step further and analyze the peer effects of cellmates in state prisons in the US. They examine the impact of a more senior cell-mate on recidivism, using as an instrument the number of times a peer has been arrested prior to observation. The identifying assumption is that prison cell-mate assignment is as good as random conditional on a variety of personal characteristics such as availability of beds, age, race and medical issues. They find null and deterrent peer effects. The results in Harris et al. (2018) could be consistent with the results in Bayer et al. (2009), considering that Harris et al. (2018) do not differentiate by crime type, suggesting that they essentially average out the effects of all crime types.

Focusing on an Italian collective pardon, Mastrobuoni and Rialland (2020) implicitly assume that co-offenders are chosen from the peer group and identify the characteristics of these peer groups. Mastrobuoni and Rialland (2020) find homophily in co-offending group formation on age, nationality and degrees of deterrence, consistent with expectations from criminology. They find no evidence of homophily with respect to education, employment status and crime types, consistent with expectations about production complementarities in criminal groups (Gavrilova, 2019).

The literature on peer effects in prison is the only subset that investigates criminal learning. This part of the literature essentially investigates a categorical outcome variable, where a criminal offends in a given crime category. This is captured in studies based on Bayer et al. (2009), where the reinforcing peer effects are estimated by crime type. However, the branching out peer effects in that study are all averaged out over the different crime categories. This framework does not allow for a thief to switch to burglary, where there is arguably a low barrier to learning. In order to identify branching out peer effects, one needs to estimate separate coefficients by crime type, allowing, for example, for a thief to impact the probability of re-offense of an individual with a criminal history of burglary. However, to identify such effects one would need to estimate a system of N equations with N × N coefficients (where N is the number of crime categories). Therefore, it would be useful to consider restrictions to this system by formally modeling types of crimes, e.g. allowing for burglary and larceny to have a similar production process. Another approach would be to distinguish between violent, property and drug crimes, and thus estimate a smaller system of equations.

This approach has been adopted in an influential criminology study by Conway and McCord (2002). They follow a set of offenders over time and find that nonviolent offenders who co-offend for the first time with violent criminals are at a subsequent higher risk of committing serious violent crime. This finding implies the existence of branching out peer effects, albeit outside of prison. It would be interesting to investigate the external validity of this claim, ideally by using some of the sources of exogenous variation proposed in the next section.

4. SOCIAL ENVIRONMENT

In this section, we focus mostly on studies where the exposure to criminal peers is exogenously determined by the availability of peers in the social environment. First, we will consider the literature on expectation formation for criminals. Most of the papers in this review do not take a stance on which variable in Becker's model is impacted through the peer effects. A small strand models the possibility that an individual's perceived probability of arrest is based on available information, where the primary sources are own past experience and the social vicinity (Sah, 1991). These predictions are tested by Lochner (2007), who uses data from the 1997 National Longitudinal Survey of Youth (NLSY). Lochner (2007) finds that respondent beliefs about the probability of arrest do not respond to changes in the arrest outcome of their siblings or other random persons. The findings by Lochner (2007) imply that deterrence policies focusing on arrest impact criminals mainly through their own perceptions of the probability of arrest, rather than peer effects. On the one hand, it would be useful to determine the external validity of this finding in other contexts. On the other hand, it is also necessary to determine which variable of Becker's model carries the strongest deterrent peer effect.

Some evidence in this direction is offered in Drago and Galbiati (2012). They examine the effects of the incentives of peers on an individual's own criminal behavior. They use identifying variation from an Italian collective prison pardon. In this reform, the residual prison sentence was suspended until a criminal re-offended and receives a new conviction. Then, the criminal would have to serve for the total time of the suspended sentence plus the total time of the new sentence, implying a large variation in the deterrent effects of punishment for each released convict. For each individual, the peer group is defined based on prison and nationality of origin (region of origin for Italians). The intuition is that when released similar inmates will tend to gather and share experience. The results show that the average residual sentence of peers has a deterrent impact on the own propensity for recidivism, with an effect size similar to an individual's own residual sentence. When defining peer groups based on age and crime committed, however, the impact of the residual sentence of the peer group is smaller.

Treating the collective prison pardon as an exogenous reform, Drago and Galbiati (2012) estimate a social multiplier of two – an exogenous shock decreasing individual recidivism by 1 percent would decrease aggregate recidivism by 2 percent. They also consider an alternative hypothesis of interactions in prison driving their result and reject it. Drago and Galbiati (2012) claim that the effect is driven by the incentives of the peer group. These findings might be consistent with the findings by Lochner (2007) if the social multiplier effect is driven by expectations about punishment, rather than expectations of being caught and arrested.

Still in the Italian context, Corno (2017) examines a network of homeless people in Milan and finds strong evidence of peer effects. She estimates a model where the probability of being imprisoned depends on the number of friends, the share of criminal friends and own background characteristics. Going back to Equation 10.1, this is equivalent to setting the coefficient on the contemporaneous outcome β_1 equal to zero and using lagged outcome variables in place of the background characteristics of the peers. Note also that these social networks are quite small relative to networks in the previous studies – on average an individual has 1.5 friends, of which 0.23 are criminal friends. Corno (2017) instruments the number of friends, thus the background characteristics of the peers in the linear-in-means model, with exogenous shifts in the supply of criminal peers. Specifically, she uses the releases of prison inmates at the monthly level, and share of rainy days in the first year of homelessness. The intuition behind the share of rainy days is that in such periods homeless people are more likely to spend their time in shelter and establish social contact with their peers. Using this empirical approach, Corno (2017) finds that one additional friend decreases the probability of incarceration by 12% percent, while one standard deviation in additional criminal friends increases the probability of incarceration by 23 percentage points. When turning to mechanisms, Corno (2017) finds that a larger network of old friends increases the probability of surviving on the streets without committing a crime. Relevant to the previous discussion on peer groups, as Corno (2017) examines an increasingly wider social network, she observes how the peer effects decrease with the more distant peers in terms of degrees of separation included in the estimation.

Focusing on potential crime-inducing interactions after imprisonment, Billings and Schnepel (2020) identify the impact of pre-incarceration peer networks on recidivism. Similar to Corno (2017), Billings and Schnepel (2020) approach the linear-in-means model through the peer's background characteristics. In their estimating equation, recidivism depends on the number of individual *i*'s neighborhood peers incarcerated during the first month of re-entry in a 1 km radius around *i*'s pre-incarceration residential location. The identifying assumption is that imprisonment status of peers is random at the moment of release of the inmate. Similar to most studies discussed above, the identification rests on a quasi-exogenous variation in the number of criminal peers to whom an individual is exposed.

Billings and Schnepel (2020) estimate the peer effect by defining an increasingly homogeneous peer group in terms of age differences, race, gender and location. They find that peer effects increase the more similar the peer group is to an individual, in line with criminology findings and previous literature. In their preferred specification with homophilic peer group, one additional peer incarcerated decreases the probability of arrest within 3 months by 3.8 percentage points, which is a 17 percent decline relative to the mean recidivism rate. Estimates for peers who are even closer, by sharing the same residential address and having co-offended with the released individual in the past, are higher, but less significant. Consistent with a mechanism of exposure to criminally minded peers, when peers are released from prison the probability of re-offending increases.

One of the broad trends in this literature is that recent studies tend to find different effects based on the definition of the peer group. A guiding principle in that regard would be to consider the idea of homophily for the peer group – individuals are likely to form social bonds with others with whom they share an identity. This implies that a peer group can be formed along gender, race, age, crime type, neighborhood or county origin. This intuition is mirrored in the definition of the peer group by Billings and Schnepel (2020). However, it is unclear which feature of the peer group provides the strongest influence. In other words, it is unclear which shared identity leads to stronger peer effects. An empirical researcher would have to try out many different specifications, leading to problems with multiple hypothesis testing. A solution for this would be to apply a machine learning routine like 'causal forest', in order to determine which covariate contributes the most to the heterogeneity in the estimation of the causal peer effect.

While much of the research on crime focuses on violent or 'street' crimes, there is scant evidence about white-collar crimes. An interesting exception is Dimmock et al. (2018), who focus on the diffusion of corporate crime, in the form of financial misconduct, among coworkers.[5] The diffusion of such misconduct may occur through several channels such as social learning, norm adherence or competitive pressure.

Identifying any of these effects, however, poses several empirical challenges. Dimmock et al. (2018) employ data on financial advisory firms that merge their branches. More specifically, they first define as 'coworkers' individuals employed during the same period at the same branch of a firm. Second, to address coworker self-selection issues, they use exogenous changes in coworkers groups caused by mergers of financial advisory firms. The idea is to use the exogenous merger to expose workers to the influence of new coworkers coming from a different location. Although the merger decision is endogenously made by the firm, conditional on merger-firm fixed effects, one can assume that coworkers are quasi-randomly assigned and identify the effect of coworker influence on individual financial misconducts. Dimmock et al. (2018) find that a financial advisor is 37 percent more likely to commit misconduct if coworkers from the merging branch have a history of misconduct. Remarkably, the coworker influence is asymmetric, as Dimmock et al. (2018) do not find any significant evidence of contagion in good conduct.

Another identification strategy uses the redefinition of borders or reference groups as a source of exogenous discontinuity. An important strand of this literature focuses on childhood exposure to 'at-risk' peers, such as other students belonging to minority groups, or whose parents have criminal records. Billings et al. (2014) use the end of the race-based school bus system of Charlotte-Mecklenburg County to assess the impact of new peers on several adult outcomes, including criminal activities. For identification, they compare students who lived in the same neighborhoods but whose pre-policy addresses placed them on opposite sides of the newly drawn school boundary. They find that males belonging to minoritarian groups who were quasi-randomly assigned to schools with a higher percentage of students belonging to a minority are more likely to be arrested and incarcerated. Their estimates suggest that a 10 percentage point increase in share minority increased the probability of arrest incarceration by about 1.3 percentage points. In a follow-up study, Billings et al. (2019) show that individuals who lived in the same neighborhood and attended the same school were more likely to be arrested for criminal partnerships. This effect was larger for individuals of the same grade, gender and race. Specifically, they find that one standard deviation increase in the number of same school-grade-race-gender students living within 1 kilometer increases the probability that a student will be arrested by 23 percent, and up to 67 percent and 41 percent for violent and property crime, respectively.

All the studies presented in this section have the advantage of exploiting a quasi-exogenous source of variation to address the well-known endogeneity issues of the linear-in-means model. In the next section, we review researchers that take this approach to the next level and use controlled experimental approaches.

5. EXPERIMENTAL EVIDENCE

Since controlled experiments cannot induce participants to commit crime, most of the studies presented in this section use a randomized controlled treatment to disentangle the effect of peers in the decision to commit a crime.

A first strand of this literature focuses on tax compliance. Boning et al. (2018) evaluate in a field experiment the direct and indirect effect of fiscal enforcement on a network of 12 172 firms under investigation by the Internal Revenue Service (IRS) – the US fiscal authority. In one intervention, treated firms received a letter from the IRS, while in a second one they received a physical visit by an IRS officer. A third group of firms, obviously, did not receive any of these treatments and serve as the comparison group. Boning et al. (2018) find that both treatments produced an increase in remitted tax, suggesting that visits or letters do have an effect on treated firms. However, the peer effect is much smaller. Indeed, the authors do not find any significant spillover effect of the letter, but only find a modest 2 percent increase in tax remitted by firms that shared a tax preparer with a visited firm. This is probably explained by the fact that, while the letter remains private information of the firm which received it, knowing that the shared tax preparer is aware of the investigation may trigger reputation concerns.

Similarly, Perez-Truglia and Troiano (2018) employ letters sent to tax delinquents to study whether shaming works as a deterrent for future tax delinquencies. More specifically, they implement a field experiment sending 34 334 letters to households found to be tax delinquent in three US states, who collectively owed half a billion dollars. The authors randomly vary the content of these letters in three different treatments with increasing levels of disclosure about the existence of tax delinquents in the surrounding areas. The overall effect of such *shaming* (i.e. being exposed in a public list of delinquents) causes a 21 percent increase of future tax compliance. The authors, however, do not find any statistically significant effect of the peer comparison mechanism, suggesting that peer pressure is a weaker mechanism to improve tax compliance compared to the introduction of a public list of delinquents *per se*.

Using a similar experimental strategy, Drago et al. (2020) study the spillover effect of letters sent to potential evaders of TV license fees in a network of over 500 000 households in Austria. In doing so, they varied the content of mail sent to potential evaders (treated) and measured the change in tax compliance of neighbor households (untreated). Unlike other studies, the experiment reveals a strong and statistically significant spillover effect. More specifically, any additional threat mail increases the likelihood of compliance for an untreated household in the network by 7 percent or, put differently, 1000 additional threats would induce 68 untreated households to start complying.

Alm et al. (2017) use instead a laboratory experiment to study the informational effect of neighbors' behavior on tax compliance. The experiment consisted of a series effort tasks, which were remunerated and then taxed at the end of each round. Subject had then to choose whether, and by how much, to comply with the tax rate. The experimental conditions varied (i) the information about other subjects' reported taxes and (ii) the information about other subjects being audited. The authors find that being informed about others' audits and reporting rates does have a statistically significant positive effect on a subject's compliance, although not in all treatments.

It is notable that the unit of treatment in these experiments is the firm or household, which is different than the individual in Sections 4 and 5. These households and firms are composed of heterogeneous individuals in terms of age and gender. Their peer group are other household and firms with similar addresses, which is a proxy for socioeconomic characteristics. From the previous sections, it is reasonable to assume that a spillover effect would be small and zero among such dissimilar peers. Thus, the non-zero effects in Boning et al. (2018) and Drago et al. (2020) are surprising and reveal that peer effects can persist among non-homophilic individuals who, however, have the opportunity for contact by living and working nearby.

6. CONCLUSION

All of the studies mentioned herein identify a different piece of the puzzle of how peers interact and contribute to the crime rate, yet there are still many pieces missing. One of the remaining open questions is on how peer effects impact criminal decision making through the Becker model variables. Another important question is on identifying crime-specific branching out peer effects or, in other words, between which crime categories do we observe the highest barriers to learning. The answer to this question can help policymakers in placing prisoners with cellmates, so as to avoid learning.

In addition, it would be of interest for future researchers to quantify the social multiplier of deterrence policies. Drago and Galbiati (2012) is the only study that attempts to identify the social multiplier; thus the question of external validity in other contexts or peer groups remains open. This question is of interest as some of the deterrence effects described in Chalfin and McCrary (2017) are likely underpinned by both individual and peer decisions. It seems straightforward to assume that the social multiplier is a sufficient statistic that can be used by a policymaker to evaluate the strength and desirability of a given deterrence policy.

NOTES

1. NoCeT Norwegian Center for Taxation; NHH Norwegian School of Economics.
2. University of Bergamo; CSEF; Webster University Geneva.
3. The concept of homophilia is popular in wider social sciences. The term comes from Greek, where *homo* means 'self' and *philia* means 'love'.
4. On a separate point, peer effects could vary by age, such that the coefficients estimated for juvenile peers could be different than the estimates for senior criminals.
5. Financial misconduct refers to the set of negligent, intentional or willful actions that result in financial fraud, theft or breach of contract.

REFERENCES

Akerlof, G. A. and Kranton, R. E. (2000). Economics and identity. *The Quarterly Journal of Economics*, 115(3):715–53.

Alm, J., Bloomquist, K. M., and McKee, M. (2017). When you know your neighbour pays taxes: Information, peer effects and tax compliance. *Fiscal Studies*, 38(4):587–613.

Bayer, P., Hjalmarsson, R., and Pozen, D. (2009). Building criminal capital behind bars: Peer effects in juvenile corrections. *The Quarterly Journal of Economics*, 124(1):105–47.

Billings, S. B. and Schnepel, K. T. (2020). Hanging out with the usual suspects: Neighborhood peer effects and recidivism. *Journal of Human Resources*, 0819–10353R2.

Billings, S. B., Deming, D. J., and Rockoff, J. (2014). School segregation, educational attainment, and crime: Evidence from the end of busing in Charlotte-Mecklenburg. *The Quarterly Journal of Economics*, 129(1):435–76.

Billings, S. B., Deming, D. J., and Ross, S. L. (2019). Partners in crime. *American Economic Journal: Applied Economics*, 11(1):126–50.

Boning, W. C., Guyton, J., Hodge, R. H., Slemrod, J., Troiano, U., et al. (2018). *Heard it through the grapevine: Direct and network effects of a tax enforcement field experiment.* Technical report, National Bureau of Economic Research.

Chalfin, A. and McCrary, J. (2017). Criminal deterrence: A review of the literature. *Journal of Economic Literature*, 55(1):5–48.

Conway, K. P. and McCord, J. (2002). A longitudinal examination of the relation between co-offending with violent accomplices and violent crime. *Aggressive Behavior: Official Journal of the International Society for Research on Aggression*, 28(2):97–108.

Corno, L. (2017). Homelessness and crime: Do your friends matter? *The Economic Journal*, 127(602):959–95.

Damm, A. P. and Gorinas, C. (2020). Prison as a criminal school: Peer effects and criminal learning behind bars. *The Journal of Law and Economics*, 63(1):149–80.

Dimmock, S. G., Gerken, W. C., and Graham, N. P. (2018). Is fraud contagious? Coworker influence on misconduct by financial advisors. *The Journal of Finance*, 73(3):1417–50.

Drago, F. and Galbiati, R. (2012). Indirect effects of a policy altering criminal behavior: Evidence from the Italian prison experiment. *American Economic Journal: Applied Economics*, 4(2):199–218.

Drago, F., Mengel, F., and Traxler, C. (2020). Compliance behavior in networks: Evidence from a field experiment. *American Economic Journal: Applied Economics*, 12(2):96–133.

Gavrilova, E. (2019). A partner in crime: Assortative matching and bias in the crime market. *Journal of Economic Behavior & Organization*, 159:598–612.

Glaeser, E. L., Sacerdote, B., and Scheinkman, J. A. (1996). Crime and social interactions. *The Quarterly Journal of Economics*, 111(2):507–48.

Harris, H. M., Nakamura, K., and Bucklen, K. B. (2018). Do cellmates matter? A causal test of the schools of crime hypothesis with implications for differential association and deterrence theories. *Criminology*, 56(1):87–122.

Lindquist, M. J. and Zenou, Y. (2019). Crime and networks: Ten policy lessons. *Oxford Review of Economic Policy*, 35(4):746–71.

Lochner, L. (2007). Individual perceptions of the criminal justice system. *American Economic Review*, 97(1):444–60.

Manski, C. F. (1993). Identification of endogenous social effects: The reflection problem. *The Review of Economic Studies*, 60(3):531–42.

Mastrobuoni, G. and Rialland, P. (2020). Partners in crime: Evidence from recidivating inmates. *Italian Economic Journal*, 6(2):255–73.

Perez-Truglia, R. and Troiano, U. (2018). Shaming tax delinquents. *Journal of Public Economics*, 167:120–37.

Sacerdote, B. (2014). Experimental and quasi-experimental analysis of peer effects: Two steps forward? *Annu. Rev. Econ.*, 6(1):253–72.

Sah, R. K. (1991). Social osmosis and patterns of crime. *Journal of Political Economy*, 99(6):1272–95.

Stevenson, M. (2017). Breaking bad: Mechanisms of social influence and the path to criminality in juvenile jails. *Review of Economics and Statistics*, 99(5):824–38.

Topa, G. and Zenou, Y. (2015). Neighborhood and network effects. In *Handbook of Regional and Urban Economics*, volume 5, pages 561–624. Elsevier.

Van Mastrigt, S. B. and Carrington, P. (2013). Sex and age homophily in co-offending networks. *Crime and Networks*, 28:51–60.

Weerman, F. (2014). *Encyclopedia of Criminology and Criminal Justice, Chapter Theories of Co-offending*, pages 5173–84. Springer.

11. New evidence on immigration and crime[1]

Paolo Pinotti[2] and Sandra V. Rozo[3]

1. INTRODUCTION

The last decades witnessed a tremendous increase in global migration. Figure 11.1 shows that the total number of immigrants in the world has almost tripled since 1960, from 93 million to 256 million. The increase is even more pronounced in high-income countries, where, during the same period, the number of immigrants increased from 33 to 190 million – 4 and 15 percent of the total population, respectively.

These massive inflows generated social and political tensions in many countries. Figure 11.2 shows the votes obtained by the main anti-immigrant parties in Europe in the last three elections for the European Parliament. In the decade between 2009 and 2019, the Italian League – possibly the prototype for all of these parties – increased its vote share from 10 percent to one-third of the total votes in Italy. UKIP reached a similar electoral share in Britain, while the Front National in France and the Freedom Party in Austria obtained one-fourth and one-fifth of the votes, respectively. Outside Europe, the Republican Party in the US moved toward more extremist positions under Trump's leadership.

Natives are concerned about migration for at least two main reasons: First, they fear immigrants' competition in the labor market, leading, in turn, to lower wages and job displacement; second, they are afraid that the presence of immigrants may increase crime (see, e.g., Zimmermann et al., 2000). Although both sentiments are extremely widespread, the latter is certainly prevalent in most countries. Figure 11.3 shows the results of a survey conducted by Eurobarometer on a sample of 28 000 European citizens. We plot the share of respondents in each country that agree with the statement 'immigrants worsen crime problems' (on the vertical axis) against the share that agrees with the statement 'immigrants increase unemployment' (on the horizontal axis). Almost all countries lie above the 45-degree line (also plotted in the graph), meaning that there are more respondents worried about crime than

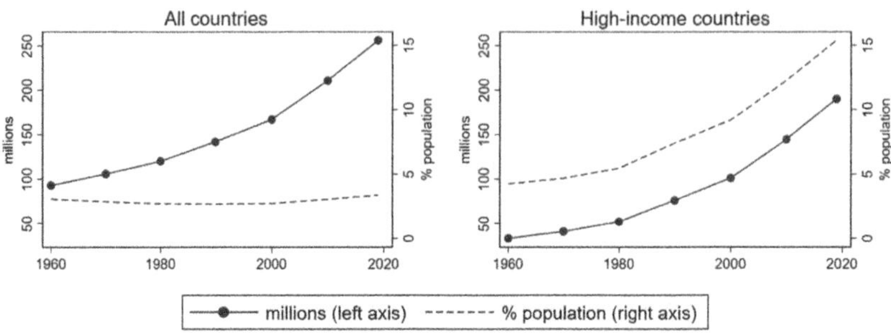

Notes: This figure shows the total number of immigrants and their ratio to the total resident population in the world (left graph) and in high-income countries, according to the World Bank definition (right graph).

Source: Global Migration Database of the United Nations.

Figure 11.1 Global migration, 1960–2019

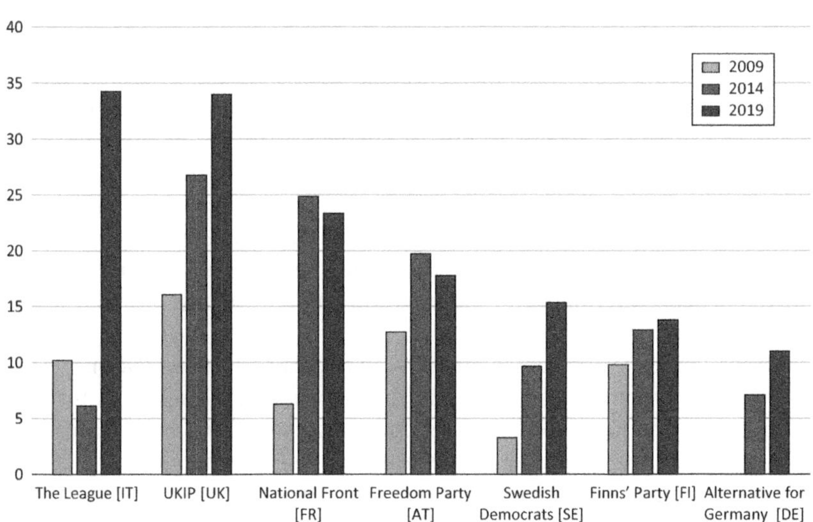

Notes: This figure shows the percentage of votes obtained by the main anti-immigrant parties in the last three elections for the European Parliament.

Source: Data have been collected from various sources.

Figure 11.2 Votes obtained by the main anti-immigrant parties in the elections for the European Parliament, 2009–19

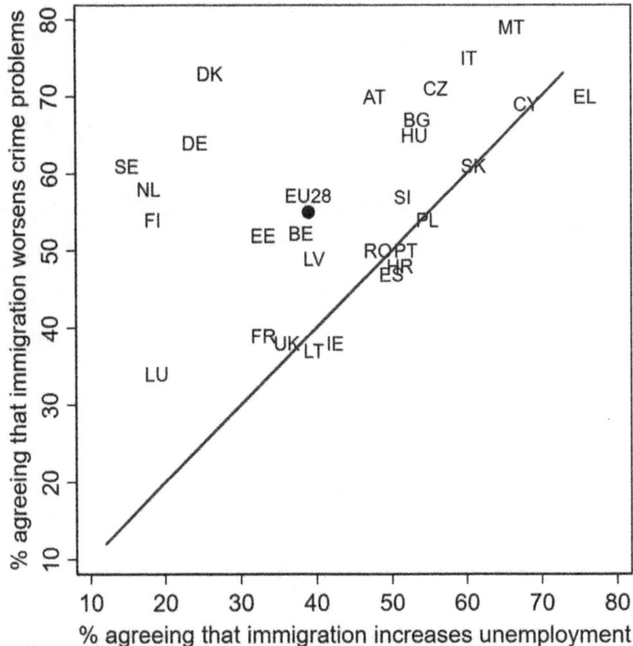

Notes: This figure plots the share of citizens across European countries concerned that immigrants increase crime (on the vertical axis) against the share concerned that immigrants increase unemployment (on the horizontal axis).

Source: Survey conducted by Eurobarometer in 2017.

Figure 11.3 Perceptions about the effect of immigration on crime and unemployment, 2017

about unemployment. In the entire sample, about 55 percent of all respondents are worried about immigrants' effect on crime, while 39 percent are worried about their effect on unemployment. Crime concerns are even higher in countries such as Italy and Germany – 75 and 64 percent, respectively. Bianchi et al. (2012) and Fasani et al. (2020) provide similar evidence using survey data covering different samples of countries and different time periods.

In light of this evidence, it is surprising that the scientific literature has paid less attention to the relationship between immigration and crime than the relationship between immigration and labor market outcomes. We document this fact using data from scholar.google.com, a popular search engine for academic articles, working papers and volumes. Figure 11.4 plots the total number of research works containing the word 'immigration' written since

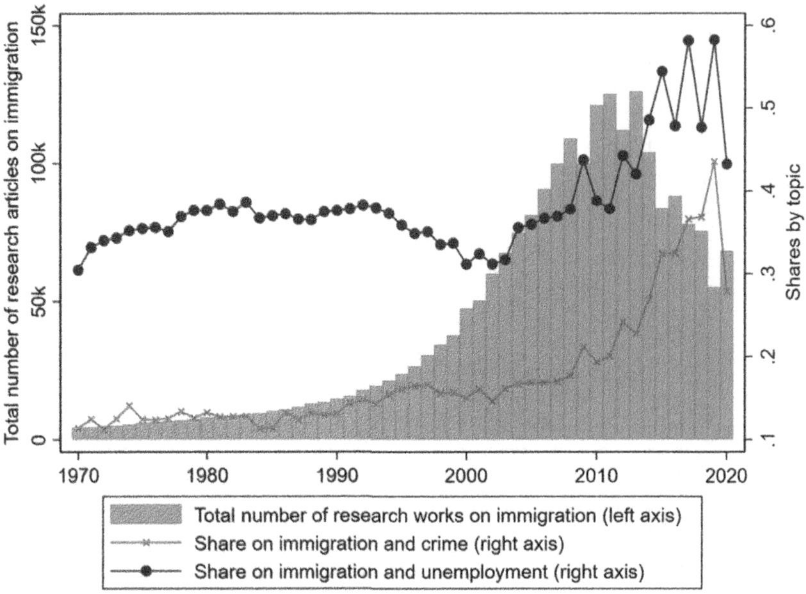

Notes: This figure plots the total number of research works mentioning 'immigration' written since 1970 (left vertical axis) and the share of those mentioning also 'crime', or any of the words 'employment', 'unemployment' and 'wages'.

Source: Scholar.google.com.

Figure 11.4 *Research on immigration, crime, and unemployment, 1970–2020*

1970, and the share of these works containing, in addition, the word 'crime' or any of the words 'employment', 'unemployment' or 'wages'. Until the early 1990s, crime and labor market effects account for about a tenth and a third of total research on immigration, respectively. The relevance of both topics increases – and the gap between them narrows – over the following decades, but research on immigration and crime remains a niche. Unsurprisingly, this is all the more true in economics, which is naturally more focused on the study of labor markets than crime. Of the 680 articles on crime published in the leading economics journals since 1990, less than a dozen address the relationship between immigration and crime (Doleac, 2020). At the same time, most of these papers were published in recent years, so, even inside academia, there is certainly a growing interest in this topic.

In this chapter, we review the body of evidence emerging from this literature. We focus primarily on recent studies employing econometric methods to uncover causal relationships, but we will also cover some earlier, descriptive analyses.

The next section starts from these earlier studies, which mainly compare the crime rates of immigrants to those of natives, and then moves to later studies describing the empirical correlation between immigration and crime across local areas within the US. Section 3 presents more recent work exploiting plausibly exogenous variation in immigration to estimate its effect on crime rates in the US as well as in other destination countries. The crucial role of immigrants' legal status is addressed in Section 4, while Section 5 reviews additional studies focusing specifically on the effect of refugees and asylum seekers. Section 6 reviews the existing evidence on the relationship between deportations and crime. Finally, Section 7 concludes.

2. EARLY EVIDENCE ON IMMIGRATION AND CRIME IN THE US

Immigration to the US reached a historical peak at the turn of the twentieth century, in the wake of massive migration flows from the Old World. Between 1860 and 1920, the ratio of foreign immigrants to the total resident population in the US hovered around 14–15 percent, a share that has remained unsurpassed since then. As has often been the case throughout history, the arrival of millions of people from different ethnicities and cultural backgrounds within a relatively short period of time resulted in widespread concerns and anti-immigrant sentiments. To make things worse, the beginning of the century also witnessed a dramatic surge in homicides across the US. The number of homicides per 100 000 inhabitants increased from just above 1 in 1903 to just under 10 at the start of the Great Depression – a tenfold increase within less than 30 years.

Some observers attributed the surge in homicides to the large presence of immigrants in that period, though, as we mentioned above, immigration had also been high in previous decades, when the homicide rate was essentially flat at 1 per 100 000 inhabitants. To address these concerns, the 'Wickersham Commission', a committee appointed in 1929 by President Hoover to investigate crime problems in the country, dedicated one of its final reports to the issue of 'Crime and the Foreign Born'. The 400 pages of the report constitute the first systematic analysis on this theme conducted using modern statistical methods. Almost a century old, such analysis appears extremely accurate and informative even by today's standards.

For starters, the report clarifies the main challenges to empirically assessing the relationship between immigration and crime:

> the difficulty of securing facts – facts about crime that are properly recorded, facts about the foreign-born element in the population, and facts about the nativity of persons charged with or convicted of crime that are likely to be even more incorrectly recorded and extremely difficult to secure. It is a subject that is clouded

with prejudice, and, although there have been many state papers prepared on this subject and many published treatises, it has rarely been subject to impartial, disinterested inquiry.

(Wickersham Commission, 1931, p. 11)

Drawing on several sources, such as police records and census data on the resident and prison population, the report compared the relative incidence of native-born whites, foreign-born whites, and blacks among offenders and the resident population, respectively. The data available for nine large cities around the year 1930 suggest that foreign-born whites were less involved in crime than natives, though with considerable heterogeneity across different foreign nationalities. Table VI of the Wickersham report, reproduced in Figure 11.5, documents this fact for any type of (serious) crime. The same

TABLE VI.—***Number of persons, per 100,000 of population of same class 15 years and over, charged with certain important offenses by the police departments of nine cities during a 1-year period, by offense, by nativity and color, and by country of birth***

Nativity and country of birth	Total number charged, per 100,000 of same population class, 9 cities [1]					
	Homicide	Rape	Robbery	Aggravated assault	Burglary	Weapons
Native white	19.4	17.8	108.1	47.5	92.2	28.7
Negro [2]	120.5	64.0	481.2	543.5	421.0	222.0
Foreign-born white	12.3	11.2	28.1	44.5	34.2	19.1
Austria	16.0	4.9	19.7	31.9	9.8	18.4
Canada	4.4	3.3	14.8	4.9	38.4	2.7
Czechoslovakia	2.1	2.1	6.4	18.0	8.5	2.1
England, Scotland, and Wales	5.6	8.1	11.8	4.3	22.9	1.2
France	7.5	7.5	18.8	18.8	11.3	7.5
Germany	3.6	2.6	2.6	14.0	10.1	4.2
Greece	0.7	20.0	22.6	164.5	32.3	58.1
Hungary	2.2	2.2	24.7	15.7	4.5	3.4
Ireland	6.0	1.3	7.3	11.3	16.0	2.0
Italy	53.6	34.8	67.0	102.3	38.7	64.7
Yugoslavia	0.0	4.9	9.9	22.3	2.5	4.9
Lithuania	21.3	18.3	36.5	101.4	39.6	24.4
Poland	8.9	12.1	37.4	52.5	25.6	9.5
Russia	7.9	3.2	13.4	20.6	14.8	5.6
Scandinavian countries	4.2	1.2	4.8	17.5	22.9	3.0
Mexico [3]	77.2	132.7	207.8	417.4	570.1	340.9
All other (white)	22.5	23.3	85.1	105.1	77.0	36.1

[1] Rates computed from figures taken from annual reports, or from special tabulations provided by the police departments, and population estimates based on census data. Cities supplying these figures were: Chicago; Detroit; Los Angeles; Cleveland; Cincinnati; Kansas City, Mo.; Rochester, N. Y.; San Francisco; and Cambridge, Mass.

[2] Separate figures for native white and negro were not supplied by San Francisco, but inasmuch as San Francisco's percentage of negro population is only 0.5 of 1 per cent it was considered safe to disregard the deficiency.

[3] All Mexican rates are of very doubtful value because of the question as to validity of population estimates.

Figure 11.5 Relative offending rate by group around 1930, from the National Commission on Law Observance and Enforcement

is true for almost all immigrant nationalities, with the notable exception of Italians, Lithuanians and Mexicans, who display very high crime rates.

Similar findings are presented in the other tables of the report. Based on this evidence, the authors conclude that, overall, immigrants were *not* disproportionately responsible for crime in the US during this period – if anything, the opposite was true. This conclusion is corroborated by several contemporaneous studies, including Sutherland et al. (1992) in his influential manual 'Principles of Criminology', and more recently by Moehling and Piehl (2009), who revisit this evidence applying modern econometric techniques.

After these first studies, academic interest in the effect of immigration on crime faded in parallel with the declining incidence of immigrants in the US, which fell from 14 percent in 1920 to 5 percent in 1970. We must wait until 1998 – incidentally, in the midst of a new migration wave – to find another systematic comparison of immigrant and native crime. Drawing on US census data, Butcher and Piehl (1998b) show that incarceration rates in 1980 and 1990 were lower for immigrants than for natives, and even more so when keeping constant socio-demographic characteristics; a follow-up paper reaches similar conclusions for the period through 2000 (Butcher and Piehl, 2007). These findings echo those of the Wickersham Commission in pointing at a *lower* involvement in crime of immigrants compared to natives.

On the other hand, this conclusion is very specific to the US context, as in most countries, immigrants are actually over-represented among offenders (see, e.g., Fasani et al., 2020). Most importantly, the fact that the foreign-born commit fewer crimes than natives does not exclude the possibility that immigration may increase crime rates, as in equilibrium, immigration may affect crime rates through several mechanisms. For instance, immigrant workers may displace natives from the labor market, leading them, in turn, to commit more crimes. Borjas et al. (2010) suggest that a 10 percent immigrant-induced increase in the supply of a particular skill group is associated with a 2.5 percent reduction in the wage of black native workers in the same skill group, a 6 percentage point reduction in their employment and a 1.3 percentage point increase in their incarceration rate. The effects on white natives have the same signs but are much weaker in magnitude. In addition, immigration could affect crime through congestion of the welfare system and the housing market. These are just examples of equilibrium adjustments through which immigration may influence criminal activity in the destination country.

In light of these issues, the focus of empirical studies progressively shifted from comparing offending rates between immigrants and natives to comparing local crime rates between cities with higher and lower immigration rates. Using census data for the period between 1980 and 2000, Reid et al. (2005), Ousey and Kubrin (2009), and Wadsworth (2010) regress crime rates on immigration across metropolitan areas. All three papers conclude that, after controlling for other area characteristics, immigration is *not* associated with higher crime rates – if anything, the relationship is often negative. Implementing a similar regression analysis across OECD countries over the period 2001–12, Fasani et al. (2020) find that the relationship between (changes in) immigration and crime across countries is flat. However, these analyses remain purely correlational, so one can hardly attach a causal interpretation to these regressions. The studies presented in the next section address this issue.

3. THE CAUSAL EFFECT OF IMMIGRATION ON CRIME RATE

Comparing crime rates in countries (or in local areas within the same country) with higher and lower levels of immigration does not identify the causal effect of immigration. The main reason is that immigrants are very mobile across potential destination countries, or across areas within the same country. For instance, they may be attracted to areas offering better employment perspectives, so comparing crime rates between high- and low-immigration areas would conflate the effect of immigration with that of positive labor demand shocks. Immigration decisions may also respond to local crime rates, so the empirical relationship between immigration and crime reflects causality going in both directions.

To address causality, the best thing would be to compare the crime rate in a destination area with the crime rate in the same area had it not received any immigration. Clearly, this is meant to be a thought experiment, as in reality, we will never be able to observe the same area under these two alternative scenarios. The next best thing would be to randomly allocate immigrants across areas and then compare average (changes in) crime rates across areas receiving and not receiving immigrants. By the virtues of randomization, these two groups of locations would be on average similar, allowing us to attribute any difference in subsequent crime rates to the causal effect of immigration. For ethical and political reasons, this experiment would also be unfeasible in practice; yet many real situations approximate such an experiment, thus allowing one to identify the causal effect of immigration separately from other confounding factors.

A popular approach exploits (i) plausibly exogenous variation in immigrant flows based on shocks in origin countries, such as conflicts or economic crises, and (ii) the geographical distribution of previous immigrants, by nationality, across different areas of the destination country. Since immigrants tend to settle in the same areas as previous immigrants from their country of origin (see, e.g., Munshi, 2020), the combination of (i) and (ii) is typically a very robust predictor of actual immigration. To the extent that shocks in the countries of origin and the geographical distribution of previous immigrants by nationality are exogenous to subsequent changes in crime rates, predicted immigration flows can then be used as an instrument for actual flows to estimate their effect on crime in a two-stage-least-squares framework. This approach has been extensively used to estimate the effects of immigrants on natives' employment and wages; see Peri (2016) for a recent survey.

Butcher and Piehl (1998a) use the same approach to estimate the effect of immigration on crime across US cities in 1980–90. They find that although the two variables are correlated in the cross-section, such correlation is driven by other omitted factors. In line with this finding, regressing changes in crime on changes in immigration, thus absorbing time-invariant differences across cities, finds no significant effects. These conclusions are partly reversed by Spenkuch (2014) when extending the sample period through the year 2000, though the estimated effect of immigration remains small. In particular, a 10 percent increase in the share of immigrants increases property crimes by 1.2 percent, while violent crimes are unaffected.

Outside the US, Bianchi et al. (2012) estimate the causal effect of immigration on crime across Italian provinces during the period 1990–2003. Similar to Butcher and Piehl (1998a), they find a positive correlation in OLS regressions, but no causal effect in instrumental variable regressions – with the exception of a small effect on robberies. A contemporaneous paper by Alonso-Borrego et al. (2012) detects significant effects of immigration on crime across Spanish provinces. However, such effects display extreme heterogeneity across different groups of immigrants – notably by education and gender – making it hard to draw general conclusions about the overall effect of immigration.

Bell et al. (2013) consider another important dimension of heterogeneity, namely, access to the labor market. Specifically, they estimate the effect of two different migration waves to the United Kingdom. The first wave consisted of asylum seekers reaching the country between the late 1990s and early 2000s as a consequence of wars and political turmoil in countries such as Iraq, Afghanistan, and Somalia. The second wave occurred in the wake of the European Union enlargement of 2004, which allowed millions of citizens from eight countries in Eastern Europe to enter and work in all other EU countries, including the United Kingdom. Bell et al. (2013) find that the first (asylum) wave brought an increase in the incidence of property crimes, while the opposite is true for the second (enlargement) wave, and that neither wave affected violent crimes. These findings are in line with the predictions of the Beckerian model of crime. Indeed, free access to the labor market increases the opportunity cost of committing (economic) crimes for new EU citizens, reducing their propensity to engage in crime, while asylum seekers faced temporary restrictions to work upon arrival in the UK. We will come back to the crucial role of labor market access in the next two sections.

A few other papers have examined the impact of different migration waves to Germany. Piopiunik and Ruhose (2017) focus on the collapse of the Soviet

Union, which triggered a migration wave of 3 million people of German ancestry. They estimate a large crime elasticity to migration (0.39), which varies significantly with local conditions. In particular, the effect is larger in regions with higher preexisting crime levels, large shares of foreigners, and high population densities. Several recent papers instead find only moderate effects, if any, of the asylum seekers' migration wave of 2014–15 on property crimes and other common types of offenses (Gehrsitz and Ungerer, 2016, and Lange and Sommerfeld, 2018). On the other hand, hate crime against immigrants increased considerably during the same period (Entorf and Lange, 2019).

Overall, the available evidence on the impact of immigration on crime rates in destination countries is mixed. The majority of papers find little or no effect, while a few papers document a significant increase in crime (e.g., Piopiunik and Ruhose, 2017, for Germany), though varying greatly with local conditions and the composition of immigrant flows. In the next section, we consider a crucial dimension of heterogeneity, namely, immigrants' legal status.

4. THE EFFECT OF IMMIGRANT LEGALIZATION ON CRIME

A relevant question in the literature on immigration and crime is whether opening labor opportunities or facilitating the regularization of undocumented migrants may impact crime in hosting locations. There are at least three main channels through which such effects could take place: First, regular migrants have access to economic opportunities in the formal sector, which likely offer higher wages and better job conditions (Kossoudji and Cobb-Clark, 2002; Kaushal, 2006; Amuedo-Dorantes et al., 2007; Devillanova et al., 2018). Better economic opportunities in official labor markets would reduce, in turn, the attractiveness of illicit activities. Next, irregular immigrants may be less willing to report crimes committed against them for fear of deportation. Finally, regularization can affect crime through a reduction of stress and depression in migrants.

Mastrobuoni and Pinotti (2015), Pinotti (2017) and Fasani (2018) examine the effects of immigrant legalization on crime in Italy. Mastrobuoni and Pinotti (2015) exploit variation in legal status across pardoned prison inmates after the EU enlargement of January 2017. They find that after the EU accession, recidivism declined markedly among inmates from new EU member countries, whereas no change occurred in the control group of inmates from EU-candidate member countries. Pinotti (2017) estimates the effect of immigrant legalization on crime by exploiting a regression discontinuity design implicit in the allocation of residence permits in Italy. Fixed quotas of residence permits are available each year, for which applications must be submitted electronically on specific 'click days'; such applications are processed on a first-come, first-served basis until the available quotas are exhausted.

Matching data on applications with individual-level criminal records, the paper documents that legalization reduces the crime rate of legalized immigrants by 0.6 percentage points on average, relative to a baseline crime rate of 1.1 percent. Finally, Fasani (2018) exploits cross-sectional and time variation in the number of immigrants legalized by repeated amnesty programs enacted in Italy between 1990 and 2005. Exploiting plausibly exogenous variation in the actual number of legalized immigrants, as driven by past amnesty applications, he finds that the amnesty enactment was reflected in lower crime rates, though the effects are small and not persistent.

For the US, Baker (2015) and Freedman et al. (2018) examine the effects of the 1986 Immigration Reform and Control Act (IRCA). IRCA represented a near-universal legalization of immigrants in the US – legalizing almost 3 million people. To identify the effects of the amnesty, Baker (2015) regresses logged crime per capita on the cumulative number of county-level IRCA legalizations per capita. He documents that an increase of one percentage point in the number of legalized IRCA applicants per capita is associated with a 4.5 percent decrease in overall crime rates. This effect was mainly driven by a reduction in economically motivated crimes, while there was only a small decline in violent crimes. Freedman et al. (2018) present similar conclusions by exploiting administrative data on the criminal justice involvement of individuals in San Antonio, Texas.

Overall, most of the evidence available for developed countries points to a strong relationship between access to legal jobs and a reduction in criminal behaviors by migrants. The effects are predominantly concentrated in property crimes or other economically motivated crimes.

The same relationship between migrants' regularization and crime is not observed in developing countries. Inside developing countries, undocumented migrants may not have the same incentives to exit the informal sector due to lower enforcement and worse employment opportunities in the formal sector compared to developed countries. Undocumented migrants, for example, may not want to assume the fiscal costs associated with legal status, as it may never provide adequate benefits to compensate for the associated contributions. For instance, they may be uncertain about the duration of their stay and, as a consequence, may not be interested in contributing to social security. Consequently, the legalization of undocumented migrants may face lower take-up rates, especially if migrants are already receiving humanitarian assistance, and associate their legalization only with tax contributions.

Ibañez et al. (2020) present evidence on the impacts of the large-scale regularization of undocumented Venezuelan migrants in Colombia. The authors combine administrative data on the location of undocumented migrants with department-monthly data from crime reports and compare crime outcomes in departments that were granted different average time windows to register for amnesty online, before and after the amnesty roll out. Their findings suggest that the regularization caused a reduction in domestic crime and an increase in sexual crime reports. Both results are in line with qualitative evidence collected by the authors during focus groups with migrants, suggesting that regularization empowered migrants to report crimes committed against them, and also improved their mental health.

In sum, the available evidence on the impacts of legalization on crime suggests that irregularity imposes a large cost on foreign immigrants in terms of poorer employment opportunities, lower incomes, lower access to social services, and lower empowerment to report violations against their basic human rights. Therefore, there are important payoffs from amnesty programs, namely, a reduction in the number of crimes committed by immigrants and a larger willingness to report crimes committed against them.

5. FORCED MIGRATION AND CRIME

Forced migration flows have been increasing dramatically in the last decade (see Figure 11.6). By the end of 2019, the combined total of asylum seekers,

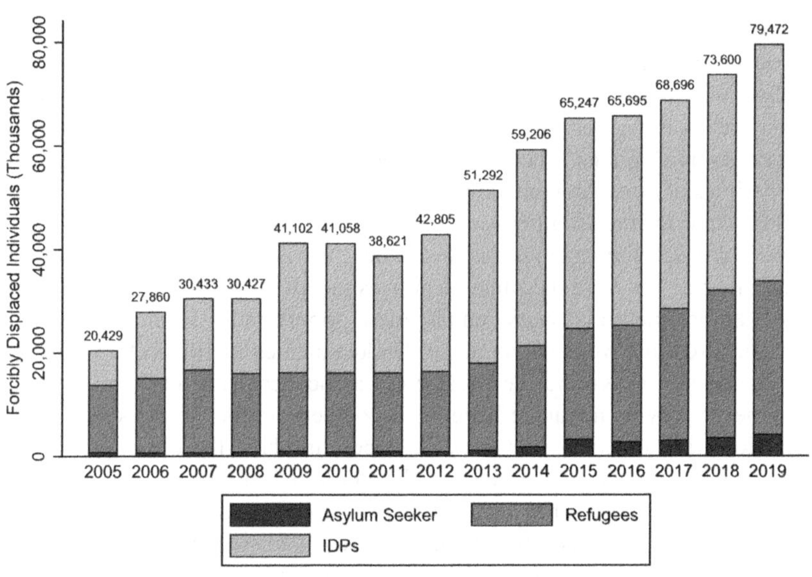

Notes: To calculate IDPs, we used data from UNHCR for 2005-2009, and from IDMC for 2010–2019.

Source: UNHCR, UNWRA, IDMC.

Figure 11.6 Forced displacement cumulative flows, 2005–19

refugees and internally displaced individuals amounted to approximately 79.5 million. Although there is no question that endemic violence and conflict are the main causes of forced migration flows, forced migration could also be impacting crime and violence in destination countries.

Forcibly displaced individuals are different from economic migrants and, as such, they may induce different effects on crime in hosting countries. Refugees typically arrive in large numbers, and, since they must move unexpectedly, they arrive with few assets and through perilous journeys. Moreover, refugees face great uncertainty with regards to their legal status and to the duration of their stay. All these factors make refugees more vulnerable relative to economic migrants, and such vulnerability may have different implications for criminal behavior.

Mejia et al. (2018) shows a strong positive correlation between internally displaced populations and crime in hosting areas in Colombia. Knight and Tribin (2020) examine the causal effects of Venezuelan migration on violent crime in Colombia. As a result of the Venezuelan crisis, more than 1.8 million individuals had arrived to Colombia by 2019. The authors exploit the closing and subsequent re-opening of the Colombian-Venezuelan border in 2016, which precipitated a massive immigration wave into Colombia, and show that homicides in Colombia increased in areas close to the border with Venezuela as a consequence. Interestingly, however, the authors document that the increase in crime was driven by homicides involving Venezuelan victims, with no evidence of a statistically significant increase in homicides involving Colombian victims. Franco-Mora (2020) also documents increases in violence associated with the arrival of Venezuelan refugees in Colombia. The effects that he documents are predominantly concentrated on theft of individuals and businesses.

Overall, the few existing recent papers suggest that forcibly displaced population inflows may be associated with higher crime rates, but that these effects are most likely driven by a higher victimization of migrant populations.

6. DEPORTATIONS AND CRIME

Although the most studied flows of forced migration move from origin to host countries, there are also deportation flows moving in the inverse direction. These flows are particularly large from the US to Central America, one of the most violent regions of the world. As illustrated in Figure 11.7, total deportation flows from the US have increased dramatically over the last century. Moreover, they display a re-composition from voluntary returns – comprised of individuals who are ordered to return based on a jury decision, but are given the choice to do it voluntarily – to forced removals – which consist of removals directly executed by migration officials.

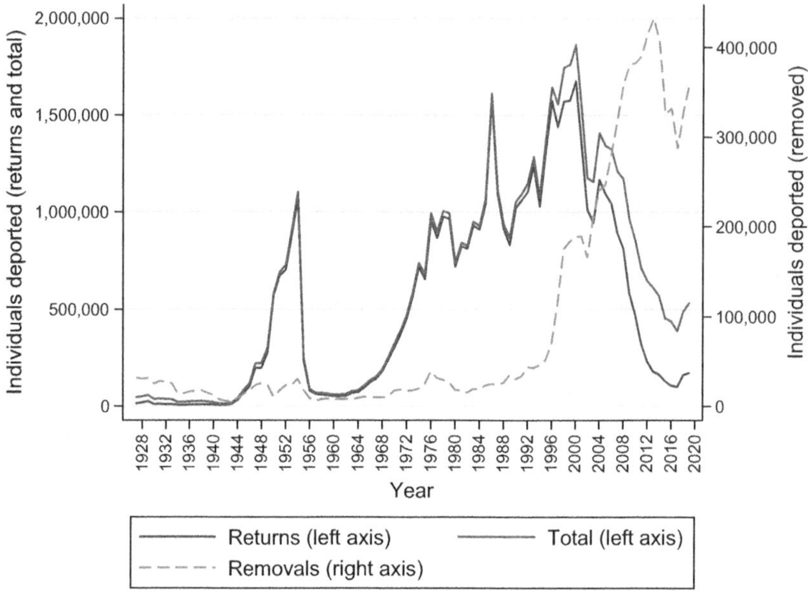

Figure 11.7 Deportation flows from the US

For most of the twentieth century, the US immigration policy related to undocumented immigration involved border enforcement, but limited enforcement within the nation's interior. After the 1980s, however, immigration enforcement gradually increased inside the US. This process involved four stages. The first stage is marked by the approval of the 1986 Immigration Reform and Control Act (IRCA), which offered a large amnesty program for migrants with strong ties to the US while making it illegal to knowingly hire an undocumented immigrant. The IRCA represented an initial intensification of enforcement of immigration law within the US interior.

The second stage coincided with the passage of the Illegal Immigration Reform and Immigrant Responsibility Act (IIRIRA) in 1996. IIRIRA streamlined the formal removal process by eliminating the requirement of judicial review for individuals apprehended at the border and individuals with a prior removal order. It also redefined the concept of 'aggravated felony' in order to make unauthorized migrants eligible for removal from the country.[4]

The third stage is marked by the September 11 attacks of 2001, after which, the US devoted large resources to increasing the enforcement of immigration law. The creation of the new Department of Homeland Security also increased the resources devoted to both border and interior enforcement.

Finally, in recent years, through cooperation between local law enforcement agencies and the federal government (287 (g) agreements) and the implementation of the Secure Communities program,[5] immigration enforcement has relied more heavily on information from local governments.

All of these policy changes from the US have increased the number of deportations, as well as changed their nature. Today, a larger proportion of deportations involve forced removal rather than voluntary returns, the proportion of deportation from the country's interior has increased and criminal deportation has grown considerably. When stratified by nationality, there is a disproportionate representation of Mexicans and nationals from Guatemala, Honduras, and El Salvador – an area known as the 'Northern Triangle' (see Figure 11.8).

Recent work has documented two main ways through which deportations from the US can impact crime in origin countries in Central America (Rozo et al., 2020). First, the selective removal of individuals with previous criminal backgrounds may create concentrated flows of deportees with weak ties to their home country, insufficient skills valued in the formal labor market, and substantial criminal experiences. Such individuals may have a higher tendency to engage in criminal activities to generate income, meaning that enforcement policy from destination countries is effectively exporting crime to origin countries. For instance, if an individual was more exposed to criminal activities while in the US (e.g., migrant youth growing up in and acculturating to the norms of very poor US neighborhoods, criminality-enhancing experiences within the US criminal justice system and developed formal ties with US street gangs), the migrant may return to their origin country more criminally prone than when he or she left for the US. Deportees with formal ties to US street gangs may seek out local gangs upon removal, start local divisions of their organization or even help expand their activities transnationally. Deportees with previous criminal backgrounds, consequently, could become perpetrators of crime upon their return to their home countries. Criminal gangs formed or joined by deportees, in turn, have direct connections to the US and even bear the names of violent US street gangs (such as the '18th Street' or the 'MS-13' gangs).

Second, mass deportation can also create a large pool of potential crime victims among deportees and individuals attempting to migrate without proper documentation. Many deported individuals are dropped at the border, or close to repatriation centers that are not necessarily close to their municipalities of origin. Many migrants stay in the areas to which they were deported in the hope of returning to the US, and may fall prey to robbery and extortion. If deportations generate violence in the deportees' origin countries, such violence can, in turn, increase migration flows to destination countries, perpetuating a vicious cycle of greater violence-induced migration to destination

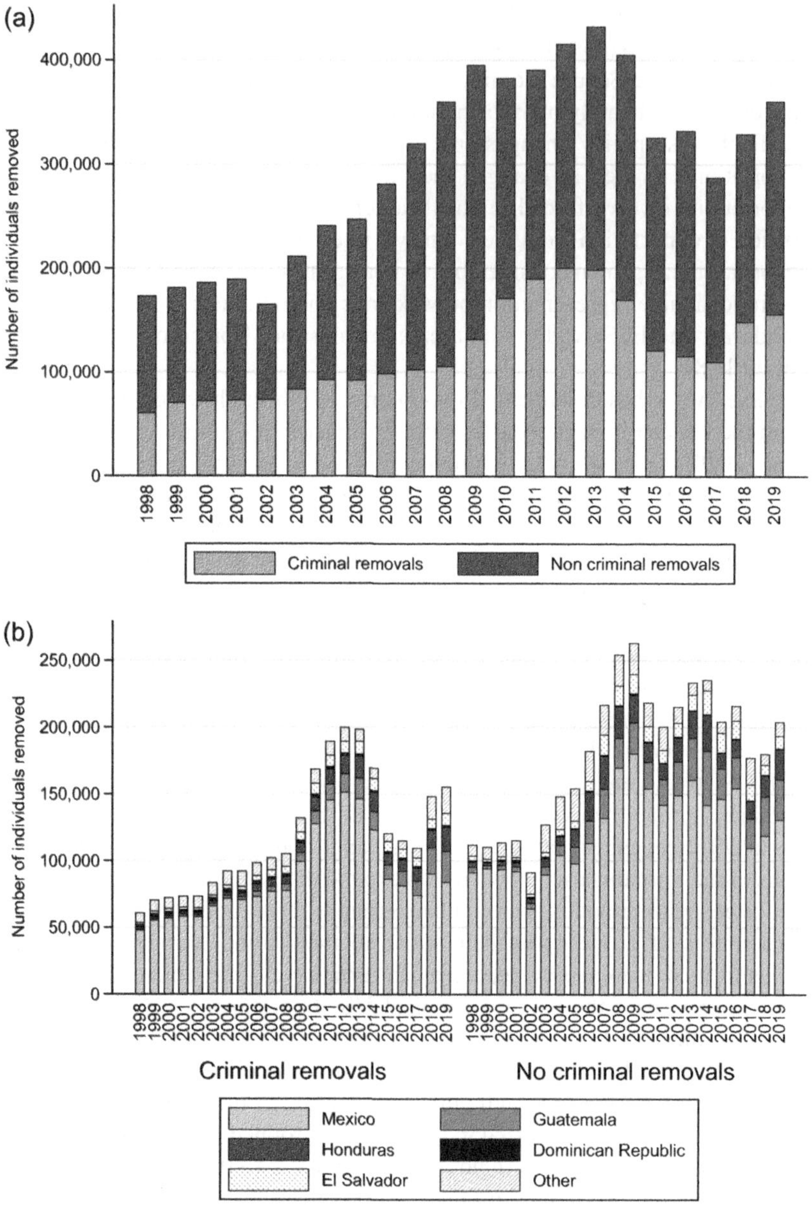

Figure 11.8 Criminal and non-criminal deportations from the US

countries, higher immigration enforcement in destination countries (i.e., more deportations), more violence in origin countries and more migration from origin to destination countries. There is ample work documenting both directions of this vicious cycle of violence and migration (Ambrosius and Leblang, 2019).

Concerning the impacts of violence in the origin countries, Clemens (2017) documents the relationship between violence in the Northern Triangle (i.e., Honduras, El Salvador, and Guatemala) and child migration to the US using US apprehensions of unaccompanied child migrants from these countries between 2011 and 2016. He finds that 1 additional homicide per year in the origin region caused a cumulative total of 3.7 additional unaccompanied child apprehensions in the US. Similar effects of higher violence on migration flows are documented by Orozco-Aleman and Gonzalez-Lozano (2018) for drug-related violence in Mexico. The authors examine the impacts of local and transit violence on migration flows from Mexico to the US. Using electoral cycles as a source of plausibly exogenous variation in violence, the authors document that higher violence in the municipality of residence increased migration. Conversely, violence on the route to the US deterred individuals from migrating.

Concerning the impacts of deportations from destination countries on violence in origin countries, earlier work has documented this relationship using cross-country variation, and more recent papers have used within-country variation. At the cross-country level, Blake (2014) relies on a cross-country panel of 38 countries over the period 1970 to 2004 and finds that an increase in the number of criminal deportees received by a country corresponds to an increase in that country's homicide rate. In the case of El Salvador, Kalsi (2018) links American criminal deportations with gang activity and reduced schooling. The author argues that regions with greater business density before the deportations are suitable for future gangs, as extortion of businesses is a gang's primary source of income. These regions are shown to become disproportionately more violent with more criminal deportations. Sviatschi (2018) exploits variation in criminal deportations from the US with geographical variation in the location of gang groups in El Salvador to document that criminal deportations from the US led to a large increase in homicide rates and gang activity, such as extortion and drug trafficking as well as an increase in gang recruitment of children, in El Salvador. Similar effects for El Salvador are reported by Ambrosius (2018). Finally, Rozo et al. (2020) document that Mexican municipalities with greater geographic exposure to deportation flows have higher rates of violent crime. To do this, the authors use municipal panel data on homicide rates matched with annual deportation flows from the US to

Mexico and assess whether municipalities with repatriation points experience higher rates of violent crime when deportation flows surge.

The evidence from these studies suggests that the current deportation system and migrant enforcement policies in the US may facilitate the creation of hardened criminals, thus inducing large unintended effects in origin countries. By deporting migrants with criminal capital and connections, the US may be facilitating the growth of future violence-induced migration flows. A more effective way to prevent larger migration flows of undocumented individuals is to improve the reintegration of migrants and ex-convicts. Assessing the effectiveness of such solutions is a promising avenue for future research.

7. CONCLUSIONS

All in all, the empirical evidence presented in this chapter suggests that migrants tend to have a lower likelihood of being involved in criminal activities relative to natives; on the other hand, migrants often appear to be disproportionately victimized by criminal groups. However, there is a large disconnect between the available evidence on the impacts of migration on crime and the perception of hosting communities on the magnitude and direction of these effects.

Some recent work addresses the gap between the hard evidence on the impacts of migration and the perception among the general public (see, e.g., Alesina et al., 2018; Hangartner et al., 2018; Steinmayr, 2021; Alesina et al., 2018; and Rozo and Vargas, 2019). As for crime effects, Nunziata (2015) shows that larger migration flows to Italy do *not* affect natives' victimization rates.

At the same time, fear of crime increases among natives, and this effect is driven by individuals reporting unfavorable attitudes toward immigrants. Ajzenman et al. (2021) extend the analysis to the implications of these perceptions on natives' behavior. They address this question in the context of Chile, where the foreign-born population almost tripled between 2010 and 2015. Using a shift-share instrument, they find that larger migration inflows are reflected in large and significant effects on crime-related concerns by natives. Most importantly, these concerns are translated into a variety of crime-preventive behaviors, such as increasing personal security, installing an alarm, and coordinating security actions with neighbors or local authorities. These changes in beliefs and behaviors took place despite the fact that immigration did not change native's victimization rates.

Unsurprisingly, media outlets play a large role in spreading (mis)information on the effects of migration on crime in hosting communities. Couttenier et al. (2020), for example, study the role of media in explaining the impacts of migration on voting behaviors. By combining violent crime data with information on crime coverage from 12 Swiss newspapers, they document a positive effect of news coverage on foreigner criminality on political support for the 'minaret ban', a referendum that aimed to ban the construction of minarets on mosques in Switzerland. Initiated by the Swiss People's Party, the referendum clearly stigmatized Islam, a religion largely practiced by a recent cohort of migrants. In the future, more work is needed to clarify whether fears of criminal behaviors by migrants explain the negative attitudes held by natives toward migrants and whether these beliefs, and subsequent behaviors, can be updated or modified.

NOTES

1. We thank María José Urbina and Caio Pedro Castro for excellent research assistance. Paolo Pinotti gratefully acknowledges ERC funding GA 861881 CLEAN.
2. Bocconi University and CLEAN.
3. Research Department, World Bank.
4. Prior to 1996, only unauthorized immigrants and legal permanent residents convicted for relatively serious felonies receiving lengthy prison sentences were eligible for deportation upon completion of their prison terms. IIRIRA rendered the definition more inclusive and made possible the retrospective application of the law for past (i.e., pre-1996) convictions for both unauthorized immigrants and legal permanent residents.
5. Secure Communities forward fingerprints normally collected in the process of booking criminal defendants following an arrest to the Department of Homeland Security (DHS). When DHS identifies a deportable alien, a 48-h hold notice is issued to the local authorities to facilitate detention and the commencement of formal removal proceedings. Participation is not voluntary, and local agencies cannot opt-out of participating. Secure Communities was discontinued in November 2014 and replaced with a more targeted deportation effort titled the Priority Enforcement Program.

REFERENCES

Ajzenman, N., P. Dominguez-Rivera, and R. Undurraga (2021). Immigration, Crime, and Crime (Mis)perceptions. IZA Discussion Papers #14087.

Alesina, A., A. Miano, and S. Stantcheva (2018, June). *Immigration and Redistribution.* NBER working papers, National Bureau of Economic Research, Inc.

Alesina, A., S. Stantcheva, and E. Teso (2018). Intergenerational mobility and preferences for redistribution. *American Economic Review 108*(2), 521–54.

Alonso-Borrego, C., N. Garoupa, and P. Vazquez (2012). Does immigration cause crime? Evidence from Spain. *American Law and Economics Review 14*(1), 165–91.

Ambrosius, C. (2018). Deportations and the roots of gang violence in central America. *Criminal Justice, Borders and Citizenship Research Paper* (3225314).

Ambrosius, C. and D. A. Leblang (2019). Immigration Demand and the Boomerang of Deportation Policies. Available at SSRN: https://ssrn.com/abstract=3491522.

Amuedo-Dorantes, C., C. Bansak, and S. Raphael (2007). Gender differences in the labor market: Impact of irca. *American Economic Review 97*(2), 412–16.

Baker, S. R. (2015). Effects of immigrant legalization on crime. *American Economic Review 105*(5), 210–13.

Bell, B., F. Fasani, and S. Machin (2013). Crime and immigration: Evidence from large immigrant waves. *Review of Economics and Statistics 21*(3), 1278–90.

Bianchi, M., P. Buonanno, and P. Pinotti (2012). Do immigrants cause crime? *Journal of the European Economic Association 10*(6), 1318–47.

Blake, G. O. (2014). America's deadly export: Evidence from cross-country panel data of deportation and homicide rates. *International Review of Law and Economics 37*, 156–68.

Borjas, G., J. Grogger, and G. Hanson (2010, April). Immigration and the economic status of black men. *Economica 77*, 255–82.

Butcher, K. F. and A. M. Piehl (1998a). Cross-city evidence on the relationship between immigration and crime. *Journal of Policy Analysis and Management 17*(3), 457–93.

Butcher, K. F. and A. M. Piehl (1998b). Recent immigrants: Unexpected implications for crime and incarceration. *Industrial and Labor Relations Review 51*(4), 654–79.

Butcher, K. F. and A. M. Piehl (2007). *Why Are Immigrants' Incarceration Rates so low? Evidence on Selective Immigration, Deterrence, and Deportation*. National Bureau of Economic Research.

Clemens, M. A. (2017). *Violence, Development, and Migration Waves: Evidence from Central American Child Migrant Apprehensions*. Working Paper (459). Center for Global Development.

Couttenier, M., S. Hatte, M. Thoenig, and S. Vlachos (2020). *The Logic of Fear: Populism and Media Coverage of Immigrant Crimes*. Working Paper, CEPR Discussion Papers 13496, C.E.P.R. Discussion Papers.

Devillanova, C., F. Fasani, and T. Frattini (2018). Employment of undocumented immigrants and the prospect of legal status: evidence from an amnesty program. *ILR Review 71*(4), 853–81.

Doleac, J. (2020). *Database of Crime-related Papers Published in Economics Journals*. Technical report, Database available at the web-address http://jenniferdoleac.com/resources/.

Entorf, H. and M. Lange (2019). Refugees welcome? Understanding the regional heterogeneity of anti-foreigner hate crimes in Germany. ZEW - Centre for European Economic Research Discussion Paper No. 19-005, Available at SSRN: https://ssrn.com/abstract=3343191.

Fasani, F. (2018). Immigrant crime and legal status: Evidence from repeated amnesty programs. *Journal of Economic Geography 18*(4), 887–914.

Fasani, F., J. Llull, and C. Tealdi (2020). The economics of migration: Labour market impacts and migration policies. *Labour Economics 67*, 101929.

Franco-Mora, S. (2020). *¿Los sospechosos de siempre? Efectos de la migracion irregular en la criminalidad*. Documentos CEDE N. 8, Universidad de los Andes.

Freedman, M., E. Owens, and S. Bohn (2018). Immigration, employment opportunities, and criminal behavior. *American Economic Journal: Economic Policy 10*(2), 117–51.

Gehrsitz, M. and M. Ungerer (2016, January). Jobs, Crime, and Votes: A Short-Run Evaluation of the Refugee Crisis in Germany. IZA Discussion Paper No. 10494, Available at SSRN: https://ssrn.com/abstract=2903116.

Hangartner, D., E. Dinas, M. Marbach, K. Matakos, and D. Xefteris (2018). Does exposure to the refugee crisis make natives more hostile? *American Political Science Review 113*, 1–14.

Ibañez, A., S. Rozo, and D. Bahar (2020). *Empowering Migrants: Impacts of a Migrant's Amnesty on Crime Reports*. IZA discussion paper N. 13889. IZA.

Kalsi, P. (2018). The impact of US deportation of criminals on gang development and education in El Salvador. *Journal of Development Economics 135*, 433–48.

Kaushal, N. (2006). Amnesty programs and the labor market outcomes of undocumented workers. *Journal of Human Resources 41*(3), 631–47.

Knight, B. G. and A. Tribin (2020). *Immigration and Violent Crime: Evidence from the Colombia Venezuela Border.* Technical report, National Bureau of Economic Research.

Kossoudji, S. A. and D. A. Cobb-Clark (2002). Coming out of the shadows: Learning about legal status and wages from the legalized population. *Journal of Labor Economics 20*(3), 598–628.

Lange, M. and K. Sommerfeld (2018). *Causal Effects of Immigration on Crime: Quasiexperimental Evidence from a Large Inflow of Asylum Seekers.* Mimeo, ZEW.

Mastrobuoni, G. and P. Pinotti (2015). Legal status and the criminal activity of immigrants. *American Economic Journal: Applied Economics 7*(2), 175–206.

Mejia, J. F., H. Velasquez, and A. Sanchez (2018). Internal Forced Displacement and Crime: Evidence from Colombia. Center for Research in Economics and Finance (CIEF), Working Papers No. 18-07, Available at SSRN: https://ssrn.com/abstract =3222807.

Moehling, C. and A. Piehl (2009, November). Immigration, crime, and incarceration in early twentieth century America. *Demography 46*, 739–63.

Munshi, K. (2020). Social networks and migration. *Annual Review of Economics 12*(1), 503–24.

Nunziata, L. (2015). Immigration and crime: evidence from victimization data. *Journal of Population Economics 28*(3), 697–736.

Orozco-Aleman, S. and H. Gonzalez-Lozano (2018). Drug violence and migration flows lessons from the Mexican drug war. *Journal of Human Resources 53*(3), 717–49.

Ousey, G. C. and C. E. Kubrin (2009). Exploring the connection between immigration and violent crime rates in U.S. cities, 1980–2000. *Social Problems 56*(3), 447–73.

Peri, G. (2016, November). Immigrants, productivity, and labor markets. *Journal of Economic Perspectives 30*(4), 3–30.

Pinotti, P. (2017). Clicking on heaven's door: The effect of immigrant legalization on crime. *American Economic Review 107*(1), 138–68.

Piopiunik, M. and J. Ruhose (2017, December). Immigration, regional conditions, and crime: Evidence from an allocation policy in Germany. *European Economic Review 92*, 258–82.

Reid, L. W., H. E. Weiss, R. M. Adelman, and C. Jaret (2005). The immigration–crime relationship: Evidence across us metropolitan areas. *Social Science Research 34*(4), 757 –780.

Rozo, S. and J. Vargas (2019, June). *Brothers or Invaders? How Crises-Driven Migrants Shape Voting Behavior.* Empirical studies of conflict project (esoc) working papers. Empirical Studies of Conflict Project.

Rozo, S. V., T. Anders, and S. Raphael (2020). Deportation, crime, and victimization. *Journal of Population Economics 34*(1), 141–66.

Spenkuch, J. (2014). Understanding the impact of immigration on crime. *American Law and Economics Review 16*(1), 177–219.

Steinmayr, A. (2021). Contact versus exposure: Refugee presence and voting for the far-right. *The Review of Economics and Statistics 103*(2), 310–27.

Sutherland, E., D. Cressey, and D. Luckenbill (1992). *Principles of Criminology. G - Reference, Information and Interdisciplinary Subjects Series.* General Hall.

Sviatschi, M. M. (2018). Making a gangster: Exporting US criminal capital to El Salvador. Working Paper.

Wadsworth, T. (2010). Is immigration responsible for the crime drop? An assessment of the influence of immigration on changes in violent crime between 1990 and 2000. *Social Science Quarterly 91*(2), 531–53.
Wickersham, G. W. (1931). National Commission on Law Observance and Enforcement: Report. Washington, D.C: U.S. G.P.O, Print.
Zimmermann, K. F., Bauer, T. K., and Lofstrom, M. (2000). Immigration policy, assimilation of immigrants and natives' sentiments towards immigrants: evidence from 12 OECD-countries. Available at SSRN 251988.

12. Females in crime

Evelina Gavrilova[1]

1. INTRODUCTION

There is a well-known decline in crime over the last decades. This decline has been driven by decreased crime participation of men. Meanwhile, women seem to have picked up the slack and started to commit more crimes. Recent evidence from several developing countries shows that female criminals are on the rise (Lauritsen et al. 2009 for the US; Estrada et al. 2016 for Sweden; Beatton et al. 2018 for Australia, Section 2 this chapter). If the general decrease in crime is driven by successful crime deterrence policies, then these policies seem to have little effect on women and there is a need to identify new policies.

Female offending has largely been overlooked in the economics on crime (Freeman 1999; Campaniello and Gavrilova 2018). Economists study the impact of policies on crime through the lens of the Becker (1968) model, where the criminal in the model could equally likely be a man or a woman. There is an implicit assumption that predictions should hold in equal measure for all sub-populations of criminals. In this chapter, I review the existing literature and show that women respond differently than men to exogeneous policies.

The emerging picture is that women are increasingly involved in crime at all ages in the US, Sweden and Australia. Women are favored in the justice process with lower probabilities of arrest, shorter sentences and lighter sentencing regimes. The possible existence of a judicial bias means that female crime cannot be curbed by the policy maker through sweeping deterrence policies that affect all criminals. Rather, the key to decreasing crime lies in the multitude of life-cycle events that impact the opportunity cost of crime. Consistent with this, females are successfully deterred by welfare policies, with effects driven by the subgroup of single mothers. However, given trends of decreasing fertility in the developed world, the group of potential criminals responding to welfare policies is dwindling. Therefore, there is a need for more research into the incentives that deter female criminals, in order to expand the set of tools that the policy maker can use to limit rising female crime.

In criminology and sociology, research is already guided by a gendered theory of offending (D. Steffensmeier and Allan 1996; Kruttschnitt 2013). This theory has its basis in the equality hypothesis, which states that as women and men become more equal in their social roles, they should become more equal in their criminal offending (e.g. Simon 1976).[2] Given initial low female crime participation, this hypothesis captured attention at the time with the stark prediction of an almost doubling of the crime rates as women start joining the ranks of criminals. More than 40 years later, it seems like the two genders are meeting in the middle – women have started to offend more and men have decreased their crime (Estrada et al. 2016). The on-going research in criminology shows that there are different pathways for men and women into crime, influenced by different policies and incentives.

Economists are well-equipped to catch up. Economists are excellent at capturing incentives, and they are no strangers to examining gender effects. There is a multitude of theories explaining and predicting the differences between male and female participation in the legal labor market. Given the broader trends in the crime market, it becomes necessary for future research to develop a gender-specific economic model of crime that can capture the incentives that influence males and females differently. The purpose would be to generate testable predictions and to guide policy with the goal of effectively deterring crime.

This paper is organized as follows. In Section 2, I show descriptive evidence about female crime participation in terms of yearly and age trends with US data. In Section 3, I examine the criminal incentives of illegal earnings, arrest and punishment. In Section 4, I present causal evidence from research on the spillover of welfare policies and labor market policies onto crime. In Section 5, I present evidence of education policies and peer effects that shift potential criminals to/from the crime path in the long term.

2. PARTICIPATION TRENDS

In this section, I quantify the trends in female crime participation, using data from the National Incident Based Reporting System (NIBRS).[3] I focus on property crimes, as previous research shows that women are most often involved in property crimes (in the US, UK and Italy, Campaniello 2019). I present descriptive evidence for the US and compare the figures with the results in the previous literature.

In Figure 12.1, I plot property crime rates for offenders of different genders in the US. In the figure, one can see an increasing trend in female crime and a decreasing trend in male crime. In relative terms, 23 percent of the crimes in 1995 were committed by women. In the next 20 years, until 2015, this rate increased by almost half to 33 percent of the offenses.

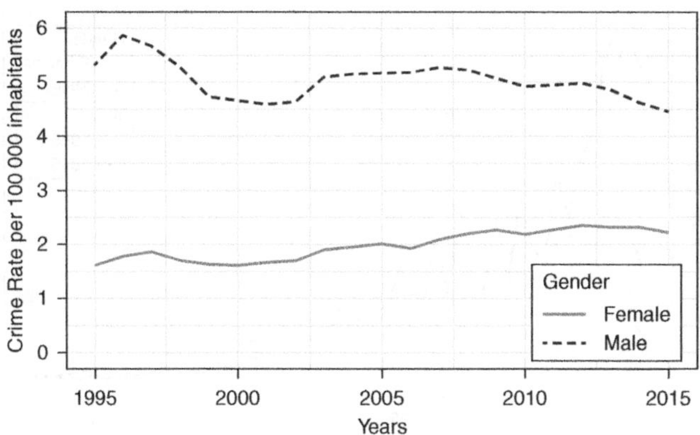

Notes: Each line shows the crime rate per 100 000 in total property crimes, including larceny/theft, burglary, motor vehicle theft and stolen property offenses.

Source: NIBRS.

Figure 12.1 *Crime participation by gender*

Under these numbers there seems to be significant heterogeneity driven by age groups and cohorts. In Figure 12.2, I plot the age gradient for males and females in the first and last year of the sample. We can see that the age gradient underwent an evolution in these 20 years. The decrease in male participation seems to be driven by a relative decrease in males aged 15–20 years, while female participation has increased throughout all ages above 18. Looking at both women and men, it seems like the cohort of criminal young men in 1995 is aging out, and in its place, there is more participation of women in all ages.

The question of the criminal career is understudied in economics, yet it might have additional bearing on the overall figures that we observe. It is unclear how many of the crimes in Figures 12.1 and 12.2 are due to single-time offenders vs career criminals. In publicly available crime data, researchers often cannot link different crimes to the same person. Therefore, it is unknown whether there are differences in the careers of criminals of different genders. For example, one could predict that female participation in crime would decrease around child-bearing age, while male participation would remain constant. This could lead to a pattern where males are likely to commit more crimes during their careers than females. Therefore, counting criminals, rather than crimes as in Figure 12.1, could result in more even criminal participation. This would be in line with the findings in Williams (2015). He uses self-reported data on property crimes from NLSY1997 in the time period

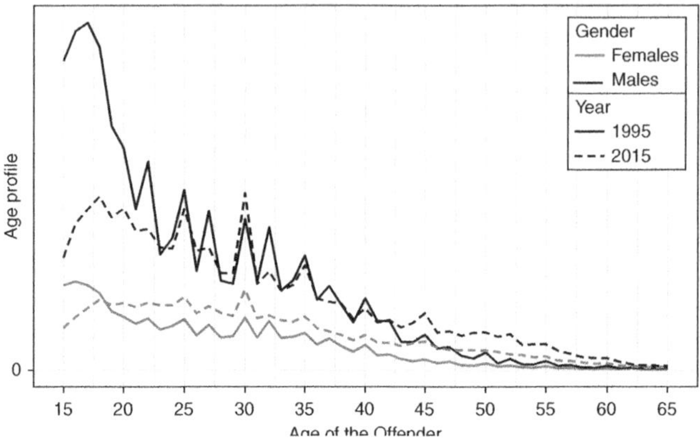

Notes: The dashed line represents reported crime counts for men; the solid line represents crime counts for women. The spikes at 20, 25, 30 etc. are consistent with witness errors. The corresponding arrest lines are smooth, not shown for brevity.

Source: NIBRS.

Figure 12.2 Age profiles by gender

1997–2011. Respondents were 12–16 years old in 1997, with retention rates for the sample over 80 percent. Williams (2015) finds roughly similar rates in thefts between the two genders. He observes that 54.4 percent of the male vs 42.5 percent of the female respondents have committed a theft. These findings speak to an equalization in the existence of a criminal career for the offender. Taken together with Figure 12.2, it could confirm the notion that men commit more crimes during their careers.

However, it is notable that for both genders age and crime participation seem to be negatively correlated. This decrease coincides with life-cycle events such as employment in the ages 25–60 years old, primary childcare in the ages 20–45 years and crime incapacitation events like incarceration. It is interesting to consider the summary statistics of the study on reoffending by Agan and Makowsky (2021). Their sample comes from 43 states, with time span 2000–14. The average age for all released inmates is 35 years, which is well beyond the most active years for criminals from Figure 12.2. Considering the average age at release, 17.7 percent males recidivate within one year and 35.5 percent within three years. For women, the figures are lower at 14.2 percent recidivate within a year, 28.4 percent within three years. Overall, as observed in Figure 12.2, the recidivism numbers are lower for women consistent with lower participation in crime in the age categories above 35.

The increase of female participation in crime is not only in property crime. Lauritsen et al. (2009) look at violent crime in the US with police reports and with victimization data. They find that in the period 1973 until 2005 female involvement in violent crime has increased by roughly 20 percent from a range of 5–15 percent to a range of 15–25 percent for robbery, simple and aggravated assault.

This pattern of increasing female participation is found also in other countries. Beatton et al. (2018) look at criminals aged 15–24, in Queensland, Australia, for a period of 20 years and find a narrowing of the gender crime participation gap. The narrowing is driven by falling male offending rates, while female rates remain stable, for both violent and property crime. Estrada et al. (2016) look at the gender gap in Sweden since the mid-nineteenth century. In addition, they follow three birth cohorts 1965, 1975 and 1985 and their convictions, in theft offenses and violent crime. They find that the narrowing of the gender gap is due to a powerful decline in the number of men convicted of theft crime and an increase in women's convictions for violence.

3. CRIMINAL INCENTIVES

In this section, I examine the main incentives to commit crime from Becker (1968) – illegal earnings, probability of arrest and punishment.

3.1. Illegal Earnings

One of the main parameters of the crime participation decision is the criminal profits. In property crimes, these profits can be quantified in monetary terms by the value of property stolen. There are few papers that have used this type of information to describe the criminal decision. Campaniello and Gavrilova (2018) look at the criminal earnings gap between men and women. When including all property crimes, they find an average earnings gap of 7 percent. This gap is notably lower than the 12.4 percent gap at the 10th percentile of the hourly wage distribution in the US (Blau and Kahn 2017).

There are many margins of dynamics that underlie this average gap. First of all, Campaniello and Gavrilova (2018) find that shoplifting is an important crime for women. Anecdotal evidence suggests that females sort into shoplifting crimes because these crimes are complementary to regular household activities. Another explanation could be that there is no uncertainty about the intrinsic value of the stolen property. Other stolen items will have to be pawned, which leads to a significant decrease and uncertainty in the value obtained from the theft. Shoplifted items can directly substitute other budgeted items, so that the budget constraint of the criminal is relaxed.

Campaniello and Gavrilova (2018) find that women prefer to commit shoplifting. They find an average earnings gap of 13 percent in the absence of shoplifting, which decreases to 7 percent once shoplifting is included in the sample. They interpret this as evidence that females sort into shoplifting to obtain higher criminal earnings. Similarly, Carr and Packham (2019) look at the impact of welfare programs on crime and find strong responses of women committing shoplifting. However, it is important to note that this crime is in no way unique to women – about 60 percent of shoplifting crimes are committed by men; it is only when comparing shoplifting to other possible ventures that it becomes apparent that it is a preferred crime for women.

Second, there is an issue of selection. Women could be less likely to select into high-profit crimes. Williams (2015) uses data on the value of the theft, volunteered by the respondents. He separates between thefts of value less than \$50 and with value of more than \$50. For the latter sample, he finds participation figures of 21 percent male vs 11.2 percent of the female respondents. Notably, this participation gap is larger than the average gap discussed above from the same paper, hinting at a distinctly different pattern of searching and sorting into criminal opportunities for men and women. In addition, this pattern could be explained by higher risk-aversion in women, where they would focus on lower-gain crimes to offset the risk of participating in criminal activities.

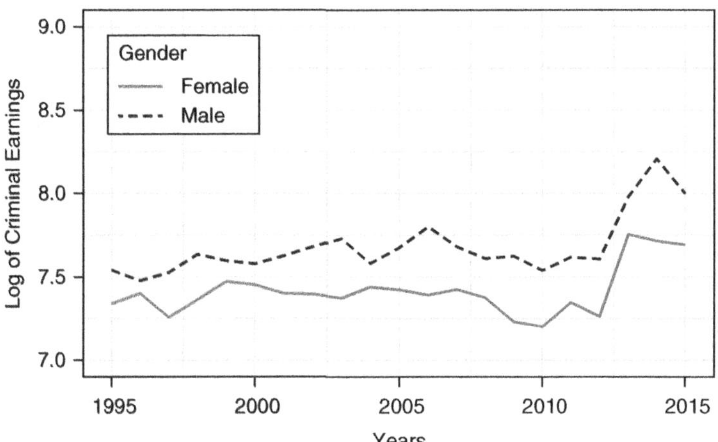

Source: NIBRS.

Figure 12.3 Criminal earnings by gender

With respect to policy incentives, it is interesting to consider whether women respond differently to earnings incentives than men. When they focus on the decision to commit a crime, Campaniello and Gavrilova (2018) find that males are more responsive to earnings opportunities with an elasticity of crime with respect to earnings of 0.36 vs 0.23 for females. In the legal market, the earnings elasticities are flipped in size with females having higher own-wage elasticities (Blau and Kahn 2017). This, taken together with the similarity in earnings gap, is interesting to explore for future research.

3.2. Arrests

Women are generally favored in the justice process. The fractions of females in each stage of the justice process are shown in Figure 12.4. Arrests are the point of entry into the justice system. In the figure we observe that for motor vehicle theft and burglary women are less likely to be arrested than men. For larceny we observe a higher arrest rate for women. Likely this figure is driven by shoplifting, which is included in the definition of larceny, and it is a crime with a high likelihood of arrest due to monitoring devices in stores.

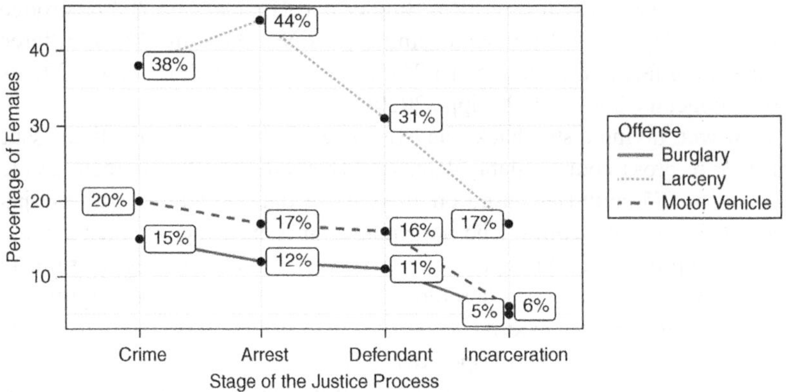

Notes: each dot shows the percentage of women within each crime type at each stage of the justice process. For example, 20 percent of motor vehicle thefts are committed by women. Seventeen percent of motor vehicle theft arrests are of women. Females are 16 percent of the defendants and 6 percent of the incarcerations in motor vehicle thefts. Note that larceny includes shoplifting. All statistics pertain to the year 2010, except for defendants – 2009.

Source: NIBRS, 2010, Department of Justice, 2012.

Figure 12.4 Fraction of women at each stage of the justice process

Overall, Campaniello and Gavrilova (2018) find that females face a 9 percent lower likelihood of arrest, conditional on crime characteristics. They find similar arrest elasticities with respect to the decision to commit a crime of –0.14 for both genders. This would imply that in the Becker framework of the criminal dilemma, both genders respond similarly to increases in the probability of arrest. A smaller baseline probability of arrest for females could contribute to explaining the gradual upward shift in female crime from Figure 12.1.

3.3. Incarceration and Sentencing

There are reasons to believe that women are favored by a bias in the justice process. In descriptive terms, in Figure 12.4 it is easily observed that for burglary, larceny and motor vehicle theft the fraction of women incarcerated is much lower than the fraction of reported and arrested women. For these crimes, on average, one in every ten incarcerated criminals is female, whereas looking only at reports, around a third of crimes are committed by females. This type of 'leaky pipeline' phenomenon is well known in the literature. Most papers have an unexplained portion of the gender gap and argue in favor of discrimination. This unexplained bias can take several forms: shorter sentences (e.g. Mustard 2001; Starr 2015; Philippe 2020), lighter sentence regimes (e.g. Freiburger and Hilinski 2013; Bindler and Hjalmarsson 2020), stronger downward departures from sentencing guidelines (Mustard 2001), different processes of fact finding (e.g. Starr 2015; Bindler and Hjalmarsson 2020) and lower monetary fines (e.g. Philippe 2020).

However, taking a step back, the existence of a bias is a contentious issue. Turning to cross-country data, Wang and Stamatel (2019) document gender gaps across 75 countries based on 10 years of data of contact with the justice system, for all crimes. The percentages of females across each stage of the justice process (contact, prosecution, conviction) are roughly the same on average, within a country.[4] Therefore, the pattern in the US from Figure 12.4 does not seem to have external validity. There are two main caveats to this claim. First, a bias could still operate at the point of first contact – the arrest. Second, the cross-country analysis can't capture the shorter spans and lighter sentence regimes that are highlighted as one of the main pathways by which the bias can be expressed.

Most studies in this strand of the literature are motivated by a large gender disparity in sentencing length. Mustard (2001) focuses on sentencing and departures from sentencing guidelines. He finds that women get 33-month shorter sentences than men, on average, in the period 1991–94. Starr (2015) looks at the whole post-arrest justice process. In the raw data, she observes that females receive sentences that are 31 months shorter than the sentences of men, in the period 2001–09. The two gaps, 33 months and 31 months, are notably similar despite being representative of two different time periods in the US. In that line of thought, Mustard (2001) finds a raw average sentence length for men of 51 months vs 18 months for women. Starr (2015) finds, respectively, 56 months and 25 months, hinting at a pattern of increasing sentence length over the years for both genders.

In more detail, Mustard (2001) shows that the gap decreases to five months, once accounting for offense level and criminal history.[5] Females are likely to receive 21 months less for bank robberies, 11 months less for drug trafficking and about a month less for larceny, fraud and immigration crimes, while the difference is not significant for firearm possession and trafficking. He finds that these differences result from departures from guidelines and account for 70 percent of the male-female differences. Conditional on receiving downward departures, females get seven months less than males on average. In addition, males are less likely to get no prison term, when the option is available, and less likely to receive downward departure and more likely to receive upwards adjustment. Mustard (2001) paints a harsh picture of how sentencing patterns favor women over men. By focusing on guideline departures, he hints that judges are partially responsible for the gap. The main caveat in this and other studies is that the judges might be privy to information that is not available to the researcher.

Starr (2015) attempts to account for how much each procedure (charging, bargaining, fact-finding, sentencing) contributes to the observed gender gap. A decomposition of the average sentencing gap shows that a new disparity favoring women seems to be introduced at every stage of the sentencing process. Accounting for pre-charge control variables explains 70 percent of the gender gap, and it reduces the gap to eight months. Charging and conviction have little influence, while fact-finding seems to explain 17 percent of the overall gender gap, reducing it to two months' unexplained gap. Most of the disparity in the justice process comes in at fact-finding – around 60 percent of the unequal treatment for the same two criminals of different genders comes at this stage.

This type of disparity at fact-finding is also observed in the historical English context by Bindler and Hjalmarsson (2020). Examining 200 years of data from the courts of London, they find a persistent gender gap in judge sentencing and jury convictions. Looking at case characteristics, they find that two witnesses are necessary to convict a woman at the same rate as males against whom one witness is testifying.

Bindler and Hjalmarsson (2020) suggest a mechanism where an all-male judiciary protected female criminals from the harshest punishments. One protection offered in the period 1715–1850 has been that females were less likely to be sentenced to capital punishment and more likely to get transportation. This type of 'lighter' sentencing regime can be also observed in current times.

Focusing on different types of sentencing, Freiburger and Hilinski (2013) look at data from Michigan and find that females are 11 percent more likely to get probation than jail with respect to males. The effect is strongest for white females. Considering the type of incarceration, the two genders are equally likely to be sentenced to prison or jail.

All of the studies until now suggest that there is an unexplained difference in sentencing that is correlated to gender. Starr (2015) exploits the available data on court cases and tests the implications of several competing theories for the source of the unexplained differences. First, she considers the role of unobservable differences in the crimes committed by women and men. Using data on drug quantity and quality which determine eligibility for mandatory minimums, she finds suggestive evidence that women benefit from disparate treatment. Second, she explores the 'girlfriend theory', which states that women are accessories to the criminal undertaking of their male partners. In this case, leniency would be appropriate. She tests the implications of this theory in multi-defendant cases and finds supporting evidence for a larger gender gap. However, this explanation is not valid for single-defendant cases, where there are still large disparities. Third, she tests the role of parental responsibilities in conviction. Female defendants are more likely to have primary custody of children. This leads to a prediction of large disparities among single parents and small disparities among childless defendants. The prediction is confirmed by the data, but still a large disparity remains among the latter defendants. Fourth, females might receive more leniency because they cooperate with the government more often. This seems to be more difficult to measure through the different case parameters, as it is endogenous to a deal being offered. Suggestive evidence explains up to 9 percent of the unexplained gap in drug cases, and it has no explanatory power in non-drug cases. Fifth, Starr considers the role of other sympathetic life circumstances such as mental health, addiction etc. The idea is that females could have a more troubled life, and thus be perceived as less culpable. Such departures from guidelines are part of the case only if cited by the judge, so it is not easy to determine their role in sentencing. Tentative evidence suggests that they might explain 1–2 percent of the gender gap but are too rare to explain more. Finally, Starr shows that the gender gap is substantially larger among black than non-black defendants (74 percent vs 51 percent). Racial disparities among men favor whites, but among women the race gap is insignificant and reversed in sign.

The sentencing gap is not only a fact of the US and the UK. Philippe (2020) uses observational data from France, for the period from 2000 to 2003.[6] He finds that women receive 15-day shorter sentences on average. One logical step in this strand of research is to account for the gender of the judge, as female judges could counter the favors extended by male judges. He finds that one standard deviation increase in the number of women in the court (in judging and prosecutor roles) decreases the gender gap by 10 percent.

In addition, Philippe (2020) finds that the gender gap persists for co-offenders in multi-defendant cases. Within a mixed gender pair, women are less likely to get prison, and if they do their sentence is 50 percent shorter, which is consistent with the findings of Starr (2015). Similar to the findings of Mustard (2001) and Freiburger and Hilinski (2013), women are more likely to get suspended prison sentences. As a dependent variable that has not been considered previously in the literature, Philippe (2020) also shows that females are likely to get lower monetary fines for their crimes.

Overall, the literature on sentencing finds that women benefit relative to men in the prosecution process. There are many pathways along which a bias could be expressed, and more causal evidence is needed. A straightforward road for this literature would be to explore new instruments and quasi-random judge assignment, in order to prove a null hypothesis of no difference in the treatment of gender. An interesting question to investigate further would be to determine the role of the gender of the judge in the sentencing gap.

4. OPPORTUNITY COST

The opportunity cost of crime is represented by the labor market outcomes in the absence of crime. This is often measured through the legal wage. Yet, implicit in this measurement are the two legal labor market decision margins: extensive, for having a job, and intensive, for how high the earnings from the job are. The predictions are that if a criminal is unemployed and has no job, then she is likely to commit a crime. If a criminal earns a low wage, then high criminal profits can sway her to commit a crime. Implicitly, if a criminal has a tight budget constraint, she is more likely to commit a crime.

Most of the literature focuses on quasi-experimental variation in labor market outcomes, or in the budget constraint of the criminal. These types of reforms come in many forms: mass layoffs (Bennett and Ouazad 2020), housing vouchers (Carr and Koppa 2020), welfare benefits (Carr and Packham 2019; Corman et al. 2013) and tax credits (Agan and Makowsky 2021). While these reforms impact the whole population of criminals, they tend to have different impacts by gender. Sometimes this impact is underpinned by requirements that are best fulfilled by female household heads. Thus, the impact of these policies hinges on working together with life-cycle events in the life of a woman.

Focusing on the extensive margin, Bennett and Ouazad (2020) estimate the impact of exogenous mass-layoffs on own criminal activity in Denmark for a sample with a strong attachment to the labor force. They find positive and significant results for men, up to three years post-job loss. In the displacement year, men have a 0.57 percentage point higher probability of committing any crime. The result for women is exactly half at 0.26 percentage point higher probability of committing crime, and the effect is only for the displacement year. Both effects are driven by property crimes. A woman who has lost her job is less likely than a man to commit a crime. One potential explanation could be that women are less likely to be the primary earners in the household; therefore their job loss does not change the household budget constraint. An alternative explanation could be along the lines of women being more forward-looking than men about the potential impact of a conviction on their job prospects. This job concern is consistent with the underlying sample which has been selected with an eye toward strong labor force attachment. Finally, the nature of the mass layoffs speaks to a mechanism with network effects, which are stronger for men than for women as described in the next section (Billings and Schnepel 2020).

Another factor that influences the extensive margin is the stigma faced by ex-convicts. Sciulli (2013) and Sheely (2020) consider the labor market opportunities for women beyond convictions using, respectively, British and US data. Sciulli (2013) uses propensity score matching and finds evidence that the employment probability of middle-aged females is about three times lower than the employment probability for males as a result of conviction (21.2 percent vs 7.1 percent). Conviction increases the inactivity by males by 4.1 percent vs 14.5 percent for females. Sciulli (2013) interprets the evidence as a strong discouragement effect and stigmatization of conviction among females. In a similar vein, Sheely (2020) uses fixed effects models to look for the separate effects of arrests, conviction and incarceration on labor market outcomes. She finds suggestive evidence that the differences between the three margins are not significant. She finds effects of 5 pp (for arrest), 7.4 pp (for conviction) and 8.3 pp (for incarceration) decreases in the probability of employment for women and 9.4 pp, (for arrest), 11.9 pp (for conviction) and 17.3 pp (for incarceration) increases in the probability of not being in the labor force. Sciulli (2013) finds larger employment effects for women, while effects on detachment from the labor force seem to be consistent between the two studies. Neither study can disentangle the effect of stigmatization for ex-convicts who find it difficult to enter the labor force due to the effect of voluntarily abstaining from participation in the labor market due to childcare responsibilities. A logical extension of this literature would be to consider the impact of 'ban-the-box'-type policies on women.

Looking at the intensive margin, Agan and Makowsky (2020) look at the impact of the minimum wage and the Earned Income Tax Credit (EITC) in the US on crime. They theorize that a change in the minimum wage impacts the labor prospects of released criminals through two channels – on the extensive margin, the likelihood of finding employment and on the intensive margin, the wage effect is underpinned by the wage they expect to earn. EITC benefits increase available income on the intensive margin and, thus, incentives to work in the labor market. They use a sample from 2000 to 2014, across 43 states. Agan and Makowsky (2020) find evidence that increases in both types of policies reduce female recidivism. On one hand, the effect of the minimum wage is the same for both genders. On the other hand, the EITC has an impact only on females, mainly in violent crimes. The availability of a state top-up to the federal EITC decreases the probability that a woman will return to prison in three years by 3 percentage points. The effect seems to be underpinned by the fact that females are more likely to have custodial responsibility for children, which is defined in the eligibility criteria for EITC.

From the perspective of policies impacting the budget constraint, Carr and Koppa (2020) identify the effects of housing vouchers on arrests of adult household heads. Housing vouchers relax budget constraints that might lead to crime, yet the prediction is ambiguous as the effect depends on the indifference curves and preferences of the household. Most importantly, voucher recipients can lose their eligibility if they are convicted of a crime. The relative value of the voucher is high enough to make this rule salient to households. Therefore, one would expect to observe a decrease in crime as potential offenders are deterred. Most of the underlying sample of applicants is composed of women, 85 percent, and most of the recipients are single mothers. Carr and Koppa (2020) find no effects for more than a year after voucher service has been received.

Another policy that impacts the budget constraint is the Supplemental Nutritional Assistance Program (SNAP, similar to 'food stamps'). Carr and Packham (2019) look at the impact of SNAP benefits on criminal activity. They find that increasing the number of disbursement days for SNAP benefits within a month leads to a decrease in shoplifting at grocery stores by 20.9 percent. They also find results consistent with increases in theft in the week before benefit receipt by women, likely in the age group above 40 years old. Note that the results for shoplifting are consistent with other evidence on crime sorting, as discussed in Section 3 on Illegal Earnings.

In addition, taking together the two studies by Carr and Koppa (2020) and Carr and Packham (2019), it seems likely that when women commit crime to relax the budget constraint they do so for small amounts. In the next section, I show evidence that women do not have access to organized crime networks, so potentially they do not have access to large criminal income opportunities the size of a housing voucher. Therefore, there is an open question as to what criminal profits influence women to commit crimes.

In a series of papers Corman et al. (2013), Corman et al. (2017), Dave et al. (2020) and Corman et al. (2018) explore the effects of a 1996 welfare reform in the US. The reform offered limited cash assistance, and eligibility was contingent on labor market involvement. Corman et al. (2013) find that the reform led to a decrease of 10–21 percent in illicit drug use among women at risk of relying on welfare. Corman et al. (2018) show that the reform influenced the offending of adult women. These two papers serve as a first stage in the subsequent intergenerational effects analyses. Corman et al. (2017) move on to the next generation and examine how maternal employment influences crime in the next generation. By filtering variation from states with more stringent work incentive policies, the authors find a decrease in arrests for minor crimes for youth aged 15–17 years by 9–11 percent. The impact is similar for boys and girls. In addition, Dave et al. (2020) find that the welfare reform led to significant increases in delinquent behavior of boys, but not for girls. The authors also find increases in drug use for both genders, more for boys than for girls. The main mechanism that seems to be at play is that boys are more responsive to disruptive events associated with the demand for welfare by the mother.

The papers reviewed in this section show that women respond to labor market incentives and welfare policies. Among the latter, the strongest responses are given by the subgroups of single mothers and older women. This is consistent with the downward age-crim profile from Figure 12.2, where crime participation decreases with age. Yet, at the same time, Figure 12.2 shows a worrying trend of increased female participation at all ages. This trend could coincide with the fall in fertility of US women,[7] which would imply that potential criminal women are less likely to have children and to be part of the subgroup that responds the strongest to welfare policies. This conjecture presents an interesting avenue for future research.

5. PATHS TO CRIME

There is an important strand in the literature that focuses on examining the impact of policies that put potential criminals on a path where they are not the marginal criminal in a Becker decision model. Such policies are related to education (e.g. Cano-Urbina and Lochner 2019) and neighborhood environment (e.g. Kling et al. 2005). By discussing education and neighborhoods, one cannot skip the topic of criminal networks and how peers influence one another. In this section, I will discuss the impact of policies and decisions that potentially sway people away from the path of crime.

5.1. Education

There is a large economic literature on the impact of education on labor outcomes. One of the most used instruments in this literature is compulsory schooling laws, which put a lower limit on the mandatory years of schooling before a pupil can drop out. Students who drop out early end up with fewer years of schooling, and so with lower earnings relative to their peers who continue their education. This implies that dropouts are more likely to face a decision *à la* Becker than their educated peers. Using this instrument, Cano-Urbina and Lochner (2019) look at the effect of education attainment on crime by females. With data from 1960 to 1990, they find that educational attainment reduces arrest rates for violent and property crime, but not for white collar crime. One additional year of schooling decreases incarceration rates for women by 0.04–0.08 percentage points, comparable to effects of 0.1–0.4 for men in the literature. In line with these results, Beatton et al. (2018) find suggestive evidence that male crime decreased more than female crime following an educational reform. Taken together, these two pieces of evidence imply that education policies seem to be more effective in deterring men than in deterring women.

Yet, Cano-Urbina and Lochner (2019) find that the effect for women corresponds to a 50–80 percent decrease of the female incarceration rate for the affected crime types. It is probable that the effect is so big because female incarceration rates are small in comparison to males, as described in previous sections. However, there is also another contribution with a large effect size in this literature. McNichols et al. (2020) look at a specific intensive margin of educational investment – sports activities in high school. They leverage exogenous variation from a reform from 1972, which required education institutions to achieve greater participation parity in sports activities. They find that a 10 percent increase in female sports participation reduced female arrests by 17.5 percent among affected cohorts.

The effects found until now in the literature are big and based on different policies; therefore it is necessary to find the policy parameters with external validity and the context-specific effects. What is ostensibly missing from this literature are more studies on other education parameters such as, for example, the impact of class size on crime. In a related note, education might not change the crime participation preferences, but rather allow criminals to sort into white-collar crime, on which there is very little research in economics.

5.2. Peers and Networks

One of the main pathways into crime is through social networks. There are separate strands in the literature on the economics of crime investigating peer effects and criminal networks. However, only a small fraction of the papers include gender as a covariate. An even smaller fraction looks explicitly at gender effects.

One of the general findings from criminology and economics is that criminal networks are described by gender *homophily*, where men tend to commit crimes with men and women tend to commit crimes with women. Preference for the same gender is observed in delinquent adolescent networks (Lee et al. 2021) and in small criminal groups (Gavrilova 2019). The presence of gender homophily is indicative of a gender bias barrier in organized crime that is difficult to cross. As an example, consider traditional organized crime structures like the mafia. With a form of reference-based initiation into crime, fathers are likely to select their sons rather than their daughters, big brothers will refer to the gang their male siblings rather than their sisters etc. This creates a path-dependence through which larger structures with more connections will be male dominated. This is consistent with the notion of 'institutional sexism' in the underworld (D.J. Steffensmeier and Terry 1986). D.J. Steffensmeier and Terry (1986) conduct interviews with 29 male criminals specializing in property crimes. The criminals reveal that they consider women as lacking important qualities to be good offenders such as trustworthiness and 'heart' for the crime. The authors conclude that women are lacking access and mentorship to big illegal opportunities. More recently, Pizzini-Gambetta (2014) discusses the role of women in organized crime, in light of the equality hypothesis. She finds that across organized crime structures women are few and they occupy roles at the lower rungs of the organization. As a wider consequence of the homophily, females would be less likely to be initiated into crime by other offenders, which is consistent with lower delinquency levels (Lee et al. 2021) and lower influence of criminal networks on their decision to participate in crime (Billings and Schnepel 2020).

The NIBRS data offers a view into the organization of small groups of criminals who offend together, *co-offenders*. Until the age of 19, more than 50 percent of the observed criminals from both genders are part of a group when committing a crime. From the age of 20 to 50 females are significantly more likely to be involved in group crimes, albeit the difference is of small magnitude – for example, at 22 years old 40 percent of the female criminals are involved in a group compared to 37 percent for males. In Gavrilova (2019), I analyze this data and find that around 75 percent of the pairs in which males are involved are homophilic. Notably, the numbers for females are lower, at 63 percent for black females and 51 percent for white females. These numbers imply that females are social criminals who could thrive within organized crime.

In Gavrilova (2019), I theorize that criminals are incentivized by the Prisoner's Dilemma and prefer to match with partners with lower probabilities of arrest. In equilibrium, this implies a pattern of positive assortative matching among criminals on the probability of arrest. Conditional on being part of a mixed group, I find that women are less likely to be arrested. I reject several competing theories, and I propose the existence of a bias where men would accept matches with women only if the women are better criminals. This would be consistent with the sexism that prevents women from entering organized crime in the first place (D.J. Steffensmeier and Terry 1986). If a female is considered to be 'bad' at offending because of her gender, then a male partner in crime would discount the features of a 'better' criminal and consider himself her equal.

However, it is necessary to point out that there is a competing explanation for the observed gender bias in organized crime. Namely, concurrent preferences of women. For example, Pizzini-Gambetta (2014) argues that females prefer to remain in the lower ranks of organized crime because they *dislike* committing violent acts to advance in the hierarchy. Yet, recent crime trends suggest that these preferences might be changing, as women become more involved in violent crime (cf. Section 2).

One of the consequences of a barrier to entry into organized crime for women is that young girls would be less likely to be initiated into crime and, therefore, they would seem less delinquent. Lee et al. (2021) use data on US teenagers from the Add Health survey to determine the key players in youth delinquency networks. They use a structural network model with a delinquency index as the dependent variable measuring the rate of rule-breaking behavior. Throughout different estimation approaches, being a female is associated with a lower delinquency level. They also find evidence of gender homophily in network formation, meaning that being of the same gender increases the likelihood of belonging to the same network.

Another consequence of the barrier to entry into organized crime is that men are more likely to rely on their criminal networks in their participation decision. This line of thought is consistent with Billings and Schnepel (2020). The article examines how the criminal decision of an ex-inmate depends on the amount of criminally involved peers in the neighborhood, in a US setting. They use information on pre-arrest criminal networks and treat the incarceration status of peers as exogenous at the time of release of a prisoner. They find that the incarceration of peers leads to a lower probability of re-offense for males, but no effect for females. Therefore, it seems like females are less influenced in their crime participation decision by their criminal network than males.

Networks could be also at the root of the findings in Kling et al. (2005). The article looks into the effects of the Moving To Opportunity (MTO) experiment on the criminal behavior of adolescents. Moving to a lower-poverty, lower-crime neighborhood led to less violent crime arrests for both boys and girls. For girls the effect extended to other crimes as well. However, several years after the move, males had an increasing rate of property crime, while females did not commit more property crime. The authors propose that there are gender differences in adaptation (consistent with Dave et al. 2020). More precisely, boys take more time to realize their advantage in scoping potential targets for property crimes. An alternative interpretation is that it takes time for boys to establish a street reputation and enter or create networks of criminal peers. Girls are less likely to be initiated into a criminal network, and if they are not influenced by a network, they are less likely to commit crimes relative to boys.

Overall, the emerging picture of women in criminal networks is hopeful for the agenda of decreasing crime. If women continue to face a barrier to entry in organized crime, then they are less likely to benefit from access to mentors, suppliers and economies of scale. Women would be less likely to be initiated into crime, and this likely dampens their increased numbers in the last decades.

6. CONCLUSION

There is little empirical research on gender in the literature on the economics of crime. Research into this gap is gaining importance given that female participation in crime has been increasing over the last decades in several developed countries. On the one hand, this trend is supported by the certainty that women face lower probabilities of arrest and favorable treatment in the justice system. On the other hand, this trend is weakened by a barrier to entry into organized crime that limits the illegal opportunities of women.

In this chapter, I review the economic literature on gender heterogeneity in crime and find that there is a need for more theoretical and empirical contributions. From the perspective of theory, there are no economics of crime contributions that consider the fact that males and females could respond to different incentives. Surveyed research in this chapter tends to find different effects for women and men, confirming that there are different incentives at play for each gender that influence the criminal participation decision. Therefore, future research can be involved in the development of a gender-specific economic model of crime, which can reflect the incentives that lead to gender heterogeneity in crime. Concurrently, from the empirical side, the surveyed causal studies are few and there is a need to learn more about gender crime effects of deterrence and labor policies.

Most of the evidence of policies on crime comes from the US. Therefore, there is a need to establish the external validity of observed effects and to expand the set of instruments available to the policy maker. There is a wide avenue open to future research dedicated to finding policies that limit female participation in crime.

NOTES

1. NoCeT Norwegian Center for Taxation; NHH Norwegian School of Economics.
2. This hypothesis became popular in the social sciences in the 1970s, concurrent with broad societal shifts in gender equality. Given the time of conception, this hypothesis is additionally referred to as the *liberation hypothesis*.

3. The NIBRS is a US-based database with records of criminal incidents. The main advantage of this database is that it provides demographic characteristics like age and gender of the criminals in reported crimes. The main drawback is that it is representative for small and medium-sized law enforcement agencies. For this exercise, I selected a balanced panel of agencies which have submitted data for the whole period 1995–2015.
4. The countries are separated into high development and middle-low development. For the first (second) group the average percentage of females at the first point of contact is 16.09 (9.64), the percentage of women in the process of prosecution is 14.93 (10.35) and for conviction 14.08 (8.09). It is also notable that data for the US are available only at the point of contact, namely 23 percent females, which is roughly consistent with the numbers in Figure 12.4.
5. Accounting for the number of dependents, age and income do not change significantly the estimate of five months (Mustard 2001, Table 6).
6. In Wang and Stamatel (2019) the average statistics for France are 14.95 percent of females at first contact, 9.43 percent in prosecution and 8.97 percent in conviction.
7. The broad trend is U-shaped. The fertility rate was 1.978 in 1995. From 1999 to 2009 it was above 2. In 2015 the fertility rate was 1.844. The two relevant years for Figure 12.2 are 1995 and 2015. Data from the World Bank, accessed at https://data.worldbank.org/indicator/SP.DYN.TFRT.IN?locations=US

REFERENCES

Agan, Amanda Y, and Michael D Makowsky. 2021. "The Minimum Wage, EITC, and Criminal Recidivism." *Journal of Human Resources* 1220–11398R1.

Beatton, Tony, Michael P Kidd, and Stephen Machin. 2018. "Gender Crime Convergence over Twenty Years: Evidence from Australia." *European Economic Review* 109: 275–88.

Becker, Gary S. 1968. "Crime and Punishment: An Economic Approach." In *The Economic Dimensions of Crime*, 13–68. Springer.

Bennett, Patrick, and Amine Ouazad. 2020. "Job Displacement, Unemployment, and Crime: Evidence from Danish Microdata and Reforms." *Journal of the European Economic Association* 18 (5): 2182–220.

Billings, Stephen B, and Kevin T Schnepel. 2020. "Hanging Out with the Usual Suspects: Neighborhood Peer Effects and Recidivism." *Journal of Human Resources*, 0819–10353R2.

Bindler, Anna, and Randi Hjalmarsson. 2020. "The Persistence of the Criminal Justice Gender Gap: Evidence from 200 Years of Judicial Decisions." *The Journal of Law and Economics* 63 (2): 297–339.

Blau, Francine D, and Lawrence M Kahn. 2017. "The Gender Wage Gap: Extent, Trends, and Explanations." *Journal of Economic Literature* 55 (3): 789–865.

Campaniello, Nadia. 2019. "Women in Crime." *IZA World of Labor, no. 105v2.*

Campaniello, Nadia, and Evelina Gavrilova. 2018. "Uncovering the Gender Participation Gap in Crime." *European Economic Review* 109: 289–304.

Cano-Urbina, Javier, and Lance Lochner. 2019. "The Effect of Education and School Quality on Female Crime." *Journal of Human Capital* 13 (2): 188–235.

Carr, Jillian B, and Vijetha Koppa. 2020. "Housing Vouchers, Income Shocks and Crime: Evidence from a Lottery." *Journal of Economic Behavior & Organization* 177: 475–93.

Carr, Jillian B, and Analisa Packham. 2019. "SNAP Benefits and Crime: Evidence from Changing Disbursement Schedules." *Review of Economics and Statistics* 101 (2): 310–25.

Corman, Hope, Dhaval M Dave, Dhiman Das, and Nancy E Reichman. 2013. "Effects of Welfare Reform on Illicit Drug Use of Adult Women." *Economic Inquiry* 51 (1): 653–74.

Corman, Hope, Dhaval Dave, Ariel Kalil, and Nancy E Reichman. 2017. "Effects of Maternal Work Incentives on Youth Crime." *Labour Economics* 49: 128–44.

Corman, Hope, Dhaval M Dave, and Nancy E Reichman. 2018. *Age Gradient in Female Crime: Welfare Reform as a Turning Point*. National Bureau of Economic Research.

Dave, Dhaval, Hope Corman, Ariel Kalil, Ofira Schwartz-Soicher, and Nancy E Reichman. 2020. "Intergenerational Effects of Welfare Reform: Adolescent Delinquent and Risky Behaviors." *Economic Inquiry* 59 (1): 199–216.

Estrada, Felipe, Olof Bäckman, and Anders Nilsson. 2016. "The Darker Side of Equality? The Declining Gender Gap in Crime: Historical Trends and an Enhanced Analysis of Staggered Birth Cohorts." *British Journal of Criminology* 56 (6): 1272–90.

Freeman, Richard B. 1999. "The Economics of Crime." *Handbook of Labor Economics* 3: 3529–71.

Freiburger, Tina L, and Carly M Hilinski. 2013. "An Examination of the Interactions of Race and Gender on Sentencing Decisions Using a Trichotomous Dependent Variable." *Crime & Delinquency* 59 (1): 59–86.

Gavrilova, Evelina. 2019. "A Partner in Crime: Assortative Matching and Bias in the Crime Market." *Journal of Economic Behavior & Organization* 159: 598–612.

Kling, Jeffrey R, Jens Ludwig, and Lawrence F Katz. 2005. "Neighborhood Effects on Crime for Female and Male Youth: Evidence from a Randomized Housing Voucher Experiment." *The Quarterly Journal of Economics* 120 (1): 87–130.

Kruttschnitt, Candace. 2013. "Gender and Crime." *Annual Review of Sociology* 39: 291–308.

Lauritsen, Janet L, Karen Heimer, and James P Lynch. 2009. "Trends in the Gender Gap in Violent Offending: New Evidence from the National Crime Victimization Survey." *Criminology* 47 (2): 361–99.

Lee, Lung-Fei, Xiaodong Liu, Eleonora Patacchini, and Yves Zenou. 2021. "Who Is the Key Player? A Network Analysis of Juvenile Delinquency." *Journal of Business & Economic Statistics*, 39 (3): 849–57.

McNichols, Drew, Joseph J Sabia, and Gokhan Kumpas. 2020. *More Sports, Less Crime: Title IX Reduced Female Arrests*. CHEPS Working Paper No. 2020902, September 18, 2020.

Mustard, David B. 2001. "Racial, Ethnic, and Gender Disparities in Sentencing: Evidence from the US Federal Courts." *The Journal of Law and Economics* 44 (1): 285–314.

Philippe, Arnaud. 2020. *Gender Disparities in Sentencing*. Economica.

Pizzini-Gambetta, Valeria. 2014. "Organized Crime: The Gender Constraints of Illegal Markets." *The Oxford Handbook of Gender, Sex, and Crime*, 448–67.

Sciulli, Dario. 2013. "Conviction, Gender and Labour Market Status." *Applied Economics Letters* 20 (11): 1113–20.

Sheely, Amanda. 2020. "Criminal Justice Involvement and Employment Outcomes Among Women." *Crime & Delinquency* 66 (6–7): 973–94.

Simon, Rita J. 1976. "American Women and Crime." *The Annals of the American Academy of Political and Social Science* 423 (1): 31–46.

Starr, Sonja B. 2015. "Estimating Gender Disparities in Federal Criminal Cases." *American Law and Economics Review* 17 (1): 127–59.

Steffensmeier, Darrell, and Emilie Allan. 1996. "Gender and Crime: Toward a Gendered Theory of Female Offending." *Annual Review of Sociology* 22 (1): 459–87.

Steffensmeier, Darrell J, and Robert M Terry. 1986. "Institutional Sexism in the Underworld: A View from the Inside." *Sociological Inquiry* 56 (3): 304–23.

Wang, Ting, and Janet P Stamatel. 2019. "Cross-National Differences in Female Offending and Criminal Justice Processing." *International Journal of Comparative and Applied Criminal Justice* 43 (3): 219–39.

Williams, Geoffrey Fain. 2015. "Property Crime: Investigating Career Patterns and Earnings." *Journal of Economic Behavior & Organization* 119: 124–38.

13. Racial bias in the criminal justice system

Jennifer L. Doleac

1. INTRODUCTION

Racial disparities have been a prominent feature of the US criminal justice system for many decades, and these persistent disparities are of concern to policymakers, advocates, and citizens. In 2019, 26.6 percent of individuals arrested were Black (FBI UCR, 2019) and 32.8 percent of sentenced inmates were Black (Carson, 2020). However, only 13.4 percent of US residents are Black (Census, 2019).

To design effective policies to reduce racial disparities in criminal justice outcomes, it's important to understand what is driving them. It's possible that a large share of existing disparities in criminal justice involvement is caused by differences in actual criminal behavior across groups – perhaps driven by differences in poverty or access to education. In these cases, addressing those root causes of differences in behavior will be required to reduce racial disparities in criminal justice outcomes.

However, it is also possible that disparate treatment by the criminal justice system – that is, racial bias from police, prosecutors, and judges – contributes to existing disparities in outcomes and should be addressed directly.[1] And when evidence of racial bias exists, understanding whether that bias represents animus (bias based on race itself), statistical discrimination (using race as a proxy for some other, unobservable, factor) or stereotyping (statistical discrimination based on inaccurate information) is similarly important for designing policies that can reduce that bias (see Doleac, 2021, for a full discussion and examples).

In this chapter, I discuss the current economics literature on racial bias at various stages of the criminal justice system (policing, prosecution, trial/sentencing, reentry). I also discuss what we currently know about what types of interventions work to reduce this bias. Throughout the chapter, I highlight the research frontier – key questions of interest for those concerned about racial bias in the criminal justice system and how to reduce it.

2. EVIDENCE ON THE EXISTENCE OF RACIAL BIAS

2.1. Policing

Police interactions with civilians come about in two ways: When on patrol, police might choose to stop a particular person (pedestrian or driver). Alternatively, they might be sent to a particular place in response to a 911 call for service. In each case, the police officer has a lot of discretion over how to handle the incident after the initial interaction occurs; the end result might be a warning or citation, an arrest, or even violence.

An important question is whether racial disparities in these outcomes are due to racial bias by officers, rather than differences in behavior by civilians. This question is difficult to answer because the researcher typically does not see everything that the officer saw in the moment – in particular, the civilian's behavior. Even obtaining detailed police reports does not solve this problem. Information recorded in police reports might – intentionally or not – be slanted to make the officer's response appear more justified than it was (e.g. claiming 'furtive movements' that seemed suspicious or, in extreme cases, lying about evidence that was planted by the officer). This would bias any analyses that condition on this information toward finding no racial bias.

A large literature attempts to address the question of racial bias in choosing whom to stop, particularly in traffic stops. The so-called 'veil of darkness' test developed by Grogger and Ridgeway (2006) compares individuals stopped during daylight and at night, with the intuition that it is more difficult to see drivers' race at night when it is dark. If there is a difference in the racial composition of stops just before and after the sun sets, but all other observable characteristics are the same, this is evidence that officers considered race when deciding whom to stop during the day. This study uses Daylight Saving Time as a natural experiment to compare the same hour of the day before and after dark; this holds other factors such as commuting patterns constant. Using data from Oakland, CA, they do not find evidence of racial bias in traffic stops.

Horrace and Rohlin (2016) note that many urban areas are well-lit even at night, and so the veil of darkness test will be more useful in areas without street lighting. They use data from Syracuse, NY, that included streetlight locations, and find that Black drivers are disproportionately more likely to be stopped during the day than at night when it is dark. This implies racial bias against Black drivers in the decision of whom to stop.

Another influential strain of this literature uses 'outcome tests' (Becker, 1957; Knowles et al., 2001) to test for racial bias in the choice of whom to stop (both pedestrians and drivers). The intuition for these tests is that officers should be stopping people based on their probability of some misconduct – for instance, carrying contraband. They should therefore choose to stop people from various groups in a way that maximizes the likelihood of achieving some outcome (finding contraband or making an arrest). This implies that the marginal white person who is stopped and the marginal Black person who is stopped should have equal probabilities of carrying contraband. If the probability of finding contraband on the marginal white person is higher, this implies that officers are acting inefficiently, and they should stop more white people and fewer Black people. If they don't adjust in this way, this implies racial bias against the group with the lower 'success' rate.

Antonovics and Knight (2009) refine this test by using the interaction of officer and driver race to determine whether racial bias is due to animus or statistical discrimination. The intuition behind this approach is that if statistical discrimination is driving behavior toward Black drivers, then it should be the same for white and Black officers alike. (This is because all officers are incentivized to use information that helps them infer criminality; if a driver's race is valuable in this way, then white and Black officers will both use it.) However, animus against Black drivers is less likely from Black officers, because individuals are unlikely to exhibit animus toward their own race.

A challenge in this literature is identifying the marginal person stopped – the so-called 'inframarginality problem'. The original theory papers that devised this test essentially assumed representative agents where the marginal person was the same as the average person.[2] They could thus compare averages across groups to test for racial bias. But of course in the real world people are not homogenous, and the marginal person will typically not be the same as the average.[3] So, while outcome tests are appealing intuitively and have been influential in policy settings, they are problematic in practice.

There is an active literature working to refine these tests and clarify their implications (see for example: Canay et al., 2020; Gelbach, 2021; and Hull, 2021). These studies highlight (at least) two additional issues with outcome tests: (1) Outcome tests may fail – thus implying racial bias – due to 'omitted payoff bias'. That is, the outcome that is the focus of the test is not the (only) outcome that officers care about. For instance, officers may stop drivers in the hope of finding contraband *or* arresting people with outstanding warrants. An outcome test based only on the former might fail, but might pass if both outcomes were considered. In practice, it is difficult for researchers to know officers' complete objective functions. (2) Statistical discrimination may be based on inaccurate information ('stereotypes' in the terminology of Bordalo, et al., 2016).

Both of these issues further complicate the value of outcome tests. Hull (2021) shows that omitted payoff bias is empirically indistinguishable from the use of stereotypes, though of course the two possibilities have very different implications (the first may not be concerning, but the second would be unconstitutional).

Another problem with outcome tests in practice is that incentivizing officers to equalize 'success' rates across groups could push racially biased officers to lie about the outcome of the search. They might plant contraband on Black drivers to make those stops look successful based on the metrics of interest or misreport other details of the incident. Indeed, Luh, 2021, shows that officers in Texas systematically misreported Hispanic drivers as white when searches failed, in order to make themselves look less biased. Thus, while outcome tests might be useful in a vacuum, they can make problems worse if used as key performance metrics in the real world.

More recent work tests for racial bias in police behavior, separate from the initial decision to stop someone. Jeremy West (2018) uses car crashes in a large unnamed state as a natural experiment. In this context, the closest officer is dispatched to the scene to provide aid and address any wrong-doing. The officer has discretion over how to handle the incident but does not have discretion over which drivers to engage with. West shows that, after controlling for the local geographic area, the race of the driver(s) involved in the crash and the race of the officer dispatched to the scene appear random. This allows him to test for racial bias by the officers based on the race of the drivers. He found substantial evidence of in-group bias (e.g. white officers favored white drivers), particularly for low-level decisions over which officers have the most discretion – whether to cite someone for an expired registration for instance. West does not find evidence of bias in more serious outcomes – whether to charge someone with a felony offense – presumably because there is more oversight there. Since the low-level offenses typically involve clear evidence of wrong-doing (the driver's registration is either expired or it's not, there's no need to guess), West argues that the bias he measures is likely racial animus rather than statistical discrimination.

Emily Weisburst (2017) uses a similar scenario to test for racial bias in the outcomes of calls for service in Dallas. She argues that unlike voluntary interactions on patrol, officers have no discretion over which calls for service to respond to. When a 911 call comes in, officers are dispatched to the scene based on who is the nearest available officer. As in West (2018), once she controls for the geographic area, the race of the officer and the race of the civilian at the scene are essentially random. She tests for racial bias in the likelihood that officers make arrests when dispatched to a call involving an other-race civilian. While there is a great deal of variation across officers in the likelihood that they make arrests (highlighting the amount of discretion they have), Weisburst does not find evidence of racial bias in this setting. Hoekstra and Sloan (2022) use the same strategy in two unnamed cities and find evidence of racial bias in officers' use of force against civilians. The different result in that paper might be due to the different outcome measure (force versus arrests) or the different context – there is surely tremendous variation in officers' behavior across cities.

Another study of note in this area is Goncalves and Mello (2020). Using data from Florida, they note a discontinuity in punishment for speeding, at 10 miles per hour (mph) over the speed limit. Those recorded as driving 9 mph over the limit receive a warning, while those recorded as driving 10 mph over the limit receive a monetary fine. However, officers have discretion over what speed they say the driver was driving. Goncalves and Mello test for discontinuities in the likelihood of being recorded as driving 9 versus 10 mph over the limit and find that white drivers are much more likely to be recorded as driving 9 mph over the limit and let off with a warning. This suggests racial animus on the part of officers against Black drivers.

All of these papers use natural experiments in clever ways to test for differences in outcomes based on race. One shortcoming in each case, however, is that the researchers are still unable to observe the drivers'/civilians' behavior. While the race-match of the officer and civilian is random, and it is plausible that the pre-interaction characteristics of the white and Black drivers are the same (given the natural experiment that produced the interaction), once the officer arrives at the scene the behavior of both the officer and the civilian, and how they respond to one another, produce the outcome (a citation, arrest, or violence). The papers described above implicitly assume that differences in the officer's behavior are what drove any observed differences; this is a plausible assumption given the power that officers have in these contexts. But it is possible that civilians' behavior is also different, perhaps in response to the race of the officer. Ultimately what these papers are measuring is the net result of the officer-civilian pair.

2.2. Pretrial Detention

After someone is arrested, they might be held in jail while awaiting trial. In many cases, cash bail may be set, and at least a fraction of that amount would need to be paid to secure the defendant's release. In other cases, bail judges or magistrates may simply decide to hold a defendant in pretrial detention because they are a flight risk or threat to public safety. A number of studies have found that, for those on the margin of pretrial detention, being held in jail while awaiting trial has substantial detrimental effects: It increases the likelihood of conviction in the current case, as well as subsequent criminal justice involvement. It also increases court debt and reduces future employment. (See Heaton et al., 2017; Leslie and Pope, 2017; Dobbie et al., 2018; and Stevenson, 2018.) So, racial bias in the pretrial detention decision could exacerbate racial disparities in criminal justice outcomes as well as employment.

Arnold et al. (2018) use the quasi-random assignment of defendants to bail judges, along with the incidence of pretrial misconduct among those who are released, to test for racial bias in pretrial detention in Miami and Philadelphia. They find that Black defendants are more likely to be detained pretrial than similar white defendants are. The authors argue that this is evidence of racial bias against Black defendants based on inaccurate stereotypes of their criminality.

Note that focusing on the incidence of pretrial misconduct as an indicator of whether someone should have been released is an outcome test, with all the problems and caveats discussed above. In this context, because pretrial detention is a function of the judge's decision to set cash bail and the defendants' ability to pay that bail, it is possible that the higher rate of pretrial detention for Black defendants is due to judges not adjusting the bail amount (enough) based on those defendants' ability to pay. That is, if they set equal bail for similar Black and white defendants, but Black defendants are poorer and less able to pay the required amount, pretrial detention rates will be higher for Black defendants. This makes it more difficult than in other contexts to be sure that racial bias is driving the observed effect. (This possibility is also raised in Gelbach, 2021, as one reason that the data from this study appear inconsistent with basic implications of the Becker model of discrimination.)[4]

2.3. Prosecution

After the police issue a summons or arrest a suspect, a prosecutor decides whether to move forward with the case. There has been a great deal of recent attention to the discretion that prosecutors have in determining the outcomes of individual cases (see for example, Pfaff, 2017, and Agan et al., 2021); this discretion makes room for racial bias to affect decisions.

A seminal paper in this space is Rehavi and Starr (2014). Using data on federal cases from arrest through sentencing, they control for a rich set of observable case characteristics and find that the race of the defendant explains substantial remaining variation in case outcomes. They show that most of the racial differences in outcomes are driven by racial differences in prosecutors' initial charging decisions; Black defendants are substantially more likely to face a charge that carries a mandatory minimum sentence than similar white defendants are.

Of course, there may be unobservable differences across cases with Black and white defendants that the researchers were unable to control for and that may be driving the case outcomes. Sloan (2022) uses the randomization of cases across prosecutors in New York County to test for racial bias in case outcomes. She finds evidence of in-group bias in property offense cases (e.g. white prosecutors are more lenient toward white defendants), driven by prosecutors' decisions to dismiss charges in some cases but not others.

Yang (2015) considers the effects of *United States v. Booker*, which struck down federal sentencing guidelines. Overall she found that this change led to an increase in racial disparities in sentences (more on this below), but part of this effect was driven by prosecutors' charging decisions: Once sentencing guidelines were removed, prosecutors became more likely to charge Black defendants with offenses that carried mandatory minimum sentences. This increased the gap between sentences received by white and Black defendants.

Along similar lines, Tuttle (2021) uses a federal policy change related to drug offenses as a natural experiment. He shows that when the mandatory minimum threshold for crack-cocaine increased from 50 grams to 280 grams, prosecutors responded by increasing the fraction of cases sentenced at 280 grams, presumably to qualify for the mandatory minimum sentence. This increase was more likely for Black and Hispanic defendants. Tuttle argues that this reflects prosecutorial discretion in the charging decision and also shows that differences in prosecutors' responses are correlated with state-level measures of racial animus.

2.4. Conviction and Sentencing

There is a large literature on the effect of individual judges on sentencing decisions, exploiting quasi-random variation in event timing or assignment of cases to courtrooms. Previous work has demonstrated that sentencing decisions – by experienced judges – are routinely affected by irrelevant information such as temperature (Heyes and Saberian, 2019), media coverage of crime (Philippe and Ouss, 2018) and the order in which cases are heard (Chen et al., 2016).

It seems likely that this variation will disproportionately harm disadvantaged defendants, including Black defendants. For instance, Eren and Mocan (2018) find that when a local football team unexpectedly loses a game (what the authors describe as an emotional shock), judges issue harsher sentences during the following week. This effect is largest for Black defendants.

There is other evidence that race itself affects judicial decisions. Abrams et al. (2012) use random variation of felony cases across judges in Cook County, IL, to consider racial gaps in sentence outcomes for similar Black and white defendants. They find significant differences across judges in these racial gaps when looking at incarceration rates. This implies that some judges are paying attention to race when deciding whom to send to prison.[5]

Alesina and La Ferrara (2014) use rates of sentence reversal in cases where defendants were initially sentenced to capital punishment, to test for racial bias in those initial sentences. They find that the sentences of minority defendants accused of killing white people are much more likely to be overturned upon appeal. This effect is confined to Southern states. The authors interpret this result as implying racial bias against minority defendants in those states.

There is surely variation across contexts in the presence and extent of such bias. For instance, Depew et al. (2017) find evidence of negative in-group bias toward juvenile defendants by judges in an unnamed US state. Juvenile defendants who are the *same* race as the judge (that is, white defendants in white judges' courtrooms) are more likely to be incarcerated than similar defendants of another race.

Park (2017b) uses administrative data on sentencing decisions in Kansas to test the hypothesis that judges become tougher on crime (sentence more harshly) during the weeks and months leading up to an election. He finds strong, robust evidence that sentencing increases during this period, but only for Black defendants and only in places with partisan judicial elections. Park argues that this change in judicial sentencing behavior is due to electoral pressures on judges themselves. These effects are larger for Democratic judges (who might be more sensitive to 'soft on crime' attacks) and in places where (based on a couple of different measures) voters are more racially biased.

Though relatively few cases in the United States go to trial, juries still play a role in case outcomes. And race matters there, too. Anwar et al. (2012) use data from Florida and random assignment of local residents to jury pools to show that juries formed from all-white jury pools are substantially more likely to convict Black defendants than are juries formed from jury pools with at least one Black member.

2.5. Reentry

After an individual leaves prison, they must reenter civilian society. A key step is finding non-criminal employment. There is extensive evidence that employers are reluctant to hire people with criminal records; there is also extensive evidence that employees discriminate against Black applicants. A more open question is how race and criminal records interact in the labor market.

Pager (2003) conducted an audit study where Black and white individuals applied for jobs in person, randomizing whether they said they had a criminal record or not (but keeping all other qualifications the same). She found that not only did employers discriminate against people with criminal records, but that discrimination was more pronounced for Black applicants. In a striking result, Pager showed that, at least in that context, white applicants with a criminal record received more callbacks from employers than did Black applicants without a criminal record.

A more recent audit study by Agan and Starr (2018) also found that employers discriminate against people with criminal records but did not find that this effect varied by race. In fact, callback rates were nearly identical for white and Black applicants with the same criminal record status. This different result might be due to the different time period or the different place (New Jersey and New York).

Most people who are convicted of a crime will spend some time on community supervision, either on probation or parole. During this period, breaking the rules of that supervision – 'technical violations' of probation/parole, such as being out past curfew, missing a meeting, or failing a drug test – can result in incarceration. Probation and parole officers have substantial discretion in when to write someone up for a technical violation. Rose (2021) considers who is incarcerated for technical violations of supervision, in the context of probation in North Carolina. He finds that technical rules disproportionately affect low-risk Black probationers. Ostensibly race-neutral rules related to the payment of fees and fines drive much of this racial disparity in who is incarcerated due to technical violations of probation.

3. WHAT WORKS – AND WHAT DOESN'T – TO REDUCE BIAS

There are many possible ways to reduce bias in decision-making, but we have very little evidence on what works. Below I discuss a few possible approaches and the current evidence (if any) on their efficacy.

3.1. Changing the Composition of Decision-Makers

It is possible that the current set of decision-makers in the criminal justice system is more biased than others might be in the same role. If so, changing who holds these positions could reduce bias in the decisions made.

Studies such as Hoekstra and Sloan (2022) and Ba et al. (2021) provide useful descriptive evidence that Black and white officers respond differently to crime incidents involving Black residents. But such descriptive evidence does not tell us whether hiring more Black officers would be helpful – the marginal Black (white) officer hired might be different from the average Black (white) officer currently on the force. To know whether changing the composition of police forces would have beneficial effects, we need an intervention that changes the composition of the force.

There is some evidence that increasing the number of Black officers on police forces reduces arrests of Black residents (McCrary, 2007), with no detrimental effects on crime rates; similarly, increasing the number of women officers reduces violence against women (Miller and Segal, 2019). These studies use court-ordered affirmative action as natural experiments. These court orders increased the share of Black and women officers in police departments, allowing researchers to measure the effects of such a change on other outcomes.

Harvey and Mattia (2021) show that litigation against police departments in response to employment discrimination appears to have reduced discriminatory behavior throughout the institution, including among rank-and-file officers. They find that after such litigation is filed (even before the composition of the police force changed), Black-white disparities in crime victimization fell, and Black residents became more likely to report crimes to police (suggesting increased trust in the police to help them).

Of course, simply saying we want a more diverse police force (or other criminal justice agency) does not make it so. Current recruitment strategies may not be effective at encouraging new and different people to join the police. Linos (2018) describes an experiment that tested different recruitment messages in Chattanooga, TN. She found that the standard messaging – about public service – had no effect on applications. However, messages emphasizing that policing is a challenging job and a long-term career increased applications, particularly from underrepresented groups. The next step in this research space will be to see if the different people hired as a result of these different messages behave in a less-biased manner on the job.

Existing rules about who is eligible to become a police officer may unnecessarily reduce diversity. Many departments require that applicants have no criminal record, have no tattoos, have a college degree, and/or not use marijuana (even if it is legal in the state). It would be useful to measure the effects of such rules on hiring as well as on policing outcomes.

There is much less work on how the composition of other criminal justice agencies affects racial disparities in outcomes. Cohen and Yang (2019) show that federal judges appointed by Republicans issue relatively harsh sentences to Black (vs. white) and male (vs. female) defendants, when compared with judges appointed by Democrats. However, as discussed above, Park (2017b) shows that judges appear to respond to the demands of their constituency – that is, they are harsher toward Black defendants leading up to an election in places where the local electorate is more racially biased. This highlights the role that the local electorate plays in determining the behavior of those who have decision-making authority.

3.2. Training

It is possible that training decision-makers to recognize their biases and change their behavior might reduce racial discrimination. Implicit bias training is often used to try to achieve this goal, but there is currently no rigorous evidence that it is effective at changing behavior (Green and Hagiwara, 2020).

Procedural justice training could reduce disparities in outcomes if it improves trust and communication between police and civilians. Owens et al. (2018) find that such training has beneficial effects, in a relatively small experiment in Seattle. Wood et al. (2020) and Roth and Sant'Anna (2021) present results from a large-scale experiment evaluating a one-day procedural justice training for police officers in Chicago. In general, this one-day training does not appear to have had effects on citizen complaints or police use of force.

It is possible that other types of training could be effective, either for new hires or as an intervention for those who have exhibited bias on the job, but we do not yet have any evidence that this approach works. The staggered roll-out model from Wood et al. (2020) and Roth and Sant'Anna (2022) will surely be useful for testing other types of trainings in the field.

3.3. Change the Amount of Information Provided

One common approach to reducing discrimination based on particular information (such as a criminal record) is to remove that information. But this can increase statistical discrimination against a broader group that is more likely to have that characteristic. See Doleac, 2021, for a full discussion.

One relevant example is Ban the Box policies, which prevent employers from asking about a job applicant's criminal record until late in the hiring process. The goal of these policies is to help people with records get their foot in the door and increase the likelihood that they'll be hired for the job. But if employers don't want to hire people with records, and this policy prevents them from asking who has a record, then they now have an incentive to guess. This could lead them to discriminate against young, Black men without college degrees – the group that is most likely to have a recent conviction that might worry an employer. Indeed, Agan and Starr (2018) and Doleac and Hansen (2020) show that Ban the Box policies do increase statistical discrimination against young Black men, which reduces employment for those without records and leads to a net decline in employment for this group. Sherrard (2021) shows that this leads to an increase in recidivism for Black people with a previous conviction. Thus, Ban the Box policies appear to increase, rather than reduce, racial disparities in employment and criminal justice outcomes.

Expunging or clearing records could have similar unintended consequences, if doing so removes information that employers care about, thus leaving them to guess who has a criminal history that they now can't see. However, if employers are most concerned about the legal liability associated with hiring someone with a criminal record, then clearing records could be helpful – since such records aren't visible to employers, those employers can't be accused of negligent hiring if the person later commits a crime on the job. Since the effects of these policies will hinge on why exactly employers discriminate against people with criminal records – which we don't yet fully understand – it will be important to evaluate their real-world effects. Doleac and Lageson, 2020, discuss the various reasons that popular record-clearing policies might fail and call for more research on this topic.

Since removing information often has important unintended consequences, it may be more productive to *add* information. This will be a useful strategy if the type of discrimination at work is statistical discrimination – where decision-makers use race (or something correlated with race, such as a criminal record) to infer other information they can't see, such as likelihood of reoffending or productivity on the job. If we can provide better information about the characteristics that decision-makers are trying to guess, they'll have less need to rely on race.

In the employment context, court-issued rehabilitation certificates seem promising for this reason (Leasure and Stevens Andersen, 2016; Leasure and Martin, 2017). Completing a rigorous job-training or rehabilitation program could also send useful signals to employers about an applicant's reliability and work-readiness; in line with this idea, there is anecdotal evidence of such programs becoming feeders for local employers, who trust that program graduates will make good employees (Piehl, 2009).

Providing more information is also a motivation for risk assessment scores. Such scores are now used throughout the criminal justice system to inform decisions. They use relevant information to predict someone's risk of misconduct or reoffense, in a standardized way across all individuals. Thus, white and Black defendants accused of the same crime and with the same criminal history, age, gender and so on would have the same risk score. This might be helpful if judges are inclined to view the Black defendant as higher risk due to racial bias. Seeing the identical risk scores across similar white and Black defendants could push them to treat the two defendants equally, if they believe that the risk scores provide more accurate measures of true risk than they (the judges) could infer on their own.

Researchers have been particularly interested in whether providing these scores to judges who make decisions about pretrial detention and sentencing might improve those decisions (targeting incarceration more efficiently) and reduce racial disparities in outcomes. Policy simulations suggest that replacing judges' decisions with the outcome of the risk assessment would have beneficial effects (Kleinberg et al., 2018), but in practice this policy does not seem effective. Judges simply don't use the additional information or use it in a racially biased manner – for instance, treating white and Black defendants with the same score differently (Stevenson, 2019; Stevenson and Doleac, 2021). The result is no net reduction in racial disparities within a place.[6]

There is also evidence that risk assessment is adopted and used in disparate ways across places, with the end result being that this policy can actually increase, rather than reduce, racial disparities in outcomes. (This is in line with Feigenberg and Miller, 2021, which shows that racial disparities can be driven by harsher policies being implemented in more racially diverse places.) For instance, in Kentucky, it appears that risk assessment changed judges' behavior most in counties with more white residents. White residents of the state thus benefited disproportionately from the lower pretrial detention rates encouraged by the risk scores, widening racial disparities in pretrial detention at the state level (Albright, 2019).

One reason that risk assessment tools may not be having the big benefits advocates hoped for is that they do not provide additional information that judges find useful. Judges might think they are just as good at determining risk as the risk score is, but risk is not the only factor they care about. In particular, judges may be releasing people who appear high-risk because of mitigating circumstances such as age (Stevenson and Doleac, 2021). Youth is a highly predictive risk factor for misconduct and criminal activity but is widely considered a reason for leniency by criminal justice decision-makers.

That said, we know that human decision-makers are easily distracted by irrelevant information, including race. Pushing them to recognize these errors and biases – with standardized risk scores or something else – still holds promise. But existing studies on the real-world effects of these tools show that we have a long way to go to figure out how to implement such policies in a way that achieves our goals.

3.4. Limit Discretion in Decision-Making

Human decision-makers are biased, and when they have more discretion there is more opportunity for those biases to affect outcomes. One way to reduce racial disparities in outcomes, then, is to limit discretion in decision-making.

We see this in sentencing guidelines for those convicted of crimes: A range of acceptable sentences given the defendant's current offense and criminal history. As mentioned above, Yang (2015) measures the effects of *United States v. Booker*, which struck down federal sentencing guidelines. She found that this change – which gave judges and prosecutors more discretion in determining the appropriate sentence – resulted in an increase in racial disparities in sentences.

In theory, risk assessment scores could work the same way, by pushing judges to make the same decision for defendants with the same risk score. But Stevenson and Doleac (2021) find that this does not happen in practice. This is likely because there is no penalty to ignoring the risk scores – if judges were required to treat defendants with the same risk score the same way, we might see a reduction in racial disparities.

West (2018) found that, in the policing context, racial disparities were largest on outcomes where there was limited oversight (e.g. whether to write someone up for an expired registration). That is, racial disparities were wider when police officers had more discretion. Finding ways to reduce police discretion is difficult but would likely reduce racial disparities in outcomes. For instance, it is possible that requiring police officers to wear body cameras and record all interactions with civilians might push them to treat people with the same observed behavior (e.g. an expired registration, shown on camera) the same way. However, we don't yet have any evidence on this.

Prosecutors also have a great deal of discretion about whether to pursue particular charges against a defendant. In addition to sentencing guidelines, which limit the range of penalties they can seek for a particular charge, restricting their ability to pursue particular charges in the first place could be helpful. Particularly for lower-level offenses like nonviolent misdemeanors, where there is lots of variation in whether prosecutors dismiss the charges or pursue a conviction (Agan et al., 2021), instituting clear office policies about how to handle such cases would likely reduce racial disparities. At the legislative level, decriminalizing particular offenses (such as minor drug possession) achieves this goal. Within prosecutors' offices, a policy that all prosecutors will decline to prosecute particular charges would reduce (or even eliminate) racial disparities in outcomes for those charges. Of course, such policies might have other effects (reducing deterrence and increasing the incidence of those offenses), so equity concerns should be weighed against the possibility of an increase in that (perhaps undesirable) behavior. Since decriminalization and decline-to-prosecute policies are increasingly popular in many US cities and counties, more research on these tradeoffs would be helpful.

3.5. Increase Oversight/Accountability

Limiting discretion will often require greater oversight and accountability, perhaps from outside the agency of interest. In the case of policing, civilian oversight boards could serve this role, though it is unclear how effective they are in practice. Ba (2020) shows that making it easier for civilians to file complaints about police misconduct has beneficial effects.

In general it seems likely that increasing the availability of data on police conduct and outcomes would help reduce racial disparities by making those disparities salient to the local community. Luh (2021) highlights that ensuring the accuracy of those data is also important. As discussed above, she found that when police were asked to record their best guess as to a civilian's race, they systematically misreported Hispanic drivers as white when a search did not turn up any contraband. This made the officers look less racially biased than they were. A policy change that required officers to ask drivers their race appears to have corrected this problem. In addition, officers that the new data revealed to be racially biased faced professional consequences: They were less likely to be promoted or receive raises. Thus, this simple change in how race data were collected and reported provided a meaningful incentive to officers to behave in a less-biased manner.

As discussed above, external pressure from the judiciary can also be important. Harvey and Mattia (2021) show that court litigation addressing discrimination in police employment appears to have reduced discriminatory behavior throughout the department, thus reducing racial disparities in crime victimization. Similarly, Rivera and Ba (2020) showed that court decisions that increased the likely consequences for police misconduct – decisions that were made salient by memos from union leadership – had big benefits in terms of reducing citizen complaints against police (implying less police misconduct) without increasing crime rates.

To the extent that racial bias by police results in lawsuits about police misconduct, changing who pays for legal settlements or requiring that individual officers carry misconduct insurance (similar to malpractice insurance for doctors) could align incentives to make sure that police unions, leadership, and officers change their behavior. Currently, these individuals and entities are typically protected from any financial consequences of such misconduct, which means they have no incentive to reduce racial bias (Schwartz, 2020).

4. DISCUSSION

At this point there is a great deal of evidence that racial bias is a problem in essentially all areas where human decision-making is at work; it is not surprising, then, that it is also a problem in the criminal justice system. As discussed above, there is evidence of racial bias at every stage of the criminal justice process, though there is variation in the presence, extent, and type of bias (animus versus statistical discrimination) in different contexts.

The primary research frontier at this point is not identifying the presence of racial bias, but figuring out how to reduce the bias that exists. That said, there is room for more work on what is driving biased behavior (animus, statistical discrimination or stereotypes), as this could help researchers and practitioners develop successful interventions.

There is some research on what works to reduce racial bias, and racial disparities more broadly, but the interventions that have been tested have mostly been unsuccessful. Many other interventions that are popular (implicit bias training, for instance) have yet to be rigorously evaluated. Experience in the criminal justice space and in other contexts shows us that many well-intentioned interventions will fail, and some will actively make the problem worse (see Doleac, 2021, for full discussion). It is crucial that practitioners and researchers work together to iterate upon new programs and policies until we find solutions that are effective and scalable.

NOTES

1. It's also possible that Black and white Americans are subject to different criminal justice policies because they live in different places. There is evidence that racial bias drives electoral preferences about the punitiveness of local criminal justice policies (Feigenberg and Miller, 2021b). In this case, Black and white residents of a particular place are not necessarily treated differently, but differences in policies across places contribute to racial disparities in outcomes at the national level. See Albright (2019) for evidence of this in the context of pretrial detention.
2. An exception is the rank-order test developed by Anwar and Fang (2006). This test considers whether the ranking of driver search rates (by race group) varies with officer race. If it does, this implies racial animus (versus statistical discrimination or no discrimination) on the part of officers.
3. This said, Feigenberg and Miller (2021a) suggest that at least in one context the average and marginal hit rates appear to be similar. More work on this, using changes in the number of people stopped to identify those at the margin, would be helpful.
4. Also see Arnold et al. (2020) for an extension of this method in the pretrial context.
5. But also see Park (2017a), which applies Anwar and Fang's (2006) rank-order test to judicial sentencing to determine whether racial animus is at work. Using data from Kansas, he cannot reject the null hypothesis of no racial animus in judicial decision-making.
6. The good news is that the use of risk scores also doesn't seem to increase racial disparities. Racial bias is 'baked in' to the data used by risk assessment algorithms – for instance, if Black men are arrested and convicted at higher rates than white men who committed the same offense, they will appear higher risk to the algorithm. Many worry that the resulting risk scores will thus necessarily push judges to treat Black defendants more harshly. But the appropriate counterfactual isn't someone's true risk level, it's the judge's perception of their risk. If judges themselves are using the same data, the risk score might not be worse than the judge's perception. And if the judge is biased in their interpretation of that data, then the risk score could be *less* biased than the judge. The policy-relevant question is whether the use of risk scores leads to larger or smaller racial disparities in outcomes in practice.

REFERENCES

Abrams, David S., Marianne Bertrand, and Sendhil Mullainathan. 2012. "Do Judges Vary in Their Treatment of Race?" *Journal of Legal Studies*, 41(2): 347–38.

Agan, Amanda Y., Jennifer L. Doleac, and Anna Harvey. 2021. "Misdemeanor Prosecution." NBER Working Paper No. 28600.

Agan, Amanda, and Sonja Starr. 2018. "Ban the Box, Criminal Records, and Racial Discrimination: A Field Experiment." *Quarterly Journal of Economics*, 133(1): 191–235.

Albright, Alex. 2019. *If You Give a Judge a Risk Score: Evidence from Kentucky Bail Decisions.* Working paper. https://thelittledataset.com/about_files/albright_judge_score.pdf.

Alesina, Alberto, and Eliana La Ferrara. 2014. "A Test of Racial Bias in Capital Sentencing." *American Economic Review*, 104(11): 3397–433.

Antonovics, Kate, and Brian G. Knight. 2009. "A New Look at Racial Profiling: Evidence from the Boston Police Department." *Review of Economics and Statistics*, 91(1): 163–77.

Anwar, Shamena, and H. Fang. 2006. "An Alternative Test of Racial Prejudice in Motor Vehicle Searches: Theory and Evidence." *American Economic Review*, 96: 127–51

Anwar, Shamena, Patrick Bayer, and Randi Hjalmarsson. 2012. "The Impact of Jury Race in Criminal Trials." *Quarterly Journal of Economics*, 127(2): 1017–55.

Arnold, David, Will Dobbie, and Crystal S. Yang. 2018. "Racial Bias in Bail Decisions." *Quarterly Journal of Economics*, 133(4): 1885–932.

Arnold, David, Will Dobbie, and Peter Hull. 2020. *Measuring Racial Discrimination in Bail Decisions. American Economic Review.* https://www.aeaweb.org/articles?id=10.1257/aer.20201653

Ba, Bocar A. 2020. *Going the Extra Mile: The Cost of Complaint Filing, Accountability, and Law Enforcement Outcomes in Chicago.* Working paper. https://www.dropbox.com/s/wpdyf463j5iyrpn/Ba%20%282020%29.pdf?dl=0

Ba, Bocar A, Dean Knox, Jonathan Mummolo, and Roman G. Rivera. 2021. "Diversity in Policing: The Role of Officer Race and Gender in Police-Civilian Interactions in Chicago." *Science*, 371(6530): 696–702.

Becker, Gary S. 1957. *The Economics of Discrimination*. Chicago: University of Chicago Press.

Bordalo, Pedro, Katherine Coffman, Nicola Gennaioli, and Andrei Shleifer. 2016. "Stereotypes." *Quarterly Journal of Economics*, 131(4): 1753–94.

Carson, E. Ann. 2020. "Prisoners in 2019." *Bureau of Justice Statistics, NCJ*, 255115. https://bjs.ojp.gov/content/pub/pdf/p19.pdf.

Canay, Ivan A., Magne Mogstad, and Jack Mountjoy. 2020. *On the Use of Outcome Tests for Detecting Bias in Decision Making.* Working paper.

Census, U.S. 2019. *Quick Facts: Black or African-American, alone*. Available at: https://www.census.gov/quickfacts/fact/table/US/PST045219

Chen, Daniel L., Tobias J. Moskowitz, and Kelly Shue. 2016. "Decision Making Under the Gambler's Fallacy: Evidence from Asylum Judges, Loan Officers, and Baseball Umpires." *Quarterly Journal of Economics*, 131(3): 1181–242.

Cohen, Alma, and Crystal S. Yang. 2019. "Judicial Politics and Sentencing Decisions." *American Economic Journal: Economic Policy*, 11(1): 160–91.

Depew, Briggs, Ozkan Eren, and Naci Mocan. 2017. "Judges, Juveniles, and In-Group Bias." *Journal of Law and Economics*, 60(2): 209–39.

Dobbie, Will, Jacob Goldin, and Crystal S. Yang. 2018. "The Effects of Pre-Trial Detention on Conviction, Future Crime, and Employment: Evidence from Randomly Assigned Judges." *American Economic Review*, 108(2): 201–40.

Doleac, Jennifer L. 2021. "A Review of Thomas Sowell's *Discrimination and Disparities*." *Journal of Economic Literature*, 59(2): 574–89.

Doleac, Jennifer, and Sarah Lageson. 2020. "The Problem with "Clean Slate" Policies: Could Broader Sealing of Criminal Records Hurt More People than It Helps?" *Niskanen Center.* https://www.niskanencenter.org/the-problem-with-clean-slate-policies-could-broader-sealing-of-criminal-records-hurt-more-people-than-it-helps/

Doleac, Jennifer L., and Benjamin Hansen. 2020. "The Unintended Consequences of "Ban the Box": Statistical Discrimination and Employment Outcomes When Criminal Histories Are Hidden." *Journal of Labor Economics*, 38(2): 321–74.

Eren, Ozean, and Naci Mocan. 2018. "Emotional Judges and Unlucky Juveniles." *American Economic Journal: Applied Economics*, 10(3): 171–205.

FBI Uniform Crime Reports. 2019. "Table 43: Arrests." Available at: https://ucr.fbi.gov/crime-in-the-u.s/2019/crime-in-the-u.s.-2019/topic-pages/tables/table-43

Feigenberg, Benjamin, and Conrad Miller. 2021a. "Would Eliminating Racial Disparities in Motor Vehicle Searches have Efficiency Costs?" *Quarterly Journal of Economics*, 137(1): 49–113.

Feigenberg, Benjamin, and Conrad Miller. 2021b. "Racial Divisions and Criminal Justice: Evidence from Southern State Courts." *American Economic Journal: Economic Policy*, 13(2): 207–40.

Gelbach, Jonah. 2021. *Testing Economic Models of Discrimination in Criminal Justice.* Working paper. https://papers.ssrn.com/sol3/papers.cfm?abstract_id=3784953.

Goncalves, Felipe, and Steven Mello. 2020. "A Few Bad Apples? Racial Bias in Policing." *American Economic Review*, 111(5): 1406–41.

Green, Tiffany L., and Nao Hagiwara. 2020. "The Problem with Implicit Bias Training." *Scientific American*. https://www.scientificamerican.com/article/the-problem-with-implicit-bias-training/

Grogger, Jeffrey, and Greg Ridgeway. 2006. "Testing for Racial Profiling in Traffic Stops from Behind a Veil of Darkness." *Journal of the American Statistical Association*, 101(475): 878–87.

Harvey, Anna, and Taylor Mattia. 2021. *Reducing Racial Disparities in Crime Victimization: Evidence from Employment Discrimination Litigation. Journal of Urban Economics*. https://doi.org/10.1016/j.jue.2022.103459

Heaton, Paul, Sandra Mayson, and Megan Stevenson. 2017. "The Downstream Criminal Justice Consequences of Pretrial Detention." *Stanford Law Review*, 69: 711–94.

Heyes, Anthony, and Soodeh Saberian. 2019. "Temperature and Decisions: Evidence from 207,000 Court Cases." *American Economic Journal: Applied Economics*, 11(2): 238–65.

Hoekstra, Mark, and CarlyWill Sloan. 2022. "Does Race Matter for Police Use of Force? Evidence from 911 Calls." *American Economic Review*, 112(3): 827–60.

Horrace, William C., and Shawn M. Rohlin. 2016. "How Dark is Dark? Bright Lights, Big City, Racial Profiling." *Review of Economics and Statistics*, 98(2): 226–32.

Hull, Peter. 2021. *What Marginal Outcome Tests Can Tell Us About Racially Biased Decision-Making*. Working Paper no 28503. https://www.nber.org/papers/w28503

Kleinberg, Jon, Himabindu Lakkaraju, Jure Leskovec, Jens Ludwig, and Sendhil Mullainathan. "Human Decisions and Machine Predictions." *Quarterly Journal of Economics*, 133(1): 237–93.

Knowles, John, Nicola Persico, and Petra Todd. 2001. "Racial Bias in Motor Vehicle Searches: Theory and Evidence." *Journal of Political Economy*, 109(1): 203–29.

Leasure, Peter, and Tara Martin. 2017. "Criminal Records and Housing: An Experimental Study." *Journal of Experimental Criminology*, 13(4): 527–35.

Leasure, Peter, and Tia Stevens Andersen. 2016. "The Effectiveness of Certificates of Relief as Collateral Consequence Relief Mechanisms: An Experimental Study." *Yale Law and Policy Review Inter Alia*, November 7.

Leslie, Emily and Nolan G. Pope. 2017. "The Unintended Impact of Pretrial Detention on Case Outcomes: Evidence from New York City Arraignments." *The Journal of Law and Economics*, 60 (3): 529–57.

Linos, Elizabeth. 2018. "More Than Public Service: A Field Experiment on Job Advertisements and Diversity in Police." *Journal of Public Administration Research and Theory*, 28(1): 67–85.

Luh, Elizabeth. 2021. *Not so Black and White: Uncovering Racial Bias from Systematically Misreported Trooper Reports*. Working paper. https://github.com/elizluh/papers/raw/master/notsoblackandwhite.pdf

McCrary, Justin. 2007. "The Effect of Court-Ordered Hiring Quotas on the Composition and Quality of Police." *American Economic Review*, 97(1): 318–53.

Miller, Amalia R., and Carmit Segal. 2019. "Do Female Officers Improve Law Enforcement Quality? Effects on Crime Reporting and Domestic Violence." *Review of Economic Studies*, 86(5): 2220–47.

Owens, Emily, David Weisburd, Karen L. Amendola, and Geoffrey P. Alpert. 2018. "Can You Build a Better Cop?" *Criminology & Public Policy*, 17(1): 41–87.

Pager, Devah. 2003. "The Mark of a Criminal Record." *American Journal of Sociology*, 108(5): 937–75.

Park, Kyung. 2017a. "Do Judges Have Tastes for Discrimination? Evidence from Criminal Courts." *Review of Economics and Statistics*, 99(5): 810–23.

Park, Kyung. 2017b. "The Impact of Judicial Elections in the Sentencing of Black Crime." *Journal of Human Resources*, 52: 998–1031.

Piehl, Anne Morrison. 2009. *Preparing Prisoners for Employment: The Power of Small Rewards*. Civic Report 57. New York: Center for Civic Innovation at the Manhattan Institute.

Pfaff, John. 2017. *Locked In: The True Causes of Mass Incarceration and How to Achieve Real Reform*. New York: Basic Books.

Philippe, Arnaud, and Aurelie Ouss. 2018. ""No Hatred or Malice, Fear or Affection": Media and Sentencing." *Journal of Political Economy*, 126(5): 2134–78.

Rehavi, M. Marit, and Sonja B. Starr. 2014. "Racial Disparity in Federal Criminal Sentences." *Journal of Political Economy*, 122(6): 1320–54.

Rivera, Roman G., and Bocar A. Ba. 2020. *The Effect of Police Oversight on Crime and Allegations of Misconduct: Evidence from Chicago*. Working paper. https://www.dropbox.com/s/ry9fgghwmv60for/Rivera%20and%20Ba%20%282020%29.pdf?dl=0.

Rose, Evan. 2021. "Who Gets a Second Chance? Effectiveness and Equity in Supervision of Criminal Offenders." *Quarterly Journal of Economics*, 136(2): 1199–253.

Roth, Jonathan, and Pedro H.C. Sant'Anna. 2022. *Efficient Estimation for Staggered Rollout Designs*. Working paper. https://arxiv.org/pdf/2102.01291.pdf

Schwartz, Joanna. 2020. "Allocating the Costs of Police Misconduct Litigation: Available Evidence and Research Agenda." *Arnold Ventures*. https://craftmediabucket.s3.amazonaws.com/uploads/Microsoft-Word-Allocating-the-Costs-of-Police-Misconduct-Litigation-12.8.20.docx.pdf

Sherrard, Ryan. 2021. *"Ban the Box" Policies and Criminal Recidivism*. Working paper. https://www.rsherrardecon.com/_files/ugd/72c9cf_6c0c69199bf34428be5d8e88891923ff.pdf

Sloan, CarlyWill. 2022. *Racial Bias by Prosecutors: Evidence from Random Assignment*. Working paper. https://github.com/carlywillsloan/Prosecutors/blob/master/sloan_pros.pdf

Stevenson, Megan. 2018. "Distortion of Justice: How the Inability to Pay Bail Affects Case Outcomes." *Journal of Law, Economics, and Organization*, 34(4): 511–42.

Stevenson, Megan. 2019. "Assessing Risk Assessment in Action." *Minnesota Law Review*, 103: 303–84.

Stevenson, Megan, and Jennifer L. Doleac. 2021. *Algorithmic Risk Assessment in the Hands of Humans*. Working paper. https://papers.ssrn.com/sol3/papers.cfm?abstract_id=3489440

Tuttle, Cody. 2021. *Racial Disparities in Federal Sentencing: Evidence from Drug Mandatory Minimums*. Working paper. https://codytuttle.github.io/tuttle_mandatory_minimums.pdf

Weisburst, Emily. 2017. Whose Help is on the Way? The Importance of Individual Police Officers in Law Enforcement Outcomes. *Journal of Human Resources*. https://drive.google.com/file/d/1yYwJ9Kl1eJHdAD8HH9HVB8QFTvkb1Sov/view

West, Jeremy. 2018. *Racial Bias in Police Investigations*. Working paper. https://people.ucsc.edu/~jwest1/articles/West_RacialBiasPolice.pdf

Wood, George, Tom R. Tyler, Andrew V. Papachristos, Jonathan Roth, and Pedro H.C. Sant'Anna. 2020. *Revised Findings for "Procedural Justice Training Reduces Police Use of Force and Complaints against Officers"*. Working paper. https://osf.io/preprints/socarxiv/xf32m/

Yang, Crystal S. 2015. "Free at Last? Judicial Discretion in Racial Disparities in Federal Sentencing." *Journal of Legal Studies*, 44(1): 75–111.

14. Gangs and organized crime

Ben Lessing and Maria Micaela Sviatschi

1. INTRODUCTION: THE PROBLEM(S) OF GANGS

Gangs, mafias, cartels and organized crime have persisted over many years in different countries. In many cases, individuals may turn to criminal organizations looking for protection and governance, but in some other cases, individuals may become prey of criminal organizations. Always of great interest to sociologists, the last 50 years have seen steadily increasing interest in gangs and other criminal organizations (COs) by economists for two related reasons: their involvement in an ever-expanding illicit drug trade and their concomitant growth and increasing use of violence. These trends are pronounced in the US and Latin America, particularly in El Salvador, Brazil, Mexico, Colombia and Venezuela, producing important streams of empirical research. Still, much remains unknown about their internal organization, their relationships with other COs, their connections to and strategies toward the state and consequently their economic impact on people's lives and social welfare in general. In this chapter, we summarize the work that has been done over the last few years and the significant advances in the economics literature.

2. THE INDUSTRIAL ORGANIZATION OF CRIME RECONSIDERED

Overall, research on the economics of crime tends to focus on individuals and individual crimes. In part, this reflects the fact that economics is deeply rooted in methodological individualism—'50 years after Becker' as the Introduction to this volume puts it—in part the fact that criminal justice systems, and hence a great deal of crime data, also operate on the basis of individual people and acts. Even when economists turn to gangs and organized crime—organizations and collections of individuals by definition—they are often drawn to individual-level questions and interventions, such as why youth join gangs, what types of programs can get them to leave gangs and whether gang membership predicts other individual-level outcomes like lifetime earnings or behavior while in prison.

However important such questions are, from a substantive point of view they pale in comparison to questions about the size and structure of and relationships among criminal organizations (COs)—what we will call the industrial organization (IO) of crime, for lack of a better term. We are hardly the first to urge such a perspective: Thomas Schelling literally inaugurated the economic study of organized crime by asking why 'the dominant approach to organized crime is through indictment and conviction, not through regulation, accommodation, or the restructuring of markets and business conditions' (Schelling 1967, p. 114). Adopting an IO perspective led to some seminal insights, including important arguments by both Schelling (1967, 1971) and Buchanan (1973) about the potential, counterintuitive benefits of criminal monopolies. Yet these authors wrote in times and contexts in which COs exercised governance, at best, over a shady and disperse criminal underworld, operating in markets of middling size and profitability like prostitution, gambling and contraceptives (really!). The interceding decades brought a war on drugs that vastly expanded potential criminal profits (Miron 2003), urban blight and increasingly violent policing, and an unprecedented turn toward mass incarceration (Raphael and Stoll 2013). These changes occurred not only in the US but throughout much of the Western Hemisphere, contributing to a profusion of COs of all shapes and sizes, many with sizeable military arsenals, and all too often wielding governing authority over civilian populations.

Today, for any given setting, be it a slum neighborhood, a whole city, an illicit market, even an international production and transshipment supply chain, the IO of crime has an overwhelming impact on the outcomes we care most about. When prison gangs or drug cartels or mafia families go to war—most often with one another but occasionally with the state itself—violence can reach levels only otherwise seen in civil or international war. Conversely, when COs reach truces, or one of them achieves an effective monopoly, homicides rates can fall dramatically, far beyond the wildest hopes of any public policy innovator (Cruz and Durán-Martínez 2016; Lessing and Denyer Willis 2019).

The foregoing claims should not be controversial among economists—after all, knowing whether markets are competitive, oligopolistic or monopolistic is basically a pre-requisite for meaningful economic analysis. If we are interested in industrial output, say, the first questions we need to ask are 'How many manufacturers are there?' 'Are they competing or colluding?' and 'What if anything is the state is doing about it?' Studying the effects of wage increases or cognitive-behavior-therapy interventions on workers' productivity or labor participation is interesting, but probably second-order.

We make the same claim with respect to crime: if what we are most interested in is the total amount of crime and violence in a given setting, then the most important questions to ask are how many COs are operating, whether they are competing or colluding (or a bit of both) and what the state is doing about it. The exception that proves this rule—settings where only the smallest, localized COs exist and hence approximate individual actors—can itself be characterized as the competitive end of the IO-of-Crime spectrum. Moreover, and critically, if research on developed-country organized crime suggests its overall negative impact on society to be minimal (Reuter and Tonry 2020), it is precisely because the IO of crime in those places, for reasons we have not yet fully understood, tends toward peaceful collusion.

This points to perhaps *the* central challenge for studying the IO of crime: organized crime tends to be oligopolistic. A handful of drug cartels dominate the cocaine trade; pulverized local street gangs band together into city- and state-wide gang confederations; a few mafia families control a city. This is a problem because oligopolies are fundamentally multiple-equilibrium phenomena: collusion is Pareto-superior, but there are incentives to cheat, free-ride and so on. In terms of modeling and predicting when COs will collude or compete, the fact that they are illegal may be of only minor importance, since licit firms are usually legally prohibited from colluding as well. (And in all cases, it is easy to write down models that produce competition or collusion in equilibrium and quite hard to know which is capturing the relevant factors.)

Where the illegality of COs does make a critical difference is that competition' among them often takes the form of armed violence—gang war. This raises additional problems for economic analysis: the externalities from violent competition are great enough to challenge the standard finding that collusion produces an overall deadweight loss for society. Such benefits to criminal monopoly go in the same direction as, but likely far outweigh, those famously identified by Buchanan: that monopolies restrict output, so encouraging monopolies in social 'bads' like drugs or human trafficking might actually reduce their incidence.

Another critical difference is the role of the state and in particular how COs and hence the IO of crime respond to state policy. States have different policy levers for intervening in licit markets versus IO of crime, though both domains can be subject to corruption and capture. On the whole, states have more coercive leverage over licit firms (which naturally want to avoid running afoul of the law) but are at liberty to use greater brute force against COs (such as incarcerating their members). Conversely, COs may have considerably less compunction about using violence against the state in response. Though far more rare than inter-gang violence, anti-state violence by COs can have deeply destabilizing effects.

In sum, the proliferation of gangs, their agglutination into larger criminal networks of different sorts, with access to lucrative illicit markets and (hence) the means and motives to acquire significant arsenals and armies of foot soldiers, makes the economic study of COs, and hence of crime in general, both more important and more difficult.

Key advances have been made, particularly in the study of drug cartels. Perhaps most importantly, a number of studies have shed light on the causes (rather than consequences) of large-scale criminal violence. Dell (2015) showed that increased state repression of drug cartels in a given municipality leads to an increase in cartel-related violence there. Critically (from our IO-inflected perspective), her proposed mechanism is that state repression weakens the incumbent cartel, lowering other cartels' barriers to (violent) market entry. Calderón et al. (2015) find that 'beheadings' (i.e. arrests or killing of cartel leaders) cause increases in both cartel-related and general homicides in Mexican municipalities. Castillo et al. (2020) find that scarcity of drug supply in Mexican municipalities (caused by upstream drug seizures in Colombia) causes increases in violence, especially along trafficking routes and near the US border; critically, though, this effect only occurs after President Felipe Calderón launched a major crackdown on cartels in 2006. Along these lines, Castillo and Kronick (2020) provide a theoretical model of cartel collusion vs. competition under state repression, finding that if seizures lead to increased profitability (due to inelastic demand), cartels may no longer be able to sustain peaceful collusion.

More qualitative accounts of Mexico's drug war point to the critical role of institutionalized corruption, or what Snyder and Durán Martínez (2009) call 'state-sponsored protection', under the Partido Revolucionário Institucional (PRI) and its breakdown in the 2000s in triggering inter-cartel war. Trejo and Ley (2018) use a mixed-methods approach to argue that opposition gubernatorial victories in Mexican states left cartels without state protection, leading them to acquire private militias, which they in turn used to conquer territory from their rivals. Future economics research on the IO of crime, both theoretical and empirical, could fruitfully seek to incorporate these and other political variables.

3. GANG ORIGINS AND TRAJECTORIES

In the English-speaking world, gangs date back at least to the seventeenth century in the United Kingdom. The Mims, Hectors, Dead Boys and some others terrorized the streets of London while wearing colored ribbons to distinguish themselves from the different factions (Pearson 1983, Berry 2008). Poor economic conditions in the Victorian Era exasperated crime. The Peaky Blinders of Birmingham became the most iconic nineteenth-century gang whose estimated membership was 50 000 approximately. Around the same time, the East Coast in the US saw the emergence of organized crime in big urban areas such as New York and Washington DC. This was mainly fueled by poverty and the struggles that immigrants had to face when arriving in the cities (Howell and Moore 2010).

Prisons have also proven to be fertile ground for the formation of gangs and eventually, with the advent of mass incarceration policies, new forms of prison-based criminal governance. Most notoriously, Hispanic inmates in California prisons, banding together to protect themselves from other predatory inmates during the 1950s and 1960s, formed the Mexican Mafia, which grew into the most powerful gang within the California prison system. According to Skarbeck (2011), the Mexican Mafia used its control over prison life to impose governance institutions on street gangs. These facilitate illicit market exchange by protecting property, enforcing agreements and adjudicating disputes. The Mexican Mafia taxes the resulting surplus, threatening those who do not pay with violence within prison.

The Mexican Mafia and other gangs cycled in and out from prison and helped in the formation of other streets gangs, including those who emerged in Los Angeles and whose origins came from the neighborhood conditions. During the 1980s, the increased demand for narcotics sparked Hispanic street gangs who found drug-trafficking their main source of income. However, one gang whose presence is still noticeable today emerged during those years: the *Mara Salvatrucha*. The origin of this gang goes back to hundreds of Salvadoran immigrants who arrived in Los Angeles, running away from a civil war and violence. As recent migrants, they were living in poor and overcrowded *barrios* in the city and often facing discrimination from natives and other migrants as well. To protect themselves from these harsh living conditions, a group of Salvadoran youth came together in what would later be called MS-13 or Mara Salvatrucha (Hayden 2005), partly as a self-defense group in response to discrimination and threats from powerful Mexican gangs (Johnson 1989). At the same time, others joined the 18th Street Gang, a gang formed mainly by Mexican youth that became one of the biggest gangs in Los Angeles (DeCesare 1998; Dunn 2007; Lopez and Connell 1996). By 1985, MS-13 had evolved; it started taking up small-scale drug trafficking and extorting money from corner drug dealers (Ramsey 2012), and they also developed a fierce rivalry with the 18th Street Gang that has persisted to this day. Whenever their members were arrested and sent to prison, they acquired criminal capital: MS-13 members learned illegal practices, gained social connections and planned future criminal activities at a more sophisticated level.

Los Angeles' gangs not only grew, but amazingly expanded beyond the US. Sviatschi (2022) documents how the US Illegal Immigration Responsibility Act in 1996 increased the number of criminal deportations, leading to these gang members' expulsion to Central America. Consequently, El Salvador experienced a large increase in homicide rates, extortion and drug-related crimes in municipalities where US gang deportees were born. What is more, children who were exposed to the arrival of gangs had higher chances of being involved in gang-related crimes in the future. The intense violence that these gangs generated also forced thousands of Salvadoreans to run away from their country and return to the US. The criminal capital of gangs does not only affect the place where they started, but it can also spread to other countries and can be sparked by immigration policies.

In Chicago, Brunh (2021) finds that gangs cause increases in violence in highly localized areas as the result of conflict over illegal markets. The arrival of gangs in city blocks increases reported batteries (6 percent), narcotics violations (18.5 percent), incidents of prostitution (51.9 percent), weapons violations (9.8 percent) and criminal trespassing (19.6 percent).

In general, there is a consensus that gangs' arrival in neighborhoods correlates with negative local outcomes for residents, but there is little evidence on the causal effect of gangs because their emergence is highly endogenous. Moreover, as we noted above, gangs do not always go to war with one another, and sometimes the rise of larger, often prison-based gang structures can have a pacifying effect. This is a critical avenue for further research. A key challenge is developing empirical measures of gang presence independent of gang violence. Too often, our measures of gang presence rely on media or police reports of gang-related violence; such data cannot tell us anything about why or when gangs peacefully coexist.

4. SOURCES OF RENTS: THE MARKET AND ORGANIZATIONAL STRUCTURE OF GANGS

While many gangs begin more as identity-based social groupings than illicit firms per se, most gangs of interest to economists are engaged in some form of rent-producing criminal activity. We can roughly but usefully divide such activities into three broad classes, based on their degree of coercion: pure property crime (such as robbery, burglary, auto theft etc), racketeering and extortion, and black markets or illicit economic exchange (drugs, prostitution, etc.). Many COs engage in more than one type of activity, to be sure. Nonetheless, identifying a CO's main source of rents is likely to illuminate aspects of its structure and behavior. Gangs dedicated to property crime, for example, are either likely to be very loosely affiliated semi-autonomous actors (because each can only rob) or a more specialized criminal outfit focusing on a niche like banks or art. Either way, this source of rents puts limits on size and provides little or no incentive for interaction with the community.

Racketeering and extortion, on the other hand, naturally put COs into ongoing relationships with those they extract from, at the same time that they incentivize gangs to develop internal structures and division of labor. For example, among Salvadorean gangs, extortion represents the largest share of gang income, and it is often described as the *economic engine* behind the gangs and violence (ICG 2017). These gangs extort about 70 percent of all the businesses in the territories where they are present, with distribution and transport being the most affected sectors (Martínez 2016). Although there is little information on gang earnings, some wiretapped conversations revealed that MS-13 earned about $600 000 in a single week of 2016 (Martínez 2016). The Salvadoran Central Bank counts the direct cost of extortion to businesses at over $700 million a year, which is equivalent to 3 percent of GDP, and the indirect costs of criminality at upwards of $4 billion a year, which corresponds to 16 percent of GDP (Peñate Guerra et al. 2016).

In Latin America, one key component of gangs' extortion success comes from their decentralized organizational structure. For example, both MS-13 and 18th Street have national leaders (*ranfleros*) who often dictate and negotiate high-level gang policies, while operations on the ground are organized by neighborhood-level cliques (*clicas*) with ties to the area. Another key component is how the business of extortion works for these gangs. In the case of El Salvador, Brown et al. (2021) used data from a major wholesale distributor and had conversations with the firm's security team, who detailed how extortion payments work during the delivery of products. Before entering a gang-controlled territory, a driver will stop and meet with a gang representative who collects extortion. The extortion payments generally give the distributor rights to deliver to retailers rather than rights to pass through a territory. Trucks are often stopped on side streets prior to a delivery rather than on a main road, implying that the distributor does not have to pay extortion if they choose not to deliver to an area. This can be contrasted with government bribes at police checkpoints which allow firms the right to pass through an area (e.g. Olken and Barron 2009).

In a more extreme case, Brown et al. (2021) shows how a controversial truce (the second one implemented in EL Salvador) between the two main gangs led to a large reduction in violence, but it increased extortion by 15 percent to 20 percent. The first truce was implemented in March 2012 but it was officially called off in June 2013, when the government intervened in response to growing opposition from civil society and the government itself. Years later, in March 2016, leaders of the main gangs unexpectedly announced the 2016 non-aggression pact. Unlike the 2012 truce, this pact was negotiated directly between gang representatives without any government intermediaries, and it was not supported by the government. For instance, the gangs set up a 12-member 'coordinating committee' that would continue to meet to coordinate action and maintain exclusive territories (Martínez 2016). After the announcement of the non-aggression pact, homicides immediately fell by almost half in the following three months due to less violence between gangs.

While extortion is particularly important for Central American gangs, drug trafficking often presents a far larger source of income for gangs and COs. This is particularly true for neighborhood-level street gangs, who often control points of sale, and for prison gangs able to govern (Skarbeck 2011) or subsume them into larger prison-based structures (Lessing 2017). During the 1980s, the Mexican Mafia in California devoted itself to fulfilling the demand for drugs in prison due to the increasing number of inmates incarcerated for drug-related crimes (Skarbeck 2011). Outside prison, this was also extended to street gangs that saw in narcotics trafficking, a lucrative business given the increasing demand from the public. Multiple Hispanic street gangs in California jumped into this business in alliance with other COs. For example, the *Sureños* aligned with Mexican drug trafficking organizations to bolster their market. In this sense, competition for control of narcotics markets has become another root cause of increased violence among these groups (Harris 2010).

In Medellín, Colombia's second biggest city, most low- and middle-income neighborhoods are occupied by one of approximately 400 criminal gangs called '*combos*'. *Combos* do not just sell drugs and collect extortion from local businesses, they even guard some commercial streets and settle disputes between neighbors. They are highly involved with everyday life: they attend calls from residents to handle noise complaints or domestic abuse. They regulate markets, including microfinance and cooking gas distribution. These Medellin gangs are usually under the patronage of one of a handful of bigger organizations similar to mafias (*razónes*). Blattman et al. (2022) detail how over the past four decades, the gangs in Medellín evolved into a hierarchical system where nearly all *combos* are allied withone or another razón in semi-permanent relational contracts. The structure of this organization goes as follows: the *razón* provides the supply of drugs, protection and investment capital, and in return, the *combos* offer a retail distribution network and an army when there is conflict among different *razones*. Besides this, most *combos* are autonomous from the *razón*, and they operate on their own terms, following a decentralized system similar to the ones in El Salvador.

The economics behind the Medellín and El Salvador criminal organizations rely on an institutional structure. *Combos* and their respective *razón* work together to increase criminal efficiency—maximizing profit—and to minimize conflict, like the truces between major gangs. As Blattman et al. (2022) document, since the state cannot enforce criminal contracts and keep peace between gangs, *razones* play this peacemaker role, in addition to supplying wholesale drugs to *combos*: they enforce contracts and regulate illegal markets. What is more, the *razones* have formed a cartel-like governing board following a common pattern similar to ones found in other criminal organizations such as the Sicilian mafia, and US street gangs and prison gangs in California and

Brazil (Dixit 2003; Gambetta 1993, Skarbek 2011, Lessing and Willis 2019). In sum, these gangs tend to be highly vertically integrated and they have a very clear organizational hierarchy with agents who assume state-like functions (Blattman et al., 2021, 2022). In El Salvador, gangs dominate territory using violence but at the same time provide protection from the possible threat from other gangs: their rents are based on the market that they create for themselves and the conflict with any other competitor that seeks profits in this market.

5. LABOR MARKET OUTCOMES: WAGES AND CAREER STRUCTURES

5.1. Choosing the Gang Life

Most of the literature has pointed out that poverty and lack of job opportunities made gangs emerge, but this is not necessarily the case in some contexts. The early work in economics from Levitt and Venkatesh (2000, 2001) provides a descriptive work that investigates the finances of a drug-selling gang in Chicago, and it also highlights the long-term effects for those who were involved in gang activity. One important aspect of this work is the lack of economic rationality of the gang member: the wage premium does not compensate for the high risk of this activity; it is driven by the high expectations of a richer future.

In this sense, the utility gained from joining a gang might not only come from future expectations but also from a high need of belonging to a group. Sviatschi (2022) documents how the US gangs that arrived in El Salvador brought not only the extortion and drug dealing business but also a sense of social identity for Salvadoran children, and this identity formation facilitated the recruitment of new members and their expansion. These criminal deportees reproduced the structures and behaviors that gave them the same support that they had when growing up in Los Angeles where status, respect and a sense of collective identity were key elements. A recent survey shows that most children join gangs out of a desire for respect and friendship and that more than 60 percent of gang members join before the age of 15 (Cruz et al. 2017; Savenije 2009; Santacruz-Giralt and Concha-Eastman 2001; Cruz and Peña 1998). This is similar in the case of Chicago, where Bruhn (2021) describes that some areas in Chicago that are controlled by gangs who are identified as Black have a majority Black population and this is similar with gangs who identify themselves as Latinos. This suggests that gangs may find it more difficult to occupy neighborhoods with different demographics but also how identity plays a role in the formation of gangs.

Another key point that the evidence suggests is that becoming a gang member can be a lifetime commitment, even though joining involves several steps and a certain amount of time. In Salvadoran gangs, it is almost impossible to leave once inside. In most cases, if MS-13 sees an attempt to leave as a form of betrayal, it is punishable by death (Insight Crime and CLALS 2018). The ritual of becoming a gang member was brought by the criminal deportees to El Salvador who spread US-style gang culture within the country. Not only did they use the same names as the original gang organizations but they also implemented the common use of tattoos, the use of hand signs to identify gang members, clothing and overall lifestyle. New members often tattoo the names of their gangs on visible parts of their bodies, including faces, as a sign of commitment. In Medellín, *combos* are known for their late-night dance parties in the street as well as daytime cookouts and festivals, which also bring a sense of community to gang members. What is more, they also hang out in private events which, according to Blattman et al. (2022), usually involve drug consumption, sex and dancing. This supports the idea that gangs not only provide monetary rewards to their members but also non-monetary ones, as the *combo* uses parties not just for fun, but to develop new members, popular support and status. However, unlike El Salvador, there is flexibility in retiring. When a *combo* member does not have valuable information for their operations, they can quit and look for another life path. If they leave the gang life, they can either move to legal businesses or start an independent criminal career.

Finally, less is known about female participation in gangs, and further research deserves to be carried out. In California, government documentation from the Department of Justice in 2010 (Harris 2010) reported an increase of women's participation in street gangs. Among Hispanic, White and Asian gangs, women were now taking a more active role than in the past. Among Hispanic gangs, even when they are not actual members, they can be associates who provide support to male members. When it comes to the tasks they perform, they usually are involved in posting graffiti, passing information, providing housing, and transporting narcotics and weapons.

5.2. Career Path and Structures

In terms of career development, when recruited as children, gang members already perform several important tasks. In California, Afro-American street gangs like the North Side Oakland street gang have, since 2007, been reported to recruit children for tasks that include shootings, murders and gun possession (Harris 2010). In El Salvador, children gang members are employed as messengers or *antennas* in their communities, and their main function is to control residents' movements, but as they gain experience and acknowledgment, they turn to collecting rents from extortion and drug dealing. As they progress in their actions, gang leaders reward them with cellphones to inform them when either the police or non-residents enter the dominated neighborhood.

One of the main reasons why children and women are recruited into the gang business is because they are presumed to be innocent and often overlooked by police. But there is also a premium for being a child gang member: according to the law, children are not subject to criminal charges and because of this, children mainly perform tasks such as transporting weapons or drug packages. For street gangs, children are considered valuable assets since they are not likely to be prosecuted in adult courts and thus return to the streets in a short time (Cox et al. 2017), and they make a good effort in recruiting them. Due to its strong reputation and young people's perception of the gang's lifestyle, the MS-13 stands out for its capacity to attract and recruit new young members (Portillo 2003). However, gang recuritment appears to be selective: children from hostile families are the most vulnerable to being targeted by recruiters (Savenije 2009; Smutt and Miranda 1998). Most children are not only looking for a source of income, but for the recognition, support and safety that they do not find at home (Cruz et al. 2017; Klahr 2006).

In Medellín, careers are typically made within a *combo* or *razón*, and not across them, as Blattman et al. (2022) highlights, since it is unusual for combo members to be promoted into the *razón*, and such promotion has declined over time. The authors argue that one reason for this decline is that, compared to the 1990s and 2000s, fewer *razón* members have been killed and, once arrested, the arrestee almost never loses his position in the *razón* and continues to play some role in prison.

6. RELATION TO STATE: NOT ONLY FILLING IN STATE VACUUM

In developed societies, criminal organizations like gangs probably have a negative effect on economic growth, as they might impede the government from providing public goods, enforcing property rights and contracts and preventing violence. But this is not always the case; when the government is weak and not able to control parts of its territory, gangs might be able to take the role of the government and fulfill essential institutional functions, potentially enabling economic growth (Arjona et al., 2019; Bates, Greif, and Singh 2002; De la Sierra 2020; Olson 1993; Tilly 1985). Some recent work finds different results. Blattman et al. (2021) shows that protection is a good that gangs provide and charge for in competition with the state and that residents view gang and state services as substitutes.

In the case of El Salvador, where two of the world's largest gangs—MS-13 and 18th Street—spread all over the country, the effects on the economic development of this country were negative. Melnikov et al. (2020) show that individuals living under gang control have significantly less education, material well being and income than individuals even when living only 50 meters away but outside of gang territory. However, gangs coexist with the state. The mechanism behind these results is that gangs restrict individuals' freedom of movement, affecting their labor market options. In particular, those who live in gang-dominated neighborhoods often cannot work outside of gang territory, and they are forced to take low-paying jobs in small firms because of their inability to work in other parts of the city, where the largest firms are located. Note that the government did not stop providing public goods in gang areas, for two important reasons. First, the government had the incentives to do so because its legitimacy in the eyes of the local population would likely be undermined, increasing support for the gangs (Zoethout 2015). Second, it could also be very costly for incumbent politicians as they might not have incentives to defund social programs in gang areas since it could significantly reduce their reelection prospects.

REFERENCES

Arjona, Ana, Julian Arteaga, Camilo Cardenas, Ana Maria Ibanez, and Patricia Justino, (2019). *The Effects of Wartime Institutions on Households' Ability to Cope with Shocks: Evidence for Colombia*, WIDER Working Paper 2019/84.

Bates, Robert, Avner Greif, and Smita Singh, (2002). "Organizing Violence," *Journal of Conflict Resolution*, 46, 599–628.

Berry, Lynne, (2008). "Hooligan: A History of Respectable Fears, Geoffrey Pearson, Basingstoke, MacMillan, 1983," *The British Journal of Social Work*, 38(4), 830–32.

Blattman, Christopher, Gustavo Duncan, Benjamin Lessing, and Santiago Tobón, (2021). *Gang Rule: Understanding and Countering Criminal Governance*, Working Paper.

Blattman, Christopher, Gustavo Duncan, Benjamin Lessing, and Santiago Tobon, (2022). State-building on the Margin: An Urban Experiment in Medellín. https://doi.org/10.31235/osf.io/3bncz

Brown, Zach Y., Eduardo Montero, Carlos Schmidt-Padilla, and María Micaela Sviatschi, (2021). *Market Structure and Extortion: Evidence from 50,000 Extortion Payments*, National Bureau of Economic Research Working Paper Series 28299.

Bruhn, Jesse, (2021). Competition in the Black Market: Estimating the Causal Effect of Gangs in Chicago. Bravo Working Paper 2021-004.

Buchanan, James M., (1973). "A Defense of Organized Crime?" In *The Economics of Crime and Punishment*, ed. Simon Rottenberg. American Enterprise Institute for Public Policy Research, 119–32.

Calderón, Gabriela, Gustavo Robles, Alberto Díaz-Cayeros, and Beatriz Magaloni, (2015). "The Beheading of Criminal Organizations and the Dynamics of Violence in Mexico," *Journal of Conflict Resolution*, 59(8), 1455–85.

Castillo, Juan Camilo, Daniel Mejía, and Pascual Restrepo, (2020). Scarcity without Leviathan: The Violent Effects of Cocaine Supply Shortages in the Mexican Drugwar. *Review of Economics and Statistics*, 102(2), 269–86. https://doi.org/10.1162/rest_a_00801

Cox, S. et al., (2017). *Juvenile Justice: A Guide to Theory, Policy and Practice*. SAGE Publications Inc., 9th edition.

Cruz, J. M. and N. P. Pena, (1998). *Solidaridad y violencia en las pandillas del gran San Salvador: mas alla de la vida loca*, Volume 9. Uca Editores.

Cruz, José Miguel, and Angélica Durán-Martínez, (2016). "Hiding Violence to Deal with the State: Criminal Pacts in El Salvador and Medellin," *Journal of Peace Research*, 53(2), 197–210.

Cruz, Jose Miguel, Jonathan D. Rosen, Luis Enrique Amaya, and Yulia Vorobyeva, (2017). "La nueva cara de las pandillas callejeras: El fenómeno de las pandillas en El Salvador." Oficina de Asuntos Internacionales de Narcóticos y Aplicación de la Ley (INL), Departamento de Estado de los Estados Unidos.

De la Sierra, Raúl, (2020). "On the Origins of the State: Stationary Bandits and Taxation in Eastern Congo," *Journal of Political Economy*, 128.

DeCesare, Donna, (1998). "The Children of War Street Gangs in El Salvador," *NACLA Report on the Americas*, 32(1), 21–29.

Dell, Melissa, (2015). "Trafficking Networks and the Mexican Drug War," *American Economic Review*, 105(6), 1738–79.

Dixit, Avinash, (2003). "On Modes of Economic Governance," *Econometrica*, 71, 449–81.

Dunn, W., (2007). *The Gangs of Los Angeles*. Iuniverse.

Gambetta, Diego, (1993). *The Sicilian Mafia: The Business of Private Protection*. Harvard University Press.

Guerra, Peñate, Margarita Isabel, Kenny Mendoza de Escobar, José Arnulfo Quintanilla Deras, and César Antonio Alvarado Zepeda, (2016). *Estimación del Costo Económico de la Violencia en El Salvador 2014*, Departamento de Investigación Económica y Financiera, Banco Central de Reserva de El Salvador.

Harris, Kamala, (2010). Organized Crime in California. California Department of Justice, Division of Law Enforcement, Bureau of Investigation and Intelligence. https://oag.ca.gov/sites/all/files/agweb/pdfs/publications/org_crime2010.pdf

Hayden, Tom, (2005). *Street Wars: Gangs and the Future of Violence*. New Press.

Howell, James and John P. Moore, (2010). *History of Street Gangs in the United States*. National Gang Center Bulletin No. 4.

Insight Crime and CLALS, (2018). MS13 in the Americas. How the World's Most Notorious GangDefies Logic, Resists Destruction. Center for Latin America and Latino Studies, American University, Washington, DC.

International Crisis Group (2017). *Mafia of the Poor: Gang Violence and Extortion in Central America*, Latin America Report No 6. International Crisis Group.

Johnson, J., (1989). "War Refugees form Deadly Los Angeles Gangs Crime: Central American Refugees Immune to Violence Are a Growing Part of L.A. Gang Culture. Retrieved from https://www.latimes.com/archives/ la-xpm-1989-12-17-me-1499-story.html

Klahr, Marco, (2006). *Hoy te toca la muerte: El imperio de las maras visto desde dentro*. Mexico City: Editorial Planeta.

Lessing, Benjamin, (2017). "Counterproductive Punishment: How Prison Gangs Undermine State Authority," *Rationality and Society*, 29(3), 257–97. https://doi.org/10.1177/104346311770113.

Lessing, Benjamin, and Graham Denyer Willis, (2019). "Legitimacy in Criminal Governance: Managing a Drug Empire from Behind Bars," *American Political Science Review*, 113(2), 584–606. https://doi.org/10.1017/S0003055418000928

Levitt, Steven, and Sudhir Venkatesh, (2000). "An Economic Analysis of a Drug-Selling Gang's Finances," *Quarterly Journal of Economics*, 115(3), 755–89.

Levitt, Steven, and Sudhir Venkatesh, (2001). "Growing Up in the Projects: The Economic Lives of a Cohort of Men Who Came of Age in Chicago Public Housing," *American Economic Review*, 91(2), 79–84.

Lopez, Robert J., and Rich Connell, (1996). *Gang Turns Hope to Fear, Lives to Ashes; Crime: The Victims of 18th Street's Violence Are not Always Rivals, but Children, Families and Workers*.

Martínez, Carlos, (2016). "Gangs Find Common Ground in El Salvador Crackdown," in *Sight Crime Analysis*.

Melnikov, Nikita, Carlos Schmidt-Padilla, and Maria Micaela Sviatschi, (2020). *Gangs, Labor Mobility, and Development*. NBER Working Paper #27832.

Miron, Jeffrey A., (2003). "The Effect Of Drug Prohibition On Drug Prices: Evidence From The Markets For Cocaine And Heroin," *Review of Economics and Statistics*, 85(3), 522–30.

Olken, Benjamin and Patrick Barron, (2009). "The Simple Economics of Extortion: Evidence from Trucking in Aceh," *Journal of Political Economy*, 117(3), 417–52.

Olson, Mancur, (1993). "Dictatorship, Democracy, and Development," *American Political Science Review*, 87, 567–76.

Pearson, G. (1983). Hooligan: A history of respectable fears. Macmillan International Higher Education.

Portillo, Nelson, (2003). "Estudios sobre pandillas juveniles en el El Salvador y Centroamerica: una revision de su dimension participativa," *Apuntes de Psicologia*, 21(3), 475–93.

Ramsey, Geoffrey, (2012). *Tracing the roots of El Salvador's mara salvatrucha*.

Raphael, Steven, and Michael A. Stoll, (2013). *Why Are So Many Americans in Prison?* Russell Sage Foundation.

Reuter, Peter, and Tonry, Michael. (2020). Organized crime: Less than meets the eye. *Crime and Justice*, 49(1), 1–16. https://doi.org/10.1086/709447

Santacruz-Giralt, Maria L., and Alberto Concha-Eastman, (2001). *Barrio adentro. La solidaridad violenta de las pandillas*, Instituto Universitario de Opinion Publica, IUOP, 1st edition.

Savenije, W., (2009). *Maras y barras: pandillas y violencia juvenil en los barrios marginales de Centroamérica*. San Salvador: FLACSO El Salvador.

Schelling, Thomas C., (1967). "Economics and the Criminal Enterprise," *Public Interest*, 7, 61–78.

Schelling, Thomas C., (1971). "What is the Business of Organized Crime?" *Journal of Public Law*, 20, 71–84.

Skarbeck, David, (2011). "Governance and Prison Gangs," *American Political Science Review*, 105(4), 702–16.

Smutt, Marcela, and Lissette Miranda, (1998). *El Fenomeno de las Pandillas en El Salvador*. San Salvador: FLACSO and UNICEF.

Snyder, Richard, and Angelica Duran-Martinez, (2009). "Does Illegality Breed Violence? Drug Trafficking and State-sponsored Protection Rackets," *Crime, Law and Social Change*, 52(3), 253–73.

Sviatschi, María Micaela, (2022). "Spreading Gangs: Exporting US Criminal Capital to El Salvador." *American Economic Review*, 112(6), 1985–2024.

Tilly, Charles, (1985). "War Making and State Making as Organized Crime." In Peter Evans, Dietrich Rueschemeyer, and Theda Skocpol (eds.), *Bringing the State Back*, 169–91, Cambridge: Cambridge University Press.

Trejo, Guillermo, and Sandra Ley, (2018). "Why Did Drug Cartels Go to War in Mexico? Subnational Party Alternation, the Breakdown of Criminal Protection, and the Onset of Large-Scale Violence," *Comparative Political Studies*, 51(7), 900–37.

Venkatesh, Sudhir Alladi, and Steven D. Levitt, (2000). "'Are we a family or a business?' History and disjuncture in the urban American street gang," *Theory and Society*, 29, 427–62.

Zoethout, Margriet Antoinette, (2015). "Recovering Government Control over Mara Salvatrucha territory: Analysis based on the 'Santa Tecla, a Municipality Free of Violence' Agreement," *Police and Public Security Journal*, 5, 179–246.

15. Organised crime, elections and public policies

Pasquale Accardo,[1] Giuseppe De Feo[2] and Giacomo De Luca[3]

1. INTRODUCTION

Organised crime produces harmful effects on various aspects of social and economic welfare (Daniele and Marani, 2011; Pinotti, 2015a, b; Acemoglu et al., 2020). And yet, when criminal organisations succeed in establishing their control over specific areas, they become extremely difficult to eradicate. A key determinant of their resilience derives from their ability to build symbiotic relationships with legal institutions. Their infiltration into public institutions (and the private sector) is an essential part of their strategies to gain control over a territory. Criminal organisations have learned how to adapt to social, economic and political transformations while, at the same time, dissimulating their criminal nature. As highlighted by the 2019 report of the Italian Antimafia Investigation Department (*DIA*), along with illicit activities (such as extortion, usury, kidnapping, drug trafficking and prostitution), organised crime undertakes other seemingly legal

> activities [which] represent the evolution of mafia's strategies and are characterised by more sophisticated and discreet methods . . . They offer the advantage to rouse lower social alarm, involving entrepreneurs, professionals and public officials. At the same time they allow criminal organisations to contaminate the legal economy and to expand outside their regions [of origin] and abroad, thus giving them the features of a real enterprise. These are complex activities, often related to money-laundering and the reinvestment of illicit funds, fed by the infiltration into public administration and the management of public contracts, of the large-scale distribution, the waste cycle and gambling.
>
> (Direzione Investigativa Antimafia, 2019)

By being part of a wide network of collusive and corruptive relationships, criminal organisations are able to offer relevant economic advantages to actors operating in the legal economy, who create a demand for criminal services that often does not even need to be coerced by criminal organisations themselves. The main implication is that the influence of organised crime becomes less visible since, thanks to the symbiotic relationships with democratic institutions, it resorts less to explicit violence. The symbiotic relationship with formal institutions complicates the quest of studying the *causal* effects of criminal organisations on democratic institutions, their strategies of influence and, ultimately, policy guidance. There are, however, special moments in the life of a democracy where some anomalous levels of organised crime activities can be observed. For instance, in electoral periods criminal organisations have the special opportunity to infiltrate political institutions and, ultimately, the legal economy, by influencing electoral outcomes and the selection of politicians. These unusually intense activities create opportunities for researchers to estimate the social and economic effects of organised crime.

Measurement is another crucial issue faced by researchers studying organised crime. Many of the standard available crime measures (such as extortions, threats or drug trafficking), usually coming from official crime statistics, can be severely affected by under-reporting. They might be endogenous to the strength of local institutions and to the propensity of the local population to report crimes by criminal organisations. Although less prone to under-reporting, even the most visible crimes, such as homicides or bombings, are problematic since they might signal a situation of power conflict between rival gangs in the same place and/or higher efforts by local institutions to fight them. Potential solutions to the measurement issue adopted in the literature include the reliance on confidential sources or the use of various instrumental variable strategies.

In this chapter we provide a review of the recent economic literature on the impacts of organised crime on an essential dimension of democratic institutions, namely elections, and on public policies. Politicians represent a major target for criminal organisations as they shape political decisions and policy implementation. There is indeed considerable judicial and anecdotal evidence suggesting that criminal organisations, through corruption and violence, enforce agreements with politicians, from whom they get various sorts of favours, ranging from the allocation of public funds and public procurement contracts towards their areas of influence or firms under their protection to lenient judicial prosecution and favourable legislation.

Mainly relying on qualitative analysis, the first seminal work in the literature to illustrate the issue of political infiltration carried out by criminal organisations is Gambetta (1993). By focusing on the Sicilian mafia, it describes criminal organisations as sellers of private protection in situations where the presence of the central state is weak, an idea which paved the way for the first wave of studies in the economics of organised crime. Such protection services are also offered to politicians, who are buyers in a market for votes where votes are the commodity, voters are the sellers and the mafia acts as an intermediary guaranteeing the enforcement of electoral deals, whereby 'politicians are linked to mafiosi by a network of exchange'. Although fraudulent electoral deals are also sealed in areas where organised crime is not present, two distinctive issues make such a market an ideal setting for mafia-type organisations: size (the costs of negotiating individually with each voter are prohibitive for politicians), and verification (both parts cannot be sure the counterpart will honour its commitments).

Following Gambetta (1993), the electoral influence of criminal organisations has been the focal point of much of the related literature (Acemoglu et al., 2013; Buonanno et al., 2016; De Feo and De Luca, 2017; Acemoglu et al., 2020; Murphy and Rossi, 2020; Accardo et al., 2021). Some studies directly analyse violence, the distinctive feature of criminal organisations, and its effects around electoral periods (Pinotti, 2012; Sberna and Olivieri, 2014; Dell, 2015; Daniele and Dipoppa, 2017; Alesina et al., 2019). Another set of studies investigates the impacts of organised crime on the allocation of public resources, which happens through the capture of politicians and in turn allows criminal organisations to infiltrate some sectors of the legal economy, such as construction or wind power, where they can reinvest profits from illicit activities (Barone and Narciso, 2015; De Feo and De Luca, 2017; Di Cataldo and Mastrorocco, 2018; Acemoglu et al., 2020; Checchi and Polo, 2020; Murphy and Rossi, 2020; Ferrante et al., 2021). Finally, a related literature deals with the perverse effects of the presence of criminal organisations on the quality of politicians (Dal Bó et al., 2006; Pinotti, 2012; Daniele and Geys, 2015).

There is a small theoretical literature identifying the mechanisms at play in this peculiar electoral market. The seminal contribution here is Dal Bó et al. (2006), who propose a model of political influence where a pressure group (potentially a criminal organisation) can constrain politicians' decisions through a combination of bribes and threats of punishment. Relatedly, Acemoglu et al. (2013) model how criminal organisations can influence electoral outcomes by means of a probabilistic voting model of electoral competition characterised by the presence of nonstate armed actors (paramilitaries in the specific case) exerting political pressure on voters. De Feo and De Luca (2017) extend the model to a political setting characterised by a proportional electoral system and to a situation when the nonstate actor does not feature any political preference. Alesina et al. (2019) build a dynamic Bayesian game model of pre-electoral violence and political competition to explain how criminal organisations strategically use violence to influence electoral outcomes ex ante and the behaviour of elected politicians ex post.

The growing empirical literature adopts various state-of-the-art econometric techniques to test the empirical implications of theoretical models or other less formalised hypotheses. Beside measurement, the key challenge in these empirical studies is the potential endogeneity of organised crime's presence. A variety of sources of exogenous variation in the presence (or intensity) of organised crime have been proposed in the literature as bases of *instrumental variables* strategies (Barone and Narciso, 2015; Buonanno et al., 2016; De Feo and De Luca, 2017; Acemoglu et al., 2020; Checchi and Polo, 2020; Murphy and Rossi, 2020; Ferrante et al., 2021). Other studies use alternative methods to address endogeneity issues. For instance, Dell (2015) adopts a *regression discontinuity* (RD) design where municipalities characterised by a small margin electoral defeat of a party adopting policies against organised crime are used as a counterfactual for municipalities where the same party wins by a small margin. Pinotti (2012) uses a *synthetic control method*, designed for small-sample comparative studies, which compares the average outcome of units under treatment after some point in time with the weighted average outcome of units in the control group (Abadie et al., 2010). Finally, Daniele and Geys (2015) and Ferrante et al. (2021) employ *propensity score matching* estimators, which compare each treated unit to its 'nearest neighbour' in the control group on the basis of the estimated propensity (to be treated) score.

The two central challenges characterising this research agenda mentioned above, namely the measurement of organised crime and its potential endogeneity, will feature prominently in this review. More specifically, whenever discussing empirical studies we will focus on *the source of identification* proposed to overcome the potential endogeneity and the specific proxy adopted to measure the presence of the mafia, along with its original sources.

The rest of this review is structured as follows. In Section 2 we review the literature on the electoral influence of organised crime, focusing on the role played by electoral competition and violence, and on the effects of organised crime presence on the quality of elected politicians. In Section 3 we describe the economic literature on the impact of organised crime on public policies. Finally, in Section 4 we offer some concluding remarks and suggest some promising venues for future research in the area.

Table 15.1 summarises the empirical findings that are discussed throughout the chapter.

2. ORGANISED CRIME IN THE ELECTORAL FIELD

Although most contributions tend to consider together several related aspects of the infiltration of organised crime into politics, we will discuss separately studies focusing on electoral results and competition, those studying electoral violence and those investigating the quality of politicians.

2.1. The Effects on Electoral Results and Competition

The first work to deal with the electoral influence of nonstate armed actors is by Acemoglu et al. (2013), who build a model of electoral competition with the presence of such actors and show that, in the context of Colombia, right-wing paramilitary groups systematically brought votes to specific political parties after 2002, when they explicitly decided to get more involved into politics. The local presence of a paramilitary group is measured by the level of their violent activities. As predicted by their model, areas under the control of paramilitary groups (as measured by paramilitary attacks per 1000 inhabitants between 1997 and 2001) consistently feature higher vote shares awarded to the 'third parties', a new political movement developed as an alternative to the two traditional parties. De Feo and De Luca (2017) tailor Acemoglu et al.'s (2013) model to apply the same logic to organised crime. In their work they highlight the role of electoral competition in shaping the incentives for political actors to establish electoral deals with organised crime. They build a probabilistic model of electoral competition in a (single-constituency) proportional system with two regions (mafia and non-mafia) and two parties (an incumbent and a rival) competing for government. The model is set up as a four-stage game of perfect information, where in the first stage there is a price competition between the two parties to obtain mafia services, in the second stage mafia chooses which party to support in the elections, in the third stage electoral campaigns by the parties (commitment to some level of public good provision if elected) take place, and in the fourth stage the mafia decides the quantity of votes to bring to the supported party. The model predicts that when electoral competition by the rival party strengthens in the region not controlled by the mafia, the incumbent party increases its demand for votes collected by the mafia in the region where the mafia itself is present. The theoretical predictions are tested in Sicily for the national elections held in the period 1946–92, the so-called 'First Republic', after which a political earthquake hit the Italian system leading to the dissolution of the main parties. More precisely, the study uses a panel of 370 Sicilian municipalities and 12 elections for the low chamber (Camera) representatives of the Italian parliament. In this period the Christian Democracy (DC) party was the undisputed leader in the political scene, and there is considerable judicial and anecdotal evidence that the party received electoral support from the Sicilian mafia, at the national and local levels. However, starting from the 1970s, the Communist Party (PCI), following the international spread of the Communist ideology, started to contest the DC's primacy. This setting is suitable to test whether during those years the mafia moved votes to DC (the incumbent party) in response to an increase in electoral competition. The measurement of organised crime presence relies on confidential information gathered by judicial police during the investigations of the Maxi Trial, allowing the mapping of the Cosa Nostra organisation across Sicily (CG Carabinieri – Comando Generale dell'Arma dei Carabinieri, 1987). The potential endogeneity of organised crime presence is instead addressed with a combination of an original instrumental variable (IV) strategy and the intuition, derived from the model, that mafia-delivered votes are more valuable at times of close competition. Formally, they estimate the following model:

$$DC\,share_{it} = \gamma\,Mafia_i \times electoral\,competition_i + X'_{it}\beta + \delta_t + \alpha_i + \varepsilon_{it} \tag{15.1}$$

where *DC share*$_{it}$ is the share of votes gained by the DC party in municipality *i* in national election *t*, *Mafiai* is a dummy measuring the presence of the mafia in 1987, *electoral competition*$_i$ is the difference between the share of votes between DC and PCI parties in the rest of Italy, X_{it}' is a set of time-variant controls, δ_t are year fixed effects, α_i are municipality fixed effects and ε_{it} is the error term clustered at the municipality level. The identification relies on the IV strategy, where the distribution of the mafia in 1900 (*mafia1900*), an ordinal variable ranging from zero to three based on a report by the police inspector Cutrera (1900), instruments the 'contemporaneous' distribution of mafia (*mafia1987*). The analysis also controls for a set of public expenditure, socio-demographic, economic, geographic and church presence controls. IV results show that, as political competition from the PCI strengthened in the rest of Italy, the mafia moved a significant share of votes to the DC (more precisely, in correspondence with the largest drop in vote shares between DC and PCI, namely 17 percentage points, there was an increase by about 13 percentage points on average in the DC share of votes in mafia-ridden municipalities). Interestingly, when using the electoral results of other political forces as alternative outcomes, a negative and significant effect is found only for the leftist parties, thus suggesting that votes were moved from those parties to the DC.

In a closely related paper, Buonanno et al. (2016) analyse the electoral influence carried out by organised crime in the subsequent period, from 1994 to 2013, when the new leader in the political scenario was Forza Italia, the party founded by Silvio Berlusconi. The study relies on a cross-sectional regression at the municipality level of Forza Italia's average vote share obtained at national elections over the period 1994–2013 on mafia presence, province fixed effects and a set of socio-economic controls. Three alternative measures for the presence of organised crime are used: a measure based on the 1987 report by the Italian military police (*Carabinieri*) (CG Carabinieri, 1987), the *mafia1900* measure of mafia prevalence as used by De Feo and De Luca (2017) and a dummy variable equal to one if by 2011 at least one asset had been confiscated from mafia in a given municipality. To address endogeneity, mafia presence is instrumented by the number of sulphur mines in 1886, soil suitability for the cultivation of cereals and the maximum difference in elevation within a municipality. These variables have been shown by Buonanno et al. (2015) to be good predictors of the mafia's early distribution at the end of nineteenth century, consistent with the hypothesis of a natural resource curse for which the emergence of organised crime groups is favoured by the abundance of natural resources in the presence of weak institutions (Pinotti, 2015a). According to IV results, mafia presence significantly increases the share of votes gained by Forza Italia at national elections by between 15 and 18 percentage points on average. The coefficient on mafia presence remains significant even when controlling for possible spatial effects. Interestingly, the study also investigates the possible role played by the electoral system, turning proportional in 2006, in a difference-in-differences (henceforth DiD) regression framework. This part of the analysis provides no conclusive evidence that electoral manipulation by the mafia depends on the electoral system.

As mentioned above, De Feo and De Luca (2017) clearly show how the level of electoral competition crucially defines the relevance of organised crime involvement in politics and the payoffs it can derive from it. In a recent paper, Accardo et al. (2021) further explore the role of electoral competition in shaping the demand from politicians for the electoral support of criminal organisations. They focus again on the Italian context. Following a referendum, a 1991 reform modified the electoral law for the Low Chamber but, crucially, not for the Senate. Italian MPs used to be elected with a proportional representation system with open lists, in which voters could vote for a party and also for up to four candidates within the list of the same party. The reform reduced the number of candidates each voter could vote for from four to one, changing the dynamics of intra-party competition. Intuitively, by preventing coalitions, the reform increased competition among candidates and therefore the relative value of organised crime's electoral services.

Exploiting the 1991 electoral reform as an exogenous source of variation in electoral competition, a series of difference-in-differences estimates confirm that the increase in competition created more scope for criminal organisations to offer their electoral support. Following the reform more votes were awarded to the DC in organised crime-prone electoral municipalities. The measurement of the municipality-level presence of organised crime relies on the judicial police data gathered during the Maxi Trial (CG Carabinieri, 1987). Triple difference estimates (DDD), exploiting the peculiar feature of the reform implemented only in one branch of the parliament, confirm that the increase in the votes awarded to the DC is concentrated in the Low Chamber, where the reform raised competition.

Complementary results, showing (for organised crime areas) an increased dispersion of votes among DC candidates in post-reform Low Chamber elections, support the interpretation that the increase in intra-party competition due to the reform created a stronger demand for electoral support by organised crime. In other words, the support of organised crime, while granted to the 'usual' party (DC), was dispersed across candidates now competing against each other. Taken together, these results clearly flag the crucial role of electoral competition in shaping the electoral influence of organised crime.

The work by Acemoglu et al. (2020) shows, however, that organised crime also contributes to shaping electoral competition. Studying the effects of the mafia in Sicily on various economic and political outcomes, they show that Sicilian municipalities in which organised crime was active in the early 1900s systematically reported lower electoral competition, measured by the Hirschman–Herfindahl concentration index (HHI), both in the medium term and in the long term. Once more the presence of the Sicilian mafia is proxied by *mafia1900*. Their identification strategy relies on an exogenous shock given by a severe drought hitting Sicily in 1893, which dramatically worsened life conditions in the countryside and contributed to the rise of a peasant socialist movement. To contrast the latter, the rural elites resorted to private protection services offered by proto-mafia organisations in a context characterised by institutional weakness, in line with the ideas of Gambetta (1993). Based on this rationale, they adopt a Two-Stage Least Squares (2SLS) regression in which the presence of the Sicilian mafia in the early twentieth century is instrumented by the relative rainfall in 1893. The paper documents a significant and sizeable (between 0.3 and 0.4) impact on HHI in the medium term, computed for each municipality by considering the share of votes obtained by each candidate in the 1909 parliamentary elections. Interestingly, the negative effect of the mafia on electoral competition is the most persistent and robust in the long term (HHI in 1963, 1972 and 1983), as compared to other socio-economic outcomes such as high school completion, literacy and infant mortality. Hence, organised crime decreases political competition by discouraging some parties and candidates from campaigning or competing for elections or by directly coercing voters into voting for whom they support at elections. These findings thus suggest that the mafia has affected electoral competition since its origins, and they corroborate the idea that such competition is an important aspect to be considered when examining the political distortions perpetrated by organised crime.

The findings in Acemoglu et al. (2020) are, however, at odds with the results in Murphy and Rossi (2020). Studying the origin and the consequences of organised crime in the Mexican context, they report an increase in political competition (measured by the Laakso-Taagepra and the Molinar indexes) in municipalities featuring activities by drug cartels. Cartel activity in a given municipality is measured by a (time-invariant) dummy indicator built on the basis of information collected by the Observatorio de Desarrollo y Promoción Social in 2011. To address potential endogeneity concerns, the presence of drug cartels is instrumented by the presence of Chinese population at the beginning of the twentieth century in a given municipality, on the grounds that the know-how of Chinese people in the trade of opium together with legislative changes in the US in the nineteenth century (drug and immigration prohibitions) led to the creation of illegal drug markets which partially persists nowadays through Mexican drug cartels. The results, contrasting with those in the Sicilian context, might be due to methodological differences as well as to the ways different criminal organisations infiltrate politics. For instance, some anecdotal evidence suggests that Mexican drug cartels have supported independent candidates not belonging to traditional parties (something that echoes the Colombian experience discussed in Acemoglu et al. (2013)). In any case, the finding of contrasting results highlights the importance of paying attention to the specific political and social features of the context at hand, as criminal organisations may act in different ways depending on the local circumstances.

2.2. The Effects on Political Violence

The distinctive resource of criminal organisations when enforcing electoral deals or exerting political pressure is undoubtedly represented by violence, which mainly differentiates organised crime from other political pressure groups. Various violent acts against politicians, ranging from threatening letters to homicides, can be used ex ante, i.e. before the elections, to drive votes towards the preferred political actors, and/or ex post, after the elections, to influence policies once politicians are in office.

Pinotti (2012) documents abnormal spikes in homicides in Southern Italy regions (Apulia, Basilicata, Calabria, Campania and Sicily) in the 12 months before national elections in the period 1956–2007, especially in 1975, 1982 and 1991, when the leftist parties reduced significantly the gap with the Christian Democrats. This is in line with the idea that a general increase in electoral competition leads to a larger demand for the mafia's electoral services (De Feo and De Luca, 2017). By means of a DiD design run on a panel of Italian provinces over the period 1983–2003, Sberna and Olivieri (2014) find evidence that regional elections have a positive and significant impact on violence (arsons and bombings), with most of the effect coming from Southern Italy (Apulia, Calabria, Campania and Sicily). Moreover, they again find that an increase in electoral competition (as measured by the Laakso and Taagepera and Golosov indexes) results in an increase of violence in Southern Italy.

Relatedly, Alesina et al. (2019) build a dynamic Bayesian game of electoral violence and political competition to explain how criminal organisations strategically use violence to influence electoral outcomes ex ante and the behaviour of elected politicians ex post. There are two political parties competing to attract voters, and one of them, the 'captured' party, is colluding with a criminal organisation. Their analysis delivers four main predictions: (1) political violence increases during pre-electoral periods, (2) violence increases in response to electoral competition, (3) violence increases the share of votes obtained by the 'captured' party, (4) violence leads to lower anti-mafia efforts of elected politicians, even outside electoral periods. Prediction 2 emphasises the role of political competition in shaping the incentives and the intervention of organised crime in the market for votes. To test these predictions, they build a dataset of victims of the Sicilian mafia including entrepreneurs, police officers, judges and political actors murdered between 1945 and 2013, on the basis of information coming from various associations and NGOs. Their results show that the number of political victims significantly increases in the year before national elections. The magnitude is sizeable, as murders more than double in the pre-electoral periods. The same result does not hold for other types of murders, such as those against entrepreneurs, police officers or magistrates. Moreover, violence against politicians does not increase significantly after the same elections. They also run the analysis at the regional level, reporting a significantly differential increase in homicides in the months preceding national elections in the regions traditionally plagued by organised crime (Campania, Sicily and Calabria). The study investigates the role of electoral competition under two different electoral systems, proportional (1948–92 with regional data) and majoritarian (1993–2004 with provincial data), by the inclusion of a triple interaction term between the period preceding elections, a dummy for regions affected by organised crime and the difference in the vote share between DC and PCI at the national level or the fraction of voters residing in 'contested' districts, and confirms Prediction 2 mentioned above: political competition leads to an exacerbation of electoral violence. The article also shows that electoral violence comes at the expense of leftist parties, which see a reduction in their vote shares at national elections, and produces a decrease in anti-mafia efforts of appointed politicians (as measured by the salience of the topic 'mafia' during parliamentary debates), thus suggesting that political violence discourages anti-mafia efforts of politicians who eventually win the elections.

In a closely related study, Daniele and Dipoppa (2017) exploit a dataset of various types of attacks against Italian local politicians between 2010 and 2014 to test whether criminal organisations strategically use violence before and/or after the elections. Differently from Alesina et al. (2019), their analysis is at the municipality level. The pre (post)-election period is defined as the 30-day period before (after) the day a municipal election occurs. More precisely, they estimate a DiD model to test whether municipalities in regions plagued by organised crime (again Campania, Sicily and Calabria) are more likely to experience violent attacks on politicians around the local electoral cycle and whether potential violence spikes are more pronounced before or after the elections. Their results show that the presence of organised crime increases the probability of an attack against politicians in the month immediately after a local election, by 9 percentage points on average. Such an increase in violence is more pronounced for those mafia-plagued municipalities which experienced a change of the mayor, a sign that criminal organisations mainly exert violent efforts to capture newly elected politicians. The study also documents a positive and significant effect of political violence on the probability of a mayor running for re-election in the following term only in municipalities of the regions highly affected by organised crime, thus suggesting that violence can be used to defend existing political control.

The finding that political violence follows, rather than precedes, elections seems at odds with Alesina et al. (2019), who instead find that violence mostly increases before the elections. The reasons for this partial divergence are directly discussed in the paper. First, while Alesina et al. (2019) focuses exclusively on homicides, Daniele and Dipoppa (2017) consider a much wider set of attacks against politicians (with only two political murders in their dataset). Second, the type of elections considered may change incentives for violence. Alesina et al. (2019) focus on national elections: once national politicians are elected, they become more visible to the public and to law enforcement institutions. This should make it harder for the mafia to threaten national politicians, a fortiori, through homicides. Criminal organisations may be more willing to exert violent forms of political pressure before the elections for national politicians, as they can signal their strength when it is less costly. Moreover, it is possible that criminal organisations are less certain on parties' and candidates' attitudes towards organised crime before local elections, so that they might find it more profitable to wait for local politicians to be elected before threatening them. In any case, the results of these two related studies highlight the importance of studying what happens around the elections at all administrative levels. Local politics is as important as national politics since it might be even easier to influence given that it is more based on local socio-economic conditions rather than on ideological perspectives.

While in Italy organised crime violence has somewhat decreased over the last few decades, a few countries in Latin America have experienced a surge of it, mainly related to the activities of drug trafficking organisations. In this context, the contribution by Dell (2015) stands out. It analyses drug-related violence following local elections in Mexico, where in 2006 the conservative Partido Acción Nacional (PAN) started a harsh war against drug traffickers. The study exploits a dataset of drug-related homicides in Mexican municipalities in 2006–11 and local electoral results for mayors in 2007–10, to study the effects of 'close' PAN electoral victories on drug-related homicides. The identification strategy to estimate the direct impact of such electoral victories on violence consists in a *regression discontinuity* (RD) design, characterised by the following specification:

$$y_i = \alpha_0 + \alpha_1 PANwin_i + \alpha_1 PANwin_i \times f\left(spread_i\right) + \alpha_3\left(1 - PANwin_i\right) \times f\left(spread_i\right) + \varepsilon_{it} \tag{15.2}$$

where y_i is either drug-related or the overall homicide rate in municipality i (in the pre-election, lame duck or post-inauguration period), $PANwin_i$ is a dummy equal to one if a PAN candidate wins the municipal election, $spread_i$ is the vote spread margin in percentage points between the PAN and the second or first party and defines the sample to include municipalities where the PAN arrived first or second in the elections by five or less percentage points, and ε_{it} is the error term clustered at the municipality level. Two samples are considered, i.e. close elections either in 2007–08 or 2007–10, with the former having a longer post-inauguration period but fewer municipalities. As in all RD designs, the idea here is to use municipalities where the PAN loses by a small margin as a counterfactual for municipalities where the PAN wins by a small margin. Results show that the drug-related homicide rate increases by 33 percentage points during the three-year term of the mayor (2007–08 sample) and by 27 percentage points during the first year of the term (2007–10 sample), after a close PAN victory. A significant increase is also observed for the overall homicide rate. The post-electoral increase in violence is concentrated in municipalities containing a drug trafficking organisation and bordering places where rival drug trafficking organisations operate, which suggests that crackdowns run by local governments generate conflicts between traffickers by weakening the incumbent organisation and giving the rival an opportunity to conquer a new municipality. The increase in violence is also larger when a PAN administration follows a non-PAN one, which echoes the results in Daniele and Dipoppa (2017) where post-electoral violence in mafia places is higher when there is a change in local government (a new mayor is elected).

The study also employs a network model of drug trafficking to estimate the (spillover) effects of PAN victories on violence in neighbouring municipalities. In the model, traffickers aim to minimise the costs of carrying drugs through the Mexican road network from producing Mexican municipalities to the US, and they want to avoid municipalities where the PAN crackdowns (electoral victories) take place. The trafficking routes predicted by the network models are then used as the independent variable of interest in an OLS regression specification, to study spillovers in drug trafficking and violence. Estimates show that municipalities on a predicted route experience a significant increase both in the value of drug confiscations and in the drug-related homicide rate. Hence, crackdowns have spillover effects, as they divert drug trafficking and related violence elsewhere. These findings importantly highlight that local governments should be aware of the unintended consequences, both in loco and elsewhere, of their well-intentioned policies that they implement to fight organised crime.

2.3. The Effects on the Quality of Politicians

A related issue concerns the possible impact of criminal organisations on the quality of politicians selected in office, which emerges as a by-product of the infiltration of organised crime into politics. Investigating this effect is of course relevant since the quality of the political class determines the quality of public policies and, as such, it might represent one of the mechanisms through which criminal organisations harm socio-economic outcomes. The idea is first formalised in Dal Bó et al. (2006), who propose a model of political influence where a pressure group can constraint politicians' decisions through a combination of bribes and threats of punishment. The model is a two-stage game where, in the first stage, citizens decide whether to enter politics and run for public office or to enter the private sector, while, in the second stage, a political pressure group chooses the levels of bribes and threats to drive the decisions of the appointed public official towards its own interests. Individuals' wages in the private sector match their quality. The key element of the model is that individuals' expected payoffs from entering politics are determined not only by the prospective public wage but also by the level of bribe and punishment delivered by the pressure group, and the cost of being arrested for corruption if caught. The expected profits of the pressure group are affected by the gains obtained by capturing the public official in charge and the costs of delivering bribes and punishments, in turn determined by institutional quality. For the sake of the present discussion, the most important prediction of this model is that the quality of the elected public official is lower when there is an active pressure group delivering both bribes and threats, whose level, in turn, depends on the quality of law enforcement.

With organised crime playing the role of the pressure group, Daniele and Geys (2015) test this prediction on a panel dataset of municipalities in Southern Italy (Apulia, Calabria, Campania and Sicily) in 1985–2011. To measure the presence of organised crime, they exploit the staggered enforcement of Law 164/1991 allowing for the dissolution of municipality governments for mafia infiltration. In other words, the dissolution is used as a 'treatment' variable in the empirical analysis, as a way to measure mafia infiltration into local governments. The plausible exogeneity of the local council dissolutions is suggested by some features of Law 164/1991. The dissolution is indeed imposed by the national government when 'evidence emerges on direct or indirect links between local public administrators and organised crime, i.e. forms of conditioning . . . that jeopardise the free will of the electoral body and the local governments'. The process requires a series of steps involving officials of different law enforcement and political institutions, and municipalities are not aware of being under investigation. When a dissolution is eventually declared, the national government appoints three external commissioners for a period of one to three years, during which the commissioners can only undertake approved measures of ordinary administration. Using the average education of all municipality council members as a proxy for politicians' quality, and adopting a DiD model, the study documents a significant increase in the average education level of local politicians following the municipality government dissolution. More specifically, when mafia infiltration of local politics is remedied through the implementation of a stricter institutional framework, the average education of local politicians increases by around four months, which becomes one year for mayors and aldermen, who are the people holding the highest power in the municipal councils. Interestingly from a methodological perspective, this chapter uses in a robustness check a *propensity score matching* method to address potential selection bias. More precisely, the propensity scores of mafia infiltration are estimated via a probit regression with log population, mafia-related homicides, unemployment rate, young-old population ratio, the share of males and entrepreneurs in the municipal council and the average year of birth of municipal council members as independent variables. Then the method compares each treated municipality to its 'nearest neighbour' in the control group in terms of propensity score, thus matching treated (dissolved) municipalities with control (never dissolved) municipalities having a similar probability of being dissolved. The coefficient on treatment comes from a weighted average of each comparison based on estimated propensity scores. Results are robust to this alternative estimation procedure.

Using a panel of Italian regions and national elections in 1956–2007, Pinotti (2012) offers further evidence of the impact of organised crime on the quality of politicians. He documents a significant relationship between upswings in pre-electoral violence and two measures of politicians' quality, i.e. the fraction of elected politicians subsequently involved in scandals (positive relationship) and the fraction of politicians holding a college degree (negative). Moreover, by focusing on the specific case of two Italian regions, Apulia and Basilicata, he reports that the human capital of politicians, as alternatively measured by the fraction of politicians subsequently involved in scandals and holding a university degree, deteriorated after the 1970s, when these regions started to exhibit spikes in the homicide rate and to experience the presence of criminal organisations according to judicial and anecdotal evidence. The analysis employs the synthetic control method, which compares the average outcome of regions under treatment after some point in time with the weighted average outcome of regions in the control group (never exposed to treatment). The idea is to build a synthetic control region that mimics the initial and potential conditions of the treated region before the exposure to treatment and approximates the unobserved counterfactual, i.e. the trend of the outcome of the treated region after treatment if the treatment had been absent. Weights for the construction of the synthetic control outcome are computed by minimising the difference between the treated and control units pre-treatment outcomes and their predictors, in some period before the treatment starts.

Overall, the existing (admittedly thin) empirical evidence seems to confirm the intuition elaborated in the model by Dal Bó et al. (2006): the infiltration of politics by organised crime negatively affects the politicians' selection process, resulting in lower quality leaders.

3. ORGANISED CRIME AND PUBLIC POLICIES

So far we have focused on the effects of organised crime on elections, the process through which the selection of administrators unfolds in democracies, and we reported on the level of violence its involvement implies. The ultimate goal of organised crime engaging in politics, however, is influencing public choices to their own advantage. Public policies are indeed a key element in the 'synallagmatic' relationship between organised crime and political actors, and their distortion allows criminal organisations to enter, in various ways, the legal economy. In the economic literature, one of the first works to investigate this issue is by Barone and Narciso (2015), who analyse the impact of organised crime on the allocation of public subsidies to firms, by using a dataset of Sicilian municipalities over the period 2004–09. In the empirical analysis they focus on the Italian Law 188/92. The law was a policy instrument especially targeted at under-developed areas, whose aim was to reduce inequalities across Italy. It gave the opportunity for businesses to be awarded project-related public grants, on the basis of various criteria, such as the potential number of jobs generated by the investment and its environmental impacts. The inflows of such public funds often attract criminal organisations, which may profitably distort their allocation towards their own actitivites of interest, using threats to public officials or fictitious firms. Barone and Narciso (2015) investigate these questions by estimating a cross-sectional model testing whether firms were receiving more Law 488/92 public funds in 'mafia municipalities'. The presence of organised crime is measured with a dummy taking a value of one if a mafia-related crime (as per article *416-bis* of the Italian penal code) occurred in a given municipality. To address endogeneity, mafia presence is instrumented by the value of land in the nineteenth century, as proxied by three determinants of land productivity, namely slope, altitude and relative rainfall (ratio of mean rainfall in 1851–60 to long-run mean rainfall in 1800–50, measured at the weather station level and interpolated at the municipality level). IV estimates document a positive and significant impact of mafia presence on both the probability of obtaining public funds and their amount. In particular, on average, the probability of obtaining public grants is higher by 64 percentage points in mafia-ridden municipalities than other municipalities, and the amount of such grants per employee is higher by 1500/1600 euros. The study also documents a positive and significant impact of mafia presence on the number of properties seized by the police due to links with organised crime (interpreted by the authors as a proxy for the number of fictitious firms created by the mafia) and the number of public administration corruption cases per capita, which might suggest that infiltration into the public administration to obtain funds partially happens through the creation of fictitious firms and the corruption of public officials.

More recently, Di Cataldo and Mastrorocco (2018) have gone one level deeper and rely on municipality budgets to assess the impact of organised crime on public resources, both outgoing (expenses) and incoming (taxes). They exploit a panel dataset of municipalities in Calabria, Campania and Sicily between 1998 and 2013, containing information on local public investments in different sectors, electoral results, criminal violence and a set of demographic and economic controls. As a way to measure the infiltration of criminal organisations into local institutions, they use the staggered enforcement of Law 164/1991, as did Daniele and Geys (2015). The study investigates whether a municipality experiencing dissolution for infiltration has some distortion in the allocation of public resources. More precisely, it uses a DiD design characterised by the following regression equation:

$$y_{it+1} = \alpha + \gamma\, \textit{inflitration}_{it} + \beta' X_{it} + \theta_i + \delta_t + + \varepsilon_{it} \tag{15.3}$$

where y_{it+1} is the amount of financial resources municipality i plans to spend over the following year, either overall or allocated to a specific spending component (construction, waste, police and so on), X_{it} is a set of controls, θ_i and δ_t are municipality and year fixed effects and ε_{it} is the error term clustered at the municipality level. The years during which an external commission is in power are excluded from the sample (as well as all municipalities experiencing a dissolution before 1998, i.e. when the panel starts). The $\textit{infiltration}_{it}$ dummy is always equal to one for the years from when a subsequently dissolved municipality held its last elections to when the dissolution took place.

While no significant effect of mafia infiltration on the total level of public spending of municipalities is found, when breaking down the components of spending decisions, it emerges that infiltrated municipalities tend to significantly invest more (by 13 per cent) in the construction and waste management sectors and less (64 per cent) in municipal police compared to other municipalities. The former are those economic sectors in which Italian mafias are well-known to have strategic interests. Moreover, infiltrated municipalities collect on average 17 per cent less waste taxes, which is one of the main sources of income for local governments.

Similar evidence of the distortion of public resources by organised crime is also found by Acemoglu et al. (2020) for early twentieth-century Sicily. The mafia, even at its early stages, had a negative impact on the public development expenditure of municipal governments and on long-term aqueduct availability. It is worth noting that these detrimental effects are not universal: Murphy and Rossi (2020), in their work on drug cartels in Mexico, find that the presence of drug cartels leads to an increase in local tax revenues and a decrease in a marginalisation index, which is built on the basis of various socio-economic indicators including essential public goods (electricity and water). These results provide a different perspective on the impacts of organised crime on communities, and they are in line with the hypothesis that drug lords receive and give support to local economies, especially where the state does not. Beyond the methodological differences, the sharp contrast between their findings and those in the literature on the Sicilian mafia might also be due to differences in the criminal organisations under study and the ways they interact with local communities.

When criminal organisations aspire to enter the legal economy, there are some sectors whose specific features make them particularly vulnerable to their infiltration. An important instance is represented by the construction industry, which has been attracting organised crime for a long time, given its high territorial specificity, low levels of innovation and a strong dependence on the public administration to carry out activities through public procurement contracts or private permissions (Lavezzi, 2008). Moreover, it requires large initial investments, and criminal organisations usually have large liquidity coming from illegal activities. The importance of the construction sector for organised crime has been investigated by De Feo and De Luca (2017), Di Cataldo and Mastrorocco (2018) and Ferrante et al. (2021). De Feo and De Luca (2017) find that, when electoral competition strengthened, the share of construction workers over the total labour force significantly increased in mafia-ridden municipalities (by about 4 percentage points in correspondence with the largest drop in electoral competition). This finding suggests that, in exchange for electoral support, the Sicilian mafia obtained favours in the construction sector, through the allocation of public procurement contracts or private permissions. These interpretations are in line with anecdotal and judicial evidence describing such events as the so-called 'Sack of Palermo', the famous construction boom involving the city of Palermo in the 1950s–60s, when many illegal building licenses were granted to entrepreneurs with close mafia connections by politicians responsible for public works. Nowadays as much as back then, rigged public tenders in the construction (and waste) sectors appear often in the presidential decrees dissolving municipalities for mafia infiltration (Law 164/1991).

As observed by Varese (2011), in the construction sector firms tend to compete locally, and the relatively low barriers to entry give an incentive to develop a demand for protection against market competition. The presence of criminal organisations available to fill such a demand consequently raises the barriers to entry. Ferrante et al. (2021) study the effects of organised crime on market competition in the construction sector, using a panel of Sicilian municipalities in 1991, 2001 and 2011. The presence of organised crime is measured by a dummy variable built on the basis of three variables, namely the distribution of the mafia in 1987 (*mafia1987* in De Feo and De Luca (2017)), a map of the Sicilian municipalities where the mafia is active drawn by a study of the University of Messina in 1992 and a measure derived by a DIA report in 2016. Their 2SLS regressions, in which the current presence of the mafia is instrumented either by its presence before 1900 (based on (Cutrera, 1900) and a report from the Sicilian Prefects contained in (Gambetta, 1993)) or by the share of mafia municipalities in the same province, document that mafia presence has a positive and significant impact on the Herfindahl–Hirschman index of market concentration in the construction industry. This finding suggests that one of the harmful consequences of the infiltration of organised crime into legal economic sectors is the dilution of market competition. Further results, obtained both by 2SLS and propensity score matching estimation, suggest that the seizure and reassignment of mafia-owned assets enacted by law enforcement authorities might be an effective anti-mafia policy in the long run, as it directly affects the financial interests of criminal organisations and fosters new entries and competition in the markets affected.

The interests of criminal organisations in the legal economy are not limited to the construction sector. Any opportunities to capture public funds or launder illegal profits through legal activities are carefully exploited. For instance, the emergence of new industries supported by public incentives, such as renewable energies, has offered criminal organisations new opportunities to infiltrate emerging economic sectors. Checchi and Polo (2020) study the infiltration of the Sicilian mafia into the wind power sector. Over the last 20 years, this sector has been promoted by public policies, in line with climate change policies at the European level. In Sicily, various judicial investigations have unveiled episodes of involvement of organised crime in the wind power business, mainly for the purpose of money laundering. As for construction activities, access to the wind power business strongly depends on public institutions, requires large initial investments and is supported through public funds. These features make wind power highly attractive for criminal organisations, which may be directly involved in the whole business or in the construction and transportation phases, act as a financial advisor to an entrepreneur, offer protection services against physical harm or competitors in exchange for a fee, corrupt and coerce public officials to assign administrative authorisations or public subsidies and soften periodic controls, and extort money from the entrepreneur. The presence of the mafia is measured by an index sourced from DIA in 2018. By using a 2SLS regression, where current presence of the mafia is instrumented by its presence in 1994 (University of Messina) and 1987 (Carabinieri), Checchi and Polo (2020) show that the probability of observing at least one wind farm is around 50 per cent higher in mafia-ridden municipalities. The effect of the mafia on wind investments is larger after 2012, when the Italian regulation changed the incentives from being based on green certificates to tariffs, which increased the incentives for the construction of wind plants of smaller size in terms of capacity in MW. The immediate response of the criminal environment also shows the adaptability of organised crime to policy changes. This should not be surprising, as criminal organisations are increasingly becoming real enterprises, with the ability to go along with institutional changes and always ready to exploit new profitable opportunities.

4. CONCLUSIONS AND FUTURE RESEARCH

This chapter provides a review of the nascent economic literature on the interactions between organised crime and political institutions, outlining the methodologies and strategies adopted to address two key issues: potential endogeneity and the measurement of organised crime presence.

It focuses on the effects of organised crime on elections and on public policies, and on the strategic use of violence to influence politics, which represents a fundamental channel through which criminal organisations infiltrate the legal economy. Organised crime produces harmful consequences for the infiltrated markets, such as the reduction of competition.

A side effect of political infiltration is represented by the reduction in the quality of the political class, which may further harm the economy as politicians are after all those who drive policy decisions.

Most of the existing literature seems, therefore, to confirm what intuition would suggest: the presence of organised crime disrupts the functioning of democratic institutions and curbs local development and welfare in the affected areas. A notable exception is Murphy and Rossi (2020) who report a positive local impact of drug-trafficking organisations on the welfare of affected communities in Mexico. An important disclaimer, discussed by the authors themselves, is that in a context where organised crime is endemic, its social costs may be more widely spread across all communities, whereas some (relative) gains are obtained in organised crime stronghold communities only.

If the overall picture is therefore relatively clear, there is still a lot we do not know, which opens opportunities for further research in the field. For instance, the mechanisms through which criminal organisations control votes during elections are a largely unexplored area. Some works, such as Alesina et al. (2019), have documented significant spikes in violence around electoral periods, but the methods through which this is done need to be studied more closely. If behind the control of votes there is only intimidation of some part of the electorate, we should observe an effect on turnout, or even a stronger effect on less motivated voters. Relatedly, it is not yet clear which factors stimulate the demand for votes by politicians and the supply by organised crime in the market for votes, or how different electoral systems or regulations might affect the manipulation of votes exerted by criminal organisations.[4] Identifying these mechanisms would ultimately offer relevant suggestions on how to keep electoral manipulation at bay.

As noted throughout the review, most existing studies focus on the case of the Sicilian mafia, or Italy in general. Other Italian criminal organisations with supposedly very strong control of the territory, such as the Camorra in Campania or the 'Ndrangheta in Calabria, have been so far almost completely overlooked. Perhaps more importantly, further work on Latin American criminal organisations, as well as the Russian or Japanese mafias characterised by relatively different historical legacies and institutional settings, will clarify whether the findings in the current review apply universally. The findings in Murphy and Rossi (2020) constitute a warning in this respect.

Finally, in the wake of De Feo and De Luca (2017), Di Cataldo and Mastrorocco (2018), Ferrante et al. (2021) and Checchi and Polo (2020), there is scope for future research on the infiltration of organised crime into various, traditional or new, economic sectors. Sectors such as waste, hospitals or catering activities have been shown to be targets of criminal organisations by judicial evidence but they are yet to be scrutinised by economic research.

Table 15.1 ***Summary of the empirical literature discussed***

Study	Dep. variable(s)	Measure(s) of OC	Method(s)	Effect(s) of OC
Pinotti (2012)	Fraction of elected politicians involved in political scandals	Homicide rate in mafia regions (ISTAT)	OLS	+***
	Fraction of elected politicians holding a college degree	Homicide rate in mafia regions (ISTAT)	OLS	–***
	Fraction of elected politicians involved in political scandals (or holding a university degree)	Mafia regions (Apulia and Basilicata)	SCM	+(–)
Acemoglu et al. (2013)	'Third parties' vote share	Paramilitary attacks per 1000 inhabitants in 1997–2001 (Centro de Estudios sobre Desarrollo Económico)	OLS	+***
Sberna and Olivieri (2014)	Arson and bomb attacks	Mafia regions (Apulia, Calabria, Campania and Sicily)	DiD	+***
Barone and Narciso (2015)	Public funds per employee assigned to businesses in 2004–09 (amount and dummy)	Mafia-type association according to article 416-bis of the Penal Code (Italian Ministry of the Interior)	2SLS	+***
Daniele and Geys (2015)	Average years of education of politicians in the local council	Municipality dissolution for mafia infiltration	DiD	–***
Dell (2015)	Confiscations of domestically produced drugs (dummy and value)	Drug trafficking route (predicted on the basis of a network model)	OLS	+***
	Drug-related homicides (dummy and rate)	Drug trafficking route (predicted on the basis of a network model)	OLS	+*** (dummy), +** (rate)
	Drug-related homicide rate	National Action Party electoral victory	RDD	+***
Buonanno et al. (2016)	Vote share of Forza Italia party	Seizure of assets to mafia before 2011 (Agenzia del Demanio), mafia in 1987 (Carabinieri), mafia in 1900 (Cutrera)	2SLS	+***

Daniele and Dipoppa (2017)	Attacks against politicians in 2010–14 (dummy)	Mafia regions (Calabria, Campania and Sicily)	DiD	+***
	Mayor re-running for election (dummy)	Mafia regions (Calabria, Campania and Sicily) and attacks against politicians in 2010–14 (dummy)	DiD	+**
De Feo and De Luca (2017)	Vote share of the Christian Democratic party	Mafia in 1987 (Carabinieri), mafia in 1994 (University of Messina) IV: mafia in 1900 (Cutrera)	2SLS	+***
	Share of construction workers over total labour force	Mafia in 1987 (Carabinieri), mafia in 1994 (University of Messina) IV: mafia in 1900 (Cutrera)	2SLS	+***
Di Cataldo and Mastrorocco (2018)	Local public spending per capita in construction and waste management	Municipality dissolution for mafia infiltration	DiD	+***
	Local public spending per capita in police	Municipality dissolution for mafia infiltration	DiD	–**
	Waste tax	Municipality dissolution for mafia infiltration	DiD	–**
Alesina et al. (2019)	Homicide rate	Mafia regions (Calabria, Campania and Sicily)	OLS	+***
	Leftist parties vote share	Number of political homicides before elections (Fondazione Progetto Legalit`a, Libera, VittimeMafia, Wikipedia)	OLS	–***
	Occurrence of the word 'Mafia' during parliamentary debates	Number of political homicides before elections (Fondazione Progetto Legalità, Libera, VittimeMafia, Wikipedia)	OLS	–***
Acemoglu et al. (2020)	HHI of political competition	Mafia in 1900 (Cutrera)	2SLS	+***
Checchi and Polo (2020)	Presence of wind farms (dummy)	Mafia in 2018 (DIA) IV: mafia in 1987 (Carabinieri) and 1994 (University of Messina)	2SLS	+*
	Investment in wind farms (dummy)	Mafia in 2018 (DIA) IV: mafia in 1987 (Carabinieri) and 1994 (University of Messina)	2SLS	+***
Murphy and Rossi (2020)	Laakso-Taagepera and Molinar indexes of political competition	Cartel presence in 2011 (Observatorio de Desarrollo y Promoción Social)	2SLS	+***
	Marginalisation index	Cartel presence in 2011 (Observatorio de Desarrollo y Promoción Social)	2SLS	–***

(*Continued*)

Table 15.1 *Continued*

Study	Dep. variable(s)	Measure(s) of OC	Method(s)	Effect(s) of OC
Accardo et al. (2021)	HHI of (intra-party) political competition of the Christian Democratic party	Mafia in 1987 (Carabinieri), mafia in 1994 (University of Messina) Mafia Index (Transcrime), mafia regions (Apulia, Basilicata, Campania, Calabria and Sicily)	DiDiD and 2SLS	–***
	Vote share of the Christian Democratic party	Mafia in 1987 (Carabinieri), mafia in 1994 (University of Messina) Mafia index (Transcrime), mafia regions (Apulia, Basilicata, Campania, Calabria and Sicily)	DiDiD and 2SLS	+***
Ferrante et al. (2021)	HHI (based on the number of employees) in the construction industry	Mafia in 1987, 1992, 2016 (Carabinieri, University of Messina, DIA) IV: mafia before 1900 (Cutrera, Gambetta) or share of mafia municipalities in the province (Carabinieri, University of Messina, DIA)	2SLS and PSM	+***

Notes: DiD stands for Difference-in-Differences estimations; DiDiD for Difference-in-Difference-in-Differences; PSM for Propensity Score Matching; RDD for Regression Discontinuity Design; SCM for Dynthetic Control Method.

NOTES

1. Leicester University.
2. Leicester University.
3. University of Bozen and LICOS KU Leuven, Belgium.
4. A first step in this direction has been taken by Accardo et al. (2021).

REFERENCES

Abadie, Alberto, Alexis Diamond, and Jens Hainmueller, "Synthetic control methods for comparative case studies: Estimating the effect of California's tobacco control program," *Journal of the American Statistical Association*, 2010, *105* (490), 493–505.

Accardo, Pasquale, Giuseppe De Feo, and Giacomo Davide De Luca, "With a little help from my friends. Political competition with interest groups," 2021. Available at SSRN: https://ssrn.com/abstract=3836462 or http://dx.doi.org/10.2139/ssrn.3836462.

Acemoglu, Daron, Giuseppe De Feo, and Giacomo Davide De Luca, "Weak states: Causes and consequences of the Sicilian mafia," *Review of Economic Studies*, 2020, *87* (2), 537–81.

Acemoglu, Daron, James A. Robinson, and Rafael J. Santos, "The monopoly of violence: Evidence from Colombia," *Journal of the European Economic Association*, 2013, *11* (s1), 5–44.

Alesina, Alberto, Salvatore Piccolo, and Paolo Pinotti, "Organized crime, violence, and politics," *The Review of Economic Studies*, 07 2019, *86* (2), 457–99.

Barone, Guglielmo and Gaia Narciso, "Organized crime and business subsidies: Where does the money go?," *Journal of Urban Economics*, 2015, *86*, 98–110.

Buonanno, Paolo, Giovanni Prarolo, and Paolo Vanin, "Organized crime and electoral outcomes. Evidence from Sicily at the turn of the XXI century," *European Journal of Political Economy*, 2016, *41*, 61–74.

Buonanno, Paolo, Ruben Durante, Giovanni Prarolo, and Paolo Vanin, "Poor institutions, rich mines: Resource curse in the origins of the Sicilian mafia," *The Economic Journal*, 2015, *125* (586), F175–F202.

CG Carabinieri - Comando Generale dell'Arma dei Carabinieri, "Relazione Del Comandante Generale dell'Arma dei Carabinieri alla Commissione Parlamentare sul Fenomeno della Mafia," March 1987.

Checchi, Valeria and Michele Polo, "Blowing in the wind: The infiltration of Sicilian mafia in the wind power business," *Italian Economic Journal*, 03 2020.

Cutrera, Antonino, *La mafia e i mafiosi*, Palermo, IT: Reber, 1900.

Dal Bó, Ernesto, Pedro Dal Bó, and Rafael Di Tella, "'Plata o Plomo?': Bribe and punishment in a theory of political influence," *The American Political Science Review*, 02 2006, *100* (1), 41–53.

Daniele, Gianmarco and Benny Geys, "Organised crime, institutions and political quality: Empirical evidence from Italian municipalities," *The Economic Journal*, 2015, *125* (586), F233–55.

Daniele, Gianmarco and Gemma Dipoppa, "Mafia, elections and violence against politicians," *Journal of Public Economics*, 2017, *154*, 10–33.

Daniele, Vittorio and Ugo Marani, "Organized crime, the quality of local institutions and FDI in Italy: A panel data analysis," *European Journal of Political Economy*, 2011, *27* (1), 132–42.

De Feo, Giuseppe and Giacomo Davide De Luca, "Mafia in the ballot box," *American Economic Journal: Economic Policy*, 2017, *9* (3), 134–67.

Dell, Melissa, "Trafficking networks and the Mexican drug war," *American Economic Review*, 2015, *105* (6), 1738–79.

Di Cataldo, Marco and Nicola Mastrorocco, "Organised crime, captured politicians and the allocation of public resources," *Trinity Economics Papers tep1219*, Trinity College Dublin, Department of Economics, September 2018.

Ministro dell'Interno, "Relazione del Ministro dell'Interno al Parlamento sull'attività svolta e sui risultati conseguiti dalla Direzione Investigativa Antimafia,"January 2019

Ferrante, Livio, Stefania Fontana, and Francesco Reito, "Mafia and bricks: Unfair competition in local markets and policy interventions," Small Business Economics 56, 1461–1484, 2021.

Gambetta, Diego, *The Sicilian Mafia: The Business of Private Protection*, Cambridge, MA: Harvard University Press, 1993.

Lavezzi, Andrea, "Economic structure and vulnerability to organised crime: Evidence from Sicily," *Global Crime*, 08 2008, *9*, 198–220.

Murphy, Tommy E. and Martín A. Rossi, "Following the poppy trail: Origins and consequences of Mexican drug cartels," *Journal of Development Economics*, 2020, *143*, 102433.

Pinotti, Paolo, "Organized crime, violence and the quality of politicians: Evidence from Southern Italy," Paolo Baffi Centre Research Paper No. 2012-124.

Pinotti, Paolo, "The causes and consequences of organised crime: Preliminary evidence across Countries," *The Economic Journal*, 2015, *125* (586), F158–74.

Pinotti, Paolo, "The economic costs of organised crime: Evidence from Southern Italy," *The Economic Journal*, 2015, *125* (586), F203–32.

Sberna, Salvatore and Elisabetta Olivieri, "'Set the night on fire!' Mafia violence and elections in Italy," *SSRN Scholarly Paper ID 2451701*, Rochester, NY: Social Science Research Network, 2014.

Varese, Federico, *Mafias on the Move: How Organized Crime Conquers New Territories*, Princeton, NJ: Princeton University Press, 2011.

16. What predicts corruption?[1]

Emanuele Colonnelli,[2] Jorge Gallego[3] and Mounu Prem[4]

1. INTRODUCTION

Policy makers around the world consider the fight against corruption to be one of the most important, and yet most challenging objectives of our society. In the presence of corruption, regulations tend to be inefficient (Djankov et al., 2002), businesses are held back (Fisman and Svensson, 2007; Colonnelli and Prem, 2020), mortality rates are higher (Fisman and Wang, 2015), public and social spending is wasteful (Olken, 2007; Bandiera et al., 2009) and growth is slower (Mauro, 1995).[5]

As a result, anti-corruption policies are ubiquitous. While all policies tend to focus on some mix of monitoring and punishment of illicit acts, central to all of them is the need to effectively target the anti-corruption activity. That is, curbing corruption requires the ability to *predict* where corruption is most likely to take place. Yet, while many studies have analyzed the consequences of anti-corruption programs, little is known about what predicts corruption.[6]

In this chapter, we attempt to fill this gap by focusing on the unique setting provided by Brazil's national anti-corruption audit program, which generated exogenous observable snapshots of corruption levels across thousands of municipalities over time. Based on these reports, we create two discrete measures of corruption, one for municipalities that reveal levels of corruption above the median and one for municipalities in the top quartile of the empirical distribution. The latter is constructed with the aim of capturing more severe cases of corruption at the municipality level. We complement our measure of corruption with a set of approximately 150 municipality characteristics that span different features of Brazilian municipalities. In particular, we include characteristics of the private and public sectors, measures of financial development, human capital, local politics, public spending, natural resources' dependency and other municipality characteristics.

Using our rich dataset and our measures of corruption, we first train a group of popular machine learning models as well as an ensemble model to assess whether corruption can be accurately predicted. We do so by performing a five-fold cross-validation procedure on a training set covering 70 percent of our data and leaving the remaining 30 percent for testing the models' out-of-sample performance.

Our analysis reveals that machine learning models exhibit high levels of performance. In particular, using different measures of model performance such as AUC (area under the ROC curve) and accuracy, we find that tree-based models, as well as the ensemble model, outperform LASSO (Least Absolute Shrinkage and Selection Operator) and neural networks. Our results prove to be robust to the use of a continuous measure of corruption, as well as to account for class imbalance in the case of the high corruption measure.

We then move to analyze which features have a higher predictive power on corruption, finding that private sector and human capital characteristics are the ones more likely to do so. The problem with this analysis is that there could be a group of features with high predictive power but with no particular feature having a high one. To account for this, we assess the importance of a group of characteristics by computing the AUC of the model for each group. We find the strongest predictors of corruption to be those related to local private sector activity. Financial development and the quality of human capital are also relevant predictors, while variables related to the size and composition of the public sector, local politics, public spending and natural resources' dependency have low predictive power. A caveat to our analysis is that we abstract away from a causal interpretation of the estimates, as it is standard in prediction-focused studies. Machine learning models have recently been proven useful in other policy-related prediction issues (Kleinberg et al., 2015), such as security (Bogomolov et al., 2014), poverty (Blumenstock et al., 2015), money-laundry (Paula et al., 2016) and conflict (Blair et al., 2017; Bazzi et al., 2019; Mueller and Rauh, 2019). More related to our work, Lima and Delen (2020) use machine learning models to predict corruption perception for 132 countries, Lopez-Iturriaga and Sanz (2018) use aggregate data and newspaper evidence from Spanish provinces to predict corruption, while Gallego et al. (2019) study malfeasance in public procurement contracts in Colombia. Also, in the context of the recent COVID-19 pandemic, Gallego et al. (2020b) use a predicted index of corruption using machine learning to study how in places of higher predicted corruption, public sector inefficiencies and corruption can emerge in the face of a large need of expenditures as the one observed during this pandemic.

Our contribution to this recent literature on the use of machine learning models in social science is two-fold. On the one hand, the ability to accurately predict corruption can inform national anti-corruption policies worldwide and help improve cost-effectiveness in a notoriously challenging and costly area to tackle. On the other hand, our results on what specific predictors matter the most shed light on the key role played by the *private* sector in the fight against corruption, which instead tends to be mostly focused on initiatives targeting the *public* sector (Hanna et al., 2011).

2. CONCEPTUAL FRAMEWORK

2.1. Corruption, Moral Hazard and Machine Learning

An important strand of the literature on corruption has understood this phenomenon as an agency problem (Besley and McLaren, 1993; Mookherjee and Png, 1992; Banerjee, 1997; Acemoglu and Verdier, 2000; Dabla-Norris, 2002; Aidt, 2016). Under this approach, it is often assumed that a benevolent government, enacting as the principal, needs to delegate many of its most important tasks and duties to self-interested bureaucrats. The goals of these two types of actors need not be aligned, as bureaucrats want to obtain personal gains from their activities (Aidt, 2016), while governments seek to correct market failures and maximize social welfare (Banerjee, 1997). Corruption arises when the principal cannot perfectly monitor the actions of its agents. Bureaucrats may exploit information asymmetries, accept bribes and engage in other forms of misgovernance, anticipating not being caught by the principal. As modeled by Acemoglu and Verdier (2000), government interventions need bureaucrats in order to collect information and implement policies, but bureaucrats are self-interested and hard to monitor perfectly.

Consequently, an evident implication of this framework is that strategies aiming to reduce information asymmetries between governments and bureaucrats, or at least affecting the agents' beliefs regarding these asymmetries, may be effective in curbing corruption. In other words, the right combination of monitoring and punishment may serve as a disciplining device (Becker and Stigler, 1974). Top-down monitoring, in which higher-level officials monitor lower-level bureaucrats, represents a popular method of accountability (Olken, 2007). In this context, anti-corruption programs based on (random) audits, like the one used in Brazil, aim to tackle corruption at least through two channels: first, as mentioned above, audits increase the amount of information available to the principal related to the agents' actions. Therefore, audits enhance the government's observability. Second, given the randomness of the process, the threat of being audited should have an effect on agents' beliefs and expectations of the probability of being caught and punished. In fact, recent evidence shows that audits are useful to curb corruption (Avis et al., 2018) and boost economic activity (Colonnelli and Prem, 2020).

However, audits are not a flawless strategy. In particular, resources are scarce and information may be so voluminous that anti-corruption agencies may easily get overwhelmed by the amount of available data. In this context, technological innovations in general, and predictive models in particular, may represent a positive shock on monitoring capacity. Random audits may be an effective strategy to alter bureaucrats' beliefs of the probability of being scrutinized but at the expense of allocating scarce resources in an inefficient way. Municipalities in which malfeasance is less likely may end up being audited, and vice versa. Consequently, machine learning models are useful because they allow agencies to identify, ex-ante, places where the likelihood of corruption is higher (Gallego et al., 2019). In fact, as we show below, the models that we estimate in this chapter are quite accurate in predicting corruption, suggesting that these strategies are useful if the goal is to reduce information asymmetries precisely in those places in which it would be most harmful.

2.2. The Role of the Public and the Private Sectors

A common feature of many anti-corruption programs that have been implemented and studied in recent years is that they target the incentives faced by bureaucrats to engage in malfeasance (Olken and Pande, 2012). Public sector wages may be a direct mechanism to discipline agents, as better-paid officials could face lower incentives to misbehave (Van Rijckeghem and Weder, 2001; Rauch and Evans, 2000; Di Tella and Schargrodsky, 2004). Higher salaries, coupled with civil service reform (Xu, 2018), may also attract better-qualified people into the public sector (Ferraz and Finan, 2011). Other pecuniary and non-pecuniary mechanisms may work as well, in such a way that additional benefits, conditioned on observable performance indicators, may discipline public officials (Glewwe et al., 2010; Muralidharan and Sundararaman, 2011; Duflo et al., 2012).

Other strategies that directly tackle the probability of being detected and punished have been implemented and studied as well. In addition to the top-down accountability strategies represented by audits that were discussed above (Olken, 2007; Ferraz and Finan, 2008; Avis et al., 2018), some other forms of monitoring have been promoted, such as grassroots participation (Bjorkman and Svensson, 2010). Moreover, both top-down and bottom-up accountability, which heavily depend on available information, may be enhanced by other mechanisms such as transparency (Djankov et al., 2010; Banerjee et al., 2012; Dunning et al., 2019), the media (Reinikka and Svensson, 2005; Ferraz and Finan, 2008) and technology (Lewis-Faupel et al., 2016; Gallego et al., 2019; Enikolopov et al., 2018).

However, these strategies reveal that the recent fight against corruption has overwhelmingly focused on bureaucrats and the public sector. Implicitly, it is assumed that features of the government, public bureaucracy, local and national level politics, electoral competition, among others, constitute the main predictors of corruption. However, corruption involves *quid pro quo* arrangements, in which the private sector is commonly involved. In fact, early cross-country studies (Laffont and N'Guessan, 1999; Svensson, 2005) underscore the importance of economic variables directly related to entrepreneurship, such as openness and competition, in explaining corruption. Our analysis represents a significant contribution on this front, for at least two reasons: first, our rich micro-data allows us to incorporate into the analysis of what predicts corruption an important set of features characterizing the private and financial sectors of Brazilian municipalities. Second, we use cutting-edge methods to quantify the *predictive power* of the different dimensions that may affect the levels of malfeasance encountered in the country. Surprisingly, we find that features associated with the public sector, local elections and public spending rank low in terms of their predictive importance, compared to variables related to the private sector and financial development.

3. BACKGROUND

In May 2003, under the administration of Luis Inácio Lula da Silva, the Brazilian central government launched a large anti-corruption program to fight the rampant corruption in the waste of public resources by local governments. The program consisted of 39 rounds of randomized audits of municipalities' expenditures—with replacement—over the 2003–14 period, followed by anti-corruption enforcement activities, such as the suspension of corrupt public officials and politicians.

The audits are conducted by the Office of the Comptroller General (Controladoria Geral da Uniao (CGU)), which is the federal agency responsible for ensuring the transparent use of public funds and is considered the main anti-corruption body in Brazil. At each audit round, approximately 60 municipalities were randomly selected, with replacement.[7] As of 2014, more than 99 percent of Brazil's 5570 municipalities were eligible, and 1881 had been selected at least once. Only municipalities below a certain population threshold were eligible for the program, and state capitals were excluded.

The audit process begins immediately after the random draw, with the federal CGU office detailing the audit to the various CGU state offices by means of a number of inspection orders. The audits investigate how the federal transfers from the central government to the municipality are spent and focus mostly on the previous three years. During an intense few weeks of fieldwork, the auditors analyze all relevant documents and receipts related to the spending of federal funds, interview local people, bureaucrats and other relevant parties, solicit direct anonymous complaints about malfeasance and take pictures to document the quality of public service delivery. Following this fieldwork, the auditors write a detailed audit report following the meticulous instructions from the federal CGU. These publicly available reports can span up to 300 pages and include organized analyses of all the information gathered during the weeks-long audit.

4. DATA

4.1. Measuring Corruption

Measuring corruption is challenging, and typical sources of information such as self-reported perceptions or malfeasance cases covered by the media tend to suffer from severe measurement error (Sequeira, 2012). To alleviate these concerns, we focus on Brazil's anti-corruption program discussed in the previous section. Since municipalities are not able to anticipate the audit, and because of the uniform criteria adopted by highly paid federal auditors in the auditing process, this setting is uniquely well-suited to the measurement of our main outcome variables.

Our primary measures of corruption intensity in a municipality are observed the year the audit takes place using administrative data collected by the anti-corruption federal agency that oversees the program, namely CGU. Out of 5570 municipalities in Brazil, 1084 have been randomly selected for at least 1 audit during the 2007–14 audit period we study. We focus on two binary definitions of corrupt municipalities, constructed using the share of the total number of irregularities over the size of the municipality.[8] Irregularity cases are extremely heterogeneous, ranging from cases of mismanagement in the allocation of public funds to outright bribery in government procurement. We consider corruption to be any case of moderate or severe irregularity as defined by CGU. 'Corrupt' ('Highly Corrupt') municipalities are those with an above-median (top quartile) share in the distribution of corruption across all municipalities audited.

4.2. Covariates

We augment our analysis with granular data on local characteristics at the municipality-year level that comes from multiple confidential and publicly available sources.

We use 147 covariates that we group into 8 categories: (i) private sector includes different measures of economic activity and sectoral distributions, (ii) public sector features include the number, relative importance and wages of public officials, (iii) financial development includes measures of credit-related variables from public and private banks, (iv) human capital includes measures of education and access to it, (v) public spending includes different types of spending as well as local procurement variables, (vi) local politics includes variables of political competition and alignment with the central government, (vii) natural resources' dependency includes the relevance of different natural resources and finally (viii) local demographics include variables related to income distribution, health statistics and crime.

The data sources and exact definitions of each variable are reported in Table 16.6. All variables, except the few in the Decennial Census, are measured as averages in the three years prior to the audit.

5. MACHINE LEARNING MODELS

In this section, we describe the machine learning models used to predict corruption as well as the training procedure and the different measures we use to assess the performance of the different models.

5.1. Models

In order to predict municipality-level corruption, we train a set of popular machine learning models, which include 'random forests', 'gradient boosting', 'neural networks' and 'LASSO'. Each model has weaknesses and strengths, and therefore we also rely on an ensemble model that combines the predictive capabilities of all individual models to optimize performance (Friedman et al., 2001). We ultimately let the data inform which model is best suited for this application based on out-of-sample performance.

5.1.1. LASSO

The LASSO regression, first introduced by Tibshirani (1996), is similar to a logistic regression but adds a penalization term based on the sum of the absolute values of the coefficients. This penalization term aims at shrinking the parameters toward zero. Hence this estimator is similar to a logit model, but it is more parsimonious, adding only those variables that are relevant predictors. One of the advantages of this model is that it is simple and less prone to overfitting. However, it is incapable of identifying complex relationships between the predictors and our outcome variable, i.e., corruption. The tuning parameter in the cross-validation is the weight of the penalization term in the objective function (λ), which is optimized over a grid of potential values.

5.1.2. Random forests

Random forests are ensembles of many decision trees, where each one of them is a sequence of rules that divides the sample into subgroups (called leaves) based on certain variable cutoffs. The prediction for each leaf, in the case of a classification task, is the most common outcome for the trained observations on that leaf, and the trees are fit so as to maximize the information gain of the resulting partitions of the data. Each tree in a random forest is constructed by sampling a random subset of the training data and a random subset of the predictors. Each of these trees generates a prediction, and the overall prediction of the random forest is the average (or the majority) of the predictions among all trees. In this application, we keep fixed the number of fitted trees (500) and use cross-validation to determine the optimal number of features available in every node.

5.1.3. Gradient boosting machine

Gradient boosting machines (GBM) are ensembles of weak learners, in this case, decision trees. Under boosting, classification algorithms are sequentially applied to a reweighted version of the training data (Friedman et al., 2000). GBM is a variant of random forests, in which trees are not fitted randomly or independently. Instead, each tree is fitted sequentially to the full dataset, in such a way that the weaknesses of trees are identified by using gradients in the loss function, allowing subsequent predictors to learn from the mistakes of the previous ones. In other words, a gradient descent procedure is used to minimize the loss when adding new trees. Consequently, as opposed to random forests, observations are not selected via bootstrapping but as a function of past errors. In this way, the addition of each tree offers a slight improvement in the model (Freund et al., 1999). In our models, we keep fixed the learning rate (shrinkage parameter) and the minimum number of observations in the terminal nodes to avoid overfitting and use cross-validation to determine the optimal number of trees and the interaction depth.

5.1.4. Neural networks

Neural networks model the relationship between input and output signals through models that mimic the way biological brains work. In particular, neural networks are composed of three basic elements: an activation function that, for each neuron, transforms the weighted average of input signals (predictors) into an output signal; a network topology, which is composed by the number of neurons, layers and connections used by the model; and a training algorithm, which determines the way in which connection weights are set with the task of activating or not neurons as a function of the input signals. This process determines the final prediction of the model. The most common activation functions include the logistic sigmoid, linear, saturated linear, hyperbolic tangent and Gaussian (radial basis) functions. In the end, the process entails an optimization problem in which the optimal weights of the input signals are determined for each node. In this analysis, we keep fixed a logistic activation function and use cross-validation to determine the optimal number of units in the hidden layer (size) and the regularization parameter (decay).

5.1.5. Super learner ensemble

Ensembles are collections of predictors which are grouped with each other in order to give a final prediction. It is usually the case that ensembles—as they result from the combination of different models—perform better than their individual components. For our analysis, we use the super learner ensemble method developed by Polley et al. (2011), which finds an optimal combination of individual prediction models by minimizing the cross-validated out-of-bag risk of these predictions. It has been shown that the super learner performs asymptotically as well as the best possible weighted combination of its constituent algorithms (Van der Laan et al., 2007). We use the super learner models not only to stack the individual predictions but also to test for the relative importance of different groups of variables to predict corruption.

5.2. Training and Testing

We use an indicator variable for corruption in year t as our variable of interest, while all predictors are measured as averages between the years $t-1$ and $t-3$, and in the case of census variables, they are all measured in 2000. In this way, we end up with a cross-sectional dataset with all the municipalities that were audited at least once between 2007 and 2014. For those audited more than once, we only use the first audit. In order to train our models, we conduct the following procedure:

1. We divide our dataset into 70 percent as our training set and 30 percent as our testing set.
2. In our training set, we perform a five-fold cross-validation procedure in order to train our models and choose the optimal combination of parameters. This method divides the training set into five different equal size samples at random. Then, a model is fit in four subsamples and then tested in the remaining one. We repeat this procedure for each of the five subsamples, so each one of them ends up being a validation set, and for each of the values of the tuning parameter grid of each model. Then, the best performing parameters are chosen.
3. The previous step is repeated ten times with different random partitions. Hence, we obtain ten 'optimal parameters', and we use as our optimal parameter the average of them. For the case of integer parameters, we round it to the closest integer.
4. Using these optimal parameters, we assess the performance of our models in the testing set that has never been used for training purposes.

We standardize the data by the mean and standard deviation of the training set. Table 16.1 shows the optimal parameters of our training procedure for each of our models.

Table 16.1 *Model's parameters*

Model	Optimal parameters	
	Corrupt	Highly Corrupt
Lasso	λ: 0.01	λ: 0.01
Random forest	Trees: 500	Trees: 500
	Mtry: 145	Mtry: 24
Gradient boosting	Trees: 50	Trees: 50
	Depth: 1	Depth: 1
	Shrinkage: 0.1	Shrinkage: 0.1
	Min obs: 10	Min obs: 10
Neural networks	Size: 5	Size: 5
	Decay: 0.1	Decay: 0.1
Ensemble weights	Lasso: 0.05	Lasso: 0.08
	Random forest: 0.22	Random forest: 0.32
	Gradient boosting: 0.55	Gradient boosting: 0.60
	Neural networks: 0.18	Neural networks: 0

Notes: This table presents the optimal parameters for each of the prediction models we implement after the training procedure described in Section 5.2.

5.3. Assessing Models' Performance

Once we have calibrated our model following the cross-validation procedure explained above, we compare the performance of the different models using the test set. We use as a first performance measure of interest the area under the receiver operating characteristic (ROC) curve (AUC). This is a measure of the trade-off between the true positive rate and false positive rate, as we vary the discrimination threshold. It can also be interpreted as the probability that, if we randomly select two observations, they will be correctly ordered in their predicted risk of corruption, i.e., the probability that the municipality at a greater risk for corruption is assigned a higher probability of corruption. We also present each model's level of *accuracy*, which corresponds to the proportion of municipalities correctly predicted as corrupt; models' *precision*, which is the proportion of positive identifications that are correct (or true positives over true positives plus false positives); models' *recall*, which is the proportion of actual positives identified correctly (true positives over true positives plus false negatives) and models' *F1*, which is the harmonic mean of precision and recall.

5.4. Identifying Best Predictors

To identify the municipality characteristics that best predict corruption, we first use *covariate* importance measures. For tree-based models, importance is measured as the information gain, or the homogeneity in the resulting partitions of our set of municipalities, achieved when splitting on each variable. In the procedure that we implement, importance is measured on a scale from 0 to 100, in such a way that each variable's information gain is expressed relative to the variable with the highest information gain. Hence, the most important predictor receives a score of 100 according to this scale and the scores start to decrease for the remaining variables. For the LASSO model the importance is determined by the estimated coefficients of the regression, where larger parameters (in absolute value) correspond to higher importance. In the case of neural networks, importance is determined by the weights that connect neurons within the network.

We then move to the analysis of the predictive performance of subgroups of related predictors in order to understand which categories matter the most. It may be the case that some groups do not have one particular variable that highly predicts corruption, but that the group as a whole has high predictive power. We perform this analysis in the following way. We estimate models including each category individually (i.e., excluding all variables that are not part of it) and compute the resulting AUC for the group. Then, we rank them according to their AUC and compare the computed AUC with a 50 percent level, which corresponds to the AUC of a random prediction 'model'. The category that increases the AUC by itself the most is the model with the highest predictive power level. We compute confidence intervals at a 95 percent confidence level by performing bootstrapping over the test set and computing the AUC for each sample. In this way, we are able to determine if there are any statistically significant differences in AUCs across categories.

6. FINDINGS

In this section, we present the results of our analysis. First, we focus on the overall performance of the predictive models and their robustness to alternative measures and specifications. Then, we identify the best individual and group predictors and their link to the corruption literature.

6.1. Models' Performance and the Predictability of Corruption

Figure 16.1 depicts the performance of our models. Using the two primary corruption measures of "Corrupt" (Panel A) and "Highly Corrupt" (Panel B) municipalities, we present the ROC curves of each individual model and the ensemble model: the models perform extremely well in predicting both corruption measures. Table 16.2 reports the AUC levels for every model, which range from a minimum of 0.95 (0.94) for neural networks to a maximum of 0.98 (0.99) for gradient boosting and the ensemble model when predicting

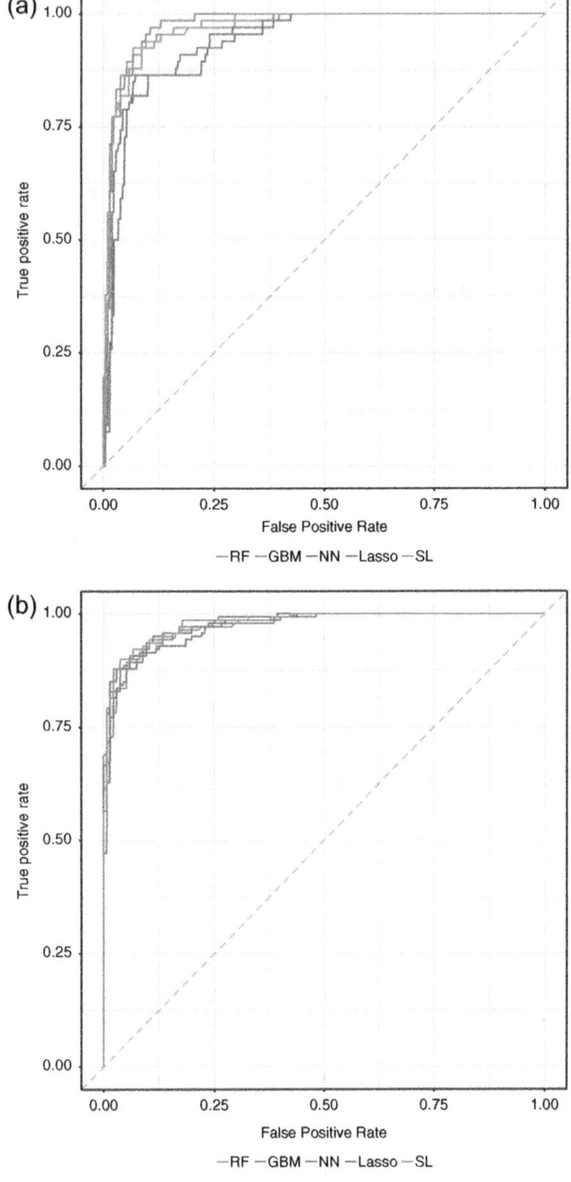

Notes: This figure presents the ROC curves for all our models.

Figure 16.1 ROC curve. Panel A: Corrupt. Panel B: Highly Corrupt

Table 16.2 Model performance

Model	LASSO	Random forest	Gradient boosting	Neural networks	Ensemble
			Panel A: Corrupt		
AUC	0.97	0.97	0.98	0.95	0.98
Accuracy	0.91	0.91	0.92	0.88	0.92
Precision	0.91	0.93	0.92	0.89	0.94
Recall	0.92	0.89	0.93	0.89	0.91
F1	0.91	0.91	0.92	0.89	0.92
			Panel B: Highly Corrupt		
AUC	0.96	0.98	0.99	0.94	0.98
Accuracy	0.91	0.94	0.94	0.90	0.94
Precision	0.80	0.88	0.86	0.79	0.89
Recall	0.82	0.88	0.90	0.82	0.85
F1	0.81	0.88	0.88	0.80	0.87

Notes: This table presents the model performance for all our prediction models. *AUC, accuracy, precision, recall* and *F1* are defined in Section 5.3.

"Corrupt" ("Highly Corrupt") municipalities. Generally, AUC levels of 0.8 and above are considered excellent.

Overall, in terms of individual models, Figure 16.1 shows that our tree-based algorithms, namely gradient boosting and random forest, outperform LASSO and neural networks. We find this to be the case not only in terms of AUC levels but also concerning precision, recall and F1, as is evident from Table 16.2. Not surprisingly, the ensemble model performs best, as it is constructed by optimizing the weights of each individual model.

In sum, these results suggest that by using fine-grained information from Brazilian municipalities, we are able to predict which areas exhibit higher levels of corruption. This is an important result from a policy perspective, as recent evidence shows that anti-corruption audits are effective tools to curb corruption (Avis et al., 2018) and boost economic activity (Colonnelli and Prem, 2020). However, at the same time they are expensive to conduct and are therefore restricted to a limited number of target areas. Risk scores estimated through machine learning models may help anti-corruption agencies optimize their resources, in such a way that audits may target those places in which information asymmetries are predicted to be more harmful.[9] In fact, recent efforts in European countries are being conducted in this direction (Petheram et al., 2019).

6.2. Robustness and Additional Analyses

We now present alternative specifications to test for the robustness of our main results. Specifically, we present the model performance for a continuous measure of corruption, i.e., the number of cases over the number of establishments. We estimate the continuous versions of our four models and compare their performance with a (naive) baseline model, in which the prediction is simply the mean value of our outcome variables. To measure performance, we use traditional metrics such as the root mean square error (RMSE), the mean absolute error (MAE) and the in-sample R-squared (see Table 16.3). Overall, our machine learning models perform better than the baseline case, with random forests and GBM usually achieving the highest levels of performance, as in the case of our discrete measure of corruption.

Additionally, we show that our findings for the 'Highly Corrupt' dummy are robust to account for the class imbalance in the outcome. Class imbalance may be an issue when the relevant category of the outcome that we want to predict, high levels of corruption in our case, is considerably less frequent than the other category. Different methods have been proposed in the literature to deal with this problem. Given the nature of our data, we use over- and under-sampling techniques to randomly increase (decrease) the number of highly corrupt (non-highly corrupt) municipalities. Table 16.4 shows that our results remain largely unchanged, suggesting that the high levels of predictive performance achieved by our original models are not driven by class imbalance.

Finally, we also estimate models for the discrete outcomes in which quadratic and interaction terms of all of our predictors are incorporated in order to account for non-linearities and more complex associations between corruption and municipality-level characteristics. In terms of model performance, the results of these estimations, available upon request, are quite similar to what we encountered for our baseline models.

6.3. What Are the Best Predictors of Corruption?

We now move to the analysis of the individual covariates that best predict corruption. Figure 16.2 presents the covariate-specific importance in predicting

Table 16.3 *Model performance for continuous outcomes*

Model	LASSO	Random forest	Gradient boosting	Neural networks	Ensemble
RMSE	8.08	6.39	4.94	0.95	0.98
MAE	4.37	3.13	1.80	0.88	0.92
R2	0.00	NA	0.92	0.89	0.94

Notes: This table presents the model performance using the share of cases over establishments. *Baseline* model is the case in which the mean of the outcome is used as the prediction. *RMSE* is the root mean square error in the testing set or the sample standard deviation of the differences between predicted values and observed values. *MAE* is the mean absolute error in the testing set or the sample absolute difference between predicted values and observed values. *R2* is the sample R-squared of the model.

Table 16.4 Model performance for high corruption accounting for class imbalance

Model	LASSO	Random forest	Gradient boosting	Neural networks	Ensemble
			Panel A: over-sampling		
Accuracy	0.90	0.96	0.94	0.93	0.96
Precision	0.89	0.94	0.92	0.92	0.94
Recall	0.92	0.99	0.98	0.96	0.99
F1	0.91	0.97	0.95	0.94	0.96
AUC	0.96	0.99	0.99	0.97	0.99
			Panel B: under-sampling		
Accuracy	0.87	0.91	0.96	0.86	0.94
Precision	0.87	0.93	0.95	0.87	0.95
Recall	0.89	0.91	0.97	0.88	0.93
F1	0.88	0.92	0.96	0.87	0.94
AUC	0.96	0.98	0.98	0.96	0.98

Notes: This table presents the model performance for the "Highly Corrupt" dummy accounting for class imbalance. In Panel A, we perform over-sampling, in which observations of the minority class (highly corrupt municipalities) are randomly replicated. In Panel B, we perform under-sampling, in which observations of the majority class (non-highly corrupt municipalities) are randomly excluded. *AUC*, *accuracy*, *precision* and *F1* are as defined in Section 5.3.

both outcome variables of 'Corrupt' and 'Highly Corrupt' municipalities and restricting the focus to the top ten features in each case. The results highlight the striking importance of a primary private sector covariate, namely the count of business establishments in the formal sector, in predicting corruption. Other important predictors are measures of market competition and human capital. These results go in line with early cross-country evidence (Svensson, 2005), which suggests that corrupt places tend to be less open to competition and regulate more the entry of firms to markets.

We also implement a variable selection procedure following Belloni et al. (2014). Table 16.5 presents the OLS from the doubly robust LASSO suggested by the authors. We find that five to six variables are selected as 'important' predictors, which suggests that our models are sparse. In this context, sparsity is a desirable trait, as it shows that our machine learning models are capable of simplifying a complex high-dimensional case into a simpler low-dimensional model that is easier to interpret (Hastie et al., 2015), something that conventional methods—such as OLS—will hardly achieve. This procedure allows us to determine which individual covariates matter the most and what is the direction of their correlations with corruption. In particular, these results show that private sector concentration (HHI) and the share of the construction sector are positively correlated with corruption. Other variables related to the

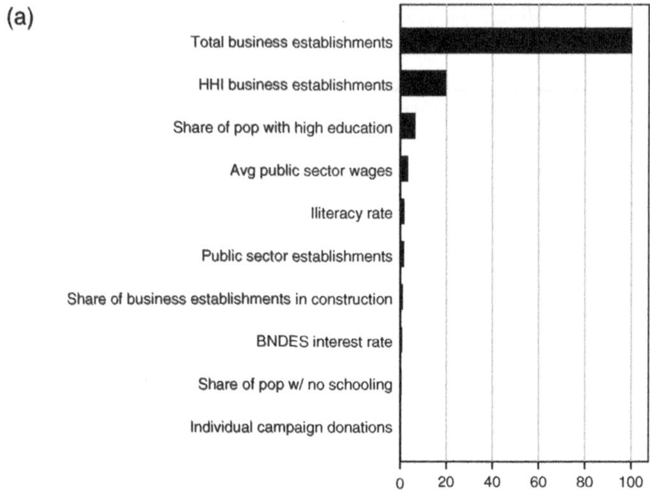

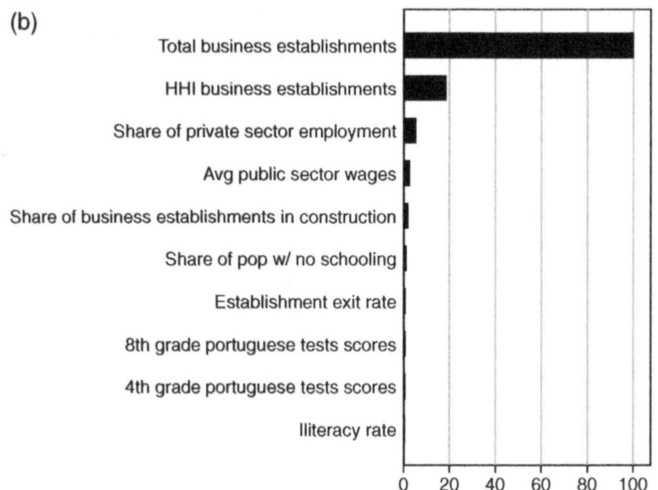

Notes: This figure presents the relative importance of covariates, as described in Section 5.4.

Figure 16.2 Covariates importance. Panel A: gradient boosting: Corrupt. Panel B: gradient boosting: Highly Corrupt. Panel C: random forest: Corrupt. Panel D: random forest: Highly Corrupt. Panel E: neural networks: Corrupt. Panel F: neural networks: Highly Corrupt. Panel G: LASSO: Corrupt. Panel H: LASSO: Highly Corrupt

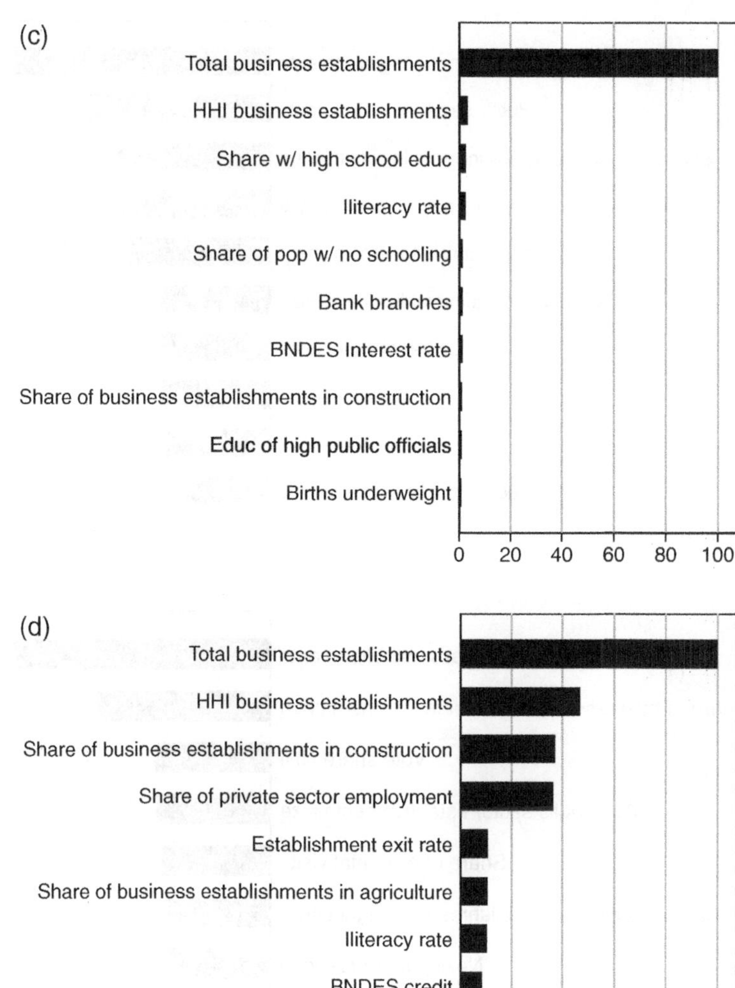

Figure 16.2 *(Continued)*

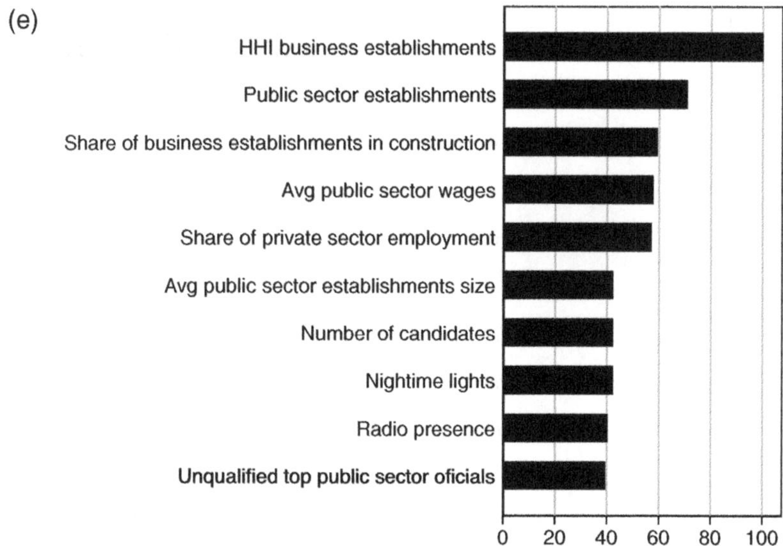

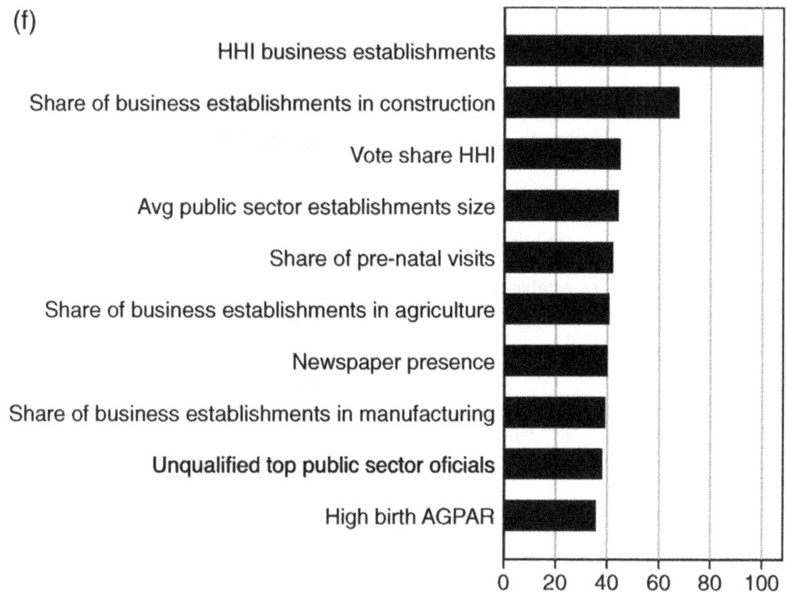

Figure 16.2 (Continued)

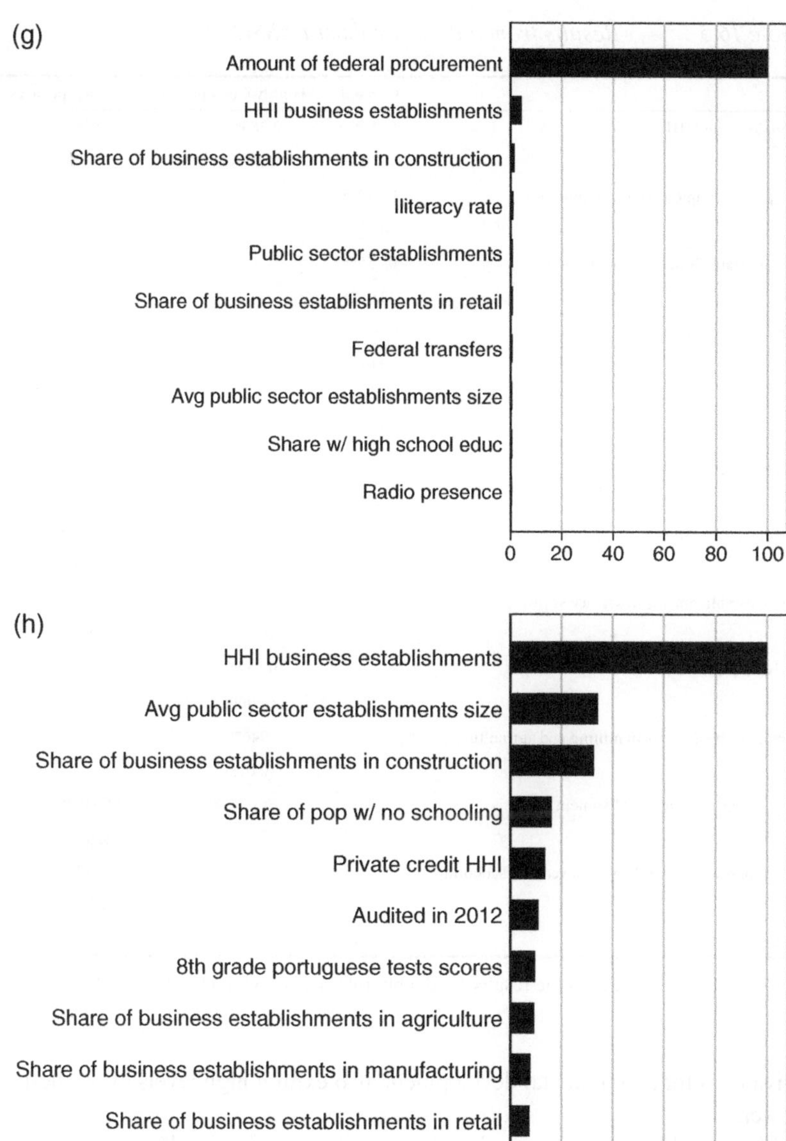

Figure 16.2 *(Continued)*

Table 16.5 *Results from a doubly robust LASSO*

	Corrupt	Highly Corrupt	Share of corrupt cases
Employment HHI	0.326***	0.265***	3.549***
	(0.013)	(0.014)	(0.398)
Sh private employees over population	−0.032***		
	(0.011)		
Sh of establishments in retail sector	−0.055***		
	(0.012)		
Sh rural population	0.035**		
	(0.014)		
Local radio	−0.030***		
	(0.011)		
Number of candidates	−0.021*		
	(0.012)		
Sh of establishments in construction sector		0.086***	1.723***
		(0.015)	(0.391)
Sh of establishments in service sector		0.042***	0.586**
		(0.010)	(0.273)
Private credit HHI		−0.059***	
		(0.009)	
Sh of establishments in mining and agriculture		0.046***	
		(0.013)	
Sh of medium size establishment			1.063***
			(0.366)
Sh of pop with more than eight years of schooling			−0.334
			(0.229)
Mean DV	0.508	0.255	3.836

Notes: This table presents the results for doubly robust LASSO model suggested by Belloni et al. (2014).

private sector and financial development also exhibit high levels of predictive power.

Motivated by this individual ranking analysis, in Figure 16.3, we perform an estimation where we categorize all 147 covariates into eight groups, as shown in Table 16.6. Sequentially and separately, adding each group to the estimation of the ensemble model, we assess the performance of each of them as measured by the AUC. We also present confidence intervals at a 95 percent confidence level by performing bootstrapping over the test set.

Consistent with our analysis of individual features, we find that the *private sector* category is the strongest predictor of corruption, followed by the

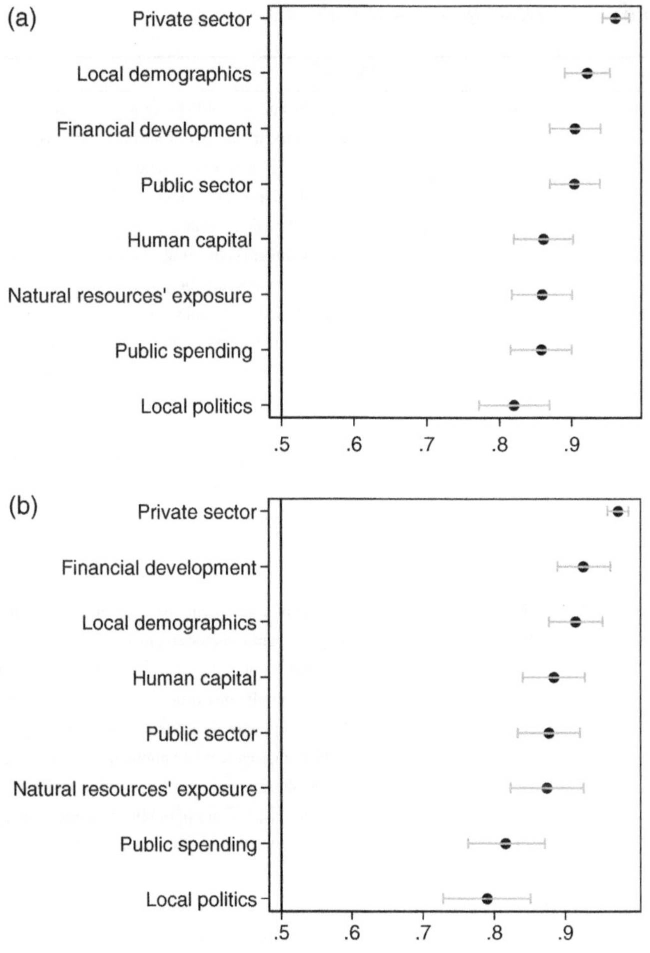

Notes: This figure presents the relative importance of group of covariates, as described in Section 5.4. Confidence intervals at 95 percent are constructed by bootstrapping over the test set.

Figure 16.3 Group importance. Panel A: Corrupt. Panel B: Highly Corrupt

categories of *financial development*, *local demographics* and *human capital* (see Panel A Figure 16.3).[10] The categories of *public sector*, *natural resources' exposure* and *public spending* are less important predictors, and *local politics* is the least important one for both measures of corruption.

These results are somewhat surprising, given the overwhelming focus of both the academic and policy literature on the latter category types. For

Table 16.6 Description of variables

Categories	Source	Variables
Private sector	RAIS	Average business establishments size based on employment, number of business establishments, payroll per employee, average business establishments payroll, share of business establishments entering, share of business establishments exiting, business establishments churning, share of private sector workers over population, Hirschman–Herfindahl index based on business establishments size, average growth in business establishments and in employment in past 3 years, share of business establishments below 5 employees, share of business establishments between 5 and 25 employees, share of business establishments above 25 employees, share of business establishments in construction, share of business establishments in retail, share of business establishments in services.
Public sector	RAIS	Share of public sector employees over population, average wage of public sector employees, share of public institutions opening, share of public institutions closing, public institutions churning, share of workers by position within the institution, average growth in public employment and public institutions in past three years, share of public sector employees from municipal institutions, number of public institutions, average public institution size based on employment.
Financial development	BNDES ESTBAN, UNICAD	Share of business establishments receiving public loans, number of public loans per business establishment, total public credit per business establishment, average interest rate in public lending, bank branches per capita, banks per capita, total private credit per capita, total deposits per capita and Hirschman–Herfindahl index based on private banks' total assets and based on private banks' credit.

(Continued)

Table 16.6 (Continued)

Categories	Source	Variables
Human capital	2000 Census, Ministry of Education, RAIS	Literacy rate, the share of population between 15 and 24 years old that finished the first, second and third cycle of primary education (Census), illiteracy rate (Census), average test scores in Portuguese and math for nationwide tests at 4th and 8th grade, average private sector employees' education, average private sector employees' education by worker position within the firm, share of unqualified public employees based on job requirements, share of unqualified public employees by position within the institution, average public employees' education, average public employees' education by position within the institution, number of higher public education institutions per capita, number of higher private education institutions per capita.
Local politics	TSE	Number of candidates, Hirschman–Herfindahl index based on the vote shares, margin of victory between the winner and the runner-up, an indicator for whether the mayor is in his second term, an indicator for whether the mayor's party is the same as the one of the governor, an indicator for whether the mayor's party is from the same party as the one of the president, an indicator if the mayor is from a right-wing party, an indicator if the mayor is from a left-wing party, average candidate campaign donations and expenditures for firms and individuals and per capita campaign donations and expenditures for firms and individuals.
Public spending	Ministry of Planning, Budget, and Management	Total expenditures per capita, personnel expenditures per capita, budget surplus per capita, total revenue per capita, federal transfers of capital per capita, federal current transfers per capita, transfers from the national tax fund per capita, share of business establishments in the municipality with public procurement, number of contracts per business establishment, federal procurement expenditure over population, share of discretionary contracts and share of competitive contracts.

(*Continued*)

Table 16.6 (Continued)

Categories	Source	Variables
Local demographics	2000 Census, NOAA, Ministry of Health	Population density, GDP per capita, share of population living in rural areas (Census), deaths by aggression, GINI coefficient for income distribution (Census), average night light intensity coverage performing deblurring, inter-calibration and geometric corrections, local radio, local newspapers, infant mortality rate, child mortality rate, average number of prenatal visits, share of abnormal births, share of underweight births, share of births with more than seven prenatal visits and share of births with more than four prenatal visits.
Natural resources' exposure	RAIS IBGE	Share of business establishments in agriculture and mining sector, share of production of each of the top seven crops in the country multiplied by the log change in international prices and share of value of production over GDP (as constructed in Bernstein et al., 2018). The crops included are sugar cane, oranges, soybeans, maize, rice, rice, banana and wheat, covering more than 98 percent of total agricultural production.

example, several studies of patronage suggest that the size of the public sector is strongly linked to corruption (Robinson and Verdier, 2013; Gallego et al., 2020a; Colonnelli et al., 2020). Similarly, an important strand of literature has focused on the key role played by public sector compensation in curbing corruption (Di Tella and Schargrodsky, 2003; DalBo et al., 2013). Other studies suggest that elections may discipline politicians, as informed voters may punish candidates who engage in corrupt activities (Ferraz and Finan, 2008; Chong et al., 2015; Dunning et al., 2019). Moreover, the resource-curse literature (Sachs and Warner, 1995) suggests that corruption may be one of the reasons explaining why resource-rich places often exhibit lower levels of development (Shaxson, 2007). The emphasis on the role of the private and financial sectors, on the other hand, remains significantly lower (Rose-Ackerman and Palifka, 2016).

7. CONCLUSIONS

The ability to predict corruption is crucial to policy. In the context of Brazilian municipalities, we show that machine learning models and rich micro-data provide a powerful combination to accurately predict where corruption in local public spending is most likely to take place. Interestingly, we find that private sector, financial development and human capital features are the most important predictors of corruption, while public sector and political features play a secondary role.

Our findings have important policy implications that may affect how we think the fight against corruption should be carried out. First, the fact that our algorithms achieve high levels of performance implies that these types of methods, coupled with recent advances on the fronts of technology and transparency, represent a positive shock on governments' monitoring capacity. Audits conducted by anti-corruption agencies throughout the world tend to follow heuristic rules or random assignment mechanisms. Randomness may have important effects on agents' beliefs and expectations but at the expense of generating inefficient allocations of scarce auditing resources. Our results suggest that a targeted distribution of monitoring, based on the risk scores that result from machine learning algorithms, may help governments distribute audits to places in which information asymmetries may be more harmful.

In addition, it is important to recognize that recent efforts to control corruption, such as the consolidation of top-down and bottom-up accountability mechanisms, salary and incentive-based interventions, civil service reforms, among others, overwhelmingly rest on the assumption that features associated with the public sector and local politics are the most important predictors of malfeasance. However, our covariate-importance metrics, both at the individual and especially at the group level, reveal that other dimensions are more important in predicting corruption. In particular, our models suggest that features associated with the private sector and financial development across Brazilian municipalities achieve the highest levels of predictive power. Hence, even though our analysis is not causal in nature, it tentatively suggests that a new generation of interventions to be tested and implemented in the future should focus more on the role that the private sector, financial institutions, competition and markets play in enhancing or curbing corruption.

NOTES

1. We are grateful to the Stanford Institute for Innovation in Developing Economies (SEED), the Private Enterprise Development in Low-Income Countries (PEDL) Initiative by the Centre for Economic Policy Research (CEPR), the Stanford Center for International Development (SCID), the Stanford Institute for Research in the Social Sciences (IRiSS), the Abdul Latif Jameel Poverty Action Lab (J-PAL) Governance Initiative and Universidad del Rosario for financial support. We are grateful for the comments and suggestions at the Corruption and Big Data Conference at Universidad del Rosario.
2. Booth School of Business, University of Chicago.
3. Department of Economics, Universidad del Rosario.
4. Department of Economics, Universidad del Rosario.
5. Some theories predict that corruption may be efficient (Leff, 1964), but these theories are mostly rejected by the empirical literature and, importantly, they refer to second-best contexts.
6. See Olken and Pande (2012), Rose-Ackerman and Palifka (2016) and Fisman and Golden (2017) for extensive reviews of the literature.

7. The randomization is linked to the draw of a popular national lottery. The implied audit probability in any given round, which is constant within a state, is therefore quite low (1 percent within a round, and 3 percent within a year). Additionally, there is a small exception to the random draw with replacement, as municipalities cannot be selected if they were selected in one of the previous three rounds.
8. Municipality size is computed as the number of business establishments in the municipality.
9. Indeed, motivated by value-for-money concerns, Brazil's anti-corruption agency recently moved to a semi- randomized audit program, where previous audit results are used with the goal of predicting the highest-risk municipalities to target. This strategy is common across several Supreme Audit Institutions around the world.
10. Local demographics include a host of health and population measures, as well as other measures such as media access which do not perfectly fit into the other seven categories.

REFERENCES

Acemoglu, D. and Verdier, T. (2000). The choice between market failure and corruption. *American Economic Review*, 90(1):194–211.

Aidt, T. (2016). Rent seeking and the economics of corruption. *Constitutional Political Economy*, 27(1):142–57.

Avis, E., Ferraz, C., and Finan, F. (2018). Do government audits reduce corruption? Estimating the impacts of exposing corrupt politicians. *Journal of Political Economy*, 126(5):1912–64.

Bandiera, O., Prat, A., and Valletti, T. (2009). Active and passive waste in government spending: Evidence from a policy experiment. *American Economic Review*, 99(4):1278–308.

Banerjee, A. (1997). A theory of misgovernance. *The Quarterly Journal of Economics*, 112(4):1289–332.

Banerjee, A., Mullainathan, S., and Hanna, R. (2012). *Corruption*. Technical report, National Bureau of Economic Research.

Bazzi, S., Blair, R. A., Blattman, C., Dube, O., Gudgeon, M., and Peck, R. (2019). "The promise and pitfalls of conflict prediction: evidence from Colombia and Indonesia." *The Review of Economics and Statistics*, 104(4): 764–79.

Becker, G. and Stigler, G. (1974). Law enforcement, malfeasance and the compensation of enforcers. *Journal of Legal Studies*, 3(1):1–19.

Belloni, A., Chernozhukov, V., and Hansen, C. (2014). High-dimensional methods and inference on structural and treatment effects. *Journal of Economic Perspectives*, 28(2):29–50.

Bernstein, S., Colonnelli, E., Malacrino, D., and McQuade, T. (2018). *Who Creates New Firms When Local Opportunities Arise?* Technical report, National Bureau of Economic Research.

Besley, T. and McLaren, J. (1993). Taxes and bribery: The role of wage incentive. *Economic Journal*, 103(416):119–41.

Bjorkman, M. and Svensson, J. (2010). When is community-based monitoring effective? evidence from a randomized experiment in primary health in uganda. *Journal of the European Economic Associarion*, 8(2):571–81.

Blair, R. A., Blattman, C., and Hartman, A. (2017). Predicting local violence: Evidence from a panel survey in liberia. *Journal of Peace Research*, 54(2):298–312.

Blumenstock, J., Cadamuro, G., and On, R. (2015). Predicting poverty and wealth from mobile phone metadata. *Science*, 350(6264):1073–76.

Bogomolov, A., Lepri, B., Staiano, J., Oliver, N., Pianesi, F., and Pentland, A. (2014). Once upon a crime: Towards crime prediction from demographics and mobile data. In Proceedings of the 16th International Conference on Multimodal Interaction, pages 427–34. Istanbul: ACM.

Chong, A., de la O, A., Karlan, D., and Wantchekon, L. (2015). Does corruption information inspire the fight or quash the hope? A field experiment in Mexico on voter turnout, choice, and party identification. *Journal of Politics*, 77(1):55–71.

Colonnelli, E. and Prem, M. (2022). Corruption and firms. *Review of Economic Studies*, 89(2): 695–732.

Colonnelli, E., Prem, M., and Teso, E. (2020). Patronage and selection in public sector organizations. *American Economic Review*, 110(10):3071–99.

Dabla-Norris, E. (2002). A game theoretical analysis of corruption in bureaucracies. In Gupta, G. T. A. S., editor, *Governance, Corruption, Economic Performance*, chapter 5, pages 111–34. The International Monetary Fund.

DalBo, E., Finan, F., and Rossi, M. (2013). Strengthening state capabilities: The role of financial incentives in the call to public service. *Quarterly Journal of Economics*, 128(3):1169–218.

Di Tella, R. and Schargrodsky, E. (2003). The role of wages and auditing during a crackdown on corruption in the City of Buenos Aires. *Journal of Law and Economics*, 46(1):269–92.

Di Tella, R. and Schargrodsky, E. (2004). Do police reduce crime? estimates using the allocation of police forces after a terrorist attack. *American Economic Review*, 94(1):115–33.

Djankov, S., Porta, R. L., de Silanes, F. L., and Shleifer, A. (2002). The regulation of entry. *Quarterly Journal of Economics*, 117(1):1–37.

Djankov, S., Porta, R. L., de Silanes, F. L., and Shleifer, A. (2010). Disclosure by politicians. *American Economic Journal: Applied Economics*, 2(2):179–209.

Duflo, E., Hanna, R., and Ryan, S. (2012). Incentives work: Getting teachers to come to school. *American Economic Review*, 102(4):1241–78.

Dunning, T., Grossman, G., Humphreys, M., Hyde, S., and McIntosh, C. (2019). *Metaketa I: The Limits of Electoral Accountability*. Cambridge University Press.

Enikolopov, R., Petrova, M., and Sonin, K. (2018). Social media and corruption. *American Economic Journal: Applied Economics*, 10(1):150–74.

Ferraz, C. and Finan, F. (2008). Exposing corrupt politicians: The effects of Brazil's publicly released audits on electoral outcomes. *The Quarterly Journal of Economics*, 123(2):703–45.

Ferraz, C. and Finan, F. (2011). Motivating politicians: The impacts of monetary incentives on quality and performance. Working Paper No. w14906. National Bureau of Economic Research.

Fisman, R. and Golden, M. (2017). *Corruption. What Everyone Needs to Know*. Oxford University Press.

Fisman, R. and Svensson, J. (2007). Are corruption and taxation really harmful to growth? firm level evidence. *Journal of Development Economics*, 83(1):63–75.

Fisman, R. and Wang, Y. (2015). The mortality cost of political connections. *Review of Economic Studies*, 82(4):1346–82.

Freund, Y., Schapire, R., and Abe, N. (1999). A short introduction to boosting. *Journal-Japanese Society For Artificial Intelligence*, 14(771–780):1612.

Friedman, J., Hastie, T., Tibshirani, R., et al. (2000). Additive logistic regression: A statistical view of boosting (with discussion and a rejoinder by the authors). *The Annals of Statistics*, 28(2):337–407.

Friedman, J., Hastie, T., and Tibshirani, R. (2001). *The Elements of Statistical Learning*, volume 1. Springer Series in Statistics.

Gallego, J., Rivero, G., and Martinez, J. (2019). *Preventing rather than Punishing: An Early Warning Model of Malfeasance in Public Procurement*. Mimeo.

Gallego, J., Li, C., and Wantchekon, L. (2020a). *A Theory of Broker-mediated Clientelism*. Mimeo.

Gallego, J. A., Prem, M., and Vargas, J. F. (2020b). Corruption in the times of pandemia. Documento de Trabajo Universidad del Rosario. No. 018178.

Glewwe, P., Ilias, N., and Kremer, M. (2010). Teacher incentives. *American Economic Journal: Applied Economics*, 2(3):205–27.

Hanna, R., Bishop, S., Nadel, S., Scheffler, G., and Durlacher, K. (2011). *The Effectiveness of Anti-corruption Policy*. EPPI Centre Report, (1909).

Hastie, T., Tibshirani, R., and Wainwright, M. (2015). *Statistical Learning with Sparsity. The Lasso and Generalizations*. Taylor and Francis Group.

Kleinberg, J., Ludwig, J., Mullainathan, S., and Obermeyer, Z. (2015). Prediction policy problems. *American Economic Review: Papers and Proceedings*, 105(5):491–95.

Laffont, J.-J. and N'Guessan, T. (1999). Competition and corruption in an agency relationship. *Journal of Development Economics*, 60(2):271–95.

Leff, N. H. (1964). Economic development through bureaucratic corruption. *American Behavioral Scientist*, 8(3):8–14.

Lewis-Faupel, S., Neggers, Y., Olken, B., and Pande, R. (2016). Can electronic procurement improve infrastructure provision? evidence from a large rural road program in India. *American Economic Journal: Economic Policy*, 8(3):258–83.

Lima, M. S. M. and Delen, D. (2020). Predicting and explaining corruption across countries: A machine learning approach. *Government Information Quarterly*, 37(1):101407.

Lopez-Iturriaga, F. and Sanz, I. (2018). Predicting public corruption with neural networks: An analysis of Spanish provinces. *Social Indicators Research*, 140(3): 975–98.

Mauro, P. (1995). Corruption and growth. *Quarterly Journal of Economics*, 110(3):681–712.

Mookherjee, D. and Png, I. (1992). Monitoring vis-a-vis investigation in enforcement of law. *American Economic Review*, 82(3):556–64.

Mueller, H. F. and Rauh, C. (2019). The hard problem of prediction for conflict prevention. *Journal of the European Economic Association*, 1–28.

Muralidharan, K. and Sundararaman, V. (2011). Teacher performance pay: Experimental evidence from India. *Journal of Political Economy*, 119(1):39–77.

Olken, B. (2007). Monitoring corruption: Evidence from a field experiment in Indonesia. *Journal of Political Economy*, 115(2):200–49.

Olken, B. and Pande, R. (2012). Corruption in developing countries. *Annual Review of Economics*, 4:479–509.

Paula, E. L., Ladeira, M., Carvalho, R. N., and Marzagao, T. (2016). Deep learning anomaly detection as support fraud investigation in Brazilian exports and anti-money laundering. In 2016 15th IEEE International Conference on Machine Learning and Applications (ICMLA), pages 954–60. Anaheim, CA: IEEE.

Petheram, A., Pasquarelli, W., and Stirling, R. (2019). *The Next Generation of Anti-corruption Tools: Big Data, Open Data and Artificial Intelligence*. Technical report, Oxford Insights.

Polley, E. C., Rose, S., and Van der Laan, M. J. (2011). Super learning. In *Targeted Learning*, pages 43–66. Springer.

Rauch, J. and Evans, P. (2000). Bureaucratic structure and bureaucratic performance in less developed countries. *Journal of Public Economics*, 75(1):49–71.

Reinikka, R. and Svensson, J. (2005). Fighting corruption to improve schooling: Evidence from a newspaper campaign in Uganda. *Journal of the European Economic Associarion*, 3(2–3):259–67.

Robinson, J. and Verdier, T. (2013). The political economy of clientelism. *Scandinavian Journal of Economics*, 115(2):260–91.

Rose-Ackerman, S. and Palifka, B. J. (2016). *Corruption and Government: Causes, Consequences, and Reform*. Cambridge University Press.

Sachs, J. and Warner, A. (1995). The big rush, natural resource booms, and growth. *Journal of Development Economics*, 59(1):43–76.

Sequeira, S. (2012). Chapter 6 advances in measuring corruption in the field. In *New Advances in Experimental Research on Corruption*, pages 145–75. Emerald Group Publishing Limited.

Shaxson, N. (2007). Oil, corruption and the resource curse. *International Affairs*, 83(6):1123–40.

Svensson, J. (2005). Eight questions about corruption. *Journal of Economic Perspectives*, 19(3):19–42.

Tibshirani, R. (1996). Regression shrinkage and selection via the lasso. *Journal of the Royal Statistical Society. Series B (Methodological)*, 267–88.

Van der Laan, M. J., Polley, E. C., and Hubbard, A. E. (2007). Super learner. *Statistical Applications in Genetics and Molecular Biology*, 6(1): 1–21.

Van Rijckeghem, C. and Weder, B. (2001). Bureaucratic corruption and the rate of temptation: Do wages in the civil service affect corruption, and by how much? *Journal of Development Economics*, 65(2):307–31.

Xu, G. (2018). The costs of patronage: Evidence from the British empire. *American Economic Review*, 108(11):3170–98.

17. Organised crime, state and the legitimate monopoly of violence[1]

Tommy E. Murphy and Paolo Vanin

1. INTRODUCTION

> A compulsory political association with continuous organization will be called a "state" if and in so far as its administrative staff successfully upholds a claim to the monopoly of the legitimate use of physical force in the enforcement of its order.
>
> Max Weber, *The Theory of Social and Economic Organization*

The definition of 'state' is notoriously elusive, but few people would contend that the one provided by Weber above – or small variations of it – is the one that comes to mind more often. Traced back at least to Hobbes's *Leviathan*, and extensively used by a myriad of scholars, the idea of 'legitimate monopoly of violence' is indelibly linked to the *nature* of states, that is, why and how they appear. Yet it is also crucial for understanding their *capabilities*. It is in the end the possibility of exercising coercion that gives states the power to extract resources from the population (giving them fiscal capacity) and to enforce their rules (giving them legal capacity). Coercion is so important that it is hard to conceive a state that does not use violence or the threat of force to rule. In fact, most other definitions of state also centre on coercion. North, for example, talks about a state as an organisation that has 'a comparative advantage in violence, extending over a geographic area whose boundaries are determined by its power to tax constituents' (North, 1981: 21). It is in taming this violence that states make their contribution to the prosperity of societies.

The 'legitimate' or 'monopoly' elements of the Weberian take are certainly not less important, but they are more problematic to analyse. Even in modern, developed democracies we can think of occasional uses of force by the government that could be considered illegitimate. And one can think of innumerable cases where the monopoly of violence of the state is seriously contested by actors that could be considered more or less legitimate. Cases abound: at the end of the twentieth century many terrorist groups and *guerrillas*, like the Irish Republican Army, *ETA*, *Sendero Luminoso* or the *Ejército Zapatista de Liberación Nacional*, received considerable attention; in recent years many consider organised crime in the form of mafias or cartels as the main agents fighting over that monopoly. Related to the latter case, it is interesting to note that at least since the 1980s Tilly was noting that many of the activities carried out by states are not necessarily too different from what we normally refer to as organised crime:

> If protection rackets represent organized crime at its smoothest, then war making and state making—quintessential protection rackets with the advantage of legitimacy—qualify as our largest examples of organized crime.
>
> (Tilly, 1985: 169)

Tilly has a point there. Save for legitimacy – and, as we pointed out, that is seriously questioned for many states – it is easy to find similarities in the behaviour of states and organised crime. And the presence of those similarities partly explains the complex relationship between these organisations.

In this essay we discuss this particular relationship through the lens of this idea of the legitimate monopoly of violence. We explore the role of violence in the appearance and development of states, in the presence of both productive and appropriative activities, organised crime as illegal organisations often claiming the legitimate use of that violence and then both states and criminal organisations fighting over the monopoly of violence.

2. ANARCHY, VIOLENCE AND THE STATE

Violence *and* cooperation are defining elements of social behaviour. Both have been invoked as key to understanding the rise of societies, and the way in which they interact contributes to explaining how these societies persist, thrive or collapse. For one, humans are exceptionally cooperative, even in very large groups of non-related individuals (Henrich and Muthukrishna, 2021). This is surprising because there are no good reasons to think this would be the case *ex ante*. Jean Jacques Rousseau famously stated in his *Second Discourse* (1755) that 'nothing is gentler than a man in his primitive state', but nothing seems to be further from the truth (Keeley, 1996). There are at least three pieces of evidence suggesting 'man in his primitive state' was *not* gentle at all: the aggressiveness of non-human primates (such as chimpanzees and bonobos), the violent nature of contemporary nonindustrial societies as it is described in ethnographic accounts and the extensive archaeological evidence that this was indeed the case for primitive societies (Seabright, 2010, Ch. 3). In this sense, Thomas Hobbes appears to have depicted a more accurate picture of life in a 'natural state' in his *Leviathan* (1651), when he described it as one of 'continual fear, and danger of violent death; and the life of man, solitary, poor, nasty, brutish, and short', not too different from the one William Golding vividly portrayed three centuries later for the children stranded in the island of the *Lord of the Flies*.

Cooperation is not necessarily to be expected *ex ante* because it usually involves making choices that help or avoid hurting other individuals at some personal cost. In that sense, cooperation is rare in mammals save for humans and normally limited to cases of close relatives or a small number of reciprocators (see, e.g., Boyd and Richerson, 2005). Kin-based altruism, which explains cooperation between close relatives, and reciprocal altruism, which relates to tit-for-tat behaviour in small groups of people that interact frequently, are quite widespread and can be rationalised in simple models of genetic and/or cultural inheritance (Henrich and Muthukrishna, 2021). That is, in small kin-related groups with only occasional interactions with individuals outside the group, cooperation can be sustained, and the level of conflict can be contained and dealt with informally (Diamond, 1997). But as societies grow in size, those mechanisms cease to be enough. By construction, both kin-relatedness and the potential for reciprocity decline with the size of population, making it difficult to rely upon informal conflict resolution. And the sources of conflict also quite likely increase. In most cases, the rise of large civilisations was made possible thanks to the appearance of agriculture, which generated a higher potential not only for economic growth but also for conflict. Agriculture created a surplus – either in the form of excess labour or an excess product in the form of a non-perishable good such as grain – that could be looted and appropriated (Allen, 1997; Mayshar et al., 2020). Here lies an interesting paradox: prosperity increases the risk of violence, and violence hinders prosperity (Dal Bó et al., 2015).

A few societies were able to solve that puzzle, and those that did relied upon institutions and social arrangements of different sorts. For authors like Acemoglu and Robinson (2016), prosperity is largely dependent on the eventual appearance of inclusive economic institutions, and these are more likely to appear in contexts with inclusive political institutions that show at least some degree of both pluralism and political centralisation. This second element is of particular relevance, because the crucial problem social orders needed to solve to regulate economic activity, impose taxes and provide public goods was that of violence (North et al., 2009). As pointed out by Bates:

> Political development occurs when people domesticate violence, transforming coercion from a means of predation into a productive resource. Coercion becomes

> productive when it is employed not to seize or to destroy wealth but rather to safeguard and promote its creation.
>
> (Bates, 2001: 101–102)

Societies have been able to domesticate violence in many different ways, and the most successful is probably that of political centralisation in the form of a state. Instead of eliminating violence, states have been able to actually tame it via somehow legitimating its monopoly:

> In most of the world, the activity of states has created a startling contrast between the violence of the state's sphere and the relative non-violence of civilian life away from the state . . . European states led the construction of that contrast. They did so by building up fearsome coercive means of their own as they deprived civilian populations of access to those means.
>
> (Tilly, 1990: 68–9)

And the state has been indeed successful in this task. Pinker (2011) provides some empirical evidence validating Hobbes' idea that the state has been able to deal with the problem of violence successfully. The comparison between states and nonstate societies in terms of deaths in warfare shows an outstanding difference in the percentage of deaths caused by violent attacks rather than natural causes. Leaving aside figures displayed by prehistoric societies for which we have limited records, the percentage of violent deaths in the worst performing state, which is pre-Columbian Mexico, is still much lower (5 per cent) than the average of the hunter-gatherers' group (14 per cent) and the hunter-horticulturalists' group (24.5 per cent). In this latter group, there is also the last European nonstate society, the Montenegrins, whose percentage is almost identical to that of the whole group. Similar results are found when comparing states and nonstates with respect to the rate of death in warfare, with an average of 524 annual war deaths per 100 000 people in nonstate polities, while twentieth-century Germany only reached 144. There is a general (mis)perception that many tribes are less prone to wars and are therefore considered pacific. The Semai, a tribe living in Malaysia, is often taken as an example of one of the least violent. Nonetheless, Semai people murder each other at a rate which is comparable to the most dangerous American cities in the 1990s and three times greater than that of the US in the twentieth century.

Yet, the state has not always meant a panacea, nor does its absence indicate incapability to deal with the problem. In fact, whereas now nearly all individuals are under the umbrella of a nation-state, not long ago self-governing peoples were the great majority of humankind (Scott, 2010). Nonstate polities developed cultural patterns and informal institutions aimed at repelling state absorption and preventing state formation, such as in the vast territory of

Zomia superbly studied by Scott (2010), the ideal zone of refuge for all those peoples who preferred to avoid coercion, conscription and taxation. These societies were characterised by extreme equality among individuals, fluid leadership and a strong aversion to authority. Specifically, in South-East Asia these features were often accompanied by religious heterodoxy and multi-ethnic demography. The inhabitants of Zomia were, in fact, quite diverse with respect to ethnicity, culture and religion. However, they shared the choice of having fled a state. The possibility to evade the extraction of agricultural surpluses by the elites, conscription during wars and *corvée* labour during peace must have been strongly appealing to many, which is not surprising as life conditions under early states were probably worse than in their self-governing counterparts.

How societies are able to achieve large-scale cooperation in the absence of a state has been explored in different studies, notably in the work of Peter T. Leeson (2014) about anarchy. Anarchy is usually referred to as a synonym of disorder, violence and primitiveness but, according to Leeson, this is not necessarily the case:

> Gover*nance* – social rules that protect individuals' property and institutions of their enforce*ment* – doesn't require government, which is but one means of supplying governance. Hobbes overlooked the possibility of *self*-government: privately created social rules and institutions of their enforcement. He also underestimated the possibility of truly horrible governments.
>
> (Leeson, 2014: 1; his emphasis)

Leeson (2014) also argues that states, especially when they appear in a predatory form, can even be outperformed by efficient anarchies, that is, one welfare maximising individuals would choose over a government. This is the case of small primitive societies, whose persistence in statelessness can be explained by their relatively small size and homogeneity. The higher level of trade provided by a well-functioning government is in this case an ignorable advantage due to the lack of exchange opportunities. Individuals' low and standardised productive abilities make these societies egalitarian and small enough not to incentivise the creation of a state power which would also need some organisational cost. Thus, stateless societies can only persist when they find themselves in a small and isolated environment and in the absence of conditions allowing economic development. A common feature of these cases of 'efficient anarchies' is that societies find somehow private order institutions to deal with the problem of violence in a context where the state is weak or entirely absent, or the society wants to actively avoid the state. What states regard as criminal organisations can sometimes provide such institutions.

3. PRODUCTION, APPROPRIATION AND THE MONOPOLY OF VIOLENCE

Organised crime resembles states in that it not only extracts resources through violence (or its threat) but also supplies protection along with other goods and services. Economic theory has long studied the emergence and development of similar institutions and organisations against the backdrop of tension between productive and appropriative activities. After an early contribution by Haavelmo (1954, pp. 91–8), this issue has been addressed in a variety of ways by the literatures on rent seeking, conflict, cooperation, crime and more generally public economics and political economics (e.g., Olson, 1993, Allen, 1997; Dixit, 2006; Konrad and Skaperdas, 2012; Dal Bó et al., 2015; Mayshar et al., 2020). It is impossible in these pages to do justice to all elements of this large debate, but three broad insights from it will be useful for our subsequent discussion.

A first insight is that *appropriative activities can be socially very costly, hence motivating a need for protection*. One cost comes from harm to the victims and their properties, as well as other potential collateral damage. But appropriative activities can generate additional social costs as they reduce production in two ways: by reducing returns to producers' effort and by creating an incentive to divert resources from production to protection. Hirschleifer (1988) and Baumol (1990) present insightful formalisations and discussions of the associated incentives and effects. Modern crime economics starts with Becker (1968) precisely as a reflection on public enforcement of law, its costs and its optimal configuration. While illuminating, this analysis presupposes the existence of a state with its laws and its capacity to punish lawbreakers. In many contexts, today and in the past, state capacity is weak at best. In the absence of the state, the presence of 'bandits', i.e., agents devoted to appropriation, may induce self-protection efforts by individuals or by a community of producers. Skaperdas (1992) and Hirschleifer (1995) investigate the tension between productive and appropriative activities, showing that anarchy may be a form of order, but a rather fragile one, and that while the absence of conflict is possible, there are also equilibria in which producers are exploited. Grossman and Kim (1995) investigate defence as a deterrent to predation. Skaperdas and Syropoulos (1995) show that under anarchy, when skills and resources are unevenly distributed, those with a comparative advantage in extractive activities or more initial resources will specialise in appropriation and extract resources from the larger productive population. As they put it, parasite gangs specialised in the use of violence emerge as primitive extractive states. Their power is based on coercion, which absorbs resources, and exploitation severely limits incentives to production. As a result, such proto states are generally poor, and although rulers are richer than subjects, they are not particularly wealthy either, because there is little surplus to be extracted.

Here comes a second insight: *individuals with the incentive and capacity to loot the producers may realise that it is in their best interest to reduce extraction and engage in the costly provision of productive public goods.* Olson (1993) proposed the idea, later formalised and extended by McGuire and Olson (1996) and others, that 'roving bandits' have incentives to become 'stationary bandits', who seek to monopolise the use of violence and supply protection to the population. By providing peace and protecting against other looters, while also enhancing their own legitimacy, they raise the amount of surplus produced and hence the overall rents they are able to extract. Perhaps surprisingly, the bandit's subjects are also better off, as those with the coercive power have the incentive to exercise it in a way that is (at least partly) consistent with the interest of the society, increasing the size of the cake. In early societies it was probably not obvious whether the most efficient solution was for producers to self-protect or to allow for 'Olsonian bandits', but as conflict (military) technology became more complex, the latter solution clearly ended up dominating and making the monopoly of violence a stable equilibrium.

But what happens if different groups compete with one another to gain this monopoly of violence over a certain territory and hence the ability to supply protection and extract rents? Here we have a third insight: while competition in private goods in legal markets is usually welfare-enhancing, *competition among providers of protection is not necessarily beneficial.* Competition among them may be transitory and result in open conflict with a final winner, which defeats opponents and becomes a monopolistic provider of protection over the whole territory, or it may be permanent, involving either territorial division or co-existence over the same territory. Konrad and Skaperdas (2012) focus on an equilibrium in which several 'lords' divide the territory. They show that competition among such lords eliminates all production gains potentially allowed by protection, because it diverts resources from production to the military apparatus: '[l]iteral anarchy is replaced by a more organised, higher-level anarchy of predatory states' (Konrad and Skaperdas, 2012: 432). A more nuanced perspective on the effects of competition emerges when different 'lords', which may be a mafia and a state, supply protection and extract resources from different sectors within the same territory, such as a 'legal' and an 'illegal' sector, as in Grossman (1995).

4. ORGANISED CRIME

Organised crime certainly takes many forms but – like states – it often deals with the problem of societal conflict, specially where there are 'lootable' resources. And, as a private organisation active in the protection business, it needs a series of resources, mainly information on potential and actual threats, the possibility and capability to use force to prevent or punish them and a reputation for being able to effectively do so, in order to charge a price for its services. It obviously gains from reducing market competition and possibly establishing itself as a monopolist, at least locally. This may lead to conflicts with other organisations or to agreements with them to divide the territory into areas of monopolistic influence. This division may also be economic as well as geographic, with different organisations specialised in different sectors, but even agreements are sustained by the threat of conflict and may unravel if the balance of power changes.

Even if criminal organisations find an agreement to peacefully co-exist, at least temporarily, the aim of achieving the monopoly of violence will naturally lead to conflict with the state, both for power and legitimacy among the population. Schelling (1971) interestingly conceptualised organised crime as seeking monopolistic rule over the underworld, similarly to what a state government does for the overworld. But both worlds are really interlinked. In fact, organised crime appears to emerge and consolidate when and where there is a combination of weak state capacity and high economic opportunities. If its presence further undermines state capacity (for instance, because it depresses economic activities and returns to investment in institutional quality, for either the elite or voters, depending on the context), it may generate a poverty trap. But, to the extent that it replaces weak public governance with a more efficient – albeit criminal – organisation, it can boost economic activities and become – at least locally and temporarily – an engine of development. The Sicilian mafia, for example, the famous and prominent criminal organisation, is portrayed by Gambetta (1993) as basically providing protection for profit. Its birth dates back at least to the time of Italian unification in 1861. In that period, state enforcement in Sicily was extremely weak, leaving many individuals and groups exposed to predation. Opportunities for appropriation were abundant after the demise of the feudal system half a century earlier, in 1812. In particular, landlords felt threatened by peasants' revolts, and booming sectors offered high returns to appropriation. Moreover, soldiers and guards previously employed by feudal lords or by the Bourbon state were looking for new employers. In such conditions, mafia lords recruited them and started a long-lasting protection racket.

There are, of course, some differences between protection supplied by the state and by private organisations. In despotic states, the coercive apparatus operates more at the ruler's discretion than in democratic ones, but in both cases, citizens cannot typically be excluded from state protection. This makes protection either a public or a common good. When supplied for profit, instead, protection becomes a private or club good, because those who do not pay for it are excluded (and potentially looted). Notice that the degree of rivalry does not depend so much on the identity of the provider, as on the kind of protection. For instance, protection of a town against foreign predators is nonrival for its citizens, whether provided by public or private organisations, but protection of a farm obtained by moving guards away from other farms makes it rival. Also, in a sort of paradoxical version of Say's law, private protection supply creates its own demand. This happens in two main ways. First, protection is provided through the use or the threat of violence, and the threat against which a private provider supplies protection may just be the use of its own violence against those who do not pay. Hence, the boundary between private protection and extorsion is blurred. Second, by deflecting appropriation activities towards those who are not protected, private protection creates negative externalities on them and raises their demand for protection. This creates strategic complementarity in protection demand, making it particularly difficult for a single individual to exit from the private protection or extorsion racket.

The empirical economic literature has explored these ideas in a variety of ways. In particular, it has tried to assess the role of two factors in the historical origins of organised crime: high demand for protection – associated with valuable lootable resources or with specific threats – and insufficient ability of the state to act as a monopolistic provider of protection. The above observation that private protection creates its own demand, poses an important empirical challenge: an increase in the demand for protection might be the effect rather than the cause of the presence of organised crime. One way of addressing this difficulty is presented by Buonanno et al. (2015), who exploit a natural experiment to measure the effect of a boom in the value of lootable natural resources on the early diffusion of the Sicilian mafia. In particular, they focus on sulphur, a mineral that was abundant in the island, especially in some areas, but until the beginning of the nineteenth century had negligible economic value. The Industrial Revolution changed the picture, as sulphur became crucial for chemical composites produced in England and France, and since in Sicily it was superficial and easy to extract, sulphur exports exploded, and Sicilian production moved from nearly zero in 1800 to more than 80 per cent of the world market in 1900. A subsequent change in technology moved international demand in the twentieth century towards sulphur extracted elsewhere, so the boom in its value was indeed temporary. The uneven distribution of sulphur over the island thus produces a natural experiment, with some locations experiencing an exogenous increase in the value of natural resources and other locations serving as a control. Estimates based on historical data on sulphur mines and mafia presence at the local level show evidence of a resource curse: mines offered new opportunities for the protection racket and the sulphur boom fostered the early diffusion of the Sicilian mafia. Acemoglu et al. (2020) investigate a different exogenous source of increase in demand for protection, again in the context of the Sicilian mafia. They exploit variations in rainfall and in the local intensity of the drought that affected Sicilian municipalities in 1893 and that set off peasants' protests. Landlords turned to mafia dons to counter the threat posed by socialist movements. They again provide evidence that an exogenous increase in demand for protection fosters mafia diffusion. While these and other contributions provide consistent evidence of the effect of protection demand on the diffusion of organised crime in the context of weak states (see also Bandiera, 2003, and Dimico et al., 2017), we know comparatively little on the supply side, namely on the conditions under which particular groups of individuals are able to organise a protection racket. Gambetta (1993) lists information, violence and reputation as crucial assets in the business, but empirical research along these lines has been limited by data availability.

Of particular relevance are the consequences of private protection for prosperity and conflict. In principle, mafia-type organisations might have positive effects, to the extent that they provide a valuable service that the state is not able to provide effectively, possibly reducing predation and violence and also generating income and employment. On the other hand, the protection racket, the use of violence and the fight for its monopoly may harm and distort economic activity and create a variety of long-lasting negative externalities. The empirical literature provides ample evidence in support of this more negative perspective. A natural case study is Italy. There the positive effects of mafia protection are clearly outnumbered by the negative ones imposed through economic distortions and violence. Pinotti provides a general overview of the causes and consequences of organised crime (Pinotti, 2015a) and specifically estimates the economic costs of mafia presence in southern Italy (Pinotti, 2015b). By constructing a synthetic control, obtained as an optimally weighted average of surrounding regions, he compares the actual evolution of regions in which the mafia entered at some point to their likely counterfactual evolution, had the mafia been absent. After 30 years of mafia presence, mafia regions show a level of GDP that is 16 per cent lower than in the counterfactual, and similarly lower levels of electricity consumption, which are harder to hide and thus suggest a real drop of economic activity rather than a mere move towards the underground economy. This drop is driven by a fall in private investment and in the productivity of public investment, due to distortion and corruption in public procurement, and it is matched by a substantial rise in homicide rates. Barone and Narciso (2015) document similar distortions in Sicilian municipalities plagued by the mafia, where fake firms are created just to appropriate public subsidies and corruption raises subsidies distracted by mafia-related firms. Here the causal identification relies on an instrumental variable strategy, based on rainfall shocks in the 1850s, slope and altitude. Using drought intensity in 1893 as an instrument for mafia presence in

Sicilian municipalities, Acemoglu et al. (2020) also document that it lowered literacy, public goods provision and political competition.

Evidence on the positive effects of criminal organisations, arising at least locally and in specific contexts, either from the supply of protection or from the employment and income they generate, is more limited but nonetheless important. For Italy, Buonanno et al. (2015), using historical sulphur mines and department fixed effects as instruments, show that the Sicilian mafia reduces thefts and car thefts, a result in line with its role as a provider of protection. Le Moglie and Sorrenti (2022) show that after the crisis of 2008, Italian provinces with higher mafia infiltration experienced a less severe drop in the number of new enterprises established, a result coherent with the mafia's investment in the legal economy. If we move outside Italy, Murphy and Rossi (2020) document a positive impact of Mexican drug cartels on local socio-economic outcomes, arising, despite violence, from the flow of income, employment opportunities and public goods they generate for the local communities. To identify such effects, they exploit an instrumental variables strategy based on historical migration patterns and on US policies of opium prohibition and migration restrictions, which induced the presence in Mexico of migrant groups with the know-how and the resources to produce and smuggle opium to the US. Needless to say, a positive impact at the local level is perfectly compatible with a negative impact at the aggregate level.

One of the reasons why it is important to consider the potential local benefits of criminal organisations is that they help explain the local support mafia groups and drug cartels often enjoy among the population. This is not dissimilar to what happens with states. In either case, obedience, acceptance and legitimacy are based on a combination of fear of punishment and recognition of benefits. The fight between state and organised crime is thus a double fight, for power (monopoly of violence) and for legitimacy.

5. FIGHTING FOR THE MONOPOLY

Even when criminal organisations provide some degree of protection and other public goods and services at the local level, and thus possibly enjoy some support from the local population, they tend to have a negative aggregate impact, due to actual or threatened violence and distortions to economic activities. A benevolent government would thus have an incentive to curb them and eliminate private competitors in the provision of protection and in the use of violence. Mafia lords would then have an obvious incentive to fight back. As each player has a number of different possible strategies, this fight can take many forms. Economists have increasingly studied them over the past two decades, both at the theoretical and empirical level. Of course, the government may pursue objectives that differ from social welfare and may find it in its best interest to tolerate criminal organisations or come to an agreement with them. Alternatively, it may just be unable to curb them, or the cost of doing so may be too high. If it fights, criminal organisations may fight back through violence, bribes or a combination of both. These may be directed towards citizens such as candidates, informants or witnesses (or just simple citizens, as in the case of terrorism), or towards state officers such as policemen, judges, bureaucrats and politicians. The general goal is to modify decision makers' behaviour in a desired direction, or to change their identity so as to have more favourable individuals in key positions. Through the provision of goods and services to the local population, criminal organisations may gain support, which makes the state's efforts even more uphill. While some of these strategies are in principle available even to individual criminals, they can be clearly pursued by criminal organisations on a completely different scale. For all these reasons, fighting criminal organisations is actually harder than individual crime, and the standard tools of public enforcement of law, namely punishment intensity and probability, may not work or may even backfire.

There has been a number of theoretical contributions that investigate corruption, violence and vote buying as tools available to criminal organisations fighting against the state. Kugler et al. (2005), for example, focus on corruption and how it can undermine or even overturn the standard incentives provided by punishment intensity and probability in public enforcement of law. Their model features criminal organisations that compete globally in the crime market and are local monopsonists in the corruption market. They show that when state governance is weak (hence the cost of bribing is low) and criminal rents are high, an increase in the intensity of punishment for lawbreakers threatened by the state induces more corruption, thus lowering expected sanctions and raising crime. In one sentence, in weak states, being tougher on crime may backfire. As a consequence, once organised crime and corruption are established, they become hard to eradicate. Dal Bó and Di Tella (2003) focus instead on the threat of violence (or more generally of punishment) against an elected politician if he or she does not choose the policy desired by a criminal organisation (or more generally a pressure group). Corruption and violence may well co-exist. Pablo Escobar, the famous head of the Colombian drug cartel of Medellín, who in the 1980s became one of the richest men in the world, used to offer *plata o plomo*, that is, a choice between his money or his bullets, to public officials involved in the antidrug war. Dal Bó et al. (2006) investigate under which conditions criminal organisations use violence, bribes or both to obtain a resource from public officials, and what implications this has for politicians' quality. They develop a model in which citizens split between the private and the public sector, with the former offering wages equal to individual productivity and the latter flat wages, so that only individuals below a certain productivity threshold are attracted to the public sector. Moving up this threshold amounts to raising politicians' quality. Just as criminal organisations have two instruments, so does the state, which may choose to make bribes or violence costlier. Improved enforcement reduces the number of active criminal organisations, but the two strategies have different implications, because bribes make the public sector more attractive, while the threat of violence makes it less attractive. As a consequence, making *plomo* costlier raises the quality of politicians, whereas making *plata* costlier has ambiguous effects. Clearly, here 'quality' refers to skills associated with productivity in the private sector, not to intrinsic honesty or public spiritedness, so being tough on violence may induce an increase in politicians' 'quality' that goes together with an increase in corruption. As mentioned above, on top of changing public officials' choices, criminal organisations may seek to change public officials themselves. In the case of democratically elected politicians, this requires some form of electoral fraud, such as vote buying or voter coercion. We refer to the chapter by Accardo, De Feo and De Luca in this volume for a discussion of these issues and the related literature.

While criminal organisations have a variety of tools to counteract the state's attempts to curb them, the same is true for the state. These include specific punishments for criminal associations, seizing goods or assets, leniency towards informants, various forms of investments in state capacity and even targeted military intervention. Yet they do not necessarily work in the expected way. Consider for instance leniency towards low-rank criminals who turn informants. Piccolo and Immordino (2017) show that it has two effects: an obvious one of raising the conviction probability of informants' bosses and an indirect one of reducing the risks incurred by criminal soldiers and therefore the cost of hiring them in equilibrium. The first aspect makes leniency always desirable *ex post*, as it provides useful incentives to collaborate with justice and reveal valuable information, but the second aspect may actually foster criminal organisations and make leniency more problematic from an *ex-ante* point of view, unless some corrective measures are undertaken.

The potential for corruption, violence and political interference, and the subtleties involved in specific targeted interventions, make the state's fight against organised crime particularly complex. While theoretical research on these topics has made substantial progress over the past two decades, many aspects are still under-investigated. For instance, we still know little about the specific temporal and spatial patterns of this fight and its interaction with different institutional, economic, cultural and social dimensions. While this remains an open and active field of research at the theoretical level, crucial advances have also been made at the empirical level.

Some contributions have looked at corruption, economic distortions and politicians' quality. Barone and Narciso (2015) provide evidence of corruption and public funds distraction in Sicilian municipalities plagued by the mafia.

Other studies focus on the *plata o plomo* effect on politicians' self-selection analysed by Dal Bó et al. (2006). In particular, Daniele and Geys (2015) show that improved enforcement in southern Italian municipalities, in the form of the dissolution of municipality councils due to mafia infiltration, raises the quality of politicians at subsequent elections, as measured by their human capital. Daniele (2019) documents that the murder of a politician by organised crime in a municipality is followed by a sharp and sizable reduction in politicians' average level of education at the subsequent elections. More broadly, the literature has produced abundant evidence of the importance of both pre- and post-electoral violence. Dell (2015) documents that in Mexican municipalities a close mayoral election won by a candidate from the PAN party, which is actively engaged in the war on drugs, is followed by an increase in violence. Interestingly, such violence is not just directed towards politicians but also towards rival drug traffickers weakened by crackdowns. Daniele and Dipoppa (2017) show that in Italian mafia regions attacks on politicians increase in the first month after local elections. Alesina et al. (2019) instead document, again for Italian mafia regions, that homicides increase in pre-electoral years and that since Italy turned from a proportional to a majoritarian electoral system, this pattern has only been present in uncertain districts.

Finally, there is evidence that mafia lords, drug cartels and paramilitary groups bring votes to some political parties in exchange for support. Acemoglu et al. (2013) document this exchange for Colombia, showing three main pieces of evidence. First, after the FARC entered into politics, areas with high paramilitary presence witnessed an increase in the vote share of parties associated with the paramilitaries. Second, politicians with more votes from these areas supported the paramilitaries in both legal and illegal ways, as documented by votes for lenient bills and arrest data. Third, paramilitary groups display higher persistence in areas where at the 2002 elections President Uribe received more votes and, based on previous elections, might have instead expected to receive fewer votes. Additional evidence for Colombia is provided by Fergusson et al. (2018), who focus on the role of media, scandals and coercion, and by Galindo-Silva (2021), who show that armed groups with more political power deter other groups from initiating certain types of violence. Evidence of a votes-for-support exchange between mafia lords and political parties is also available for Italy. De Feo and De Luca (2017) and Buonanno et al. (2016) document the first side of this exchange, namely the positive impact of mafia presence on the vote share of the main centre-right party during the First and Second Republics, respectively. In particular, the first paper shows that, coherently with their theoretical model, the effect of the mafia on votes is more pronounced when political competition is higher and also provides suggestive evidence on the other side of the exchange, namely what mafia lords obtain from politicians, showing that construction activities significantly increase in mafia municipalities. Di Cataldo and Mastrorocco (2020) expand in this direction and document that local governments infiltrated by the mafia spend more on construction and waste management, less on municipal police and public transport, and collect fewer taxes for waste and garbage.

While evidence from Italy and Latin America has grown significantly over the last decade, we still know little about other parts of the world. We also know little, both at the theoretical and empirical level, on two relevant aspects: the fight between states and criminal organisations may involve several actors on either side, which may cooperate or fight in many ways; and, as already mentioned, this fight is not just about power but also legitimacy, so that the degree of success of different strategies may crucially depend on the cultural aspects of this battle.

6. FIGHTING FOR LEGITIMACY

Many state rulers, today and in the past, rise to power through violence and claim their rule to be legitimate, but the extent to which they are able to exercise their power crucially depends on the degree to which that legitimacy is recognised among the population, which can be more or less inclined to accept the rules and abide by them. Just as a well-functioning state is recognised by its citizens as having a legitimate monopoly on violence, a prosperous criminal organisation needs some degree of legitimacy or popular support. This may be based on a combination of fear, identification or even idealisation. In any case, expectations about other people's behaviour play a fundamental role here. This is because institutions are by nature an equilibrium phenomenon and, as such, beliefs need to support that equilibrium (Greif, 2006). The source of this legitimacy in the classic Weber (1994) description could be tradition (since the political or social order has been there for a long time), charisma (we have faith in the rulers) or a rational legal element (we trust its legality). In more normative terms, legitimacy could come from whether the coercive power is justified. In many cases organised crime can rely on the products it provides as a direct justification, be that protection (in the case of mafias) or, say, job opportunities (in the case of illicit drug trade organisations). But sometimes they need to rely upon other strategies.

Just as nation states have an incentive to invest in nationalism, so as to make their population more cohesive, criminal organisations have an incentive to establish their legitimacy in a variety of ways, including the use of religion, the provision of private and public goods, the magnification of career prospects inside the organisation and the discrediting of outside options. Economic theory has so far explored these aspects more in the context of states than in that of organised crime. Alesina et al. (2020, 2021) recognise that governments, whether democracies or dictatorships, may have an incentive to foster nationalism at the cultural level, for instance through public education programs, so as to make their population less heterogeneous and more cohesive. They also document that governments indeed pursue this goal in a variety of ways. As with other cultural traits, nationalism can evolve over time through different channels, including intentional transmission efforts by elites or parents, and reinforcement or imitation mechanisms, giving rise to an evolutionary dynamic as in Besley (2020), where civic culture is complementary to state capacity and public goods provision. While an extensive analysis of the reasons for and ways of fostering national identities would take us too far, what is interesting in the present context is that criminal organisations have similar incentives to establish their legitimacy in a variety of ways, including the use of codes of honour, the magnification of career prospects inside the organisation and the discrediting of outside options. These aspects are particularly interesting in light of the evidence provided by Levitt and Venkatesh (2000), who document choices by low-rank members of a drug-selling gang, who are paid roughly minimum wage but face a death probability around 7 per cent per year: such choices are hard to reconcile with standard preferences, unless one brings non-economic considerations into the picture. A systematic theoretical and empirical investigation of the functioning of these mechanisms in the case of organised crime is still largely a fascinating avenue for future research.

Religion has traditionally played a central role in the legitimisation of the political powers of European monarchies and the Chinese empire, so it is not surprising that religious imagery and rituals also appear to be very much related to some forms of organised crime and might well be related to sources of legitimacy. Although this is a topic that is largely understudied, there are many suggestive elements in the history of the rise of the Sicilian mafia and its relationship with the Catholic Church (Gambetta, 1993). The Italian Unification in 1861 generated a certain degree of hostility between church and state, which lasted at least until the late 1920s. In that period, 'the local church in all likelihood found in the mafiosi a more cooperative and respectful secular power' (Gambetta, 1993: 49), and despite the mafia being such an important disruptive feature of Sicilian life, there are virtually no records of interventions or complaint from the church till World War I. The mafiosi, in turn, tended to use the language of Catholicism to enhance their reputation, as with the use of saint celebrations (Gambetta, 1993: 47–8).

Since legitimacy entails a dimension of coordination, an individual may consider a power legitimate as long as other people do so too and stop recognising its legitimacy if she expects other people to stop as well. This creates the possibility of sudden changes in popular support, provided one is able to coordinate a critical mass of individuals. For instance, news about relevant corruption scandals may depress tax morale; news about other people reporting racket attempts may induce more victims to do the same; and news about the mafia killing children, running against its own proclaimed code of honour, may substantially reduce its acceptance. Also, the state may come to an agreement with criminal organisations, implicitly and sometimes even explicitly providing mutual recognition to one another. But even when this is not the case, and there is in fact a fight for legitimacy among the population, convincing people tends to be the result of a patient and systematic work at different levels, from schools to neighbourhoods, from firms to public administration and so on. When this work is coupled with short-run triggers such as the above-mentioned scandals or particular trials or assassinations, new possibilities suddenly open up. Victories in the fight for legitimacy may be hard, because expectations and social norms do not change if one falls short of moving the necessary critical mass. At the same time, they may be self-reinforcing if one passes such threshold. Sudden changes are then possible, in one direction or the other.

NOTE

1. Tommy E. Murphy is Associate Professor at the Department of Economics, Universidad de San Andrés, Argentina, and Paolo Vanin is full Professor at the Department of Economics, Università di Bologna, Italy.

REFERENCES

Alesina, Alberto, Paola Giuliano and Bryony Reich [2021]; "Nation-Building and Education," *The Economic Journal*, Vol. 131, No. 638, pp. 2273–303.

Alesina, Alberto, Salvatore Piccolo and Paolo Pinotti [2019]; "Organized Crime, Violence, and Politics," *Review of Economic Studies*, Vol. 86, No. 2, pp. 457–99

Alesina, Alberto, Bryony Reich and Alessandro Riboni [2020]; "Nation-Building, Nationalism, and Wars," *Journal of Economic Growth*, Vol. 25, No. 4, pp. 381–430

Allen, Robert C. [1997]; "Agriculture and the Origins of the State in Ancient Egypt," *Explorations in Economic History*, Vol. 34, pp. 135–54

Acemoglu, Daron and James A. Robinson [2016]; "Paths to Inclusive Political Institutions," in J. Eloranta, E. Golson, A. Markevich and N. Wolf (eds.), *Economic History of Warfare and State Formation* (Springer), pp. 3–50

Acemoglu, Daron, Giuseppe De Feo, and Giacomo De Luca [2020]; "Weak States: Causes and Consequences of the Sicilian Mafia," *Review of Economic Studies*, Vol. 87, No. 2, pp. 537–81

Acemoglu, Daron, James A. Robinson and R. J. Santos [2013]; "The Monopoly of Violence: Evidence from Colombia," *Journal of the European Economic Association*, Vol. 11, No. s1, pp. 5–44

Bandiera, Oriana [2003]; "Land Reform, the Market for Protection and the Origins of the Sicilian Mafia: Theory and Evidence," *Journal of Law, Economics and Organization*, Vol. 19, No. 1, pp. 218–44

Barone, Guglielmo and Gaia Narciso [2015]; "Organized Crime and Business Subsidies: Where Does the Money Go?" *Journal of Urban Economics*, Vol. 86, pp. 98–110

Bates, Robert H. [2001]; *Prosperity and Violence: The Political Economy of Development* (W. W. Norton & Company)

Baumol, William J. [1990]; "Entrepreneurship: Productive, Unproductive, and Destructive," *The Journal of Political Economy*, Vol. 98, No. 5 Part 1, pp. 893–921

Becker, Gary S. [1968]; "Crime and punishment: An economic approach," *Journal of Political Economy* Vol. 76, No. 2, pp. 169–217

Besley, Timothy [2020]; "State capacity, reciprocity, and the social contract," *Econometrica*, Vol. 88, No. 4, pp. 1307–35

Boyd, Robert and Peter J. Richerson [2005]; *The Origin and Evolution of Cultures* (Oxford University Press)

Buonanno, Paolo, Ruben Durante, Giovanni Prarolo, and Paolo Vanin [2015]; "Poor Institutions, Rich Mines: Resource Curse in the Origins of the Sicilian Mafia," *Economic Journal*, Vol. 125, Feature Issue, pp. F125–F202

Buonanno, Paolo, Giovanni Prarolo and Paolo Vanin [2016]; "Organized Crime and Electoral Outcomes: Evidence from Sicily at the Turn of the XXI Century," *European Journal of Political Economy*, Vol. 41, pp. 61–74

Dal Bó, Ernesto and Rafael Di Tella [2003]; "Capture by threat." *Journal of Political Economy*, Vol. 111, No. 5, pp. 1123–54

Dal Bó, Ernesto, Pedro Dal Bó and Rafael Di Tella [2006]; ""Plata o Plomo?": Bribe and Punishment in a Theory of Political Influence," *American Political Science Review*, Vol. 100, No. 1, pp. 41–53

Dal Bó, Ernesto, Pablo Hernández and Sebastián Mazzuca [2015]; *The Paradox of Civilization: Pre-Institutional Sources of Security and Prosperity*, (National Bureau of Economic Research, NBER Working Paper, No. 21829).

Daniele, Gianmarco [2019]; "Strike One to Educate One Hundred: Organized Crime, Political Selection and Politicians' Ability," *Journal of Economic Behavior & Organization* Vol. 159, pp. 650–62

Daniele, G. and G. Dipoppa [2017]; "Mafia, Elections and Violence against Politicians," *Journal of Public Economics*, Vol 154, pp. 10–33

Daniele, G. and B. Geys [2015]; "Organized Crime, Institutions and Political Quality: Empirical Evidence from Italian Municipalities," *Economic Journal*, Vol. 125, No. 586, pp. F233–F255

De Feo, G. and G. D. De Luca [2017]; "Mafia in the Ballot Box," *American Economic Journal: Economic Policy*, Vol. 9, No. 3, pp. 134–67

Dell, Melissa [2015]; "Trafficking Networks and the Mexican Drug War," *American Economic Review*, Vol. 105, No. 6, pp. 1738–79

Di Cataldo, Marco and Mastrorocco, Nicola [2020]; *Organised Crime, Captured Politicians, and the Allocation of Public Resources* (University Ca' Foscari of Venice, Dept. of Economics Research Paper Series No. 04/WP/2020)

Diamond, Jared [1997]; *Guns, Germs, and Steel: The Fates of Human Societies* (W. W. Norton & Company)

Dimico, Arcangelo, Alessia Isopi and Ola Olsson [2017]; "Origins of the Sicilian Mafia: The Market for Lemons," *Journal of Economic History*, Vol. 77, No. 4, pp. 1083–115

Dixit, Avinash K. [2006]; *Lawlessness and Economics: Alternative Modes of Governance* (Oxford University Press)

Fergusson, Leopoldo, Juan F. Vargas and Mauricio A. Vela [2018]; *Sunlight Disinfects? Free Media in Weak Democracies*, The Latin American and Caribbean Economic Association-LACEA Working Paper, No. 016174)

Galindo-Silva, Hector [2021]; "Political Openness and Armed Conflict: Evidence from Local Councils in Colombia," *European Journal of Political Economy*, Vol. 67, p. 101984

Gambetta, Diego [1993]; *The Sicilian Mafia: The Business of Private Protection* (Harvard University Press)

Greif, Avner [2006]; *Institutions and the Path to the Modern Economy: Lessons from Medieval Trade* (Cambridge University Press)

Grossman, Herschel I. [1995]; "Rival Kleptocrats: The Mafia Versus the State," in G. Fiorentini and S. Peltzman (eds.), *The Economics of Organised Crime*. pp. 143–56

Grossman, Herschel I. and Minseong Kim [1995]; "Swords or Plowshares? A Theory of the Security of Claims to Property," *Journal of Political Economy*, Vol. 103, No. 6, pp. 1275–88

Haavelmo, Trigve [1954]; *A Study in the Theory of Economic Evolution* (North-Holland)

Henrich, Joseph and Michael Muthukrishna [2021]; "The Origins and Psychology of Human Cooperation," *Annual Review of Psychology*, Vol. 72, pp. 207–40

Hirshleifer, Jack [1988]; "The Analytics of Continuing Conflict," *Synthese*, Vol. 76, No. 2, pp. 201–33

Hirshleifer, Jack [1995]; "Anarchy and its Breakdown," *Journal of Political Economy*, Vol. 103, No. 1, pp. 26–52

Keeley, Lawrence [1996]; *War before Civilization: The Myth of the Peaceful Savage* (Oxford University Press)

Konrad, K. A. and S. Skaperdas [2012]; "The Market for Protection and the Origin of the State," *Economic Theory*, Vol. 50, No. 2, pp. 417–43

Kugler, M., T. Verdier and Y. Zenou [2005]; "Organized Crime, Corruption and Punishment," *Journal of Public Economics*, Vol. 89, No. 9–10, pp. 1639–63

Le Moglie, M. and G. Sorrenti [2022]; "Revealing 'Mafia Inc.'? Financial Crisis, Organized Crime, and the Birth of New Enterprises," *Review of Economics and Statistics*, Vol. 104, No. 1, pp. 142–56

Leeson, Peter T. [2014]; *Anarchy Unbound: Why Self-Government Works Better than You Think* (Cambridge University Press)

Levitt, Steven D. and Sudhir Alladi Venkatesh [2000]; "An Economic Analysis of a Drug-Selling Gang's Finances," *Quarterly Journal of Economics*, Vol. 115, No. 3, pp. 755–89

Mayshar, Joram, Omer Moav and Luigi Pascali [2020]; *The Origin of the State: Land Productivity or Appropriability?* (MIMEO)

McGuire, Martin C. and Mancur Olson [1996]; "The Economics of Autocracy and Majority Rule: The Invisible Hand and the Use of Force," *Journal of Economic Literature*, Vol. 34, No.1, pp. 72–96

Murphy, Tommy E. and Martín A. Rossi [2020]; "Following the Poppy Trail: Causes and Consequences of Mexican Drug Cartels," *Journal of Development Economics*, Vol. 143, p. 102433

North, Douglass C. [1981]; *Structure and Change in Economic History* (Norton)

North, Douglass C., John J. Wallis and Barry R. Weingast [2009]; *Violence and Social Orders: A Conceptual Framework for Interpreting Recorded Human History* (Cambridge University Press)

Olson, Mancur [1993]; "Dictatorship, Democracy, and Development," *American Political Science Review*, Vol. 87, No. 3, pp. 567–76

Piccolo, S. and G. Immordino [2017]; "Organised Crime, Insider Information and Optimal Leniency," *Economic Journal*, Vol. 127, No. 606, pp. 2504–24

Pinker, Steven [2011]; *The Better Angels of Our Nature: Why Violence Has Declined* (Viking)

Pinotti, Paolo [2015a]; "The Causes and Consequences of Organised Crime," *Economic Journal*, Vol. 125, No. 586, pp. F158–74

Pinotti, Paolo [2015b]; "The Economic Cost of Organized Crime: Evidence from Southern Italy," *Economic Journal*, Vol. 125, No. 586, pp. F203–32

Schelling, Thomas [1971]; "What Is the Business of Organized Crime?," *The American Scholar*, Vol. 40, No. 4, pp. 643–52

Scott, James C. [2010]; *The Art of Not Being Governed: An Anarchist History of Upland Southeast Asia* (Yale University Press)

Seabright, Paul [2010]; *The Company of Strangers: A Natural History of Economic Life –Revised edition–* (Princeton University Press)

Skaperdas, Stergios [1992]; "Cooperation, Conflict, and Power in the Absence of Property Rights." *The American Economic Review*, Vol. 82, No. 4, pp. 720–39

Skaperdas, Stergios and Constantinos Syropoulos [1995]; "Gangs as Primitive States," in G. Fiorentini and S. Peltzman (eds.), *The Economics of Organised Crime*. pp. 61–82

Tilly, Charles [1985]; "War Making and State Making as Organized Crime," in P.B. Evans, D. Rueschemeyer and T. Skocpol (eds.), *Bringing the State Back In* (Cambridge University Press), pp. 169–91

Tilly, Charles [1990]; *Coercion, Capital, and European States, AD 990–1992* (Blackwell)

Weber, Max [1994]; "The Profession and Vocation of Politics," in P. Lassman and R. Speirs (eds.), *Political Writings* (Cambridge: Cambridge University Press), pp. 309–69. (ed. orig. 1919)

Index

Printed and bound by CPI Group (UK) Ltd, Croydon, CR0 4YY
16/04/2025
14658493-0002